Business and Corporate Law

By the same author:

1. Business and Industrial Law
2. Mercantile Law
3. Modern Business Law
4. Principles of Management
5. Organisational Theory and Behaviour: Text and Cases (2nd Edition)
6. Organisational Behaviour (UPTU)

Business and Corporate Law

Dr. B.S. Moshal
Associate Professor
Department of Commerce
Zakir Husain Post Graduate Evening College
(Delhi University)
Founder Director, D.C.A.S
(I.P. University)
Former Visiting Faculty), ICAI

Ane Books Pvt. Ltd.
New Delhi ♦ Chennai

Business and Corporate Law

B.S. Moshal

Published by

Ane Books Pvt. Ltd.

4821, Parwana Bhawan, 1st Floor, 24 Ansari Road, Darya Ganj,
New Delhi - 110 002, Tel.: +91(011) 23276843-44, Fax: +91(011) 23276863
e-mail: kapoor@anebooks.com, Website: www.anebooks.com

Branch Office:

- Avantika Niwas, 1st Floor, 19 Doraiswamy Road, T. Nagar,
  Chennai - 600 017, Tel.: +91(044) 28141554, 28141209
  e-mail: anebookschennai@gmail.com, rathinam@anebooks.com

ISBN : 978-93-8116-202-6

Printed at : Sagar Colorscan, New Delhi.

Preface

This book has been written primarity to cater to the needs of M.B.A. students and students of other professional courses. In this book attempts have been made for presenting contents of the various relevant provisions of the different acts in more effective and simplified manner.

Many authors have made impressive attempts to write on the various Acts of *Business and Corporate Law*. But subject matter of law needs regular updating. Thus the concept of 'latest is the best' holds good. While writing the book, the latest amendments, modifications and changes taking place in many Acts including Indian Companies Act, 1956, the Consumer Protection Act, 1986, have been fully taken care of. Due care has also been exercised in providing precise and easy interpretation of the various provisions of the Acts.

The use of simple class teaching language, suitable examples and the leading cases make subject matter more interesting. It may help to generate an understanding on the part of prospective managers about the various Acts of Business Law.

The subject matter of the book has been organised into four major units. The first unit which consists of the Indian Contract Act, 1872, gives full account of formation, essentials, performance of a contract including certain special contracts. The second unit contains the Indian Partnership Act, 1932 and the Indian Sale of Goods Act, 1930. Unit third comprises the Negotiable Instrument Act, 1881 and the Indian Companies Act, 1956. The last unit provides detailed account of the Consumer Protection Act, 1986 and the Information Technology Act, 2000.

I shall be obliged to solicit and take care of comments and suggestions from the readers.

Dr. B.S. Moshal

Syllabus for
Uttar Pradesh Technical University
Gautam Buddha Technical University
Mahamaya Technical University

Year I, Semester–II

MBA 022 : Business Laws

UNIT 1 **(10 SESSIONS)**

Contract Act, 1872

Definition of a Contract and its Essentials, Formation of a Valid Contract—Offer and Acceptance, Consideration, Capacity to Contract, Free Consent, Legality of Object, Discharge of a Contract by Performance, Impossibility and Frustration, Breach, Damages for Breach of a Contract, Quasi-Contracts, Contract of Indemnity and Guarantee, Bailment and Pledge, Agency.

UNIT II **(12 SESSIONS)**

Partnership Act, 1932

Definition of Partnership and its Essentials, Rights and Duties of Partners, Types of Partners, Minor as a Partner, Doctrine of Implied Authority, Registration of Firms, Dissolution of Firms.

Sale of Goods Act, 1930

Definition of a Contract of Sale, Conditions and Warranties, Passing of Property, Right of Unpaid Seller against the Goods, Remedies for Breach.

UNIT III **(10 SESSIONS)**

Negotiable Instrument Act, 1881

Definition and Characteristics, Kinds of Negotiable Instruments, Promissory Note, Bill of Exchange and Cheques, Holder and Holder in Due Course, Negotiation, Presentment, Discharge from Liability, Noting and Protest, Presumption, Crossing of Cheques, Bouncing of Cheques.

Companies Act, 1856

Nature and Definition of a Company, Registration and Incorporation, Memorandum of Association, Articles of Association, Prospectus, Kinds of Companies, Directors: Their Powers and Duties, Meetings, Winding up.

UNIT IV **(8 SESSIONS)**

Consumer Protection Act, (1986)

Aims and Objects of the Act, Redressal Machinery under the Act, Procedure for Complaints under the Act, Remedies, Appeals, Enforcement of Orders and Penalties.

Information Technology Act, 2000

Definition, Digital Signature, Electronic-Governance, Attribution, Acknowledgement and Dispatch of Electronic Records, Sense Electronic Records and Sense Digital Signatures, Regulation of Certifying Authorities, Digital Signature Certificates, Duties of Subscribers, Penalties and Offences.

Syllabus for
Uttarakhand Technical University

Semester–IV

MBA 401 : Corporate Legal Environment

Objective: The objective is to provide knowledge about important business laws relevant to Business and Corporate World.

Course Contents

(*i*) Meaning and Importance of Business Laws; Laws and Business Managers; Government and Business Relationships in India.

(*ii*) Indian Contract Act, 1872; Definitions, Characteristics, Essentials of Valid Contract; Detailed Exposure to the Provisions; Discharge of Performance of Contract; Consequences of Breach of Contract.

(*iii*) Types of Contract – Indemnity, Guarantee, Contingent, Bailment, Pledge, Agency.

(*iv*) Negotiable Instrument Act – Meaning and Types of Different Negotiable Instrument and the Provision Applicable to them.

(*v*) Sales of Goods Act.

(*vi*) Indian Arbitration Act.

(*vii*) Indian Partnership Act.

(*viii*) Indian Companies Act, 1956 – Definitions, Characteristics, Types and Formation of a Company. Shares Debentures, Borrowing Powers, Provision Relating to Company Liquidation.

(*ix*) Company, Management – Directors, Managing Director and Their Appointment, Qualification, Duties, Rights, Liabilities, Position, Remuneration and Removal; Company Meetings and Proceedings; Prevention of Oppression and Mismanagement.

Detailed Contents

UNIT I CONTRACT ACT, 1872

UNIT II INDIAN PARTNERSHIP ACT, 1932 SALE OF GOODS ACT, 1930

UNIT III NEGOTIABLE INSTRUMENT ACT, 1881 COMPANIES ACT, 1956

UNIT IV CONSUMER PROTECTION ACT, 1986 INFORMATION TECHNOLOGY ACT, 2000

Unit 1

Contract Act, 1872

1

Contract: Definition, Essentials and Types

LEARNING OBJECTIVES

- Develop conceptual clarity about the terms, contract and agreement.
- Understand essentials of a valid contract.
- Remember various types of a contract.
- Be clear about formation of a contract.
- Understand legal consequences of offer acceptance, agreement, promise and obligations.

INTRODUCTION

In order to conduct business operations, many transactions are made by the parties. Mostly these transactions are made in the form of contract. In these transactions certain rights and obligations are created. The rights of one party would be obligations of other party and vice-versa. It is therefore to regulate and settle these transactions Indian Contract Act 1872 has been enacted. The law of contract deals with those transactions or promises which create legal rights and obligations. This act lays down legal rules relating to promises, their formation and enforceability. In case of non-performance of the promise by one party, it also provides legal remedies to an aggrieved party.

Indian Contract Act came into being in September 1872. The Act is extended to the whole of India except the state of Jammu and Kashmir. It contains 266 sections. Out of these, Sections 1 to 75 are related to formation and performance of the contract. Sections 124 to 238 deal with some special contracts such as agency, bailment guarantee etc. Section 73 to 123 and Sections 239 to 266 have been repealed and merged into Indian Sale of Goods Act and Indian Partnership Act.

In brief Indian Contract Act can be studied in following phases:

1. Formation of contract and essentials of a valid contract.
2. Performance of a contract or promises made in a contract.
3. Special contracts including contracts of indemnity and guarantee, bailment and agency.

The Contract Act has the following limitations.

Firstly Indian Contract Act creates right *in personam*, which is available only against particular party or particular person. (Parties or person making a contract). For example, A lends sum of Rs. 10,000 to B. In this transaction A gets right to recover the money only from B and not from any one else. Secondly the Law of contract is not the whole law of agreements or the whole law of obligations. Agreements and obligations which are not contractual in nature do not come within the purview of this Act. For example, A borrows sum of Rs. 5000 from his friend B. If A does not repay money, B gets right to sue upon him. But if A invites B his friend for a dinner at his home. B agrees to it but, does not turn up for dinner, A has no legal remedy against him. It is because in this case relationship created between A and B is personal and social in nature not covered by Indian Contract Act. According to Salmond, Law of Contract is the law of those agreements which creates obligations and those obligations which have their source in agreement. In other words, provisions of this Act are applicable only on those obligations which are contractual and legal in nature.

CONTRACT DEFINED

It is clear that the legal provisions of Indian Contract Act are applicable only on those transactions which are made in the form of contract.

Therefore, it is necessary to define and understand the meaning of the term contract.

Generally, contract may be defined as an agreement which creates rights and obligations between the parties. These rights and obligations must be of such a nature that these can be claimed in the court of law.

In the words of Sir William Anson, "Contract is a legally binding agreement made between two or more persons by which rights are acquired by one or more to acts forbearances on the part of other."

Salmond has defined contract "As an agreement creating and defining obligation between the parties." According to Section 2 (h) of the Indian Contract Act, "Contract is an agreement which is enforceable by law."

Analysis of these definitions of contract reveals that contract has three major components:

(*a*) Agreement

(*b*) Obligation

(*c*) Enforceability

(*a*) *Agreement:* In order to form a contract at first instance there must be an agreement between parties.

(*b*) *Obligation:* Agreement made between the parties must give a rise to rights and obligations. These rights and obligations must be legal in nature. Such obligations form a central part of a contract.

(*c*) *Enforceability:* Rights and obligations created in agreement must be contractual in nature. In other words, these must be legal in nature which can be claimed in the court of law. It is the legal consequences involved in these obligations and rights which make them enforceable in the court.

Agreement defined: Agreement is a foundation stone of a contract. The contract is formed only on the basis of agreement. It is a combined effect of offer and acceptance. One party makes an offer for doing or not doing anything and other party accepts it. Agreement is formed between them.

Agreement = Offer + Acceptance. According to Section 2 (e), agreement is a promise or a set of promises forming consideration for each other. The offer itself is of no legal consequences unless it is accepted. On acceptance the offer is converted into binding promise. The party making an offer becomes promisor and acceptor becomes promisee. As a legal consequence of acceptance, the acceptor becomes promisor and offeror becomes promisee. In this way there is a mutual exchange of promises between offeror and acceptor resulting in formation of an agreement. It is, however to be noted that in an agreement the promisee is always in a position of benefit. It is because the promisor has to perform the act for the benefit of promisee.

Example: A offers to sell out his bike to B for Rs. 30,000; B accepts the offer. Agreement is formed between A and B. In this agreement A is a promisor for transferring the possession and ownership of the bike to B. B, is a promisee in the position of benefit. On acceptance of the offer B also becomes promisor for making payment of Rs. 30,000 to A who has come in a position of promisee.

Agreement creating rights and obligations between the parties become enforceable subject to fulfillment of some conditions. These conditions are mentioned in Section 10 of Indian Contract Act.

ESSENTIALS OF A VALID CONTRACT

An agreement to be enforced in the court has to satisfy certain conditions. On satisfying these, the agreement becomes a contract, and these conditions become essentials of a valid contract. According to Section 10 of Indian Contract Act, "all agreements are contracts if they are made by free consent of parties, competent to contract, for a lawful consideration and with a lawful object and are not expressly declared to be void." In brief essentials of a valid contract are as under:

(*i*) ***Agreement:*** To form a contract, there must be an agreement between the parties. Agreement is created by offer and acceptance. It is a result of mutual exchange of promises between the parties. One party makes a promise for doing or not doing anything to another and that another makes similar promise to first one.

Agreement is created by lawful offer and valid acceptance. It is only by an agreement a contractual relation is established between the parties.

(*ii*) ***Creation of legal relationship:*** Agreement made between parties must create legal relationship. Legal relationship consists of rights and obligations which can be claimed by the parties in the court of law. Sometimes, there may be an agreement between the parties, which creates relationship other than legal one such as social, personal and religious etc. Such, agreement is not enforceable, thus will not become a contract.

Examples: A invites his friend B to his birthday party. B accepts the offer. But he fails to turn up for the party. This agreement creates social and personal relationship between A and B. It cannot be enforced in the court. Thus A has no legal remedy against B. Therefore, the very base of a contract is a legal relationship.

A borrows sum of Rs. 500 from his friend B for three months. B gets legal right to sue upon A if he fails to return money. It is because this agreement creates legal relationship, which can be enforced in the court. Therefore, the parties make an agreement with an intention to create legal relationship.

BAL FOUR *vs* BAL FOUR (1919) 2 K.B 571: In this case a husband just makes a promise to pay his wife monthly allowance of £ 30 for her maintenance. Later on they separated and husband failed to pay stipulated amount to his wife. She filed suit for that allowance. But it was held by the court that such arrangements are not contracts or do not result in a contract. Because parties did not intend to create legal relationship. And finally the suit was dismissed.

(*iii*) ***Lawful consideration:*** Agreement is a mutual exchange of promises between parties. Each party making a promise gets something in return of his promise. It constitutes a consideration for his promise. An agreement to be enforced must be supported by lawful consideration. The consideration may be defined as a price for which, a promise of the promisor is bought. Generally, consideration will be given by the promisee But in some cases even if it is given by other party on behalf of promisee it is valid.

According to English Mercantile Law consideration may be defined as, "any benefit, interest or right which one party gets at the cost of loss, detriment or obligation on the part of other party."

Any act or promise or abstinence will constitute lawful consideration which is legal, moral and not against the public policy.

(*iv*) ***Contractual capacity:*** Parties making an agreement must have contractual capacity. Lack of contractual capacity would invalidate contract. Contractual capacity of the party means he or she must be legally competent for making a contract.

Section 11 of Indian Contract Act states that every person is competent to contract who is of age of majority, of sound mind and is not disqualified from contracting by any law to which he is subject.

In other words, the person to have contractual capacity must satisfy the following conditions:

(*a*) He must be of a major age and not a minor.

(*b*) He must be of a sound mind and not lunatic, idiot or drunkard.

(*c*) He must not have been declared disqualified by law from contracting such as insolvent, convict and alien enemy etc.

Agreement made by the parties not fulfilling the above conditions cannot be enforced in the court of law and will not become contract.

(*v*) ***Free consent of the parties:*** State of mind of the parties is involved in making offer and giving acceptance for it. As soon as offer is accepted it becomes a binding promise having a legal consequences. Thus both the parties entering into agreement must have their consent for it and that consent must be free. Consent may be defined as an identity of two or more minds on a particular subject matter. Two or more persons are said to have consent if they agree upon same thing in the same sense. And their consent is said to be free if it has not been induced by any one of the following factors: (*a*) Coercion (*b*) Undue influence (*c*) Misrepresentation (*d*) Fraud and (*e*) Mistake.

When consent is caused by any of the first four factors the contract becomes voidable and if it is induced by mistake it would be void and cannot be enforced in the court of law.

(*vi*) ***Lawful object of agreement:*** Agreement is made for some object or purpose such object is formed on the basis of promises made by the parties. These promises are made either for doing or not doing anything. The object of an agreement must be to do some act which is legal. Contrary to it, agreements made for doing something illegal, immoral or against public policy, cannot be enforced in the court of law.

Example: A and B make an agreement for smuggling out some goods from India to another country. This agreement cannot be enforced in the court. Similarly A in consideration of Rs. 1 lakh from B makes promise to kill C. This agreement has been made for doing some illegal act and therefore cannot be enforced.

(*vii*) ***Agreement, not declared expressly void:*** There are certain agreements which have been expressly declared void by the law. Thus an agreement made by parties should not fall in that category. If it is so it would also meet same fate and cannot be enforced in the court of law.

Briefly, agreement expressly declared void are agreements in restraint of marriage, trade, legal proceedings and wagering agreements etc. In spite of having all other features of regular agreement these cannot be enforced.

(*viii*) ***Certainty in the meaning of agreement:*** Agreement made by the parties must be certain or capable of being made certain in its meaning. It is because agreement would result in creating rights and obligations between the parties. These rights and obligations will be claimed in the court of law. Agreement with uncertain meaning will bring uncertainty in the rights and obligations created by it. And uncertain rights and obligations cannot be enforced in the court of law.

Example: A is a dealer of kerosene oil and coconut oil. B makes an agreement with him for buying 10 litres of oil. Meaning of this agreement is uncertain and therefore it cannot be enforced.

Example: A has agriculture land in Delhi. He makes an agreement with B for selling entire produce of wheat crop of next year @ Rs. 1000 p.q. Although on the face of it, meaning of agreement seems to be uncertain, but it can be made certain on the production of wheat crop next year.

(*ix*) ***Other legal formalities:*** Agreement to be enforced, needs to satisfy other conditions of being in writing, registered and duly stamped. Generally Indian Contract Act does not make any discrimination between written and oral agreement. Oral agreements are as good as written agreement. Reasons being that oral or verbal agreements creates similar rights and obligations between parties as being created by written agreements, and oral agreements can be enforced in the same manner as written agreements. But some agreements to be enforced in the court need to be made in writing and got to be registered with appropriate legal authority and must have adequate stamp duty.

Example: All insurance agreements, arbitration agreements, and those related to transfer of immovable properties, negotiable instruments like cheque, bill of exchange and promissory note, articles of association and memorandum of association must be made in writing and must be registered. Some of these must carry required stamp duty such as promissory notes, and agreements for transferring immovable properties etc.

To acquire status of a valid contract, the contract must possess these mentioned features. The contracts meeting these requirements are known as 'regular' or 'valid contracts'.

CLASSIFICATION OF CONTRACTS

Contracts made by the parties can be classified into different types on the following bases:

1. Formation of Contract.
2. Performance of Contract.
3. Extent of Validity of Contract.

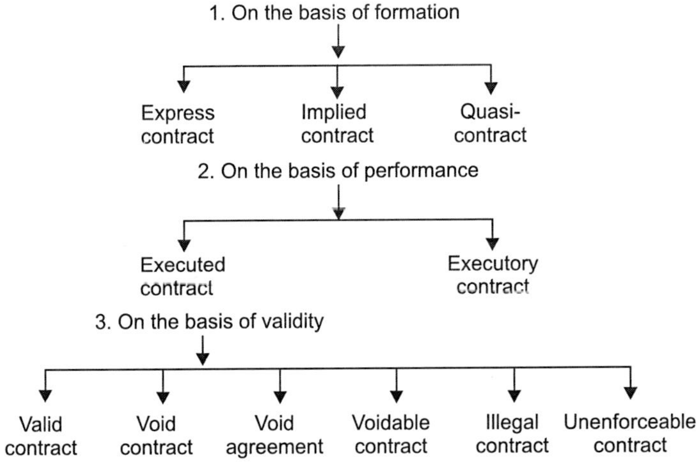

Fig. 1.1 Classification of Contracts

1. On the Basis of Formation

The contracts may be grouped into three groups as:

(*i*) ***Express contracts:*** Generally the contracts are made in this form. These contracts results from express agreements. Express agreement is formed by making offer and giving acceptance in the words spoken or in writing. According to Section 9 of Indian Contract Act, insofar as the proposal and acceptance of any promise is made in words, the promise is said to be express. An express promise leads to the formation of express contract.

Example: A, who is in front of B, makes an offer to sell out his bike to B by the words of mouth. B gives his acceptance verbally. Express contract is formed between them. Similarly B sends offer for selling out his bike to B by post and B gives his acceptance by sending letter by post. It would also result in express contract.

(*ii*) ***Implied contracts:*** Implied contracts are formed on the basis of implied promises on the part of parties. Implied promises are those which are not made by the parties in writing or by the words of mouth. Rather these promises are inferred from the conduct of the parties or from the circumstances. In an implied contract, one of the party conducts himself or does some act which is being accepted by other party either by his conduct or course of his dealing or circumstance. Thus in implied contract, making of an offer and giving acceptance to it is manifested by the act on the part of party.

Example: City transport company has plied various buses on the different routes. A, a commuter, is standing at a particular bus stop on a particular route. Bus bearing specific number meant for that route comes to halt at that stop. A gets into the bus and travels on that route for his destination. He is bound to pay freight charged by the company for that distance. Contract between city transport company and A is implied in nature.

(*iii*) ***Quasi-contracts:*** Quasi-contracts are based on the principle of justice and equity. In spite of not having any contract between parties, the rights and obligations are created. These are resembling to rights and obligations as created by a formal contract. In such contracts, obligations between parties are created by operation of law rather than offer and acceptance. The legal base of quasi-contract is that a person shall not be allowed to enrich himself unjustly at the cost or expense of other. If he does so he comes under legal obligation to pay cost or expense without any formal contract.

Example: A has lost his dog. B finds it and takes it into custody. He spends on the maintenance of the dog. On tracing real owner, B can claim reimbursement of expenses incurred by him without any contract. Similarly

A is under legal obligation to take reasonable care of the dog. Such rights and obligations which are quite resembling with that of formal contract are considered as quasi-contracts.

Sections 68 to 72 of Indian Contract Act deal with the cases of quasi-contract.

2. On the Basis of Performance

The contracts may be grouped up as:

(i) ***Executed contract*:** Contract consists of certain legal obligations. On the complete discharge of these obligations, the contract is said to have been executed. In other words, executed contract is one that has been performed. It means, both the parties have fulfilled their respective promises, which they have made in contract. Nothing more remains to be done by either of the parties.

Example: A makes an agreement for buying one hundred cotton bales from B @ Rs. 5,000 per bale. B delivers these cotton bales to A and in return of it A makes payment to B. This contract becomes executed one.

(ii) ***Executory contract*:** Executory Contract is one that has not been yet performed. In other words, parties having made promises for doing or not doing anything have not fulfilled their respective promises.

Till such promises are fulfilled the contract remains to be executory one. Not only this, but also if one party has performed his promises and an other party has yet to perform his promise, the contract remain executory in spite of partial performance.

Example: A makes an agreement for buying a car from car dealer. A has made payment. The car has been delivered to him. But ownership of that car is yet to be transferred to him. The contract remains executory.

3. On the Basis of Extent of Validity

The contracts may be classified as:

(i) ***Valid contract*:** Contract is said to be valid if it satisfies all conditions required for its enforceability. In other words, valid contract is enforceable in the court of law. Lack of any element as prescribed by Section 10 would change legal status of a contract and it may not be permitted to be enforced.

(ii) ***Void contract*:** A contract which ceases to be enforceable by law becomes void. No party has right to claim it in the court of law. The contract may become void either from beginning when it was made or may later on discovered to be void.

Example: A was elected as a managing direct or of X Company by its board of directors. After six months it is found that one of the directors who have elected A has not purchased qualification share. He was not a bona fide director. Thus service contract made with A is discovered to be void.

Sometimes validity of a contract may adversely be affected by supervening impossibility or by the element of free consent.

Example: A makes an agreement with B for buying 500 quintal of wheat @ Rs. 1000 p.q. But before the date of performance the Central Government enacts new legislation debarring an individual to buy more than 10 quintal at a time. The contract becomes void on account of supervening impossibility which arises after the formation of a contract.

Example: A, by causing consent of B by coercion makes agreement with him for buying his bike for Rs. 50,000. Later on, B who is an aggrieved party declares it as void this contract becomes void due to lack of free consent.

(*iii*) ***Void agreement*:** Agreement which is not enforceable by law is void agreement. In other words, if an agreement lacks any one of essentials of a valid contract 'except free consent' it becomes void. Such agreement does not create any legal right and obligation between the parties and cannot be enforced in the court either by the parties. Void agreements do not have any legal consequence and it is null and void in the eyes of law. Not only this, but also such agreements remain void from the time at which these are made. For example, agreement with a minor, agreement without lawful consideration, agreement having uncertain meaning or declared as void by law etc.

Major points of distinction between void agreement and void contract are that void agreement is void from the beginning, but void contract becomes void later on. Similarly, void agreement does not create any legal right and obligation between the parties while void contract creates such rights and obligations.

(*iv*) ***Voidable contract*:** According to Section 2 (*i*), an agreement which is enforceable by law at the option of one or more parties, but not at the option of other or others is a voidable contract. In a voidable contract consent of one of the parties has been caused by other party either by using coercion, or undue influence or misrepresentation or fraud. Such contract lacks element of free consent. Voidable contract has the following features:

(*a*) Consent of one of the parties is not free. It has been caused by using coercion, undue influence, misrepresentation or fraud.

(*b*) It is voidable only at the option of aggrieved party whose consent had not been free but not at the option of other party.

(*c*) Voidable contract remains valid till so far, it has not been declared void by an aggrieved party.

(*d*) Aggrieved party can avoid it, can enforce it and if other party compels him to perform he can seek protection on the ground of his not having free consent.

Example: A, by causing consent of B at gunpoint makes an agreement with him for buying his bike for Rs. 50,000. This contract is voidable at the option of B only (whose consent had not been free). He can declare it as void or can enforce it against A or if A compels him, he can seek protection.

(*v*) ***Illegal contract*:** Every contract carries some object or purpose. It is formed on the basis of promises made by the parties in that contract. The contract is said to be illegal if its object is illegal. Illegal agreement has the following features:

(*a*) The contract becomes illegal if it is made for doing something illegal, immoral or against public policy. Such contracts defeat provisions of law.

Example: A, in consideration of Rs. one lakh from B agrees to kill C. Contract is illegal.

(*b*) Illegal contracts are necessarily void contract not creating any legal rights and obligations between the parties.

(*c*) Illegal contracts cannot be enforced either by the parties.

(*d*) Any transaction or agreement which is based on illegal contract would also be void having no legal substance.

(*vi*) ***Unenforceable contract*:** Sometimes, a contract may be good in the eyes of law. But due to some technical reasons it may not be allowed to be enforced in the court. Technical reasons affecting validity of contract may be that contract is not made in writing or is not registered or has no adequate stamp duty on it. Such contracts are good in substance. But due to non-fulfillment of prescribed legal formalities these cannot be claimed in the court. As soon as the technical reason is looked into and rectified such contracts may be allowed to be enforced.

Table 1.1 Distinction between void agreement and voidable contract

Base	Void agreement	Voidable contract
Definition	Agreement not enforceable by law is void agreement.	Agreement which is enforceable by law at the option of one party only is voidable contract.
Cause	Agreement becomes void if it lacks any one of the essentials of a valid contract.	Agreement becomes voidable if the consent of one of the party had not been free (Except mistake).
Time	Void agreement is void when it is made.	Voidable contract becomes void only when it is declared to be so by an aggrieved party.
Right	In void agreement if the party has suffered any loss he cannot claim any compensation.	If aggrieved party in voidable contract caused by fraud suffers any loss he has a right to claim compensation from other party.

Table 1.2 Distinction between void and illegal agreements

Base	Void agreement	Illegal agreement
Cause	Agreement becomes void if it lacks any one of the essentials of a valid contract. Such as agreement with minor, agreement without consideration and agreements, and having uncertain meaning.	Agreement becomes illegal if the very object or purpose of it is to do some act which is illegal or immoral or against public policy.
Scope	Void agreement is wider in scope, because it also includes illegal agreement.	Illegal agreement are used in a narrow sense and less wider, because agreement becomes illegal when its object is illegal.
Time	Though void agreements are void from the beginning, sometimes, valid contract may become void or may be discovered to be void later on.	Illegal agreements are void from the beginning.
Punish-ment	Void agreements do not attract any punishment for the parties.	In an illegal agreement if the party has done act which is illegal, immoral or against public policy, he may be prosecuted or punished.
Effect	Void agreement has no effect on other transaction or agreement which is based on it.	In case of illegal agreement, any transaction or agreement based on illegal agreement will also be affected and will be void.

Example: A makes out promissory note in favour of B for Rs. 1000. It has stamp duty of Rs. 5 only. While as as per requirement of law it must have stamp duty of Rs. 10. Such promissory note is invalid. But if stamp duty is raised up to required level it may be allowed to be enforced.

REVIEW QUESTIONS

1. Define the term contract. Explain essentials of a valid contract.
2. 'All contracts are agreement, but all agreements are not contract.' Comment.
3. Distinguish between agreement and contract.
4. 'All agreements enforceable by law are contract.' Comment.
5. 'Law of Contract is not a whole law of agreement nor the whole law of obligations.' Comment.
6. Distinguish between:
   (*a*) Void agreement and voidable contract
   (*b*) Void agreement and illegal agreement
   (*c*) Express and Implied contracts
   (*d*) Agreement and contract
7. Write notes on:
   (*a*) Quasi-contract
   (*b*) Void agreement
   (*c*) Illegal agreement
   (*d*) Voidable contract

PRACTICAL PROBLEMS

1. A has applied for a licence of liquor. In the meanwhile he starts selling liquor. What is the legal position of A in the eyes of law?
2. A, borrows sum of Rs. 1000 from his friend B for three months. At the expiration of that period A refused to repay. Can B sue upon his friend B for the recovery? (Hint: Yes).

3. A makes a promise to his friend B for giving him a ring on his coming birthday. A fails to do so. Can B sue upon him? (Hint: No).
4. A was appointed managing director in a X Coy by board of directors of the company. After three months it was discovered that one of the directors of the coy who was member of selection committee has not purchased qualification shares. Can A claim benefits mentioned in a service contract which is void? (Hint: Yes).
5. A in consideration of Re one lakh from B agrees to kill C. B, borrows this amount from D. Who knowingly lends money to B. Can D recover this amount from B. (Hint: No, agreement based on illegal agreement is also void.)

2

Offer and Acceptance

LEARNING OBJECTIVES

- Get a clarity about the basic concepts of offer and acceptance.
- Examine legality of a valid offer.
- Remember legal provisions regarding communication of offer, acceptance and revocation.
- Understand the factors which make acceptance valid and effective.
- Analyse both offer and acceptance separately and jointly.

INTRODUCTION

Offer and acceptance are the two basic elements which comprise an agreement. One person makes an offer to another person, when the other person accepts that offer, it becomes a binding promise or an agreement. The person making the offer is a promisor and the other person becomes the promisee. The point to be noted here is that an offer gets legal sanction and acquires legal consequences when it is accepted. It means that every agreement is an accepted offer or proposal.

OFFER

Offer is one of the essential elements of a contract. Making an offer is giving a proposal for doing or not doing a thing. The term proposal has been defined under Section 2(a) "As when one person signifies to another his willingness to do or to abstain, from doing anything with a view to obtaining, the assent of that other to such act or abstinence, he said to make a proposal."

Elements of Offer

The offer has following elements:

(*a*) In an offer one party expresses his willingness for doing or not doing a thing.

(*b*) The person giving an offer expresses his willingness to another person whom he wants to give his offer.

(*c*) Offer is made with a view to know assent of the other person to the proposed act or abstinence (will he accept offer?).

According to the definition of proposal given in the Act it is clear that the mere expression of willingness for doing anything will not constitute offer.

Example: A desires to sell his bike to B for Rs. 30,000. It does not constitute an offer, because A has merely expressed his desire. On the other hand if A asks B would you buy my motorbike for Rs. 30,000, this makes an offer, because in this expression A wants to get B's consent for the proposed act.

Thus the expression of willingness for doing or not doing anything will constitute offer if it is followed by the intention of getting the assent of the other party to such act or abstinence.

An offer may be made for 'doing' (positive act) or 'not doing' anything (negative act).

Example: A cricket star makes a promise to X Sports goods company not to use bats manufactured by the coy other than X Sports goods coy. The offer is made for not doing something.

The person who makes an offer is known as 'offeror' and the other person to whom to the offer is made is known as 'offeree'.

Classification of Offer

(*i*) ***Specific offer:*** Sometimes an offer is made to a particular person, party or organisation, such offer is known as 'specific offer'. The specific offer can be accepted only by that particular person or organisation.

Example: A makes an offer for selling out his car to B for Rs. 1,00,000. Similarly, A offers to supply 50 cotton bales to B @ Rs. 500 per bale to X & Coy. These are specific offers.

(*ii*) ***General offer:*** It is an offer which is made to a group of people or public at large. Such offer can be accepted by any member of that group or public.

Example: A is student of B.Com (H) has lost his bag in a class. He offers to pay Rs. 500 to whosoever gets it and gives it back to him. This is general offer, any student of that class may accept it.

(*iii*) ***Cross offer:*** Two parties exchange identical offers with each other. They are ignorant about the offer made by each other. Such offer is known as 'cross offer'. Such offers do not amount to valid acceptance for each other and therefore may not result in a binding contract with each other.

Example: A makes an offer to sell out his bike to B for Rs. 20,000. B is ignorant of this offer and makes a similar offer for buying A's bike for Rs. 20,000. These two offers are known as 'cross offers' and none of these will Constitute as an acceptance.

(*iv*) ***Counter offer:*** Incomplete and conditional acceptance of an offer is known as 'counter offer'. In other words, the acceptor, instead of accepting the offer as such along with all its terms and conditions deviates from it. Such acceptance becomes a counter offer.

Example: A makes offer to B for selling 100 quintals of wheat @ Rs. 1,000 per quintal on cash down basis. B gives his acceptance stating that he will make 50 per cent payment on cash down and remaining by instalment or B gives his acceptance for buying 80 quintals only. In both these cases, acceptance given by B is known as a counter offer.

Essentials of Valid Offer

The offer to be legally valid must be subject to certain rules which are prescribed in Indian Contract Act.These rules are:

(*i*) ***Offer must create a legal relationship and consequence*****:** The whole concept of contract is based on legal relationships or obligations of legal consequences. Thus the formation of a contract which starts with an offer, its acceptance followed by the legal relationship and its consequences means the party making an offer must have a clear intention to establish the legal relationship with other party. He should ensure that the offer made by him gives a rise to legal foundation. Lack of such intention on his part may invalidate the offer. Similarly if the party is engaged in creating a social relationship through an offer and its acceptance, then such offer will have no legal value in the eyes of law.

Example: A promises to pay a particular amount per month to his mother on completion of his graduation and subsequently getting a suitable job. On his failure to do so his mother will not get legal right to sue upon him for the recovery of that payment. It is because mother and son were engaged in creating social and personal relations. Thus the promise on the part of the son will have no legal consequence.

(*ii*) ***Offer may be express or implied:*** The offer may be made either by the words of mouth or in writing. Such an offer is known as an 'express offer'. On the other hand if the offer is inferred, or indirectly understood either from the conduct of parties or from the circumstances. Such offer is known as 'implied offer' (implied by conduct of parties or circumstances).

Example: Delhi Transport Corporation has plied many buses in different routes of Delhi. A who is a commuter, is standing in a particular bus stop. When a bus comes and A gets into it. He is bound to pay the prescribed freight for specified destination travelled by him. In this case Delhi Transport Corporation has made an implied offer, which is being accepted by A and it results in an agreement between them.

(*iii*) ***Offer may be specific or general:*** The offer being made to a particular individual or organisation is known as 'specific offer'. It can be accepted only by that individual or organisation. On the other, if an offer has been made to a group of people or public at large, such offer is known as 'general offer'. General offer can be accepted by any member of that group or public.

(*iv*) ***Offer must be communicated:*** An offer is made with a view to create, legal relationship so it must be communicated to the person to whom it is made. In other words, it must be brought to the notice of that person, so that he may do what is necessary at his end to accept it. Without communication an offer is incomplete so it cannot be accepted.

LALMAN SHUKLA *vs* **GAURI DUTT (1913 all L.J.389).** In this case G sent S, his servant, in search of his missing nephew. Meanwhile G made an announcement that anyone who traces his missing nephew and brings him back home will be suitably rewarded. S found the boy and brought him back. He claimed for reward. It was held that he cannot claim a reward because he reached out and brought that boy home in ignorance of that reward (there is no communication of offer to S, he cannot accept it and it would not result in agreement between S and G).

(*v*) ***Offer must be distinguished from a mere expression of intention or invitation:*** Sometimes, one party merely shows his intention for making an offer or invites other party for making it. Such intention or invitation for making an offer will not be considered as a valid offer, such as price list, advertisement for vacant position, goods price marked in showroom, customer enquiries and quotations etc., cannot be stated as offers.

Examples: A bookseller has published a pricelist for the various books being sold by him. But legally he is not bound to supply any particular book at the price mentioned against it. It is because the price list is a mere declaration of his intention and not an offer.

In a showroom of readymade garments a particular shirt is displayed which is price marked, again, in this case the showroom owner has not given any offer for selling that shirt at the price marked on it because he is not making an offer, rather desires to sell that shirt for the marked price.

HARVEY *vs* FACIE (1893 A.C 552). This case explains a distinction between an offer and an invitation to offer. In this case, the plaintiffs telegraphed to the defendant writing that will you sell us bumper hall pen. Telegraph lowest cost price, the defendant replied by telegram, lowest cost price for bumper hall pen $ 900. The plaintiff immediately sent this last telegram stating, we agree to buy bumper hall pen for $ 900 asked by you. The defendant however refused to sell pen at that price. The plaintiff contended that by quoting their minimum price in response to the enquiry, the defendant has made an offer to sell at that price, but the judicial committee turned down the suggestions. Their lordship pointed out that in their first telegram the plaintiff has asked two questions, as to the willingness to sell and second as to lowest price. They reserved their answer as no willingness to sell, thus they had made no offer, the lordship were of the opinion that the mere statement of lowest price at which vendor should sell contained no implied contract to sell at that price to the person making the enquiry.

Following this case, it was held in another case where the owner of property says that he will not accept less that Rs. 6,000 as price. So he does not make an offer but mearly invites to make an offer **MAC PHERSO *vs* APPANNA (1951, A.S.C 184).**

(*vi*) ***Offer may be conditional:*** While making an offer the offeror may impose conditions for the acceptor, such conditional offer is valid subject to the following conditions:

(*a*) Offeror cannot impose any such condition the non-fulfillment of which would lead to acceptance of that offer.

Example: A offers to sell out his bike to B stating that if B does not reply with in a week, he will assume that he has accepted the offer. This is not a valid offer, because failure on the part of B to reply would result in an acceptance.

(*b*) The terms and conditions imposed by the offeror must be mentioned in the offer in such a way that a person of a reasonable prudence may find indication for those conditions and those conditions must be readable with reasonable eyesight.

Example: A has delivered some woollen clothes for dry cleaning purpose to B and B issued receipt to A for it. At the back of receipt some terms and conditions are laid down. In the absence of the indication B is not supposed to go through them and they are not binding on him. But if at the bottom of receipt it is mentioned that for conditions see reverse side, B is bound by these conditions even if these are mentioned in the language other than known to him, he is expected to take the help of the person who knows that language. Finally if those conditions are not readable because of printing defect B is not bound by those conditions.

REICHADSON *vs* ROWN TREE (1894, A.C 217). In this case, the passenger booked his passage on a ship and received a ticket, it was folded in such a way that no writing was visible until it was opened. It was held that the passenger is not bound by conditions which limited ship-owners liabilities to $ 50 in case of any loss.

Standing Offer or Tender

Standing offer is an offer which is continuous in nature. It is made for supplying certain goods on a particular price up to a specified period of time. It is also known as a tender, In this offer it is not necessary to mention the quantity of the goods to be supplied over that period of time. Such type of offer is suitable for those who need regular supply of specified goods or services for a particular period of time.

On the acceptance of a standing offer or tender, order may be placed as and when the goods and services are required. In this regard it is to be noted that each time distinct contract is made for the goods and services, by giving notice of revocation to the offeror standing offer may be put to an end for the remaining period.

GANILATIF *vs* MANILAL (1916, 18 BOMBAY, L.R 227). In this case A agrees to supply coal to B in any quantity up to 1,000 tonnes @ 150 per tonne as and when required by B over a period of 12 months. This is a continuous offer or tender. Each order placed by B will amount to the acceptance of offer. A can revoke this offer regarding future supply at anytime by giving notice of revocation to B.

It is also to be noted that in a standing offer the offeree has a right not to place any order even after having approved this tender, it is because a tender becomes an offer only when it is approved. The agreement is formed, when an order is placed to the party accepting the tender according to the terms of a tender.

ACCEPTANCE

Offer has no legal consequence or value unless it is accepted. It is only by acceptance that the offeror and the acceptor come into a legal relationship and formation of an agreement becomes complete on the acceptance of offer.

Meaning

According to Section 2(*b*) "A proposal or offer is said to have been accepted when the person to whom the proposal is made, signifies his assent to the proposal. In other words, when a person to whom the offer is made gives his assent for the act or abstinence accordingly, it amounts to an acceptance."

Sir **WILLIAM ANSON** has rightly defined relationship between offer and acceptance by clarifying their legal consequences. According to him, acceptance is to offer what is a lighted match is to a train of gun powder.

According to this statement it is clear that an offer has little or no legal consequences. Once it is accepted it creates binding legal relationship between an offeror and an acceptor. The legal consequence of a valid acceptance cannot be undone. Though an offer or proposal lays down the foundation of a contract, it becomes complete only through a valid acceptance. On the other hand, if the offer has lapsed or revoked before acceptance it has no legal consequences. Thus an offer is considered a lighted match and its acceptance is considered a train of gun powder. The gun powder will explode when it gets lighted, so offer without an acceptance will not form an agreement. Similarly a train of gun powder will not explode without a lighted match, and once an offer is accepted it becomes a promise which cannot be withdrawn or cancelled.

Rules Regarding a Valid Acceptance

An acceptance to be legally valid and effective must be subject to the following rules:

(*i*) ***Acceptance must be absolute and unconditional:*** Offer may be made for a specific quantity, volume and price. It may also contain terms and conditions. It is necessary for the acceptor that he must give his acceptance for the entire quantity and volume offered. Similarly he must accept each and every term and condition, of the offer. If he deviates on minor condition the acceptance will not be legally effective. In this regard the general rule is that the offer must be accepted and the acceptor must not impose any condition for the offeror. Partial and conditional or qualified acceptance will not be valid. Thus an offer must be accepted without any variations, conditions and reservations.

Example: Ram offers to supply 100 tonnes of wheat to Shyam @ Rs. 1,000 per tonne Shyam gives his acceptance for buying only 50 tonnes of wheat at that rate. Acceptance is partial therefore it is not valid. Similarly if Shyam gives his acceptance for entire quantity but puts condition that the payment will be made after a month. This acceptance is conditional and therefore is not valid.

ROUTLEDGE *vs* GRANT (1828, 4 BING 653). In this case, a party offered to purchase another's house with vacant possession from 25 July. The vendor of the house sent his acceptance suggesting possession from 1 August. It was held that the acceptance is not valid; therefore it will not conclude to valid contract.

(ii) Acceptance must be given in a prescribed mode or manner: While making an offer, the offeror may prescribe a particular mode or manner of acceptance and the acceptor must abide by it. If the acceptor does not follow that particular mode for sending his acceptance, the offeror may further insist on the acceptor to abide by it. But if still it is not followed, the offeror can reject that acceptance.

On the other, if no mode is prescribed, by the offeror then the acceptor can follow the usual mode of acceptance.

Example: A offers to sell out his car to B and asks him to send his acceptance through a registered post. B accepts the offer and sends his acceptance through e-mail. A may further insists upon B to use the prescribed manner for sending his acceptance. On this if B fails to comply with prescribed manner A can reject the acceptance.

Section 7(2) of the Indian Contract Act states that acceptance must be expressed in some usual manner, unless the proposer prescribes the manner in which it is to be accepted.

Example: A sends an offer by ordinary post to buy a television set from B. On acceptance B may also send his acceptance by ordinary post because no manner or mode was prescribed.

SURINDERNATH *vs* KEDARNATH (1936 A.I.R, Cal 87). In this case, an offer was made to a person to sell a house at Rs. 7,000 and it was specifically mentioned that in case the offer is accepted he should write to X at his address. The intended purchaser sent his representative to X, in place of writing him for accepting the offer, here this acceptance was not given in the prescribed manner, so it was held that the acceptance is not valid.

(iii) Time of acceptance: To make it valid acceptance, it must be given within stipulated period of time if any. When no time is specified, acceptance must be given within reasonable period of time.

Reasonable time in each case is a question of fact which varies from person to person depending on the intention of party, nature of transaction and circumstances. In case acceptance is not sent within the prescribed time or reasonable time (which is applicable), the offer is deemed to lapse.

> ***Example:*** A is a student of B.Com. He placed an order in the last week of June with X bookseller of Meerut for the supply of books on Business Law, Accounting and Economics. Time has not been stipulated and bookseller is supposed to supply these books within reasonable period of time. According to circumstances, the intention of the party and nature of transaction, he must supply these books, latest by middle of July. It is because by this time academic session starts and the student may be in need of these books.
>
> **RAMSGATE VICTORIA HOTEL COY. *vs* MONTEFIORE 1866 L.I.R EX 109).** In this case, a person applied for certain shares in a joint stock company in the month of June. But the company made an allotment in the month of November. That person refused to accept the shares, so allotted on the plea of delayed acceptance. He was allowed to withdraw the offer.

(iv) Acceptance must be communicated: As the offer needs to be communicated, so does the acceptance. Acceptance to be legally effective must be communicated and brought to the knowledge of the offeror. Even if the acceptor has accepted the offer but if it is not communicated properly it would not result into an agreement.

In this regard it is however to be noted that mental acceptance is no acceptance. If the offeree mentally accepts the offer or decides to accept it but does not communicate it, it will not be considered as legally effective acceptance.

> **BROGDEN *vs* METROPOLITAN RAILWAY COY (1877, A.C 66).** In this case, the manager of railway coy received a draft agreement relating to the supply of coal. He wrote the word approved on it and put it is his drawer. It was held that there was no contract because the acceptance has not been communicated.
>
> Thus mere mental expression to an offer, not backed by spoken or written words or conduct of the party will not constitute acceptance.

POWELL *vs* LEE (1908, 99 LT 284). In this case, P applied for the post of principle of a school. Management of the school decided to appoint him but the announcement was withheld. One of the member of management informed P about the decision. But later on the management changed decision. P filed suit for breach of contract, but the suit was rejected on the ground that the management of the school has never communicated their decision to P, thus there is no contract.

(*v*) ***Acceptance may be express or implied:*** The acceptor may give his assent for the proposed act by the words of mouth or in writing. Such acceptance is known as 'express acceptance'. In addition if the acceptance is directly understood either from conduct of the party or from circumstance, it is known as 'implied acceptance'. In other words, when party does some act as being intended by the offeror, it amounts to implied acceptance.

CARLILL *vs* CARBOLIC SMOKE BALL COY. In this case carbolic smoke ball coy had been producing smoke balls. The company made an announcement whosoever buys these balls from the market and uses in the given direction, even then if he or she gets influenza the coy will suitably reward him. Lady Carlill got these balls purchased and used them in the given direction. But unfortunately got influenza, she claimed reward. It was held that there is contract between the coy and Carlill through implied acceptance on the part of Carlill and therefore she can claim reward.

(*vi*) ***Acceptance must be made before offer is revoked:*** Acceptance implies mental readiness of the person for proposed act or abstinence. Therefore, it must be given before the offer lapses or is withdrawn or cancelled. Once the offer is dead due to any reason it is dead forever, and to revive it, such offer is to be made afresh.

Example: A made an offer to B for selling 100 cotton bales @ Rs. 2,000 per bale and prescribes week time for acceptance. B fails to accept it on time, the offer is lapsed. Afterwards B gives his acceptance, such acceptance is not legally valid.

(*vii*) ***Acceptance is not implied from silence of the party:*** Acceptance of offer is not implied from silence. The offeror cannot impose condition on offeree that his silence will amount to acceptance. It is very clear that it should be given either by spoken words or in writing or by performing any act which amounts to implied acceptance. Thus silence on the part of offeree regarding the offer in no case may amount to acceptance. But in practice, this rule is subject to following exceptions:

(*a*) When offeror has been dealing with offeree in the past and the offeree has given reasons to understand that his silence amounts to acceptance.

(*b*) Communication of acceptance has been dispensed with by the offeror as per conditions of offer. So silence on the part of offeree may amount to acceptance.

(*c*) Where performance or fulfillment of all terms and conditions of the offer without communication of acceptance is regarded sufficient acceptance.

(*d*) Where the offeree gets reasonable opportunities to reject the offer. But takes the benefits of that offer it will also amount to acceptance of offer. The acceptor need not do anything for it.

Examples: A subscribes particular magazine for a period of one year. At the end of the year contract automatically comes to an end. But the company continued to supply that magazine to A. And he gets benefit of this offer and continues to accept it, without giving any intimation to the coy. A, would be liable for paying subscription.

Ram offers to sell out his house in Delhi to Shyam, if he comes to Delhi, gets house repaired and starts living in that house. Shyam does all these, without communicating acceptance to Ram. There is a contract between Ram and Shyam.

COMMUNICATION OF OFFER AND ACCEPTANCE

It is very necessary to know that whether the offer and acceptance has been properly communicated because without communication of offer it cannot be accepted. Similarly acceptance to be legally valid and effective must have been communicated properly. Communication of offer and acceptance can be made either by spoken words or in writing or it may be inferred from the conduct of the party. According to Section 3 of Indian Contract Act, that the communication of proposal, the acceptance of proposal, and the revocation of proposal and acceptance respectively are deemed to be made by any act or omission of the party proposing, accepting or revoking by which he intends to communicate such proposal, acceptance or revocation or which has the effect of communicating it.

Communication of Offer

Offer is communicated to the party to whom it is made. Unless it is communicated it cannot be accepted. According to Section 4 of the Act, communication of offer is complete when its comes to the knowledge of the person to whom it is made. It means even if the letter of offer has reached to offeree, unless he goes through it the communication will not be complete.

Example: Ramesh makes an offer to his friend Mahesh in Bombay for selling his car to him. The offer is sent though registered post and reaches Mahesh. But Mahesh did not open it and go through. Its communication is not complete.

Communication of Acceptance

According to Section 4 of the Act, communication of acceptance is complete:

(*a*) As against the proposer, when the letter of acceptance is put in a course of transmission, so as to be out of the power of the acceptor.

(*b*) As against the acceptor, when it comes to the knowledge of proposer.

Example: A applied for 100 equity shares of X and Coy. Face value of each share was Rs. 100 per share. The Coy demanded Rs. 10 per share on application and Rs. 20 per share on allotment. Remaining balance would be obtained through various calls. In the meeting of broad of directors 100 shares were alloted to A and a letter of allotment was sent to him for demanding allotment money. The letter was duly stamped and correctly addressed. In the meanwhile the Coy went into liquidation and official receiver found that a sum of Rs. 9,000 was due on the account of A to whom 100 shares were allotted. He sent a notice for the recovery of the amount along with interest. A pleaded that he never received letter of allotment. But it was held against A, who is a proposer that communication of acceptance is complete and he is bound to pay. But he cannot claim rights of a shareholder because letter of allotment had not been reached to him.

Thus communication of acceptance against the coy in not completed therefore he cannot be treated as a shareholder.

ADAM *vs* LIND SELL, (1818 1.B & Alal 68). In this case, A proposes to sell a house to B at a certain price thorough a letter which was posted on 10 March. It reaches to B on 12 March. Communication of offer was complete when B received a letter on 12 March. B sent his acceptance through post on 13 March which was received by A on 15 March. Communication of acceptance as against A is complete on 13 March and as against B on 15 March.

Revocation of Offer

Offer is made with an intention of seeking the assent of offeree for proposed act or abstinence. But before it is accepted by offeree, the offeror can withdraw it, or can cancel it or the offer may be lapsed on account of other reasons, it is known as 'revocation of offer'.

Briefly revocation of offer means withdrawal, cancellation or lapse of offer. According to Section 6 of this Act offer can be revoked under the following circumstances:

(*a*) ***By notice:*** Offer can be revoked by giving a notice to this effect. Such notice will be given by the offeror. The offeror after having made offer, can withdraw or cancel it. But such notice of revocation must be given before the communication of acceptance is put in the course of transmission. After that point of time notice of revocation will have no legal value.

(*b*) ***By lapse of time:*** The offer must be accepted well in time as prescribed by the offeror. And if no time in prescribed, acceptance must be made within reasonable period of the time. On the expiration of stipulated or reasonable period of time, the offer is lapsed.

(*c*) ***Death or insanity of offeror:*** In case of death or insanity of offeror, the offer is revoked, provided information regarding death or insanity reaches to offeree before he puts letter of acceptance in a course of transmission. If it reaches after words, there is a binding agreement which may be enforced, against the legal representative of deceased offeror.

(*d*) ***Non-fulfillment of prerequisite conditions:*** When the offeror has put some conditions, which are prerequisite to acceptance. Such conditions must be fulfilled before accepting offer. Non-fulfillment of such conditions will lead to revocation of an offer.

Example: A offers to sell his house to B who stays in Bombay, provided B comes Delhi and starts living in that house. To accept the offer B has to come Delhi and start living in that house. If he does not do so the offer given to him will automatically be revoked.

(*e*) ***By counter offer:*** To form an agreement the acceptor must give absolute and unconditional acceptance. Contrary to it, partial or conditional acceptance becomes counter offer and leads to revocation of offer.

Example: Ram offers to sell his bike to Shyam for Rs. 20,000 on the basis of cash down payment, Shyam accepts the offer on a condition that he will make payment in two instalments, such acceptance is a counter offer and initial offer is revoked.

(*f*) ***Non-compliance of prescribed mode or manner:*** Sometimes the offeror may prescribe particular mode or manner in which offeree must send his acceptance. Non-compliance of prescribed mode may lead to rejection of acceptance provided the offeror once insists upon offeree to use prescribed mode only.

Communication of Revocation

According to Section 4 of this Act, communication of revocation is complete:

(*a*) As against the person who makes it when he puts letter of revocation in a course of transmission for sending it to another party.

(*b*) As against the person to whom it is made, when the letter of revocation reaches and comes to the knowledge of that person.

Example: A, makes an offer to B for selling 200 cotton bales @ Rs. 2,000 per bale on 1March. It reaches B on 2 March, who accepts it and sends his acceptance on 5 March which reaches A on 6 March. A revokes his offer on 4 March, communication of revocation is complete against A on 4 March and against B it will be complete when it reaches B.

REVIEW QUESTIONS

1. What do you mean by the term 'offer'? Explain the rules regarding a lawful offer?
2. 'Binding relationship between two parties is the result of a valid offer and acceptance.' Comment.
3. Define the term 'acceptance'. Explain requirements of a valid acceptance.
4. What is revocation of offer? Explain those circumstances under which offer can be revoked.
5. Explain rules regarding communication of an offer and communication of acceptance. Give suitable examples.
6. Comment on the following:

   (*a*) An offer is quite different from a mere expression of intention and an invitation to offer.

   (*b*) Acceptance is to an offer, what a lighted match is to train of gun powder.

   (*c*) There cannot be a contract to make contract.

   (*d*) Mere mental acceptance is no acceptance.

   (*e*) An offer cannot be accepted, without communication and without communication of acceptance, there cannot be an agreement.
7. 'Acceptance cannot implied from silence.' Explain this rule and discuss the various exceptions to this rule with suitable example.

8. Write notes on:
   (*a*) Communication of acceptance.
   (*b*) Standing offer.
   (*c*) Counter offer.
   (*d*) Revocation of offer.

PRACTICAL PROBLEMS

1. A desires to sell his horse to B for Rs. 5,000. B accepts the proposal of A is this agreement, (no, mere expression of desire made by A is not valid offer.)
2. Ram makes an offer to Shyam for selling 200 tonnes of wheat @ Rs. 1,000 p.t. Shyam accepts the offer, prepare a letter of acceptance and forgets to post it, does it constitute agreement, if not so why? (Hint: Communication of acceptance.)
3. A offer to sell out to his house to B who is staying in Bombay for Rs. 5 lakh provided B comes to Delhi, repairs the house and starts living in it. B accepts to buy house from Bombay itself. Is acceptance valid? (Hint: No).
4. Ramesh visits showroom of Maruti car in Delhi, he finds a particular car which is price marked and is displayed in showroom. He asked showroom owner to sell that car for the price mentioned on it. Can Ramesh compel showroom owner to sell that car for that price? (Hint: It is not offer, but intention to make an offer).
5. A has agricultural farm in Delhi. He offers to sell out 50 tonnes of wheat to B at the price of Rs. 1,500 per time on cash down basis. B accepts the offer and states that payment will be made through instalments. Is acceptance valid? (Hint: No condition has been put by B).
6. Mohan applied for 200 shares in particular company. The company allotted shares after more than six months from submitting application by Mohan. Mohan refused to accept delivery of shares on the plea that his offer has lapsed after a reasonable period of time. Has he right to do so? Discuss. (Hint: Yes).
7. A has lost his pet dog. He made an announcement that whosoever traces his dog and gives this information to him he will be suitably rewarded. B finds the dog in ignorance of the reward, he hands over dog to A. Can he claim for reward? Substantiate your answer with reasons.

8. Ram sends an offer for selling his bike to Shyam on 4 March. It reaches to Shyam on 6 March. Shyam gives acceptance and puts it in a letter box at 10 a.m. on 10 March. Immediately after that he receives letter of revocation from Ram. Is there any agreement between Ram and Shyam? (Hint: Communication of acceptance.)
9. A reputed pharmaceutical company in Delhi is manufacturing drug to be used as anti-malaria drug if used in the given direction. The company made an announcement that anyone who uses that drug in the given direction and even if he gets contacted with malaria the coy will pay Rs. 2,000 to him as compensation. Manoharlal purchased drug and used it in the given direction. But he contacted malaria and he claimed reward. Is he entitled to reward? Give reason and discuss entire case.
10. A was appointed as managing director in X coy by board of directors. After 6 months it was found that one of the directors in the board had not purchased qualification shares. What is the legal status of agreement made by the coy with A? Is he entitled to all benefits mentioned in the agreement? Give reasons why.
11. Manohar offers to give some presentation to Shoran on his marriage. But he failed to do so. Can Shoran has any legal remedy against Manohar? (Hint: No).
12. B has given woollen garments for dry cleaning to shopkeeper. The shopkeeper issued a receipt for that. In the back of that receipt terms and conditions were laid down in Bengali language, B does not know that. Is he bound by that condition? Give reasons. (Hint: Yes).
13. A sends telegram to B 'Would you sell your car? Quote lowest price.' B replied that lowest price is Rs. 20,000. A sent another telegram stating 'I would buy your car for that price'. B refused to sell the car. Can A compel him? Give reasons (Hint: No).
14. Ram borrows a sum of Rs. 1,000 from his friend Shyam for three months. At the expiration of that period Ram refused to repay. Can Shyam sue upon him for recovering that amount? (Hint: Yes).

■■■

3

Consideration

LEARNING OBJECTIVES

- Understand the concept of consideration in the context of validity of a contract.
- Examine, essentials of a lawful consideration.
- Remember the rule of 'No consideration, no contract along with exceptions to it.
- Analyse the role of stranger to consideration regarding validity of a contract.
- Analyse case study of 'Chinaiya *vs* Ramayya' and find out the guideline given by the court.

INTRODUCTION

Consideration is one of the essential element of valid contract. Every agreement must be supported by lawful consideration as to get legal validity.

Agreement is a mutual exchange of promises. One party makes a promise for doing or not doing anything to another party. And another party also makes similar promise. In such mutual exchange, every promisor gets something in return of his promise from another party. Whatever he gets will constitute consideration for his promise.

Example: A offers to sell his car to B for Rs. two lakh. B accepts the offer. There is a mutual exchange of promises between them. A is a promisor for handing over possession and ownership of that car to B. In return of his promise he gets right to recover Rs. two lakh from B which constitute consideration for his promise. Similarly B is a promisor to pay two lakh to A. And in return of it he will get possession and ownership of that car which will constitute consideration for his promise.

CONSIDERATION DEFINED

Consideration is regarded as a price for which promise of the promisor is bought. The term consideration has been defined by British court in one of the leading cases.

CASE RE CURRIE *vs* MISA (1875. L.R, 10 EX 153)

"A valuable consideration in the sense of law may consist either in some right, interest, profit or benefit accruing to one party or some forbearance, detriment, loss or responsibility given, suffered or undertaken by other."

It is clear from the definition that in agreement right, benefit or interest got by one party will constitute consideration for his promise. It is at the cost of loss or responsibility or detriment on the part of other party.

According to Section 2 (*d*) of this Act, "when at the desire of promisor, promisee or other person has done or abstained from doing, does or abstains for doing or promises to do or to abstain from doing something, such act, abstinence or promise is called consideration for the promise."

In the words of J. Patterson "consideration means something which is of some value in the eyes of law, moving from the plaintiff. It may be some benefit to the plaintiff or some detriment to the defendant."

Example: A promises to compensate B for the losses which he may incur in the suit filed by C against him. B pays Rs. 10,000 to A. In this example, A is benefited by Rs. 10,000 which is consideration for his promise to B who loses this amount. Similarly B gets right to be compensated by A which is an obligation of A and consideration for B.

RULES REGARDING CONSIDERATION

An analysis of the above definitions of consideration reveals some legal requirements of a valid consideration. These are:

(*i*) ***Form of consideration:*** The consideration will always be in the form of some act or abstinence or a promise for doing or not doing something.

Example: In return of Rs. two lakh from a Sports Goods company a super star of cricket makes a promise not to use bats other than manufactured by that company. In this case consideration for the company is in the form of abstinence. A superstar has promised to abstain from using other bats.

It is however to be noted that any act, abstinence or promise may result in benefit, right or interest for one party and loss and obligation for another party.

(*ii*) ***Consideration must be moved or given at the desire of promisor:*** In agreement there are two parties i.e., promisor and promisee. The consideration is generally given by the promisee to promisor. According to this, rule any act or promise will be valid consideration if such act has been done or promise is made at the desire or request of the promisor.

In other words, if the act is done voluntarily or at the request of the person other than promisor, it will not constitute valid consideration.

Example: A buys a book for his friend B. Later on B promises to pay Rs. 100 to A. Since A has bought a book voluntarily without the desire of B, it cannot be valid consideration for the promise of B.

DURGA PRASAD *vs* BALDEV (1880, 3, All, 221). In this case, Deputy Collector has requested A, who is an influential person of that area to develop market in that area. A did so at the desire of Deputy Collector. On the development of market, B promised to pay commission to A in return of some space in that market.

It was held that to get space in the market will not constitute consideration for B's promise. It is because market has not been developed at the desire of B. Rather it is developed at the desire or request of Deputy Collector.

(*iii*) ***Consideration may be past, present or future:*** Promisor makes a promise and consideration is given to him for his promise. If these two act of making promise and getting consideration are done simultaneously, the consideration is known as 'present consideration'.

Example: A buys a book on Business Law from the bookseller and makes payment of the price simultaneously. In this agreement consideration given to bookseller is 'present consideration'.

In addition if the consideration has been given to the promisor before he makes a promise, it is known as 'past consideration'. But even in case of past consideration desire or request for that act which constitute consideration must have been made by promisor.

Example: A buys a book on Business Law for his friend B at his request on 1 January. Later on after two months B promises to pay Rs. 100 to A. In this case, consideration for the promise of A is past consideration.

Similarly, consideration may be in the form of promise to be performed in future. Such consideration is known as 'future consideration' or 'executory consideration'. In other words, when consideration is to be moved at some future date it is known as 'future consideration'.

Example: A makes an agreement for buying raw material from B on 1 January. The raw material is to be supplied by B on 20 January and payment is to be made by A on 15 March. In this agreement consideration is future consideration for both parties.

It is however to be noted that according to English Mercantile Law consideration may be present and future consideration only. And past consideration is not recognised by English Law.

(*iv*) ***Consideration may be moved or given by promisee or by any other person:*** Generally in every agreement consideration is given by promisee to the promisor. But it is not necessary. Any other person on behalf of promisee may give consideration. Such consideration will also be valid. According to Indian Contract Act, it is not important that who has given a consideration, because it can be given by any person who is not even party to a contract. But the English law differs on this point. According to it consideration must be given by the promisee himself.

In this regard, question arises that who may be that person who is not party to a contract, but gives consideration to promisor. The court has given following two guidelines in the case **CHINAYYA *vs* RAMAYYA.**

(*a*) If there is a contract between A and B, no other person gets any right unless he is made party to contract.

(*b*) Stranger to consideration, but party to a contract can sue upon that contract. It is also known as 'Doctrine of constructive consideration'.

In other words, if someone does not know anything about consideration or he has not given consideration, but he is party to a contract will get rights in that contract.

Example: A distributes his property between his two sons C and D makes agreement with them that they will bear all expenses of his daughter's marriage.

In this case C and D are promisors and the daughter is a promisee. Though the daughter has not given consideration to C and D (She is stranger to consideration), yet she can claim expenses of her marriage from them because she is party to a contract.

CHINAYYA *vs* RAMAYYA, (1881, 4 MAD, 137). In this case A transfers part of his property to his daughter B and makes agreement that she will pay a particular amount, out of that property annually to his brother C. Later on B refused to pay stipulated amount to C on the plea that there is no consideration form C for supporting B's promise. But it was held that it is not necessary that consideration should have been given by the C (promisee). It has been given by A on behalf of C. Thus B is bound to pay.

It is however to be noted that any person can claim his right in a contract only if he is a party to that contract, irrespective of the fact that he is stranger to consideration.

(*v*) ***Consideration need not be adequate:*** In agreement, promisor makes promise for doing or not doing something. Such promise will have some value. He gets consideration for his promise, that will also have some value. According to Indian Contract Act, it is not necessary that the value of promise should be equal to the value of consideration. Even if the value of consideration is less that value of promise, the contract is valid.

Inadequacy of consideration does not invalidate contract provided the consent of the party getting lesser consideration has been free.

Example: A has got house in Delhi which is valued at Rs. 10 lakh. He makes agreement to sell out this house to B for Rs. 5 lakh. Agreement is valid provided consent of A has been free.

Thus, in a contract, presence of consideration is necessary (Barring exceptions given under Section 25). But its adequacy is not needed for making contract valid one. Rather inadequacy of consideration may be taken into account to ensure that party has free consent for the contract. Therefore, the concept of consideration is a mere technicality for validity of contract. Its presence is essential, but its inadequacy does not matter.

(*vi*) ***Consideration must be real and not illusory:*** Inadequacy of consideration does not affect validity of contract. But whatever consideration is being given it must be real. In other words, it must have some value in the eyes of law. It must not be illusory, fictitious, fraudulent, uncertain and illegal.

Examples: A in consideration of some money from B promises to bring gold for him from sun or convert copper into gold with the help of magic. The consideration is illusory and fictitious on account of impossibility and uncertainty.

Ram borrows sum of Rs. 5,000 from his friend Shyam for six months. After three month Ram promises that if Shyam returns money immediately he will allow discount of Rs. 500 to him. The promise of Shyam for allowing discount is not backed by consideration having real value. It is because consideration must be something more than what the promisee is already bound to do.

The performance of an act by a person who is legally bound to perform, the same cannot be a consideration for a contract.

RAMACHANDRA CHINTAMAN *vs* KALU RAJU, (1877, 2 BOM.362). In this case it was promised by the party to pay an additional amount to the lawyer above his service charges, if the suit was successful. Held the promise is void, since the consideration being illusory due to pre-existing legal obligation on the part of the lawyer to render required services under the original contract.

(*vii*) ***Consideration must be lawful:*** Agreement to be enforced in the court must be made for lawful consideration. Any act which is illegal, immoral and against public policy will not constitute valid consideration for the contract.

It is to be noted that in a contract if any part or whole of consideration is illegal, the contract is void if illegal part cannot be separated from legal part.

Example: A agrees to supply 100 cotton bales of quality X and 50 cotton bales of quality Y to B at certain rate. But sale and purchase of Y quality of cotton bales is prohibited. In this case sale of X quality cotton bales can be separated from the sale of Y quality cotton bales. Former part is legal and later part is illegal.

NO CONSIDERATION, NO CONTRACT

To form a valid contract, there must be an agreement between the parties. That agreement must be enforceable by law. In order to enforce agreement in the court it must be supported by lawful consideration. Contrary to it, any agreement which lacks consideration cannot be enforced in the court and therefore will not become a contract. In the words of Salmond, a promise without consideration is a gift, and a promise made for consideration is a bargain.

Section 25 of Indian Contract Act states that, "subject to certain exceptions, agreements without consideration are void; leaving aside these exceptions, agreement to be enforced needs consideration." Under exceptional situations which are contained in Section 25, the agreement or promise without consideration is valid in the eyes of law. These exceptions are:

(*i*) ***Any agreement, which satisfy the following conditions can be enforced by law without consideration:***

(*a*) Agreement between the parties must be made in writing.

(*b*) Agreement must be registered.

(*c*) Agreement must have been made on account of natural love and affection between the parties.

(*d*) Agreement must be made between the parties, standing in near relationship.

Example: A agrees to transfer part of his property to his son. This agreement is valid provided it is made in writing and made registered. It is assumed that father has done it on account of natural love and affection for the son and both are having near relationship. Agreement is valid without consideration.

RAJLUKHEE DEBEE *vs* BHOOTNATH (1900, 4 CWN, 488). In this case, there was a marital disagreement and discard between husband and wife. Husband executed registered document in favour of his wife agreeing to pay for her maintenence. But there was no consideration from the side of his wife. It was held that agreement was void for the want of consideration. It was not made out of natural love and affection.

(*ii*) ***Promise to compensate for past voluntary services:*** A person renders some services or does some act for other person voluntarily in the past. Another person who gets benefit of these services or act makes promise to compensate wholly or partially, such promise is valid without consideration. (Services rendered in the past voluntarily do not constitute consideration).

Thus in order to make such promise legally binding the following conditions must be satisfied:

(*a*) Services must have been rendered voluntarily.

(*b*) These services must have been rendered for the promisor only and he must have got benefit of these services.

(*c*) The promisor must have been in existence at that when services were rendered.

(*d*) The promisor must have clear intention to compensate the promisee for those services rendered by him.

(*e*) The service rendered by the promisee must be legal.

(*iii*) ***Promise to repay time-barred debt:*** While lending money, relevant provisions of Banking law, Money Lenders Act and Indian Limitation Act are applied. Provisions of Indian Limitation Act provide time period (if not determined by debtor and creditor) within which, the lender must give notice of demand or must have got debt recovered. Failure to do so will make that debt time-barred. On being debt time-barred, the creditor of such debt has no legal authority to recover it. But if the debtor of such debt makes a promise to repay part or whole of it to the creditor, such promise is valid without consideration provided the following conditions are satisfied:

(*a*) Promise made by debtor should be in writing.

(*b*) It should be signed by the promisor or by his agent.

(*c*) There must be express promise to pay.

Example: A has borrowed sum of Rs. 10,000 from B for the period of 2 years. Till the expiration of that period neither A served notice of demand to B nor B repaid the debt. Debt becomes time barred which A cannot legally recover. B makes promise to repay Rs. 5,000 after a month. This promise is valid without consideration provided B makes it in writing and signs on it with a clear intention of making partial payment.

(*iv*) ***Completed gifts and donation:*** Explanation 1 to Section 25 states that nothing in this Section shall affect the validity as between donor and donee of any gift actually made. In case of completed gift or donation the rule of no consideration and no contract does not apply. In this connection the following points must be taken care of:

(*a*) Promise to donate money or give some gift to any charitable organisation or friend is not valid without consideration.

(*b*) But, if money has been donated or goods have been gifted, these cannot be taken back on the plea that there was no consideration.

(*c*) Although promise to donate money is not valid, but if the promisee of such promise undertakes some liability on the basis of such promise, the promisor is bound to donate money.

KEDARNATH *vs* GAURI MOHAMMED (1886, 14Cal, 54). In this case, Kedarnath was a secretary of Town Hall. He approached Gauri Mohammed to give some donation for the construction of Town Hall at Howrah. Gauri Mohd. promised to give Rs. 100 as donation. On the faith of this promise, Kedarnath engaged contractors and thus incurred liability to pay them. Gauri Mohd. refused to pay donation. It was held that since Kedarnath has incurred liability on the basis of promise to donate, made by Gauri Mohd., thus he is liable to pay to the extent of liability subject to maximum amount of Rs. 100.

(*v*) ***Contract of a agency:*** According to Section 185 of this Act, contract made for creating relationship of agency between parties does not require any consideration.

Without consideration such contracts are valid. Thus a promise made by the person to act as an agent of another person is enforceable without consideration. Similarly if the person makes an agreement with another to appoint him as his agent for a particular period of time. It is also a valid agreement.

Example: A appoints B as his agent for the period of one year on the basis of 10% commission on sale. There is no consideration for supporting A's promise. As an exception, such promise is valid.

(*vi*) ***Remission by the promisee of performance of the promise:*** Promise made by the party for accepting lesser performance for the whole promise is valid without consideration. Similarly, an agreement to extend time of performance of a contract does not require any consideration.

According to Section 63 of this Act, a creditor can agree to give up part of his claim and there need be, no consideration for such an agreement.

Examples: A owes Rs. 5,000 to B. B makes an agreement with A that in receiving Rs. 4,500 from A it will be treated for the discharge of whole debt. Agreement is valid, B has a right to give up a part of claim in favour of A.

Ram agrees to deliver raw material to Shyam on 12 March and Shyam is to make payment on 20 March. Ram supplied raw material on time but Shyam is unable to pay on time. Ram extends date of payment by month. This promise is also valid without consideration.

STRANGER TO CONSIDERATION AND STRANGER TO CONTRACT

It has been made clear by the court in 'Chinayya *vs* Ramayya' case that the consideration may also be given by someone else on behalf of promisee. In this case it was held that contract cannot confer rights or impose obligations on any person other than the party to it. And moreover, it is cardinal rule of law that only the person who is party to a contract can sue upon that contract.

The party who does not know anything about consideration or who has not given consideration or who is stranger to consideration. But if he is party to contract he will get the rights. Contrary to it, the person who is not a party to contract or who is stranger to it cannot sue upon that contract. Thus stranger to consideration can sue upon while stranger to contract cannot.

DUNLOP PNEUMATIC TYRE CO. *vs* SELFRIDGE & CO. (1915, A.C. 847). In this case, a dealer buys tyres from Dunlop Coy and sold them to a retailer on the condition that he shall not sell the tyres below the listed price of the company. If this condition is violated he will be penalised with £5 for each tyre sold below the list price. But retailer, in one case did not comply with this condition. Dunlop Company sued him for breach of contract. It was held that there is no contract between Dunlop Company and the retailer. Thus the Company does not get any right and cannot sue the retailer for breach of contract.

DOCTRINE OF PRIVITY OF CONTRACT

This doctrine states that to get rights and obligations in a contract one must be party to it or there should be privity of contract between that person and another party. One cannot sue upon simply because contract is made for his benefit or consideration has been given on his behalf. On the other, if that person is stranger to consideration but stays in the privity of contract, he will gets the rights in that contract.

In the above case since there is no privity of contract between Dunlop Company and a retailer, thus the Company was not allowed to sue the retailer for breach of contract.

In practice there are certain exceptions to this doctrine. Under these exceptional situations, person who is stranger to a contract made for his benefit can sue upon that, contract. These exceptions are:

(i) Beneficiary of a trust: Trust is an arrangement whereby some property is handed over to trustees by the owner. This property is to be managed by the trust or trustees for the benefit of party known as 'beneficiary'. In this arrangement of trust, the beneficiary can sue to enforce his rights under the trust, though he is not a party to a contract.

Umanath Baksh Singh *vs* Jang Bahadur (Air, 1938, P.O, 245). In this case A appointed his son B his successor and was put in possession of his entire estate and made an agreement with him that B would give certain sum of money to C, an illegitimate son on attaining majority. It was held that trust was created for the benefit of C and therefore he is entitled to maintain a suit for the recovery of that benefit.

(ii) Marriage settlement, partition or other family arrangement: Agreements may be made with regard to marriage of a family member, partition of properties and other family arrangements. In such agreement provision may be made for the benefit of a particular member. Such person, who is beneficiary in the agreement can maintain a suit, though he is not in privity of a contract.

> ***Example:*** Agreement was made by the family members for setting aside particular part of property of family for meeting marriage expenses of female member. Such female member gets right to sue for that benefit, without being party to a contract.
>
> **Rose Fernandez *vs* Joseph Gonslaves (1950, A.I.R Bom, 97).** In this case, father of a girl made an agreement with Joseph for the marriage of

her daughter. Later on Joseph refused to marry. It was held that after attaining age of majority she can maintain a suit against Joseph for breach of promise of marriage, though she was not a party to the contract.

KHWAJA MOHD. *vs* HUSSAINI BEGUM (1910, 32 All 410). In this case a muslim lady filed suit against her father-in-law to recover Rs. 15,000 being the arrears of allowance (Petel box Expenses) payable to her by him under an agreement made between him and father of that lady at the time of her marriage. It was held that she was entitled to recover the money, though she was stranger to contract, made by her father and father-in-law.

(iii) Contract made by an agent: Agent makes an agreement on behalf of his principal. His main role is to bring third party into contractual relationship with the principal. In all such contracts made by agent, there is no direct privity of contract. But as an exception, principal gets rights in such contract, can file suit against third party or can be sued by third party.

Example: A is an agent working on behalf of his principal B. A makes an agreement for selling goods on behalf of B to C. Later on C refuses to pay to B. B, though is not a party to a contract made between A & C, is an exception as he gets right to sue C for the recovery of sale price.

(iv) Estoppel to acknowledgement: When a party acknowledges or admits liability in a contract to third party. Later on if he denies or refuses it on any ground, he will be stopped from doing so. His liability would continue towards third party, though there may be no privity of contract between party admitting liability and third party.

Example: Ram gives sum of Rs. 1,000 to Shyam to be paid to Mahesh. Shyam informs to Mahesh that he is holding that amount to pay him. Later on Shyam refuses to pay. Shyam will be stopped from denying his liability to pay and Mahesh is entitled to recover it from Shyam.

(v) Charges created on immovable property: Agreement creating charge on immovable property in favour of third party for his benefit can be enforced by third party. Although third party is stranger to contract but can sue upon that contract.

Example: A Public Limited Coy issues debentures and creates charge on its immovable property in favour of debenture holders. These debenture holders are beneficiary and in case company fails to repay them, they can maintain suit against coy for enforcing charge created on immovable property.

(*iv*) ***Agreements relating to land:*** The owner of land is subject to certain rights and obligation to some authority of land. Buyer purchases that land and gives notice to the authority that owner of a land is bound by those rights and obligations. Although, buyer is stranger to a contract between seller and land authority, he will be subject to those rights and obligations.

Example: A, possesses, piece of land on lease basis which he gets from Delhi Development Authority. He is subject to some rights and obligations to Delhi Development Authority. B buys this piece of land from A and gives notice to the authority that he will be bound by those rights and obligations. Later on if that land becomes free hold A will get benefit of it, though he was not party to a contract entered into between A and Delhi Development Authority.

REVIEW QUESTIONS

1. Define the term 'consideration'. Explain various rules regarding lawful consideration.
2. 'No consideration and no contract.' Discuss this rule and explain various exceptions to this rule.
3. What do you mean by 'Doctrine of Privity of Contract'? Explain various exceptions to this doctrine.
4. Agreement without consideration is void. Are there any exceptions to this rule? Discuss.
5. 'Consideration as an essential element of valid contract.' Discuss.
6. 'Stranger to consideration but party to a contract can sue upon that contract.' Explain it by giving suitable examples.
7. Under what circumstance can stranger to a contract enforce it?
8. Can consideration be given by a person other than promisee?
9. Comment on:
   (*a*) Inadequacy of consideration does not invalidate the contract.
   (*b*) Consideration must be given at the desire or request of promisor.
   (*c*) Stranger to contract cannot sue upon that contract.
   (*d*) Law does not confer rights and obligation on the person who is not a party to contract.
   (*e*) Valid consideration is legal and real.

(*f*) Past consideration is as good as present and future consideration.

(*g*) Insufficiency of consideration is immaterial, but agreement without consideration is void.

(*h*) Stranger to contract can enforce it provided it is made for his benefits.

10. Can gratuitous promises be enforced? Give suitable examples.

PRACTICAL PROBLEMS

1. A buys book for his friend B without his request. Later on B promises to pay the price of the book. Is the promise of B is valid? (Hint: No).
2. Ram has lost his bag in the college. He makes an announcement that whosoever finds the bag and returns it to him will be suitably rewarded. Shyam made a search voluntarily for a bag without any intention of getting reward. He found it and returned it to Ram. Has he got legal claim for reward? (Hint: No).
3. A developed a shopping Mall in Delhi at the request of B who is a Municipal Corporator. C makes agreement to pay Rs. 5,000 p.m. to A for some space in that Mall. Judge the validity of an agreement made between A and B.
4. Mahesh has got a house in Delhi costing Rs. 10 lakh. He makes agreement for selling this house to Ramesh for Rs. 5 lakh. Is this a valid agreement? (Hint: Consent of Mahesh should be free.)
5. A gives sum of Rs. 5,000 to B to be given to C. B informs C that he is holding that money which is to be paid to him. Later on he refuses to pay it to C on the plea that he has no obligation to pay. Can C recover this amount from B? (Hint: Yes).
6. A makes trust arrangement with B, C and D (Trustees), and transfers a part of his property to the trust. As per agreement it is to be managed for the benefit of E. Can E enforce his right for the benefit? (Hint: Yes).
7. Manohar made a promise to donate sum of Rs. 5,000 to the secretary of RamLila committee, New Delhi. The secretary of committee hires a contractor for constructing stage for RamLila and incurs a liability of Rs. 2,000. He does it with a hope that he will get donation from Manohar. Is Manohar liable to pay donation? If yes, to which extent he is liable? (Hint: He is liable to pay Rs. 2,000 only).

8. A pays sum of Rs. 2,000 as donation to a charitable institution. Can he take this money back on the plea that there has been no consideration from the side of that institution? (Hint: No).
9. Ram borrows a sum of Rs. 10,000 from B for one year. After three months, B promise to allow a discount of Rs. 1,000 if Ram repays that money immediately. Is the promise of B is valid? (Hint: No, preexisting obligation on the part of Ram to repay.)
10. There is a constant quarrel and marital discord between husband and wife. As a part of settlement the husband agrees to pay sum of Rs. 5,000 per month as maintenance allowance to his wife provided she stays separately. Does a wife has claim to get that amount? (Hint: No).
11. Ram borrows Rs. 5,000 from Shyam @ 10% interest for one year. He fails to repay and makes an agreement with Shyam that if Shyam does not move to court Ram will pay higher rate of interest *i.e.* 15% p.a. Ram agrees to it. Can Ram enforce the promise made by Shyam? (Hint: Yes).

■■■

4

Contractual Capacity

LEARNING OBJECTIVES

- Note the various ingredients of incapacity to contract.
- Remember legal position of minor's agreements.
- Examine those situations in which minor's agreements are enforceable and minority does not matter.
- Analyse legal qualification of various special parties in the light of contractual capacity.

INTRODUCTION

Contractual capacity is an essential ingredient of a valid contract. According to Section 10 of this Act, parties making an agreement must have the contractual capacity. Contractual capacity means they must be legally competent for making a contract.

Meaning

The legal competence of the party is determined by Section 11 of this Act.This Section states that "every person is competent to contract who is of a age of majority according to law to which he is subject, and who is of a sound mind and is not declared disqualified from contracting by law to which he is subject."

Briefly speaking the age, soundness of mind and legal qualification of a person constitute his contractual capacity.

To have a contractual capacity, one must fulfil the following conditions:

Elements

I. ***Factor of Age:*** The person to have a contractual capacity must be of a major age and not a minor.

II. ***Soundness of mind:*** The person must be of sound mind to possess contractual capacity and must not be lunatic, idiot and drunkard.

III. ***Legal qualification:*** Contractual capacity implies that the person must not have been declared disqualified by law for making contract.

I. FACTOR OF AGE

Section 11 of this Act provides that an age of majority of a person is determined by law to which he is subject.

According to Section 3 of the Indian Majority Act 1875, every person in India who has completed 18 years of his age becomes major. This rule is subject to the following exceptions:

(*i*) When the guardians of the minor are appointed by the court, such minor will have to complete 21 years of his age, to become major.

(*ii*) When the property of minor has been handed over to court of ward for its management, minority will continue till completion of 21 years of age.

Legal Position of Minor's Agreements in India

Generally it is assumed that mental faculties of a minor are in a developing state. He is not mature enough to understand what is good and what are its implications on his interest. In the light of it, law protects a minor, so that any person by making an agreement with him cannot exploit him.

The Indian Contract Act 1872, has also granted privileged position to a minor with regard to agreements made by him. In any agreement he does not incur personal liability. He is allowed to get benefit in an agreement entered into by him. Not only this, but entire judicial mechanism helps him. Judges are their councellors, jury are their servants and law is their guardian. But at the same time, it is ensured that while protecting interest of minor, unnecessary hardships should not be created for the persons who deal with a minor.

Legal position of minor's agreement can be understood clearly with the help of following instances:

(*i*) ***Agreement made by minor is absolutely void and inoperative:*** A minor does not have the contractual capacity. When he makes agreements, such agreements are void and cannot be enforced in the court of law. Even if he has got some benefit in that agreement, before declaring that agreement as void, he may not be compelled to return that benefit.

Mohiri Bibi *vs* Dharmodas Ghosh (1930, 30 cal is 539, 1 A 114). In this case, a minor borrowed Rs. 8,000 from a moneylender and executed a mortgage bond of Rs. 20,000 in his favour. Later on, the minor filed a suit for setting aside the mortgage on the plea that he is a minor. It was held that the agreement of mortgage is void *ab initio* and the money lent by mortgagee could not be recovered.

(*ii*) ***Minor can be a promisee or beneficiary:*** Although, an agreement entered into by a minor is void, but he can be a promisee or beneficiary in an agreement. Simple rule of law is that a minor cannot be stopped from getting benefits in an agreement. By being in position of a promisee means to be in the position of getting benefit. When the minor is promisee or is to get some benefit in the agreement, he can enforce agreement against other party in the court of law.

Example: A is a minor. He draws a cheque in favour of B. B cannot recover the payment of that cheque from the bank. But, if B draws a cheque in favour of A, who is a minor, A can get payment of this cheque from bank.

There is nothing in law, which debars a minor from becoming a promisee or beneficiary.

Collector of Meerut *vs* Hardian (1954, All 156). In this case, minor purchased certain property and has paid price for it to a vendor. Vendor declined to give possession of that property to a minor. It was held that minor has performed his obligation in the agreement. He is allowed to enforce it against the vendor. The minor was given decree for possession of the property purchased.

(*iii*) ***Rule of Estoppel is not applicable in case of minor:*** Rule of Estoppel is a branch of law of evidence. According to rule of estoppel, when the person has made any statement by the words spoken or in writing or by his conduct, which induced other persons to believe that a particular event has happened; later on if the person denies happening of that event, he will be stopped from doing so.

But in case of minor, this rule is not applicable. A minor who makes an agreement by representing himself to be a major and gets a benefit in that agreement can still plead his minority for declaring agreement as void.

Gadigeppa Bhimappa Mets *vs* V. Balangowda Bhiman Gowda (Air, 1931, Bom 561). In this case, a minor represented himself to be a major and induced another for making an agreement. The court was of the opinion that where an infant represents fraudulently or otherwise that he is of age and thereby induces another to enter into contract with him then on an action founded on the contract, the infant was not stopped from setting up infancy.

(*iv*) ***Doctrine of restitution is not applied against minor:*** Accordingly to this doctrine, if a person obtains property or goods by making false representation he can be compelled to restore it to the person from whom he has obtained it. But earlier this rule was not applicable on minor. As it was held in **Mohiri Bibi *vs* Dhamodar Ghosh** case. Sections 64 and 65 of the Indian Contract Act which deals with restitution will not be applicable on minor's agreements.

With the passage of time many developments took place and it was made clear that the law gives protection to a minor but does not give him the liberty to cheat others.

R. LESLIE *vs* SHEILL (1941, 3, K.B, 607). In this case **Sheill**, a minor misrepresented his age and made an agreement for selling his property to **Leslie** and received Rs. 10,000 as consideration from him. Out of this amount he spent Rs. 6,000 in purchasing a car and the balance on a pleasure trip. When he attained majority **Leslie** applied to the court for the performance of this contract. It was held that an aggrieved party had no legal remedy against the minor because, agreement was void *ab initio*. But on account of misrepresentation the court was at its discretion to order him to handover the car to the aggrieved party.

However, the situation was changed after the enforcement of the Specific Relief Act 1963.

Section 33 of this Act provides:

(*a*) Where void or voidable contract has been cancelled at the instance of a party thereto, the court may require him to restore such benefits which he may have received from the other party and to make any compensation to him which justice may require.

(*b*) Where defendant successfully resists any suit on the ground that the agreement sought to be enforced against him in the suit, is void by reason of his not having been competent to contract. Under Section II of this Act the court may if the defendant has received any benefits under the agreement, from the other party requires him to restore the benefit obtained by him under the agreement, but only to the extent to which he or his estate has benefitted thereby.

Sub-section (*i*) of the above provision states that 'he who seeks equity must do equity'. Under this rule courts have discretion to require minor plaintiff to return benefits obtained under void agreement. But the court will not compel minor to restore benefit, where other party was aware of infancy or where false representation did not influence decision of other party.

According to Sub-section (*ii*) of the above provisions where the minor is defendant successfully resist any suit on the ground that contract is void by reason of his being a minor he may be required to return benefit obtained by him by the court. But court will allow restitution only to the extent to which he or his estate has been benefited.

(*v*) ***Agreements for basic necessities of life:*** Although agreements entered into by minor are void. But if he makes an agreement for buying goods of basic necessities of life on credit such agreements carry different legal consequences. In these agreements, the person who has supplied those goods will be reimbursed provided:

(*a*) Goods were basic necessities of life for a minor.

(*b*) Re-imbursement will be made only for reasonable cost of those goods and not a contracted price.

(*c*) Such reimbursement will be made only from property of a minor if any. But minor will have no personal liability.

The goods of basic necessities of life of a person will differ from person to person depending on social status and economic position of that person. It is to be noted that the goods which are of a the basic necessities of life for one person (high income bracket) may be goods of extra comfort for another person (low income bracket).

On the basis of decisions of the courts from time and again, the following have been considered to be necessaries of life:

(*a*) Fund supplied to a minor for the marriage of a female member in the family.

(*b*) Funds required for performing funeral obsequies of the father of minor.

(*c*) Expenses incurred in connection with litigation regarding his property.

(*d*) Funds required for the education and training of a minor.

In addition to these necessaries it would also include, items of food, clothings, shelter, education and training, medical treatment etc.

ROBERTS *vs* GRAY, (1913, I K.B 520). In this case, a minor who was intended to become a billiards player entered into contract with R, a famous billard player. He agreed to pay him fees to learn the game and play matches with him during his world tour. It was held that G was liable to pay, as it was an agreement for necessaries related to education, training and employment.

(*vi*) ***Ratification of minor's agreement is not allowed:*** Agreements made by a minor during minority are void. On attaining age of majority he cannot ratify those agreements for making them valid. Ratification implies subsequent authorisation of the act done earlier.

Example: A, who is a minor makes promissory note in favour of B. Such Promissory note is void. After sometime A attains age of majority and gives new promissory note in place of old one. Second promissory note is also invalid, because it is a subsequent approval of first one.

RAMASWAMY *vs* A CHETTIAR (1906, 16 MC, J 422). In this case, a minor borrowed a sum of money and executed bond for it. After attaining majority he executed second bond in respect of original bond and interest therein. It was held that second bond was not maintainable, since it was without consideration.

(*vii*) ***Agreements made by the guardian of a minor:*** Agreements made by a minor are void. But if the guardians of a minor make an agreement on behalf of a minor, such agreement is valid provided:

(*a*) Agreement has been made for the benefit of a minor.

(*b*) It is made on behalf of a minor.

(*c*) It is made by the guardian within the scope of authority given to them.

It is however to be noted that a guardian cannot purchase an immovable property on behalf of a minor without the consent of the court.

(*viii*) ***Minor cannot be declared insolvent:*** Agreements made by minor are void. In these agreements, he does not incur personal liability. At the most, in some cases he may be compelled to return benefit or pay reasonable cost only from the property if any. Thus he cannot be adjudicated as an insolvent by the court.

(*ix*) ***Minor as agent:*** A minor can be appointed as an agent. He can work on behalf of principal. It is because the main job of agent is to bring third party into contractual relationship with his principal. As soon as relationship is established, his role is over. And third party can sue upon the principal for that transaction, made by the agent. Thus minor agent binds principal without incurring any liability.

Example: A appoints B as his agent. B is a minor. He was appointed for selling goods. He sells goods to C. C refuses to pay to B. A can file suit against C for the payment of price.

(*x*) ***Minor as shareholder:*** A minor cannot be shareholder in a Joint Stock Company because he is not legally competent for making a contract. But if he has been allotted shares due to some mistake, both he and the company may continue to enjoy a benefit of such holding. But he would not be liable to pay calls, which are due on his holding.

Minor can become a shareholder in a company, through his guardian who will act as his trustee. Trustee's name will be recorded in the Register of member, and he shall be a member of the company for all purposes.

PALANIAPPA *vs* OFFICIAL LIQUIDATOR: In this case, shares were allotted by a company to a minor under an application signed by his guardian. When company went into liquidation, neither minor, nor his guardian was found liable for paying unpaid call. It is because the name of a minor was written in the register of members. By being incompetent to contract he cannot be sued.

(*xi*) ***Minor as a partner:*** Relationship of a partnership arises out of a contract and minor has no capacity to contract. Therefore he cannot become partner in a partnership firm. But if all partners do agree, he can be admitted to the profits or benefits of the firm. His liability for the acts of the firm will be limited up to his share which he has got in assets and profits of the firm.

(*xii*) ***Surety for a minor:*** A person who stands guarantor for the debt borrowed by the minor is known as 'surety'. Though the creditor cannot sue upon minor, but directly he can file suit against surety. The liability of surety arises out of a different contract which he makes with creditor.

KASHIBA *vs* SRIPAT (1894, Bom, 697): In this case, it was held that contract between surety and third party (creditor) is a direct and independent contract, thus the minor will be saved from his liability.

II. SOUNDNESS OF MIND

To have contractual capacity one must be of a sound mind. According to Section 12 of this Act, a person is said to be a sound mind for the purpose of making contract, if at the time, when he makes it he is capable of understanding it and forming a rational judgement as to its effects upon his interest.

To determine soundness of mind for making a contract one has to ensure that:

(*a*) The person at that time of making contract is capable of understanding the contract.

(*b*) He is also capable of understanding implications of that contract upon his interest. He knows how that contract can affect his interest.

Section 12 of this Act further states that a person who is usually of unsound mind, but occasionally of sound mind may make contract when he is of a sound mind.

Soundness of mind of a person is adversely affected by certain factors including use of intoxicants and mental disease etc. These factors are as under:

(*i*) ***Lunacy:*** Lunacy is a mental disease which is curable. In this disease mental faculties of a person start working above or below the normal prescribed range. So long as these faculties operate within a prescribed range, the person is of a sound mind. When those faculties starts moving out of range, he becomes of unsound mind.

It is however to be noted that the lunatic, when he is of sound mind has a contractual capacity. All agreements made by him are valid and enforceable except those made by him when he becomes of unsound mind.

(*ii*) ***Idiocy:*** It is also a mental disease which is not curable. In this disease the mental faculties of a person have not been developed since birth or he has lost his mental faculties forever due to some accident or shock etc. Such person will never come to the state of understanding contract and its impact on his interest. Idiots do not have a contractual capacity and therefore agreement made by them are absolutely void. Such person can be beneficiary in an agreement for supplying necessaries of a life to him or to his dependents and money is recoverable from his property if any.

(*iii*) ***Drunkards or intoxicated person:*** A person who takes any intoxicants like alchohol, marijuna and cannabis, etc., is temporarily incompetant for making an agreement. The mental faculties of such persons are clouded for sometime. Thus so long as he remains under the influence of intoxicant or drug he has no contractual capacity. Agreement made by such person are void. But for the supply of necessaries, reasonable cost of it can be recovered from his property and he has no personal liability for it.

III. LEGAL DISQUALIFICATION

In addition to these, there are certain parties whose contractual capacity has been restricted by law to which they are subject. Such incompetancy may arise by the status of a person. And law may debar him from making an agreement. The following persons have been included in this category:

(*i*) ***Alien enemy:*** A person who lives in and is a citizen of foreign country is known as an alien. He may be friend or enemy to the citizen of our country. Alien friend can make an agreement with Indian citizen. But if war is declared between the two countries, the citizens of those countries become alien enemy to each other. And agreements made with alien enemy are void.

In other words, after the declaration of war, citizens of those countries become alien enemy and agreement cannot be entered into by them. When they make agreements, such agreements are void. But agreements made before the declarations of war will be either declared as void or may be suspended so long as war continues. Such agreements can be revived, when the war is over and can be re-enforced in the court of law with prior approval of the Central Government.

(*ii*) ***Foreign sovereign and ambassadors:*** Ambassadors, High Commissioners or foreign diplomatic staff do represent their country. Therefore they have been provided some immunities. They can make an agreement with Indian citizen and can enforce those agreements against Indian citizens in India. But Indian citizens to sue upon them for the rights arising out of an agreement has to seek prior permission of Central Government.

It has been done with a view to ensure that for personal gain no one is allowed to spoil relationship of the country with the country to which that diplomatic official belongs.

ENGELKE *vs* MUSMAN (1928, A.C, 433). In this case, Engelke was in the diplomatic staff of foreign embassy. He was tenant of Musman, Engelke did not pay rent regularly and it causes into arrears. It was held that he cannot be sued upon for the recovery of rent, because he was protected under diplomatic immunities.

(*iii*) ***Married woman:*** Indian Constitution does not discriminate between man and woman, and grants equal rights to them. But after marriage, status of woman is slightly changed. With regard her contractual capacity the following guidelines should be taken care of:

(*a*) Married woman has no right to make agreements regarding joint property of husband and wife, unless she is authorised to do so by her husband.

(*b*) Married woman is free to make any agreement to deal with her personal property such as bank balance in her name and jewellries, etc.

(*c*) On the failure of husband, to fulfil the basic necessities of her life, she becomes 'agent of her husband by necessity'. For the supply of such basic necessities she can make agreements binding on the property of her husband.

(*iv*) ***Corporation and joint stock company:*** Corporation is a body corporate which is brought into existence by passing special legislation in the Parliament. Joint Stock Company comes into being after fulfilling legal formalities prescribed in the Indian Company Act. Once such corporation or company comes into existence, legal status is granted to them, and they are considered as separate legal entity.

Such corporation or company can enter into an agreement, can sue third party or can be sued upon. Not only this, but also they can own properties and transfer it.

Since Corporation or Company has no physical existence, some official is to be authorised for using these rights on behalf of the corporation or company. Contractual capacity of such corporation or company will be limited up to the provisions of the law which brings them into existence. Any agreement or any other act beyond the provisions of that Act would be *ultra vires* and void.

Similarly the corporation or company exists only in the eyes of law, thus no agreement of personal nature can be entered into on behalf of the corporation.

(*v*) ***Insolvent:*** Generally, when the assets of a person fall short of liabilities and liabilities cannot be paid fully. Such state of affair is known as 'insolvency'. The person is declared as an insolvent by the court, his property handed over to the 'Official Receiver'. The insolvent cannot make any agreement regarding that property. The Official receiver realises the property and distribute the cash among creditors ratably. It is only when the court issues 'order of discharge' in favour of that person he becomes competent to make agreements.

(*vi*) ***Convict:*** A convict is a person who has been found guilty for some legal offence. He may be prosecuted and may be sent to imprisonment. So long as he remains in the imprisonment he has no contractual capacity. On his release from imprisonment on bail or parole, he becomes competent for making agreement, when such convict is finally released from imprisonment he becomes competent. But in case of barbaric offences such person may be declared disqualified for a particular period of time, even after being released from imprisonment.

However in England, Barristers are not permitted to enter into agreement relating to their profession. They cannot be sued upon or cannot file a suit against the client for theirs dues. But in India an advocate can sue upon his client for the recovery of fees and other dues.

REVIEW QUESTIONS

1. Define the term 'contractual capacity'. Explain its elements in brief.
2. 'Agreements entered into by a minor are void.' Discuss exceptions to this rule.
3. Explain legal position of minor's agreement in India.
4. What is soundness of mind? Discuss the contractual capacity of various categories of people whose mental state is affected either by illness or by intoxicants.
5. Explain with suitable example, the law relating to validity of contract made by a minor.
6. Comment on:
   (*a*) Minor is not allowed to cheat others.
   (*b*) Agreements for minor's benefit can be enforced by him.
   (*c*) Minor as an agent.
   (*d*) Lunatic can make agreements.
7. Discuss the legal competence of the following for making an agreement:
   (*a*) Corporation
   (*b*) Married woman
   (*c*) Alien enemy
   (*d*) Insolvent

PRACTICAL PROBLEMS

1. Ram is a minor. He falsely represents himself to be a major makes agreement with Shyam, gets benefit in that agreement and finally sets aside it as void. Can Ram be compelled for returning the benefit to Shyam? (Hint: Yes, Specific Relief Act.)
2. A 'who is a minor' had borrowed a sum of Rs. 5,000 from B. He has spent that money for paying fee towards a computer course being pursued by him. Is A liable to repay? (Hint: Yes, from his property for basic necessaries.)

3. A shoe merchant has supplied 10 pairs of shoes to C who is minor at a particular price. Is he entitled to recover that price? (Yes, but reasonable price for 2, 3 pairs of shoes from the property if any.)
4. A is a lunatic. He has a wife and two children. He makes an agreement to borrow a sum of Rs. 5,000 from B. The money is utilised on fooding and clothing of his family members. Can B recover this amount? (Hint: Yes, from the property.)
5. Mahesh, who is a minor makes an agreement for borrowing Rs. 10,000 from Ramesh. To borrow this amount he is signing mortgage deed of his property for Rs. 20,000. Later on he wants to get his property free from mortgage. Can he do it without returning Rs. 10,000 to Ramesh? (Hint: Yes, as per Sections 64 and 65 of Indian Contract Act.)
6. A is a minor. His guardian opens a bank account jointly in the name of minor. Discuss the legal status of this account.
7. Ram is a minor. His father was a partner in a partnership firm. He dies. Shyam and Manohar agree to give his share to his son, Ram. What is the limit of liability of Ram for the acts of the firm?
8. X, a minor, has been allotted shares in a Joint Stock Company by mistake. Is he liable to pay calls which are due on shares? (Hint: No).
9. A is a minor draws cheque of Rs. 2,000 in favour of B. After attaining the age of majority he replaces the cheque and instead gives new cheque for it. Can B get payment of the cheque? (Hint: No).
10. A foreign diplomatic official got a house in rent from an Indian citizen in Delhi. He refused to pay the agreed amount of rent to the Indian citizen. Can he sue upon the foreign diplomat? What is the legal remedy available to him? (Hint: No, without permission of Central Government he may approach to the House of Parliament.)
11. A got married with B and A does not fulfil the basic necessities of his wife. Can B make a binding agreement on the joint property? (Hint: Yes, Agency by necessity.)
12. A is Managing Director of X corporation. He is authorised to make an agreement on behalf of the corporation. He makes an agreement beyond the powers of Managing Director mentioned in the Act. Is this agreement binding on the corporation? (Hint: No, *Ultra vires*.)

13. A minor falsely represents himself to be a major, enters into an agreement for selling his property to B. A receives Rs. 20,000 a part of price in advance out of this amount he buys car for Rs. 15,000 and spends remaining amount on a pleasure trip. After A gets the majority age, B files suit against him for transferring possession and ownership of that property. Will he succeed, or will he get Rs. 20,000 back from A? (Hint: Refer to R Leslie *vs* Sheill case. He cannot succeed, the court may allow him to repay Rs. 15,000 to B).
14. Y, a minor, who wants to become a professional magician, makes an agreement with a musical company and agrees to pay a certain sum of money for attending classess of music. Is he liable to pay the fee? (Hint: Yes, from his property as a case of basic necessaries).

■■■

5

Free Consent

LEARNING OBJECTIVES

- Examine the consequences of free consent and lack of consent in the formation of a contract.
- Get familiar with the concept of 'consensus-ad-idem', in the formation of contract.
- Analyse the consequences of various elements of free consent.
- Make distinction between fraud and misrepresentation, and coercion and undue influence.
- Understand the role and consequences of various types of mistakes on the validity of a contract.

INTRODUCTION

Free Consent is equally important for the validity of a contract. Formation of an agreement involves two parties. One party makes an offer on particular subject matter to another party and that another party accepts it. Both the parties must ensure that they have consent on that subject matter of an agreement and that consent is free. Without free consent of the parties an agreement does not acquire legal sanctity and consequences.

Generally, consent of the parties means, both of them have understood subject matter of an agreement in the same sense. Other way around, both of them have identical minds on that subject matter.

Section 10 of this Act states that, all agreements are contracts if they are made by the free consent of the parties. According to Section 13 of this Act, two or more persons are said to consent when they agree upon same thing in the same sense.

Section 14 of this Act states that consent is said to be free when it is not caused by:

I. *Coercion*—Application of physical force.

II. *Undue influence*—Use of mental pressure.

III. *Misrepresentation*—Innocent false representation.

IV. *Fraud*—Cheating or deceiving.

V. *Mistake*—Wrong impression about anything.

However, it is to be noted that, the use of any one of the four factors to seek consent will make that contract voidable one. While as use of mistake in causing consent will make contract void. But when the parties make fundamental mistake regarding subject matter or identity of party or a nature of agreement, either there will be no agreement or agreement will be void. Simple rule is that a contract does not arise in the absence of consent. This point was made clear in the following case.

CUNDY *vs* LINDSAY. In this case, while placing an order for the goods, with Cundy, Blenkiron an individual closely imitated address and signature of well-known firm Blenkiron & Coy. Cundy sent goods to him thinking that the order came from Blenkiron & Coy, who in turn sold them to Lindsay. Cundy on discovering his mistake filed a suit against Lindsay for the recovery of goods. It was held by the House of Lords that as Cundy thought that he was dealing with Blenkrion & Coy and knew nothing about Blenkiron and had no intention to deal with him. Thus there was no contract between Cundy and Blekiron.

BOULTON *vs* JONES (1857, E.R.232). In this case, A sold his business to B without disclosing this fact to his customers. C sent an order for goods to A. B received order and without intimating change of ownership supplied the goods to C. It was held that there was no contract between B and C, because C intended to make contract with A only and not with B.

In practice, it is difficult to distinguish between case of fundamental error or mutual mistake. It is made clear that fundamental error means there is no consent of parties, thus there is no agreement. But in case of mutual mistake on the part of the parties agreement will become void.

Example: A has got two scooters *i.e.*, Vespa and Bajaj. He made an agreement for selling a scooter to B for Rs.10,000 believing that he is selling Vespa but B thought that he is buying Bajaj scooter. Agreement between A and B is void on account of mutual mistake regarding identity of subject matter.

ELEMENTS OF FREE CONSENT

1. Coercion

Coercion implies use of some kind of physical force by doing some act forbidden by law to seek consent of other party. For example, one may put another into physical injury to cause his consent or may threat to retain physical possession of his property.

According to Section 15 of this Act, "Coercion is, committing or threatening to commit any act forbidden by Indian Penal Code or unlawful detaining or threatening to detain any property, to the prejudice of any person, whatever, with the intention of causing any person to enter into an agreement."

On the basis of above definition of coercion, the following features of it may be pointed out as under:

(*i*) ***Coercion:*** Coercion includes committing or threatening to commit any of the following acts:

(*a*) To commit any act which is forbidden by Indian Penal Code or any act which is punishable under I.P.C.

(*b*) Threatening to commit such forbidden or punishable act.

(*c*) Unlawful detention of the property of that another person.

(*d*) Threatening to detain that property of another person.

Example: A is seeking consent of B for an agreement at revolver point or A has fired one round and then forcing B to sign on agreement. A withholds possession of B's car unless B gives his consent for agreement. In all these cases, coercion has been used for causing consent of other party.

(*ii*) ***Intention of the party:*** Committing or threatening to commit forbidden acts will amount to coercion provided those acts would have been done with a view to cause consent of other party for an agreement. Thus intention of the party doing those act is very important for determining use of coercion. By committing such act another party must have been compelled to give his consent for an agreement. Then only it will amount to coercion.

(*iii*) ***Direction of coercion:*** It is not necessary that the act of coercion must be directed against the person whose consent is being caused for agreement. It may be directed upon any other person even who is not a party of agreement. Coercion may be directed upon A to cause consent of B.

BANSRAJ *vs* THE SECRETARY OF STATE (1939, A.W.R 242). In this case, the Government imposed a threat of attachment against the property of A for the recovery of a fine due from B, the son of A. A had to pay fine. It was held that payment of fine was induced by coercion and therefore A was entitled to recover the money paid to remove wrongful attachment.

(*iv*) ***Place of coercion:*** The explanation of Section 15 of this Act makes it clear that, it is not necessary that the place at which the act of coercion is done is subject to jurisdiction of Indian Penal Code. Even if coercion is used in the aeroplane going in the sky or ship going in the ocean, it will amount to coercion. It cannot be pleaded that in the sky or ocean, the provisions of Indian Panel Code are not applicable.

Case: A and B were on the board of ship. A caused B to make a contract by an act of criminal intimidation. Later on B did not perform contract. A sued B at Calcutta for breach of contract. B's argument that the contract was caused by coercion was accepted and it was held that it was immaterial whether at the place of making a contract Indian Penal Code was applicable or not.

(*v*) ***Threat to commit suicide amounts to coercion:*** As per the provisions of Indian Penal Code it is only an attempt to commit suicide, which is punishable. But in many decisions of the courts it was held that if the person seeks consent of another for agreement by threatening to commit suicide it will also amount to coercion.

CHIKKAM AMIRAJU *vs* CHIKKAM. In this case a person threatened to commit a suicide if his wife and son did not contract with his brother to release certain disputed property in his favour. The court held that the contract was caused by threat to commit a suicide, which amounts to coercion.

(*vi*) ***Effect of coercion:*** According to Section 19 of this Act, if one person seeks consent of another by using coercion such contract is voidable at the option of aggrieved party whose consent had not been free. He can repudiate or avoid a contract, or he can enforce it against another party. And if other party compels him to perform it he can refuse it on the plea that his consent has been caused by coercion.

Generally, burden of proof that consent was obtained by coercion lies on the party who alleges coercion. And who wants to set aside contract on the plea of coercion.

Duress and coercion: In English Mercantile Law, the term 'duress' has been used for coercion. Duress is defined as causing or threatening to cause bodily violence or imprisonment with a view to obtain the consent of other party for a contract. Main point of difference between duress and coercion is that duress does not include unlawful detaining property of other to cause his consent. Secondly, coercion may be used by any person even by a person stranger to contract, but duress must be used by the party to the contract.

2. Undue Influence

Undue influence implies unfair use of dominating position to cause the consent of other party for a contract. In undue influence some kind of mental and moral pressure is brought upon the party to cause his consent.

According to Section 16(1) of this Act, "A contract is said to be induced by undue influence where the relation subsisting between the parties are such that one of the party is in a position to dominate the will of other and uses the position to obtain an unfair advantage over the other." According to this definition it is clear that undue influence involves the following elements:

(*a*) Two parties making a contract are somehow related to each other.

(*b*) One of the party is in dominating position who can dominate or influence will of other party for making contract.

(*c*) The party who is in dominating position gets unfair advantages of his position by causing the consent of other party.

Example: A who is a doctor makes an agreement with B who keeps poor eyesight and health to pay for his professional charges. The amount to be paid by B is unreasonably very high. In this example, the doctor who is in a dominating position must have used his position to get unfair advantages by causing consent of B for the agreement.

Legal presumption of undue influence: According to Section 16(2) of this act "it is legally assumed that under the following situations one party who is in dominating position must have caused undue influence to cause the consent of other for the agreement."

(*i*) ***Relationship of real and apparent authority:*** One party holds real and apparent authority over other party. They make an agreement. It will be legally assumed that the party who is in a superior position, in terms of authority must have used undue influence for causing the consent of other party. Pre-existing relationship of authority means the relationship of superior and subordinate.

Example: A and B are working in the same department. A is a section officer and B is an assistant. Both of them enter into contract. It will be legally assumed that A who is in a superior position to dominate will of B must have exercised undue influence to cause the consent of B for a contract.

(*ii*) ***Fiduciary relationship:*** Fiduciary relationship is a relationship, which is based on a mutual trust and confidence between two parties. In such relationship one of the parties is thought to be in a dominating position. When parties standing in fiduciary relationship make an agreement, legally it will be presumed that the party in a dominating position must have caused the consent of other through undue influence.

Some of the cases of fiduciary relationship are as under:

(*a*) Father and Son/Guardian and Ward

(*b*) Teacher and Disciple

(*c*) Doctor and Patient

(*d*) Advocate and Client

(*e*) Trustee and Beneficiary

RHODES *vs* DATE (L.R.I, Ch. 257). In this case, the court has made it clear that the doctrine of undue influence applies to all varieties of fiduciary relations in which domination may be exercised by one person over another. A test is to be applied whether one party is able to dominate the will of other.

(*iii*) ***Mental distress:*** Sometimes, mental capacity or a strength of a person may be adversely affected either by age, illness or other bodily and mental strain. Such person is said to be in a mental stress. Anyone who makes an agreement with such person is assumed to have exercised undue influence to cause his consent for an agreement. In these cases, status of a party is enough to prove the existence of undue influence.

Example: An old man of 80 years who is being looked after by his relatives may be influenced by the relative for making an agreement regarding the property of old man.

Similarly the person who meets with an accident and gets serious injury, is in a dire need of money to get necessary treatment makes an agreement for borrowing money. He may also be easily influenced by the moneylender for paying higher rate of interest.

(*iv*) ***Inadequacy of consideration:*** Though, it is not necessary that value of consideration given to the promisor must be equal to the value of a promise made by him. If he gets consideration of lesser value than the value of promise. In this case, it will be assumed that consent of the party getting lesser consideration has been caused by exercising undue influence. Thus inadequacy of consideration is also considered as an evidence of use of undue influence.

Burden of proof: In all above cases, cited under Section 16(2) there is a legal presumption that the party in a dominating position must have used it, in an unfair manner to cause the consent of another. In these cases, burden of proof for not using undue influence lies on the party who is in a dominating position. He can rebute the presumption by showing that:

(*i*) He had made full disclosure of facts relevant to the contract to that another party.

(*ii*) Consideration was adequate and transaction is not unreasonable.

(*iii*) The weaker party was in a position to receive independent advice and his consent was free.

Effects of undue influence: Where the consent is caused by exercising undue influence, contract is voidable at the option of aggrieved party whose consent had not been free. Such contract may be set aside by an aggrieved party. He can also enforce it against another party. And if he is compelled to perform it he may refuse it on the plea that his consent has not been free.

According to Section 19A of this Act, if the party who is entitled to avoid the consent has received any benefit there under may be called upon to restore it upon such terms and conditions, as the court may consider just and equitable.

Unconscionable transactions: Where the party in dominating position, makes an agreement with weaker party to make exhorbitant profit, such agreements are known as unconscionable transactions or agreements. In these transactions, the party in dominating position makes unreasonable profit from weak position of another party. In such agreements, the burden of proof is shifted to the dominant party. He has to prove that he did nothing to dominate the will of other party.

Mostly, money-lending transactions and gifts belong to this category. But to declare transaction unconscionable the parties of a transaction must have unequal position so that one can dominate the will of other.

Sometimes, high rate of interest may be charged by the moneylenders. If he is in a position of dominating will of the borrower and uses his position to get unfair advantage, the transaction may be declared as unconscionable one, and the court may intervene. In one of the case, where a poor widow borrowed Rs.1,500 from a moneylender @ 100% interest per annum, for filing a suit to establish her right to maintenance. The rate of interest was reduced to 24% per annum by Madras High Court. This relief was granted only on the basis of undue influence.

The court while dealing with the cases of undue influence normally takes four factors into consideration:

(*i*) Whether the transaction is righteous i.e., whether it is an act a right-minded person could be expected to carry out.

(*ii*) Whether it manifest so much improvidence as to suggest the idea that executant was not master of himself and not in a state of mind to sit and weigh as to what he was doing.

(*iii*) Whether intention of making the gift originated with the donor.

(*iv*) Whether it was a matter, which requires legal advice.

***Pardanashin* women:** Any women who observes 'parda' system is known as *pardanashin* woman. She does not come into contract with any person, other than her family members. She remains within four walls of the house and does not interact with outside world. Due to lack of outside exposure, the law grants protection to her. Thus anyone making a contract with *pardanashin* woman, can enforce such contract provided he proves that:

(*i*) She was in receipt of independent advice.

(*ii*) She has free consent for that contract.

(*iii*) She understood the nature of the contract as explained by another party.

Such protection is also granted to illiterate and ignorant women who are equally exposed to the danger and risk of unfair deal.

Table 5.1: Distinction between Coercion and Undue Influence

	Coercion	Undue Influence
Meaning	It includes committing or threatening to commit unlawful act or unlawful detention or threatening to detain property of others, to cause his consent.	A person in dominating position gets unfair advantage of his position to cause consent of other person.
Contents	It implies use of physical force or threat to cause consent.	It involves use of moral or mental pressure to cause consent.
Pre-existing Relationship	It is not required for using coercion.	Pre-existing relationship between parties is required to use undue influence.
Party of contract	It is not necessary for the party to direct coercion against the other party of contract and he may use it against the person who is stranger to contract.	Party using undue influence and against whom it is used, both of them must be parties of contract.

Contd...

	Coercion	Undue Influence
Burden of Proof	In coercion an aggrieved party who is entitled to set aside contract has to prove the act of coercion.	In undue influence burden of proof shifted on dominant party making unfair use of his position and getting consent of other party.
Restoration	In the use of coercion if an aggrieved party repudiates contract he has to restore benefit received in that to other party (Section 64).	In case of undue influence the court is at a discretion to direct an aggrieved party to return whole or part of benefit received, to other party (Section 19A).

3. Misrepresentation

While making contract, one of the party may make any statement regarding the subject matter of a contract. Such statement, if turns to be untrue it amount to misrepresentation. It is a misstatement of material facts.

Misrepresentation of facts is always innocent in nature. The party making untrue statement believes that the statement is true, but in reality statement turns to be incorrect. The party making misrepresentation has no intention for making untrue statement. And at the same time he may not have sufficient ground to believe that the statement was true.

According to Section 18 of Indian Contract Act, misrepresentation means and includes the following:

(*i*) ***Assertion of facts:*** The positive assertion in a manner not warranted by information of the person making it which is not true, though he believes it to be true. In other words, in misrepresentation, the person asserts on untrue statement, however innocently. And he has no sufficient ground to believe that it is untrue. But really it turns to be untrue.

Example: A has a Maurti Car. He believes that his car runs 20 km by using one litre of petrol. He make this statement to B believing that it is true. B makes an agreement to buy the car. And it appears that the car hardly gives mileage of 12 km with one litre of petrol. It amounts to misrepresentation on the part of A, by making positive assertion of facts.

(*ii*) ***Breach of duty:*** Any breach of duty which without an intention to deceive, gains an advantage to the person committing it or anyone claiming under him, by misleading another to his prejudice or anyone claiming under him. There are certain case in law, where one party is under legal obligation for making full and correct disclosure of material fact related to contract to another party. In such case, if the party makes breach of duty however, innocently without an intention to deceive other, it amounts to misrepresentation on his part. It happens in all contracts of 'utmost good faith'.

In these contracts, one party knows material facts related to subject matter of a contract, which other party does not know and has no reasonable means to know. The party having knowledge of material facts is under legal obligation to make full and correct disclosure of those facts to other party. These contracts include: contracts based on a fiduciary relationship, insurance contracts, contracts to buy shares in joint stock company, partnership contracts and contracts related to family matters etc.

Example: A makes a contract with Fire Insurance Company to get his house insured against the risk of fire. This is a contract of utmost good faith. In this contract A is in a position to know each and every material facts about the house, which insurance company does not know or does not have reasonable means to know. Thus A is under legal obligation for making full and correct disclosure of these facts to insurance company. If he does not do so however, innocently which means innocent breach of duty, it amounts to misrepresentation.

(*iii*) ***Untrue statement made innocently:*** Causing, however innocently, a party to an agreement to make a mistake as to substance of the thing which is the subject matter of the agreement.

Sometimes, the person innocently makes untrue statement regarding particular subject matter before another person. That another person makes mistake on the basis of that statement and enters into a contract for buying that subject matter. Later on, it appears that contract was made on the basis of untrue statement. The person making such untrue statement however, innocently will be liable for misrepresentation.

Example: A & B are sitting in coffee house. A however innocently says to B that his house is fit for dwelling purpose. B, makes mistake on the basis of this statement and buys A's house. Later on it appears that there are big cracks on the walls and foundation of the house is very weak. A will be liable for misrepresentation.

DERRY *vs* PEEK (1889,14 App. Cas: 337). In this case, in the prospectus of a company there was an assertion that it had statutory powers to run its tramways by steam, provided the consent of Government is obtained. The director issued prospectus stating therein that the company has a right to use steam power. They believed that the company would be given permission for using steam power. The permission was refused and company had to wound up. It was held that the directors were liable for misrepresentation.

Effects of misrepresentation: In a contract, when consent of the party is caused by misrepresentation made by another party. Such contract is voidable at the option of an aggrieved party whose consent was caused by misrepresentation. He has the following rights:

(*i*) He can avoid or rescind the contract.

(*ii*) He can insist on the performance of a contract with a condition that he shall be placed in the same position, as he would have been if there had been no misrepresentation.

Example: A had rented his house to B and has given a notice to him for vacating the house. Believing that it will be vacated soon he makes a statement to C that his house is free from tenancy. C is induced to make mistake and finally he makes the agreement for buying that house. It is found that house is not vacated. This contract is voidable at the option of C and he can insist on A to perform the contract by getting house vacated and making it free from tenancy of B.

In case of misrepresentation, the aggrieved party can avoid the contract provided he proves that he had no reasonable means of knowing truth.

Example: A owns a factory of plastic goods at Okhla. He gives statement to B that his factory produces 1000 units of particular plastic item. He does it however, innocently. By mistake B gets induced to buy his factory. After buying factory it appears that factory can produce only 700 units of that plastic item. There is a misrepresentation. But B has no right to rescind or avoid a contract, because by inspecting production records of the factory he would have discovered truth of statement made by A.

Thus an aggrieved party whose consent has been caused by misrepresentation loses the right to avoid or rescind contract under the following situations:

(*i*) Aggrieved party has reasonable means for discovering truth of a statement.

(*ii*) Right to avoid or rescind a contract must have been used within reasonable period of time. In case of undue delay he may lose his right.

(*iii*) If the parties cannot be restored to their original position, the contract cannot be rescinded.

(*iv*) If third party has purchased goods in good faith for valuable consideration which were brought in by using misrepresentation the aggrieved party will lose the right to avoid or rescind the contract.

4. Fraud

An intentional misrepresentation of the facts amounts to fraud. Fraud is always committed with a view to deceive or cheat another person. Thus, when one person does anything or makes false statement knowingly to induce other for causing his consent, it is known as 'fraud'.

According to Section 17 of Indian Contract Act, "Fraud means and includes any of the following acts committed by a party to a contract or with his connivance or by his agent with intent to deceive other party thereto or his agent to enters into a contract."

(*i*) The suggestion as to a matter of fact, of that which is not true, by one who does not believe it to be true.

(*ii*) The active concealment of a fact by one having knowledge or belief of the fact.

(*iii*) A promise made without an intention of performing it.

(*iv*) Any other act fitted to device other.

(*v*) Any such act or omission as the law specially declares to be fraudulent.

Elements of fraud: According to the definition of fraud the following elements are included in a fraud:

(*i*) ***False representation:*** Most important element of fraud is false representation or untrue statement made by the party intentionally. The party, while making agreement, makes untrue statement regarding subject matter of a contract with an intention to cause the consent of another party, it amounts to fraud. The person giving untrue account of material facts has a knowledge of it, he does it to cheat or mislead another party. Thus, to constitute fraud, false statement must be accompanied by intention to mislead.

Example: A has purchased second hand scooter from B. He makes an agreement to sell it to C by saying that it is brand new scooter. A has committed a fraud with C by causing his consent for the agreement.

(*ii*) ***Active concealment of facts:*** A person may also commit a fraud by hiding certain material fact related to subject matter of contract. It also amounts to fraud if he does it to deceive other by causing his consent.

Example: A buys a second hand car from car dealer. He gets it repaired and painted it, as it looks new one. Later on he agrees to sell it to B as a new one car. A has made willful concealment of material facts regarding the car, it amounts to fraud. He has done it by covering up defects of old car by getting it painted.

However, if some businessman makes any untrue statement in making self-praise or commendation of his own goods it will not amount to fraud. It is because businessmen are supposed to speak optimistically about their products.

Example: A is a manufacturer of coloured television sets. He gives an advertisement that television set manufactured by him is the best available in the market. Such statement will not amount to fraud, because it is a mere expression of opinion for making self-praise of his own goods.

(iii) ***Making promise without an intention to perform:*** When a person makes a contract with another person, without an intention of performing it. It will also amount to a fraud. It is because the promisor carries an intention to deceive other party by making such contract right from the beginning.

Example: A buys some goods from B on credit. A carries an intention of not making payment to B. It will amount to fraud, because A has made a promise with an intention not to perform it.

(iv) ***Any other acts fitted to deceive:*** In order to extend coverage of fraud this clause has been added. According to this clause, acts other than covered under Section 17, if performed with an intention to mislead other, it will also amount to a fraud. It makes clear that all other acts which are not covered under Section 17 will also be considered as fraud if such acts are done to deceive another.

(v) ***Act or omission declared fraudulent by law:*** In addition, law has declared many acts or omission as fraudulent. If these are done it will also amount to fraud. Such acts or omissions have been cited in Insolvency Act, Indian Company Act and Transfer of Property Act etc. Under Section 55 of Transfer of Property Act, transferor of immovable property is required to disclose to the buyer or transferee all material defects in a property to be sold and non-disclosure of such defects amounts to a fraud.

Briefly speaking to constitute fraud the following conditions must be satisfied:

(a) Untrue or misleading statement has been made or any other device or technique is used or act is performed.

(b) Such misleading statement or fraudulent act or technique must have been used knowingly.

(c) Intention of giving misleading statements doing acts or using technique must be to deceive another person.

However, mere non-disclosure of the facts or mere expression of opinion or statement by a businessman in making self-praise of his goods will not amount to fraud.

Silence as fraud: Mere silence or mere non-disclosure of facts normally does not constitute fraud unless party keeping silence is under legal obligation to speak or his silence is equivalent to speech.

According to Section 17, mere silence as to fact likely to affect the willingness of a person to enter into a contract is not fraud unless the circumstance of the case are such that regard being made to them, if it is duty of a person keeping silence to speak or unless silence is equivalent to speech.

Example: A and B are traders. A enters into an agreement with B for buying some raw material. B has got private information regarding change in the price level of that raw material. He does not disclose it to A, because it may affect A's willingness to make an agreement. Such non-disclosure on the part of B will not amount to fraud. So, as per law, that a person before entering into a contract or while entering into it need not disclose material facts which he knows to the other party. But he must refrain from making active misstatement.

Thus generally silence, maintained by the party on material facts of subject matter does not amount to fraud. But this rule has certain exceptions. Under these situations, silence maintained by the party will amount to fraud. These situations are as follows:

I. ***Party keeping silence is under duty to speak:*** In a contract of utmost good faith, one party who has complete knowledge of subject matter is under legal obligation to make full and correct disclosure of that information to the another party. That another party may not be knowing it or may not have reasonable mean to know it. So if the party under legal obligation does maintain silence it will amount to fraud.

Duty to speak and make disclosure of material facts arises when parties entering into contract repose trust and confidence on each other. It happen in all contracts based on fiduciary relationship. Obligation to speak and make disclosure arises in the following contracts:

(*a*) Contracts of insurance.

(*b*) Contracts of allotment of shares in joint stock company.

(*c*) Contracts of family settlement.

(*d*) Partnership contracts.

(*e*) Contract between parties having fiduciary relationship.

(*f*) Contracts of marriage.

(*g*) Contracts of transferring immovable property.

II. ***Silence maintained by the party is equivalent to speech:*** In all such cases, where silence maintained by the party is equivalent to his speech. Such silence will also amount to fraud.

Example: A makes an agreement for buying B's motorbike. While making an agreement A says to B that if you do not refuse I believe that motorbike is in operational condition. B keeps silent. Later on it appears that motorbike is out of operation. B's silence is equivalent to his speech, thus he will be liable for a fraud.

III. ***Half truth:*** While making an agreement when one party discloses a portion of information or relevant fact, in the mean time he stops to disclose remaining facts. Disclosure of half truth amounts to fraud. It has been treated worse than misleading statement, by the court. Thus silence regarding unspoken facts will amount to fraud.

Table 5.2: Distinction between Fraud and Misrepresentation

	Fraud	**Misrepresentation**
Meaning	It includes any act, technique or misstatement to deceive other.	It includes misstatement of facts made honestly believing it to be true.
Intention	In case of fraud, intention of a party making it is to cheat another.	There is no such intention on the part of the person making misstatement.
Nature	It is intentional in character and is made deliberately.	It is however innocent in nature.
Remedy	Aggrieved party can avoid the contract and claim for compensation for the loss.	Aggrieved party can avoid the contract.
Silence	Under certain circumstance, silence maintained by the party amounts to fraud i.e., duty to speak, and if silence is equivalent to fraud.	But silence maintained by the party does not constitute misrepresentation.
Discovery of truth	In case of fraud, aggrieved party can avoid contract and except in case of silence as fraud he has to prove that reasonable means for discovering truth were not available.	In case of misrepresentation, aggrieved party can avoid or rescind a contract provided he had no reasonable means to discover truth.
Criminal Act	Fraud is a civil wrong or criminal act which is punishable under Indian Penal Code.	But misrepresentation does not amount to criminal act.

Effects of fraud: When the consent of a party has been caused by fraud, such contract is voidable at the option of an aggrieved party. Aggrieved party has the following legal remedies:

(*i*) He can avoid or rescind the contract.

(*ii*) He may insist on other party to perform a contract on the condition that he must be placed in that position, as there would have been no fraud.

(*iii*) Aggrieved party can also claim for compensation if he has suffered any loss due to fraud.

5. Mistake

Last element which affects the free consent of the party is the mistake. The consent cannot be said to be free if it is caused by mistake.

Mistake may be defined as a wrong impression or erroneous opinion in the mind of a person about any subject matter, event or instances.

According to Section 20 of this Act, "where both the parties to an agreement are under mistake as to the matter of fact essential to an agreement, the agreement is void." Thus it is clear that in case the consent of the party is induced by mistake the contract becomes void.

In the words of Salmond, error in consensus prevents existence of any contract. It means, in some cases of fundamental error, a contract does not even exist between parties.

SURAT CHANDER *vs* KANAI LAL (1921, Cal. 786). In this case Surat Chander was induced to sign a sale deed by Kanai Lal on representation that it was power of attorney. It was held that there was no contract due to error in consensus.

Mistake may be of two types:

(*i*) Mistake of law

(*ii*) Mistake of fact

Mistake of law again can be of two types:

(*a*) Mistake of law of own country.

(*b*) Mistake of law of foreign country.

(*i*) Mistake of Law

Sometimes the person may carry wrong impression in his mind regarding related provisions of law of his country. He may commit a mistake on the basis of that wrong impression and makes a contract. Such contract is binding. It is because, being citizen of the country he is expected to know the law of that country related to him. There is a general rule of law that 'ignorance of law is no excuse' and a person must be punished if he breaks the law—no matter he knows or does not know the law.

Example: A lends money to B and does not know Law of Limitation Act under which debt becomes time barred. Till the expiration of particular period of time he did not recover or made a notice of recovery of debt. That debt becomes time barred. So A cannot claim innocence of not knowing relevant provisions of the Act. Had he known it, he would have recovered it. The law will not excuse him for his ignorance.

But mistake related to law of foreign country renders a contract as void. According to Section 21 of this Act, a mistake as to a law not in force in India, has the same effect as the mistake of fact has and, on account of mistake of fact contract becomes void.

(*ii*) Mistake of Fact

Mistake of fact may also be of two types:

(*a*) Bilateral mistake

(*b*) Unilateral mistake

When both the parties of a contract are under mistake and mistake is related to material facts of subject matter of a contract, such mistake is known as mistake of fact. The contract affected by mistake of fact is void. Thus the contract will become void on account of mistake of fact provided the following conditions are satisfied:

- Both the parties of a contract must be under mistake.
- Mistake must be of facts.
- Mistake must be of a material fact of subject matter of a contract.

Bilateral mistakes of fact, related to material facts of subject matter of contract, are as under and the contracts are void under these situations:

Existence of subject matter: Both the parties of a contract are mistaken regarding existence of subject matter, the contract is void on account of mistake of fact. Such mistake occurs if at the time of making contract, the subject matter of contract ceases to exist, but the parties do not have knowledge of it.

Example: A agrees to buy some cargo from B which is being brought by a ship of B. But at the time of making a contract ship was sunk in the ocean. This fact was not known to them. The contract between A and B is void.

Identity of subject matter: Identity of subject matter is also a material facts. When both the parties of a contract make mistake regarding identity of a subject matter, such contract will also be void.

Example: A has two cars Maruti 800 and Honda City. He makes an agreement for selling a car to B. A believes that he is selling Honda City and B thinks that he is making a contract to buy Maruti 800. Both of them are mistaken on the identity of subject thus the contract is rendered to be void.

Ownership of subject matter: Where both the parties of contract commit a mistake regarding ownership of subject matter. Such contract is void due to bilateral mistake of fact.

Example: A has purchased a machine 10 years back on higher purchase basis. He is yet to pay last instalment. Believing that he has become owner of the machine he makes a contract to sell it to B. B thinks that A has been using that machine for the last 10 years, therefore he will be real owner of that machine. The contract is void.

Quantity of subject matter: The quantity of subject matter to be supplied is also an essential fact of a contract. Therefore common mistake on the part of both parties will render such contract as void.

HANKEL *vs* PAPE (1870, L.R.6 EX 7). In this case, A inspected 50 rifles in a shop. Later on he telegraphed 'send three rifles'. But due to a mistake of the telegraph department it was made as, 'Send the rifles'. The shopkeeper sent 50 rifles. But A refused to accept delivery. It was held that, the contract is void because both the parties are under mistake regarding quantity of subject matter.

Price of subject matter: When there is mutual mistakes on the part of both the parties regarding price of a subject matter, the contract is void. It is because price is also a material fact related to subject matter.

Example: A buys certain grocery items from B. While preparing a bill, the price of a particular item has been added twice by mistake. Contract is void on account of bilateral mistake of fact.

DAGADU VS. BHAN. (1904, 38, BOM.42). In this case, A agreed to hire B's auditorium at Rs. 800. But while writing an agreement the figure was written as Rs.1,000 by mistake. Agreement is void.

However, it is to be noted that when both parties of a contract make mistake regarding value of subject matter, the contract will not be void. It is because value of a particular subject matter differs from person to person depending on ones outlook, attitude, interest, hobby etc.

Unilateral Mistake: Mistake regarding subject matter on the part of one party only, is known as 'unilateral mistake'.

According to Section 22 of this Act, "A contract is not voidable merely because it was caused by one of the party to it being under mistake as to a matter of fact."

In other words, while entering into a contract one of the party carries erroneous opinion about essential facts of subject matter. But another party understood those facts correctly. The contract will not be void.

SMITH *vs* HUGHES (1871). In this case, a party bought oats from a vendor. A sample of which has already being shown to him. He erroneously thought that the oats were old. However the oats were new one. It was held that he had to suffer due to his own mistake and he could not avoid the contract.

Exceptions: But this rule is subject to certain exceptions, which are as under. In these exceptional cases, though the mistake is unilateral but agreement would be void.

(*a*) ***Mistake regarding nature of contract:*** When the party of a contract gives his consent under a mistake as to nature and character of a written document, such mistake may render the contract void.

In this regard, it is made clear that according to the judgement of Supreme Court if there is a fraud about character of document agreement is void.

Example: A is an old man who is being looked after by his relative B who has also been managing A's property. B states to A that part of his property is being given on lease to C and asks him to sign a document, which is in fact a gift deed in favour of B. A signs on it by mistake. Such deed is void, because there is fraud about a character of document.

(*b*) ***Mistake regarding identity of a party:*** This is when one of the party of a contract is under mistake regarding an identity of another party, which is essential for performing a contract. Such contract is also void. Thus mistake regarding identity of party renders contract void provided such identity is essential for the performance of a contract.

Example: A agrees to sell his motor bike to B on credits believing that he is C. Contract is void, because A is under mistake regarding B's identity and identity of B is essential for performing a contract *i.e.*, recovery of price from him.

LAKE *vs* SIMMONS (1927, A.C. 487). In this case a woman by falsely representing her to be the wife of well-known Baron, obtained two pearl neckless from a firm of jewellers on the pretex of showing them to her husband for the approval. She pledged them with a pawn broker who in good faith paid the

$ 10,000. It was held that here was no contract between the jeweller and woman thus even an innocent buyer did not get good title and must return them to the jewellers.

In this connection Sir William Anson has rightly pointed out that, 'If a man accepts a offer which is plainly meant for another or if he becomes a party to a contract by falsely representing himself to be another, the contract in either case is void.'

Effects of mistake: When the consent of the party is caused by mistake for a contract. Such contract is void and the following legal remedies are available to the parties.

(*i*) Any person, who gets any advantage in such contract, is bound to restore it or to make compensation for it to the person from whom he has received it (Section 65).

(*ii*) A person to whom money has been paid or any thing delivered by mistake must repay or return it to the party delivering it (Section 72).

REVIEW QUESTIONS

1. Define free consent and explain various elements of free consent in brief.
2. 'Free consent is one of the essential of a valid contract.' Comment.
3. Explain with suitable examples that how free consent and its various element affect validity of contract.
4. What is coercion? Explain various elements of coercion.
5. Distinguish between coercion and undue influence.
6. Define undue influence. Discuss those situations in which it is legally assumed that one party must have exercised undue influence to cause consent of another party.
7. What is misrepresentation? Explain various components of misrepresentation with suitable examples.
8. What do you mean by fraud? Explain contents of fraud with suitable examples.
9. Distinguish between fraud and misrepresentation.
10. What do you mean by 'Silence as fraud'? Explain its exception.
11. Define 'mistake'. Discuss various types of mistakes and explain the effect of mistake on the validity of a contract.

12. What is 'mistake of fact'? Under which situations contract becomes void on account of bilateral mistake regarding material facts of subject matter?
13. Define 'unilateral mistake'. Discuss the circumstances in which contract becomes void by unilateral mistake.
14. Comment on:
    (*a*) Making untrue statement regarding subject matter of contract is not fraud.
    (*b*) Unilateral mistake does not affect validity of contract.
    (*c*) Mere silence on the part of the party is not fraud.
    (*d*) Fundamental mistake regarding subject matter may not give a rise to contractual relation.
    (*e*) Place at which coercion is used may not necessarily be within the jurisdiction of IPC to prove it as coercion.
    (*f*) Mistake of law is no excuse.
15. Write notes on:
    (*a*) *Pardanashin* woman
    (*b*) Contract of utmost good faith
    (*c*) Effects of fraud
    (*d*) Unconscionable transaction
    (*e*) Bilateral mistake
    (*f*) Free consent
    (*g*) Duress and Coercion

PRACTICAL PROBLEMS

1. A makes an agreement with B for buying his house and seeks the consent of B by threatening to file a suit against him. Is this a valid contract? (Hint: Yes).
2. A kidnaps B's son and demands a ransom of Rs.10,000. B agrees to pay this amount to A. Does it amount coercion on the part of A? (Hint: Yes).
3. Ram sold his business to Shyam. Ram did not disclose it to his customers. Manohar sent an order of goods to Ram. But Shyam received an order and without informing change of ownership he supplied goods to Manohar. Is there a contract between Manohar and Shyam? (Hint: No, because of fundamental error about identity of the party).

4. X has two horses, one is black and another is white. He makes an agreement to sell one horse to Y. X believes that he is a making an agreement for selling white one, while as Y thinks that he is buying black horse. Is there any contract between X and Y? (Hint: Yes, but the contract is void on account of bilateral mistake regarding materiel fact *i.e.*, identity.)
5. A has delivered some goods to B by mistake. Can he recover those goods from B? (Hint: Yes, under Section 72.)

   B has consumed those goods. What legal remedy is available to A?
6. A has agricultural land in Delhi. He makes statement to B that he produces 100 tonnes of wheat per harvest from this land. B, by mistake enters into an agreement with A for buying that land on the basis of that statement. Later on it appears that hardly 50 tonnes of wheat can be produced in that land. Is contract between A and B valid? Can B avoid this contract? (Hint: Contract is voidable but B can avoid it because he had no reasonable means for discovering truth of the statement.)
7. A applies for a loan to a banker at a time when there is stringency in the money market. The banker declines to sanction the loan except at an exceptionally high rate of interest. A accepts the loan on those terms. Is the contract induced by undue influence? (Hint: No).
8. A agrees to buy some raw material from B at a particular price. B has got private information regarding change in the price level of that raw material. He does not disclose it to A, because it may affect A's willingness to make contract. Is this contract valid? (Hint: Yes).
9. A has advanced money to B during his minority. Upon B becoming of major age A obtains a bond from B by using influence of B's parents for a greater amount than the sum due in respect of his advance. Can A enforce the loan? (Hint: No, because ratification of minor's agreement is not allowed.)
10. A is already indebted to B, the moneylender of his village. A seeks fresh loan from him. B grants loan at unreasonably high rate of interest. Is there any use of undue influence? (Hint: Yes, unconscionable transaction.)
11. Manohar is manufacturing coloured television sets. He gives an advertisement in the newspaper that the television sets being produced by him are the best available in the market. However he knows that there are many other companies, which are manufacturing television set better than produced by him. Does it amount to fraud? (Hint: No, Businessmen are supposed to make self-commendation of their products.)

12. A is enfeebled by disease of age is induced by B who is his attendant to pay B unreasonable amount for his professional services. Can B enforce agreement)? (Hint: No, use of undue influence.)
13. A young widow was forced to adopt a boy, under threat of preventing the dead body of her husband from being removed and getting cremated. Can widow set aside adoption deed? (Hint: Yes, use of coercion.)
14. A enters into an agreement with B believing that he is C for selling goods on credit. Is there is any agreement between A and B? Can A enforce the agreement? (Hint: No).
15. Life Insurance Agent gives proposal to B for getting his life assured for a specific amount. B just thinking that he is 18 years old fills up it in the column of age. But actually he is 19 years old. Can LIC avoid this contract? (Hint: Yes, misrepresentation, innocent breach of duty.)
16. A purchased shares in a company on the basis of information given in the prospectus. The prospectus contained a false statement that B was a director of the company. A never heard of B earlier. Can A rescind the contract? (Hint: No, because false statement given in the prospectus is not a material fact for making contract of buying shares.)
17. A threatened his wife and son to commit suicide if they did not agree to transfer A's house to his brother C. His wife and son agreed to it. Later on they file a suit to set aside the contract. Can they do it? (Hint: Yes).

6

Legality of Object

LEARNING OBJECTIVES

- Get familar with the various objects of a contract.
- Examine legality of object.
- Be clear about legal object and lawful consideration.
- Develop conceptual clarity regarding Public Policy and agreements opposed to it.

INTRODUCTION

Every contract is made for an object or a purpose. The object of a contract is formed on the basis of promises made by the parties. The contract to be legally valid, must contain lawful object. When the contract is made for doing something illegal defeating provisions of the law such contract is not valid in the eyes of law.

According to Section 10 of this Act, "All agreements are contract if they are for lawful consideration and with a lawful object. Lawful object means, intention to do something permissible within the provisions of law."

However, it is to be noted that in many cases the consideration and the object of a contract may be the same. But in all cases it is not necessary. But the object and consideration of an agreement must be lawful.

Examples: A in consideration of Rs. one lakh from B agrees to kill C. The object of this agreement is killing of C, which is illegal and punishable under Indian Penal Code.

A, B and C agree to smuggle out some goods to D outside India. Again agreement is illegal.

According to Section 23 of this Act, consideration or object of an agreement is unlawful under the situations discussed below.

1. IT IS FORBIDDEN BY LAW

There are many acts, which are forbidden, *i.e.*, punishable under Indian Penal Code or under other laws. Thus if the object or consideration of any agreement is to do any of such act which is in contravention of provisions of the law such agreements are void on account of being illegal one.

Example: A is working at a higher capacity in some Government organisation. In consideration of Rs. 50,000 he ensures employment to B in this organisation. Agreement is void because of its illegal object.

BIGGS *vs* LAWRENCE (1789, 3, T.R. 454). In this case, a dealer agrees to sell certain goods to the buyer, knowing well that the goods are to be smuggled out of the country. It was held that the contract is unlawful.

2. IT DEFEATS THE PROVISION OF ANY OTHER LAW

If it is of such a nature that if permitted it would defeat the provision of any other law, it will be illegal one. When the agreement made by the parties is of such a nature that if it is permitted to continue it may lead to violation of the some provision of the law of land. Such agreements in fact involve indirect violation of the provisions of law. These agreements do not defeat the provisions directly, rather provisions of the law get defeated, when such agreements are allowed to continue.

Example: A has got house in Delhi. He pays house tax every year, which is calculated on the basis of rental value of that house. A, rents out his house to B for Rs. 5,000; as rent per month and makes another agreement with B that of Rs. 5,000; Rs. 2,000 will be considered rent and remaining amount has been charged for other amenities. If this agreement is allowed to continue the house rent comes down from Rs. 5,000 to Rs. 2,000 and simultaneously rental value of the house is reduced which ultimately reduce amount of house tax to be paid to Municipal Corporation. Thus the agreement is void, because of unlawful object.

Example: Agreement by the person who has been declared insolvent to pay full amount to any of his creditor in preference to other creditors is void on account being unlawful under Insolvency Act.

NAPIER *vs* NATIONAL BUSINESS AGENCY LTD. (1951, 2 ALL.E.R. 264). In this case, X agrees to enter Y's service in consideration of a weekly wage of Rs. 100 and weekly expense allowance of Rs. 20. Both parties are aware that the expense allowance is a device to conceal the revenues. It was held that agreement is void, because it defeats the provisions of law.

3. IT IS FRAUDULENT

Fraud is considered as civil wrong or tort, which is punishable under the provisions of law. Thus any agreement made with an object of defrauding or deceiving anothers will be void on account of illegality of object.

SCOTT *vs* BROWN. In this case, T agrees to buy shares at premium in a joint stock company through a broker S who has given as impression to the public that shares were useful of being purchased at a premium. Later on, he found that broker has sold his own shares to him and not purchased any shares from the market. It was held that agreement was aimed at cheating the public and therefore is void.

Example: An agreement between A and B to defraud government department by submitting tender in their names though they were both partners in transaction, is void as object is fraudulent.

4. IT INVOLVES AN INJURY TO A PERSON OR PROPERTY OF OTHER

Agreements made with an object or consideration of putting some person into criminal or wrongful harm or damaging his property or reputation is void. It is because in all such cases intention is to harm to someone or his property.

Examples: A promise to repay his debt by doing manual labour daily for a particular period of time and agrees to pay interest at an exorbitant rate in case of default. Such agreement is void, because consideration is illegal as it imposes slavery on the part of A.

A in consideration of Rs. 10,000 from B agrees to publish defamatory material against C. Agreement is void, because it involves injury to the reputation of C.

5. IT IS IMMORAL

When the object or consideration of an agreement is considered as immoral in the opinion of the court, such agreement will be void on account of unlawful object.

Among others, the immoral acts involve interference in a marital relationship, and the act of promoting or encouraging prostitution.

Example: A lets his house to B (a prostitute) knowingly that she will display her character there. Agreement is void A cannot recover rent from B.

P had advanced money to D a married woman to enable her to obtain divorce from her husband. D agreed that as soon as she gets divorced she will marry with P. Agreement between P and D is void on account of immorality.

6. IT IS AGAINST PUBLIC POLICY

The term public policy has not been defined under this Act. But in the name of public policy freedom of making a contract has been restricted by law only for the good of public.

Any agreement which goes against public policy and adversely affect public welfare, public decency, public cause and interest will be void.

It is therefore desirable to invoke 'doctrine of public policy' only in those areas where the damage to public interest and welfare is substantial. An attempt to enlarge scope of public policy will result in curtailment of individual's freedom to contract.

The courts have declared the following agreements oppose to public policy:

(i) ***Trading with alien enemy:*** In the event of war declared between two countries, citizens of those countries become alien enemy to each other. Taking into account national interest, no one is allowed to make an agreement with the citizens of enemy country. It is because it may help that country. The contracts made with that country before declaration of war will remain suspended till war continues. When the war is over such agreements can be enforced only with the permission of Government.

It is however to be noted that an agreement, which promote or encourage hostility with a friendly country is also considered oppose to public policy and therefore is void.

(ii) ***Trafficking in public office:*** Agreements, which interfere with the functioning of the public office and encourage corruption and inefficiency, are considered against public policy. Thus such agreements are void on account of illegality of object. The word trafficking is used in the sense of doing business with public office for private again.

Example: A is a manager in public sector bank. He makes an agreement with B that in consideration of money he will provide employment to him in the bank. Such agreement is void, because in public office if there is any employment opportunity, everyone whosoever is eligible has a right to avail it.

A is a businessman who is to pay Rs. 2 lakh income tax for a particular financial year. He makes an agreement with some official in Income Tax department. As a result of that agreement, A will pay Rs. 50,000 income tax and remaining part will be shared by A and income tax officer. Such agreement being opposed to public policy is void.

(iii) ***Interfering with course of justice:*** Impartial and independent functioning of judiciary is necessary. No one is allowed to interfere with an administration

of justice. In every situation, it is ensured that law takes its own course. Any agreement which interferes in the administration of justice either by influencing judge or the process of judgement is void as being against public policy. Agreements interfering with course of justice include following:

(*a*) ***Stifling prosecution:*** When someone commits a legal offence, he must be suitably punished under the provisions of law. An agreement, which protects the person from being prosecuted or reduces quantum of punishment in consideration of money is void.

General rule of law regarding it is in public interest criminal should be prosecuted and punished. Any agreement not to prosecute the offender or to withdraw a pending prosecution is void if the offence is of a public nature.

BHAWANIPUR BANKING CORPORATION LTD. *vs* DURGESH NANDANI (1941, A.I.R., P.C., 95). In this case, a mortgage was executed by Durgesh as a part of consideration for a promise by the bank to withdraw the criminal proceedings instituted against her husband by the bank. It was held that mortgage deed was void.

(*b*) ***Reducing period of limitation:*** Agreement made by the parties which reduces period of limitation within which an aggrieved party can enforce his right, is void. It defeats the object of law of limitation. According to law an action against the party making breach of contract must be taken within three years from the date of breach. An agreement which makes this period shorter less than 3 years will be void.

(*c*) ***Maintenance and champerty:*** These two terms are related to promotion of litigation between the parties. Maintenance includes those agreements, which are made with a view to promote litigation in which a person has no interest of his own. On the other, Champerty includes an agreement whereby one party agrees to assist another in recovering property in a suit and to share such proceeds.

In England both agreements of maintenance and agreement of champerty are void if they are found against public policy.

NUTHAKI VENKATSWAMI *vs* KATTA NAGI (1962, A.I.R. A.P. 457). In this case it was decided that an agreement to transfer ¾ share in the property if recovered has been held champertous and therefore void.

(*iv*) ***Marriage brokerage agreements:*** Marriage, being matter of one's life must be founded on mutual understanding between the parties. When the marriage is procured by some middleman, in consideration of money, such agreements are considered against public policy and thus are void.

Agreements to pay money as marriage brokerage that brings two parties into matrimonial relationship are void, because these agreements hinder exercise of free choice by the parties.

PITAMBER *vs* JAGJIVAN (13, BOMBAY 131). In this case a Purohit was promised Rs. 200 as consideration for procuring wife for a defendant. It was held that agreement is invalid and the money could not be recovered.

(v) Agreement creating interest against professional duty: In every profession the person who is engaged in it is subject to some obligations and duties. He is supposed to perform these to the best of his knowledge and capacity. Any agreement made by him, which goes against his duty and brings some personal gain to him, is void.

Example: A and B are partners in a partnership firm. A has been authorised to manage business of the firm. A makes secret profits in the business for him. Agreement of earning such profits is void because it creates interest against duty of a partner for not making personal gain.

(vi) Agreement interfering with parental duties: Parents and guardian have an authority and duty over their children. They are supposed to use it for the maximum welfare of their child. The authority of the parents cannot be transferred absolutely to another person. Agreements made for restricting parental authority or transferring such authority or interfering with such authority are void on account of being against public policy.

Example: A agrees to place his daughter at the disposal of B to be married according to her choice. This agreement is void and illegal because it interferes with a parental duty of A to find out suitable husband in the best interest of his daughter.

However, agreements of adoption duly made under Hindu Adoption and Maintenance Act are valid as an exception.

(vii) Agreements restraining personal freedom: Article 21 of Indian Constitution has guaranteed personal freedom to the citizens. Any agreement which takes away such personal liberty partially or completely is void being as oppose to public policy.

HARDWOOD *vs* MILLARS TIMBER AND TRADING COY (1917, I.K.B., 305). In this case, A has borrowed some money from B who is a moneylender and entered into an agreement with him that he will not change his residence, and employment or will work for the moneylender at reduced salary. It was held that agreement is void and illegal, because it interferes with personal liberty of the person.

(viii) Agreement interfering with marital duty: After the marriage husband and wife owe certain duties to each other. Agreement which stops them from performing marital duties is void on the ground of being against public policy. Some of these agreements are as under:

(*a*) A promise by a married person to marry during the lifetime of the spouse or after his or her death.

(*b*) An agreement in contemplation of divorce *e.g.*, an agreement to lend money to a woman in consideration of her getting divorce and marrying the lender.

(*c*) An agreement that husband and wife will always stay at the wife's parent's house or the wife will never leave her parental house.

UNLAWFUL *vs* ILLEGAL AGREEMENTS

Unlawful agreement does not create any rights and obligations between parties and therefore cannot be enforced in the court of law. It is absolutely void and does not have any legal sanctity and consequences. In such agreements only the parties making agreements are affected.

On the other, illegal agreement is one, which cannot be enforced in the court and does not have any legal consequences. In such agreements not only the immediate parties are affected but collateral transaction which is based on illegal agreement will also be void.

Example: A in consideration of Rs. one lakh from B agrees to kill C. For making payment to A, B borrows this amount from D, and D knowingly lent the amount to B that it is to be paid to A who is to kill C. Agreement between A and B is void and illegal. Another agreement between B and D is a collateral transaction based on first one will also be void.

All illegal agreements are unlawful, but all unlawful agreements are not illegal. Distinction between unlawful and illegal agreements can be made on the basis of the intention of the competent authority of making law.

When the law is made for protecting public and public interest any agreement which defeats provision of such law is illegal agreement on the other hand, if law is made for protecting revenue and administrative convenience and any agreement which violates the provision of such law is unlawful agreement.

Examples: A agrees to sell 20 carats of liquor to B at a specified price. A does not possess licence for it. Such agreement is illegal and void. It is because sale of liquor without license is illegal and the object of prohibition is to protect the public.

A has purchased a DDA flat. He constructs second floor on it without permission of DDA. He is liable to pay penalty. Such agreement is unlawful and void because it makes breach of law, which intended to protect revenue and administrative convenience.

CONSEQUENCES OF ILLEGAL AGREEMENT

(*i*) When the object of an agreement is to do something illegal which defeats provisions of the law, such agreement is void *ab initio*. Such agreements do not create any right and obligation between parties and cannot be enforced in the court either by the parties.

(*ii*) No legal remedy is available to any party and nothing can be recovered under illegal agreement. In other words, no action can be taken for the recovery of money paid or for the breach of agreement. In the example given above if A kills C and B does not pay to A. A has no legal remedy for recovering Rs. one lakh from B. And if B has paid money to A and A did not kill C, B cannot recover this amount from A.

(*iii*) Collateral transaction based on illegal agreement will also be void.

(*iv*) Any party who has done illegal act will be prosecuted as per relevant provisions of the law.

REVIEW QUESTIONS

1. 'Agreement can be enforced only with lawful object and consideration.' Comment.
2. Discuss those situations under which object is considered to be unlawful.
3. Define 'illegal agreement'. Explain its effect with suitable examples.
4. What is Public Policy? Explain the agreements, which are declared against public policy.
5. Comment on:
   (*a*) Every illegal agreement is unlawful, but every unlawful agreement is not illegal.
   (*b*) Consideration and object of agreement must be lawful to be enforced in the court.
   (*c*) No action is allowed in an illegal agreement.

6. Write notes on:
   (*a*) Maintenance and Champerty.
   (*b*) Illegal agreements.
   (*c*) Agreements oppose to public policy.
   (*d*) Effects of illegal agreement.
   (*e*) Agreement of marriage brokerage.

PRACTICAL PROBLEMS

1. X is a section officer in a bank. He makes a promise in consideration of Rs. 20,000 from Y to procure suitable employment for him in the bank. Is agreement valid? (Hint: No).
2. A rented out his house to B at Rs. 10,000 per month. In order to reduce municipal taxes A makes another agreement with B for reducing rent to Rs. 5,000 and remaining amount will be charged for other services. Explain the validity of second agreement.
3. A borrows some money from B and makes an agreement that he will remain in employment with him unless he pays back money to B. Is it a valid agreement? (Hint: No).
4. Manohar agrees to kill Shyam in consideration of Rs. one lakh from Hari. Hari borrows this amount from Shohan who knowingly lent money to Hari. Can Shohan recover this amount from Hari? (Hint: No).
5. A lent a sum of Rs. 50,000 to B who is to seek divorce from her husband and agrees to marry A. Can A recover this amount from B? (Hint: No).
6. Mohan has rented his house to a prostitute at certain amount of rent. Mohan knew that the prostitute will display her character over there. Can he claim rent from her? (Hint: No).
7. A in consideration of Rs. 1,000 from B enters into an agreement with him for publishing same objectionable material against C. Can A recover this amount from B? (Hint: No).
8. A is a businessman. He has a tax liability of Rs. 2 lakh in Income Tax Department makes an agreement that he will deposit Rs. 50,000 as a tax and remaining balance will be shared equally by them. Is agreement valid? Why? (Hint: No).

9. A has got a claim of Rs. 20,000 against B, he files suit against B for the recovery of his claim. C makes an agreement with A to help him financially. And in consideration of such promise A also makes a promise to give him ½ of proceeds recovered from B. A wins cause and refuses to pay any thing to C. Can C recover his share from A? (Hint: Yes).
10. A has two daughters. After the marriage of second one he makes an agreement with her husband that both of them will stay with him and look after him so long he is alive. Is it a valid agreement? (Hint: No).

■■■

7

Agreement Expressly Declared Void

LEARNING OBJECTIVES

- Understand the basic concept of agreements which are expressly declared void.
- Get knowledge about agreements in restraints of marriage, and legal proceedings.
- Examine agreements in restraint of trade.
- Understand difference between wagering agreements and other agreements.

INTRODUCTION

In general, an agreement becomes void if it does not satisfy anyone of the essentials of a valid contract. Such as agreements with minor, agreement without consideration, agreement with illegal object and agreement by the parties having no contractual capacity, etc.

Void agreements do not create any rights and obligations between parties and cannot be enforced in the court either by the parties.

In addition, there are many agreements, which have also expressly been declared as void by the law. Thus if agreement made by the parties falls in this category, such agreement will also become void. These agreements are as under:

1. Agreement in restraint of marriage (Section 26).
2. Agreement in restraint of trade (Section 27).
3. Agreement in restraint of legal proceedings (Section 29).
4. Agreement meaning of which is uncertain (Section 29).
5. Agreement by way of wager (Section 30).
6. Agreement to do impossible act (Section 56).

1. AGREEMENT IN RESTRAINT OF MARRIAGE (SECTION 26)

Every individual is at a liberty of getting married and enjoy marital status. For every reason law gives due recognition to such status.

An agreement which prevents the person from getting married or puts any hindrance in the process of marriage is void. Restrictions on marriage may be either absolute or partial in nature. In both the cases agreement will be void. When the person is prevented from marrying at all it is known as general restraint. On the other when he is restrained to marry particular person or person from particular community such restraint is particular. But the restraints will be void in both the cases.

This rule is subject to following exceptions:

(*i*) A promise to marry a particular person does not imply restraint of marriage.

(*ii*) Penalty imposed upon marriage under the provisions of law does not amount to any restraint.

(*iii*) Agreement, which prevents a minor from getting married, is valid.

However it is to be noted that in English Mercantile Law it is only an absolute restraint which is void and partial one is valid.

LOWE *vs* PEERS (1768, 98, E.R. 160). In this case, P promised to marry Miss L and in default pay her $ 1000. Later on, he got married to someone else. Miss L sued upon P for the recovery of that amount. It was held that the contract was in restraint of marriage and thus void.

2. AGREEMENT IN RESTRAINT OF TRADE (SECTION 27)

As per the Indian Constitution every citizen has a right to start and conduct any lawful trade, industrial work or vocation. He can earn profit out of it. Thus an agreement which prevents the person from carrying such business is void. Not only this, but also an agreement that creates any hindrance in that process is void.

According to Section 27 of this Act, "Every agreement is restraint of trade is to that extent void."

Example: A and B are doing business of timber at Kirti Nagar. Both of them are rivals to each other. To protect him from this rivalry A agrees to pay a sum of money to B provided B closes his business from this area. B closed his business but A refused to pay him. Agreement is void, *ab initio* and therefore money cannot be recovered.

Agreement in restraint of trade may be either absolute or partial. But in both cases agreement will be void. However, it is to be noted that if an agreement is divisible and partial restraint is upon particular part of an agreement only that part will be void.

There are certain exceptions to this rule. Some of them are statutory in nature and others are arising out of judicial interpretation of Section 27.

(i) Sale of goodwill: Goodwill is known as name and fame of the firm. It refers to capacity of the firm to earn super profits on and above reasonable rate of return of the industry to which the firm belongs.

According to Section 27(I), one who sells the goodwill of a business may agree with the buyer to refrain from carrying on a similar business, within specified local limits so long as the buyer or any person deriving title to the goodwill from him carries on, a similar business therein.

In other words, when the owner of a business has earned a goodwill and makes an agreement for selling it to other. The buyers of the goodwill may prevent the seller from being in similar business. Such agreement as an exception is valid provided:

(*a*) Seller of goodwill is being prevented from doing similar business of which he is selling goodwill.

(*b*) Seller is prevented from carrying similar business within specified local limits only.

(*c*) Such restraints have been imposed on the seller only for a reasonable period of time, *e.g.*, so long as buyer derives benefits of goodwill.

Example: A is doing a business of steel goods at Moti Nagar, Delhi. A makes an agreement for selling goodwill of his business to B for Rs. one lakh. In that agreement B prevents A from doing business of steel goods for two years in Moti Nagar. Such agreement is valid because restraints have been imposed on A only for Moti Nagar. He can do similar business in other local areas of Delhi; secondly restriction is imposed for a particular period of time *e.g.*, two years, which seems to be reasonable one.

(ii) Restrictions under Partnership Act: The Indian Partnership Act also provides certain exceptions to the rule of agreement in restraint of trade is void. These are:

(*a*) At the time of admission of a partner in the firm he makes an agreement with the firm that so long as he remains partner will not conduct similar business. Such agreement is valid though it restricts right of partner for doing business. [(Section 11(II)].

(*b*) Agreement made by outgoing partner for not doing business similar to that of firm for reasonable period of time within specified local limits is also valid. [(Section 36(2)].

(*c*) In anticipation of dissolution of the firm, agreement made by the partners for not carrying a business similar to that of firm for a particular period of time and within specified local limits. Such agreement is also valid. (Section 54).

(*d*) Any partner or firm on sale of goodwill enters into an agreement with the buyer for not doing business similar to that of firm for a particular period of time within local limits. Such agreements are valid. [(Section 55(3)].

Exceptions under judicial interpretation

(*i*) ***Trade combinations:*** In practice, many agreements are made by the firms doing similar business. Agreements made with a primary objective of regulating business or conditions of a business are valid. Reasons being that such agreements are in the interests of all firms belonging to that business.

Such agreements may take a form of trade association, chamber of commerce and pools, etc. These are made by the firms voluntarily for reducing cut throat competition by dividing market, fixing prices and standardising goods. These agreements restrict liberty of the firms in conducting business, but by being in a larger interest these are valid as an exception.

On the other hand, agreements made by the various firms doing similar business with a view to create monopoly in the market are void. It is because monopolistic practices in the market may lead to exploitation of customers.

Examples: There are four dealers of Maruti car in Delhi. They make an agreement for distributing entire market of Delhi among them. Each of them will function within boundaries of the market allotted to him. An agreement among them is valid, because they made it to regulate the market of their product.

In anticipation of huge sale of sweets during Diwali festival all sweet meat makers of Delhi make an agreement that they will not sell sweet below Rs.100 per kg. This agreement tends to create monopoly in the market, thus it is void.

It is governed and regulated by the provisions of the Monopoly and Restrictive Trade Practices Act, 1969.

(ii) ***Sole-selling agreements:*** In practice manufacturers appoint agents for selling their products. They may give this right only to a particular agent on distributor who may be refrained from dealing in goods of other manufacturers. Such agreements are valid, though freedom of sole-selling agent or distributor is restricted. These agreements are considered part of common commercial practice among businessmen for promoting their business.

Example: Tata Tele Services Ltd. appoints A as their sole-selling agent, making an agreement with him that he will not deal in the goods of other Teleservice companies. Such agreement is valid.

It is however, to be noted that such agreements should not create hardship either for manufactures or purchasers by creating monopolistic trends in the market. In such cases, such agreement may be declared void.

S. KALLU *vs* RAMSARAN BHAGAT. In this case a person agreed to buy all combs manufactured by all the manufacturers in Patna. Such agreement was declared to be oppressive and monopolistic. Thus it is void.

(iii) ***Service contracts:*** When the person is appointed as an employee in a particular organisation. As a matter of condition of service agreement he may be restricted by his employer from doing similar job outside. Such agreement is valid. For instance, doctors of government hospitals are usually debarred from conducting private practice, so long as they remain in the employment with government hospitals.

But such restraint on the employee is valid only during his employment. When he leaves the organisation or is terminated from the service he may be engaged in similar job outside the organisation.

It is to be noted that the service restraint put on the employee must be reasonable one, which differs from case to case depending on nature of job and other factors.

LUMLEY *vs* WAGNER (1852, I.D.M.C., 604). In this case Miss Wagner agreed to sing at the theatre of Mr. Lumley for three months and not sing elsewhere. It was held that she can be restrained from singing elsewhere during the period of three months.

CHARLESWORTH *vs* MCDONALD (1898, 23, BOM.103). In this case, M agreed to work with Dr. C at Zanzibar for a period of three years. The contact provided that during the term of agreement M will not practice on his own account at Zanzibar. However, after one year of service, M left the service and started his own practice at Zanzibar. It was held that agreement was valid and Dr. C was entitled to get injunction, restraining M from practising at Zanzibar during the period of agreement.

3. AGREEMENT IS RESTRAINT OF LEGAL PROCEEDINGS (SECTION 29)

Jurisdiction of court or law cannot be restricted by any agreement. Everyone who is entitled to a legal course can adopt it. And let the law take its own course.

Thus any agreement, which interferes with the course of justice or prevents the person from taking legal course, is void. Similarly, any agreement which limits time period within which one can enforce his right arising out of contract is void.

According to Section 28 (a) of this Act, "Every agreement by which any party thereto is restricted absolutely from enforcing his rights under or in respect of any contract, by the usual legal proceedings in the ordinary tribunal's or which limits the time with in which he may thus enforce his rights is void to that extent."

It is clear that the access to normal course of law for enforcement of agreement cannot be denied to themselves by the parties.

However, it should be noted that restraints to legal proceedings must be absolute. If it is partial, agreement will not be void.

Following are the exceptions to Section 28:

(*i*) ***Arbitration of present dispute:*** When some dispute is going on between the parties, they make an agreement that instead of going to the court, they refer to an arbitration. Such agreement is valid, though they cannot agitate for the same dispute in the court.

(*ii*) ***Arbitration of future dispute:*** In anticipation of some dispute, the parties enter into agreement that in case any dispute arises, it will be referred to an arbitration. Such agreement is valid.

However an agreement that the validity of an award shall not be objected on any ground, by any party entitled to, in an appropriate court is void.

4. AGREEMENT MEANING OF WHICH IS UNCERTAIN (SECTION 29)

To enforce an agreement in the court its meaning must be certain or capable of being made certain. Any uncertainty in the meaning of agreement will create uncertainty regarding rights and obligations. Such uncertain rights and obligations cannot be claimed in the court of law.

Thus, an agreement, which is ambiguous or vague in its meaning, creating confusion about basic nature of it, cannot be enforced in the court of law.

Examples: A agrees to buy 10 litres of oil from B who is a dealer of kerosene oil and mustard oil. Agreement is void on account of uncertain meaning.

A has got agricultural land in Delhi. He agrees to sell entire crop of wheat next year to B at specified rate. Agreement is valid, because its meaning would become certain with the passage of time when the crop of wheat will mature.

MONTREAL GAS COY *vs* VASEY (1900, A.C. 595). In this case, Gas coy agreed with Vasey that at the expiration of Vasey's existing contract of service, the company would favourably consider the renewal of the contract. It was held that agreement was void, it is because there is uncertainty in the meaning of agreement, and thus no obligation will arise.

Example: A agrees to sell his motorbike to B for a price which will be determined by C. Agreement is valid, because the price can be very well determined by C.

5. AGREEMENT BY WAY OF WAGER (SECTION 30)

Wagering agreement is one in which money is to be paid by one to another party or vice versa on the happening or non-happening of future uncertain event. If the event turns in one way one party is to pay to another and on the turning of event in another way, another party will pay to first one. But in every case, whether event happens or does not happen, payment of money is to be made.

In the words of William Anson, wager may be defined as, "A promise to give money or moneys worth upon the determination or ascertainment of an uncertain event."

In wagering agreement either of the party is to win or to lose. Thus if one loses another will win or vice versa.

Essential of wagering agreement

The essentials of wagering agreement are:

(*i*) ***Mutual gain or losses:*** There are two parties in wagering agreement. One of the parties will win and another party will lose. Their gain or loss depends on the happening or non-happening of future uncertain events. That party will lose if event happens who has promised payment of money on the happening of the event and vice versa.

Example: Cricket match is going on in Pakistan, between India and Pakistan. A agrees to pay a sum of Rs. 20,000 to B if India wins and if India loses B will pay same amount to A. This is wagering agreement made by the parties for their mutual loss or gain.

(*ii*) ***Uncertain event:*** The performance of wagering agreement depends on happening or non-happening of a future uncertain event. The event is not uncertain because it is to happen in future, but it is more uncertain because its result is not at all known to the parties. Both the parties of an agreement keep on guessing about happening or non-happening of future event.

(*iii*) ***Interest of the parties:*** Parties of wagering agreement do not have any interest on the happening or non-happening of that event. They simply look at the possibility of happening of the event for their gain or loss. They contemplate the determination of the uncertain event as sole condition of their contract.

(*iv*) ***Control over the event:*** In wagering agreement, there is no control of the parties, on the happening of the event. Event is an independent one, which may or may not happen, but its own way. There is no influence of the parties on it. If any of the party has a control over the event, it will not be considered as wagering transaction.

According to Section 30 of this Act, "Agreement by way of wager are void. And no suit shall be brought for recovering anything alleged to be won by any wager or entrusted to any person to abide by the result of any game or other uncertain event on which any wager is made."

Effect of wagering agreement

The effect of wagering agreement are:

(*i*) Wagering agreement are void. Therefore the winner cannot recover amount which other party had to pay.

(*ii*) Agreement by way of wager is just void and unenforceable. The collateral transaction based on such agreement are not affected and thus are valid.

However, in the state of Maharashtra and Gujarat, such wagering agreements are not only void, but illegal also.

Example: A agrees to pay Rs. 5,000 to B if cricket player Dhaumi makes out century in the match going on between India and West Indies. A borrows this amount from C who knowingly lent this amount to him. In the state of Maharashtra and Gujarat C cannot recover this amount from A, but in other states he can recover it.

Transactions included in wagering agreement

The following transactions are included in wagering agreement:

(*i*) ***Speculative transactions:*** These transactions are made in stock exchanges. These transactions are related to purchase and sale of shares and other securities of the companies. In these transactions, parties are intended to buy or sell securities with a prime motive of making profit out of changes in the market value of these securities. In speculative transactions, payments of price, delivery of securities and transfers of ownership do not take place. Simply on the date of settlement of transaction, a difference in market value of the securities is calculated and paid either to the party. Though such transactions are allowed in stock exchanges, they are void.

Example: A agrees to buy 100 shares of X coy at the price Rs. 250 per share from B on 1st of January. On due date of transaction no real sale or purchase takes place, rather difference between agreed price and market price is calculated and paid to the party accordingly.

(ii) ***Transactions of lotteries:*** A lottery is a game of chance. An agreement to buy a lottery ticket is void. Thus if someone buys lottery ticket and wins the prize, legally he cannot recover it from the party conducting the business of lottery. But in fact various state governments have permitted government departments or other agencies for conducting this business. Still transactions of lottery remain void. Only effect of such authorisation is that persons conducting business of lotteries are not to be prosecuted.

(iii) ***Horse race and gambling transaction:*** These transactions are also included in wagering transactions and therefore void. Gambling is an offence under Indian Penal Code, thus any transaction on gambling will be void.

So far as transactions of horse race are concerned, agreement to pay less than Rs. 500 to the winner of the horse race is void. But to subscribe Rs. 500 or more to the winner of the horse race is valid.

(iv) ***Crossword puzzle:*** In a crossword puzzle, winning of the puzzle may be the matter of chance and involves manipulation of words and does not require special skills. Such puzzles are considered as lottery transaction and thus are void.

However, the following transactions are resembling with wagering transactions, but are not of a wagering nature:

(i) ***Purchase of shares and debentures:*** Transaction of real and genuine sale and purchase of shares and other securities in stock exchange is not of wagering nature. In these transactions shares are actually delivered, ownership is transferred and payment of price is made. These transactions are absolutely valid.

(ii) ***Competition and crossword puzzles:*** To win a prize in any competition including athletic competition or debate competition, etc., or crossword puzzle is a valid transaction. It is because such competitions do require

special skill and talent on the part of participants. Thus if someone wins a prize, he can legally recover it from the party organising such competition.

(*iii*) ***Insurance contract:*** Insurance contract is a contract whereby the insurance company in consideration of payment of premium from the insured promises to compensate his losses arising out of insured cause. These contracts are valid.

Such contracts differ from wagering agreements on the following grounds:

(*a*) In insurance contract, the party (insured) has insurable interest on subject matter. It is only to protect such interest he makes an agreement. But in wagering agreements parties have no interest on the event. They are only interested in winning.

(*b*) In insurance contract, on the happening of uncertain event actual losses of the party are compensated by the insurance company. But in wagering agreement only stipulated amount will be paid to the winning party.

(*c*) Insurance contracts are considered in the interest of the society and therefore encouraged. But wagering transactions do not serve any interest of the society, rather encourage gambling.

(*d*) In insurance contract, the amount of premium is determined on scientific way, keeping in view degree of risk involved. But in a wagering agreement, to determine amount of loss or gain has no basis at all.

ALMAI *vs* POSITIVE, GOVERNMENT SOCIETY LIFE ASSURANCE COMPANY (1889, 23, BOM. 191). In this case, Almai insured the life of Mrs. X, a wife of his employee for a term of 10 years and for Rs. 25,000 with an insurance coy. The policy was assigned to Almai. Mrs. X died a year later. A filed suit for the recovery of the amount of policy. It was held that it was a wagering transaction, because A had no insurable interest in the life of Mrs. X, therefore A cannot recover the amount.

6. AGREEMENT TO DO IMPOSSIBLE ACT (SECTION 56)

Section 56 of this Act states that "an agreement to do an act impossible in itself is void."

When the parties make an agreement to do something impossible, such agreement has been expressly declared void by law.

Example: A in consideration of Rs. 10,000 agrees to discover treasure with the help of magic. Agreement is void due to impossibility of act.

Impossibility may arise in the contract, after its formation, due to change in law or any other reason, beyond the control of parties. Such impossibility is known as 'supervening impossibility' and the contract affected by it, will be void.

When one party makes a promise for doing something which he knew or must have known with reasonable diligence that is impossible and promisee did not know it. Such promisor must pay compensation to the promisee for any loss, which he suffers, because of non-performance of contract.

Example: A contracts to marry B who is already married to C and being prohibited by law to practise polygamy. A must pay compensation to B for a loss caused to her by non-performance of a promise.

Right of restitution in void contract: According to this right, when contract becomes void, the party who has received any benefit under it must restore it to the other party. In case, restoration is not possible he must compensate to another party. This right is claimed by the party from whom other party has got benefit. It is based on the principle of justice and equality.

Sections 64 and 65 of this Act deal with this right. According to Section 64, "a party who is entitled to avoid contract if does so, he shall restore any benefit received by it to the person from whom it was received."

Section 65 gives a right of restitution to the party concerned under the following situations:

(*i*) ***When an agreement is discovered to be void:*** When parties make an agreement but it is not enforceable, such agreement does not become a contract. Thus in such an agreement one party who has received some benefits must return it or compensate other party.

(*ii*) ***When a contract becomes void:*** A contract has been entered into between the parties. But due to impossibility of performance arising after a formation of contact it cannot be performed. Such contract becomes void. A party who has received any benefit under it, must restore it to the party from whom such benefit has been received.

However when the agreement has been expressly declared void by the law under various sections, no restitution is allowed in these cases.

Example: A agrees to sell his car to B for Rs. one lakh. B pays Rs. 50,000 as an advance. Before sale takes place the car has been stolen. The contract becomes void on account of impossibility of performance. Thus A should return Rs. 50,000 to B.

Example: A in consideration of Rs. 10,000 from B agrees to discover treasure by magic. B has paid Rs. 2,000 as an advance. A fails to discover treasure. B cannot recover money given in advance, because this agreement has expressly been declared void by law.

REVIEW QUESTIONS

1. Discuss agreements that have been expressly declared as void by the law.
2. 'Agreements in restraint of trade are void.' Explain exceptions to this rule.
3. 'Agreements interfering with legal course are void.' Explain exceptions to this rule.
4. Distinguish between wagering agreements and insurance contracts.
5. What do you mean by the term 'wagering agreement'? Discuss various wagering transactions with suitable examples.
6. Comment on:
   (*a*) Agreement in restraint of marriage are void.
   (*b*) Meaning of an agreement must be certain.
   (*c*) Transactions which resemble with wagering transaction are valid.
   (*d*) Agreement in restraint of legal proceeding are void.
   (*e*) Void agreement are different from void contracts.
7. Write short note on:
   (*a*) Wagering agreement.
   (*b*) Right of restitution.
   (*c*) Uncertain agreements.
   (*d*) Characteristics of wagering agreements.

PRACTICAL PROBLEMS

1. A agrees to marry B and no one else except her. If A defaults he will pay a sum of Rs. one lakh to B. Later on, A got married with someone else. B filed a suit for the recovery of that amount. Will she succeed to get it? (Hint: No, agreement is void.)
2. A and B are doing business of computer spare parts in Delhi separately. They are rivals to each other. In order to reduce cut throat competition they agree to divide market of Delhi in two parts and allot these parts to themselves. Later on A sells computer spares in one of the areas of the market belonging to B. Suggest legal remedy to B.

3. Ram made an agreement with B to sell all his produce at a specified rate with a condition that B was bound to accept the whole quantity. Is it a valid agreement? (Hint: Yes).
4. Ram and Shyam are two rival shopkeepers in a particular colony of Delhi. They make an agreement that if Ram closes his shop from the colony, Shyam will pay him Rs. 20,000. Later on Shyam refused to pay. Can Ram recover this amount from Shyam? (Hint: No, agreement is void *ab initio*.)
5. While admitting A into partnership as a partner the firm makes an agreement with him that so long he is a partner in the firm he will not do business similar to that of partnership firm. Is it a valid agreement? (Hint: Yes, exception to the agreements in restraint of trade are void.)
6. A was employed with B as an assistant. B makes an agreement with him that so long as he is working with him, he will not be allowed to get engaged in similar work, but A takes up a similar kind of job outside on part time basis. Suggest legal remedy to B.
7. All dealers of a particular commodity in a particular market enter into agreement that they will not sell the product for less than agreed price. Is it a valid agreement? (Hint: No, it tends to create monopoly.)
8. Manohar was appointed as an agent for selling the goods produced by Sohan. On a condition that Manohar will not deal in goods of any other manufacturer. Is such restraint valid? (Hint: Yes, the principle can put such restraints on his agent.)
9. A agrees to pay Rs. 5,000 to B if it rains today. And if it does not rain B will pay some amount to A. Is it valid agreement?
10. Ram agrees to pay a sum of Rs. 1,000 to the winner of horse race at Race Course Delhi. Examine validity of this agreement.
11. A agrees to discover treasure with the help of magic and B pays Rs. 2,000 to A for his promise. A fails to do so. Can B recover this amount from A? (Hint: No, agreement is void *ab initio*).

8

Quasi-Contracts and Contingent Contracts

LEARNING OBJECTIVES

- Try to understand logic behind quasi-contract.
- Compare quasi-contract with other contracts.
- Examine various types of quasi-contracts.
- Get familiar with contingent contracts.
- Compare contingent contract with wagering agreements.
- Analyse on enforceability of contingent contracts.

QUASI-CONTRACT: MEANING AND DEFINITION

Quasi-contract implies creation of legal rights and obligations between parties without making any formal contract. In quasi-contracts, the parties do not go into the process of offer and acceptance, rather a relationship resembling with that of a contract is established between them from the circumstances or by operation of law. The law imposes such obligations on the parties, which are similar to that created by contract. Thus such cases are known as 'quasi-contractual obligations' or 'quasi-contracts'.

Briefly speaking, a quasi-contract is created by law or circumstances. The obligation created by quasi-contracts can be enforced in the court in similar manner as in case of a formal contract. Therefore quasi-contracts are known as 'relations resembling those created by contracts' in Indian Contract Act.

The term quasi-contracts has been used in English Law. In the words of Pollock,

"Quasi-contracts are a contract in law but not in fact, being the subject matter of fictitious extention of the sphere of a contract to cover obligations which do not, in reality, fall within it."

This definition makes it clear that quasi-contracts are simply an extention of formal contract.

WHY QUASI-CONTRACTS

The concept of quasi-contracts is based on the principle of equity and justice. According to this principle, nobody will be allowed to be enriched at the expense or cost of another person. If he gets benefit unjustly he must pay its cost to the person from whom he derives it.

Sometimes he may not so easily be paying its cost, in such situations law will impose obligation upon him to pay the cost.

Lord Mansfield has rightly pointed out that "Law as well as justice should try to prevent unjust enrichment of one person at the cost of another; in one word, the gist of this kind of action is that the defendant, upon the circumstances of the case, is obliged by ties of natural justice and equality to refund the money."

Lord Wright has stated that, "It is clear that only system of law is bound to provide remedies for cases of what has been called unjust enrichment or unjust benefits, that is, to prevent a man from retaining the money of or some benefit derived from another which is against conscience that he should keep."

On the basis of these statements it is clear that:

(*i*) If the person has got payment of money or any other benefit unjustly under any circumstances, he must not retain it.

(*ii*) Such benefit or payment should be returned back to the person from whom it has been received.

(*iii*) In case benefit has been consumed, its cost should be paid or should be compensated for that loss.

(*iv*) Both parties should be put in equal footing. One should not unjustly get benefit and another unjustly should not suffer a loss.

Section 73 of this Act provides that, "when an obligation resembling those created by contract has been incurred and not been discharged, any person injured by the failure to discharge is entitle to receive same compensation from the party in default as if such person has contracted to discharge it and has broken his contract."

From this it is clear that, when the person fails to discharge his obligation arising out of Quasi-contract, another party will get legal remedies as if the contract in broken.

TYPES OF QUASI-CONTRACTS

The Indian Contract Act provides for five types of quasi-contracts, which are contained in Sections 68 to 72 of this Act.

(*i*) ***Supply of necessaries to the person having no contractual capacity or to his dependent (Section 68):*** Agreements made by the person who has no contractual capacity are void. These agreements cannot be enforced in the court of law. But agreements made by such person to procure necessaries for him or for his dependent carry different legal consequences. And supplier of necessities is legally entitled to recover the cost of such supplies provided:

(*a*) Articles supplied or money paid is basic necessity of life.

(*b*) It was supplied to him or to the person whom he is bound to support.

(*c*) Reasonable cost of such supplies is recoverable and not a contracted price.

(*d*) Necessaries should have been supplied with an intention of getting payment for it.

Example: A is lunatic having no contractual capacity. B, a grocery merchant, has supplied grocery items for five months to fulfil the basic needs of the family of such person. Agreement is void, but B is entitled to recover reasonable cost of these items from the property of lunatic if any.

NASH *vs* INMAN (1908, 2 KBI). In this case, a minor studying at Cambridge was supplied with clothing including 11 waistcoats. He already had sufficient clothing with him. It was held that waistcoats were not basic necessities of the life. It is because he was adequately provided with articles of that kind. Thus he is not liable to pay for them.

To determine the basic necessities of life, facts of individual case, such as social status and financial position will be taken care of.

(*ii*) ***Reimbursement of payment made by a person who is interested but which another person is legally bound to pay (Section 69):*** In many cases it happens that one party makes a payment, because he is interested in that payment. But liability for making that payment lies on another person. Thus on making such payment, the person liable to pay has to reimburse it to the person who has made the payment.

For making that person liable, the following conditions must be satisfied.

(*a*) Plaintiff must have some interest in making the payment. That interest must be legal, recognisable and bona fide.

(*b*) Plaintiff must have made payment for protecting his bona fide interest. And payment should have been made by him to another person or organisation.

(*c*) But that payment must be liability of defendant. He should be bound to pay. Such liability may be either contractual or statutory in nature.

Example: A has got a house in Delhi. He has rented it to B. Regarding that house; municipal taxes have not been paid by him. And due to huge arrears of taxes, Municipal Corporation has proposed auction of that house if arrears are not paid by a stipulated date. On being aware of this fact, A makes payment of the arrears.

Though there is no formal agreement between A and B, B is legally bound to reimburse A. In this case B was under legal obligation to pay municipal taxes. But A who is a tenant in that house has interest in protecting it from being auctioned. It is therefore to protect this interest he makes payment. He is entitled to recover it from B.

(*iii*) ***Obligation to pay for non-gratuitous act or service (Section 70):*** Sometimes, a person may render some services or do some act for another person. That person does such act voluntarily with an intention of getting its return. Thus the person who gets benefit of such acts or services is liable to compensate the person doing such act or rendering services. But the following conditions must be satisfied:

(*a*) The service rendered or act done by the party must be lawful. It is clear that for unlawful act, no payment can be recovered.

(*b*) Services must have been rendered voluntarily without any request. The intention of the person rendering services must be to get compensation for those services. If he renders services gratuitously, he is not entitled for the payment.

(*c*) The person for whom services have been rendered or act has been done must have got its benefit. If he is not benefited he is not bound to pay for.

Example: A's house is on fire. B who is passerby helped A in extinguishing fire without A's request. B did it with an intention of getting compensation for his services. A is under legal obligation to compensate B for the services rendered by him.

However, Section 70 of this Act is not applicable on the person having no contractual capacity. If such person gets benefit of services rendered by other, he is not bound to pay.

(*iv*) ***Rights and duties of the finder of lost goods (Section 71):*** A person who finds goods lost by another person. On his being taken custody of those goods, certain rights and obligations are created on his part without any formal contact. These rights and obligations are against the person who has lost goods or who is owner of the goods. Such rights and obligation are resembling with that of a formal contract and can be enforced in a similar manner. Obligations of finder of goods are as under:

(*a*) To take reasonable care of goods, as he would have taken in case of his own goods.

(*b*) To make reasonable efforts for tracing owner of those goods.

(*c*) Not to make use of those goods.

(*d*) On finding real owner to return goods to him.

Rights of finder of goods:

(*a*) To make claim for expenses paid by him for the maintenance of goods.

(*b*) To keep possession of goods.

(*c*) To claim for reward if any.

(*d*) To exercise lien over the goods for expenses and reward.

(*e*) To sell goods under certain circumstances.

Example: A has lost his pet dog. Not being able to find it out he announces that whosoever finds it and returns it back to him, he will suitably reward him. D found that dog and took custody of it. By making reasonable efforts he could find owner of that dog. On tracing him B claimed expenses which he incurred for the maintenance of dog and reward. A is bound to pay both expenses and reward to B.

(*v*) ***Liability of person to whom money is paid or things delivered by mistake or under coercion (Section 72):*** Where the person has delivered some goods or has made payments of money to another person either by mistake or under coercion. Such person is under legal obligation to return it to the person delivering. In case he has consumed it, he will pay compensation.

Example: A Railway company refuses to deliver certain goods to the consignee, except upon the payment of illegal charge of carriage. And the consignee was bound to pay such charges to get goods released from the

Railway company. He is entitled to recover these charges from Railway coy. Money paid under mistake is recoverable. Mistake may be mistake of the fact or law. It implies equitable restitution. When the person makes payment believing that it is due, but in reality it is not. He has right to recover it.

SALES TAX OFFICER *vs* KANHAIYA LAL MUKUNDWALA SARAF (1959, S.C.J. 53). In this case, levy of sales tax imposed on forward transaction having been held to be *ultra-vires* by Allahabad High Court. The respondent claimed refund of money paid under mistake of law. It was held that the party paying such levy is entitled to get the refund.

However it is to be noted that for applying Section 72 of this Act undue pressure on the party is enough to prove coercion. And an interpretation of this term is not same as it is under Section 15 of this Act. In other words, coercion, in this context, has been used in more popular and practical way.

Section 72 of this Act does not apply on the following cases:

(*a*) Natural obligation demands that if it discharged, party discharging it has no right to recover it. Repayment of time barred debt is a suitable example of it.

(*b*) When the party makes payment by making deliberate disregard to law, such payment cannot be recovered. For example, if the party makes the payment voluntarily and knowingly well that the contract is void he cannot recover such payment.

CONTINGENT CONTRACTS: MEANING AND DEFINITION

Contract is a mutual exchange of promises between the parties. These promises are got to be performed on the due dates. But in many cases the performance of a contract instead depends on the happening or non-happening of some future uncertain event. Such contracts are known as 'contingent contracts'.

According to Section 31 of this Act, "A contingent contract is a contract to do or not to do something, if some event, collateral to such contract does or does not happen."

It is clear from this definition that contingent contracts are conditional in nature. The condition is related to the performance of such contract. In other words, the performance of a contract is dependent on the happening or non-happening of future uncertain event.

However it is to be noted that the collateral event must be independent and ancillary to the contract. It should not be a performance of promise by the promisor or consideration given to him.

Example: A agrees to pay sum of Rs. 20,000 to B; if his house is on fire. Contract between A and B is a contingent contract. The performance of it depends on breaking of fire in B's house.

FEATURES OF CONTINGENT CONTRACTS

The features of contingent contracts are as follows:

(*i*) It must satisfy all essential conditions of a valid contract, such as consideration, contractual capacity and free consent.

(*ii*) The performance of a contingent contract depend on the happening or non-happening of an event in future.

(*iii*) That event must be uncertain, and contingency will arise only if its happening or non-happening is quite uncertain.

(*iv*) That event must be collateral to the main contract. Collateral event means neither it is performance of a promise on the part of a promisor nor it constitutes any consideration for the promise of the promisor. Rather the event is independent and ancillary to a contract.

In the example of contingent contract given above, payment of money by A will be made on breaking of fire in the house of B. Fire in B's house is not a consideration for A's promise and nor it is a performance of a promise on the part of A. It is an independent event which is ancillary to the contract between A and B.

RULES REGARDING CONTINGENT CONTRACT (SECTION 32 to 36)

(*i*) ***Contingency on happening of an event:*** The contract, which is contingent on the happening of the future uncertain event, will be performed only when the event occurs. Its performance is conditional on the happening of an event. Thus it cannot be enforced unless such event occurs. Due to any reason if the happening of that event becomes impossible or it does not occur, such contract becomes void.

Example: A agrees to sell some goods to B, which are being brought by ship coming to Bombay. But the ship sinks in the ocean. Agreement becomes void, because happening of an event upon which performance of contract depends has become impossible. And this agreement will be performed only if ship returns to Bombay.

(*ii*) ***Contingency on non-happening of an event:*** When the performance of contingent contact depends upon non-happening of future uncertain events; on the occurrence of that event, agreement becomes void. The obligation to perform it will arise only when that event does not happen or its happening has become impossible.

Example: A promise to pay sum of Rs. 2,000 to B if B's ship does not return from the United Kingdom. On the return of ship agreement becomes void. The liability of A to pay will arise only when ship does not return on it has sunk in the ocean, as to make it impossible to return.

(*iii*) ***Contingency of human conduct:*** When the performance of a contingent contract depends upon the happening of the future uncertain event, which is contingent on the behaviour or conduct of the third party at the specified time. When that third party does any act, which renders happening of that event impossible; such contract will become void.

Example: A agrees to rent out second floor of his house to B, provided DDA gives him permission for constructing second floor. DDA refused to give him the permission, contract becomes void. The performance *e.g.*, renting out of second floor of the house depends on the construction of that floor. This is contingent on the permission to be given by DDA and on the refusal, of permission such contract becomes void.

(*iv*) ***Contingency on the happening of an event within stipulated time:*** The contract, which is contingent on the happening of some future uncertain event within stipulated time. Such contract can be enforced only if that event happens within that stipulated period of time. In case happening of such event becomes impossible even before that time, such contract becomes void.

Example: A has taken final examination of graduation. Provisionally, he has been allowed to appear in bank examination subject to passing of examination of graduation within two months. If he fails in that examination even before two months, he ceases to be eligible for that job. And if the result is not declared within two months, his eligibility for a job comes to an end.

(*v*) ***Contingency on non-happening of an event within the stipulated time:*** Contrary to earlier one, when the performance of a contract depends on non-happening of some event with in stipulated period of time, if the event occurs within that, contract becomes void. And the contract can be enforced if till the expiration of that time, that event does not occur. When, before that time happening of that event becomes impossible, the contract can be enforced.

Example: A agrees to pay a sum of Rs. 5,000 to B if B's ship does not return to Bombay with in three months. When the ship returns to Bombay within that time the promise of A becomes void. But if ship sinks into ocean before that time or does not return to Bombay A will be liable to pay.

(*vi*) ***Contingency on the happening of impossible event:*** Contingent contract to do or not to do something if an impossible event happens is void. It is insignificant that the impossibility was known or not known to the parties at the time of making a contract. Impossible event cannot happen, thus contract based on it will also be void.

Example: A agrees to pay Rs. 20,000 to B if he discovers treasure with magic. This agreement is void, because its performance is based on happening of impossible event.

Table 8.1: Difference between wagering transaction and contingent contract

	Wagering agreement	**Contingent contract**
Meaning	It implies promise to give money upon the determination of an uncertain event.	It is a contract to be performed on the happening or non-happening of some uncertain event, collateral to it.
Validity	Wagering agreements are void.	Contingent contracts are valid subject to conditions.
Mutual Promise	It consists of mutual promises. Money will be paid either in case and to either party.	It is to be performed on happening or non-happening of some uncertain event.
Interest of party	In wagering agreement, parties do not have any interest on the happening or non-happening of that event.	In contingent contract, one or both the parties may have some interest on the event.
Nature of event	In wagering agreement, future event is determining factor.	In a contingent contract, future event is collateral to a contract.

REVIEW QUESTIONS

1. What is a 'quasi-contract'? Explain rationale behind quasi-contract.
2. Discuss the various types of quasi-contracts with the help of suitable examples.
3. 'Quasi-contracts are not formal contracts, but these are the obligations created by law.' Discuss.
4. 'In certain cases, law imposes an obligation and allows an action to be taken on it, as if it arises out of a contract.' Explain it with examples.
5. Discuss rights and duties of finder of goods.
6. 'A person shall not be allowed to enrich himself at the cost of others.' Comment.
7. Does the law of contract impose any obligation on the person enjoying benefits of a non-gratuitous act of another person done for the former? Explain it by citing suitable examples.
8. Comment on:
   (*a*) Quasi-contracts are based on the principal of equity and justice.
   (*b*) Obligation resembling that of a formal contact carry some legal consequence.
   (*c*) Gratuititous acts are to be compensated.
   (*d*) Money paid by mistake is recoverable.
9. What is 'contingent contract'? Explain essential features of contingent contract.
10. Discuss the rules regarding contingent contract.
11. Performance of contingent contract depends on happening or non-happening of some future uncertain events.
12. Distinguish between wager agreements and contingent contract.

PRACTICAL PROBLEMS

1. A in consideration of Rs. 10,000 from B promises to bring gold for him from the sun. Examine validity of this agreement.
2. A has offered his bike to B. A makes an agreement with C that if B refuses to buy his bike he will sell it to him at particular price. Is it a valid agreement?
3. A, who is a minor, purchases grocery items regularly for three months from a grocery merchant on credit. Later on, A refuses to pay the bills. Suggest legal remedy to grocery merchant.
4. Ram hails from lower income class. He buys 5 pairs of Woodland shoes from Shyam on credit @ Rs. 2,000 p.p. Can Shyam recover this amount from Ram?
5. X, a minor, had been studying at Cambridge brought 10 waistcoats on credit from a merchant. In fact, X had adequate stock of such clothing with him. Is he liable to pay for waistcoats?
6. An insurance company makes payment of claim to the policy-holder on fire insurance policy. While making the payment the company was under mistake to believe that goods have been destroyed by insured cause. In fact, goods were stolen. Is company entitled to recover this payment from the policy-holder?
7. A agrees to sell a part of specific crop of wheat to be grown on his agricultural land to B at a specific price. Crops were being delivered after two months. But before delivering B paid a part of the contracted price. The crop of wheat was destroyed. Examine the legal consequences of an agreement between A and B.
8. Fire broke out in the godown of Ram. Shyam who was passing by rendered his services in extinguishing that fire. He did it with an intention of getting compensation for it. Has he a legal right to recover it from Ram?
9. A has lost his horse. B finds it and takes it into his custody. By the time he could trace owner of the horse, B incurred some expenses on the maintenance of that horse. Explain rights and duties of B with regard to that horse.
10. A stays in the house of B. Regarding that house municipal authorities made an announcement that if the taxes are not paid by the stipulated date, the house will be sold in auction. A makes payment, can he recover it from B?

9

Discharge of Contract

LEARNING OBJECTIVES

- Develop conceptual clarity about discharge of contract and its consequences.
- Examine various modes of getting a contract discharged.
- Analyse, discharge of contract by breach of contract.
- Remember meaning and nature of supervening impossibility.
- Learn how contract is discharged by supervening impossibility and compare it with other similar situations when contract is not discharged.

INTRODUCTION

Formation of a contract results in the creation of certain rights and obligations on the part of the parties. These rights and obligations can be claimed in the court of law. These are also known as contractual relationship between the parties making a contract. The rights on the part of one party becomes obligations for another and vice versa.

MEANING

Discharge of a contract implies termination of the contractual relationship between the parties. On the termination of such relationship the parties are released from their obligations in the contract. And in this way contract comes to an end. In other words, a contract is said to be discharged, when rights and obligations created by it come to an end.

Broadly the contract may be discharged either by the act of the parties or by operation of the law. The parties of a contract may be released from the obligations either by fulfilling or discharging them or the law may exempt them from their obligations in the contract.

MODES OF DISCHARGING CONTRACT

The contract may be discharged in any one of the following ways which are known as modes of discharging contract:

1. By performance.
2. By mutual agreement.
3. By supervening impossibility.
4. By operation of law.
5. By lapse of time.
6. By material alteration.
7. By breach of contract.

1. Discharge of Contract by Performance

This is the most popular and usual way of discharging contract. The contract is a mutual exchange of promises between two parties. They make a promise either for doing or not doing anything. Both the parties are promisors as well as promisees. When both the promisor do what they have promised to do, the contract is said to be performed. And this way both parties get released from their obligations in that contract, and contract comes to an end.

Example: A agreed to supply 200 cotton bales to B at particular price. On due date A delivers cotton bales and makes payment. Both of them get released from their obligations in the contract, and contract comes to an end.

Performance of a contract may be of two types:

(*i*) Actual performance

(*ii*) Attempted Performance

(*i*) **Actual performance:** Generally at the time of making a contract, parties to it decide about the point of time on which both parties will perform their respective promises. In actual performance, both the promisors perform the acts, which they have promised to perform on the decided point of time. Actual performance brings the contract to an end.

Example: Ram agrees to deliver 50 tonnes of wheat to B on 1 September at a particular price. B was to make payment on 5th September. A delivers wheat to B on the due date (1Sept.). And Simultaneously B makes payment on 5 Sept. The contract is said to be discharged by actual performance.

(*ii*) **Attempted performance or tender:** When the promisor is ready and willing to perform his promise but he cannot do it, because the promisee does not accept the performance, this is known as 'attempted performance' and it is legally treated equivalent to actual performance except in case of payment of money.

Section 38 of this Act provides that "Where a promisor has made an offer of performance to the promisee, and the offer has not been accepted, the promisor is not responsible for non-performance, nor does he thereby lose his rights under the contract."

Example: Ramesh was to supply 50 tonnes of coal to Mahesh on 15 October and Mahesh is to pay for it on 20 October. On the due date of performance Ramesh made an offer to supply coal to Mahesh. But he refused to accept delivery of specified quantity of coal. It amounts to attempted performance and Ramesh gets released from the obligation of supplying 50 tonnes of coal to Mahesh. But his rights against Mahesh will remain intact e.g., he can proceed against Mahesh for breach of contract.

Example: A has borrowed sum of Rs. 10,000 from B for two months. On the due date, A makes payment, but B does not accept it. In this case, A will not be released from his liability of making that payment to B. However, he will not be liable for paying any interest on that after two months.

Essentials of Valid Attempted Performance or Tender

An attempted performance, to be legally valid must meet the following requirements:

(*a*) ***It must be unconditional:*** While making an attempted performance, the promisor cannot put any condition, regarding that, for the promisee. Conditional offer to perform is not valid.

Example: A agrees to supply 100 tonnes of wheat to B and subsequently, B was to make the payment. A offers to deliver wheat to B provided he makes half of the payment in advance. Such attempted performance is conditional and thus is not valid.

(*b*) ***It must be made at reasonable place and time:*** Attempted performance to be legally effective, must be made within usual business hours and at a reasonable place.

Example: Ram agreed to supply 100 tonnes of iron ore to B on 1 January. On the due date of supply he took stipulated quantity of iron ore to B's residence at midnight. Place and time of supply is not reasonable, thus making attempted performance invalid.

(*c*) ***Reasonable opportunity to ascertain capability:*** The person to whom attempted performance is being made, should be given reasonable opportunity to ascertain that the person giving attempted performance is able and willing to fulfil whole of the promise, then and there. A person offering to perform the promise must have necessary stock of goods to be delivered along with required man-power.

(*d*) ***Inspection of goods*:** When the attempted performance is made to supply the goods, the promisee should be given reasonable opportunity to ascertain that the promisor really possesses the goods of contracted quality.

Example: A agreed to supply 100 cotton bales of X trademark to B on 2 February. A attempts to supply these to B on the due date. B is not willing to accept delivery. He should be given reasonable opportunity to inspect quality of cotton bales to be delivered.

(*e*) ***Proper person:*** In case of valid attempted performance it must have been made to the promisee or any other person duly authorised by him.

(*f*) ***Joint promisees:*** In case there are two or more than two joint promisees, an attempted performance can be given to any one of them. It is not necessary that it should be given to all promisees.

Example: A made a promise to supply specific quantity of wheat to B and C. On the due date he can offer to supply either to B or to C.

2. Discharge of Contract by Mutual Agreement

A contract is formed when the parties mutually agree. In the same way, both the parties of a contract by mutual agreement can discharge that contract.

Sections 62 and 63 of this Act provide for the following methods of discharging a contract by mutual agreement:

According to Section 62 of this Act, "If the parties to a contract agree to substitute a new contract for it or to rescind or alter it, the original contract need not be performed."

(*i*) **Novation:** Under the method of novation, existing contract is replaced by new one either between same parties or between new parties. It discharges an existing contract and brings new contract into existence.

Examples: A borrows sum of Rs. 10,000 from B on promissory note for six months. On the due date A is unable to pay and makes out another promissory note along with the amount of interest. It amounts to novation and existing promissory note is terminated and new one of Rs. 10,000 + interest is made.

A owes Rs. 5,000 to B and B also owes same amount to C. On the due date they agree that A will pay Rs. 5,000 to C. In this case, two agreements, one between A and B and another between A and C have been replaced by third agreement which is between A and C (new parties) will exist.

(*ii*) **Alteration:** Parties of an agreement are at liberty to alter or change any one or more terms of it mutually. When they make any change regarding any terms of contract by mutual consent, such contract need not be performed and is discharged. Mutually agreed alteration discharges the original contract and the parties become legally bound by new contract. In this context, new contract means the contract with altered terms and conditions.

Example: A agrees to sell his bike to B for Rs. 50,000 on cash down payment. Before the due date of performance A and B mutually agreed that B will make payment in instalments. Thus original agreement of making cash down payment is discharged. And now A and B are bound by the new agreement in which payment will be made in instalments.

(*iii*) **Rescission:** When the parties of a contract, by mutual agreement cancel all or some of the terms of a contract, it is known as 'rescission'. As a result of rescission, the contract whose terms have been cancelled is discharged. In brief rescission means cancellation of terms of a contract.

Rescission may be either partial or absolute. In an absolute rescission, entire contract is cancelled and need not be performed. But in partial rescission, some of the terms may be cancelled, but contract will be performed with remaining terms.

Example: Ram agreed to supply 100 units of plastic goods to Shyam at a particular price. Later on they agree that Ram will supply only 50 units of plastic goods to Shyam. It is known as 'partial rescission'. On the other hand, if they agree that Ram will not supply any unit of plastic goods to Shyam, it is absolute rescission. This leads to termination of the whole contract.

Rescission of a contract takes place under the following circumstances:

(*a*) Rescission may take place by mutual agreement between the parties of contract.

(*b*) When one party of a contract fails to perform his promise, another party can rescind the contract without losing his rights for breach of contract.

(*c*) In voidable contract, an aggrieved party whose consent had not been free has a right to rescind contract.

(*iv*) **Remission:** Sometimes, the promisor may perform only a part of his promise and promisee accepts it for the performance of the whole promise. It is known as 'remission' and that contract is discharged.

In other words, remission means acceptance of lesser performance than what was actually due is a contract. Section 63 of this Act provides that "a party may dispense with or remit, wholly or in part the performance of the promise made to him. He can also extend the time of such performance or accept, instead of it any satisfaction, which he deems to be fit."

However, acceptance of lesser performance does not require any consideration.

Example: A has borrowed sum of Rs. 10,000 from B for two months. B promises that if A refunds Rs. 9,000 immediately after a month he will accept it for the settlement of whole debt. Agreement is discharged on account of remission on the part of B.

KAPUR CHAND GODHA *vs* NAWAB HIMAYATALI KHAN (1963, 2, S.C.R, 168). In this case, M was to pay a sum of Rs. 27 lakh to K. Since Hyderabad had been taken over by the Indian Government, a committee was appointed to clear the matters. It offered Rs. 20 lakh to K who accepted it in full satisfaction of the claim of Rs. 27 lakh. Later on K filed a suit for the recovery of the balance. The Supreme Court held that K could not do so as he had accepted Rs. 20 lakh in full satisfaction.

(*v*) **Waiver:** In a contract, every party is at liberty to give up some of his rights in favour of other party. When a party agrees to give up his rights the another party will get released from his obligation and the contract comes to an end. But the waiver on the part of one party must result in release of the other party from obligation. Then only the contract will be discharged. It is because waiver of rights by one party means discharge of the other party from his obligations.

Example: A draws a Bill of Exchange on B, who accepts it and gives it back to A. Later on A indorses it in favour of C who further indorses it to D. While indorsing it to D, C waives right to get notice of dishonour in favour of indorsee. Thus if B/E gets dishonoured, C will become liable without getting notice of dishonour.

3. Discharge of Contract by Supervening Impossibility

Contract is made between parties either for doing or not doing some act. The act, for which promise has been made, must be capable of being performed. When the parties enter into an agreement for doing something impossible, such agreement is void *ab initio*.

In many occasions, the contract at the time of formation is capable of being performed. Subsequently after the formation, its performance becomes impossible or illegal. Such impossibility may arise due to the reasons beyond the control of both parties. This kind of impossibility which crops up in a contract after its formation is known as 'Supervening Impossibility' and the contract is discharged.

An impossibility whether it is there at initial stage of making a contract or arises subsequently after the formation of a contract will render contract as void.

At the initial stage of formation of contract such impossibility may be known or unknown to the parties. If an impossibility was known to the parties that agreement is void *ab initio*. In case the parties were not aware of impossibility and come to known about it afterwards, such contract becomes void.

Example: A agrees to sell his motor bike to B for a specific price. Later on they come to know that motor bike has already been stolen. Contract is void.

However, the contract becomes void on account of subsequent impossibility provided the following conditions are satisfied:

(*a*) The act which is to be performed in a contract must have become impossible.

(*b*) Impossibility should have been caused by circumstances beyond the control of parties.

(*c*) Impossibility must not be the outcome of some acts on the part of the parties.

In this regard, Section 56 of this Act provides that, "A contract to do an act, which after the contract is made, becomes impossible or by reason of some event which the promisor could not prevent, unlawful, becomes void, when the act becomes impossible or unlawful."

A contract is discharged due to supervening impossibility under the following situations:

(*i*) **Destruction of subject matter:** Every contract has same subject matter. When the subject matter is destroyed due to any cause beyond the control of the parties, before the performance of a contract; such contract is discharged on account of supervening impossibility.

TAYLOR *vs* CALDWELL (1863M 122, A.R, 299.): In this case, a music hall was let out on rent for a series of concerts on certain days. The hall gets destroyed by fire before the date of first concert. The plaintiff filed a suit against the defendant for damage arising out of breach of contract. It was held that the contract had become void and defendant was not liable to pay compensation.

(*ii*) **Discontinuation of particular state of thing, which is essential for performance:** When the contract is made by the parties, on the ground that, certain state of things will continue till the performance of a contract, but that state of things gets changed or discontinued due to any reason beyond the control of the parties; such contract becomes void on the basis of supervening impossibility. It is because the very object of contract is defeated due to discontinuation of that state of things.

KRELL *vs* HENRY (1903, 2, K.B, 740). In this case, Henry hired a room from Krell for two days to witness the coronation procession of King Edward VII. Owing to illness, the procession was cancelled. It was held that Henry was excused from the obligation of paying rent for the room. As an existence of coronation procession was necessary to continue for the performance of a contract. But it was discontinued, due to the reasons beyond the control of both parties.

(*iii*) **Change of law:** Change of law, after the formation of a contract, if renders performance of contract unlawful; such contract is discharged on the ground of supervening impossibility. However, change of law should go into the root of contract as to defeat its object.

Example: A entered into an agreement with B for selling 100 tonnes of wheat at specified price to him on 15 March. But, before due date of delivery the Government of India has passed an ordinance debarring the individual from supplying more than 5 tonnes of wheat. The contract between A and B comes to an end due to reason that its performance has become unlawful.

However legal intervention on the part of the Government, which is of a temporary nature and which does not adversely affect foundation of a contract, will not render it as void.

SATYABRATA GHOSE *vs* MUGNEERAM BANGUR & COY. (A.I.R., 1954, S.C. 44.). In this case, the company started a scheme for developing a land into housing colony. S was one of the purchasers of the land. The Coy undertook the construction of roads and drains necessary for making land suitable for residential purpose.

But before anything could be done regarding transfer of land to S, the State has acquired substantial part of that land for military purpose. The requisition order was temporary, and therefore it was held that the contract will not be discharged due to supervening impossibility.

(*iv*) **Death or personal incapacity of the party:** In a contract of personal nature, if the promisor dies or becomes incapable of performing contract, such contract will be discharged. Such personal contracts are formed, on personal considerations and may require personal skill and talent to perform the contract. So death of promissor may create vacuum and contract cannot be performed.

ROBISON *vs* DAVISON (1871M L.R.6, EX 269). In this case, an artist promised to perform some concert for a certain price. Before she could do so, she was taken seriously ill. It was held that she was discharged from her obligation due to physical incapacity.

(*v*) **Declaration of war:** On the outbreak of war between two countries, the citizens of those countries cannot make any contract. If they make contract it will be void *ab initio*. The contracts, made by the parties before the declaration of war will remain suspended during the war. When the war is over, an enforceability of such contracts depends on the discretion of the Central Government. The Government may either abrogate them or may allow to enforce them on some conditions.

Example: Ram agrees to supply some raw material to Shyam in another country at a specific price. Before due date, war is declared between the countries. It makes contract void, because Ram cannot deliver that raw material to Shyam.

Exceptions to doctrine of supervening impossibility: In a contract when the person makes promise for doing or not doing anything, he must perform it. But on becoming performance impossible, due to reasons beyond his control, the contract is discharged. There are certain situations, resembling to supervening impossibility, but are not included in supervening impossibility.

Under these situations, contract will not be discharged and the parties are liable to perform it. Though the performance may be more difficult, expensive, less profitable or cumbersome, but the parties concerned have to perform it. These situations may be considered as exceptions:

(*a*) ***Difficulty of performance:*** Generally, difficulty is no excuse for performance. When the performance of the promise becomes more expensive, difficult and cumbersome due to any reason, the promisor has to perform it. He cannot seek any excuse on the ground of performance becoming difficult.

Example: A agreed to supply huge quantity of iron ore to B at a particular price. Before, due to steep hike in the prices of petroleum products, cost of transport has been doubled. But A has to supply iron ore in spite of increased transportation cost.

BLACKBURN BOBBINNS COY. LTD. ***vs*** **ALLEN & SONS (1918, 2, K.B, 467).** In this case, A sold certain quantity of Finland timber to B to be delivered between June and September 1914. No delivery was made before August when war broke out and transport was disorganised so that A could not bring any timber from Finland. Held impossibility of getting timber from that country could not excuse performance.

(*b*) ***Commercial difficulties:*** When the performance of a promise becomes costlier, non-profitable and more risky, such contract will not be discharged. Such difficulties are known as 'commercial difficulties'. These may arise due to sudden change in price line, economic policies of the Government, non-availability of raw material, deep drastic change in exchange rate and outbreak of war, etc.

Example: A agreed to supply certain goods to B. Before due date, due to sudden outbreak of war, the market price of goods shot up. And supply of goods has become costlier. But A is liable to supply even if he suffers a loss.

(*c*) ***Strikes, lockout, riots and civil disturbances etc:*** When the performance of a contract becomes very difficult or practically impossible due to strike of labourers, lockout in the business premises, or riots etc., the contract will not be discharged. These events have not been included in Section 56 of this Act.

HARI LAXMAN ***vs*** **SECRETARY OF STATE OF INDIA (1928, 30, BOM. L.R. 49).** In this case, the lessor of certain salt pans failed to repair them, as per the terms of the contract on the ground of strike of workmen. It was held that, a strike by workmen was not sufficient reason to excuse performance, of a contract.

(*d*) ***Difficulty arising out of conduct of third party:*** When the party of a contract relied on third party for the performance of his promise, failure of third party or his inability will not be considered sufficient ground for discharging a contract.

Example: A is a wholesaler of some goods which are manufactured by B. A agreed to supply some goods to C, which he will procure from B. But goods have not been manufactured by B. Even then A is liable to supply these goods to C. Failure on the part of B for producing those goods is not sufficient ground to discharge the contract.

ALLOPI PARSAD ***vs*** **UNION OF INDIA (1960, S.C. 588).** In this case, A was acting as an agent of Government of India for procuring edible oils for the use of Army personnel. The rates of oil were fixed by the

Government. But due to outbreak of IInd World War, there has been steep rise in the price of oils. A maintained a supply at higher prices. But it was held that A was not entitled to claim more than the price as fixed by the Government.

(*e*) ***Partial impossibility:*** When the contract has been entered into for achieving single objective and achievement of which becomes impossible, that contract will be discharged. But in many case, the contract may be made for achieving more than one objectives. In case one object fails contract will not bc dischargcd. Rathcr thc partics will pcrform it for achieving another object.

H.B. STEAM BOAT COY *vs* HUTTON (1903, 2, K. 683). In this case, stream Boat Coy agreed to let a boat to Hutton to view; (*i*) the navel review at the coronation of King Edward VII and (*ii*) to cruise round the fleet. Due to illness of the King, the navel review was cancelled, but the fleet was assembled and the boat could have been used to cruise round the fleet. It was held that the contract is not terminated, because it will continue for another object.

4. Discharge of Contract by Operation of Law

Contract may also be discharged by operation of law. In these cases, law comes into force and the parties are released from their obligations in the contract. These cases are:

(*i*) **Death of promisor:** After having made a contract, if the promisor dies, the contract of a personal nature comes to an end. It is because such contracts require special skill and talent on the part of promisor to perform the promise. Thus in case of his death, contract is discharged.

Example: A, who is singer has agreed to perform certain programmes on a particular date. But before that date A dies, such contract which is of a personal nature will come to an end.

However in case of other contracts, if the promisor dies, his legal representative will be called upon to perform the promise. But his liability will be limited only to the extent, he inherits properties from such deceased promisor.

(*ii*) **Insolvency:** In case the person is declared as an insolvent by the court of law, he is released from performing his part of contract by law. His rights and liabilities are transferred to the official Assignee or official Receiver appointed by the court.

After getting certificate of discharge he is discharged from all obligations prior to his declaration as an insolvent. And he gets new lease of life.

(*iii*) **Merger:** Two parties make two contracts on the same subject matter. In one contract one of these two parties get superior rights. And in another contract this party gets inferior rights. When these two contracts, merge or coincide on that same subject matter, the contract containing superior rights will exist and another contract which carries inferior rights will vanish and discharged by operation of law.

Example: A acquires a piece of land from Delhi Development Authority for doing some industrial work on lease basis for 10 years. Before 10 years, A could manage the fund, and by making another agreement he buys that same piece of land on ownership basis. Thus agreement of lease and agreement of ownership merge on that particular piece of land. An agreement of lease will be discharged by law and agreement of ownership will remain in force.

5. Discharge of Contract by Lapse of Time

While making a contract, the parties prescribe a time within which it is to be performed. When no time of performance is fixed, the contract must be performed within reasonable period of time. Reasonable period of time is a matter of fact which differs from case to case depending on nature of agreement, circumstances and intention of the parties.

Thus the contract must be performed within stipulated period of time or reasonable period of time. Till the expiry of such times, if the contract is not performed it will be discharged.

Relevant provision of Indian Limitation Act provide that "A contract should be performed within a specified period i.e., period of limitation. If the contract is not performed and if no action is taken by the promisee within the period of limitation, he is deprived of his remedy at law." In case of contracts, the period of limitation is three years. After the expiry of this period the court will not allow to enforce the contract and it will be discharged.

Example: Ram agreed to supply raw material worth Rs. 10,000 to Shyam on credit. The period of credit has not been fixed. In this case, Ram must file suit for the recovery of payment within three years. In case Ram fails to do so at the expiry of three years period, that amount will become time barred and Ram will not be legally entitled to recover it.

6. Discharge of Contract by Material Alterations

Sometimes, the contract and its terms and conditions may be contained in a particular document. When the promisee or his agent make any material alteration without the consent of other party in that document of contract, such contract is treated to be discharged. Such alteration to be legally effective must satisfy the following conditions:

(*i*) Alteration or change in the document must be related to a contract.

(*ii*) Consent of other party has not been taken for such alteration, it is unilateral in nature.

(*iii*) Alteration made with regard to a contract must be material alterations. Material alterations include all those alterations which in a significant way affect rights and duties of the parties in that contract. Such as change in the name of payee, change in the date of payment, and change in the amount which is payable, etc. After the material alterations, the contract no longer, continues to be the same, thus no party can sue upon it. However, alterations which are not material and do not affect rights and duties of the parties or which are made to carry out common intention or protect common interest will not affect validity of a contract. Such alterations may include correction of clerical mistake, correction of spelling of the name or place etc. It is to be noted that the party who makes material alterations in the document of contract will have no right to claim performance of contract as it stood before alteration.

Example: A borrows a sum of Rs. 10,000 from B, for one year at 10 per cent interest per annum. All these terms are put in a document which is known as 'promissory note'. B, who is having promissory note makes a change in the rate of interest by increasing it to 15 per cent without consent of A. This alteration is material one and affect right and duties of the parties. Thus the contract of promissory note is discharged. Since B has made material alteration, he is deprived of his right to claim interest of 10 per cent. However, the altered promissory note may be used as an evidence by B for proving debt covered by it.

ANANTH RAO *vs* KANDIKANDA (1920): In one of this leading case, it was held that the document, though altered, could be used as proof of the transaction and the creditor might be allowed to claim refund of money actually advanced by him.

Therefore, the promissory note becomes invalid due to material change in it made by one of the parties without the consent of other. Nevertheless, such promissory note may be used as a proof of debt covered under it.

7. Discharged by Breach of Contract

Contract can also be discharged by not performing it. Breach of contract means refusal of performance on the part of the parties. When a party to a contract refuses to perform it, or does not perform it or makes himself unable to perform it, other party may put such contract to an end.

Example: A, enters into a contract with B for supplying spare parts of a machine on particular date at specified price. On the due date of performance A fails to supply. B, has a right to put this contract to an end, thus the contract comes to an end because A fails to perform it. It amounts to breach of contract.

Breach of contract may be of two types:

(*i*) Actual Breach

(*ii*) Anticipatory Breach

(*i*) **Actual breach:** Generally, the time of performance of a contract may be determined by the parties at the time of making a contract. In such case, the parties must perform their promises on that time. Failure on the part of the party to perform his promise on due date is regarded as actual breach of contract.

Thus, actual breach of a contract occurs when the party does not perform his promise on due date or refuses to performs it on that date. On such refusal, another party of a contract is entitled to treat the contract discharged and can move against the party making breach of contract.

Example: Mahesh agreed to supply one hundred cotton bales to Suresh on 10th March at specified price. On 10th March he refused to supply. Suresh has a right to treat this contract as discharged and sue upon Mahesh for breach of contract.

CORT *vs* AMBERGATE RAIL COY. (1851, 17, Q.B. 527). In this case, Cort contracted with Railway company to supply 3,000 tonnes of railway timber at a certain price to be delivered in instalments. After supplying 1,787 tonnes; the Railway Coy asked to Cort not to supply more. It was held that Cort could bring an action for breach of contract.

(*ii*) **Anticipatory breach:** When, before due date of performance of a contract the promisor refuses to perform or disabled himself from performing his promise; it is known as 'anticipatory breach of a contract'. In anticipatory breach, the promisor refuses to perform before due date of actual performance. The promisor either informs the promisee regarding his refusal or may do some act which is inconsistent with the contract or which renders him disabled from performing his promise.

Example: A, agrees to marry B on 1st January. Before this date A gets married with C. As a result of it, he has disabled himself from getting married with B, before due date. It amounts to anticipatory breach of contract.

REVIEW QUESTIONS

1. What is 'discharge of a contract'? Discuss various ways in which the contract gets discharged.
2. Explain the various modes of discharging a contract by mutual agreement and give suitable examples.
3. Define the term 'supervening impossibility'. Discuss various circumstances under which contract is discharged due to supervening impossibility.
4. Explain various exceptions to supervening impossibility.
5. What is material alteration? How does the contract comes to an end by material alteration?
6. Define 'attempted performance'. Explain requirements of a valid attempted performance.
7. 'Impossibility of performance is as rule, not an excuse for non-performance of contract.' Discuss it with suitable examples.
8. Explain different ways in which the contract is discharged by operation of law.
9. Comment on:
   (*a*) Discharge of a contract releases the parties from their obligation.
   (*b*) Performance as a usual mode of discharging contract.
   (*c*) Difficulty of performance may not lead to discharge of contract.
   (*d*) Attempted performance is equivalent to actual performance.
   (*e*) Impossibility which is known to the parties at the time of making a contract is one and the same thing as subsequent impossibility.
10. Write notes on:
    (*a*) Merger (*b*) Supervening impossibility
    (*c*) Material alterations (*d*) Breach of contract
    (*e*) Rescission (*f*) Discharge of contract by lapse of time

PRACTICAL PROBLEMS

1. A borrows a sum of Rs. 10,000 from B for one year @ 10 per cent per annum. A did not make demand for repayment before the expiry of one year and B did not repay it. Can A recover this sum from B after the expiry of that period of time? (Hint: No, debt has become time-barred.)
2. Ram agrees to supply some furniture to Shyam in two instalments. Shyam was to pay stipulated price to Ram on a particular day. Identify rights and obligations of Ram and Shyam.
3. Akhilesh, agreed to supply 200 tonnes of coal to a Railway company at specified price. On the due date of performance, Akhilesh took required quantity of coal to the godown of Railway coy, but they refused to accept delivery. Is Akhilesh released from his obligation of supplying coal. What is the legal status of his rights against Railway coy?
4. X, owes Rs. 5,000 to Y. On due date he offered to repay this amount to Y, but Y refused to accept payment. Is X released from his obligation of repaying that amount to Y; (Hint: No; monetary obligation.)
5. S, a singer, makes a contract with R to sing at his musical theatre every night for one month. R has agreed to pay her Rs. 2,500 for each night show. On 15th night S, willfully absents from the musical show. Can Y put this contract to an end? (Hint: Yes, breach of contract by S.)
6. X and coy was in agreement with Russell, a citizen of foreign country for supplying certain goods at a particular price on 25th December. But before due date of supply war is declared between two countries. Is X and coy legally bound to supply the goods. What will be legal position of this contract when the war is over?
7. A, an eminent piano player, promised B to perform at a concert. In the morning of that day A informed B that she is too ill to attend the concert. Explain legal status of this contract.
8. Manohar hired a room at Connaught Place in some hotel to witness Republic Day parade on 26th January. But due to some emergency the parade show was cancelled. Examine legality of this contract.
9. A, is a wholesaler of particular item of plastic goods to be manufactured by B. A enters into a contract for supplying 50 items of plastic good to C who is a retailer. But due to labour strike B could not manufacture plastic goods. Is A liable to supply that quatity of plastic good to C? (Hint: Yes, otherwise he will be liable for breach of contract.)

10. Contract was entered into between London based merchants, for the sale of certain goods which were to be imported from Algeria. Due to riots and civil disturbances the goods could not be imported. Is seller liable for the supply of those goods? (Hint: Yes; commercial difficulty).
11. A, borrows Rs. 2,000 from B and writes a promissory note in his favour for three months. After three months A goes to B and expresses his inability to repay that amount and gives new promissory note to him. Is old promissory note cancelled or discharged?
12. Mahesh took piece of land from Delhi Development Authority (DDA) on lease basis for 10 years. At the end of 5th year of lease he makes another agreement with DDA for buying the same piece of land. Explain this contract with the help of rule of merger.
13. Y, draws a bill of exchange on Z for Rs. 10,000 at three months. Z accepts the bill and returns it back to Y. Y, who is a drawer makes change in the amount of that bill and raises it to Rs. 20,000. Can Y claim this amount from Z? (Hint: No, material alteration.)
14. Suresh is sugar mill owner at Lucknow. He makes an agreement for supplying 200 tonnes of sugar to Mahesh in Delhi on 25th December. In the meanwhile, the Central Government has brought a notification that no one can transact for more than 5 tonnes of sugar. Explain legal remedies available to Mahesh, if any.

10

Performance of Contract

LEARNING OBJECTIVES

- Understand basic concept of performance of contract.
- Examine performance of joint promises.
- Remember rules regarding appropriation of payment.
- Get familiar with that who can perform and who can claim performance.
- Examine time as an essential factor for performing contract and its implications on appropriation of payment.
- Learn basic concept of reciprocal promises and their performance.

INTRODUCTION

Contract is a mutual exchange of promises between parties. They make promises for doing, or not doing something. After having made such promises, they are legally bound to fulfil what they have promised to perform. If they do so, it is known as 'performance of a contract'. Subsequently, on the performance of a contract the parties are released from their obligations and the contract comes to an end.

Briefly, performance of a contract means fulfillment of legal obligations created by a contract. And the performance of a contract is a natural mode of discharging a contract. According to Section 37 of this Act, "The parties to a contract, must either perform or offer to perform their respective promises, unless such performance is dispensed with or excused under the provisions of the Act."

As per the interpretation of this Section, the performance of a contract may be of two types actual performance and attempted performance. In actual performance, both the promisors of a contract do an act which they have promised to do. And it leads to peaceful ending of a contract. Sometimes, one of the promisor may be ready and willing to perform his promise, but fails to do so, because another party does not accept it. It is known as 'attempted performance'. Legally valid attempted performance releases such promisor from his obligation in that contract. But his rights against another party will remain intact.

Example: A agrees to supply 100 bags of tea to B @ Rs. 500 per bag on a particular date. B was to pay subsequently after the supply of tea. On due date A supplies tea and B makes payment. It lead to actual performance of a contract and the contract comes to an end. But, if on due date, A takes the contracted quantity of tea to B's godown and B refuses to accept the delivery. Thus, it is regarded as attempted performance and as a result of it A gets released from the obligation of supplying tea to B.

However under both ways of performance, the promisors get released from their obligations in that contract and the contract comes to an end. It is to be noted that in case of attempted performance for the payment of money the promisor, making it, does not get released from the obligation of making payment. But from the date of attempted performance he would not be liable for any interest.

With regard to performance of a contract, many questions arise as to who must perform the contract, who can demand such performance and what should be the time and place of performance. The Indian Contract Act contains various provisions to deal with these questions.

WHO MUST PERFORM CONTRACT

Contract is nothing but a bundle of promises. These promises are made by the promisors and these are made for doing or not doing something. The promisors are under legal obligation and they have to fulfil that obligation, unless it is dispensed with by law. The liability of performing a contract basically lies on the promisors. Sections 37 to 41 of this Act lays down the basic rules regarding legal status of the person who is to perform the contract. The contract may be performed:

(*i*) **By the promisor himself:** Simple rule of law is that the person who makes a promise must perform it. Sometimes, law may permit him to get his promise performed through another person.

But in case of a contract of personal nature, which is based on personal considerations and requires special skill and talent to perform, must be performed by the promisor himself. In case of his death, such contract will come to an end. Section 40 of this Act provides that, "where the contract is of a personal nature only the promisor can perform it and no one else."

Example: A, who is painter, enters into a contract for preparing painting piece for B at a particular price. This contract is of a personal nature and therefore A must perform his promise, he cannot get it performed by anyone else.

But in case of general contract the promise may be either performed by promisor himself or he may get it performed by another person.

(ii) **By the agent of promisor:** In case of a contract of impersonal nature, the promisor may appoint someone as his agent for performing his promise. Such agent will act on behalf of a promisor and the promisor will be bound by the acts of his agent. If an agent does not perform the promise according to the terms and conditions of a contract, ultimate liability will be on the part of promisor. Section 40 (Para II) states that the promisor himself or his agent may perform the contract.

Example: A, appoints B as his agent for selling goods. B enters into a contract with C for selling goods on credit. C makes default in payment. This contract is binding on A, therefore he can sue upon C for the recovery of payment.

(iii) **By legal representative:** According to Section 37 (Para II) of this Act, a contract which involves the use of personal skill or is founded on personal considerations comes to an end on the death of the promisor. As regards any other contract, the legal representatives of the deceased promisor are bound to perform it, unless contrary intention appears from the contract. But their liability under a contract is limited to the value of property they inherit from the deceased.

Example: A borrowed sum of Rs.1,00,000 from B for two years. After one year A dies and C, who is a legal representative, inherits property of Rs. 60, 000 from him. On the due date of repayment B will call upon C to repay. But the liability of C is limited up to the value of Rs. 60,000. He cannot be liable for more than that.

(iv) **By third person:** Thc promise may also be performed by a stranger on behalf of promisor, provided promisee agrees to it. When the promisee accepts performance of promise by third person, he cannot enforce it against the promisor.

According to Section 41 of this Act, "Performance by a stranger accepted by promisee produces the result of discharging promisor."

KAPUR CHAND *vs* MIR NABAB HIMAYAT ALI KHAN. In this case, A, who has to recover Rs.15,000 from B, accepts Rs.11,000 from a third person C in full settlement of account with B. It was held that A cannot enforce this contract against B.

WHO CAN DEMAND PERFORMANCE

Contrary to the obligation of performing contract, the right to claim lies with anyone of the following:

(*i*) **Promisee:** There is direct privity of contract between promisor and promisee. Therefore, the promisee, in a natural way, has a right to demand performance of the contract.

(*ii*) **Legal representative:** In a contract, in case of death of promisee, right to demand performance is shifted to his legal representative; unless contrary intention appears from the contract or the contract is of personal nature.

Example: Y agrees to marry Z. Before the marriage Y dies. Contract comes to an end. Because it is of personal nature and legal representative of Y cannot demand performance of contract from Z.

(*iii*) **Third person:** The general rule of law is that a person cannot acquire rights under a contract to which he is not a party. But this rule is subject to exceptions. Under these exceptional situations, stranger to a contract can demand performance of a contract. Such exceptional situations are:

(*a*) Third person, who is beneficiary in an agreement of trust can demand performance of a contract.

(*b*) If the party, as per rule of estoppel, is stopped from denying his liability toward third party, third party gets right to demand performance.

(*c*) In a contract of family settlement, if the provision is made for the maintenance of female member or for her marriage expenses, she has right to demand performance, though she is stranger to a contract.

PERFORMANCE OF A JOINT PROMISES

When two or more person jointly make a promise for doing or not doing some thing to two or more persons such promise is known as 'joint promise'. Promisors become joint promisors and promisees are known as 'joint promisees'. Joint promises may take any of the following forms:

(*i*) Two or more promisors jointly make a promise to the promisee.

(*ii*) One promisor makes a promise to two or more promisees.

(*iii*) Two or more promisors make a joint promise to two or more promises.

Rules Regarding Performance of Joint Promises

Rules regarding performance of joint promise are:

(*a*) ***Joint liability:*** When two or more promisors make joint promise for doing or not doing something; both the promisors are jointly liable to perform it. In case of death of any one of them, his legal representative along with remaining promisors will perform the promise. When both of them or all joint promisors die, their legal representatives will be called upon to perform the promise jointly.

Example: A and B have borrowed sum of Rs. 10,000 from C. On due date both A and B are jointly liable to pay. If A dies, his legal representative with B and if both of them die, their legal representatives will jointly repay the amount to C.

(*b*) ***Individual liability:*** When two or more joint promisors make promise and there is no express contract contrary to it, both of them are individually liable to perform. So in addition to joint liability they are individually liable to promisee. Hence liability of joint promisors is 'Joint and Several'. In case of individual liability, the promisee of a joint promise can compel any one of the joint promisors to perform whole of the promise.

Example: A and B are joint promisors to repay Rs. 5,000 to C. He can compel either A or B to repay entire amount.

(*c*) ***Right of contribution:*** Joint promisors have joint and several liability. Any of them can be compelled to perform whole of the promise. When one of the joint promisors has been compelled to perform entire promise, he has a right to claim contribution or share of other promisors, unless contrary intention appears from the contract.

Example: X, Y and Z are joint promisors. They have promised to pay sum of Rs. 20,000 to R. On the due date R compels X to pay entire amount. Later on, X has a right to claim respective share or contribution of Y and Z.

However, it is to be noted that ratio of contribution may be decided by them. In case it is not decided they are expected to contribute equally.

(*d*) ***Default in making contribution:*** When any one of the joint promisors could not contribute his share, remaining joint promisors will bear the loss arising from such default. The loss will be shared by them equally.

It is to be noted that this principle is also applied in case of recovery of loan from the legal representatives of deceased debtor, who become joint promisors by operation of law after the death of debtor.

(*e*) ***Release of one of the joint promisors:*** According to Section 44 of this Act, "A release by the promisee of any one of the joint promisors does not discharge other joint promisors from liability. The released joint promisor also continues to be liable to other joint promisors."

Application of this Section does not allow that released joint promisor to gain anything out of it. Rather, after release he will be liable for his share or contribution to other joint promisors who will perform the promise.

Rights of Joint Promisees

In case of joint promise, all joint promisees have a joint right to demand performance of a contract. Unless it is agreed, one promisee cannot claim performance of a joint promise.

According to Section 45 of this Act, "When a promise is made to several persons jointly, then, unless the contrary intention appears from the contract, the right to claim performance, rests with all promisees jointly and a single promisee cannot demand performance. When any one of the promisee dies, right to claim performance rests with the legal representative of such deceased person jointly with the surviving promisees. When all the promisees are dead, the right to claim performance rests with legal representatives of all promisees jointly."

Thus, so long as, all joint promisees survive, they have joint right to claim performance. In case of their death such right is shifted to their legal representative and they can jointly claim performance.

TIME AND PLACE OF PERFORMANCE

Generally, while making a contract, the parties, by mutual agreement decide about time and place of performance. And both the parties are expected to perform their respective promises accordingly. When time and place, are not determined, they should perform their promises within a reasonable period of time and place. Reasonable time and place is a matter of fact which varies from situation to situation depending on intention of the parties, nature of contract and circumstances of the case.

In order to facilitate performance of contract without any dispute, certain rules are laid down regarding time and place by the Indian Contract Act. These are:

(*i*) **Time is not prescribed and performance is not to be applied:** Time of performance has not been stipulated and the promisor has to perform his promise without the request or application of promisee. In such case, the promisor must perform his promise within reasonable period of time. Reasonable period of time depends upon the intention of the parties, nature of contract and circumstances (Section 46).

(ii) **Time is specified, performance is not to be applied for:** When a promise is to be performed on a certain day, the promisor may undertake to perform it without application or request by the promisee. In such a case, the promisor may perform the promise at any time during usual business hours on such day (Section 47).

Example: A agrees to supply 200 bags of sugar to B on 1st October at a particular price. A should deliver these bags to B during usual business hours on 1st October.

(iii) **Application for performance by promisee:** When date of performance is specified and the promisor has to perform his promise on the application or request of promisee. Thus it is the duty of promisee to apply for performance on that day. He must apply during usual business hours.

Example: A agreed to supply 50 bags of tea to B on 8th September. As per the terms of a contract B would apply for performance. Thus on due date, within usual business hours, B must inform A regarding time and place of supply of tea bags to him.

(iv) **No application of performance and no place is fixed:** When, the place of performance is not fixed and promisor has to perform his promise without application or request of promisee. Thus, it is a duty of promisor that he must contact with promisee as to decide about place of performance and accordingly perform the promise (Section 48).

In case, the place of performance is fixed in a contract, promisor is bound to perform at that place. The place which is fixed in a contract must be reasonable for both the parties. Place of performance implies both place for delivery of goods and place of payment.

Example: Ram entered into a contract for supplying 100 quintals of jute to Shyam on 5th September at a specific price. On due date of performance, Ram must apply to Shyam for determining reasonable place and must deliver the jute to him at that place.

(v) **Promisee prescribes the manner and time of performance:** According to this rule, the promisor must perform his promise in any manner and at any time, being prescribed by the promisee (Section 50).

Example: B owes to A, Rs. 10,000. A asks B to deposit this amount in A's bank account. B deposits the amount in A's account. After sometime bank fails and A has no information regarding transfer of money to his account. There has been good payment by B and in this way he is discharged from his obligation.

In another case, A owes Rs. 5,000 to B. B agrees to accept some goods supplied by A in the deduction of the debt. The delivery of goods will be considered as a part of payment.

Time as the Essence of a Contract

It is usual on the part of the parties to decide about the time of performance at the time of making a contract. In this case, the promisor must perform his promise within such stipulated time. In other cases, reasonable time must be followed for the performance.

The time of performance stipulated by the parties does not become an essence of a contract unless the parties have an intention to do so.

According to Section 55 of this Act, "When the party to a contract, promises to do certain things at or before the specified time and fails to do any such thing at or before the specified time the contract or so much of it, has not been performed, becomes voidable at the option of the promisee, if the intention of the parties was that, the time should be of essence of the contract."

The contents of this section make it clear that when the parties decide about time of performance and have an intention to make it essence of a contract, such stipulated time becomes the essence of a contract. And the promisor must fulfil his promise within that stipulated time. If he fails to do so, the contract becomes voidable at the options of promisee.

HITKARI SINGH *vs* A.I.R. (1952, J.K.10): It was held in this case that in mercantile contracts, where once a particular time is specified, the presumption is that the time is of the essence of the contract, unless a contrary intention appears from the terms of the contract and other surrounding circumstances.

Thus time is an essence of a contract, provided:

(*a*) Time of performance has been decided about by the parties.

(*b*) Parties are intented to make it the essence of a contract, either by the words of mouth or in writing.

(*c*) Surrounding circumstances are also in favour of making it as the essence of a contract.

It is to be noted that when time is an essence of a contract and promisor fails to perform his promise on time, such contract becomes voidable at the option of the promisee.

Keeping in view the various judicial decisions, stipulated time is considered as essence of contract under the following situations:

(*a*) When the parties of a contract have expressly agreed that stipulated time will be the essence of a contract.

(*b*) In a contract of sale, stipulated time for the delivery of goods and payment of price has been considered as the essence of the contract.

(*c*) Again, in a contract of sale, time of shipment is of the essence of the contract.

WASOO ENTERPRISES *vs* J.J. OIL MILLS (1968): In this case, the goods were to be shipped by August 1954. On failure to ship in August, time was extended to 10th September. Even then the supplier failed to ship the goods. The buyer repudiated the contract. It was held that time was of essence of the contract. Thus supplier is liable for breach of contract.

(*d*) In all commercial transaction, time of performance, as determined by the parties is considered as an essence of the contract.

When the stipulated time is not the essence of a contract and the promisor fails to perform his promise on due date, the promisee can only claim for compensation, if he has suffered any loss.

Even if the time is an essential factor in a contract, the promisee is free to accept delayed performance. If he wants to claim compensation for delayed performance, he must give notice of his intention to the promisor.

PERFORMANCE OF RECIPROCAL PROMISES

Generally, a contract is a mutual exchange of promises. The promise made by one party forms consideration for the promise of another party. Such promises are known as 'reciprocal promises'. According to Section 2(*f*) of this Act, "when one party gives a promise in consideration of other party's promise, both the promises are called reciprocal promises."

Example: A promises to deliver raw material to B, B promises to pay for that. There is a mutual exchange of promises between A and B. These are known as 'reciprocal promises', because one promise forms consideration for another promise.

Lord Mansfield, in **JONES *vs* BARKLY** case classified reciprocal promises as:

(i) Mutual and dependent: Such promises are interdependent. The performance of one promise depends on the prior performance of other promise. In other words, performance of one promise depends on other.

(ii) Mutual and concurrent: When both reciprocal promises are got to be performed simultaneously these are known as 'mutual and concurrent promises'.

(iii) Mutual and independent: Such promises are independent but forms consideration for each other. These promises are performed independently without waiting for other.

Rules Regarding Performance of Reciprocal Promises

Sections 51, 54, 57 and 58 deal with the performance of reciprocal promises.

(*a*) **Simultaneous performance of reciprocal promises:** When a contract consists of reciprocal promises to be performed simultaneously, no promisor needs to perform his promise unless promisee is ready and willing to perform his promise. This is so, because both the promisors have to perform their promises simultaneously with each other (Section 51).

Example: A agrees to deliver 200 tonnes of rice to B. And B is to make payment on delivery. Thus A has to give delivery and B is to make payment. A need not give delivery unless B is ready and willing to pay.

(*b*) **Order of performance:** When the parties making reciprocal promises, determine the order of performance expressly, they must perform in that order (Section 52).

Example: A makes promise to build a house for B at fixed price. A must build house first for B as to get payment from him. A can claim payment from B only when the house is built, because order of performance of both promises is determined.

(*c*) **Effect of one party preventing another from performing promise:** In a contract consisting of reciprocal promises if one party prevents another from performing a promise, the contract becomes voidable at the option of the party so prevented. He can claim compensation if he has suffered any loss (Section 53).

Example: A promises to sell standing timber to B. As per the terms of a contract A will cut and cord the timber, where upon B will take it away and pay for it. A cords only a part of timber and neglects to cord the rest. In this contract, B may avoid contract and claim compensation from A.

(*d*) **Effect of default as to promise to be performed first:** When the contract consists of reciprocal promises, such that one promise cannot be performed or its performance cannot be claimed till other promise has been performed. In case of default on the part of promisor who is to perform first, he cannot claim performance from another promisor and if other promisor has suffered a loss due to non-performance, he is entitled for compensation (Section 54).

Example: B, a ship owner agrees to convey A's cargo from Calcutta to Mauritius for a certain amount of freight. A fails to provide cargo to B. B is entitled to avoid contract and claim compensation for the loss if any.

(*e*) **Reciprocal promise to do something legal and also some other things which is illegal:** When a person reciprocally promise first to do certain things which are legal and secondly to do certain other things which are illegal, the first set of promise is a contract and second set is void agreement.

Example: A and B agree that A will sell a house to B for Rs. 50,000 and also that if B uses it as gambling house A will further pay him Rs. 75,000—the first set of reciprocal promise for selling a house is a valid contract, but the object of second one is illegal therefore if it is void.

This rule is applicable, where reciprocal promises can be separated out. Legal part of promise can be enforced provided it can be separated from illegal part of the promise.

APPROPRIATION OF PAYMENT

Appropriation of payment implies to apply or use particular payment for discharging debt. It is related to time and place of performance of a contract. The person may borrow money from the creditor many times. Each borrowing may be of distinct amount and repayable on different dates. It means various debts are different in terms of amount and date of payment. In such case, if the borrower makes payment which is not sufficient for discharging all debts. The question arises, how to apply or use that payment and against the discharge of which debt should be used.

In this regard, the following rules, which are give under Sections 59 to 61 of this Act are as follows:

(*i*) By express instructions of debtor: While making payment, generally, the debtor gives necessary instructions to the creditor for the application of that amount. In such case appropriation must be made according to those instructions. It has been rightly pointed out by Lord Campbell, in '**RAFT *vs* LUMELY**' case that 'there is an established rule of law that, when money is paid, it is to be applied according to express will of the payer, not of the receiver'.

(*ii*) Implied by intention of debtor and circumstance: In case the debtor does not give express instructions for the application of payment, it can be used according to an intention of debtor and the circumstances.

Example: A owes three debts to B. One of Rs. 5,000 for two months, another of Rs. 2,000 for one year and third one of Rs. 1,000 under Bill of Exchange which is due on 5th January. A makes payment of Rs. 1,000 to B on 4th January, but does not give any instruction for application of that payment. In this case, it is implied, both from intention of A as well as circumstance that the payment must have been made by A to discharge that Bill of Exchange which falls due on 5th January.

(*iii*) Discretion of creditor: When the debtor does not give any instruction and nothing is indicated by his intention and circumstances, the creditor has a discretion to apply such payment for discharging any lawful debt due against the debtor. The creditor can apply such payment, even for discharging debt which, otherwise has become time-barred under the provisions of Indian Limitation Act.

Example: Ram owes several debts to Shyam, which are of distinct amount and payable on different dates. One of the debts has become time-barred which Shyam cannot legally recover it from Ram. On a particular date Ram makes a payment, does not give any instruction and its application is not implied from intention of Ram and circumstances. In this case, Shyam has a right to apply this payment for discharging even that time-barred debt.

(*iv*) Order of time: When the parties do not make appropriation and it is not implied from the circumstances, the payment shall be applied for discharging debts in order of time. The debt which falls due first will be discharged first. But, if two or more debts fall due on same date, the amount of payment shall be applied to those debts in the ratio of principal amount.

Example: A owes many debts to B. Two debts fall due on the same date prior to others. The principal amount of these two is Rs. 5,000 and Rs. 10,000. A pays Rs. 4,000. In the absence of all other rules this amount will be applied against these two debts in the ratio of 1 : 2.

ASSIGNMENT OF CONTRACTS

Assignment of a contract is a process, whereby rights and liability of a contract are transfered to a third party. As a result of assignment, such third party can bring an action, against another party of a contract at his own. Though Indian Contract Act does not contain any provision to deal with assignment of a contract, the following rules are followed by the courts of law:

(*i*) **Assignment may take place by the act of the parties of a contract:** By making agreement of assignment they can transfer contractual rights and liability to a third party. Assignment of contract, by the act of the parties is subject to the following rules:

(*a*) According to Section 40 of this Act, contractual obligations involving personal skill or ability cannot be assigned *e.g.*, contractual obligation by a singer to sing, or by film actor to act or a contract of marriage, etc.

(*b*) In a contract, promisor cannot assign his liability or obligation without the consent of the promisee. On giving such consent by the promisee, it becomes case of novation. The promisee is entitled to know that, in a contract who is to provide satisfaction to his right.

Example: A owes Rs. 2,000 to B. A can assign his liability of paying the debt to C, only with the consent of B and C. This is so because B as a promisee has a right to know that who is to pay him.

(*c*) Rights and benefits under a contract can be assigned, except in a contract which involves personal skill and ability. But such assignment must be subject to all equities between original parties of a contract. For example, an actionable claim (right to take legal action) can be assigned only by making an instrument in writing. And it is in the interest of assignee to give notice of assignment to the debtor, though it is not legally required.

KEMP *vs* BAERSELMAN (1906, 75 L.J.K.B., 873): In this case, B agreed to supply eggs to a cake manufacture. The eggs were to be delivered at three different places and payment to be made through Bill of Exchange drawn upon him. The business of cake manufacturer was taken over by a company in which he was main shareholder. B refused to deliver eggs to the company. It was held that the contract was based on personal considerations, therefore it cannot be assigned.

(*ii*) **Assignment by operation of law:** In many instances, rights or benefits in a contract automatically devolve upon third party by operation of law. As it happens in case of death or insolvency of the party, the rights and liabilities are transfered to their legal representatives (except in case of a contract of personal nature) or official assignee. (in case of insolvency).

CONTRACTS WHICH NEED NOT BE PERFORMED

According to the Indian Contract Act, a contract need not be performed, in the following cases:

(*i*) When the performance of a contract becomes impossible due to any reasons beyond the control of the parties, such contract becomes void and need not be performed (Section 56).

(*ii*) When the parties of a contract, substitute to new contract, or alter it or cancel it by mutual agreement, such contract need not be performed (Section 62).

(*iii*) When the promisee of a contract accepts lesser performance of the whole promise or extend the time of performance, such contract is discharged (Section 63).

(*iv*) When the party who is entitled to rescind the contract or at whose option the contract can be declared as void, avoids such contract, it need not be performed (Section 64).

(*v*) When the promisee neglects or refuses to afford the promisor reasonable facilities for the performance of his promise, such contract comes to an end (Section 67).

REVIEW QUESTIONS

1. What do you mean by 'performance of a contract'? Explain actual and attempted performance.
2. Explain who can demand performance of a contract and from whom it can be demanded.
3. Discuss the rules regarding performance of a joint promises.
4. Explain the various rules regarding time and place of performance of a contract.
5. Explain time as an essence of a contract. Discuss the various instances in which time is considered as an essential factor of a contract.
6. Can rights and liabilities of a contract be assigned? Discuss the rules regarding it.
7. Define reciprocal promises with suitable examples. Explain various legal provisions related to the performance of these promises.
8. What is appropriation of payment? Explain the legal provisions regarding it.
9. Comment on:

   (*a*) Performance is a natural mode of discharging a contract.

   (*b*) Contract of a personal nature cannot be assigned.

   (*c*) Time as an essence of a contract.

   (*d*) Contract for doing something impossible need not be performed.

   (*e*) Joint promisors are liable jointly and severally.

PRACTICAL PROBLEMS

1. A, who is a painter, agrees to make a painting for B. Before the due date, A dies. Can B claim performance? (Hint: No).
2. Ram borrows a sum of Rs. 20,000 from Shyam for six months. Two months, after having borrowed the money, Ram dies. Manohar, who is a legal representative of Ram inherits a property worth Rs. 15,000 from him. Examine the legal consequences of this contract.
3. X and Y jointly promise to pay Rs. 5,000 to Y. Before the due date X dies and Y becomes insolvent. What is the legal remedy available to Z?
4. A owes Rs. 10,000 to B. B asks A to deposit the amount in the account of B. A does so. Before B knows about the transfer of money to his account the bank fails. Can B recover this amount from A? (Hint: No).
5. A agrees to get B's house repaired, provided B vacates the house. But B does not vacate the house and as a result of it A fails to repair his house. Is A liable for breach of contract? (Hint: No).
6. A enters into an agreement with B for selling his house to B at Rs. 50,000. But if B uses this house for gambling purpose he shall pay Rs. 75,000 for it. Can B avoid both sets of promises? (Hint: No).
7. In a contract, A has to recover Rs. 25,000 from B. Later on, A accepts a sum of Rs. 15,000 from C in full settlement of account with B. Can A claim the remaining balance from B? (Hint: No).
8. Manohar was to deliver 200 bags of cement to Sohan on 5th September. As per the terms of a contract Sohan would apply for performance. On the due date Sohan forgets to apply for performance. Can the contract be enforced? (Hint: No).
9. A was to supply 100 cotton bales to B on 10th October. Both the parties are intented to make it an essential factor of a contract. A fails to deliver cotton bales. What is the legal remedy available to B. Explain if time fixed by the parties of contract is not an essence of a contract can B avoid that contract. (Hint: No).
10. X owes several debts of distinct amount and payable at different period of time to Y. One of the debt has become time barred. Meanwhile X makes payment at random and does not instruct Y for applying it. Y gets an opportunity and uses this payment for discharging the debt which has become time barred. Is appropriation of payment valid? (Hint: Yes).

11. A agrees to marry B. Before marriage A becomes unsound mind. Can B claim compensation from the legal representative of A?
12. Ram agreed to supply eggs to Shyam who manufactures cakes. Eggs were to be supplied at different places and payment was to be made through Bill of Exchange drawn upon Shyam. The business of Shyam was taken over by newly formed private company in which Shyam is main stockholder. Ram refuses to supply eggs to the Company. Can the company take any legal action against Ram? (Hint: No).

■■■

11

Breach of Contract

LEARNING OBJECTIVES

- Understand meaning and concept of breach of contract.
- Compare legal consequences of actual breach and anticipatory breach of contract.
- Get familiar with legal remedies of an aggrieved party in breach of contract.
- Develop clarity about damages and their types.
- Examine suitability of each legal remedy.
- Analyse rule of '*quantum meruit*' and its applications.

MEANING AND TYPES OF BREACH OF CONTRACT

Formation of contract results in creating contractual obligations between the parties. These contractual obligations are to be fulfilled by the parties on the due date as per terms and conditions of a contract. When the party does not fulfil his obligation or refuses to fulfil it or disabled himself from fulfilling it is known as 'breach of contract'. Such contract comes to an end, and another party gets certain legal remedies to be used against party making breach of contract.

Breach of contract may be of two types: (*a*) Actual breach (*b*) Anticipatory breach.

Actual breach of contract takes place when the promisor fails to perform his obligation or refuses to do so on the due date of performance.

Example: A was to deliver 100 bags of sugar to B on 5th September at a specific price. On the 5th September A does not make supply or refuses or becomes untraceable. It amounts to actual breach of contract and the contract is discharged.

In ***Anticipatory breach*** of contract, the promisor either refuses to perform or makes himself unable to perform a promise before due the date of performance. Anticipatory breach of contract takes place before the date of actual performance.

The promisor may either inform promisee that he is not going to perform his promise or does any act, which is inconsistent with terms and conditions of a contract.

According to Section 39 of this Act "when a party to a contract has refused to perform or disable himself from performing his promise in its entirely, the promisee may put contract to an end; unless he has given his acquiescence in its continuance by words or conduct."

In other words, on the refusal of promisor if the promisee condones breach of contract or waives his rights the contract will continue.

Anticipatory breach of contract also takes place if the promisor does an act, which renders performance of his promise impossible or illegal.

Example: A enters into an agreement to marry B on 15th January. But on 15th December he marries C. This act on the part of A has rendered the performance of his promise illegal; thus A will be liable for anticipatory breach of contract by impossibility.

On anticipatory breach of contract the promisee or aggrieved party has the following options:

(*a*) The promisee can wait till the due date of performance. And on that date, anticipatory breach will be automatically converted into actual breach and the contract will be discharged.

During intervening period between anticipatory breach and actual breach if supervening impossibility takes place and contract is discharged; the promisee or aggrieved party loses his right to claim for compensation.

Avery *vs* Bowden (1885,5 E&B, 714). In this case B chartered A's ship and agreed to load it with a cargo at Odessa within 45 days. On the arrival of the ship at Odessa, B was unable to supply cargo. A did not accept the refusal and continued demanding the cargo. Before the expiry of 45 days war was broken and performance of the contract became impossible. It was held that, contract was discharged and A is not entitled to sue upon B for compensation.

(*b*) On getting information regarding anticipatory breach, the promisee can immediately rescind or avoid the contract. And without waiting till due date of performance he can use legal remedies against the promisor *e.g.*, sue upon the promisor for compensation or specific performance.

HOCHSTERV *vs* DE, LA, TOUR (1953, 2E&B, 678). In this case, defendant agreed to engage the plaintiff as his attendant on a continental tour, which he will start from 1st June for three month at a particular salary. The defendant later on changed his mind and informed plaintiff before 1st June that he would not require his service. It was held that the plaintiff can put contract to end even before 1st June and bring a suit for compensation. He was not bound to wait till the date of performance.

LEGAL REMEDIES FOR BREACH OF CONTRACT

There are two parties in a contract. They make mutual exchange of promises between them. These promises are known as 'contractual obligations'. When a party does not fulfil his promise or refuse to perform it, breach of contract takes place. In that contract, another party is technically known as 'aggrieved party'. Such aggrieved party has got various legal remedies, which he can use against the party making a breach of contract.

These legal remedies are as under:

- Rescission of the contract.
- Suit for damages.
- Suit for specific performance.
- Suit injunction.
- Suits upon '*Quantum meruit*'.

1. Rescission of the Contract

When a party makes breach of contract by not fulfilling his obligation, the aggrieved party has a right to rescind such contact. To exercise this right, the aggrieved has to file a suit for rescission of a contract. On granting rescission, the aggrieved party gets released from his obligation in that contact. He is no more liable to perform his promise. The net legal effects of rescission are:

(*a*) Aggrieved party is discharged from his obligation in that contract.

(*b*) Right of restitution comes into force and the party who has got benefit in that contract will be liable to restore it or give it back to the party from whom he has received it (Section 64).

(*c*) It would also clear the way for aggrieved party to use other legal remedies against the party making breach of a contract.

Example: Manohar was in an agreement with Sohan for supplying 200 bags of cement on 5th January. On the due date Manohar does not supply bags of cement to Sohan. It amounts to breach of contract by Manohar. Sohan, before taking any legal remedy against Manohar, has to get himself absolved from his obligation of making payment. It is only by getting rescission from the court he gets free from his obligation and it also clears the way for using other legal remedies against Manohar.

2. Suit for Damages

On making a breach of contract by a party, the aggrieved party may suffer monetary loss. In the event of breach he may be put in a disadvantageous position or in a position of discomfort. In such case, the aggrieved party has a right to claim for compensation. The basic idea of providing compensation to the aggrieved party is to put him in the same financial position, as he would have been if the contract had been performed.

However due to breach of contract the aggrieved party may suffer variety of losses such as loss of profit, loss of reputation, loss of payment of expenses and loss due to change in price line etc. Not only this, but aggrieved party may also exaggerate his losses as to get benefit of the situation.

Thus in this regard the courts make judicious assessment of the losses suffered by an aggrieved party and grant compensation accordingly. The amount of compensation granted by the court is technically known as 'damage'.

In one of the leading case, the court has observed that, "the role of common law is that where a party sustains loss by reason of breach of contract, he is to be placed in the same situation, with respect to damages as if the contract has been performed".

According to Section 73 of this Act, "when a contract has been broken the party who suffers by such breach is entitled to receive from the party who has broken the contract compensation for any loss or damage caused to him thereby:

(*a*) Which naturally arose out of breach of contract.

(*b*) Which the party knew when they make contract to be likely to result from the breach of it.

(*c*) Such compensation is not to be given for any remote and indirect loss or damage sustained by reason of the breach." In this connection there had been very interesting case in which certain rules regarding damages were made clear. **HADLEY *vs* BAXENDALE (1854, 9, EX, 341):** In this case, the plaintiff had delivered a crankshaft to the manufacturers who were to make a new shaft on the basis of old one. The servant of plaintiff had informed the carrier that the working of the mill was stopped and the crankshaft must be sent to the manufacturers immediately. The carrier made delay in sending crankshaft as a result of which new shaft was received very late and the mill could not work. The plaintiff filed a suit against the defendant claiming damage for the loss of profit, because of the stoppage of the mill due to non-availability of crankshaft. Defendant pleaded that these were remote damages and they were not liable to pay.

Justice B. Alderson observed that, "where two parties have made a contract, which one of them has broken, the damage which the other party ought to receive in respect of such breach of contract should be as such as fairly and reasonably be considered either arising naturally, that is, according to the usual course of thing from such breach of contract itself or such as may reasonably be supposed to have been in the contemplation of both parties, at the time they made contract as the probable result of breach of it."

This decision lays down the following two rules:

(*a*) Only those losses may be compensated which are fair, reasonable and directly and naturally arising out of breach of contract.

(*b*) Indirect or remote losses such as loss of profit may be compensated provided such loss would have been in contemplation or consideration of both parties at the same time of making the contract.

Example: A agreed to supply spare parts of machine to B on 5th September at a particular price. A fails to deliver spare parts on due date. There is a breach of contract and B filed a suit against A for the compensation of losses. B claimed that due to non-delivery of spare parts, the machine could not function, as a result of which the following losses were incurred:

(*a*) Depreciation on machine.

(*b*) Fixed expenses such as salary paid to permanent staff, rent of premises and other rate and taxes.

(*c*) Loss of profit which would have been earned through contract which could not be done due to non-functioning of machine.

In this case, taking note of **HADLEY *vs* BAXENDALE,** compensation may be granted to B only for depreciation, fixed expenses and salary paid to permanent staff. The loss of profit from government contract is a remote and indirect loss, therefore it can be compensated provided A and B could have considered it at the tine of making contract.

Types of Damages

Damages can be of the following types:

(*i*) Ordinary damages

(*ii*) Special damages

(*iii*) Exemplary or vindictive damages

(*iv*) Nominal damages

(*i*) ***Ordinary damages:*** When breach of contract takes place, the aggrieved party is entitled to claim for compensation for the losses caused to him. Ordinary damages are those damages, which will be sanctioned by the court for those losses, which do arise in the natural and ordinary course from the breach of contract. These damages are granted for the losses, which are directed and general in nature. The calculation and quantum of ordinary damages depend upon the circumstances, which were prevailing at the time of breach of contract.

According to Section 73 of this Act, "general damages is referred to, compensation for any loss caused to him thereby which naturally arose in the usual course of things from such breach."

Natural and direct losses resulting from breach of contract may vary situation-to-situation depending on nature of transaction and prevailing circumstances. The following examples may help in understanding such losses.

Difference between contract price and market price: *Example:* A agrees to sell 200 bags of cement to B on 5th September at Rs. 500 per bag. B is to make payment on the delivery of cement bags. Before due date the price of cement has increased to Rs. 600 per bag. A refused to supply cement to B. There is breach of contract B is entitled to claim for compensation for the loss arising out of change in price *e.g.*, Rs. 100 per bag of cement (Rs. 2,000).

Principal amount and interest for delayed payment: *Example:* X borrows sum of Rs. 1,000 from Y @ 10 per cent interest per annum. On due date X fails to repay. As a result of it Y could not fulfil his obligation and totally ruined. X liable only for the payment of Rs. 1,000 plus interest @ 10 per cent for delayed payment.

Medical expenses and financial losses caused by death: *Example:* A's wife brought tin fish from the merchant. After consuming it the poisoning was caused and she died. A is entitled to recover from the merchant (*a*) expense for employing servant during her illness, (*b*) medical expenses, and (*c*) financial loss caused by the death of his wife.

Cost of hiring another ship: *Example:* A hires B's ship for going to Mumbai and boarding cargo on 1st January which is to be brought to Calcutta at particular fright. B does not send his ship to Mumbai and made a breach of contract. A is entitled to receive compensation for such troubles and expenses which will be incurred by him for hiring another ship.

Cost of rebuilding the house, loss of rent and compensation to third party: *Example:* A entered into an agreement for constructing house for B and to give complete possession on 1st January. B makes agreement with C for renting out that house to him from 2nd January; this fact is very much in the knowledge of A. The house was badly constructed and collapsed before 1st January. B is entitled to get compensation for (*a*) cost of reconstructing the house. (*b*) loss of rent, and (*c*) compensation; which B was to pay to C for not renting out the house.

Not responsible for the losses due to closure of the mill: *Example:* A made a contract for supplying 100 cotton bales to B at a particular price. A knows nothing about the nature of business, being contracted by B. As a result of non-availability of cotton bales, B's mill is closed. B entitled to get compensation for the loss expenses, price difference to be incurred for arranging supply from other sources. But A is not liable to pay compensation for the loss caused by closure of the mill.

Losses arising out of breach of conditions and warranties in a contract of sale: *Example:* A agrees to sell washing machine on a warranty of particular quality to B. B who relies on that warranty sells it to C. But C does not find the machine of that quality on which warranty has been given. B pays compensation for breach of warranty to C. Later on, B is entitled to recover it from A.

(*ii*) ***Special Damages:*** Special damages are granted by the court for compensating special losses caused to the party due to breach of contract. Special losses are those losses, which do arise from special circumstances, which are attached to a contract. These special circumstances, which may cause special loss to the party in case of breach of contract, must have been informed to another party at the time of making a contract.

According to Section 73 of this Act, "special losses refer to those that may be caused by breach of contract, which the party knew, when they made a contract, to be likely to result from breach of it."

Thus the special damages imply:

(*a*) Compensation for special losses arising out of the breach of contract.

(*b*) These special losses do arise from the special circumstances, which were attached to the contract.

(*c*) These losses must have been in consideration of the parties at the time of making a contract. It means such probable loss must have been properly communicated to the other party.

(*d*) Special losses are in addition to ordinary losses. Special losses are remote and indirect in nature, not directly arising from breach of contract. Rather, these arise out of special circumstances attached to the contract.

The basic nature of special losses can be understood on the basis of the following examples.

Loss of profit: *Example:* A was in agreement to supply spare parts of machine to B latest by a particular date. While making agreement B has properly informed to A that in case he does not get that part of machine on time, in addition to other losses, he will also suffer a loss of a particular amount per day due to non-execution of government contract. A fails to deliver part of machine on time. B is entitled to claim for compensation both for ordinary losses and special loss, *e.g.*, loss of profit regarding non-execution of government contract.

Loss of income: *Example:* Ram, who is a taxi driver gives his taxi to Shyam for getting it repaired and informs him that unreasonable delay in repairing will result in loss of income of Rs. 100 per day. Shyam makes unreasonable delay in repairing. He is bound to pay compensation for the loss of income, which is a special loss.

(iii) ***Exemplary or vindictive damages:*** When the amount granted by the court is more than ordinary and special losses, it is known as exemplary or vindictive damages. Such damages are granted by the court, for the disapproval of conduct of the party making a breach of contract.

These damages are the exceptions to the general rule that damages are not to be in the nature of punishment but only compensation for the losses incurred by the party.

Exemplary damages are generally awarded to deter the person from making breach of contract on the one hand, and on the other, the idea of awarding such damages may also be to compensate the aggrieved party to some extent, for mental pain, loss of reputation and sense of humiliation etc.

These damages are awarded by the court, under the following situations:

(*a*) When there is a breach of contract of marriage, aggrieved party is entitled to claim such damages. The quantum of damage depends on the extent of mental injury and loss of reputation caused to him.

(*b*) When a bank, wrongfully dishonours a customer's cheque drawn upon it on the plea of insufficient credit balance in his account, the customer is entitled to claim exemplary damages for compensating the loss of credit.

WESTERN *vs* OLATHE STATE BANK (1925,78, col.217): In this case, a banker agreed to advance money to Western's trip to California, by putting credit balance in his account. But the bank wrongfully failed to put that amount in the credit of customer's account. As a result of it, the cheques drawn by the customer were dishonoured. It was held that Western was entitled to claim for exemplary damages for humiliation and mental suffering.

It is interesting to note that, in such cases, the rule of determining damages is, 'the smaller the cheque, the greater the damage.'

(*iv*) ***Nominal damages:*** Nominal damages are awarded, when the court is of the opinion that aggrieved party has not suffered real loss due to breach of contract. The basic idea of granting such damages is to bring the party making breach of contract to record and to recognise the right of aggrieved party. In other words, such damages are awarded just to establish the right to decree for the breach of contract.

According to the recent decision of Delhi High Court "no damage can be allowed under Section 73 of this Act unless the aggrieved party has suffered some loss."

UNION OF INDIA *vs* TRIBHGUWAN DAS JI PATEL. (1971, A.I.R. Delhi 120). In this case, T agreed to supply sleepers to Railway Administration. As per the terms and conditions of the contract, T was required to pay damages to the Railways on his failure to supply, regardless of the fact that whether the railways suffer any loss or not. T failed to supply and Railways did not suffer any loss. Thus Delhi High Court disallowed the suit filed by the Railways for compensation.

How to calculate damages: In order to calculate amount of damage, to be sanctioned to the aggrieved party, the courts normally follow the following guidelines:

(*i*) Damages are allowed only to compensate the aggrieved party for the losses, which are direct, fair, natural and reasonable.

(*ii*) Remote or indirect losses of aggrieved may also be compensated provided such losses were in contemplation or consideration of the parties at the time of making a contract.

(*iii*) Only in a very specific case, exemplary damages may be granted for compensating loss of reputation and mental suffering.

(*iv*) While calculating the amount of damage the court takes into account that the aggrieved party is being put in such a financial position, in which he would have been, if the contract had been performed.

(*v*) The court will also recognise that there is duty on the part of aggrieved party to mitigate the loss arising out of breach of contract. He cannot claim compensation for that amount of loss which would have been mitigated by making reasonable efforts.

(*vi*) The aggrieved party is also entitled to get the cost of getting decree for damages.

(*vii*) Damages can also be recovered for physical inconvenience and discomfort.

(*viii*) While calculating amount of damage in case of breach of contract of sale, generally the difference between contract price and market price is taken into consideration. And any change in the price taking place after date of breach will not be considered.

JAMAL *vs* MOOLA DAWOOD & SONS. In this case, A agreed to sell 23,500 shares to B, to be delivered and paid for on 30 December 1911. On that date, B refuses to accept delivery. The market price, on the date of breach was such as to cause loss of Rs. 1,09,218. But A sold those shares much later and suffered a loss of Rs. 79,862. The court allowed damage of Rs. 1,09,218 to A.

Liquidated damage and penalty: The concept of liquidated damage and penalty is relevant in connection with calculation of damage. Sometimes, the parties while making a contract, may fix the amount of damage, which may be either liquidated damage or penalty depending on the manner of fixing it defined as:

(*i*) When the amount of damage to be paid to the aggrieved party has been fixed by the parties, on the basis of probable losses which may arise out of breach of a contract, such amount is known as liquidated damage.

(*ii*) When the parties fix the amount of damage to be paid not on the scientific basis, but with a view to put some kind of punishment on the party who will make breach of contract, such amount is known as 'penalty'.

These two terms are used in English Mercantile Law. The courts in England, usually allow 'liquidated damage' without any regard to the actual loss suffered by the party due to breach of a contract. And the court will make assessment of actual loss and grant damage for compensating that loss.

The distinction between penalty and liquidated damage has been made clear in the following case.

DUNLOP PNEUMATIC TYPE *vs* NEW GARAGE AND MOTOR COY. (1914, A.C. 79). The essence of penalty is payment of money stipulated as '*in terrorum*'. and the essence of liquidated damage is a genuine covenated pre-estimate of damage.

But, Indian courts do not recognise difference between liquidated damage and penalty. Rather, in case of breach of a contract, the court makes assessment of actual loss and grants compensation for it. While granting damage, amount fixed by the parties will be taken as maximum limit of damage.

According to Section 74 of this Act, "when a contract has been broken, if a sum is named in the contract as the amount to be paid in case of breach or if the contract contains any other stipulation by way of penalty, the party complaining breach is entitled, whether or not actual damage or loss is proved to have been caused thereby, to receive from the party who has broken the contract, reasonable compensation not exceeding the amount so named, as the case may be, the penalty stipulated for."

Stipulation regarding payment of interest: When the creditor charged increased rate of interest from the date of default, such stipulation for increased rate of interest will be regarded as penalty. And if the debtor makes default in repaying the debt, such increased rate will be disallowed by the court provided increased rate of interest seems to be unreasonable.

Example: A borrows sum of Rs. 20,000 from B @ 10 per cent interest per annum for 2 years. A signs promissory note with a stipulation that in case of his default in repaying that sum B will be allowed to charge @ 50 per cent interest from the date of default. The stipulation of increased rate of interest seems to be unreasonable thus B will be allowed to get compensation as court regards reasonable.

In connection with a stipulation for increased rate of interest, the following rules should be taken care of:

(*a*) Unless, the parties make express or implied agreement interest cannot be recovered as a damage.

(*b*) Stipulation for increased rate of interest will be regarded as penalty. Thus only reasonable amount of compensation may be granted by the court in such cases.

(*c*) Increased rate of interest, which the party is supposed to pay from the date of default must be unreasonable in the eyes of law.

(*d*) When the contract provides that the amount should be paid without interest by a particular date and on default it will be payable with reasonable rate of interest, it may be allowed by the court.

(*e*) Payment of compound interest on default is allowed provided it is not at an increased rate.

3. Suit for Specific Performance

When breach of contract takes place and aggrieved party suffers a loss, these losses may be of such a nature that damage granted for these by the court may be inadequate. It is because such losses cannot be measured in terms of money. In such cases, the aggrieved party is entitled to claim for order of specific performance. Specific performance means actual carrying out of a contract as agreed.

The order of specific performance is an order issued by the court directing upon the party making breach of contract and instructing him to perform what he has undertaken to perform. Such order is a discretionary order, which is allowed by the court in a limited number of cases.

The rules for granting order of specific performance are contained in Chapter II of Specific Relief Act, 1963. The order of specific performance, at the discretion of the court may be granted in the following cases:

(*a*) Where monetary compensation is not an adequate remedy for breach of contract.

(*b*) Where there is no standard for ascertaining the actual damage, caused by non-performance of promise by the party.

(*c*) When it is probable that compensation in terms of money on non-performance of contract cannot be obtained.

(*d*) In a contract of sales of goods such order can be granted for specific goods, which are unique, rare and cannot be easily purchased from the market, such as rare articles and antiques etc.

But order of specific performance will not be granted in the following cases:

(*a*) Where monetary compensation is an adequate remedy for the breach of contract.

(*b*) Where the court cannot supervise performance of contract, particularly when it is continuous in nature.

(*c*) To enforce a contract of personal nature based on personal consideration and which requires special skill and talent to perform it, such as contract of marriage, contract with singer and painter etc.

(*d*) Contracts made by a company beyond its powers as laid in its Memorandum of Association.

(*e*) Contracts, which are made by trustees which amount to breach of trust.

4. Suit for Injunction

In a contract if the party has made a promise for not doing something and the party makes a breach of contract by doing that thing, to prevent such party from doing that act an order of injunction may be claimed by an aggrieved party.

It is an order, passed by the court of law, directing upon the party and refraining him from performing what he has promise not to perform.

An injunction is a preventive relief, which is provided to an aggrieved party where damages would not be an adequate relief. It is a negative form of order of specific performance.

The power of the court for granting injunction is discretionary in nature. The court may grant such order either on temporary basis or for an indefinite period of time.

Example: Superstar of a cricket makes an agreement with some sports goods company for not using the bats except manufactured by that company. On some occasions the company finds him using cricket bats manufactured by some other company. There is a breach of contract on the part of superstar of cricket.

To grant damage for compensating losses of the sports goods company is an inadequate remedy. Thus the company may get an injunction from the court for preventing cricket star from using bats of other company.

LIMLEY *vs* WAGNER (1852, 5 De, GM & coy 604). In this case, W agreed to sing at L's theatre during certain period of time to sing nowhere else. Later on W made an agreement with Z to sing at his theatre and refused to perform the contract with L. It was held that W could be restrained by injunction from singing at Z's theatre.

5. Suit upon *Quantum Meruit*

In a contract the promisor may be in the process of performing his promise. Before he completes it, the promisee makes a breach of contract. Among other remedies, the aggrieved party can also claim for *quantum meruit*.

Quantum meruit is a Latin dictum, which means "as much as earned or merited". That means under *quantum meruit* aggrieved party can also claim for the reasonable cost of work done by him in the contract.

This legal remedy is claimed by an aggrieved party where in the performance of a contract, he has done some work or rendered some services. In case other party makes a breach of contract he can recover reasonable cost of work done or services rendered.

According to Section 70 of this Act, an aggrieved party can claim right of *quantum meruit* under the following situation:

(*i*) ***Breach of contract:*** One party is in the process of performance of a contract, but other party makes a breach of such contract. In such case if an aggrieved party has done some work or has rendered services, he is entitled to claim reasonable cost of work done services rendered.

Example: In an agreement A was to construct three-storey building for B. He was to make payment of particular amount at the completion of each storey. A completed first storey of the building, but B fails to make stipulated payment. Among other remedies, A can also claim reasonable cost of constructing first storey of building.

(*ii*) ***When contract is discovered to be void:*** When the person has done some work or rendered services in a contract, which was discovered to be void. Another person who gets benefit of such work or services must pay its cost to the person who has done the work in that contract.

Example: A was appointed as CEO of a company by the board of directors. After six months, it is found that one of the directors of the board who was a member of selection committee has not purchased qualification shares and therefore he was not a bona fide director. Thus service contract of CEO was discovered to be void. But he is entitled to get all benefits under that contract for a period of six months.

(*iii*) ***Something done voluntarily, but with an intention of getting consideration:*** When the person delivers some goods or renders some services for another person with an intention of getting consideration for it. The person who gets benefits of such services or goods is bound to pay reasonable cost or compensation to that person.

Example: A's godown gets into fire. B who is passersby helps A in extinguishing that fire. B has an intension of getting something in return of his services. Thus he is entitled to get reasonable compensation for his services.

(*iv*) ***Divisible contract:*** Where a contract made by the parties is divisible. And a party to that contract has completed a part of his obligation, even if he has made breach of contract he can claim right of *quantum meruit.*

The right of *quantum meruit* is subject to following limitations:

(*a*) A person who has made breach of contract is not allowed to claim right of *quantum meruit.*

(*b*) In a contract which is not divisible into part and lump sum payment is to be made for the complete work the party making part performance is not entitled to claim this right.

REVIEW QUESTIONS

1. Define the term 'Breach of Contract'. Explain how the contract is discharged by Breach. Give suitable example.
2. Discuss the various legal remedies, which are available to an aggrieved party in case of breach of contract.
3. What are 'damages'? Discuss the various types of damages which can be claimed by an aggrieved party for compensating his losses.
4. Explain various rules regarding calculation of damages which are followed by the court.
5. Define the term '*quantum meruit*'. When this right can be claimed by aggrieved party. What are its limitations?
6. What is 'specific performance'? In which situations the court grants order of specific performance? Explain when this order is not applicable.
7. Explain various rules regarding damages, which were laid down in Hadley *vs* Baxendale case. To what extent these rules are applicable in India?
8. Distinguish between 'liquidated damages' and 'penalty'. Explain it in the context of English and Business law.
9. Write notes on:

   (*a*) Anticipatory breach

   (*b*) Liquidated damages

   (*c*) Order of specific performance

   (*d*) *Quantum meruit*

10. Comment on:
    (*a*) Liquidated damage and Penalty are one and same.
    (*b*) Anticipatory breach does not discharge contract automatically.
    (*c*) Nominal damage is granted only for recognising decree for damage.
    (*d*) Specific performance can be claimed when compensation is not a adequate remedy.
    (*e*) Stipulation regarding increased rate of interest after default is also a penalty.
    (*f*) Damages are not to be in the nature of punishment.
    (*g*) Injunction is a preventive relief.
    (*h*) Exemplary damage is awarded by the court for compensating loss of reputation and mental pain etc.

PRACTICAL PROBLEMS

1. Ram agrees to supply 200 bags of rice to Shyam on 5th September at a particular price. Shyam was to make payment on 10th September. On the due date of performance Ram refuses to deliver rice. Examine nature of Shyam's obligations in this contract and how can he be released from it.
2. A was in agreement for supplying furniture to B on 1st January. On 15th December A informs to B that he will not make supply of furniture to him. What is legal remedy available to B? When can he use it against A?
3. A enters into an agreement to marry B on 15th September. But before 15th September A married with C. Examine legal validity of the contract between A and B.
4. Mohan was to supply 500 bags of sugar to Sohan. On the 18th January and Sohan subsequently was to pay for that. On the due date Mohan refused to supply sugar to Sohan. But Sohan did not accept Mohan's refusal and continuously demanded performance. On 5th December the Government makes a law debarring the individual from buying or selling more than 10 bags of sugar at a time. Is contract discharged? Suggest legal remedies to Sohan, if any.
5. X was in contact to pay Rs. 10,000 to Y on a particular date. X does not pay that money on the due date. As a consequence of it, can Y claim for any compensation for being ruined?

6. A, who is a tailor, delivered a sewing machine and some cloth to Railway Coy, to be delivered at a place, where festival was to be held. He was expecting to earn more profit at the festival, but did not bring this fact to the notice of Railway authorities. The goods were delivered by Railway Coy after the festival. Can A claim, the loss of profit which he would have earned during festival by selling those goods? (Hint: No, he has not informed Railway Coy of the special circumstance of festival).
7. Banker agreed to advance loan to A on a particular day by crediting amount of A. After that date A draws two cheques, which were dishonoured, because the banker had not credited amount of loan sanctioned to the account of A. Can A claim for exemplary damages? Explain with reason.
8. A made an agreement for hiring B's shop on rent and paid one months rent in advance. B could not give possession of that shop to A. As a result of it, A could not do any business for 6 months and filed suit for damages as to compensate his loss. Will he succeed in getting it? (Hint: No, he will not get more than refund of his advance, because it was his duty to mitigate loss, which he did not do).
9. A agrees to lend sum of Rs. 10,000 to B @ 10 per cent per annum for one year on a condition that if B does not refund money on the due date, he will have to pay interest @ 30 per cent per annum from the date of default. B defaults in repaying money. Is A, entitled to recover increased rate of interest?
10. A agrees to deliver 50 Maunds of salt petre to B on 1st January at a certain price. Before 1st January B makes an agreement with C to sell salt petre at the price, which is higher than market price of January. A does not deliver salt petre to B. Can B recover loss for that price from A which is higher than contract price? (Hint: No, only the difference between market price on 1st January can be recovered as compensation.)
11. A agreed to sell 500 cotton bales to B, on 5th September at a particular price. A knows nothing about the business of B. A fails to deliver cotton balls. Having no cotton bales B was forced to close the mill. Is A responsible for the loss caused to B on account of closure of the will?
12. A, a builder agrees to construct two floors on condition that B will make payment in two instalments *e.g.*, first on the completion of 1st floor of building and second on the completion of second floor. A constructed 1st floor and B refused to pay. Suggest suitable legal remedies to A which he can use against B.

■■■

12

Contract of Indemnity and Guarantee

LEARNING OBJECTIVES

- Understand the meaning and concept of Indemnity and Guarantee.
- Compare these two contracts in terms of their basic features.
- Examine limit and nature of surety's liability.
- Enumerate various types of losses for which the contract of Indemnity can be made.
- Analyse the surety's legal position in terms of his rights and liabilities.

INTRODUCTION

Contracts of indemnity and guarantee are very much a part of general contract, but with some special features. It is therefore special provisions from Sections 124 to 147 that have been provided in Indian Contract Act to deal with these special contracts.

MEANING AND DEFINITION OF CONTRACT OF INDEMNITY

A contract of indemnity is entered into for compensating losses of other party. These losses may or may not occur in future. Thus a contract of indemnity in a part of contingent contract. The performance of it depends on happening or non-happening of certain event in future which may cause the losses to another party.

Thus, a contract of indemnity is a contract in which one party promises to compensate or protect other party from the losses arising in future.

According to Section 124 of Indian Contract Act, "a contract of indemnity is a, contract by which one party promises to save the other from loss caused to him either by the conduct of the promisor himself or by the conduct of any third party."

The definitions of contract of indemnity given under this Section seems to be very narrow. This is so because according to this definition a contract of indemnity is made only for compensating:

(*i*) losses arising out of a conduct of the promisor.

(*ii*) losses arising out of conduct of third party.

(*iii*) losses which are express in nature.

Example: A has filed a suit against B in the court of law. C makes a promise to A that whatever the losses A will suffer on that suit he will compensate him for the same. A contract between A and C is a contract of indemnity.

However, the definition of a contract of indemnity given in English Mercantile Law is an exhaustive one. According to this definition, a contract of indemnity also includes losses caused to the party by an event or accident.

According to English Law a contract of indemnity has been defined as, "a promise to save another harmless, from loss caused as a result of a transaction entered into at the instance of the promisor."

It is therefore in our country that broader interpretation of a contract of indemnity is followed by the courts. And a contract of indemnity can be made for compensating the following losses:

(*i*) Loss arising out of a conduct of parties.

(*ii*) Loss arising out of an event or accident.

(*iii*) Express losses.

(*iv*) Implied losses.

In this context, in a case **Regional Manager Oriental Fire and General Insurance Coy. *vs* Saving Solvent Oil Extractions, Ltd, (1997)6, Andh, L.D 1, DB, A.P.** The court observed that, the English definition of indemnity is wide enough to include a promise of indemnity against loss arising from any cause whatsoever *e.g.*, loss caused by fire or by some other accident. Indeed every contract of insurance, other than life insurance is a contract of indemnity. Similarly in **GAJANAN MORESHWAR *vs* MORESHWAR MADAN (1942)**

A.I.R Bom. 302, 304 case, the court has made it clear that, "Sections 124 and 125 of Indian Contract Act are not exhaustive of the law of indemnity and the court here would apply same equitable principles that the courts in England do."

Characteristics of Indemnity

(*i*) A contract of indemnity is entered into between two parties namely indemnifier who makes a promise to indemnify loss and indemnity holder whose losses are made good by the indemnifier.

(*ii*) A contract of indemnity is a special contract, thus it must satisfy all essential conditions of a valid contract, such as contractual capacity, lawful object, consideration and free consent etc.

(*iii*) According to judicial interpretations, contract of indemnity includes losses arising out of a conduct of the party and happening of an event or accident. It also includes not only express promise but also an implied promise for compensating losses.

Example: A hires a taxi for the purpose of going to Bombay. On the way he meets with an accident and the taxi is badly damaged. The owner has a right to get compensation for this loss from A, because there was an implied promise of indemnity on the part of A.

(*iv*) A contract of indemnity is made primarily for compensating losses of another party which may be caused to him either by the conduct of party or by any event or accident. Thus all insurance contracts except life insurance contracts are considered as a contract of indemnity.

Rights of Indemnity Holder (Section 125)

In a contract of indemnity, the indemnity holder who is to be compensated for the loss has the following rights:

(*i*) **Damages:** An indemnity holder is entitled to recover the amount of damage which he has been compelled to pay to another party in a suit to which contract of indemnity is applicable.

(*ii*) **Costs:** An indemnity holder is also entitled to claim all costs which he has incurred for defending himself in a suit to which the promise of indemnity is applicable. Such costs may include all incidental charges and legal expenses paid in that suit.

(*iii*) **Other payments:** In a contract of indemnity if the indemnity holder has made any payment to another party on the compromise of that suit to which contract of indemnity is applicable, he is entitled to recover such payment from the indemnifier provided he has acted as a person of reasonable prudence or such compromise has been allowed by the indemnifier.

When Does Liability of Indemnifier Arise?

A contract of indemnity is made for the purpose of indemnifying losses. In this contract, indemnity holder has got some rights against indemnifier such as to claim damage, costs and other payments. Now the question arises that at what point of time the liability of indemnifier commences? Is it after having made payments by the indemnity holder or just when the liability of payment arises on his part.

Indian Contract Act does not contain any provision regarding commencement of indemnifier's liability. And the courts are divided on this issue. Judicial interpretations given by various high courts can be summarised as:

(*i*) High courts of Bombay and Nagpur have held that the indemnifier is not liable until and unless the indemnity holder has suffered actual loss or has discharged the liability. It means the liability of indemnifier commences after the indemnity holder suffers actual loss or he has made payments which he is entitled to recover from the indemnifier.

(*ii*) But, the high courts of Calcutta, Allahabad, Patna and Madras have held that the indemnity holder can compel indemnifier to compensate his losses even before he has actually discharged the liability or has made the payment. It means it is enough for making the indemnifier liable that the liability of indemnity holder has arisen in a suit to which contract of indemnity is applicable.

(*iii*) On the review of whole subject, the Bombay high court held that as soon as the liability of indemnity holder arises and becomes absolute, he may call upon the indemnifier to protect him from losses. This point of view is considered to be more equitable and acceptable.

OSMAN JAMAL & SONS *vs* GOPAL (1919), 56, C.1, 262.

In this case it was held that the official liquidator of the company was entitled to recover the amount, even though the company had not actually paid the supplier. The court observed that indemnity is not necessarily given by repayment after payment. Indemnity requires that the party to be indemnified shall never be called upon to pay. Thus liability on the part of indemnity holder must be absolute to call indemnifier to pay off.

DEFINITION AND MEANING OF CONTRACT OF GUARANTEE

According to Section 126 of this Act, "A contract of guarantee is a contract to perform the promise or discharge the liability of third person in case of his default."

Thus the contract of guarantee is made to ensure performance of a contract or discharge of obligation by the promisor. In case if he fails to do so, the person giving assurance or guarantee becomes liable for such performance or discharge.

In a contract of guarantee there are three parties namely *the principal debtor*, who is primarily liable to pay debt or discharge obligation, *the creditor* to whom the principal debtor is liable to pay; and *the surety* who takes responsibility that if the principal debtor fails, he will discharge the obligation.

Example: A borrows a sum of Rs. 10,000 from the bank. B gives guarantee to the bank that in case A defaults in repayment, he will repay to the bank. This is a contract of guarantee. A is a principal debtor, the bank is creditor and B is surety.

Characteristics of Contract of Guarantee

(*i*) ***Essentials of a valid contract:*** The contract of guarantee is a special contract. It must possess all essentials of a valid contract like contractual capacity, free consent, lawful consideration and lawful object etc.

(*ii*) ***Concurrence of the party:*** In a contract of guarantee, there are three parties—principal debtor, creditor and surety. To be legally valid there must be concurrence of all parties to a contract of guarantee and to its terms and conditions. In case, if someone becomes surety to the creditor without the consent of principal debtor, the contract is not enforceable.

(*iii*) ***Consideration:*** Like all other contracts, the contract of guarantee must be supported by lawful consideration. But there is little difference regarding consideration for the promise of surety. It is not necessary that the surety must get some consideration directly from the creditor. Rather, the benefit enjoyed by the principal debtor is considered sufficient consideration to support the promise of the surety.

Example: A agrees to sell goods worth Rs. 5,000 to B on credit provided C becomes surety for the payment. C agrees with the consent of B to give guarantee to A. In this contract, A who is a principal debtor gets benefit of credit sale. And it is sufficient consideration to support the promise of C to A. There is no need that C should get separate consideration for his promise.

(*iv*) ***Primary liability:*** In a contract of guarantee there is a primary liability on the principal debtor to repay or to discharge obligation. It is only at his default, the surety may be called upon to repay. Thus the liability of surety is secondary in nature and will arise only in case the principal debtor fails to repay. The surety gives a guarantee for the debt which exists on the part of principal debtor.

(*v*) ***Implied indemnity:*** In every contract of guarantee, there is an implied indemnity. The surety gets benefit of it. In case if the surety is called upon to discharge the obligation of the principal debtor, the surety after having done so is entitled to claim compensation for the losses sufferred by him, from the principal debtor.

(*vi*) ***Disclosure of facts:*** Though the contract of guarantee is not a contract of utmost good faith it is a duty of the creditor that, he must disclose to the surety all those facts likely to affect the degree of his responsibility. Sections 142 and 143 of this Act state very clearly that the guarantee obtained by means of misrepresentation or concealment of material facts by the creditor is invalid. Thus validity of contract of guarantee depends upon mutual trust and good faith on the part of creditor.

(*vii*) ***Form of a contract*:** According to Section 126 of this Act, the contract of guarantee may be made in writing or by the words of mouth. Similarly, it may be implied contract directly understood from the conduct of the parties.

DIFFERENCE BETWEEN CONTRACT OF INDEMNITY AND CONTRACT OF GUARANTEE

Though these two contracts are species of a general contract, they are distinct from each other on the following grounds:

Basis	Contract of indemnity	Contract of guarantee
Meaning	It is a contract made for compensating losses of another party caused to him either by the conduct of the parties or from an event or accident.	It is a contract to perform the promise or discharge liability of third party in case of his default.
Number of parties	There are two parties in a contract of indemnity namely indemnity holder and indemnifier.	In a contract of guarantee, there are three parties, the principal debtor, creditor and the surety.
Number of contracts	In indemnity there is only one contract that is between indemnity holder and indemnifier.	There are three contracts in guarantee. One between principal debtor and creditor, another between surety and creditor, and third one between principal debtor and surety.

[Contd...]

Basis	Contract of indemnity	Contract of guarantee
Nature of liability	In a contract of indemnity, the liability of indemnifier who makes promise to compensate the loss, is primary in nature.	In a contract of guarantee, the the liability of the surety is secondary in nature. This is so because his liability will arise only if the principal debtor defaults.
Object of contract	The main purpose of a contract of indemnity is to protect the indemnifier from losses.	The contract of guarantee is made with an object of providing security or ensuring discharge of liability.
Existence of liability	In a contract of indemnity the liability or loss to the indemnity holder is contingent, which may or may not arise.	But in a contract of guarantee, the liability or debt being guarantee is already in existence.
Interest	A person who promises to indemnify loss may have some interest in the contract or in that transaction.	But in a contract of guarantee the surely should have no other interest apart from guarantee given by him.
Right of the Party	In a contract of indemnity, even after having compensated losses; the indemnifier cannot sue third party in his own name, because, there is no privity of contract.	In a contract of guarantee, after having discharged, a liability of principal debtor, the surety can sue principal debtor in his own name.

Kinds of Guarantee

A contract of guarantee may be made for the various purposes as to enable a person to get loan, employment or goods on credit etc. More commonly a guarantee may be given for (*i*) securing loan, (*ii*) getting goods on credit, and (*iii*) procuring employment.

A contract of guarantee may be of the following kinds:

(*i*) Prospective and Retrospective.

(*ii*) Specific and continuing: In case, a contract of guarantee is made for existing debt, it is known as 'prospective guarantee'. As against it, if a guarantee is given for a future debt or future transaction it is known as 'retrospective guarantee'.

Similarly, contract of guarantee is made for a particular transaction and is known as 'specific or simple' and it covers only that single transaction.

Example: A borrows a sum of Rs. 5,000 from the bank. B gives guarantee for repayment by A. This is an example of specific or simple guarantee. As A repays that debt, B ceases to be liable.

But if a contract of guarantee is made for a particular transaction having many series or parts thereof it is known as 'continuing guarantee'. In such case, the liability of the surety extends to all those series which are involved in that transaction. However, after having completed a few series, the surety may withdraw himself from a contract of guarantee.

Example: A employs B as his employee for recovering rent of A's premises on monthly basis. C gives guarantee to A for the collection and payment of monthly rent by B, for the period of one year. In this contract collection of rent is a particular transaction having 12 series, thus it is a continuing guarantee.

Revocation of Continuing Guarantee

Continuing guarantee may be revoked in any one of the following manners:

(*i*) **By notice:** After having completed some series of transaction for which guarantee has been given, the surety by giving notice of revocation to the creditor may revoke a contract of guarantee. In such case, the surety will be liable for all those series which have been completed till that notice.

(*ii*) **By death of surety:** A continuing guarantee may also be revoked in case of death of the surety. However for the series completed prior to the death of surety, the estate of surety will be liable even without giving a notice of death to the creditor.

(*iii*) **By other modes:** In addition to notice by the surety or his death, a contract of continuing guarantee will be revoked under all circumstances in which the surety is discharged from his liability. These circumstances are being discussed ahead.

NATURE AND EXTENT OF SURETY'S LIABILITY

In the eyes of law the surety is considered as a 'Favoured Debtor'. His liability arises only when the principal debtor defaults. The following provisions of law are related with the extent and nature of his liability:

(*i*) Liability of the surety is secondary: In a contract of guarantee, the principal debtor is primarily liable to pay or discharge liability. It is only at his default, the liability of the surety arises and he may be called upon to discharge it. And the creditor is not required to give any notice to this effect to the surety.

***(ii)* Liability of the surety is contingent:** In a contract of guarantee, liability of the surety is contingent or conditional in nature. It may or may not arise. It will arises only when the principal debtor commits default. And it is not certain that he will default. In practice, generally he discharges his liability to the satisfaction of the creditor.

***(iii)* The liability of the surety is immediate in nature:** Once the principal debtor commits default, immediately the creditor may proceed against the surety. It is not necessary that he should first exhaust his remedies against the principal debtor. Thus, on default by the principal debtor, the creditor instead of suing the principal debtor, can file suit against the surety.

***(iv)* The liability of surety is co-extensive:** In a contract of guarantee, the liability of the surety is co-extensive with that of the principal debtor. He is liable for those sums that the principal debtor is liable for. His liability cannot be more than that of principal debtor. In case, the liability of the principal debtor is scaled down or extinguished by the creditor or by operation of law, either in whole or in part, the liability of the surety would also be reduced or extinguished to the same extent.

***(v)* Surety may limit his liability:** Although the liability of the surety is co-extensive with that of principal debtor, he has a right to limit his liability. He can do it by declaring it expressly at the time of making a contract of guarantee. In such a case, irrespective of all other factors, the liability of the surety will not go beyond that limit as declared by him.

***(vi)* Liability in continuing guarantee:** In case of continuing guarantee, the liability of the surety extends to a series of transaction over a period of time, not to a specific number of series but to any number of them. It makes the surety liable for unpaid balance.

***(vii)* Liability of the surety where original contract between the principal debtor and the creditor is void or voidable:** In a contract of guarantee, there are two independent contracts, one between principal debtor and creditor and another between the creditor and the surety. And law does not treat, principal debtor and surety as one person. Thus if a contract between the principal debtor and the creditor is void, the surety will be liable as if he is principal debtor.

> ***Example:*** A, who is a minor, borrows a sum of Rs. 20,000 from the bank. B gives guarantee to the bank. The contract between A and the bank is void, because A has no contractual capacity. The bank cannot sue the minor A. But B will be liable to discharge A's liability towards the bank.
>
> Similarly if the creditor does not sue principal debtor within a period of limitation, or the principal debtor is discharged from his liability by operation of law or death, the surety will remain liable.

Rights of Surety

In a contract of guarantee, the surety is considered as favoured debtor and he has the rights:

I. against the principal debtor.

II. against the creditor.

III. against the co-sureties (if any).

I. Rights Against Principal Debtor

The surety has got the following rights against the principal debtor:

(*i*) **Right of subrogation:** The surety will get right of subrogation when he fulfils the obligation of the principal debtor fully. In other words, if the principal debtor commits default, and the surety pays the debt to the creditor, the surety steps into the shoes of creditor. The surety will be invested with all the rights which the creditor has against the principal debtor. It has been held by the courts that the surety is entitled to every remedy which the creditor has against the principal debtor including securities held by the creditor and all means of payment by the principal debtor.

Example: A has borrowed Rs. one lakh from the bank. B stands surety to the bank for the repayment. On due date A defaults and the banks calls upon B to repay. B makes repayment to the bank. The bank was also holding assets worth Rs. 20,000 as a security for this loan. On repayment B is entitled to recover assets held by the bank as security and will further proceed against A for the balance.

(*ii*) **Right of indemnity:** In every contract of guarantee, there is an implied promise by the principal debtor that any loss caused to him will be indemnified by the principal debtor. Thus the surety is entitled to recover from the principal debtor whatever sum he has rightfully paid under the contract of guarantee.

In other words, indemnity is applicable only on those payments made by the surety in connection with guarantee, which are just and equitable. It covers, principal amount, interest thereon, legal expenses if any and the cost of the suit.

Example: Ram was indebted to Shyam for Rs. 20,000 and Mohan stood as surety for the repayment. Ram defaulted repayment and Shyam filed suit against Mohan. Finally Mohan was asked to pay the amount along with interest and cost of suit which was around Rs. 5,000. After making payment, Mohan is entitled to recover Rs. 20,000 + Rs. 5,000 from Shyam.

II. Rights of Surety Against the Creditor

The surety has the following rights against the creditor:

(*i*) **Right to claim securities:** Where the principal debtor has given securities in addition of guarantee of the debt, and in case he fails to repay, the surety becomes liable to pay. The surety is entitled to those securities which are held by the creditor. If the creditor loses or without the consent of surety, parts with, any security, the surety is discharged from his liability to that extent.

Example: A borrows sum of Rs. 10,000 from B for three months. C stands surety, in addition to securities worth Rs. 5,000. Without the consent of C, B returns security worth Rs. 2,000 to A. In case A defaults and C makes repayment, he is entitled to get back security of Rs. 5,000 from B.

(*ii*) **Right of set off:** In a contract of guarantee, if the principal debtor has got any cross claim against the creditor, the surety becomes entitled to that claim against the creditor. And the surety may have a benefit of set off while determining the extent of his liability.

Example: A has borrowed sum of Rs. 30,000 from B. C stands as surety in the transaction. B has purchased goods worth Rs. 5,000 from A on credit. A defaults in repayment and C was called upon to pay. C is entitled to a right of set off and his liability will be limited to Rs. 25,000 only.

(*iii*) **Right to share reduction:** In a contract of guarantee if there has been some reduction in the amount of debt being guarantee by the surety, the surety is entitled to such reduction and his liability will also be reduced to that extent.

Example: A who is a farmer borrows sum of Rs. 20,000 for buying tractor from the Agriculture Deptt. B becomes surety for that loan. Later on, the state government declares 25% subsidy on that loan. B is entitled to share the reduction in the amount of debt.

(*iv*) **Right to demand termination of employee:** In a contract of fidelity guarantee regarding honest behaviour on the employment, the surety has a right to demand dismissal of the employee if he defaults in his behaviour.

III. Rights Against Co-sureties

Where the debt is guaranteed by two or more persons, they are known as co-sureties. The surety has following rights against other co-sureties:

(*i*) **Right of contribution:** Where two or more persons stand sureties for the same debt either jointly or severally, the co-sureties are liable themselves to pay equal share of the whole debt. In case if any one of them has been compelled to pay the whole debt, the person is entitled to get contribution in equal ratio from other co-sureties.

Example: A, B and C have guaranteed a loan of Rs. 45,000 taken by D from E. D defaults in repayment. A, B and C are liable to the extent of Rs. 15,000 each.

(*ii*) **Co-sureties giving guarantee for different amount:** Where the same debt is guaranteed by two or more co-sureties, offering guarantee for different amount, they will be liable in equal ratio subject to the maximum of the amount of guarantee given by them.

Example: A, B and C stand sureties to the extent of Rs. 10,000; Rs. 20,000 and Rs. 40,000 respectively to D. In case he makes default of Rs. 50,000 and the liability of A, B and C will be Rs. 10,000; Rs. 20,000 and Rs. 20,000 respectively.

DISCHARGE OF SURETY

In a contract of guarantee, the surety has a liability parallel to that of principal debtor, which arises in case of default of principal debtor. The surety is said to be discharged from his liability when his liability comes to an end—he is no more liable to the creditor. The liability of the surety comes to an end in the following manners:

I. By revocation.

II. By the conduct of creditor.

III. By invalidation of contract of guarantee.

This can be well understood with the help of following chart.

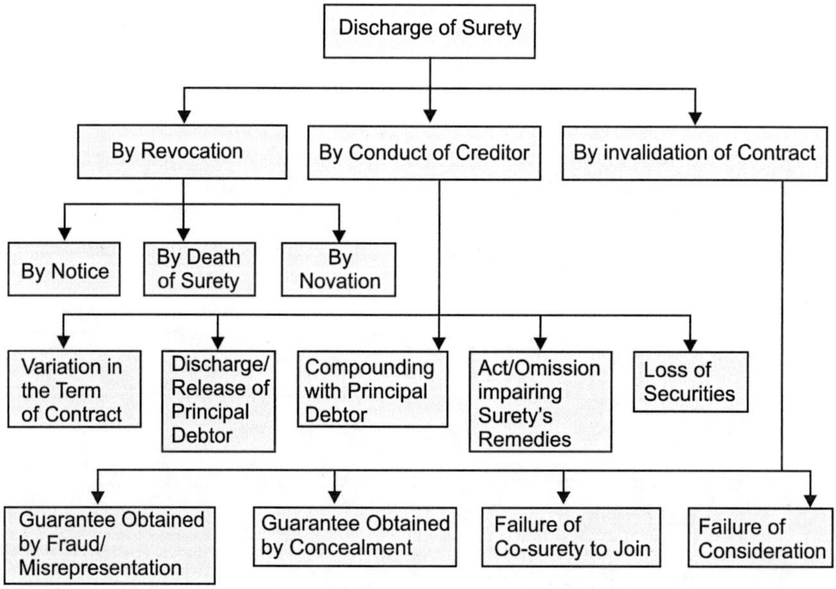

I. By Revocation

The surety gets released from his liability in a contract of guarantee by revocation under the following situation:

(*i*) **By notice of revocation:** In a contract of continuing guarantee the liability of surety extends to various series of a transaction. In such case, the surety by giving notice to thc crcditor may revoke the contract for remaining series. But he will be liable for the series which have been completed before such notice.

(*ii*) **By death of surety:** A contract of continuing guarantee is also revoked at the death of the surety for the remaining series of that transaction. The legal representative of the surety will be liable for the series which have been completed by the time of death of surety.

(*iii*) **By novation:** By mutual consent of all parties, original contract of guarantee may be replaced by new contract. In such case the surely will be discharged from his liability in the original contract.

II. By Conduct of Creditor

The surety will be discharged from his liability in a contract of guarantee by the conduct of creditor under the following circumstances:

(*i*) **By variation in the terms of contract:** Any material variation or change regarding terms of a contract of guarantee by the creditor and principal debtor without consent of the surety will discharge him from his liability as to transaction subsequent to such change. Material variations means the variations which effect interest of the surety in a significant way.

Example: A is appointed as salesman by B. C gives guarantee for his honest behaviour during employment. Later on, A and B agree that A would also be liable for realising debtors and B will pay him higher salary. C is no more liable as a surety in a contract.

(*ii*) **By release or discharge of principal debtor:** The liability of the surety is secondary in nature. Thus, if the principal debtor is released or discharged from his liability by any act or omission of the creditor, the liability of the surety will also come to an end.

Example: A who is a farmer has borrowed sum of Rs. 20,000 for buying some agriculture tools on the guarantee given by B. Later on, as a part of the state government policy towards agriculture, A has been exempted from repaying that loan. B would get discharged from his liability as a surety.

However, in case of death or insolvency of the principal debtor or failure of the creditor to sue within period of limitation, it would not lead to discharge of liability of the surety.

(*iii*) **By compounding with principal debtor:** A contract between the creditor and principal debtor whereby the creditor extends time of payment or makes promise not to sue the principal debtor in case of his default. The surety will be discharged from his liability in that contract of guarantee.

Example: X has borrowed Rs. 5,000 from the bank on the guarantee provided by Y. On the date of repayment X becomes unable to repay and enters into an agreement with the bank for extending period of repayment. The bank agrees to it. Y will get discharged from his liability as surety.

(*iv*) **By impairing surety's remedy:** Any act or omission of the creditor which damages the rights of surety would lead to his discharge from liability.

Thus if the creditor does any act which is inconsistent with the rights of surety or omits to do any act which is his duty to do and the eventual remedy of the surety against the principal debtor is impaired, the surety is discharged.

Example: A was appointed as a cashier in the bank on the guarantee given by B for the recovery of loans. It was also agreed that, the bank would provide performance report of A to B on monthly basis. But the bank does not do so, B will be discharged from his liability.

(*v*) **By loss of security:** While making a contract of guarantee, in addition to guarantee, some security has also been given to the creditor. In case the creditor loses that security or part with it without consent of the surety, the surety will be discharged from his liability to that extend.

Example: X borrows Rs. 20,000 from bank on a guarantee given by Y. X has also pledged assets worth Rs. 5,000 as security. Due to fire in the premises of the bank that asset was also destroyed. Y will be released from his liability to the extent of Rs. 5,000.

III. By Invalidation of Contract of Guarantee

The surety will be discharged from his liability in the following cases on account of a contract being invalid:

(*i*) **Guarantee obtained by misrepresentation:** Where the guarantee has been obtained by creditor by using misrepresentation or fraud, a contract of guarantee will be invalid and the surety will be discharged.

(*ii*) **Guarantee obtained by concealment:** Where the creditor obtains guarantee by means of keeping silent or concealing material facts, a contract of guarantee is invalid and provides sufficient ground for the surety to get discharged.

(iii) **Failure of consideration:** Lawful consideration is required in a contract of guarantee. In case of failure of such consideration, a contract becomes invalid and leads to discharge of surety from his liability.

(iv) **Failure of co-surety to join:** Where a person agrees to be surety in contract on a condition that the creditor shall not act upon unless co-surety joins. In case such a person does not join as the co-surety, the surety will be discharged from his liability.

REVIEW QUESTIONS

1. Define a 'contract of indemnity'. Discuss its characteristics.
2. Explain various rights of indemnity holder.
3. Define a 'contract of guarantee'. Discuss various features of it.
4. Distinguish between 'contract of indemnity' and 'contract of guarantee'.
5. Explain various kinds of guarantee and discuss those situations when the continuing guarantee is revoked.
6. Who is surety? Discuss his right, as against principal debtor, creditor and co-sureties.
7. Explain various situations in which the surety will be discharged from his liability in a contract of guarantee.
8. Discuss the nature and extent of surety's 'liability in a contract of guarantee'.
9. 'Liability of surety is coextensive with that of principal debtor.' Comment.
10. 'Surety is a 'favoured debtor' in a contract of guarantee.' Comment.

PRACTICAL PROBLEMS

1. A hired car from B for going to Calcutta. While on the route the car collided and it was badly damaged. Is A responsible for loss to B? (Hint: Yes, implied indemnity.)
2. A forged a signature of B and presented forged transfer of shares for registration to a company. The company registered the transfer. Is company entitled to recover loss arising from the act of A? (Hint: Yes, implied indemnity.)

3. X makes an agreement with Y for killing Z in consideration of Rs. 50,000 and Y promising to indemnify X for his act. As a consequence of this act X was fined Rs. one lakh. Can he recover it from? (Hint: No, object of an agreement is unlawful.)
4. Ram borrows sum of Rs. 20,000 from the bank and Shyam stands surety to the bank for repayment. But Ram does not know about guarantee given by Shyam. On due date Ram refuses to pay. Can a bank recover this amount from Shyam as surety? (Hint: No, there is no concurrence for the agreement of guarantee among Ram, bank and Shyam.)
5. A borrowed sum of Rs. 20,000 from the bank and pledged assets worth Rs. 10,000 along with guarantee given by B. On due date A fails to repay. Can the bank sue B without returning assets to him? (Hint: Yes).
6. P got house from M on rent. N provided guarantee to M for the payment of rent by P on the condition that, the rent was paid initially for three months and thereafter from week to week. After 4 months N gave notice to M revoking his guarantee. Examine the extent of N's liability as a surety.
7. A was in agreement with B for building a ship for a stipulated amount paid by B when the work reaches to certain stages. C provides guarantee for A's due performance. B without the knowledge of C makes advance payment of two instalments to A. Is C discharged from his liability? (Hint: Yes).
8. A borrows sum of Rs. 80,000 from the bank. B, C and D stood as co-sureties for the payment to the extent of A–Rs. 20,000; B–Rs. 30,000; C–Rs. 30,000. A makes default of Rs. 50,000. How it would be shared by B, C and D?
9. X borrowed Rs. 20,000 from Y for three months on the guarantee furnished by Y. On due date X failed in repayment and Y extended date of payment for next two months without consent of Z. Is Z liable as surety? (Hint: No).

■■■

13

Contract of Agency

LEARNING OBJECTIVES

- Develop an understanding about basic nature of agency.
- Understand implications and difference between a contract of agency and a general contract.
- Remember various modes of creating agency, especially agency by ratification.
- Learn duties and right of both agent and principal.
- Understand the basic concept of agent's liability.
- Analyse the position of the principal in relation to the third party.

INTRODUCTION

In business no one can do everything on his own. He needs to delegate part of his authority to others to get things done. He may do so either by appointing someone as his employee or as his agent. Where someone is appointed an agent, he acts on behalf of the person appointing him. Legal status of an agent is quite different from employee. An agent acts as an employee, but on behalf of that other person makes him liable by his acts.

MEANING AND DEFINITION

The person who is appointed to work for another person on his behalf is technically known as 'agent'. According to Section 182 of this Act, "an agent is a person employed to do any act for another or to represent another in dealing with third person." The person who does act or represent other is known as the 'agent' and the person who is so represented is called the 'principal'. And the contract through which relationship of agency is created between the agent and the principal is known as 'contract of agency'. The contract of agency is also a species of a general contract with some distinct features.

Thus a contract of agency is made for creating relationship of agency between principal and agent.

The relationship of agency is based on the following rules:

(*i*) '*Qui facit per alium facit per se*' *i.e.*, one who does through another does by himself. It means that acts done by an agent are binding on the principal who appoints him. And these acts will have same legal consequences as would have been done by the principal himself.

(*ii*) The person may appoint someone as his agent for doing those act which he is expected or authorised to do. But this rule has many exceptions in practice such as in a contract of personal nature involving personal services, skill and qualification an agent cannot be appointed for performing the promise.

(*iii*) An agent is basically a representative of his principal. It is a representative character of his functioning which distinguishes him from other employees. In fact, an agent represents his principal in dealing with third party.

(*iv*) The main job or role of an agent is to bring third party into contractual relationship with his principal. As soon as this relationship is established he is no more in picture.

Essentials of Contract of Agency

The contract of agency has the following distinct essential features:

(*i*) ***Agreement:*** To form a contract of agency, there must be an agreement between principal and agent, which leads to creation of relationships of agency. Thus the contract of agency is based on true nature of relationship. Such agreement may be express or implied by circumstances, by operation of law and intention of the parties.

(*ii*) ***Contractual capacity:*** In a contract of agency there are two parties—namely the principal and agent. The principal must have contractual capacity. According to Section 183 of this Act, "any person who is of age of majority according to law to which he is subject, and who is of a sound mind may employ an agent."

However, agent need not to have contractual capacity. According to Section 184 of this Act, "as between principal and third person, any person may become an agent." This is so because an agent does not make contracts on his own. In case an agent has no contractual capacity, such as minor agent, the interest of third party is not going to be affected. Rather such agent will not be responsible to his principal, but third party will be bound by that act to the principal.

Thus the principal must have contractual capacity, but it is not necessary to have such capacity for the agent.

(*iii*) ***Consideration:*** Although the relationship of agency is created by agreement, but it is not necessary that such agreement must be supported by a lawful consideration. According to Section 185 of this Act, no consideration is required to create an agency.

(*iv*) ***Privity of contract between principal and third party:*** An agent acts on behalf of his principal. He establishes privity of contract between principal and third party. Whatever he does on behalf of his principal, within the scope of authority given to him, all such acts will be binding on the principal in relation with third party.

Example: A has been appointed as agent of B. A buys raw material for B on credit from C. In case B refuses to pay, C can sue him for the recovery of payment. It is because there is a privity of contract between B and C.

CREATION OF AGENCY

Relationship of agency is created in the following manners:

I. Agency by express agreement

II. Agency by implied agreement

I. Agency by Express Agreement

This is very popular and usual mode of creating relationship of agency between two persons. Anyone, who has a contractual capacity can appoint another as his agent, either by the words of mouth or by making written agreement, the agency is known as agency by express agreement. Agreement for appointing an agent is made by executing 'deed of power of attorney'. It authorises an agent to act on behalf of his principal within the scope of authority mentioned in the agreement. Where an agent is appointed for doing some specific job or dealing with third party on that job, a special power of attorney is executed. But, to give an authority to an agent for doing all acts on behalf of the principal or to represent him in all dealings, a general power of attorney is executed in his favour.

II. Agency by Implied Agreement

A relationship of agency is also created by conduct of parties and circumstances. Such agency is known as 'implied agency'. Implied agency arises when a person is placed in such situation, that he is bound to act as an agent of other without making formal agreement with him.

Agency may be implied from the circumstances, conduct of the parties, ordinary course of dealings and business traditions and customs. It mainly includes the following:

(*i*) ***Agency by estoppel:*** Where the person, either by the words of mouth or in writing or by his conduct induces another person to believe that someone is working as his agent, in reality he is not his agent. Any person who is so induced if makes any transaction with so-called agent, such transaction will be binding on the person inducing so and he will be liable as principal. Such agency is known as 'agency by estoppel'.

Example: Y, in the presence of X tells to Z that Y is working as X's agent. But really he is not an agent and at the same he is not contradicting the statement of Y. Z makes contract with Y believing that he is an agent of X. This contract is binding on X; because there exists agency by estoppel between X and Y.

According to Section 234 of this Act, "when an agent has, without authority, done acts or incurred obligation to third parties on behalf of his principal, the principal is bound by such acts or obligations if he has by his words or conduct induced such third parties to believe that such acts and obligations were within the scope of agent's authority."

However, it is to be noted that in case of agency by estoppel the principal remains passive giving an impression to third party that he is the principal.

Example: A consigns some goods to B for sale and gives an instruction to him not to sell them below a fixed price. C who is unaware of this instruction, makes contract with B to buy the goods at a price lower than a fixed one. This contract will be binding on A.

Thus agency by estoppel is created under the following situations:

(*a*) A person who is not really an agent, but is being considered as an agent.

(*b*) A person is being considered as an agent, though he ceases to be an agent.

(*c*) A person is being considered as an agent, for having more authority than actually he has.

(*ii*) ***Agency by holding out:*** In fact agency by holding out is a branch of agency by estoppel with a little difference that in case of holding out, the relationship of agency is created by some positive or affirmative act on the part of the principal. In this case, the principal himself holds out that someone is his agent. Here, there is some active assertion or representation by the principal to induce another person for believing that someone is his agent or has been given more authority than actually he has.

Example: A allows his servant B to buy the goods on credit from C and pays for them. On one occasion. A has asked his servant to buy the goods for cash. But he bought the goods on credit and misappropriated cash given to him. The principal is bound by this transaction as he has held out his servant to buy the goods on credit in the past, giving impression that the servant is his agent having authority to buy goods on credit for the principal.

(iii) ***Agency by Necessity:*** Under certain situations, it becomes necessary for the person to act as an agent of another person without his authority. Such agency is known as 'agency by necessity'.

In other words, an agency by necessity is conferred by law in certain cases, where a person is faced with an emergency in which the property or interest of another person may be in danger, and it becomes necessary to act in order to preserve the property or interest, before the instructions of the owner can be obtained. In such case, law assumes, the consent of the owner to the creation of the relationship of principal and agent, which is known as 'agency by necessity'. For creating relationship of agency by necessity the following conditions must be satisfied:

(*a*) There must be an emergency situation, which makes it necessary for the person to act as an agent.

(*b*) It should be impossible for the person who is acting as an agent to communicate with another person for whom he is acting.

(*c*) The person must have acted as an agent on behalf of another person, bona fide in the interest of that another person.

(*d*) The person, acting as an agent must have acted with reasonable prudence taking into account, danger, expense and time factor.

Example: A sends a consignment of oranges to B in Bombay asking him to send to C at Calcutta. When the consignment reached in Bombay B found that the oranges are getting spoiled and may perish totally by the time consignment reaches Calcutta. Therefore B sells oranges for the best obtainable prices without an authority of A. The transaction of sale will be binding on A, because B has acted as an agent by necessity for A.

Agency by necessity may be established under the following situations:

(*a*) ***Emergency situations:*** In an emergency situation the agent is entitled to do all such acts for saving principal from losses as a person of reasonable prudence would have done to save himself under such situations. All those acts will be binding on the principal, because agency by necessity has been created.

(*b*) ***Husband and wife:*** In case, the husband fails to provide for basic necessities of life of his wife, the wife may act as an agent of husband, in necessity, and can pledge his credit and the husband will be bound such acts.

(*c*) ***Protection of property:*** Where, the person is entrusted with the property of another person, which he has to protect or preserve. The person so entrusted is entitled to do all necessary acts for protecting the property of the owner and such owner will be bound by those acts under the relationship of agency by necessity.

GREAT NOTHERN RAIL COY. *vs* SWAFFIELD (1874, L.R-9, Ex-132): In this case, a horse was sent through railway company. On reaching to its destination, no one could receive it. Due to lack of proper accomomdation for it, the railway company put it in stable for horses on rent. In was held that the railway company has acted as an agent in necessity on behalf of the owner of a horse, therefore rent for putting horse in stable will be paid by the owner.

(*iv*) ***Agency by ratification:*** Ratification implies an approval of the acts which have been done without an authority of the person approving them. In other words, where the person has done some act for another person without his prior authority or consent. Later on the person for whom such acts have been done can either reject them altogether or may accept those acts. In case he accepts, he becomes bound by such acts as these acts would have been done by his authority or consent. The relationship of agency arising out of such approval or acceptance is known as 'agency by ratification'.

According to Section 196 of this Act, "where acts are done by one person on behalf of another, but without his knowledge or authority, he may elect to ratify or to disown such acts. If he ratifies them the same effect will follow as if, they have been performed by his authority."

Section 197 of this Act states, "ratification may be expressed or may be implied by the conduct of the person on whose behalf the acts are done."

Example: Ram buys some raw material for Shyam, but without his authority. Later on Shyam makes use of that raw material, which have been purchased without his authority, in the production process. Thus it is implied by his conduct that he has accepted or ratified the act of Ram. And as a result of it relation of agency will be created by implied ratification.

Requirements of valid ratification: A ratification to be valid and effective must fulfil the following conditions:

(*a*) ***Acts done on behalf of principal:*** An act to be ratified must have been done on behalf of the person ratifying it. Thus, if the act is done not in the name of the principal, but in the name of agent himself, such act cannot be ratified.

Example: A authorised B to purchase wheat for him at specified price. But B purchased wheat at a higher price that too in his own name. A cannot ratify this transaction, because if has been done in the name of B who is acting as an agent.

(*b*) ***Existence of the principal:*** The principal must be in existence at the time when the act was done on his behalf by an agent. Thus if an agent does some act on behalf of the principal, but the principal was non-existing at that time. Later on, he cannot ratify those acts.

KELNER *vs* BAXTER (1866, LR-2, CP-174): In this case, the promotors of the company to be formed for managing a hotel, made an agreement on behalf of the proposed company, for buying wine from a plaintiff. On the formation of a company, the company intended to ratify that agreement. It was held that the promotors of the company were personally liable for that agreement, because the company was not in existence at that time and thus could not be made liable for the agreement made by the promotors.

However, under Section 15 of Specific Relief Act 1963, "if a pre-incorporation contract is within the object of the company, the company can ratify it and it becomes binding on the company and third party."

(*c*) ***Contractual capacity:*** The person on whose behalf the act is being done, at that time he must have contractual capacity. Thus an act done on behalf of the minor cannot be ratified by him on attaining age of majority. Because at the time when act was done he was not competent to contract.

(*d*) ***Full knowledge of principal:*** The principal who is to ratify an act must have full knowledge about that act. Section 198 of this Act clearly states, "no valid ratification can be made by a person whose knowledge of the fact is materially defective."

(*e*) ***Whole transaction:*** The ratification to be legally valid must relate to whole transaction or act. Partial ratification is not valid. Section 199 of this Act states that a person ratifying an unauthorised act done on his behalf ratifies the whole of the transaction of which such act formed a part.

(*f*) ***Lawful act:*** The principal can ratify only lawful acts which have been done by an agent without his authority. An act which is void or unlawful cannot be ratified.

(*g*) ***Reasonable time:*** To be valid, the ratification of an act must have been done within reasonable time. After the expiry of reasonable time, an act cannot be ratified.

(*h*) ***Damage or loss to third party:*** Where the ratification of an act results in any injury or damage or loss to third party, such ratification is not valid. According to Section 200 of this Act, "ratification which has the effect of subjecting a third person to damage or terminating any right or interest of a third person, cannot be made."

Example: A has hired a car from B for one month. C on behalf of B takes back that car from A after 15 days. A suffers a loss due to mature return of the car. B cannot ratify the act of C, because it results in loss to A.

(*i*) ***Communication:*** A ratification to be valid must have been communicated to third party involved in that transaction as to make transaction binding upon him.

Duties of Agent

Duties and rights of an agent are largely determined by the mutual agreement between the agent and the principal. The main duties of an agent are as follows:

(*i*) ***Duty to perform the work:*** An agent is appointed to do work or to act for the principal. Therefore, he must perform that act in satisfactory manner. If he fails to do so, he will be liable to the principal for any loss or damage arising out of it.

(*ii*) ***To exercise reasonable skill, care and diligence:*** An agent must perform the acts related to the business of agency with a reasonable care, and diligence. He must exercise reasonable degree of skill which the person of average skill would have done in his own case. In case, loss or damage caused to the principal due to his negligence, want of skill and misconduct, will be compensated by him.

Example: A was appointed an insurance agent by B to effect an insurance on a ship. He omits to see that the usual clauses of marine insurance are inserted in the policy. Later on, the ship was lost. Due to omission of clauses nothing can be recovered from the underwriting firm A is bound to compensate the loss caused to B due to his negligence and carelessness.

(*iii*) ***To render proper accounts:*** An agent is bound to render proper accounts to his principal on demand. He must explain those accounts to the principal and produce the vouchers in support of the entries made therein. Once necessary accounts have been rendered and accepted by the principal, and the same cannot be reopened by the principal.

(*iv*) ***To follow directions of the principal:*** An agent is bound to conduct the business of his principal according to his directions. In the absence of necessary directions or instructions, an agent must follow usual practice of the trade which prevails in similar type of business. If he does not do so, he will be liable to compensate the principal for the losses.

(*v*) ***To communicate with principal:*** It is the duty of an agent to use all reasonable diligence in communicating with his principal and in seeking his instructions, in case of difficulty. But in case of emergency when he cannot communicate with the principal he should take all reasonable steps to protect interest of his principal.

(*vi*) ***Not to act on his own:*** An agent is appointed to act on behalf of the principal. He must not act at his own, while dealing with third party. But if an agent is personally interested in the transaction, his duty towards the principal and his personal interest may come in conflict with each other. In consequence of such situation, if he gets unfair benefit the principal is entitled to: (*a*) rescind the transaction, and (*b*) recover compensation from the agent.

(*vii*) ***Not to make secret profits:*** An agent is expected to work for the principal. Thus it is his prime duty not to earn any secret profit in any transaction made by him with third party. According to Section 216 of this Act, "if the agent deals in the business of agency on his own account without the knowledge of the principal, the principal is entitled to claim from the agent any benefit which may have resulted to him from the transaction."

(*viii*) ***To pay sums received for the principal:*** The agent is bound to pay to his principal, all sums received on his account. He may deduct therefrom all money due to himself in respect of advances made or expenses-incurred by him in conducting such business and also such remuneration as may be payable to him for acting as agent.

(*ix*) ***Not to delegate authority:*** As a matter of rule, the agent cannot delegate authority to a third person without the consent of the principal except in case where the nature of business requires such delegation.

(*x*) ***Not to set up adverse title:*** The agent should not set up an adverse title to the property in his hands against the principal. It means he must not set up his own title or the title of the third party to the goods or property received by him from his principal in the capacity of an agent.

(*xi*) ***To protect interest of principal on his death or insanity:*** In case an agency is terminated on the principal becoming insolvent or dying, the agent is bound to take all reasonable steps on behalf of the representative for the protection and preservation of the interest of deceased principal.

(*xii*) ***Not to use information against the principal:*** In the course of business of agency, the agent may get information regarding various transaction. It is his duty not to use that information against the interest of principal. In case he does so, he will be liable to compensate the losses suffered by the principal.

Right of Agent

The agent has the following rights against the principal:

(*i*) ***Right to receive remuneration:*** An agent has a right to receive agreed remuneration on the completion of his work. And in absence of an agreement reasonable remuneration will be paid to him. According to Section 219 of this Act, "in the absence of any special contract, payment for the performance of any act is not due to the agent until the completion of such act." Though the completion of the work depends on the terms of contract and nature of work, an act is deemed to be complete when the agent has done whatever was necessary on his part.

Example: A was appointed as an agent for buying 100 tonnes of raw material for B at specified price. A made an agreement for buying that raw material from C. On making an agreement he becomes entitled to get his remuneration regardless of the fact that when that raw material is actually supplied by C.

However, the agent who is guilty of misconduct in the business of agency is not entitled to any remuneration in respect of the business which he has misconducted.

(*ii*) ***Right to retain money:*** An agent works on behalf of the principal. In the business of agency he may receive any sums on account of the principal. He has a right to retain which he has spent and which he has advanced in the operation of business of agency.

According to Section 17 of this Act, "an agent may retain, out of any sums received on account of the principal in the business of agency, all moneys due to himself in respect of advances made or expenses properly incurred by him in conducting such business, and also such remuneration as may be payable to him for acting as an agent."

However, it may be noted that an agent cannot retain sums received by him in one business for his remuneration or commission in other business. And this right can be exercised only on sums received on account of the principal, in the business of agency.

(*iii*) ***Right of lien:*** It is a right to retain the property of other unless certain claims or debts are satisfied. According to Section 221 of this Act, "in the absence of any contract contrary to it, an agent is entitled to retain goods, paper and other property, whether movable or immovable of the principal received by him until the amount due to him for commission, disbursement and services in respect of the same has been paid or accounted for to him."

Section 171 of this Act states that in the absence of contract, contrary to it factors, bankers and attorneys of high court have the right of general lien. Thus besides these, all other agents have right of particular lien. Under this right an agent can retain only those goods in respect of which charges or claims are due. The right of lien can also be claimed by the sub-agent appointed properly.

(*iv*) ***Right of indemnity:*** An agent has a right to get compensation for all losses caused to him in discharging his duty as an agent. According to Section 222 of this Act, "an agent has a right to indemnify against the consequences of all lawful act done by him in exercise of authority conferred upon him."

According to Section 223 of this Act, "where one person employs another to do an act and the agent does the act in good faith, the agent has a right to be indemnified against the consequences of the act, even though it causes injury to the right of third person."

Example: X who possesses some goods belonging to Y requests Z to sell these goods. Z is not aware of ownership of goods sells those goods to A and hands over proceed of sale to X. Later on, Y who is a real owner of the goods sues upon A and recovers value of the goods sold. X is liable to indemnity Z for these losses.

However, the right of indemnity does not extend to those acts which are known to the agent to be unlawful.

(*v*) ***Right of compensation:*** The right of compensation is available to the agent for the injuries caused to him by the neglect and want of skill, on the part of the principal. But if such injuries are caused to him by his own neglect and want of skill, he cannot claim compensation from the principal.

Similarly an agent is also entitled to compensation for the losses caused to him due to premature revocation of agency.

According to Section 205 of this Act, "where there is an express or implied contract that the agency should be continued for any period of time, the principal must make compensation to the agent for any premature revocation of the agency without sufficient cause."

(*vi*) ***Right to appoint sub-agent:*** An agent has a right to appoint sub-agent under the situation when it is necessary by the nature of business of agency or when he has got implied or express authority to do so.

Duties of Principal

The principal has the following duties towards an agent:

(*i*) The principal has a duty to pay the agent his commission and remuneration as per the terms of agency on the completion of the work.

(*ii*) The principal is under duty to indemnify the agent against the consequences of all lawful acts done by the agent in the business of agency.

(*iii*) The principal is under obligation to compensate an agent for all losses caused to him due to neglect and want of skill on the part of the principal.

(*iv*) The principal is also under duty to indemnify an agent against the consequences of acts done by the agent in good faith even if it causes an injury to third party.

Rights of Principal

The principal has a right to enforce duties of an agent against him which are:

(*i*) The principal has a right to ensure that the agent follows his instructions while conducting business of agency. In case the agent deviates from given instructions and the principal suffers loss, he has a right to claim compensation for it.

(*ii*) In case an agent misconducts or neglects or due to want of skill on his part, the principal suffers a loss, he can claim compensation for it.

(*iii*) The principal has a right to demand books of account and seek necessary explanation regarding entries made therein.

(*iv*) In case the agent deals on his own in the business of agency and makes personal gain out of it, the principal has a right to claim such benefit from the agent.

(*v*) Where the agent, without the knowledge and permission of the principal makes any secret profit out of business transactions of agency, the principal is entitled to recover such profits from the agent.

(*vi*) In case the agent makes breach of contract or breach of duty, the principal can refuse to admit the rights of an agent and if the principal suffers any loss, he can claim compensation from the agent.

AUTHORITY OF AGENT

An agent acts on behalf of the principal. Whatever he does within the scope of authority given to him, such acts will be binding on the principal. The right of an agent to bind the principal by his act is known as an 'authority of agent'.

According to Section 226 of this Act, "contracts entered into through an agent and obligation arising form the acts done by an agent, may be enforced in the same manner and will have same legal consequences, as if the contracts had been entered into and the acts done by the principal in person."

The contents of the above Section make it clear that the acts done by the agent on behalf of the principal will have same legal consequence as would have been done by the principal himself provided such acts had been done within the scope of authority given to him.

The scope of authority of an agent can be determined by taking into account the following types of authority of agent:

I. Actual authority.

II. Apparent or ostensible authority.

III. Emergency authority.

I. Actual Authority

Actual authority of an agent means an authority which has been conferred upon him by the principal. It may be either express or implied authority. An authority is said to be express if it is given to him in writing or by the words of mouth. On the other hand, implied authority means an authority which is inferred either from circumstances or from conduct of parties, business usage and intention of the parties.

Example: A in Delhi manages shop of B who lives in Mumbai. A habitually buys goods for the shop on credit on behalf of B. And B occasionally comes to Delhi and pays for it. Thus it implies from the conduct of both A and B that A had an authority to buy the goods on credit.

Apparent Authority

An agent is appointed for doing some act or all acts in the business of agency. And actual authority is given to him for doing those acts. In addition to those acts for which authority has been given, the agent has to perform many other necessary acts which may be incidental to the main acts. Authority to bind the principal by such acts is known as 'apparent authority'. Apparent authority is an authority which appears to others and may coincide with actual authority. Sometimes, it may be in excess of actual authority.

According to Section 188 of this Act, "an agent having an authority to do an act or to carry on business has authority to do every lawful things which is necessary in order to do such act or which is usually done in the course of conducting such business."

The contents of the above Section reveals that an apparent authority is used by the agent for doing all necessary lawful acts for conducting business of agency. And the principal will be bound by those acts.

RAYN *vs* PILKINGTON (1959, 1WL.R, 403): In this case, estate agent was appointed and instructed by the owner to find buyer for a property. Accordingly an agent did so and accepted deposit from a prospective purchaser as an agent. It was held that estate agent was not given authority to accept deposits, but he had acted within the scope of his apparent authority.

Emergency Authority

While conducting the business of agency an agent may meet some emergency situations. In such situations it is his duty to do needful for protecting the principal from a loss. Authority to do such needful acts is known as 'emergency authority'.

According to Section 189 of this Act, "agent has also authority in an emergency, to do all such acts for the purpose of protecting his principal from loss as would be done by a person of reasonable prudence in his own case, under similar circumstances."

To bind the principal, by the act of agent done under emergency authority, the following conditions should be satisfied:

(*i*) There should have been an emergency.

(*ii*) The principal must have been suffering from loss.

(*iii*) An agent must have acted with reasonable prudence.

(*iv*) He must have done all needful things to protect the principal from loss, which a person of reasonable prudence would have done in his own case under similar circumstances.

Example: A sent consignment of fruits of B, his agent at Calcutta to forward it to Bombay. When the consignment reached to Calcutta, B finds that fruits are getting spoiled and by the time the consignment reaches Bombay, the entire lot will be spoiled. Thus B sells the consignment for best obtainable prices without an authority from A, but under emergency authority.

DELEGATION OF AUTHORITY BY AGENT

As a matter of rule 'a delegate cannot further delegate'. Thus an agent to whom authority has been delegated by the principal cannot delegate it further to another person.

According to Section 190 of this Act, "an agent cannot lawfully employ another to perform acts, which he has expressly or impliedly undertaken to perform personally unless by the ordinary custom of trade a sub-agent may, or from the nature of agency, a sub-agent must be employed."

The above Section makes it clear that generally an agent cannot appoint another person as his agent and delegate authority to him. But under certain circumstances, he may delegate part of his authority to another person. These circumstances are:

(*i*) Where ordinary custom of trade permits the appointment of sub-agent.

(*ii*) Where the nature of business of agency is such that it cannot be carried out without appointing sub-agent.

(*iii*) Where the acts to be done are purely ministerial in nature can be delegated.

(*iv*) Where, there would have been some unforseen emergency which requires the appointment of sub-agent to cope with the situation.

(v) Where the principal agrees to the appointment of sub-agent.

Sub-Agent

According to Section 191 of this Act, "sub-agent is a person employed by and acting under the control of the original agent in a business of agency."

Thus sub-agent is appointed by the agent. And by appointing sub-agent, the original agent delegates part of his authority to him. Sub-agent acts under the control of original agent and there exists a relation of principal and agent between original agent and sub-agent.

Where the appointment of sub-agent is proper within above mentioned situations, he bears the following relations with the principal and original agent:

(*i*) In all transactions and agreements made by sub-agent with third party, the principal will be represented. Though there is no privity of contract between the principal and sub-agent, the principal would be liable for the acts of sub-agent as those would have been done by the original agent appointed by him.

(*ii*) The original agent will be liable to the principal for the acts of sub-agent. It is because for the work delegated to sub-agent, the original agent will have ultimate liability.

(*iii*) The sub-agent will not directly be liable to the principal. He is appointed by, and works under the control of original agent, thus will be liable to him only. In brief, the sub-agent will be liable to original agent and the original agent will be liable for the acts of sub-agent to the principal.

However where an agent, without having authority to do so, has appointed a person as sub-agent, (*i*) the principal will not be represented by the acts of sub-agent, and (*ii*) the original agent will be liable for the acts of the sub-agent both to the principal and to third person.

Substituted Agent

A substituted agent is a person who is named by the agent and holds express or impled authority from the principal to act for the principal. There is a direct privity of a contract between the principal and substituted agent for such part of business of agency which is entrusted to him. Although a substituted agent is an agent of the principal, he is named by the original agent at the request of principal.

While naming substituted agent for the principal, an agent is bound to exercise same amount of discretion as a man of an ordinary prudence would exercise in his own case. If the agent does so, he is not responsible to the principal for the acts or negligence of the substituted agent.

Example: A appoints B as his agent for selling his property in auction and request B to name some reliable solicitor for that purpose. B has named C as a solicitor. There is a direct privity of contract between A and C, thus C is a substituted agent.

Difference between sub-agent and substituted agent

	Sub-agent	Substituted agent
Appointment	Sub-agent is appointed by the original agent.	Substituted agent is named by the original agent and appointed by the principal.
Privity of contract	There is no privity of contract between sub-agent and the principal.	There is a direct privity of contract between the principal and substituted agent.
Liability	A original agent is liable for the acts of sub-agent towards the principal.	An original agent is not liable to the principal for the acts of substituted agent.
Direction and control	Sub-agent works under the control and direction of a original agent.	Substituted agent works under the direction and control of the principal.
Relationship	Sub-agent is an agent of a original agent.	Substituted agent is an agent of the principal, thus is also known as co-agent.

POSITION OF PRINCIPAL IN RELATION TO THIRD PARTY

All acts done by an agent on behalf of the principal within the scope of his authority are binding on the principal. In fact, the principal is being represented by his agent to deal with third party. The legal position of the principal in relation to third party may be understood with the help of following situation:

I. Agent acts for named principal.

II. Agent acts for unnamed principal.

III. Agent acts for undisclosed principal.

I. Where an Agent Acts for Named Principal

The legal position of the principal whose name and existence are disclosed by the agent, is as:

(*i*) ***Liability of the principal for the acts within the authority of agent:*** The principal will be responsible for the acts and contracts of agent with third party provided such acts or contracts are within the scope of his authority and in the course of his employment as an agent.

According to Section 226 of this act, "agent's acts and contracts will have the same legal effect as if the contract had been entered into and the acts done by the principal in person."

Example: A is appointed as an agent to buy raw material for B. A buys raw material from C on credit on behalf of B. This transaction is binding on B as well as on C.

(*ii*) ***Liability of the principal when agent exceeds authority:*** Where an agent does acts, some of them fall within the scope of authority and others are beyond the scope if:

(*a*) The acts within and beyond the scope of authority can be separated, the principal will be bound by those acts which are within the scope of authority of the agent.

(*b*) The acts cannot be separated, the principal will not be bound by such acts and he is entitled to repudiate all acts done within or beyond the scope of agent's authority.

Example: X was appointed as an agent for buying a horse for Y. But X buys a horse and carriage for Rs. 10,000. The acts of this transaction cannot be separated, thus Y will not be liable for this transaction.

(*iii*) ***Liability of the principal for the notice given to agent:*** Any notice given to the agent in the course of business of agency transacted by him with third party and any information obtained by the agent shall have same legal consequences as if, it had been given or obtained by the principal. Thus, notice to the agent is the notice to the principal and the principal will be liable to third party for such notice or information.

(*iv*) ***Liability of the principal for misrepresentation or fraud by agent:*** The principal is liable for the misrepresentation made or fraud committed by the agent in the course of the business. Such misrepresentation or fraud will have same effect on agreement made by agent as if, these had been made or committed by the principal.

Example: A is working as an agent of B for selling goods. For inducing customers. A makes misrepresentation about the quality of goods and sells goods to C. B will be liable to C for misrepresentation made by A.

(*v*) ***Liability of the principal for agents unauthorised acts:*** Where the principal by his words or conduct induces third person to believe that the unauthorised acts of an agent are within the scope of agents's authority, the principal shall be bound by such acts.

Example: X is appointed as an agent by Y for buying goods for him. On one occasion X buys goods on credit and Y pays for it though X had no authority to buy goods on credit. Again X buys goods on credit from Z. Y is responsible to Z for the payment.

II. Agent Acts for Unnamed Principal

It is a rule of law that once an agent discloses that he is acting as an agent the contract made by an agent binds the principal, though the principal has not been named by agent. On being discovered the legal position of unnamed principal is the same as where the principal is named. However, if the agent declines to disclose the identity of the principal, he becomes personally liable on that contract to third party.

Example: A is working as an agent of B for selling his goods. For making a contract of sale with C, A writes 'for the principal' without mentioning name of the principal. B is liable for this contract, though his name has not been mentioned.

III. Agent Acts for Undisclosed Principal

An agent acts on behalf of the principal. His role is to bring third party into contract with the principal. He simply represents the principal in dealing with third party.

However, if the agent does not disclose the existence of his principal, he is personally liable on that contract. Third party can sue upon him and he can also sue upon third party. But agent's right of action comes to an end with the intervention of undisclosed principal.

The undisclosed principal can intervene and may ask third party to perform contract. The rights of undisclose principal are protected by Section 231 of this Act.

This Section provides, "if an agent makes a contract with a person, who neither knows nor has reason to suspect that he is an agent, his principal may require performances of the contract; but other contracting party has, as against the principal, the same rights as he would have against the agent if the agent had been the principal."

The contents of the above Section make it clear that:

(*i*) Undisclosed principal may require third party to perform the contract.

(*ii*) Third party has a right to sue upon agent in that contract.

(*iii*) Third party has a right to claim performances of a contract as against the undisclosed principal.

However the right of undisclosed principal to intervene and sue third party is subject to the following conditions:

(*i*) An undisclosed principal may require the performances of a contract, subject to rights and obligations between the agent and third party of a contract.

(*ii*) If the principal discloses himself before the contract is completed, the other contracting party may repudiate the contract, if he can show that, if he had known, who the principal was or had he known that the agent was not a principal, he would not have entered into the contract.

(*iii*) An undisclosed, principal has no right to intervene if he has been excluded from the contract by express or implied terms of the contract made by the agent.

PERSONAL LIABILITY OF AGENT TO THIRD PARTY

An agent is appointed to represent the principal in dealing with third party. As soon as third party comes into contractual relation with the principal, the role of agent is over. Neither he can enforce that agreement against third party nor he is personally liable in that agreement to third party.

Thus, in ordinary course of business of agency, an agent does not become personally liable. It is the principal on whose behalf the agent acts can enforce that agreement against third party.

But, under certain situations an agent who has a representative role incurs personal liability in the agreements made by him on behalf of the principal. These situations are:

(*i*) ***Foreign principal:*** An agent who acts for the principal or buys and sells the goods on behalf of the principal residing abroad, will be held personally liable for all transactions made by him.

(*ii*) ***Undisclosed principal:*** When an agent acts for the undisclosed principal, the agent incurs personal liability. An undisclosed principal means the name and identity of the principal is not being disclosed by the agent while dealing with third party.

(*iii*) ***Non-existing principal:*** When the agent acts for non-existing or fictitious principal, the agent will be personally liable for that act, because it would be presumed that he has acted personally.

(*iv*) ***Express agreement:*** When an agent, while contracting with third party expressly agrees to be personally liable on the contract, he can be held personally liable in that contract.

(*v*) ***Where principal cannot be used:*** When the agent acts on behalf of the principal, though name and identity has been disclosed, but cannot be sued, the agent will be personally liable in such a case. But if it is in the knowledge of third party that the principal cannot be sued, the agent will have no personal liability.

(*vi*) ***Agent exceeds his authority:*** At the time of appointing an agent, generally, authority is given to him. And he is expected to act within the scope of his authority. Thus, if an agent exceeds his authority while dealing with third party, the agent will be personally liable for those acts.

(*vii*) ***Agency coupled with interest:*** The business of agency may have subject matter. When an agent has some personal interest in that subject matter, the agency is said to be coupled with interest. In case of agency coupled with interest, the agent will be personally liable to third party to the extent of his interest.

Example: A owes sum of Rs. 20,000 to B. A appoints B as his agent for selling his property in auction and recover a sum due to him. In this case B has got personal interest for selling property of A in auction. Thus agency is said to be coupled with interest and to the extent of Rs. 20,000 B will be personally liable.

(*viii*) ***Trade usage and customs:*** Sometime, it may be customary in the business of agency that whatever an agent does for his principal, the agent is held personally liable for those acts to third party. In all such case, the agent incurs personal liability.

(*ix*) ***Agent acts on his own:*** An agent is expected to act for the principal on his behalf. When an agent does some acts or makes contract in his own name, may be for the principal, the agent will be personally liable for such acts or contracts.

TERMINATION OF AGENCY

Agency is said to be terminated, if the relationship between agent and principal comes to an end. Agency may be terminated in any of the following manners:

I. Termination of Agency by the act of parties.

II. Termination of Agency by operation of law.

I. Termination of Agency by Act of Parties

The relationship of agency may be terminated by the acts of the parties under following situations:

(*i*) ***By agreement between principal and agent:*** The relationship of agency is generally created by mutual agreement between the principal and agent. They are free to terminate relationship of agency by mutual agreement at any time.

(*ii*) ***Revocation by the principal:*** The principal can revoke authority of an agent at any time, before the authority has been exercised so as to bind the principal. Such revocation may be either express or implied by the conduct of the parties.

The principal shall have to pay compensation to the agent in case he revokes agent's authority without assigning sufficient cause, before the period for which it was delegated to him.

However, the principal cannot revoke agent's authority under the following situation and such agency is known as 'Irrevocable Agency':

(*i*) ***Agency coupled with interest:*** According to Section 202 of this Act, "where the agent has himself an interest in the property which forms the subject matter of agency, the agency cannot, in the absence of an express contract, be terminated to the prejudice of such interest."

(*ii*) ***Where agent has incurred personal liability:*** While exercising an authority in the business of agency, if the agent has incurred personal liability, the principal cannot revoke authority of the agent.

(*iii*) ***Partial exercise of authority by agent:*** According to Section 204 of this Act, "where the agent has partly exercised his authority, it becomes irrevocable, so far as regards such acts and obligations as arise from the acts already done in the agency."

It is to be noted that an agent after giving reasonable notice to the principal may also renounce the business of agency.

II. Termination of Agency by Operation of Law

The relationship of agency, between the principal and agent may be terminated by operation of law in the following situations:

(*i*) ***Completion of business:*** Where the relationships of agency has been created for doing particular business, as soon as the business is completed, agency will be terminated automatically.

(*ii*) ***Expiry of time:*** Where the agent has been appointed for a particular period of time, at the expiry of that period, he ceases to be an agent.

(*iii*) ***Destruction of subject matter:*** An agency which has been created to deal with particular subject matter will be terminated on the destruction of that subject matter.

Example: A was appointed as an agent for selling a house of B in auction. Before auction, the house gets fire and destroyed. Agency will get terminated.

(*iv*) ***Insolvency of the principal:*** In the business of agency, if the principal is declared as an insolvent, as soon as the fact of insolvency comes to the knowledge of an agent, the relationships of agency will be terminated.

(*v*) ***Death of the principal or agent:*** An agency will get terminated on the death of the principal or an agent. In case, the principal dies, the agent is bound to take all reasonable steps for the protection and preservation of principal's interest on behalf to his representative.

(*vi*) ***Insanity of the principal or agent:*** Where, the principal or his agent becomes of unsound mind, the relationship of agency will be terminated. In case, the principal becomes of an unsound mind, the agent is bound to take reasonable steps for protecting and preserving the interest of the principal.

(*vii*) ***Dissolution of a company:*** Where the principal or agent is a body corporate or incorporated company, on the dissolution of such company, an agency will get terminated.

(*viii*) ***Termination of sub-agents authority:*** In case, the principal revokes, the authority of his agent, it will lead to automatic termination of sub-agent's authority appointed by original agent.

Effect of Termination of Agency

According to Section 208 of this Act, "as between the principal and the agent, termination of agency is effective only when it becomes known to the agent. But as far as third parties are concerned termination of agency takes effect when it is known to them." It is therefore relationship of agency between the principal and the agent ceases to exist when notice of such termination comes to the knowledge of the agent. To make termination of agency effective as against third parties the principal must give a public notice regarding termination of agency.

Even in case of death or insanity of the principal, termination of agency becomes effective when the fact of death or insanity comes to the knowledge of the agent.

REVIEW QUESTIONS

1. Define the term 'agent'. Discuss the nature of his role.
2. Explain various modes of creating relationship of agency in brief.
3. How the agency is created by ratification? Discuss various requirements of a valid ratification.
4. 'One who does through another, does by himself.' Comment.
5. Explain the various duties of an agent against the principal.
6. 'Rights of agent are duties of the principal.' Explain it.
7. Explain nature and scope of authority of an agent.
8. 'Delegate of authority cannot further delegate it.' Comment.
9. Define sub-agent. Discuss his role with regard to principal and original agent.
10. Define sub-agent and substituted agent. Distinguish between these two.
11. Discuss the legal position of the principal in relation with third party.
12. Explain the circumstances under which an agent is personally liable for the acts done by him on behalf of the principal.
14. What is termination of agency? When the agency is terminated by operation of law.
13. Write notes on:

    (*i*) Agency by holding out. (*ii*) Agency by necessity.

    (*iii*) Irrevocable agency. (*iv*) Sub-agent.

    (*v*) Undisclosed principal. (*vi*) Authority of agent.

PRACTICAL PROBLEMS

1. A, who is a minor has been appointed as an agent by B to buy raw material for him. A buys 10 tonnes of raw material on behalf of B on credit from C. Later on, C refused to pay because A who has made transaction is minor. Can C claim the price from B (Hint: Yes, agent may be a minor.)
2. Ram appoints Hari as his agent on specific commission for selling some goods. Hari agrees to it. There is no consideration in this agreement between Ram and Hari. Is this agreement is enforceable? (Hint: Yes, agency does not require consideration.)

3. A tells to B in the presence of C that A is B's agent, in fact he is not an agent. B does not refuse it. Later on, C makes a contract for buying goods with A, believing that he is B's agent. Is B bound by this contract? (Hint: Yes, there is an agency by estoppel.)
4. X has been working as an agent of Y for the last one year. Now his services have been terminated by Y, but no notice was given to this effect by Y. X subsequently purchased some goods on credit in the name of Y from Z. Is Y liable to pay the price? (Hint: Yes).
5. A allows his servant to purchase goods for him in the past on credit from B. On one occasion he pays cash to his servant for buying the goods. But the servant misappropriated that money and bought the goods on credit form B. Is A liable to pay for the goods? (Hint: Yes, there is an agency by holding out.)
6. A railway company has carried a horse from Bombay to Delhi, appointed destination. On the arrival at Delhi no one comes forward for getting delivery of the horse. The railway company has handed over the horse to stable keeper on rent. On tracing real owner of the horse, the railway company claimed for the rent. Is this claim valid? (Hint: Yes, there is an agency by necessity.)
7. A got married to B. After sometime A fails in providing basic necessities of life to his wife. His wife for the fulfillment of basic necessities pledges the property of her husband. Is an agreement of pledge valid? (Hint: Yes, there is an agency by necessity).
8. A purchased one hundred tonnes of wheat in his name for B without B's authority. Later on, B ratifies the transaction. Is ratification valid? (Hint: No, A has acted at his own.)
9. A is a managing director in a particular company. He accepts the offer made by B for buying goods purporting to act as an agent on behalf of the company. Later on, B withdrew his offer and ratifies the act of managing director. Examine legal position of the offer and acceptance.
10. A has rented his car to B for one month to be used for carriage purpose. C gets the car back from B without A's permission after 15 days. As a result of it B suffers a loss. A ratifies C's act. Does it amount to a valid ratification? (Hint: No, it implies loss to B.)

11. R has been appointed as an agent to sell one house of B. R finds out buyer of the house and gets an advance of Rs. 20,000 from him. Later on, he misappropriates this amount. Can buyer of the house claim this amount from B? (Hint: Yes, the act of R was within his scope of authority.)
12. A made an agreement with a stock broker for buying 500 equity shares of a particular company named as Blue and Green Coy Ltd. The broker did not buy these share in an open market, rather sold 500 equity share of that company which he owned, to A. Is A bound by this agreement? (Hint: No, the broker has worked in contradiction to his duty.)
13. A appoints B as his agent to recover Rs. 20,000 from C and invest it on good securities. B recovered the amount and 50% of it was invested on the good securities and remaining balance was invested on the securities which B knew to be bad securities. A suffers a loss of Rs. 1,000 from bad securities. Is B entitled to a remuneration on Rs. 20,000? Who shall be liable for a loss of Rs. 1,000 on bad securities.
14. A at the request of B sells goods being possessed by B without having right to sell the goods. A, not knowing this, sells the goods and hands over the proceeds to B. Later on, C who is a real owner of the goods sues A and recovers value of goods as well as legal cost. Is B liable to A to reimburse payments? (Hint: Yes).
15. Ram was appointed as an agent by Shyam for selling Shyam's property in auction and made out sum of Rs. 20,000 out of the proceeds which Shyam owes to Ram. Can Shyam revoke authority which he has given to Ram? (Hint: No, agency is coupled with interest of Ram.)

■■■

14

Contract of Bailment and Pledge

LEARNING OBJECTIVES

- Get familar with the concept of bailment of goods and types of bailment.
- Analyse rights and duties of bailor and bailee.
- Remember the rights and duties of finder of goods.
- Compare bailment of goods and pledge of goods.
- Get an idea on when non-owners can create valid pledge of the goods.

INTRODUCTION

Sometimes, the owner transfers physical possession of goods to another person without affecting the right of ownership. Such transfer of physical possession or delivery of goods may be made for various purposes i.e., for safe custody, as a security and in some cases for the use of that another person etc. But in all these case, that person to whom the goods are delivered will have very limited right that too only for a short period of time. Such types of transaction are made in the form of a contract of 'bailment'.

DEFINITION

According to Section 148 of the Indian Contract Act, "bailment is, the delivery of goods by one person to another of same purpose, upon a contract that, they shall, when the purpose is accomplished, be returned or otherwise disposed of according to the directions of the person delivering them."

Thus bailment is a contract where upon the physical possession of goods is transferred by one person to another for some purpose which may vary from situation to situation. The person who transfers possession of the goods is known as 'bailor' and to whom it is transferred to is known as 'bailee', and the contract between them is known as 'bailment'.

ESSENTIAL FEATURES OF BAILMENT

The contract of bailment has the following important features:

(*i*) ***Delivery of goods:*** The contract of bailment implies delivery of goods by one person to another. Delivery of goods involves transfer of physical possession. According to Section 149 of this Act delivery of goods may be either 'actual' or constructure. When the bailor hands over the goods physically to the bailee it is known as 'actual delivery' and on the other hand, if the bailor does some act which has an effect of putting goods in the possession of another person, it is known as 'constructure delivery'. As a result of such act another person gets authorisation or control over the goods without removing the goods physically.

(*ii*) ***Agreement:*** In case of bailment there is an agreement between bailor and bailee. It is under such agreement that goods are delivered by the bailor to the bailee. Such agreement may be either express or implied from the circumstances.

(*iii*) ***Purpose:*** In a contract of bailment the bailor delivers the goods to the bailee for some purpose. The purpose may vary situation to situation depending upon the need of the person and circumstances. Delivery of the goods may be given for the purpose of safe custody, forth security of loan or may be for the use of the bailee. The goods delivered by one person to another either by mistake or without purpose will not be included in the contract of bailment.

(*iv*) ***Return of goods:*** The contract of bailment implies that when the said purpose for which the goods have been delivered is accomplished, the goods will be returned back to the bailor or will be disposed of according to the directions of the bailor. It is however to be noted that goods may be returned either in original form or in an altered form.

***Example*:** A has given a piece of cloth to the tailor for making a shirt out of it. The tailor stitched it for making a shirt and when it is completed, he becomes bailee and will return in an altered form.

Besides the above features, it is also to be noted in bailment that the ownership of the goods is not transferred to the bailee.

KINDS OF BAILMENT

The contract of bailment may be entered into for various purposes. Sometimes is may be for the benefit of bailor or bailee and sometimes it may be made for the mutual benefits of both the parties. Broadly the bailment can be classified as:

(*i*) ***For the benefit of the bailor:*** Delivery of the goods exclusively for the benefit of the bailor will be included in this category. For example, bailment for safe custody without any charge or hire.

(*ii*) ***For the benefit of the bailee:*** Sometimes, the goods may be bailed only for the benefit of bailee such as bailment for use of bailee without any hire or rent.

(*iii*) ***For the mutual benefits:*** In majority of the cases, the contract of bailment is made for the mutual benefit of both bailor and bailee. For example, bailment of the goods as security for processing loan, or bailment of the goods to which some value is added for reward such as cloth is altered into specific garment for charges.

(*iv*) ***Bailment for reward:*** Where the transaction of bailment involves payment of remuneration either to the bailor or to the bailee, it is known as 'bailment for reward'.

Example: A lends his car to B for carriage on rent. A will get remuneration. Similarly A deposits his valuables in the bank for safe custody and the bank takes charges for it. In this case, the bailee is entitled to a remuneration.

(*v*) ***Gratuitous bailment:*** Wherein a transaction of bailment neither the bailor or the bailee is entitled to any remuneration, it is known as 'gratuitous bailment', such as lending a car to a friend without any rent or delivery of goods to a friend for safe custody without any charge, etc. In such transactions of bailment, the detriment suffered either by bailor or by bailee, as the case may be, is enough consideration for supporting validity of a transaction.

RIGHT AND DUTIES OF BAILOR AND BAILEE

In a contract of bailment, the bailor and the bailee have got certain rights and duties against each other.

Right of Bailor

The bailor has got the following rights in a contract of bailment against the bailee:

(*i*) ***Right to terminate bailment:*** The bailor has right to terminate the transaction of bailment if the bailee makes unauthorised or wrongful use of the goods bailed to him. An unauthorised use of goods means the bailee is using that goods without having the right to do so or he has a right to use goods for specific purposes but he is using it for the purpose other than specific one.

(*ii*) ***Right to seek return of goods:*** In a transaction of gratuitous bailment, the bailor has a right to demand return of goods even before the expiry of specific period or accomplishment of specific objective for which the goods have been bailed. But in case of such immature return, if the loss suffered by the bailee is greater than the benefit derived from the use of goods, the bailor has to compensate him for the excess of loss.

(*iii*) ***Right to demand any natural increase in goods bailed:*** In a contract of bailment, if there is an increase in the goods bailed to the bailee, the bailor is entitled to demand return of such increased portion along with goods originally given on bailment. Such as if a pregnant cow is given on bailment and she gives a birth to a baby cow, the bailor has an equal right of return against that calf along with a cow.

(*iv*) ***Right to enforce duties of bailee:*** In fact, the duties of the bailee are the rights of the bailor. And the bailor can enforce those duties of bailee even by filing a suit against him.

Duties of Bailor

In a contract of bailment the bailor has got the following duties regarding the goods bailed towards the bailee:

(*i*) ***Duty to disclose faults in the goods:*** The bailor is under legal obligation to disclose all defects or faults lying in the goods bailed to the bailee. But in case of gratuitous bailment, the bailor's duty is limited only for disclosing known defects. In a bailment for reward he is liable for both known as well as unknown faults in the goods. Thus if the bailee suffers any loss due to these faults the bailor will be liable to compensate him.

(*ii*) ***Duty to bear expenses incurred by the bailee:*** In case of a gratuitous bailment if the bailee has carried out some work on the goods bailed as per the terms of bailment or has spend some money for the reasonable maintenance of the goods, such expenses will ultimately be borne by the bailor. And in case of bailment for reward, the bailor will be liable only for extraordinary expenses.

(*iii*) ***Duty to indemnity losses of bailee:*** In case of gratuitous bailment, due to immature return of goods if the bailee has suffered losses which are more than the benefit derived, it is the duty of the bailor to indemnify those losses suffered by the bailee.

(*iv*) ***Duty to compensate loss of the bailee due to defective title:*** Where the bailor has no right to bail the goods or his title of those goods is defective, and the bailee suffers any loss due to such defective title, the bailor is under legal obligation to compensate those losses of the bailee.

Example: A has stolen car from B. A gives it to C on rent. In the meantime B comes to know about it and gets the car recovered from C. In this process C suffers a loss, he is entitled to get compensation from A who is the bailor of that car.

(*v*) ***Duty to take goods from the bailee:*** Bailment is made for a specific purpose. On the completion of that purpose, the goods bailed should be returned to the bailor. If the bailor refuses to take those goods and the bailee suffers a loss, he is entitled to get compensation from the bailor. Thus the bailor must accept the return of goods from the bailcc on time.

Rights of Bailee

The bailee has got the following rights against the bailor:

(*i*) ***Right to enforce bailor's duty:*** The duties of the bailor are the rights of the bailee. Therefore, the bailee is entitled to sue upon the bailor for enforcing the bailor's duties.

(*ii*) ***Right to be indemnified:*** In a contract of bailment, if the bailee suffers any loss due to defective title of the goods on the part of the bailor, he is entitled to get indemnified. These losses many arise, because the bailor was not entitled to make bailment or to receive back the goods or to seek the disposal of goods, etc.

(*iii*) ***Right to claim compensation:*** Where the bailee suffers a loss due to the faults lying in the goods bailed, he has a right to claim compensation. In case of gratuitous bailment his liability is confined only up to those faults which were known to him, but in a bailment for reward he will be liable for both known or unknown faults.

(*iv*) ***Right to sue the wrongdoer:*** As long as the goods are in the possession and use of the bailee as per the terms of bailment, he has all rights against any wrongdoer which are enjoyed by the owner of the goods. It means if the bailee has been deprived of the use of goods or an injury has been caused to him by a third party he is entitled to sue him.

(*v*) ***Right to return goods to any one of the joint bailors:*** In a contract of bailment in which two or more bailors jointly make a bailment. On the accomplishment of the purpose of the bailment, the bailee can return the goods to any one of the joint bailors. And it is necessary for him to inform another joint bailor.

(*vi*) ***Right to recover expenses:*** The bailee is entitled to recover general expenses or charges for his services which he has rendered as per the conditions of bailment or under any logical obligation, he can recover these from the bailor. But in case of bailment for reward he is entitled to recover only extraordinary expenses incurred by him.

(*vii*) ***Right against third party or owner:*** In case, the purpose of the bailment is accomplished and the bailee returns the goods to the bailor in good faith. The bailee has a right against third party who has a claim against goods to protect himself. Thus the bailee will not be liable to such third party.

(*viii*) ***Right of lien:*** It is a right to retain possession of the property of another person until some debt or claim against that person is paid. This right is known as possessory lien and therefore as soon as possession of the property is lost, this right will also be lost. The right of lien may be of two types 'particular lien' and 'general lien'.

In a particular lien, the person exercising this right can retain the possession of that property in respect of which debt or claim is due. But in general lien any property may be retained unless and until any of the debts or claim against that another person is satisfied. This right is available only to special type of bailees such as banker, factor, warmfinger, attorneys of high courts, *etc.,* and policy brokers. And all other bailees enjoy right of particular lien. According to Section 170 of this Act, the right of particular lien has been conferred upon the bailee. This Section further provides "where the bailee has in accordance with the purpose of the bailment rendered any service involving the exercise of labour or skill in respect of the goods bailed, he has, in the absence of a contract to the contrary, a right to retain such goods, until he receives due remuneration for the services he has rendered in respect of them."

Thus the right of particular lien is available to the bailee subject to the fulfillment of the following conditions:

(*i*) The bailee must have rendered some services on the goods bailed.

(*ii*) Such services must involve use of labour and skill of the bailee.

(*iii*) Such services have been rendered by the bailee according to terms and conditions of the contract of bailment.

(*iv*) There must not be any contract contrary to the above conditions such as condition to pay service charges at future data, etc.

(*v*) The bailee can exercise this right only for the payment of due remuneration for the services rendered by him.

(*vi*) Services rendered by the bailee must be complete.

Example: A has delivered a car to B for making necessary repair on it. B did it as per the terms and conditions of the bailment. In this case, B is entitled to retain the possession of the car until A makes payment of service charges to B provided B has repaired the car. But, as per the term of a contract, if the payment of charges is to be made after two months, B is not entitled to the right of lien.

It is however to be noted that the right of lien comes to an end under the following circumstances:

(*i*) The person who is entitled to this right has lost the possession of goods.

(*ii*) There is a term in a contract which is contrary to this right.

(*iii*) Right of lien is terminated as soon as the payment of debt or claim is made or tendered.

(*iv*) Right of lien available to the bailee may be waived by him voluntarily.

Duties of Bailee

In a contract of bailment, the bailee is subject to following duties:

(*i*) ***Duty to take reasonable care:*** In all cases of bailment, most important duty of the bailee is to take reasonable care of the goods bailed to him. Reasonable care of goods means that much care as person of reasonable prudence would have taken in case of his own goods and under similar circumstances.

According to Section 151 of this Act, "in all cases of bailment, the bailee is bound to take as much care of the goods bailed to him, as a man of ordinary prudence would, under similar circumstances take of his own goods of the same bulk, quality and value as the goods bailed."

In case the goods are damaged or destroyed due to lack of reasonable care, the bailee will be liable for the loss. In spite of taking reasonable care if the goods are damaged, the bailee will not be liable for such losses.

Martin *vs* London Country Council (1947, K.B., 628) In this case, plaintiff was brought as a patient to a paid hospital. On entry she handed over two pieces of jewellery and a cigarette case to the hospital authorities. These were stolen by a thief. The hospital authorities were held liable as a bailee, because they had failed in taking as much care as the nature of articles demanded.

(*ii*) ***Duty not to make unauthorised use of the goods bailed:*** The transaction of bailment may be made for the use of goods by the bailee. The bailee is under obligation to use the goods in the manner as prescribed and for the purpose as mentioned in the contract. And he must not use the goods in a manner which is inconsistent with the terms of a contract. In case, he makes an unauthorised or inconsistent use of the goods and the goods are damaged, he shall be liable to pay compensation to the bailor.

Example: A hired his horse to B, who shall use it for the purpose of riding. But B used for carriage purpose and the horse got injured. B will be liable for the loss. Similarly, A rented his car to B for going to Mumbai. But B goes to Lucknow and on the way meets with an accident and car was damaged. B shall be liable for unauthorised use of the goods.

(iii) ***Duty not to mix the goods with his own goods:*** There is a duty on the part of the bailee that he must not mix the goods bailed with his own goods. In case, he mixes them with his own goods with the consent of the bailor, both of them will have same interest as they had before mixing the goods. But, if the goods are mixed without the consent of the bailor and goods can be separated out, all expenses and damage arising out of it shall be borne by the bailee.

In case the goods are not separable, the bailee shall be liable to compensate the bailee for a loss.

(iv) ***Duty to return the goods:*** The transaction of bailment is always made for some specific purpose. And as soon as the purpose is accomplished it is the duty of the bailee to return the good to the bailor. In case, delay occurs in returning the goods and in the meantime, the goods are destroyed, the bailee will be liable for the loss to the bailor.

In case of gratuitous bailment, the bailor has a right to demand immature return even before the specific period for which the goods are bailed. If, the loss suffered by the bailee on account of immature return is more than the benefit derived by him, the bailor will compensate the loss.

(v) ***Duty to return any natural accretion to the goods:*** In case there has been a natural accretion to the goods bailed, it is his duty to return it along with the goods to the bailor.

Example: A leaves a pregnant cow with B to be taken care of. Later on, the cow gives birth to a calf. B is under duty to return both the cow as well as calf to A.

(vi) ***Duty not to set up adverse title:*** Section 117 of the India Evidence Act provides that, "no bailee shall be permitted to deny that his bailor had, at the time of bailment authority to make such bailment." In other words, the bailee cannot deny the title and right of the bailor. Thus if the bailee return the goods to the bailor in good faith he shall have no liability towards third party who may be real owner of the goods.

Right of Bailor and Bailee against Wrongdoer

(*i*) In case, the bailee is deprived of the use or possession of the goods bailed or does any injury, the bailee is entitled to use such remedies as the owner might have used in the like case if bailment had not been made.

(*ii*) Either the bailor or the bailee may bring a suit against the wrongdoer for such deprivation or injury (Section 180).

(*iii*) Whatever is obtained by way of relief or compensation in any such suit is to be apportioned as between the bailor and the bailee according to their respective interest (Section 181).

TERMINATION OF BAILMENT

A contract of bailment stands terminated under the following situations:

(*i*) ***Expiry of specified period:*** In case the contract of bailment is made for a specific period of time; as soon as that period expires, a contract of bailment gets terminated.

(*ii*) ***Specific purpose:*** The goods are generally bailed to the bailee for a specific purpose. On the accomplishment of such purpose, the contract of bailment will automatically be terminated.

(*iii*) ***Termination of gratuitous bailment:*** In a contract of gratuitous bailment, the bailor has got right to demand return of the goods even before the accomplishment of purpose or expiry of specific period of time. On the return of the goods, the bailment will come to an end.

(*iv*) ***Inconsistent use of the goods:*** In case the bailee makes unauthorised or inconsistent use of the goods bailed, the bailor may demand return of the goods and can seek termination of the bailment.

(*v*) ***Death of bailor or bailee:*** A contract of the gratuitous bailment will come to an end in the event of death of the bailor or the bailee.

FINDER OF THE GOODS

Where the person who finds the goods lost by another person, and takes custody of those goods, he gets same legal position in the eyes of low as a bailee in a gratuitous bailment. Thus he is subject to some rights and obligations.

According to Section 71, "a person who finds goods belonging to another and takes them into this custody is subject to same responsibility as a bailee."

Rights of Finder of Goods

The finder of the goods who takes custody of those has the following rights against the owner of the goods:

(*i*) ***Right to possess the goods:*** The finder of the goods is entitled to possess those goods until he traces the real owner, against everyone except the true owner.

(*ii*) ***Right to claim for reward:*** Generally the real owner of the lost goods declares some reward for the finder of the goods. The finder of goods may sue the real owner for such reward.

(*iii*) ***Right of lien:*** According to Section 168 of this Act, a finder has a right to retain possession of the goods until he receives reasonable compensation for expenses, incurred in connection with preservation of goods and finding out of the owner.

(*iv*) ***Right of sale of goods:*** In spite of making reasonable efforts if the bailee does not succeed in tracing real owner of the goods, he has a right to sell off those goods, but under the following situations:

   (*a*) when the thing is in danger of perishing or losing greater part of its value, or

   (*b*) when the lawful charges of the finder in respect of things found, amount to two third of its value.

Duties of Finder of Goods

Finder of goods is subject to the following duties for preserving the goods and protecting an interest of true owner:

(*i*) A finder of goods must take reasonable care of those goods. Due to lack of reasonable care, if the goods are destroyed he shall be liable to the real owner for the loss.

(*ii*) A finder of goods must make all reasonable efforts to trace the real owner of the goods.

(*iii*) On tracing the real owner he must return the goods to him.

(*iv*) A finder of goods is also under obligation for returning natural accretion to the goods like the bailee.

PLEDGE

The contract of bailment is made for various purposes. A pledge is a special kind of bailment which is made for providing security to the lender against the loan given by him.

According to Section 172 of this Act, "pledge is the bailment of the goods as security for payment of a debt or for performance of promise. The person who delivers the goods is known as 'pawnor' and to whom the goods are bailed known as 'pawnee'."

Thus pledge is bailment of goods as a security for procuring loan or for performance of promise.

Characteristics of Pledge

Pledge is a special kind of bailment. It has the following characteristics:

(*i*) ***Delivery of goods:*** As a kind of bailment, the transaction of pledge involves transfer of physical possession of goods to the 'pawnee'. Such transfer may be in the form of 'actual delivery' or in the form of constructure delivery.

(*ii*) ***Purpose of delivery:*** In a pledge, the goods are delivered to the pawnee for a specific purpose *i.e.*, as a security for payment of debt. Thus so long as debt is not paid, goods will be in the possession of the pawnee.

(*iii*) ***Return of goods:*** In a transaction of pledge, as soon as the debt or loan procured by the pawnor is paid, the goods will be returned by the pawnee to him.

(*iv*) ***Transfer of special interest:*** While pledging the goods, the pawnor transfers special interest with regard to those goods to the pawnee. But general interest remains with the pawnor.

DIFFERENCE BETWEEN BAILMENT AND PLEDGE

Though the pledge is a special kind of bailment, it differs on the following points:

(*i*) ***Purpose:*** The pledge is a bailment of the goods as a security for paying debt or for performance. But the bailment can be made for varieties of purposes other than those two, such as safe custody, for the use of bailor or for creating additional value in the goods, etc.

(*ii*) ***Use of good:*** In pledge, the pawnee is not entitled to use the goods bailed to him. Rather he has a special interest on the goods of retaining possession so long as debt is not paid. But in many other transactions of bailment the bailee may enjoy not only the possession but also the use of goods.

(*iii*) ***Sale of goods:*** In case of pledge, if the pawnor fails in repaying debt or performing promise, the 'pawnee', by giving reasonable notice to the pawnor can sell those goods. But in bailment, the bailee has no right to sell the goods bailed to him.

(*iv*) ***Scope:*** All transaction of pledge are bailment, but all transaction of bailment are not pledge.

RIGHTS AND DUTIES OF PAWNOR AND PAWNEE

Rights of Pawnor

The pawnor has the following rights:

(*i*) ***Right to redeem goods:*** As stated earlier, if the pawnor fails to pay debt, the pawnee has a right to sell the goods. But before the actual sale of goods by the pawnee, the pawnor has a right to redeem the goods.

(*ii*) ***Right to receive accretion:*** In case some increase or accretion takes place to bailed goods, the pawnor has a right to receive back that increase or accretion.

Example: A company has borrowed sum of Rs. 10 lakh from the bank and as a security for the loan the company pledged equity shares of another company with the bank. Meanwhile, some bonus shares accrued on account of pledged shares. Thus on repayment of that loan the company has a right to get original shares along with bonus shares.

(*iii*) ***Right to enforce duty of the pawnee:*** The pawnor, as a bailor has a right to get all duties of pawnee enforced by filing a suit against him.

Duties of Pawnor

The pawnor has the following duties:

(*i*) ***Duty to meet obligation on time:*** The pawnor is under duty to pay debt on time according to terms of a pledge and comply with other conditions of the pledge.

(*ii*) ***Duty to bear extraordinary expenses:*** In case, the pawnee incurs some extraordinary expenses with respect to goods pledge, it is the duty of pawnor to compensate the pawnee for those expenses.

(*iii*) ***Duty to compensate pawnee for defective title:*** Where the pawnee suffers any loss due to some defects in the title of pawnor, it is the duty of pawnor to compensate the pawnee for those losses.

Rights of Pawnee

The pawnee has following rights as against the goods pledged and the pawnor:

(*i*) ***Right of retainer:*** The pawnee has a right to retain the goods pledged with him until his debt or dues are cleared or paid. He can exercise this right not only for the debt, but also for an interest due on the debt and all other necessary expenses incurred by him. This right may be known as 'pledger's right' of particular lien.

(*ii*) ***Right of retainer for subsequent advances:*** When the pawnee lends money to the pawnor after the date of pledge without taking any further security, it shall be presumed that, right of retainer over the pledged goods extends to subsequent advance made.

(*iii*) ***Right to recover extraordinary expenses:*** Where the pawnee incures some extraordinary expenses for preserving the goods pledged, he is entitled to recover these expenses from the pawnor. But the pawnee cannot exercise right of retainer for the recovery of such expenses.

(*iv*) ***Right to sue the pawnor or sell the goods at his default:*** In case the pawnor fails to pay debt or perform promise the pawnee can exercise any of the following rights:

(*a*) He may retain goods as collateral security and file a suit against the pawnor for the recovery of amount.

(*b*) After giving reasonable notice to the pawnor, he can sell the goods pledged.

Duties of Pawnee

The pawnee is subject to the following duties and obligations in a contract of pledge:

(*i*) ***To take reasonable care:*** The pawnee is under legal obligation to take reasonable care of the goods pledged to him.

(*ii*) ***Not to use goods:*** The pawnee generally is not entitled to use the goods pledged to him. In case the pawnor allows him, he must make authorised use of the goods.

(*iii*) ***Not to mix the goods:*** The pawnee is under duty to keep goods pledged separately and not to mix them with his own goods.

(*iv*) ***To return goods:*** On the payment of debt of performance of a promise, the pawnee must return the goods to the pawnor. Any under delay which causes damage or loss to goods will be the liability of the pawnee.

(*v*) ***To return increase in goods:*** In case there has been any natural increase in the goods pledged, it is a duty of the pawnee to return such increase to the pawnor.

(*vi*) ***Not to set up an adverse title:*** It is also a duty of the pawnee that he must not deny the title and right of pawnor. And he must not set up his own title or title of third party on the goods pledges.

PLEDGE BY NON-OWNERS

As a rule of law, it is the real owner of the goods or the person duly authorised by him can create a valid pledge of those goods. But in practice, there are many situations under which even a non-owner or the person who is not authorized to pledge can create a valid pledge. These exceptions are:

(*i*) ***Pledge by mercantile agent:*** The mercantile agent, who has got the possession of goods or documents of title with the consent of owner pledges those goods without any authority, even then such pledge will be valid provided the following conditions are fulfilled:

(*a*) The goods or document of title of goods are in the possession of a mercantile agent with the consent of owner.

(*b*) He pledges the goods in an ordinary course of business of agency.

(*c*) The pawnee has acted in good faith believing that the mercantile agent has a right to pledge the goods.

(*ii*) ***Pledge of goods obtained in voidable contract:*** In case the person obtains possession of the goods in a voidable contract in which the consent of another party has not been free. If these goods are pledged before the contract is declared as void by an aggrieved party, such pledge is also legally valid provided the pawnee has acted in good faith.

(*iii*) ***Pledge by the person having limited interest on the goods*****:** When the person has limited interest on the goods and he pledges those goods, such transaction of pledge will be valid up to the extent of his interest.

Example: A has pledged the goods as a security for the payment of loan of Rs. 10,000 which he has taken from B. B further pledges these goods to C for the payment of loan to Rs. 15,000. The pledge of goods by B to C is valid to the extent of Rs. 10,000.

(*iv*) ***Pledge by one of the joint owners:*** In case the goods are owned jointly by two or more persons, and one of the joint owners pledges those goods, such pledge is valid provided.

(*a*) He has got possession of goods with the consent of other joint owners.

(*b*) The pawnee must have acted in good faith believing that the joint owner is authorised to pledge the goods.

(*v*) ***Pledge by the seller having possession of goods after sale:*** When the seller has sold the goods, but he is still possessing those goods. In case he pledges those goods, the pledge is valid provided the pawnee has acted in good faith and had no notice of earlier sale.

(*vi*) ***Pledge by the buyer in possession of goods in agreement to sell:*** Where the buyer buys the goods under agreement to sell. Before he gets ownership he pledges those goods. Such pledge is valid provided the pawnee has acted in good faith.

Example: A buys a machine worth Rs. 2,000 on hire purchase basis. The payment is to be made in 20 equal instalments. After having paid a few instalments he pledges that machine with B, the pledge is valid provided B has acted in good faith having no notice of hire-purchase.

REVIEW QUESTIONS

1. What is 'bailment'? Discuss its essential features.
2. Explain the various types of bailment.
3. What is 'lien'? Explain the various types of lien and discuss, bailees particular lien.
4. Distinguish between bailment and pledge.
5. Explain various rights and duties of the bailor.
6. Discuss the rights and duties of the bailee.
7. Explain rights and duties of the finder of the goods.
8. Can a non-owner create a valid pledge? Explain the exceptions.

PRACTICAL PROBLEMS

1. A went to see an exhibition. A parked his car in a field belonging to a farmer who has permitted the parking of vehicles in his field. After sometime A returned to the field and found that the car has been stolen. Is the farmer liable for the loss of car to A? (Hint: No, he is not a bailee.)
2. M is going out of station and leaves his car with N for safe custody. N does not charge anything from M. Is it a contract of bailment? (Hint: Yes).
3. A customer visited a restaurant for having dinner. As soon as he entered the restaurant, a waiter took his coat without being asked to do so and hung it on a hook behind him. When the customer after finishing dinner

was to leave, he found that the coat was missing. Is the owner of that restaurant liable for a loss of a coat? (Hint: Yes, he has acted in the position of the bailee.)

4. A has borrowed a sum of Rs. 50,000 from a bank and pledged some shares of joint stock company. Later on the company issued bonus share on those pledged shares. Is A entitled to receive those bonus shares? (Hint: Yes).
5. M found a car. He took it in his custody. He has only one car garage in which he used to park his car. Thus he parked the found car outside the garage. That car has been stolen. N who is a owner of that car claimed compensation from M. Is he entitled to it? (Hint: Yes).
6. A has taken a horse from B on hire for riding purpose. But A used it for carriage purpose. The horse got injury while doing the job of carriage. Is A liable for this loss to B? (Hint: Yes, A has made unauthorised use of that horse.)
7. Ram has given a piece of cloth to a tailor for making a suit out of it. The suit was half stitched. Ram refused to pay tailoring charges. Can a tailor exercise right of lien over the half stiched suit? (Hint: No).
8. A has pledge some goods with B and secured loan of Rs. 10,000 against it. B further pledged these good with C as a security for paying a loan of Rs. 15,000. Can A take his goods from C without making any payment to him. (Hint: Yes, by making payment of Rs. 10,000.)

■■■

Unit 2

Indian Partnership Act, 1932
(Ch 15–17)

Sale of Goods Act ,1930
(Ch 18–21)

INDIAN PARTNERSHIP ACT, 1932

15

Definition and Registration of Partnership

LEARNING OBJECTIVES

- Develop your understanding on partnership.
- Examine those factors, on the basis of which the relationship of partnership between two or more persons can be judged.
- Compare, the partnership with Joint Stock Company, Co-ownership and Joint Hindu Family.
- Remember legal consequences of registration and non-registration of partnership.
- Get clarity about types and role of various partners in terms of capital contribution, liability, participation and sharing in profit and loss.
- Get familiar with the position of minor beneficiary in the firm both after attaining majority and during minority.

INTRODUCTION

The Partnership Act is merely one of the branches of Special Contract Act. The law relating to partnership was contained in Sections 239 to 266 of the Indian Contract Act 1872. These Sections have been repealed and separate Act was enacted, known as the Indian Partnership Act, 1932. It came into force on 1 October 1932 (except Section 69, which came into force one year later).

The Indian Partnership Act 1932 contains 74 Sections, which are applicable to the whole of India except the state of Jammu & Kashmir. Section 3 of this Act provides that the unrepealed provisions of the Indian Contract Act, 1872, shall continue to apply to firms, where the provisions of the Indian Partnership Act are silent.

This Act is specially meant for governing business of partnerships in India. The Act mainly contains necessary provisions relating to the formation of partnership, the right, duties and liabilities of partners and the procedure for its dissolution, etc.

MEANING OF PARTNERSHIP

Simply speaking, a partnership is an association of persons who conduct some business activity and agree to share profits earned out of it.

In the words of Dixon, "partnership is a voluntary unincorporated association of individuals standing to the another in the relationship of principals for carrying out joint operation or undertaking for the purpose of joint profit."

According to Section 4 of the Indian Partnership Act, "partnership is the relation between two or more persons who have agreed to share the profit of a business carried on by all or any of them acting for all."

CHARACTERISTICS OF PARTNERSHIP

The definition of partnership reveals the following characteristics:

1. Association of Two or More Persons

To form a partnership at least two or more persons are required. In case the number of partners are reduced to one due to any reason such as death, insolvency or retirement of a partner, it would cease to be a partnership. But the Indian Partnership Act is silent about the maximum number of partners. However Section 11 of the Indian Companies Act, 1956, lays down maximum number of partners in case of banking business at 10 and 20 in case of any other business. If the number of partners exceed this maximum limit, the partnership becomes an illegal association.

Two partnership firms cannot enter into partnership but all the partners of the two firms can form a separate partnership.

2. Agreement or Contract Between Persons

The relationship of partnership is contractual in nature. It arises out of a contract or agreement made by the persons. In other words, those who are willing to form a partnership come together and make an agreement and become partners. Section 5 of this Act states that the relationship between partners arises out of a contract and not from status. The Act further makes it clear that the members of a Joint Hindu Family carrying a business and a Burmese Buddhist husband

and wife carrying on business as such are not partners in such business. Similarly, in case of death of a partner, his legal representative will not automatically becomes a partner, unless there is an agreement between them to carry on business as partners.

Justice Sulaiman of Allahabad High Court has made it clear in **Habib Bux** *vs* **Samiuel Fitz & Coy Ltd.** case that, "when the sole proprietor of a firm dies, his heirs certainly inherit the stock in trade, the outstanding dues, and even the goodwill, but such heirs do not '*ipso facto*' become partners of the firm. When there was a sole proprietor there was no question of partnership, which must be between more than one person. On the death of a sole proprietor, his heirs do not automatically become partners of the old firm, but are merely heirs to the assets of the deceased. Before a partnership can come into existence, there must be an express or implied agreement between the heirs that the firm was allowed to carry on business even after the death of a sole proprietor."

From the above observation it is clear that:

(*a*) When there is a sole proprietor, there is no question of partnership.

(*b*) In case of a death of sole-proprietor, his heirs do not automatically become partners of the firm.

(*c*) There must be an express or implied agreement between them for creating relationship of partnership.

3. Business

Partnership is an important form of business organisation. It is formed to conduct some business activity. The business to be carried out must be lawful. According to Section 2 of this Act, "business includes every trade, occupation and profession of course which is lawful and conducted with a profit motive." Thus mere holding of a property in common does not create partnership. However, in case of partnership the business may include professions like architecture, legal practice and chartered accountancy, *etc.*, in addition to other industrial trading activities.

Govind Nair *vs* **Maga (1948, 1, MAD. 343).** In this case, G and M jointly purchased a restaurant and incurred an additional expenses for purchasing pottery and utensils for it. They contributed equally and subsequently leased that restaurant on rent basis. The rent was equally shared by them. It was held that, they were only co-owners and not partners as they never carried on any business.

In another case, the court held that the existence of a business must be in continuance which is also one of the most important ingredients of partnership.

4. Sharing of Profit

The partnership is formed for doing some business, and the business is conducted with a profit motive. Thus sharing the profits of a business is the essence of partnership. Unless otherwise agreed upon, sharing of profits of business implies sharing of its losses also. However, the person can become a partner on the understanding that he will not share losses.

Generally, the ratio in which profit and losses will be shared is a matter of agreement between the partners. In absence of any ratio, profits and losses will be shared equally by the partners.

However, it should be noted that, though sharing of profits of business is an essential element of partnership, it does not follow the rule that anyone who is sharing profits of a business is essentially a partner in the firm. A manager, who as a part of his remuneration shares the profit of business, is only an employee of the firm and not a partner.

However, there is nothing to stop a partner from agreeing to receive a fixed annual or monthly amount by way of profit, whether profits are earned or not.

5. Mutual Agency

All partners of the firm have a right to participate in the management of the business. But all of them may not have a required managerial knowledge and talent. It is therefore in practice that only some partners may be given the authority for managing business of the firm. The partners who manage business perform various activities as an agent. They actually act on behalf of other partners who have authorised them to manage. Thus every partner of the firm is an agent and principal for himself and for other partners. He can bind the other partners by his acts and is also bound by the acts of other partners.

In a nutshell, the partners have a relationship of mutual agency. The law of partnership is regarded as an extension of the general law of agency. This is so because, the partner is bound by the acts of other partners and simultaneously he can also bind other partners by his acts which he or they are doing for managing business in the ordinary course of dealing.

According to Section 18 of this Act, "that subject to the provisions of Partnership Act a partner is a agent of the firm for the purposes of the business."

The partner assumes role of both agent and principal as:

(*a*) He is an agent of the firm, so far as his dealings with outside world, for the purpose of business of the firm are concerned. He can bind the firm by his acts.

(*b*) He is a principal so far other partners are concerned. The relation between the partners '*inter-se*' is that of principals.

TEST OF PARTNERSHIP

In order to test the relationship of partnership between two or more persons, the above discussed essentials of a partnership are to be given a serious thought. In many cases, it is found that the persons more or less behave as a partner or act as a partner, but may not be a partner in reality.

According to Section 6 of this Act, "in determining whether a group of persons is or is not a firm or whether a person is or is not a partner in a firm, regard shall be had to the real relation between the parties as shown by all relevant facts taken together."

To determine and judge the relationship of partnership following essentials of partnership are to be valued once again:

(i) Contractual relationship: To be in the relationship of partnership, there must be a contract or agreement between or among the persons. The agreement may be express or implied. To distinguish the relation of partnership with that of other similar relation, existence of a contract or agreement must be proved. Other relation which arise out of status or by operation of law do not have an agreement at their root. The Section 5 of this Act makes it clear that, members of Joint Hindu Undivided Family who are doing business are not a partners, rather they are co-owners of the business. Similarly Burmese Buddhist husband and wife doing business and working more or less as a partner are not actually partners. This is because the source of their relationship is not an agreement. In this regard, it is safely concluded that relation of partnership arises out of a contract not by a status.

(ii) Existence of business: To prove relation of partnership existence of business is also one of the important factor. The partners, come into relationship for conducting some business including professional activities. Two or more persons sharing income from any property are not partners rather they may be co-owners of that property.

In this regard, Nagpur High court held that continuity in business is one of the most important ingredients of partnership, rather isolated business venture. However, it must be noted that business being conducted by partners must be a legal one.

Example: A and B enter into an agreement for smuggling out some banned goods to other country. They will not be considered as a partners, because the purpose of that agreement is illegal.

(*iii*) *Profit sharing:* Profit sharing is regarded as an important element of partnership. But it may not be taken as the sole criteria for determining relation of partnership.

Thus sharing of profits is a *prima facie* evidence but it is not a conclusive test of partnership. So, where two or more persons are sharing profits in the firm, it does not necessarily mean that they are partners. There may be persons who are receiving a share in profit of business or they are getting payment contingent upon earning a profit, but are not partners. Such person may be:

(*a*) Creditor of the firm, who has lent money to the firm, may agree to take a share in profits.

(*b*) The widow or a child of deceased partner, who receives share of profit of business as annuity.

(*c*) A person receiving a share of profit in consideration of sale of business or good will of business that he has sold to the firm.

(*d*) Employee or an agent receiving share in the profit of the business in consideration with the firm.

Examples: A and B are partners in a firm. They borrow money from C on a condition that C will get 10 per cent share in profits and will have the right to inspect books of accounts. Despite these, C cannot be regarded as a partner because his position is more of a creditor.

Ram is a contractor, who appoints B as his manager for managing a business of loading and unloading of railway wagons. He was to be given 50 per cent of the profits of this business and also bear the losses if any. B is simply working as an employee so, getting share in profit alone does not make him a partner.

COX *vs* COULSON (1916, 2, KB.M.). In this case, the leasee of a theatre entered into an agreement for the performance of a play at his theatre with the manager of a theatrical company, under which the former was to provide and pay the lighting and wage bill and to receive 60 per cent of the receipts, while latter was to receive remaining 40 per cent and to provide actors and scenery. It was held that, there being sharing of returns and not profits, thus there was no partnership between them.

(iv) ***Relationship of agency:*** The underlying principal which governs partnership is the relation of agency with the partners. It provides basic criteria for judging the relation of partnership. It implies that as far as the business of partnership is concerned that every partner is the agent of all others and all others are his agent.

Thus to test the relation of partnership between two or more persons, it is essential to know that whether the person can bind others by his acts and becomes bound by the acts of others. If it is so, they are partners provided many other factors discussed earlier also support it. This is so because the law of partnership is an extension of law of principal and agent. This relationship of principal and agent, distinguishes a partnership from co-ownership and simple agreements of sharing profits.

In addition to these, many other factors may also be taken into consideration while determining relation of partnership. These factors may include, clear intention of the parties, mode of conducting business, maintaining books of accounts, relationship among them and with third parties and other relevant factors. In this regard, Section 6 of this Act clearly states that, "in determining whether a group of persons is or is not a firm, regard shall be had to the real relation between the parties as shown by all relevant facts taken together."

PARTNER, FIRM AND NAME OF THE FIRM

Partnership is basically an association of the persons. They enter into an agreement to create the relation of partnership. These persons, individually known as 'partners' and collectively a 'firm'. The name under which their business is carried on is called 'firm's name'.

The partnership firm is not a separate legal entity distinct from its members. It is only a collective name of the individuals who are forming partnership.

There is a difference between partnership and the firm. Partnership implies and describes relationship between partners. While as the firm is a collective name or body of those partners.

The partners are at liberty to select name of the firm under which their business will be carried on. But it is subject to the following limitations:

(*a*) The name must not be identical or similar to the name of another existing firm which also carries similar business. It is done to protect the interest of public who deals with firms and to protect the firm having goodwill.

(*b*) The name of the firm should not violate provisions relating to trade names and goodwill.

(*c*) A partnership firm cannot use the word 'Limited' at the end of its name.

(*d*) As per Section 53(3) of this Act, "a firm name shall not contain any of the following words namely Crown, Emperor, Imperial, King, Queen, Royal or words expressing or implying the sanction, approval or patronage of the government. However state government, by an order in writing, may signify its consent to the use of such words as part of firm name."

DISTINCTION BETWEEN PARTNERSHIP AND CO-OWNERSHIP

Sharing of profit or gross return arising from property owned and held by those persons does not make them partners rather they are called 'co-owners'. Sons who inherit some property from the father are not partners though the property is being managed jointly and its income is being shared by them, such relationship is regarded as co-ownership. However, if the sons enter into an agreement to run coffee house in that building and share its income, they will be considered as partners.

Thus co-ownership is an essential element of partnership. But every co-owner is not necessarily a partner. Difference between these two can be understood on the basis of the following points:

(*i*) ***Formation:*** Partnership is formed on the basis of an agreement, but co-ownership is formed by operation of law.

(*ii*) ***Business:*** Partnership is formed obviously for conducting lawful business activities, while as co-ownership is not necessarily created for doing business.

(*iii*) ***Profit sharing:*** Profit sharing is an essential element of partnership, but it is not necessary in case of co-ownership.

(*iv*) ***Mutual agency:*** There exists relation of mutual agency in partnership and partners are both agent as well as principal. There is no mutual agency in co-ownership.

(*v*) ***Transfer of interest:*** In partnership, partner has no right to transfer his interest to an outsider without consent of other partners. While as in co-ownership, the co-owner can transfer his share to third person.

(*vi*) ***Right of lien:*** Partner has a right of lien for the expenses which he incurs with regard to the property of the firm. But co-owner has no such lien on the joint property for any expenses or debts incurred in that regard.

(*vii*) ***Maximum limit:*** In partnership maximum limit of partners in banking business is at 10 and ordinary business at 20, but there is no such limit applicable in co-ownership.

(*viii*) ***Partition of property:*** Partners cannot demand partition of property of the firm. It is only in the event of dissolution of the firm, they can get surplus, if any, distributed among them. But the co-owner has a right to claim partition of property being owned by co-owners.

(*ix*) ***Vesting of property:*** During the tenure of partnership, no partner is allowed to deal with properties as if these were his own. But co-owners are at liberty to deal with their share of property the way they like.

PARTNERSHIP AND JOINT HINDU FAMILY

Joint Hindu family is one of the forms of business organisation in India. It is governed by the provisions of Hindu law. According to Section 5 of the Indian Partnership Act, "the members of Hindu Undivided Family carrying on a family business are not partners in such business." Partnership differs with joint Hindu family on the following grounds:

(*i*) ***Formation:*** Partnership is formed by an agreement, but joint Hindu family is created by status or operation of law.

(*ii*) ***Governance:*** Partnership is governed by the provisions of Indian Partnership Act 1932, but a joint Hindu family business is governed by Hindu Law.

(*iii*) ***Female member:*** Female member can become a partner in the firm, but female member cannot become member in joint Hindu family business. Even after the passage of Hindu Succession Act 1956, the female member does get co-sharer interest, but cannot become co-partner herself.

(*iv*) ***Status of minor:*** Minor cannot become partner in a partnership business, but he may be admitted to the benefits of the partnership. In a joint Hindu family, male minor is as good as any other member of the family.

(*v*) ***Number of members:*** There is limit on the number of partners in a firm, but there is no such limit as to maximum number of the members in a joint Hindu family business.

(*vi*) ***Right to manage:*** Every partner of a firm has a right to participate in the management of business of the firm. In joint Hindu family, this authority rests with *karta* only; but he may allow other members to participate.

(*vii*) ***Admission of new partner:*** No person can be admitted as a partner without consent of all other partners. But a person becomes a member just by virtue of having birth in the family.

(*viii*) ***Liability of members:*** In partnership, the liability of all partners is unlimited. They are jointly and severally liable for the debts of the firm. But in joint Hindu family, business the liability of '*karta*' is unlimited and other members have limited liability.

(*ix*) ***Dissolution:*** A partnership is dissolved on the death or insolvency of a partner, but such events do not lead to dissolution of joint Hindu family.

(*x*) ***Right to demand accounts:*** Every partner has a right to inspect and copy books of accounts. A member of joint Hindu family has no right to ask for account pertaining to the past dealings.

(*xi*) ***Profit sharing:*** Partners share profit in the ratio as determined by agreement. But no such ratio is predetermined in joint Hindu family business.

(*xii*) ***Mutual agency:*** In partnership, every partner can bind other partners by his acts done in the ordinary course of business of the firm. But in joint Hindu family, it is only a '*karta*' who can bind other members by his acts.

PARTNERSHIP AND JOINT STOCK COMPANY

A joint stock company is also one of the important forms of modern business organisation. It is a body corporate which is brought into existence by fulfilling legal formalities which are prescribed in Indian Company Act 1956. Once the company comes into existence it acquires legal separate status in the eyes of law. It also gets certain rights, such as right to sue, to be sued, right to own and transfer property *etc.* It differs from partnership organisation on the following grounds:

(*i*) ***Formation:*** A company is formed by fulfilling legal formalities laid down in Indian Coy Act 1956, while as partnership is created by an agreement among the persons who are willing to form it.

(*ii*) ***Number of members:*** In a joint stock company, for the private one maximum number may go up to 50, and in case of public limited coy it is unlimited. But in partnership, for doing ordinary business it is 20 and for banking business it is 10 only.

(*iii*) ***Separate legal entity:*** After the formation of the company it gets legal entity which is separate from the entity of its members. But in partnership, the firm has no separate legal entity, rather it is a collective entity of all partners.

(*iv*) ***Liability:*** In joint stock company, the liability of members is generally limited up to face value of their holding. But the liability of partners is unlimited.

(*v*) ***Transfer of share:*** In joint stock company, the members are free to transfer their shares subject to the provisions of Indian Company Act. But no such transfer of interest is allowed in a partnership.

(*vi*) ***Dissolution:*** The company enjoys perpetual succession, it goes on and goes on, irrespective of status of the members but in partnership, if the partner dies or becomes insolvent it is dissolved.

(*vii*) ***Management of business:*** In a joint stock company, an authority to manage the business, is vested in the board of directors, while as the business of partnership is managed by the partners.

(*viii*) ***Mutual agency:*** A member of the company does not stand in any relation of agent and principal with the company. But in a partnership, relation of mutual agency exists. Every partner is an agent as well as principal.

(*ix*) ***Ownership of property:*** In a joint stock company the members are owners of the company but do not own the property of the company, while as the partners are co-owners of the property of a firm.

Types of Partnership

A partnership may be of the following types:

(*i*) ***Partnership at will:*** While entering into partnership agreement, if no provision is made regarding duration of partnership and determination of partnership relation, such partnership is known as 'partnership at will'. According to Section 7 of this Act, partnership at will is a "partnership, where no provision is made in the contract between the partners for the duration of their partnership or for the determination of their partnership."

In other words, an existence of partnership depends on the will of the partners. Such relation of partnership is created for indefinite period of time. And at any point of time, by giving a notice to other partners, partnership can be dissolved. Thus with regard to partnership at will, no provision in the agreement is made:

(*a*) regarding the period for which partnership is formed.

(*b*) regarding when the relation of partnership will come to an end.

(*ii*) ***Partnership for fixed period:*** When the relation of partnership has been created for a particular period of time, it is known as 'partnership for fixed period of time'. At the expiration of that fixed period, the partnership will automatically come to an end.

(iii) Particular partnership: When the relation of partnership is created for doing or completing particular venture, the partnership is known as 'particular partnership'. On the completion of such venture relation of partnership will come to an end.

(iv) General partnership: When the scope of partnership has not been made clear in partnership agreement, it is known as 'general partnership'. Such partnership is formed for carrying on business of general nature.

Types of Partners

The relation of partnership is purely contractual is nature. The rights, liabilities and the role of a partner may be subject to terms and conditions of the agreement. Thus the partners in a partnership firm may be put in the following categories:

(i) Active or actual partner: A partner who participates in the management of business of a firm is known as 'active partner'. He deals with outsiders in various transactions. He remains so active that everyone dealing with the firm knows him as partner. It is therefore, in case of his retirement from the firm he is required to give public notice to this effect. Failure to do so, will make him liable to outsiders for the acts of other partners even after his retirement. Active partner binds himself and other partners of the firm by his acts, which he does in the ordinary course of dealing.

(ii) Dormant or sleeping partner: The partner, who does not take active part in the conduct of business of the firm, is known as 'sleeping partner'. Since he is not involved in the management of a firm, he is not known as a partner to outsiders, dealing with the firm. Like other partners, he invests capital and shares the profits of the business. He is equally liable along with other partners for the acts of active partner and debts of the firm. His position is similar to that of an undisclosed principal. Though he does not participate in the conduct of business, he is entitled to have an access to books and accounts of the firm and can have a copy of them.

At the time of retirement he is not required to give public notice. He will be not liable for the acts of the firm after his retirement.

(iii) Nominal partner: A nominal partner is one, who does not have real interest in the business of partnership firm. This is so because he does not invest capital, does not share profits, and does not participate in the management of a business. He is partner of the firm, simply because he has allowed the firm to use his name. As a result of it, he becomes liable as a partner towards third party for the acts and debts of the firm. Such partner who is dormant in all other respects except his liability is well known to the outsiders. It is because his name is being used in the firm.

(iv) Partner in profit only: By incorporating necessary clause in a partnership agreement, if the partner is allowed only to share profits not a loss, he is known as 'partner in profit'. Such partner does not have a right to participate in the management of a business. He invests the capital like other partners. He is equally liable for the acts and debts of the firm towards third party. As a partner he has joint as well as several unlimited liability. For all other practical reasons, the outsiders who deal with the firm believe that he is partner of the firm, therefore the level of his liability is same as of other partners.

(v) Partner by estoppel or holding out: When the person, who is not really a partner but induces other person to believe that he is a partner in a particular firm, and the person so induced makes transaction with the firm. The person inducing will be liable as a partner to the person making transaction. Such partner is known as 'partner by holding out' or 'partner by estoppel'. This is so because, later on if he denies his being a partner, he will be stopped from doing so.

According to Section 28 of this Act, "Anyone, who by the words spoken or written or by conduct represents himself to be a partner in a firm, is liable as a partner in that firm to anyone who has on the faith of any such representation given credit to the firm, whether the person representing himself or represented to be a partner does or does not know that the representation has reached the person so giving credit."

To become partner by holding out or estoppel, the following conditions must be satisfied:

(*a*) The person must have represented in terms of written or oral statement or by his conduct to be a partner.

(*b*) Third party must have made a transaction with the firm on the belief that, the person making representation is a partner of the firm.

A retiring partner, who has not given a public notice of his retirement can also be held liable on the grounds of holding out, if his name is being used by other partners in the firm. It is because, third party may continue to believe that he is still a partner.

However in the event of death of a partner, if firm continues a business, and uses deceased partner's name, the legal heir of deceased partner will not be held liable for the acts of the firm done after the death of a partner.

Example: Shyam was doing a business in the name of Shyam & Ram Company. He employed Ram as a manager of the business. The third parties dealing with the firm treated him a partner of the firm, Ram neither objected nor disclosed his true status in a business. Thus, Ram was considered as a partner by estoppel.

LEGAL POSITION OF A MINOR IN PARTNERSHIP

Minor has no contractual capacity and the relation of partnership arises out of a contract. Therefore a minor cannot become partner in a partnership firm.

According to Section 30 of this Act, "though, a minor cannot be a partner in a firm, but with the consent of all partners for the time being, he may be admitted to the benefits of partnership by an agreement executed through his guardian with other partners."

Minor on being made beneficiary in the firm, the following points with regard to his position must be taken into account:

(*i*) Minor can be admitted to the benefits of a partnership, only with the consent of all partners.

(*ii*) The partnership must be in existence, before a minor is admitted to benefits.

(*iii*) If the minor is made full-fledged partner in a partnership deed such deed or agreement would be invalid and cannot be even enforced *vis-a-vis* the remaining partners.

Rights of Minor

Such minor beneficiary has got the following rights:

(*i*) In accordance with agreement, the minor has a right to share profits and the property of the firm.

(*ii*) He has a right to have an access to, inspect and copy any of the accounts of the firm. But he does not enjoy this right in respect of the books which may contain confidential matters like trade secrets *etc.*

(*iii*) If the due share of profit and property is not being given to him, he has a right to file suit against the firm. However, he can exercise this right only when he leaves the firm.

(*iv*) He can become partner in the firm on attaining age of majority and shall be entitled to the same share which he was getting as a minor.

(*v*) On attaining majority he has also an option to leave the firm and if necessary he can sue the firm for accounts and his share in profits and property of the firm.

Liabilities of a Minor

The minor beneficiary is liable only to the extent of his share in profits and property of the firm. He is not liable personally to the third parties, so his private property cannot be used for paying debts of the firm.

However, on attaining majority, if he becomes a partner in the firm, he shall be personally liable to third parties for all acts of the firm since he was admitted to the benefits of the firm.

Position on Attaining Majority

Within six months of his attaining majority, such minor beneficiary has to decide and give a public notice that whether he will remain in the firm as a partner or leave the firm. Failing which, it will be legally presumed that, he has chosen to become a partner in the firm.

(i) When he becomes a partner: According to Section 30(7) of this Act, if a minor, on becoming major becomes a partner his rights and liabilities are:

(*a*) He becomes personally liable, to third parties for all acts of the firm done since he was admitted to the benefits of the firm.

(*b*) His share in the property and profits of the firm will remain same as he was getting as a minor beneficiary.

(ii) When he leaves the firm: According to Section 30(8) of this Act, if such minor, on becoming major decides to leave the firm his liabilities and rights are:

(*a*) His rights and liabilities will continue to be those of minor beneficiary up to the date of making public declaration that he is leaving the firm.

(*b*) His share in profits and property is not liable for any acts of the firm done after such public declaration.

(*c*) He is entitled to sue the partners for his share of profits and property in the firm.

REGISTRATION OF FIRMS

Registration implies getting the firm's name and other particular recorded with the registrar of the firm of the area in which the place of business of the firm is situated.

The Partnership Act does not provide for compulsory registration of firms. It is rather optional for the firms to get themselves registered. By getting the firm registered its existence is recognised. But indirectly by putting certain disabilities and disqualifications on the unregistered firm, the law has made registration of the firm desirable one.

These disabilities are such that, sooner or later, every firm gets itself registered. However, registration does not create partnership. It is only a reliable evidence of existence of a partnership. It provides protection to the outsiders dealing with the firm.

Time of Registration

Indian Partnership Act does not provide anything about the time of registration. The firm may get itself registered at any point of time during its existence. But the firm must ensure that it gets registered before filing any suit in the court.

Prithvi Singh *vs* Vazir Khan (1950, 52, BOM. L.R.862). In this case, the firm filed a suit against A, on 10 October, 1944, but the firm was unregistered. Subsequently the firm got registered on 16 March 1945. It was held that the subsequent registration could not rectify defect in the suit which existed at the time of filing it.

Procedure of Registration

Since registration of the partnership is not legally compulsory, it can be done at any stage of its existence. The procedure of registration is very simple. In order to get the firm registered, the partners are required to submit duly filled application in the prescribed form along with prescribed fee. Such application has to be submitted to the registrar of the firm of the state in which any place of business of a firm is established.

Application form, must be signed by each partner or by their authorised agents. It must contain the following informations:

(*a*) Name of the firm.

(*b*) The place or principal place of business of the firm.

(*c*) The name of other places, where the firm carries on business.

(*d*) The date when each partner joined the firm.

(*e*) The name in full, and permanent addresses of the partners.

(*f*) The duration of the firm.

When the registrar is satisfied that the provisions of Section 58 of this Act have been duly complied with, he shall record an entry of the statement in a register and will issue certificate of registration.

Registration is affected, as soon as application in the prescribed form with the prescribed fee is submitted to the registrar.

Effects on Non-Registration

Though the registration of partnership firm is not legally compulsory, but for all practical purposes it is equally desirable. If the firm does not get registered it suffers from the following legal disabilities (Section 69):

(i) No civil suit against the firm or partners: While conducting business of a partnership firm, any dispute may arise among the partners of the firm. And the disputes may be related to right and obligations arising from partnership agreement or Partnership Act. A partner of unregistered firm cannot file suit against the firm or a partner in the civil court for enforcing his rights. Thus if a partner is not paid his share of profit, he cannot claim it through the court. He can do it if: (*a*) the firm is registered, and (*b*) the names of the persons suing appear as partners in the register of firms.

(ii) No civil suit against third parties: Unregistered firm or partner of such firm cannot file a suit against third parties dealing with the firm, in the civil court, for enforcing rights arising from a contract. But as against it, the right of third parties to sue upon unregistered firm is not at all affected.

(iii) No claim of set-off: On filing a suit by third party, against the unregistered firm, in the court, the firm cannot claim right of set-off in that suit. The set-off is a process of mutual adjustment of the debts of two parties against each other. Section 69(3) of this Act provides that, "if a suit is filed, against an unregistered firm for a claim, the firm cannot take an advantage of a set-off for its own claim on the same party."

However, the right of set-off is not affected if the claim of set-off is less than Rs.100 in value [Section 69(4b)].

Rights not Affected by Non-Registration

Non-registration does not affect the following rights:

(*i*) Right of third to sue the firm or its partner.

(*ii*) The right of firm or partners of a firm having no place of business in India.

(*iii*) The right of the firm to file a suit for claiming set-off of less than Rs.100.

(*iv*) The right of partner to sue for dissolution of the firm or for the account of dissolved firm or right to realise property of dissolved firm or for recovering money from the firm's debtors.

(*v*) The right of official assignee or court to realise the property of insolvent partner and to bring an action on behalf of insolvent partner.

(*vi*) The right of firm or partners to file suit to enforce rights arising other than from a contract.

REVIEW QUESTIONS

1. Define 'partnership' and describe essential characteristics of it.
2. How would you test and determine whether a group of a persons are having relationship of partnership?
3. Explain briefly the procedure of registration of firms. Discuss various consequences of non-registration.
4. 'Registration of firms is not legally compulsory but in practice it is desirable for all practical purposes.' Comment.
5. Describe the various types of partners.
6. Can a minor be admitted to a partnership? If so, what are his rights and liabilities during minority and after he has attained age of majority?
7. Explain the circumstances under which a person can be made liable as a partner, even if he is not a partner.
8. Write notes on:

   (*a*) Partner by holding out and estoppel.

   (*b*) Partnership at will.

   (*c*) Minor as a partner.

   (*d*) Effects of non-registration.

9. Distinguish between:
   (*a*) Partnership and Co-ownership.
   (*b*) Partnership and Joint Hindu family business.
   (*c*) Partnership and Join stock company.
10. Comment on:
   (*a*) Indian Partnership Act has effectively ensured the registration of firms without making it compulsory.
   (*b*) Sharing profit is an essential feature but not a conclusive proof for testing relation of partnership.
   (*c*) Relation of partnership is contractual and does not arise from a status.
   (*d*) Minor can be beneficiary in a partnership firm.
   (*e*) Mutual agency is a core of relation of partnership.

PRACTICAL PROBLEMS

1. G and M, purchased a restaurant jointly and incurred additional expenses for purchasing pottery and utensils for it. They contributed money for that equally. Later on, they leased out restaurant on rent basis. The rent is also being equally shared by them. Are they partners, if not why?
2. Ram and Shyam agree to work together as interior decorators, but that Ram shall receive all profits and shall pay remuneration to Shyam. Are Ram and Shyam partners? (Hint: No).
3. A and B are running a business jointly. They took a loan from C on the condition that he will get 25% of profits of business over and above normal rate of interest. This sharing of profit could make him partner in the business. Examine it. (Hint: No).
4. A, B and C carried on a business for a profit. C did not contribute capital, and labour and does not share a profit. But he has lent his name to be used in the firm. Is he liable to every outsiders who provided credit to the firm, believing that he is a partner in that firm? (Hint: Yes).
5. A is a partner in the firm along with B and C. He has invested capital, and shares profit with them in equal ratio. He is equally liable like other partners for the acts of the firm. But he does not take any part in the conduct of the business therefore not known to outsiders dealing with firm. After sometime he gets retired from the firm. Is he required to give public notice to this effect? (Hint: No).

6. A is a sole proprietor of the firm. He admits B as a partner on the following conditions:

   (*a*) B will not bring any capital, and (*b*) He will not be responsible for any loss. (*c*) He is to receive Rs.1,000 p.m. in lieu of profits, and (*d*) He is not to make any contract on behalf of the firm. Discuss legal position of B.

7. A and B purchased a taxi to use it in partnership. They plied the taxi for about a year. A without the consent of B disposed of the taxi. B brought an action to recover his share in the sale proceeds. A resisted B's claim on the plea that the firm was unregistered, will B succeed in his claim? (Hint: No).

8. Ram and Shyam were partners in an unregistered firm which carries on a business of manufacturing sugar. For the supply of sugarcane the firm paid sum of Rs. 5,000 in advance to C. Due to shortage of supply of sugarcane C could supply sugarcane of Rs. 4,000 only. Later on, the partnership firm was dissolved. In a division of assets of the firm debt of Rs. 1,000 was allotted to A. Can A file suit to recover the amount? (Hint: No).

9. A, B and C run an unregistered firm. The firm has borrowed a sum of Rs.10,000 from D. And the firm has also supplied goods worth Rs. 2,000 on credit to him. D, files a suit against the firm for the recovery of Rs. 10,000. Can firm, claim a debt of Rs. 2,000 to be adjusted against it? (Hint: No).

10. A tells B in the presence of C that C is a partner with him in the firm. C does not contradict the statement. B, believing that C is a partner lends Rs. 50,000 to A. Is C liable for this debt? (Hint: Yes).

11. Ram is a minor. He was admitted to the benefits of the partnership firm. On his attaining age of majority he intends to become a partner in the firm. But other all partners of the firm do not allow him to be a partner. Can Ram become full-fledged partner by giving public notice? (Hint: No).

12. A and B are partners in the firm. C is working with them as a manager. C represents himself as a partner before D. D believing on his representation, sells goods to the firm for Rs. 10,000 on credit. The firm fails to repay this amount, can D recover it from C? (Hint: Yes).

■■■

16

Rights, Duties and Relation of Partner

LEARNING OBJECTIVES

- Understand the mutual rights and duties of partners.
- Analyse the basic concept of property of the partnership firm.
- Remember various types of authority being enjoyed by a partner.
- Analyse the concept of implied authority of a partner and implications of restrictions imposed on it.
- Develop clarity regarding rights and duties of incoming and outgoing partners.

INTRODUCTION

Partnership is formed by an agreement between two or more persons. The rights and duties of partners are usually determined in accordance with terms and conditions of an agreement. But partnership agreement may not provide for all duties and rights of partners. In such case relevant provisions of Indian Partnership Act apply automatically.

To understand mutual rights and duties of a partner, mutual agency which exists among them must be considered. A partner is both a principal as well as an agent. He is therefore bound by the acts of other partners and also binds other partners by his act. The mutual rights and duties of a partners are governed by:

(*a*) Terms and conditions of an agreement.

(*b*) Relevant provisions of Indian Partnership Act.

(*c*) Mutual agency *i.e.*, nature of relationship.

The provisions of the Indian Partnership Act governing mutual rights and duties of a partners are:

RIGHTS OF A PARTNER

Unless otherwise agreed by the partners every partner has the following rights as prescribed in the Act.

(i) ***Right to take part in the conduct of business:*** Every partner of the firm has a right to take part in the conduct and management of the business. But to promote common interest of the firm, the right to manage business may be given only to those partners who are willing and capable of managing it.

(ii) Right to be consulted: All partners have a right to be consulted in all important matters which affect the business of the firm. Every partner can express his opinion on the matter concerning the business. But all decisions, however will be made by majority except certain matters, such as change in the nature of business, reconstitution of the firm etc.

(iii) Right to have access to books: Every partner has a right to have an access to and inspect and copy of the books of the firm.

However minor beneficiary has an access only to the books of account. He has no right to inspect other books of the firm which contain confidential matters like trade secrets, etc.

(iv) Right to share profits: Generally at the time of making agreement, the ratio of sharing profits is determined. In the absence of it, partners are entitled to share profits in equal ratio.

(v) ***Right to interest on capital and advance:*** Normally, no interest is allowed on the capital contributed by the partners. However the partnership agreement may provide for the payment of interest on capital. Such interest shall be payable only out of profits.

If the partner has provided loans and advances over and above the capital, he is entitled to interest on such advances @ of Rs. 6 per cent per annum. Such interest shall be paid even if there are losses.

(vi) Right to indemnity: The partner is entitled to right of indemnity in the following two situations:

- (*a*) A partner has to be indemnified by the firm for all expenses and liabilities incurred by him in the ordinary and proper conduct of business.
- (*b*) He will also be entitled to claim reimbursement of all payments made by him in an emergency for protecting the firm from losses provided he acted in a manner as a person of ordinary prudence would have acted in a similar circumstance in his own case.

(vii) Right to use property of partnership: Every partner is a joint owner of partnership property. He is entitled to hold and use that property exclusively for the purpose of business of the firm.

(viii) Right to stop admission of a new partner: Relation of partnership is fiduciacy in nature. Thus every partner has a right to stop admission of a new partner into the firm. New partner can be admitted only with the consent of all other partners.

(ix) Right to retire from the firm: Each partner has a right to retire from partnership either as per the terms of partnership agreement, or with the consent of all other partners.

(x) Right to share profit after retirement: Unless otherwise agreed, an outgoing partner has the right to claim a share in profits of the firm or claim interest @ 6 per cent per annum finally settled. This rule will also be applicable in case of death of a partner.

(xi) Right not to be expelled: Every partner has a right to continue in the partnership. He cannot be expelled from partnership by majority of partners, unless such power is conferred by partnership agreement and exercised in good faith for the benefit of the firm.

(xii) Right to do competing business: Every outgoing partner has a right to carry on a competing business, but he cannot (*a*) use the firms name, (*b*) solicit firm's customers, and (*c*) represent the firm.

(xiii) Right in emergency: In any emergency situation, every partner has a right to do all such acts which are reasonably necessary for protecting the firm from the losses.

DUTIES OF PARTNER

Duties of partner may be put into two categories:

1. Mandatory duties, and 2. Duties subject to agreement.

1. Mandatory Duties

Relation of partnership is based on mutual trust and confidence. Each partner is expected to act in good faith and carry on the business of the firm for mutual benefit and common interest of all partners.

Section 9 of this Act clearly states that all partners of the firm are bound:

(*a*) to carry on the business of the firm to the greatest common advantage.

(*b*) to be just and faithful to each partner.

(*c*) to render true accounts and full information of all things affecting the firm, to any partner or to his legal representative. Section 10 of this Act lays down that every partner shall indemnify the firm for loss caused to it by his fraud in the conduct of the business of the firm.

These duties of a partner are absolute provisions of the Act, and are therefore mandatory. These cannot be changed by an agreement among the partners.

2. Duties Subject to Agreement

In addition to the duties laid down under Sections 9 and 10 of this Act, there are some other duties of partners as given in the Act which are subject to agreement made by partners. The partners can change these duties by making necessary provisions in the partnership agreement. These duties are:

(a) Duty to attend work diligently: In the conduct of the business, whatever duty is assigned to the partner, he must attend those diligently. It means he must perform assigned job in a reasonable manner with full care and required efforts. The partner, who takes part in the conduct of business is known as 'managing partner'. And he is under obligation to perform assigned work without any remuneration unless the provision contrary to it is made in the agreement.

(b) Duty to share losses: In the absence of any agreement, every partner is liable to contribute equally for the losses arising in the business.

(c) Duty to indemnify for willful neglect: It is the duty of partner to indemnify the firm for any loss caused to it by his willful neglect in the conduct of the business of the firm. The willful neglect implies an act of neglect done deliberately and intentionally. However, the partner will not be liable for mere error of judgment or for the acts done in good faith.

(d) To hold and use property of the firm for the firm: It is the duty of every partner to use the property of a firm exclusively for the purpose of business of the firm. In any case, such property is not to be used for any purpose other than firms business. In case, the partner makes use of property for his own purpose, he will have to give full account of profits to the firm, arising out of that purpose.

(e) Duty to account for personal profit: In case the partner makes out any profits or gain from any transaction of the firm or from the use of firms property or business connections of the firm, *etc.,* he has to account for that profit and pay it to the firm.

(f) Duty not to do any competing business: The partner may be restrained from carrying similar business to that of the firm, so long as he is partner in the firm. If partner does such business he is bound to account for and pay to the firm all profit made out of such business.

(g) Duty not to assign interest: A partner cannot assign his rights and interests which he has got in the firm to an outsider without the consent of all other partners.

(h) Duty to be liable jointly and severally: Every partner of the firm is jointly and severally liable for the acts of the firm so long as he is a partner in the firm.

Relation of Partner with Third Party

Each partner in the firm acts both as an agent and the principal. His relationship with third party dealing with the firm is governed by this relationship of mutual agency. Section 18 of this Act clearly states that from the point of view of the third party, a partner is an agent of the firm for the purpose of business of the firm. In that capacity he binds all other partners by his acts done on behalf of the firm provided such acts are done in the ordinary course of the business and in the name of firm. So all partners are liable for such acts to third parties.

AUTHORITY OF PARTNER

The law of partnership is nothing but an extension of law of agency. Every partner has an authority to bind other partners by his acts. Such authority may be either express authority or implied authority.

(i) Express authority: An authority which a partner derives from express agreement, among the partners is known as 'express authority'. The partners of the firm are free to give any authority to any of them by a mutual agreement. And the acts done by the partner within his express authority are binding on the firm.

(ii) Implied authority: In addition to express authority, the partner has implied authority. The partner derives implied authority from his position in the firm. Implied authority of a partner is an authority to bind the firm by his act which are done beyond the extent of express authority. In other words, where there is no agreement or it is silent, the acts of partner for doing routine business of the firm come under implied authority.

According to Section 19 of this Act, "the act of a partner which is done to carry on in usual way, business of the kind carried on by the firm, fall within the scope of implied authority and therefore are binding on the firm." The firm will be bound by such acts provided the following condition are satisfied:

(*a*) The act done by the partner must relate to the normal business of the firm. If such acts are usually not done in that type of business the firm will not be bound by such acts. Such as an exporter of a readymade garments places an order for a huge quantity of liquor in the name of firm. This act does not relate to normal business of export of readymade garments, therefore will not fall within the scope of implied authority of partner.

(*b*) The act must have been done in a usual way of carrying on the firms business. In order to decide which act is usual or unusual to the business, the nature of business and the usage of trade will be taken into account.

Example: A and B are partners in a retail business. Goods were sold on credit to C. Later on, A received the amount of credit sale from C on behalf of the firm. B does not know of this receipt. A utilises this amount for his personal use. The firm cannot claim the amount from C, because receiving money from debtor is an act done in usual course of business being conducted by A and B, thus this act done by A is binding on the firm.

(*c*) The act must have been done in the firm's name or implies an intention to bind the firm. The act to be within implied authority must have been done in the name of the firm and of course on behalf of the firm otherwise it will not be binding on the firm.

Acts within implied authority of a partner: The implied authority of a partner shall normally include the following acts:

(*a*) Purchasing, on behalf of the firm, goods in which the firm deals or which are used in the firms business.

(*b*) Selling the goods of the firms.

(*c*) Receiving payment of debts due to the firm and giving receipts.

(*d*) Settling accounts with third parties dealing with the firm.

(*e*) Employing servant necessary for carrying on firm's business.

(*f*) Borrowing money in the credit of the firm.

(*g*) Pledging goods of the firm as security for the purpose of getting loans.

(*h*) Drawing, accepting and indorsing negotiable instruments on behalf of the firm.

(*i*) Employing solicitor to defend action against the firm.

Restriction on Implied Authority

Section 19(2) of this Act has restricted the scope of implied authority of a partner. According to this Section, in the absence of any usage or custom of trade contrary to implied authority of a partner does not allow him to:

(*a*) Submit to arbitration a dispute relating to the business of the firm.

(*b*) Open bank account on behalf of the firm in partner's own name.

(*c*) Compromise or relinquish any claim or portion of a claim by the firm.

(*d*) Withdraw a suit or a proceeding filed on behalf of the firm.

(*e*) Admit any liability in a suit or proceedings against the firm.

(*f*) Acquire immovable property on behalf of the firm.

(*g*) Transfer immovable property belonging to the firm.

(*h*) Enter into partnership on behalf of the firm.

However, the partners, by mutual agreement can restrict or extend the implied authority of a partner. According to Section 20 of this Act "that the partner in a firm may by contract between themselves, extend or restrict the implied authority of a partner. However any act done by a partner on behalf of the firm which falls within his implied authority binds the firm unless, the person with whom he is dealing knows of the restrictions or does not know or believe that partner to be a partner."

Thus any restrictions on the implied authority of a partner imposed by an agreement will not be applicable against a party who have no knowledge of it. However according to Section 19(2) of this Act restrictions given under this provisions are effective against every party dealing with the firm whether he has knowledge of it or not.

(iii) Partner's authority in emergency: In addition to express and implied authority the partners also enjoy special authority in emergency situations. According to Section 21 of this Act, "In an emergency a partner will have an authority to do all such acts to protect the firm from a loss as a prudent man would undertake under similar circumstances in his own case." These acts do not form part of the implied authority but, nevertheless, would bind the firm.

Example: The partners of the trading firm by an express agreement, have decided that no partners would have the authority to sell goods of the firm above the value of Rs. 5,000 without the consent all other partners. Due to decrease in demand the prices have come down. And one partner to save the firm loss sold whole stock of Rs. 50,000 without consent of other partners. The firm is bound by such act of partner because he has acted reasonably to protect the firm from further losses.

Implied Authority and Third Party

All partners are liable towards third party for the acts of partner which fall within the scope of his express and implied authority. The liability of a partner to third party for such acts can be understood on the basis of following points:

(i) Extension or restriction of partner's implied authority: The scope of an implied authority can be changed by extending or restricting it. It can be done by a mutual agreement among the partners. But third parties are not bound by such restrictions unless they have knowledge of these restrictions.

Example: A and B are partners in the firm. A has authority to sell the goods up to the extent of Rs. 2,000 on credit. C is an outsider who buys the goods worth Rs. 5,000 on credit from the firm without any knowledge regarding the limit which has been fixed for A. Later on, when it comes to his knowledge that A has an authority to sell the goods on credit up to only Rs. 2,000. He refuses to pay. But he is bound to pay entire amount because he knew nothing about the limit of credit sale fixed for A at the time of buying the goods.

(ii) Effect of admission by a partner: For the purpose of conducting business of the firm a partner is considered as an agent. Thus any admission or representation made by a partner about affairs of the firm is sufficient evidence against the firm, provided an admission is made in ordinary course of business of the firm and is made regarding an affair related to firms business.

(iii) Effect of notice to an acting partner: General rule of agency states that notice to an agent is a notice to the principal on the matters regarding agency. It is equally applicable on partnership. Thus a notice on any matter or affairs related to the firm's business to a partner who habitually receives it in the ordinary course of business of the firm is taken to be notice to the firm.

However, this rule is not applicable in case of a fraud committed by a partner and third party against the firm.

(iv) Liability of a partner for the acts of the firm: Every partner is jointly and severally liable to third party for all acts of the firm while he is a partner. In other words, for the acts of the firm third party can sue each partner individually or jointly with other partners. To apply this rule following conditions must be satisfied:

(*a*) Liability of the partners is joint as well as several.

(*b*) Partners are liable only for the acts of the firm.

(*c*) Partners are liable only for those acts of the firm which were done while they were partners.

(v) Liability for wrongful acts of a partner: On committing any wrongful act by the partner, the firm will be liable for such act to the third party. Section 26 of this Act clearly provides that if on account of wrongful act or omission of a partner, acting in ordinary course of business or with the authority of other partners, some loss or injury is caused to any third party or other partners, or any penalty is incurred, the firm is held liable to the same extend as the partner.

Example: A, B and C are partners in a newspaper business. A who is the editor of a newspaper publishes defamatory article against D without checking its validity. The firm will be liable for this act of editor, partner to D, because the act was done in the usual course of business.

(vi) Liability of firm for misappropriation by partner: The firm will also be held liable for misapplication on the part of a partner. According to Section 27 of this Act "that the firm is liable to the third parties where (*a*) a partner acting within his apparent (express) authority, receives money or property from third person and misapplies it, or (*b*) the firm in the course of its business receives money or property from third party and money is misapplied by any of its partner while it is in the custody of the firm."

Example: A, B and C are partners in the firm D who is a debtor of the firm repays his debt of certain value to C. C does not inform A and B about it and misuse the money so received. The firm will have no claim against D, and D will be discharged of his debt.

POSITION OF INCOMING AND OUTGOING PARTNERS

When there is any change in the composition of partnership either by incoming and outgoing of partner, it is known as 'reconstitution of the partnership firm'. The reconstitution takes place when:

(*i*) A new partner is admitted.

(*ii*) A partner retires.

(*iii*) A partner is expelled.

(*iv*) A partner is declared insolvent.

(*v*) A partner dies.

(*vi*) A partner transfers his interest to another person.

Incoming Partner (Section 31)

Admission of a partner: A person can be admitted as a partner in the existing firm with the consent of all other partners. This is so because the relation of partnership is based on mutual trust and confidence. This rule is, however, subject to provisions of partnership agreement.

The liability of newly admitted partner will start from the date of his admission. Such partner is not liable for any act and debt of the firm before his admission. But this rule has the following exceptions:

(*a*) By mutual agreement, such partner may undertake to share liability for the past acts of the firm. But this does not give any entitlement to the creditor to proceed against him for the recovery of old debts, unless (*i*) the new firm (after reconstitution) has assumed liabilities of old firm. (*ii*) the creditors have accepted the new firm as their debtor and discharged the old firm from its liabilities. (*b*) A minor, admitted to the benefits of the firm, who on attaining age of majority elects to become a partner in the firm shall be personally liable to third parties for all acts of the firm done since he was admitted to the benefits of the firm.

Outgoing partner: An outgoing partner is one who ceases to be a partner in the firm in the event of his retirement, expulsion, insolvency, death or transfer of his share.

I. Retirement of a partner (Section 32): Any partner may retire from the firm in any of the following ways:

(*a*) with the consent of all other partners.

(*b*) in accordance with an express agreement among the partners.

(*c*) where the partnership is at will, by giving notice in writing to all other partners of his intention to retire.

Liability of retiring partner: A retiring partner continues to remain liable for all acts of the firm done before his retirement or acts pending at the time of his retirement. However, he may be discharged from his liability to third parties by mutual agreement. He may be discharged only if the creditors agree.

A retiring partner also continues to remain liable for the act of the firm even after his retirement until public notice is given to this effect of the retirement.

Similarly, partners of reconstituted firm continue to remain liable for the acts of retired partner even done after retirement until public notice is given to this effect. Such public notice may be given either by retiring partner or by the firm.

However, dormant or sleeping partner need not give such public notice at his retirement.

SCARF *vs* JARDINE (1872, APP CAS.145). In this case, A, B, C and D are partners. A and C are active partners and D is sleeping partner. C and D retire from the firm without giving public notice. And A and B take E into partnership continuing old firms name. F gives credit to the firm as newly constituted without having notice of change. F, can sue either the old partners or the new partners. But D who is sleeping partner is not liable for it.

Rights of retiring partner: A retiring partner has two rights:

(*a*) He may carry on a business competing with that of the firm and may advertise such business. But in the absence of any agreement contrary he cannot:

(*i*) use the name of the firm.

(*ii*) represent himself as carrying on the business of the firm.

(*iii*) solicits the old customers.

By mutual agreement some more restrictions can also be imposed on the retiring partners.

(*b*) In case, after the retirement of a partner, the remaining partners continue to carry on business with the property of the firm, without making final settlement of account, the retiring partner is entitled to claim either:

(*i*) such share of profits earned after his retirement which is attributable to the use of his share of property of the firm.

(*ii*) interest of @ 6 per cent per annum on the amount of his share in the property.

II. Expulsion of a partner (Section 33): The general rule of partnership is that a partner cannot be expelled by his co-partners. However the expulsion of a partner is possible if following three conditions are satisfied:

(*a*) The power to expel a partner is available by an express agreement between the partners.

(*b*) The power has been exercised by majority of partners.

(*c*) The power has been exercised in good faith and for the benefit of the firm.

A partner who is getting expelled from the firm will have same liability and rights as those of a retiring partner.

III. Insolvency of a partner [Section 42(*d*)]: To declare the person insolvent, order of adjudication is passed by the court. Thus as soon as such order is passed for declaring partner as an insolvent he ceases to be a partner from that date. The legal effects of insolvency of a partner are:

(*a*) Insolvent partner ceases to be a partner from the date of passing order of adjudication by the court.

(*b*) Unless there is a contract to the contrary the firm will be dissolved on the date of order of adjudication.

(*c*) The estate of insolvent partner is not liable for any act of the firm after the date of order of adjudication.

(*d*) The firm will not be liable for any act of insolvent partner after the order of adjudication.

The share of insolvent partner in the assets of the firm will be used for paying the debts of the firm first, remaining part will be used for the personal debt of insolvent partner.

IV. Death of partner [Section 42(*c*)]: On the death of partner, partnership firm will automatically be dissolved. But according to Section 42 (c) of the Act, "partners by contract may agree that the firm shall not be dissolved on the death of a partner."

In case the firm is not dissolved by the death of partner the estate of deceased partner is not liable for any act of the firm which is done after his death. No public notice is required to absolve deceased partner from the liability. But other partners continue to be liable for the act done on behalf of the firm.

BAGEL *vs* MILLER (1903, 2, K.B,212). In this case, M was a partner in the firm. The firm had ordered some goods during M's lifetime. But those goods were delivered after the death of M. It was held that M's estate is not liable for the price in an action for goods sold, because there was no debt due in respect of goods during lifetime of M.

V. Transfer of partners interest (Section 29): A partner can transfer his interest in partnership to an outsider. Such transferee will not become a partner without the consent of other partners. Neither he can participate in the conduct of business nor inspect books of account. He can simply claim his share in the profits of the firm.

According to Section 29 of this Act, the transferee of partner's interest becomes entitled to the following rights:

(*a*) He is entitled to get share of profit of the transferring partner as per the agreement between transferring partner and his co-partners.

(*b*) On dissolution of the firm, he has a right to get share in the assets which transferring partner was entitled to.

(*c*) On dissolution, he can claim an account from the date of dissolution for finding out his share.

With regard to reconstitution of the firm, it is to be noted that, whenever some change takes place in the constitution of the firm, the mutual rights and liabilities of the old partners in the reconstituted firm continue to remain same as they were before reconstitution.

PROPERTY OF THE FIRM

All partners of the firm are joint owners of its property. They have a right to hold and use the firm's property exclusively for the purpose of business of the firm. Thus it becomes necessary to ascertain, what constitute the property of the firm.

Generally the partners are free to determine property of the firm and separate property of individual partners. They can do it by mutual agreement. In absence of such agreement, the source from where it has been acquired and the purpose and the manner it is being used for, will determine whether it belongs to the firm or not.

According to Section 14 of this Act, where there is no contract, contrary to it, the property of the firm includes:

(*a*) All properties, rights and interests originally brought to the stock of the firm.

(*b*) The property acquired by purchase or otherwise by or for the firm.

(*c*) The property acquired with money belonging to the firm.

(*d*) The goodwill of the business of the firm.

(*e*) Personal profits earned by the partners.

Section 16 of the Act provides that subject to contract between the partners:

(*a*) If a partner derived any profits for himself from any transaction of the firm or from the use of property or business connections of the firm or the firm's name, he shall account for that profit and pay it to the firm.

(*b*) If a partner carries on competing business, he shall account and pay to the firm all the profits made by him in that business.

Therefore, whatever is brought to the common stock of firm and whatever is added to or obtained by means of this common stock during the lifetime of partnership either directly or by conduct of the business, is included in the property of the firm.

However, if the property of a partner is used for the purpose of the business of the firm, it does not become firm's property, unless partners express an intention to make it so.

Example: A, B and C are partners in the firm. The firm purchases a piece of land in the name of A, but payment is made by the firm. The piece of land will be deemed to be the property of the firm, unless there is contrary intention to it.

REVIEW QUESTIONS

1. Explain various mutual rights and duties of partners in the absence of express agreement between them.
2. What do you mean by 'implied authority'? Describe the contents of implied authority of a partner.
3. Can implied authority of a partner be restricted? Are third parties affected by restriction placed on an implied authority?
4. Discuss express authority, implied authority and authority of a partner in emergency.
5. Explain various provisions of the Indian Partnership Act with regard to transfer of interest by a partner to an outsider.
6. What is extent of implied authority of a partner? How far is a firm liable to third parties for the acts of an individual partners?
7. Explain rights and duties of (*a*) incoming partner and (*b*) an outgoing partner.
8. Define 'partnership property'. Explain how far is the partnership property liable for separate debts of the partner.
9. Discuss the rights and liabilities of a retiring partner.
10. Write notes on:
    (*a*) Implied authority
    (*b*) Expulsion of a partner
    (*c*) Partnership property
    (*d*) Mandatory duties of a partner
    (*e*) Transfer of partner's interest
    (*f*) Reconstitution of the firm
11. Comment on:
    (*a*) Relation of a partner with the third party is governed by mutual agency.
    (*b*) Scope of implied authority of a partner can be changed by mutual agreement.
    (*c*) Liability of a partner is joint and several.
    (*d*) Partner is an agent of the firm for the purpose of the business of the firm.

PRACTICAL PROBLEMS

1. Ram and Shyam are partners in a firm. Ram was asked to buy sugar for the firm. Without informing Shyam he sold entire sugar at market price to the firm and earned huge profits. Is he liable to account for this profits to the firm? [Hint: Yes, Section 16(*a*)].
2. A and B are partners in a firm. A purchases shares in his name by utilising money of the firm. Later on, other partner ratifies this act. Are the shares included in the property of the firm? (Hint: Yes, Section 14).
3. A, B and C are carrying on a partnership business. A is authorised to manage cash. A habitually comes late and as a result of it firms business is suffering. B and C want to expel A and admits D as a new partner. Are they entitled to do so? (Hint: Yes, under special circumstances A's misconduct.)
4. A, B, C and D are carrying on their business in the name of Hindustan Minerals. C is a sleeping partner. C and D get retired from the business without giving public notice. E joins as a new partner. Examine the liability of C, D and E for the acts and debts of the firm.
5. A, B and C are partners in a trading firm. By an agreement between them, they decide that no partner shall have a right to buy or sell goods beyond the limit of Rs. 5,000 without the consent of other partners. Ignorant of this restrictions, T sells goods worth Rs. 10,000 to C who does not consult his partner for this transaction. Examine the liability of partners in this regard.
6. A, B and C are partners in a business. D, a debtor of the firm, repays his debt of Rs. 5,000 to A who does not inform B and C about this payment and misuse the money. Would D be discharged from his debt? (Hint: Yes).

17

Dissolution of Partnership Firms

LEARNING OBJECTIVES

- Get conceptual clarity of dissolution of partnership firm and compare it with dissolution of partnership.
- Examine the various modes of dissolving partnership firm both with an intervention of court or without court's intervention.
- Enumerate and remember various rights, duties and liabilities of partners on the dissolution of a firm.
- Be clear about how the accounts are settled among partners on the dissolution of a firm.
- Analyse legal implications of various grounds on which partnership firm gets dissolved such as fraud and misrepresentation etc.

INTRODUCTION

Relation of partnership arises out of a contract. By making such contract the partners stand in the relationship of a mutual agency. A partnership is said to be dissolved if the relationship among partners gets changed. Such change in relationship occurs when the firm is reconstituted. In other words, partnership is dissolved if a new partner is admitted or a partner get retired or becomes insolvent, dies or is expelled.

Thus dissolution of partnership means breakdown of the relation of partnership between some of the partners. In case of dissolution of partnership, the firm may not be dissolved if some of the partners agree to continue the business in the name of the same firm.

On the other hand, dissolution of partnership firm means there is complete breaking up of relationship which existed between all the partners of the firm, business is closed and its affairs are wound up.

According to Section 39 of this Act, dissolution of partnership between all partners of the firm is called 'dissolution of the firm', and follows that partnership may be dissolved without dissolving the firm. Dissolution of partnership involves a change in the relation of the partners but it does not end partnership.

Distinction between Dissolution of Partnership and Dissolution of Partnership firm

(*i*) In a dissolution of partnership, the relationship between some of the partners gets changed or broken. In this case firm is reconstituted and business continues. But in the event of dissolution of partnership firm, there is complete breakdown of partnership relation between all partners. Thus no question of reconstitution arises.

(*ii*) In a dissolution of partnership, the business of the firm is carried by the reconstituted firm, may be in the same name. But dissolution of partnership firm implies breaking down of relation among all partners and closing down the business of the firm.

(*iii*) Dissolution of partnership firm has wider legal implication as compared to dissolution of partnership. Thus dissolution of a firm necessarily involves dissolution of partnership, whereas dissolution of partnership does not necessarily involve dissolution of a firm.

Meaning of Dissolution of Firm

Dissolution of a firm implies the dissolution of partnership between all the partners of firm. It occurs when there is complete breakdown of relationship between all partners. In such situation, the business of a firm is completely stopped, affairs of the firm wound up, assets are realised, liabilities paid off and surplus is distributed among the partners.

Sections 40 to 44 deal with the various modes of dissolution of a firm. A firm may be dissolved with or without the intervention of the court.

I. Dissolution Without the Order of Court

A partnership firm may be dissolved without the intervention of the court in any one of the following manners:

(i) Dissolution by mutual agreement (Section 40): Partnership is created by an agreement. In the same way if all partners agree they can also dissolve it.

Generally the required provisions in this regard, are incorporated in a partnership agreement. In addition to it, the partners can enter into new agreement for dissolving the firm.

Example: A, B and C are partners in a firm. At a certain point of time some kind of misunderstanding develops among them, which seriously affects their relationship. By a mutual agreement among all of them they can dissolve the firm.

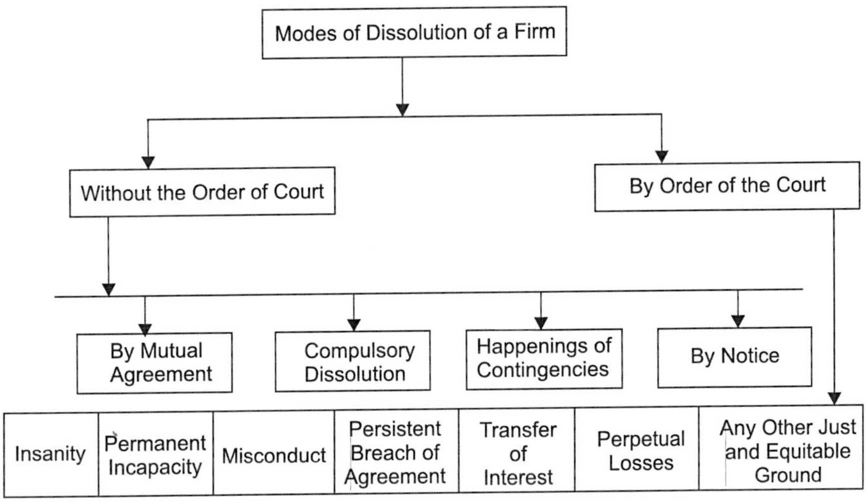

(ii) Compulsory dissolution (Section 41): A firm gets compulsorily dissolved in the following cases

(*a*) If all partners, or all but one partner, of the firm are declared insolvent or,

(*b*) On the happening of any event, the business being carried out by the partners becomes illegal.

Example: A, B and C are partners in a firm doing wholesale trading of wheat. At a particular point of time due to scarcity of the wheat, the government has enacted a law debarring the trading firms from wholesale trade of wheat. The firm has to be dissolved compulsorily.

In case the firm engaged in doing more than one business (Section 42), the illegality of one business shall not necessitate dissolution of the firm.

(iii) Dissolution on the happening of certain contingencies (Section 42): In the absence of any contract, contrary to it, a firm will be dissolved on the happening of the following contingencies:

(*a*) Where the firm is constituted for a fixed term it would automatically be dissolved at the expiration of that period.

(*b*) Where the firm is constituted for completion of one or more adventures or undertakings, the firm is dissolved when those adventures or undertakings have been completed.

(*c*) Death of partner in all cases dissolved the firm provided there is no intention contrary to it in an agreement. But generally the required provisions are made in the agreement, not to dissolve the firm, but to continue it in the form of newly constituted firm.

(*d*) Insolvency of all partners would also lead to compulsory dissolution of the firm. In case, if any one of the partner is declared insolvent, other partners reconstitute the firm provided nothing contrary to it is there in agreement.

(iv) Dissolution by notice (Section 43): In case of partnership at will, the firm may be dissolved by any partner by giving a notice to all other partners of his intention to dissolve the firm. The notice must be explicit, absolute, precise and final. It must not be ambiguous, must be made in writing, and must be duly communicated to all partners. The notice once given cannot be withdrawn, unless the consent of all partners is obtained. The firm is deemed to be dissolved from the date mentioned in the notice as the date of dissolution if no date is so mentioned in the notice as the date of communication of the notice [Section 43(2)].

However, a partnership which is not at will cannot be dissolved by notice.

II. Dissolution by Court

Partnership firm may also be dissolved by the order of court. Section 44 of this Act deals with those situations in which the court may pass an order for the dissolution of the firm. Such order may be passed by the court on receipt of petition filed by a partner. Before passing an order, the court must be satisfied that it is in the interest of justice to dissolve the firm.

The court has got discretionary power to dissolve the firm, even before the expiration of that fixed period for which it was formed. While admitting petition for dissolution, the court will give opportunity to other partners to put forward their defence against passing an order of dissolution. It is only after evaluating all evidences before the court that the court shall pass order for dissolution. The court may order dissolution of a firm on any of the following grounds:

(i) ***Insanity:*** A partner on becoming insane, is not capable of understanding the contract and forming rational judgment. In such case, the court may allow dissolution. The court may ensure that it is in the interest of both insane partner and other partners to dissolve the firm. The court may not issue such order of dissolution, if the sleeping partner of the firm become insane. This is so because, such partner does not participate in the management of firm's business [Section 44(*a*)].

The estate of insane partner would be liable for the acts and debts of the firm, until the firm is dissolved.

(ii) ***Permanent incapacity:*** When a partner has become permanently incapable of performing his duties as a partner, any other partner can file petition for the dissolution of firm. In case of temporary incapacity on the part of partner, the court will not pass an order for the dissolution [Section 44(b)].

WHITWELL *vs* ARTHUR. In this case, a partner in a firm had an attack of paralysis. Another partner of the firm filed a petition for the dissolution of the firm. The court refused to pass an order of dissolution because as per the opinion of doctor paralysis was of temporary nature and the patient's condition was improving.

(iii) ***Misconduct:*** The court has discretionary power to dissolve the firm on the ground of misconduct of a partner. To provide sufficient ground for dissolution, the misconduct must be of such a nature, as to affect adversely the conduct of firm's business.

However it is not necessary that the misconduct which provides ground of dissolution should be connected with partnership business. Conviction for travelling without ticket or the adultery by one partner with another partner's wife are good grounds for the dissolution of the firm [Section 44(c)].

ABBOTT *vs* GRUMP (1870,5 BANG,L-R-109). In this case a partner committed adultery with the wife of another partner of the firm. It was held that immoral conduct can be ground for dissolution of the firm, as it can be said to be against the concept of partnership which requires utmost good faith and mutual confidence among the partners of a firm.

(iv) ***Persistent breach of agreement:*** Relation of partnership arises out of an agreement. Every partner is expected to follow all provisions of that agreement in the larger interests of partnership.

A partnership may be dissolved by the court on the ground that the partner other than the partner filing a suit:

(*a*) willfully or persistently commits breach of agreement relating to the affairs of the firm, or

(*b*) otherwise so conducts himself in matters relating to the business that, it is not reasonable or practicable for the other partners to carry on the business in the partnership with him.

However, the court may not interfere when the breach of agreement is occasional. But when the partner conducts in such a way that to carry on business has become impracticable for other partners, the court will interfere in it.

The following are the reasonable grounds for ordering dissolution of a firm on the ground of persistent breach of agreement:

(*a*) Refusal and neglect of the duties by a partner.

(*b*) Persistent breach of partnership agreement.

(*c*) Keeping erroneous accounts and not accounting for receipts.

(*d*) Misappropriation of partnership income by a partner.

(*e*) Continuous quarrelling and such a state of animosity as precludes all reasonable hopes of reconciliation.

(*f*) The act of one partner habitually charging other with gross misconduct in the business of the firm [Section (44(*d*)].

(v) *Transfer of interest:* The relation of partnership is of utmost good faith and mutual confidence. Thus the partner is not allowed to transfer his interest to an outsider.

The court at the instance of any other partner, may dissolve the firm when a partner, in any way has:

(*a*) transferred the whole of his interest in the firm to a third party, or

(*b*) allowed his share to be charged on account of a decree passed by court towards payment of liabilities of that partner, or

(*c*) allowed his share to be charged on account of a decree passed by court towards payment of liabilities.

(vi) *Perpetual losses:* The court may dissolve a partnership firm, when it is of the opinion that, the business of firm cannot be carried on except at a loss. In other words, the firm might be suffering continuous losses and it is apparent that even in future losses are inevitable. Thus the very basic purpose of earning profits gets defeated. In such situation, the court may order dissolution at the instance of any partner [Section 44(*f*)].

(vii) ***Any other just and equitable ground:*** The court may also pass an order of dissolution on any other grounds which seem to be just and equitable to the court. The court has been given widest possible discretion to dissolve the firm. The power of the court is based on principles of natural justice, equity and good conscience. Therefore while ordering dissolution on this ground, the court must ensure that the above principles are fully taken care of. The court may use its discretion to dissolve the firm, if there is a complete deadlock in the management, there is a want of mutual confidence and good faith among partners, or the partner can no longer perform their duties and so on.

The partnership firm will be considered as dissolved from the date of judgment unless the judgment provides otherwise.

Consequence of Dissolution

Dissolution of partnership firm is a long process. It involves winding up of a affairs of partnership, closing up its business and dismantling its functional structure. In this process, the assets of the firm are realised, liabilities are paid out and surplus, if any is distributed among the partners or their legal representatives.

Consequent to the dissolution of a partnership firm, the partners have the following rights and liabilities.

I. Rights of Partner on Disssolution

(i) ***Right to have business wound up:*** Every partner or his representative has the right as against all other partners or their representatives to have business wound up and the property of the firm to be applied in the payment of debts and liabilities of the firm and also as distribution of surplus among the partners or their representatives according to their rights.

This right of the partner is called 'Partner's lien' and is available to a partner only on the surplus of the assets of the firm (Section 46).

(ii) ***Right to have the debts of the firm settled out of the properties of the firm on the dissolution of the firm:*** The debts of the firm are settled out of the properties of the firm and if there is any surplus it is utilised towards the payment of the private debts of the partners. In the similar manner, the private estate of the partner is first utilised for paying private debts and if there is a surplus it may be utilised for the settlement of the debt of the firm (Section 49).

(iii) Right to personal profits earned after dissolution: So long as the proceedings of the dissolution continue, it is the duty of the partner not to earn any personal profit or to make private gain out of any transaction related to the firm. In case he makes out such gains or profits he must share it with other partners.

(iv) Right to return of premium on premature dissolution: Any partner who joins the firm for a fixed period of time and had paid a premium (Goodwill) and the firm is dissolved before that fixed time, has a right to the return of the whole or part of the premium. The amount of premium depends on the terms of the admission and the length of time for which he had been partner in the firm.

However, such partner is not entitled to claim any return of the premium when the premature dissolution is (*a*) due to death of a partner (*b*) due to misconduct of partner, who paid premium, and (*c*) where there is no provisions for the return of premium or any part of it.

AIREY *vs* BARBAM (1861,29,BEAV, 620). In this case A and B entered into a partnership for five years. A paid premium to B. The partnership was dissolved within two years as a result of mutual disagreement due to A's failure to devote time to the business as agreed. It was held that no part of premium was payable because the dissolution has been caused by the misconduct on the part of A.

(v) Right where partnership contract is rescinded for fraud or misappropriation: Like general contract, the contract of partnership can also be rescinded on the ground of fraud and misrepresentation. The use of fraud and misrepresentation by a partner gives a right to another aggrieved partners to claim for damages. Section 52 of this Act provides the following rights to partners, where the partnership contract is rescinded on the ground of fraud or misrepresentation. These rights are available to the partners who is entitled to rescind the contract:

(*a*) *Lien on surplus assets:* He has a right of lien on the surplus assets, which are left after the debts of the firm have been paid. This right can be used with regard to sums paid by him for purchasing share in the firm or for the capital contributed by him.

(*b*) *Right of subsogation:* The partner who is rescinding a contract has a right to become creditor of the firm for the payments which he makes out of his personal assets to payoff the debts of the firm.

(*c*) *Right to be indemnified:* The partner, rescinding the contract has a right to be indemnified by the partner or partners who made use of the fraud or misrepresentation against all the debts of the firm.

However after having discovered fraud if the right of rescinding the contract is not used within reasonable period of time, such right will be lost.

(vi) ***Right to restrain partners or their representatives from the use of the firms name or property:*** During the time gap between dissolution and final winding up, the partners can restrain each other from using any property of the firm or name of the firm for his own benefit. But to make such restraints effective, agreement is to be made by the partners to this effect.

However on the dissolution of a firm if, such agreement has not been entered into among the partners, any partner can use the name of the firm.

Similarly, if any partner or his representative has purchased the goodwill of the firm, he cannot be restrained from using firm's name for his own purpose.

(vii) ***Right to restrain from carrying on similar business:*** In anticipation of dissolution, if all partners make an agreement for not doing business similar to that of firm for a particular period of time within local limits, such restraint is also valid provided such restrictions are reasonable.

II. Liabilities of Partners on Dissolution

On the dissolution of the partnership firm, the partners have the following liabilities:

(i) ***Continuing liability of partners after dissolution:*** On the dissolution of a firm, public notice to this effect must be given. It is only after such public notice, the partners are absolved of the liability to third party.

Thus in the absence of such notice every partner of the dissolved firm continues to be liable to third party for any act done, by any of them after the dissolution. And such acts are deemed to be acts done before dissolution.

However, it should be noted that the following shall not be liable for the acts done after the dissolution of the firm, even though, public notice of dissolution has not been given:

- (*a*) The estate of partner who has died.
- (*b*) The estate of a partner who has been declared insolvent.
- (*c*) The sleeping or dormant partner who has retired from the firm (Section 45).

Example: A, B and C are partners in a firm engaged in trading of rice. They decide to dissolve the firm on 7 August 2001, but fail to give public notice to this effect and continued the business of the firm even after that date.

On 10 August, A enters into contract with D in the firm's name to deliver 10 quintals of rice to D. The firm is liable for the consequence of the contract, because public notice on dissolution has not been given.

(ii) Liability for winding up the affairs of the firm and completing unfinished transaction: According to Section 47 of this Act, after the dissolution of the firm the authority of each partner to bind the firm and other mutual rights and obligations of the partners continue so far as, may be necessary for the following two purposes:

(*a*) To wind up the affairs of the firm *e.g.*, disposing of the property, realising the amount due from the debtors and paying to creditors and so on.

(*b*) To complete transactions begun but unfinished at the time of the dissolution *e.g.*, taking delivery of goods ordered before dissolution and paying for them.

Thus the partner's liability in respect of the above matters continues even after the dissolution of the firm. The firm, however, is not bound by such acts of a partner who has been declared insolvent.

III. Settlement of Accounts

After the dissolution of partnership firm, accounts of the firm are settled. The manner for settling accounts is usually provided in the partnership contract. If however, partnership contract is silent on the matter, the accounts of the dissolved firm shall be settled according to the rules given under Sections 48, 49 and 55 of this Act. These rules are:

(i) Sharing of deficiency: According to Section 48(*a*) "the losses including deficiencies of capital shall be paid first out of profits, next out of capital and lastly, if necessary, by the partners individually in proportion in which they were entitled to share profits."

This implies that if the assets of the firm are insufficient to discharge the liabilities of the firm, the deficiency arising out of it will be shared by the partners in their profit, sharing ratio and they will payout from their private estate.

Example: A, B, C and D are partners in a business sharing profits and losses equally. A dies and the firm is dissolved. On the date of dissolution it was found that the capitals of partners were Rs. 20,000 each of A and B, and C and D at Rs. 10,000 and Rs 5,000 respectively. The outside liabilities stood at Rs. 6,000 and total value of assets at Rs. 41,000. That the deficiency worked out at Rs. 20,000 (20,000 + 20,000 + 10,000 + 5,000 + 6,000 = 61,000 – 41,000).

This would be equally shared by B, C, D and A's legal heir Rs. 5,000 each.

(ii) Application of assets: The assets of the firm including any sum paid by the partners to make up deficiency of capital shall be applied in the following order:

(*a*) In paying off the debts of third parties.

(*b*) In paying to each partner ratably what is due to him from the firm for advance distinguished from capital.

(*c*) In paying to each partner ratably what is due to him on account of capital.

(*d*) The surplus if any shall be divided among the partners in the proportion in which they were entitled to share profits.

Example: A, B, C were partners in a firm. They share profits and losses equally. The accounts of the firm shows that on the date of dissolution partner's capital was A: Rs. 20,000 B: Rs. 10,000 and C: Rs. 2,000. A had advanced Rs. 2,000 as a loan to the firm. The outside liabilities were at Rs. 13,000. On dissolution the assets could realise at Rs. 50,000. This amount shall be utilised first to pay Rs. 13,000. For third party liability next Rs. 2,000 to A for the repayment of his loan and then Rs. 32,000 to A, B and C for their capital (20,000 + 10,000 + 2,000). And the remaining amount of Rs. 3,000 will be shared equally by A, B and C (profit sharing ratio).

Suppose the assets realised at Rs. 42,500 only resulting a loss of Rs. 4,500 (47,000 – 42,500). This loss will be shared by A, B and C equally reducing their capital balances to Rs. 18,500 Rs. 8,500 and Rs. 500 respectively. Thus the amount of Rs. 42,500 will be utilised as:

(*a*) Rs. 13,000 to pay outside liabilities.

(*b*) Rs. 2,000 to pay A's loan.

(*c*) Rs. 27,500 to pay the capital balances to A, B and C.

(iii) Partners of firms are jointly and severally liable to pay the debts of the firm: It makes clear that even the private property of the partners can be utilised for the payment of debts of the firm, if necessary. Not only this, the third party has the right to realise the whole amount of the debt from any partner. But this rule is subject to the provision of Section 49 of this Act which clearly states that the private assets of any partner shall be applied first to pay his private debts and then if their is any surplus it can be applied to pay the debts of the firm if necessary.

Thus partner's private assets can be used for the payment of firm's debts provided:

(*a*) His private liabilities have been paid off.

(*b*) That firm's assets are insufficient to pay firm's debts.

However it should be noted that the assets of the firm are first used for the payment of firm's liabilities and surplus, if any can be utilised for the payment of private debts of a partner only to the extent of his share in the property of the firm.

(iv) Loss arising from insolvency of partner: After having distributed loss on dissolution if a capital account of a partner shows some deficiency he shall bring necessary amount of cash so that other partners can be paid balance standing in their capital account. But if the partner whose capital accounts shows deficiency becomes insolvent and he may not be capable of bringing necessary amount, it would result in additional loss to the partners. Now the question may arise that in which ratio other partners will share the loss.

In the absence of any contract contrary to it the rules laid down in **GARNER *vs* MURRAY** case will be applicable. These are:

(*a*) That the loss of realisation of assets shall be borne by all partners in their profits sharing ratio.

(*b*) That the loss on account of deficiency of capital of insolvent partner shall be borne by solvent partners in the ratio of their capital standing just before dissolution.

Example: A, B and C are partners in business. They share profits and losses equally. On the dissolution of a firm the assets were realised at Rs. 35,000 liabilities at Rs. 47,000. Partner's capital was A: Rs. 20,000; B: Rs. 10,000 and C Rs. 2.000. A has advanced a loan of Rs. 2,000, a loss of Rs. 12,000 will be borne by A, B and C equally and their capital will be reduced to A: Rs. 16,000, B: Rs. 6,000 and C Rs. (–2,000). On becoming insolvent C could bring only Rs. 500. Thus the deficiency of Rs. 1,500 will be shared by A and B in the ratio of their capital just before dissolution; *e.g.* (2 : 1).

(v) Sale of goodwill: Section 55 of this Act provides that on the dissolution while settling accounts goodwill shall be, subject to contract between the partners be included in the assets and it may be sold either separately or along with other property of the firm.

After dissolution of the firm, if the goodwill of the firm has been sold a partner may:

(*a*) Carry on the business of old firm.

(*b*) Solicit the business from the customers of dissolved firm.

(*c*) Advertise such business.

But subject to an agreement between him and buyer he may not (*a*) use the firm's name, (*b*) represent himself as carrying on the business of old firm, and (*c*) solicit the business from the customers of dissolved firm.

However, any partner may enter into an agreement with the buyer of goodwill that such partner will not carry on any business similar to that of dissolved firm within local limits for a particular period of time.

Public notice: A public notice is to be given under Section 72 of this Act in the following cases:

(*a*) On the retirement or expulsion of a partner of registered firm.

(*b*) On the dissolution of registered firm.

(*c*) On the election of minor beneficiary to become or not to become partner on attaining age of majority in a registered firm.

The public notice relating to the above situations is given:

(*a*) to the registrar of firms.

(*b*) by publishing it in a Official Gazette and at least in one vernacular newspaper circulating in the district, where the firm to which it relates has its place or principal place of business.

Besides the above, public notice must be given when any change takes place in the constitution of the firm or nature of firm affecting interest of third party.

Consequences of failure to give public notice: It includes:

(*a*) When the minor beneficiary attains age of majority and fails to give public notice within six months whether he will remain in the firm as a partner or leave the firm. He will be liable as partner at the expiration of 6 months period.

(*b*) In case of retirement, expulsion or dissolution, if public notice is not given so retired, expelled and other partners continue to be liable as partners to third party for any act done by them.

REVIEW QUESTIONS

1. What do you understand by 'dissolution of a firm'? How can a firm may be dissolved?
2. Under what circumstances the court can order dissolution of a firm on a suit by a partner?
3. Explain rights and liabilities of partners on the dissolution of partnership.
4. Distinguish between dissolution of partnership and dissolution of partnership firm.
5. Describe the rules regarding settlement of accounts of a firm after dissolution.
6. Where goodwill has been sold after dissolution of the firm, what are the rights of a partner in relation to business of the firm?
7. How would deficiency arising out of dissolution and in the event of insolvency of a partner be made good?
8. Describe rights of a partner when the firm has been dissolved on the ground of fraud or misrepresentation of a partner.
9. Write notes on:
   (*a*) Dissolution of partnership firm
   (*b*) Public notice
   (*c*) Dissolution without the order of court
   (*d*) Firms debts *vs* Private debts
   (*e*) Garner *vs* Murray rules

PRACTICAL PROBLEMS

1. Ram and Shyam are in a partnership business. They decide to dissolve partnership by mutual agreement from 1st January. They do not give public notice to this effect but continue their business. In the month of February, Mohan sells some goods on credit to Ram in the name of the firm. Mohan was not aware of dissolution. Is he entitled to recover the amount from the firm? (Hint: Yes).

2. A, B and C are partners in the firm engaged in trading of sugar. A is a sleeping partner and does not participate in the conduct of business. After a year, A gets retired but does not give public notice to this effect. D who makes some transaction with the firm believing that A still is a partner. Is A responsible for this transaction? (Hint: No).

3. A and B entered into partnership agreement for 5 years. A paid Rs. 50,000 as premium to B. The partnership was dissolved after 2 years by mutual agreement resulting from A's failure to devote time to business as agreed. Can A claim return of premium on the grounds of premature dissolution? (Hint: No).
4. A was doing a timber business. He enters into partnership agreement with B on a condition that the goodwill of a business will be the sole property of A alone. After the death of A, his wife joined partnership on same conditions. When the term of partnership was about to expire, Mrs. A found that B was preparing a list of firm's customers. She brought an action to restrain him from doing so. Examine legal consequences of such action.
5. A was admitted into a firm as a partner and brought a sum of Rs. 20,000 as premium. The partnership firm is 'partnership at will'. After the period of 2 years the firm is dissolved on the grounds of misconduct of another partner. A demands return of premium paid to the firm. Will he succeed? (Hint: No).
6. A, B, C and D are four partners in a firm sharing profits and losses equally. On March 2005, D becomes insolvent and the partners decide to dissolve the firm. On that date their capital balances were at Rs. 30,000; Rs. 20,000 and Rs. 5,000 respectively. The outside liabilities were at Rs. 40,000. The assets of the firm realised Rs. 81,000. Calculate how much will be paid to A, B and C assuming that nothing is realised from the property of D.
7. A, B and C were partners in a firm. They were sharing profits and losses in the ratio of 4 : 3 : 3. After working together for 5 years, they agreed to dissolve the firm. After having paid off third party debts and repaying capitals of the partners, there was a surplus of Rs. 50,000. What shall each partner will get?
8. A, who is a minor admitted to the benefit of partnership by B and C. After sometime A attains age of majority but fails to give public notice within 6 months. He was not interested in remaining in the firm as a partner. Examine his liability for the acts of the firm.

SALE OF GOODS ACT, 1930

18

Law of Sale of Goods

LEARNING OBJECTIVES

- Understand the meaning of contract of sale and compare it with hire-purchase agreement and bailment.
- Develop conceptual clarity regarding subject matter of contract of sale.
- Get familiar with various types of goods and find out their suitability for sale and agreement to sell.
- Examine legal consequence of getting goods destroyed.

INTRODUCTION

Sale and purchase of goods is a common transaction in business. Sale of goods in business fetches revenue which is further used in the process of business. Sale and purchase of goods cannot be separated from each other because same transaction is a sale for one party and purchase for another. Transactions in the nature of sale of goods form the subject matter of the Sale of Goods Act, 1930 (applicable to whole of India except Jammu & Kashmir).

The Act covers topics such as the concept of sale of goods, warranties and conditions arising out of sale, delivery of goods and passing of property and other obligations of the buyer and the seller, the documents of title to goods and the transfer of ownership on the basis of such documents. The Act came into force on 1 July 1930. It extends to the whole of India, except the state of Jammu & Kashmir.

Certain minor amendments were made in this Act in 1963. This Act closely follows the provisions of English law on the contract of sale. Since contract of sale is a specific contract, thus general provisions of Indian Contract Act are also applicable on it, provided they are not inconsistent with the express provisions of Sale of Goods Act.

This Act contains rules and regulations relating to various types of contracts of sale of goods. It provides definition of various terms and covers detailed rules to the effect of destruction of goods, conditions and warranties applicable on this contract, transfer of ownership and delivery of goods and position and remedial measures available to an unpaid seller.

DEFINITION AND ESSENTIALS OF A CONTRACT OF SALE

Section 4 (1) of this Act defines a contract of sale "as a contract, whereby the seller transfers or agrees to transfer the property in goods to the buyer for a price."

From the definition the following essentials of a contract emerge:

(*i*) ***There must be at least two parties:*** Contract of sale is a specific contract. It is formed by offer and acceptance. To form it, either the buyer will give an offer to buy goods to the seller or the seller gives an offer to buyer. On acceptance of such offer the contract of sale is formed. The buyer is a person who will make payment of price to the seller and will get ownership as well as possession of goods. And the seller transfers or promises to transfer ownership and handsover the possession to the buyer in consideration of money.

However, it is to be noted that a person cannot buy his own goods or cannot sell his goods to himself.

C.M. TRANSPORT COMPANY *vs* ITO (1966). In this case a company resolved to transfer some buses to a partnership firm consisting of certain persons who were also the members of the company. Income Tax officer considered such transfer as a sale, because the company has a legal entity and can be a seller. This decision was upheld by the Supreme Court.

BELL *vs* LEVER BROTHERS LTD. In this case X is the owner of certain good, but he is not aware of this fact. Y pretends to be the owner of goods makes contract to sell them to X who is already owner of those goods. There is no contract between X and Y. However, a part, owner of goods can sell those goods to other part owner as to make him sole owner (Section 4).

Thus two parties having genuine legal entity are needed for making a contract of sale.

(*ii*) ***Subject matter of contract of sale:*** The subject matter of a contract of sale is goods. It includes all types of movable properties such as stock, shares and growing crops *etc.* Sale and purchase of immovable property is not covered by this Act. But it is regulated by the provision of Transfer of Property Act. Similarly, contracts relating to services are not treated as contract of sale.

(*iii*) ***Transfer of property:*** Transfer of property or ownership of goods is an essential feature of the contract of sale. The ownership of goods is transferred from seller to buyer. According to Section 2 (II) of this Act, property or ownership means general property in goods and not a merely special property, which means special interest in goods.

Example: A borrows a sum of Rs. 10,000 from B and pledges his property against this loan to B. In this case, A transfers special property to B by handing over possession, but retains its ownership. Thus it is not a contract of sale.

However, for transfering ownership of goods physical delivery of goods is not necessary.

(*iv*) ***Price consideration:*** In a contract of sale payment of price is made by the buyer to the seller. It constitutes consideration for the promise of the seller. The consideration in a contract of sale must be in money. However, it may be partly in money and partly in goods.

ALDRIDGE *vs* JOHNSON (1857, 7, E & B. 885). In this case, A agrees to exchange with B 100 quarters of barle at $2 p.q. and, for 52 bullocks valued at $6 p.d. and pay the difference in cash. The contract was held a fit contract for sale.

(*v*) ***Essentials of valid contract:*** The contract of sale must possess all essential elements of a valid contract such as lawful consideration, contractual capacity and free consent etc. This is so because, the contract of sale is a species of a general contract.

SALE AND AGREEMENT TO SELL

Every contract of sale involves transfer of ownership of goods, of course, it is transferred from seller to buyer. Where the ownership is transferred just at the time of making a contract it is known as 'Sale'. And if the seller promises to transfer it at some future date, it is known as 'agreement to sell'. Distinction between these two is of a prime importance. The points of distinction between these two are:

(*i*) ***Nature of contract:*** Sale is an executed contract, because ownership has been transferred. While as agreement to sell is an executory contract, because it is yet to be performed.

(*ii*) ***Transfer of property:*** In a 'sale' the property in goods passes to the buyer immediately at the time of making the contract. But in an 'agreement to sell', transfer of property in goods takes place at some future date, may be subject to fulfilment of certain conditions. Till that date seller continues to be the owner of those goods.

(*iii*) ***Nature of rights:*** In a 'sale' general property in goods is transferred to the buyer. And the buyer can exercise all ownership rights in respect of those goods. He gets rights on those goods, which is known as '*jus-in rem*'. The net legal effect of this right is that if something goes wrong with those goods, it is only the owner who has got all sort of rights to deal with those goods such as if the seller would resell those goods, the buyer can recover those from the second buyer. While as, in an agreement to sell, the buyer gets very specific rights which is known as '*jus-in personam*' *e.g.,* right against particular individual. In a nutshell, the buyer has rights regarding those goods only against the seller and nonelse.

(*iv*) ***Risk of loss:*** The golden rule of law is that risk follows ownership. It implies that whosoever is a real owner of goods will bear the risk of getting goods destroyed. Therefore, in a 'sale' when the goods are destroyed even in the possession of seller without his fault, the buyer of those goods will bear the loss. On the other, in an agreement to sell, in case the goods are destroyed, in transit, or in the possession of buyer without his fault, the loss of goods falls on the seller.

(*v*) ***Breach of contract by buyer:*** In a 'sale' if the buyer wrongfully refuses to accept the goods and pay the price, the seller can file a suit against the buyer for the price even if the goods are in his possession. The seller can also exercise right of lien, stoppage in transit and resale. But in an agreement to sell, only remedy available to seller is that he can claim for damage if the buyer fails to accept delivery and pay for goods.

Example: A sells 100 bags of rice to B for Rs. 5,000. B refuses to accept delivery of rice bags. A can file suit against B for price, even the goods are in the possession of A. But if it was an agreement to sell, A is entitled only to claim for compensation on the breach of contract by the buyer.

(*vi*) ***Breach of contract by the seller:*** In a 'sale', if seller makes breach of contract, the buyer gets two rights. The buyer can file suit against seller for damages and can also use the rights to follow property in the hands of subsequent buyer. While as, in an agreement to sell, the buyer can only claim for damages.

Example: Ram agreed to sell a particular horse to Shyam for Rs. 10,000. Subsequently Ram sells same horse to Mohan for Rs. 12,000. In this case, there is an agreement to sell, Shyam can only claim for damages. But had there been a 'sale', Shyam would have recovered horse from Mohan along with a claim for damage.

(*vii*) ***Insolvency of a seller:*** In a 'sale', seller becomes insolvent, while the goods are lying in this possession, the buyer is entitled to claim goods from official receiver, because ownership of those goods is with the buyer. But in case of agreement to sell, the buyer cannot claim goods even if he has paid the price. Buyer's only remedy in this case is to claim rateable dividend for the price paid to seller.

(*viii*)***Insolvency of the buyer:*** In case of 'sale' if the buyer becomes insolvent, price has not been paid, and the goods are in the possession of seller; the official receiver of the buyer will recover those goods from the seller and for the unpaid price, the name of seller will be included in the list of creditors of the buyer. But in an agreement to sell, if buyer becomes insolvent, before paying price, the seller may refuse to hand over the good to the official receiver. This is so because the ownership has not been transferred to the buyer.

SALE AND HIRE-PURCHASE AGREEMENT

Hire-purchase agreement resembles with contract of sale in many respects, but it is distinct from it. A hire-purchase agreement is an agreement for hire, with an option to purchase. Here, buyer agrees to make payment of price in fixed number of instalments. Till the payment of last instalment, ownership of those goods remains with the seller. And the payment made by the buyer till that date is considered as hire-charges for the goods. In case the hire-purchaser makes default in paying any instalment, the seller can recover the goods from buyer and payment of instalment till that will be treated as hire-charge, which cannot be recovered by the buyer.

Thus the hire-purchase agreement, is more likely to be an agreement to sell. It becomes sale after the fulfilment of certain conditions such as payment of last instalment *etc*.

Example: A buys a machine worth Rs. 50,000 on hire-purchase basis from B. Payment is to be made in 10 monthly instalments of Rs. 5,000 each. This is an agreement of hire-purchase. A will become owner of that machine on the payment of the 10th instalment. In case A makes any default regarding payment of any instalment, B has the right to recover the machine from A and treat the payment of instalment as hire-charge.

Hire-purchase agreement is also distinct from sale by instalment payment. In sale by instalment payment, ownership is transferred from seller to buyer on the payment of the first instalment. As the buyer pays instalment it is reduced from the price of goods. Sale by instalment payment is more likely to be a 'sale' for all practical purposes.

Distinction between sale and hire purchase

Basis	Sale	Hire-purchase
Transfer of ownership	In a 'sale' ownership is transferred at the time of making a contract.	In hire-purchase agreement ownership is transferred at some future date, e.g., payment of last instalment.
Nature	Sale is an executed contract.	Hire-purchase is an executory contract.
Contents	Sale includes sale and an agreement to sell.	Hire-purchase includes agreement to sell and bailment.
Termination of contract	In case of a sale, the buyer cannot terminate a contract by returning goods to the seller.	In hire-purchase, the hirer can terminate a contract by returning the goods to the owner.
Transfer of possession	In sale it is not necessary to transfer the possession of good immediately with ownership.	In hire-purchase, physical possession of goods is transferred immediately.
Sales Tax	In a sale, tax is levied at the time of making a contract.	In hire-purchase, sales tax cannot be levied unless it becomes a sale.
Resale	In a sale, the buyer can resell the goods, because he is the owner.	In hire-purchase, the hirer can not resell those goods unless last instalment is paid.
Right	In a sale, the buyer gets the ownership right from the point of time of making a contract.	Hire-purchaser gets rights of ownership only after the payment the final instalment.
Application of Act	In a sale, all provisions of Indian Sale of Goods Act are applicable.	Hire-purchase agreements are governed and regulated by the provisions of the Hire Purchase Act 1972.

SALE AND BAILMENT

Bailment is a contract to deliver goods by one person to another for some purpose on the condition that when the purpose is over, the goods will be returned to the person delivering them. The bailment contract differs with 'sale' on the following grounds:

(*i*) ***Transfer of property:*** In a sale, the general property in goods is transferred to buyer at the time of making a contract. But in bailment specific property in goods passes to bailee, and that too for a temporary period of time such as right to use goods right to possess them and to deal with them according to the instructions of the bailor.

(*ii*) ***Transfer of possession:*** In a sale, possession of goods may or may not be transferred immediately at the time of making a contract. While in bailment, goods are immediately handed over to the bailee.

(*iii*) ***Return of goods:*** In a sale, goods are not returned to the seller. But in bailment, when the purpose is over, the goods are returned to the bailor or disposed of according to his instructions.

(*iv*) ***Consideration:*** In a sale, consideration is given to the seller in the form of money *e.g.*, payment of price. But in bailment, consideration may or may not be present in the form of money such as in gratuitous bailment (without charge) money is not a consideration.

(*v*) ***Use of goods:*** In a sale, the buyer is entitled to possess and use the goods at his own. But in bailment goods will be used according to instructions and terms and conditions of bailment.

SALE AND CONTRACT FOR WORK AND LABOUR

In a contract of sale, physical possession and ownership of goods are transferred from seller to buyer. This differs from contract of 'work and labour', wherein one party supplies some raw material to another, who applies his skill and labour on that raw material. Here, the substance of the contract is the exercise of skill labour and the delivery of the goods is only a subsidiary component. The major element or an essence of a contract for work is the application of skill and labour. In any case the contract for 'work and labour' does not amount to a contract for sale of goods.

Distinction between these two can be understood with the help of following cases.

ROBINSON *vs* GRAVES. In this case, A is engaged as an artist for painting a portrait. B has supplied the necessary materials such as canvas, paint *etc.*, to the painter. A will apply his skill and labour to paint that portrait. Since production of that portrait was considered as a substance of the contract, it was held that it is a contract for work and labour, and not a contract of sale.

LEE *vs* GRIFFIN (1861, 30 L.J.B. 252). In this case a dentist agreed to supply a set of artificial teeth to fit the mouth of a patient. The necessary material was wholly supplied by the dentist. It was held to be a contract of sale.

Example: A supplied a piece of a woolen cloth to B who is tailor for stitching it and making a coat. B used all other necessary materials for stitching that coat. It is a contract of work and labour, because material had been supplied by A and B provided his services. In case, A without supplying that piece of woolen cloth, asked B to make a coat for him, it would have been a contract of sale.

SUBJECT MATTER OF CONTRACT OF SALE

Like other contracts, the Contract of Sale has a subject matter which is 'goods'. The term 'goods' includes all kinds of movable properties including things which can be detached from the earth such as crop of cereals and fruits and grass *etc.*

According to Section 2 (7) of the Sale of Goods Act, the goods includes: "every kind of movable property other than actionable claims and legal tender money, and also includes stock and shares, growing crops, grass and things attached to or forming part of land, which are agreed to be severed before sale or under the contract of sale."

Thus, the following points should be remembered regarding subject matter of contract of sale:

(*a*) Subject matter of contract is 'goods'.

(*b*) The terms 'goods' includes all kinds of movable properties, except legal tender money and actionable claims. Actionable claims implies—claims which can be enforced through the court of law such as claim to recover debt *etc.*

(*c*) Rare, old and antique coins may form subject matter of contract of sale.

(*d*) Immovable properties are not covered under this Act.

(*e*) Things which are attached to land and can be severed from it may also become subject matter of contract of sale, such as growing grass, trees, crops *etc.*

(*f*) Stock and shares have expressly been included in 'goods'.

(g) Similarly things like goodwill, copyright, trademark, patents, water, gas and electricity are all goods and may be the subject matter of contract of sale.

TYPES OF GOODS

The goods forming the subject matter of a contract of sale may be classified as:

(*i*) ***Existing goods:*** Goods, which are in existence at the time of making a contract of sale are known as 'existing goods'. Such goods are in the ownership and physical possession of the seller when hc makes contract of sale. However, in case of sale by an agent or pledgee, goods are possessed by an immediate seller but not owned by him. Rather, the seller may have the authority to sell the goods. Sometimes, bailee or an agent may hold goods on behalf of the owner. Existing goods may be specific, unascertained or ascertained goods.

(*a*) *Specific goods:* According to Section 2 (4) of this Act, 'specific goods means goods identified and agreed upon at the time, when contract of sale in made.' In other words, specific goods must have been separated out from the lot of goods. However, the goods will not become specific, merely because the source of supply has been identified.

Example: A has two horses, one black and another one white. He agrees to sell white horse to B. In this case, the subject matter is specific. But if A has two white horses, unless that particular horse is identified and individualised from the remaining horses it will not become a specific one.

(*b*) *Ascertained goods:* The goods which are ascertained and identified after the formation of contract, are known as ascertained goods. However in practice, specific and ascertained goods are used interchangeably. The only point of difference is that specific goods are ascertained before or at the time of making a contract, but ascertained goods are identified and individualised after the formation of a contract of sale.

Lord Atkia has rightly observed that ascertained goods probably means, 'identified in accordance with agreement after the time a contract of sale in made.'

Thus, when the quantity contracted for is set aside for a given contract, out of whole stock, the goods are said to be ascertained.

(*c*) *Unascertained goods:* The goods which are not, identified separately at the time of making a contract of sale are known as 'unascertained goods'. In fact, at the time of making contract, those goods have been identified only by description. Such goods are also known as, 'generic goods' because unless these are physically and individually separated from the lot, they are part of it.

Example: College has booking counter for HMT watches. Ram makes an agreement for buying a particular wristwatch. He identifies it by description. Next day he visits the showroom of these watches and individualises particular wristwatch. Thus before separating the watch from the lot it remains unascertained goods and on being separated out from the stock it becomes ascertained goods.

(ii) Future goods: Future goods are goods, which will be owned and possessed by the seller at some future date. Though, necessary arrangement must have been made to procure them but, these are yet to be owned and possessed by the seller.

According to Section 2 (6) of this Act, "goods to be manufactured, produced or acquired by the seller after making contract of sale" are future goods. These may be the goods which are not existing or are to be procured by the seller. Since, these goods are not in the ownership and possession of the seller, he cannot make sale for these goods. Rather agreement to sell may be made for such goods.

Example: A agrees to sell entire crop of wheat grown by him next year to B at a particular price. It is an agreement to sell for future goods.

(iii) Contingent goods: Contingent goods are type of future goods the acquisition of which depends on the happening or non-happening of future contingency. According to Section 6 (2) of this Act, there may be a contract for the sale of goods, the acquisition of which by the seller depends upon contingency, which may or may not happen. Such goods may be subject matter of 'agreement to sell'.

The contract of sale for contingent goods can be enforced only on the happening of that contingency upon which acquisition of goods by the seller depends. In case contingency does not happen, the seller will not get possession and ownership of those goods and contract will become void.

Example: A agrees to sell the cargo of ship to B which is being brought from London to Mumbai. The ship may or may not arrive. Acquisition of goods on the part of A depends upon the arrival of the ship. In case that ship sinks in the ocean, contract between A and B becomes void.

EFFECTS OF DESTRUCTION OF GOODS

In a contract of sale, the 'goods' constitute the subject matter of contract. In case the subject matter gets destroyed, the contract of sale will become void. In a contract of sale, the goods may perish or be destructed before the sale is complete. Effect of destruction of subject matter of a contract of sale may be studied under the following two heads.

I. Goods Perishing Before Making a Contract (Section 7)

Where the contract of sale in made for specific goods, the contract is void, if at the time, when the contract was made, the goods have without the knowledge of the seller, perished to become so damaged as no longer answer to their description in the contract.

To make the contract void, under this Section, the following conditions must be fulfilled:

(*a*) The contract of sale must have been made for specific goods.

(*b*) The goods must have been damaged or perished before entering into a contract of sale.

(*c*) It was not in the knowledge of the seller that goods have been perished or destructed.

(*d*) The goods must have been damaged as no longer they are answers to the description.

(*e*) Perishing of goods includes loss of goods by theft and loss of their commercial value.

ASFAR COY LTD *vs* BLUNDELL (1896, 1.Q.B., 123). In this case, contract was made for selling a cargo of dates. The dates were contaminated with sewage, so as to be unsaleable as dates. It was held that contract was void, because the dates have lost their commercial utility.

BORROWLANE ETC. *vs* PHILLIPS (1929, 1.K.B. 574). In this case, it was agreed to sell 700 bags of groundnuts lying in a particular warehouse. But it was found that 109 bags had been stolen before contract was made but both the parties were not aware of it. It was held that contract was void.

II. Goods Perishing After Agreement to Sell, But Before Sale (Section 8)

In an agreement to sell specific goods, the goods without any fault on the part of buyer and seller perish, before the risk passes to buyer, the contract of sales becomes void and both parties are excused from performance of a contract.

The contract of sale can be avoided on this basis, provided the following condition are fulfilled:

(*a*) The contract of sale must have been made as an 'agreement to sell' and not a 'sale'.

(*b*) The subject matter of an agreement to sell must be specific goods.

(*c*) The goods must have been damaged or perished before the risk passes to buyer.

(*d*) The goods have been perished or destructed without any fault on the part of buyer and seller.

Example: A has 300 cotton bales in his godown. He makes an agreement to sell 50 cotton bales to B at a particular price. At the time of making contract, the godown catches a fire and the whole stock gets destroyed. The contract of sale is not void, because 50 cotton bales which constitute subject matter of a contract, have not been identified and separated from the stock, and are not specific goods.

Sections 7 and 8 of this Act are applicable only in case of loss of specific goods, and that too without any fault of buyer and seller.

PRICE FIXATION

In a contract of sale, fixation and payment of price is also an important feature. No sale can take place without a price. The term 'price' has been defined under Section 2 (10) of this Act, 'the money consideration for a sale of goods'. However where goods are sold for a fixed amount, that amount is paid partly in terms of cash and partly in terms of valued goods.

In a contract of sale, the payment of price is made by the buyer. It may be paid either at the time of making contract or at some future date.

Modes of fixing price: With regard to price fixation, Sections 9 and 10 of this Act are applicable. According to these provisions, there are five methods of fixing price:

(*i*) ***Expressly mentioned in the contract:*** It is a usual way of fixing the price in a contract of sale. Both parties by mutual agreement may determine the price of goods. But the price fixed by the parties must be a definite sum.

(*ii*) ***In a manner provided by contract:*** The manner, in which price of the goods will be fixed may be mentioned in a contract itself such as 'market price', 'cost plus' and 'how much other customers pay' *etc.*

(iii) ***By usage:*** Where the price is not mentioned in the contract or the manner to fix the price has not been laid down in a contract, it will be fixed by prevailing business usage. These usage may be well-established practice for fixing the price in that kind of business such as 'price advertised', 'price marked on goods' and 'discount on sale price' etc.

(iv) ***By third party:*** The price to be paid by buyer may be fixed by third party provided third party accepts it. In casc he fails to fix price, agreement will become void. Where, the third party has been prevented from fixing price either by the seller or buyer, party at default will be liable to pay compensation to other party.

(v) ***Reasonable price:*** Where the price is not fixed by any one of the foregoing methods the buyer is liable to pay reasonable price which depends on the circumstance of each case.

However, after making a contract sale, if there is any increase in custom, excise duty or any tax on sale or purchase it will be added to the price. Similarly, any decrease in these will be deducted from the price to be paid by the buyer.

As far as mode of payment is concerned, the seller is not bound to accept any kind of payment except in legal tender money. He is not bound to accept payment by cheque.

EARNEST MONEY OR SECURITY DEPOSIT

Sometimes, the buyer may make part of payment in advance to the seller. Such payment may be earnest money or security deposit. When such payment is made as a part of price in advance, in case contract was not performed either by buyer or seller, it is to be refunded to the buyer. In case the contract is performed it will be deducted from the total price of the goods purchased. But it is paid as a guarantee for the performance of a contract by the buyer on his failure to perform, the seller has a right to forfeit that advance.

S.II. COTTON MILLS *vs* TATA AIRCRAFT LTD (1970, 2,S.C. 482). In this case, the purchaser deposited Rs. 2.5 lakh as earnest money being 25 per cent of the value of goods. A term of contract provided that full value of the goods will be paid before taking delivery of the goods. The purchaser failed to pay the value of goods by the stipulated time. It was held that seller was entitled to forfeit the earnest money, because the buyer makes a breach of contract.

REVIEW QUESTIONS

1. Define the term 'contract of sale'. Discuss essential features of a valid contract of sale.
2. Distinguish between 'sale' and 'agreement to sell'.
3. Make distinction between:
   (*a*) Sale and Hire purchase agreement.
   (*b*) Sale and Contract of bailment.
   (*c*) Sale and Contract for work and labour.
4. How is a contract of sale performed? Explain the various modes in which a contract of sale can be made.
5. What is the subject matter of a 'Contract of Sale'? Discuss the various types of goods which constitute the subject matter of a contract of sale.
6. Explain Section 788 of Sale of Goods Act in connection with destruction of subject matter of a contract.
7. Explain various mode of fixing price of goods in a contract of sale.
8. Write notes on:
   (*a*) Goods.
   (*b*) Existing goods.
   (*c*) Earnest money or security deposit.
   (*d*) Future goods.
9. Comment on:
   (*a*) Risk follows ownership.
   (*b*) Contract of sale is a specific contract.
   (*c*) Payment of price as consideration in a contract of sale.
   (*d*) Transfer of property in goods is an essence of contract of sale.
   (*e*) Earnest money may be paid either as a part of price or security for performance.
   (*f*) 'Sale' is made only for existing goods.

PRACTICAL PROBLEMS

1. A agrees to sell a Maruti car to B for Rs. 1.5 lakh. Before making agreement the car was stolen and it was not in the knowledge of the parties. Is A bound to deliver Maruti car to B? (Hint: No).
2. Ritesh makes contract of sale for selling heavy machine costing Rs. 2 lakh to Hitesh on a condition that Hitesh will pay Rs. one lakh in cash and will deliver a second hand car valued at Rs. one lakh. Is contract of sale valid? (Hint: Yes, payment of price is made partly in cash and partly in goods.)
3. Ram enters into a contract of sale with Shyam for selling photostat machine to him for Rs. 30,000. Invoice of the machine has been made in favour of Shyam, payment has not been made. The machine is lying in the godown of the seller. Meanwhile, his godown sets on fire and the machine is destroyed. Can Shyam claim loss of machine from Ram? (Hint: No, ownership of machine has been transferred to Shyam and machine gets destroyed without any fault of Ram.)
4. A transport company has resolved and transferred 10 buses to a partnership firm, which consists of certain people who are owners of the company. Transfer was made at a particular price. Is it a contract of sale? Examine the validity of this contract. (Hint: No, person can sell his goods to himself.)
5. A is an agent of foreign currency. B makes an agreement with him for purchasing 100 pounds for Rs. 7,500. Is contract of sale is valid? (Hint: No currency cannot be sold or purchased.)
6. Mohan and Sohan agree that Mohan will sell his second hand car to Sohan at a price which will be determined by a particular car mechanic. But the car mechanic refused to do the job of price fixation. On such refusal can Sohan compel Mohan to sell that car for any other price? (Hint: No).
7. A purchased a machine for Rs. 50,000 from B on instalment payment basis. The payment is to be made in five equal monthly instalments. A defaults in making the 3rd instalment. Is B entitled to get back the machine from A? (Hint: No). What is the legal remedy available to him?

8. X agrees to sell a horse to B on a condition that B will keep it for six days on trial basis and have the option to return on the expiry of 6 days period, if he does not find it suitable. Three days after, the horse dies due to some illness without the fault of A or B. Can this agreement be avoided? (Hint: Yes).
9. A agrees to sell the entire crop of wheat to be grown in his farm to B at a particular price. Before the crop was ready for harvesting, it was totally destroyed due to natural calamities. Is A bound to deliver wheat to B? (Hint: No).
10. A sold a piano to B for Rs. 2,000 on hire-purchase basis to be paid in 10 equal instalments. After paying the 5th instalment B refused to pay remaining instalments. Can A recover the piano from B? (Hint: Yes).

19

Conditions and Warranties

LEARNING OBJECTIVES

- Understand the meaning and application of conditions and warranties in a contract of sale.
- Apply these two concepts in practice when you buy the goods.
- Compare conditions with warranties.
- Learn implied conditions and warranties applicable on the seller.
- Apply the rule of '*Caveat Emptor*' and remember the consequences of not following this rule in practice.

INTRODUCTION

We are all consumers in one way or the other. We buy goods for satisfying our needs or for producing other goods. While making a decision to buy we take into account the various claims made by the seller regarding those goods. In a contract of sale, parties make certain stipulations or statement i.e., agree to certain terms. All stipulations or statements cannot be treated on the same footing. Some may be intended by the parties to be of a fundamental nature e.g., quality of goods to be supplied, the breach of which, therefore, will be regarded as a breach of the contract. Some may be intended by the parties to be binding, but of a subsidiary or inferior character, *e.g.*, time of payment, so that a breach of these terms will not put an end to the contract but will make the party comitting the breach liable to damages. The former stipulations are called 'conditions' and the latter 'warranties'.

CONDITION AND WARRANTY

Condition: Condition is that stipulation which goes into the root of contract of sale and forms the basis of such contract.

It is so important for the contract that, without fulfilling such stipulation, the contract of sale cannot be performed. It is essential and fundamental to the main purpose of a contract. Thus, non-fulfillment of such stipulation may result in breach of contract.

According to Section 12 (2) of Sale of Goods Act, "a condition is a stipulation, essential to the main purpose of a contract, the breach of which gives rise to a right to treat the contract as repudiated."

BALDRY *VS* MARSHALL. In this case, B consulted M a motor car dealer, for a car which is suitable for touring purpose. M suggested 'Buqatti' car and B accordingly purchased it. The car turns out to be unfit for touring purpose. It was held that suitability of a car for touring purpose is a condition. It was so vital that, if it is not fulfilled, it would defeat the very purpose of contract for which B bought the car. He was, therefore, entitled to reject car and get his money back from the dealer.

Warranty: According to Section 12 (3) of this Act, "a warranty is a stipulation, collateral to the main purpose of a contract, the breach of which gives a rise to a claim for damages, but not to a right to reject the goods and treat the contract as repudiated."

It becomes clear from the definition that, the warranty is also a stipulation, but supportive or subsidiary for the main purpose of the contract of sale. It is therefore, if the party makes breach of such stipulation, another party has a right only to claim for compensation. He cannot avoid the contract.

The basic concept of **condition** and **warranty** can be understood with the help of following example.

Example: A is willing to buy a car. He visits a nearby dealer of a car and tells him that he needs a car which runs 20 km/litre one litre of petrol. The car dealer supplies a car to him on a contract of a sale. Later on, it appears that the car can hardly run 10 km/litre petrol. A can avoid this contract, because stipulation made by him regarding fuel consumption was a condition, essential for the purpose of contract. If A visits dealer to buy a car and the dealer suggests that he has a car which runs 20 km/litre. A makes an agreement to buy that car. Later on it turns out that the car can run 10 km/1itre petrol. It amounts to breach of warranty, because stipulation made by the dealer is supportive one. Thus A can only claim for compensation. He is not entitled to avoid the contract.

DISTINCTION BETWEEN CONDITION AND WARRANTY

The use of the term condition or warranty in a contract of sale is immaterial, unless and until parties are intended to make it or not to make it basis of a contract. Distinction between the two can be made on the following points:

(*i*) ***Nature of stipulation:*** Condition is a stipulation which is essential and fundamental in nature. It is so significant for the main purpose of contract that non-fulfillment of it leads to breach of contract. While as, warranty is a stipulation which is supportive and collateral in nature. Though it is also related to the main purpose of contract, but to a small extent. It is therefore the contract of sale can be performed, even without fulfilling it.

(*ii*) ***Consequences of breach:*** In a contract of sale, if the party makes breach of condition, the other becomes entitled to avoid the contract. It is because condition is essential for the major purpose of a contract. But in case of breach of warranty, another party can only claim for compensation, if he has suffered any loss.

(*iii*) ***Treatment of stipulation:*** Breach of a condition has much wider implications on the contract as compared to breach of warranty. Thus breach of condition can be treated as a breach of warranty; but breach of warranty cannot be treated as breach of condition.

Difference between condition and warranty

	Condition	Warranty
Nature	It is fundamental in nature and essential for main purpose of contract.	It is supportive and collateral for the contract.
Breach	Due to breach of condition the contract may be avoided.	Its breach may give a rise to a right to claim for compensation.
Treatment	Breach of condition can be treated as breach of warranty.	Breach of warranty cannot be treated as breach of condition.

When a breach of condition is to be treated as breach of warranty. Section 13 of this Act provides for certain circumstances where a breach of a condition may be reduced to the status of warranty. And consequently, the buyer loses his right to reject the goods and avoid the contract. In such case, his only remedy is to claim for compensation. Breach of condition can be treated as a breach of warranty under the following circumstances:

(*a*) ***Voluntary waiver by the buyer:*** Where a contract of sale is subject to certain conditions to be fulfilled by the seller, the buyer may, waive the condition, or elect to treat breach of condition as a breach of warranty. The conditions in a contract of sale for the seller are for the benefit of the buyer, therefore this option of waiver has been given to the buyer. In case when he waives the condition, later on he cannot compel the seller to fulfil it.

Example: A agrees to supply 100 bags of wheat of a particular quality to B at the rate of Rs. 1,500 p.q. But he supplies wheat of somewhat inferior quality, the price of which is Rs. 1,200 p.q. There is a breach of condition on the part of seller. B has an option to treat it as a breach of warranty and instead of avoiding contract, he can claim for compensation of Rs. 300 p.q. of wheat.

(*b*) ***Compulsory treatment by buyer:*** When the contract of sale is not severable and the buyer has accepted the goods or part thereof, the breach of any condition by the seller can only be treated as a breach of warranty.

According to Section 42 of this Act, a buyer is deemed to have accepted the goods:

- When he intimates to the seller that he has accepted goods.
- When the good have been delivered to him, he does any act in relation to them which is inconsistent with ownership of the seller such as he has pledged the goods or, when after the lapse of reasonable period of time he retains the goods without intimating to the seller that he has rejected them.

However if the contract is severable, the buyer has accepted part of the goods, he can still exercise his right to reject the remaining goods.

HARDY & COY *vs* HILLERPS & FLOWER (1923, 2.K.B. 490). In this case, a buyer took delivery of consignment of wheat, and resold and despatched a part of it to a sub-buyer. Later on, it was discovered that wheat supplied was not of a contracted quality and he gave the seller notice of rejecting remaining quantity of wheat. But it was held that transferring possession to sub-buyer, was an act inconsistent with the ownership of seller, and therefore, the buyer was deemed to have accepted the goods.

EXPRESS AND IMPLIED CONDITIONS AND WARRANTIES

The contract of sale may be based on many conditions and warranties. These condition and warranties may be either express or implied. Both the parties of a contract of sale, are free to include any condition or warranty in that contract. They may attach any degree of significance to these terms and conditions. When the conditions and warranties, provided in a contract of sale, have been made in writing or have been explained to each other by the words of mouth, such conditions and warranties are known as 'express conditions and warranties'. Thus, where the buyer desires to buy white Maruti car, the colour of the car becomes express condition.

Similarly, buyer and seller by mutual agreement may provide for any condition and warranty.

In addition to express conditions, there are certain conditions and warranties, which are applicable in a contract of sale by operation of law. These are known as 'implied conditions'. Unless, there is a contrary intention which appears from contract, these conditions would be applicable automatically.

However, such implied conditions can be altered or negated by an express agreement or by a custom or tradition prevailing in that business. In this regard following two guidelines seem to be very important:

(*a*) *Expressum facit ceassare tacitum, i.e.,* what is expressed makes what is *facit* or implied to cease.

(*b*) *Modes. et. conventio vincent legem, i.e.,* custom and agreement over rule law—implied conditions and warranties.

Thus implied conditions and warranties are applicable, provided there is no contrary intention of the parties to it.

Sale of Goods Act provides the following implied conditions and warranties, applicable for the seller.

IMPLIED CONDITIONS

Following implied conditions are laid down by law for a contract of sale:

(*i*) **Condition as to title:** The contract of sale involves transfer of title or ownership. Therefore in every contract of sale, there is an implied condition for the seller that, in case of a sale he has ownership and right to sell. And in an agreement to sell, he will get this right in future at the time of transfering ownership to the buyer.

This condition clearly states that no one can sell what is not being owned by him or on which he has no right to sell. In this regard, the rule of law is 'one cannot give, what one does not have'. Thus if the seller has no valid title of the goods he cannot sell them to buyer. The condition of title is very essential for protecting the interest of innocent buyer.

When the seller sells the goods without ownership and right to sell, it will amount to breach of condition on his part. The buyer is entitled to return goods and get the money back from the seller.

RAWLAND, *vs* DIVALL (1923, 2,K.B. 500). In this case, A purchased second hand motor car from B and used it for sometime. Later on it was discovered that the car had been stolen by B. Consequently, A had surrendered the car to real owner. It was held that A could recover, in full, the price of the car from B.

With regard to condition as to title it is to be noted that to sell the goods it is not enough to have ownership. Rather the owner of the goods must have a right to sell those goods. Sale of goods without right will also amount to breach of condition.

NIBLETT LTD *vs* CONFECTIONERS MATERIAL COY. In this case, certain tins of condensed milk bearing the label "NISSLY BRAND" were sold by A to B. Another manufactures of condensed milk under the brand name of 'Nestle' claimed that it was an infringement of their trademark. In order to save themselves from any liability under trademark law B had to remove the labels and sold the naked tins at loss. A was held liable for breach of implied condition that they had a right to sell.

(*ii*) **Condition in a sale by description:** Sometimes the contract of sale of goods is made by description. Such description may be related to various physical as well as chemical characteristics of the goods. In such a contract, there is an implied condition for the seller that he must deliver the goods which are corresponding to given description. In other words, goods supplied must be same as were described by the party. If it is found that the goods are not corresponding to given description, the buyer has a right to reject the goods.

In this regard, Lord Blackburn has rightly observed, "if you contract to sell peas, you cannot oblige a party to take beans. If the description of an article tendered, is different in any respect, it is not the article bargained for, and the other is not bound to take it."

The term 'sale of goods' by description is wide and includes the following situations:

(*a*) It includes a case, where the buyer has never seen the goods and buys them only on the basis of description given by the seller.

Example: A makes contract of sale for selling a reaping machine by describing it to be only one year old and had been used only to cut 50 to 60 acres. On the delivery of machine, the buyer found that the machine was extremely old. It is breach of condition, and the buyer is entitled to reject the machine, because it does not correspond with given description.

Similarly, if the buyer agrees to buy a 'Phillip-juicer made in Japan,' and the seller supplies him Phillip-juicer made in Hong Kong, it does not correspond to given description.

(*b*) Buyer has already seen the goods, but he purchases them on the basis of description of those goods given by the seller.

Example: In an auction sale, the buyer purchased a set of liner napkins and table cloths, which were described by the seller as 'dating from 17th Century.' The buyer was a dealer in antiques, he purchased these after seeing them. But later, that set appeared to be an '18th Century set.' Since the buyer has relied on the description, even after seeing the goods. It is breach of condition and he can return goods.

(*c*) The method of packing goods may also form part of description.

Example: A agrees to buy 500 tins of canned fruit to be packed in cases. Each case contains 50 tins. On the supply of cases containing more or less than 50 tins, the buyer is entitled to reject the goods. In this case, sale was made by describing goods in terms of quantity in packed form. Therefore packing of goods must be according to given description.

(*iii*) Condition in a sale by sample: When the contract of sale is made by showing sample of goods to the buyer, there is an implied condition for the seller that:

(*a*) Bulk of goods supplied to the buyer shall correspond with the sample in quality.

(*b*) Buyer shall be given reasonable opportunity of comparing bulk with the sample.

(*c*) The goods shall be free from any defects which may render them unmerchantable (to be sold under that sample). Such defects may be either 'latent' or 'patent'. The latent defects are those, which cannot be discovered by making reasonable examination of sample and implied condition applies only to these defects. On the other hand, patent defects can be discovered by the buyer by making reasonable examination of the sample, and the condition does not apply to such defects.

Example: A sold to B certain quantity of worsted coating equal to sample. The coating supplied by A was equal to sample, but had a latent defect. As a result of which, the cloth was found to be unfit for making coats. B has a right to reject the goods. Reason being that the defect was latent which could not be discovered by making reasonable examination.

(*iv*) **Sale by sample as well as by description:** When goods are sold by showing sample and giving description, there is an implied condition for the seller that the bulk of goods supplied to the buyer shall correspond both with sample and the description. When the goods supplied do correspond only with sample and not with description, the buyer is entitled to reject the goods.

Example: A agreed to sell B some oil described as 'Foreign-refined rapeseed oil', equal to sample.

A supplied the oil though, corresponded with the sample, but was adulterated with palm oil. Thus it amounts to breach of condition, because the oil supplied is not according to description given at the time of making a contract.

WALLIS *vs* PRATT (1911, A.C. 394). In this case, seeds were sold by sample as 'English sainfoin seeds' and described as 'common English Sainfoin'. The seeds supplied were found to be 'Gaint Sainfoin'. It was held that there was a breach of condition as to description and therefore the buyer could recover damages.

(*v*) **Condition as to quality and fitness for purpose:** The general rule with regard to contract of sale is that a buyer is supposed to satisfy himself about the quality and suitability of goods for his purpose. Thus later on, if the goods purchased are found unsuitable or unfit for the purpose of the buyer, he will have no legal remedy against the seller:

However, there are certain exceptions to this rule. Under these exceptional circumstances, implied condition as to fitness for the purpose is applicable on the seller. And the seller is bound to supply the goods which are suitable for the purpose of the buyer provided:

(*a*) At the time of buying the goods, a buyer must have disclosed his purpose to the seller, expressly or in an implied manner.

(*b*) The buyer must have relied upon the skill and judgment of the seller for supplying goods fit for the purpose of the buyer.

(*c*) The goods sold must be of description which the seller deals in the ordinary course of his business.

It means the seller is not a casual seller, rather it is his business to sell those goods.

Example: A draper wanted to buy hot water bottle. He visited chemist shop and asked him to supply hot water bottle and made it clear that for what purpose he is buying that bottle. The chemist supplied hot water bottle and told him to use it only for hot water because it may not stand boiled water. While using the bottle, it did burst and A was injured. A is entitled to claim damage for breach of implied condition because the bottle was unfit for the purpose of the buyer.

However, it is to be noted that, when the goods can be used only for one particular purpose, the buyer need not tell his purpose to the seller.

Example: A purchased refrigerator from B. Later on, it was discovered that it failed in making ice. Thus B is entitled to avoid the contract on the ground of breach of condition.

The condition as to fitness shall not be applicable in the following cases:

(*a*) The buyer suffers from some abnormality with respect to use of goods but does not disclose it to the seller at the time of making a contract of sale.

Example: A's skin is allergitic to some cosmetic. She buys that cosmetic without disclosing this fact to the seller. On the use of cosmetic she gets her skin damaged due to allergy. The seller is not liable for damages.

(*b*) When the buyer buys the goods, under some patent or trademark, the condition as to fitness will not be applicable.

Example: A buys 'Bournvita' from a chemist as a health drink. He uses it, but does not get any improvement in his health. He has no claim for damage against the chemist.

(*vi*) **Condition as to merchantable quality:** Merchantable quality implies that, goods should be resaleable in the market under the particular description by which they are known.

According to Section 16 (2) of this Act, "where goods are bought by description from a seller, who deals in the goods of that description (whether he is manufactures or not) there is an implied condition that the goods shall be of merchantable quality."

Example: A made an agreement to sell 50 tyres to B at a particular price. On the supply of tyres, it was discovered that all tyres are carrying small holes in the tube inside tyre. B has a right to reject the goods due to unmerchantable quality of the tyres.

JACKSON *vs* ROTEX MOTORS & CYCLE COY LTD, (1910, 2, K.B. 937). In this case R placed an order for 600 motor horns of varying description. Some of the horns were dented and badly polished. R, rejected entire consignment. It was held that the defects in the horns had rendered them unmerchantable, thus R is entitled to reject them.

(*vii*) **Condition to wholesomeness:** In a contract of sale of eatables and provisions, there is an implied condition on the part of the seller that the goods shall be wholesome. It means, the goods supplied by the seller must not be dangerously adulterated and must be fit for human consumption.

Example: A bought milk from a dairy owner. The milk was contaminated with germs of typhoid fever. By consuming that milk A's wife got infected and died. A is entitled to claim damages from the dairy owner.

JACKSON *vs* WESTON & SONS (1909, 9,R.B. 193, C.A). In this case, a grocer sold tinned salmon which was poisonous. It resulted in the death and illness of many persons. It was held that the grocer was liable for damages because of breach of condition of wholesomeness.

IMPLIED WARRANTIES

Implied warranties are those stipulations which are supportive or collateral to the purpose of contract. These warranties are applicable in a contract of sale by operation of law, provided there is nothing contrary to them. These warranties are related to the implied 'condition as to title'. These are:

(*i*) **Warranty as to quite possession:** In every contract of sale, unless contrary intention appears, there is an implied warranty that the buyer shall have and enjoy quite possession of the goods. The right of peaceful use and possession may be disturbed due to defective title or ownership.

This warranty may be considered as an extension of implied condition of title which is provided under Section 14 (A) of this Act.

If the possession or use of goods by the buyer is disturbed by a person having superior rights than that of seller, the buyer may hold seller responsible for breach of warranty.

Example: A purchased second hand car from B. A thereafter spent some money on its repair and used it for sometime. The parties were not aware of the fact that the car was stolen one. Consequently, A was forced to return the car to its real owner. He is entitled to recover cost of car and the amount spent on its repair from B. This is so because B is liable for breach of warranty.

(*ii*) **Warranty of freedom from encumbrances or economic charges:** After having purchased goods, the buyer is entitled to assume that the goods are free from any economic charge or encumbrance in favour of third person. If the goods are found subject to some charge in favour of third party, the seller will be liable to pay compensation for it to the buyer.

However, this warranty will not be applicable where the buyer has been informed of such charge or has a notice of the same.

Example: A agrees to sell some goods to B which are already hypothecated to bank against a loan of Rs. 5,000. B was not aware of this fact at the time of making a contract of sale. B had to pay Rs. 5,000 to the bank to free them from charge in favour of the bank. B is entitled to claim this amount from A, because it is a breach of warranty.

(iii) Warranty to disclose dangerous nature of goods: Sometimes, the goods sold by the seller may be dangerous in nature. In such case there is an implied warranty for the seller that while selling such goods he must warn the innocent buyer regarding probable dangers which may arise out of its use. If the seller fails to do so, and buyer suffers loss due to dangerous nature of goods the seller will be liable to compensate the buyer.

CLARKE *vs* ARMY & NAVY COOPERATIVE SOCIETY LTD. (1903, 1, K.B. 155, C). In this case, C purchased a tin of disinfectant powder from A. A knew that the tin was to be opened with special care, otherwise it may prove dangerous. He also knew that C was ignorant about it, but he did not warn C. While opening that tin the disinfectant powder flew into her eyes and caused injury. It was held that A was liable to pay damage to C.

DOCTRINE OF *CAVEAT EMPTOR*

It is a fundamental principle of law relating to sale of goods. It implies that while buying the goods, the buyer must be cautious. The term *caveat emptor* means 'Let the buyer beware.' This principle states that at the time of buying goods the buyer must make reasonable examination of the goods as to satisfy himself regarding suitability of goods for the purpose he buys for and as to discover the defects.

After having purchased goods, if any defects appears on those, which could have been discovered through reasonable examination of goods, the seller shall not be liable for such defects.

It is very clear that when seller displays goods in open market it is up to the buyer to make proper selection. If goods turn out to be defective, the seller cannot be held liable. When the buyer makes bad choice, nonelse, except him will be blamed and liable for.

WORD *vs* HOBBS (1878, 4. A.C. 13). In this case, certain pigs were sold, "with all faults." The pigs were suffering from typhoid fever. They also infected other pigs of the buyer. It was held that the seller was not bound to disclose that pigs were unhealthy. *Caveat emptor*, being the rule, the buyer is not entitled to claim damage from the seller.

The doctrine of *caveat emptor* is, however, subject to the following exceptions:

(*i*) **Misrepresentation by seller:** Where the seller makes misrepresentation, the buyer relies on that and makes a contract of sale. The rule of *caveat emptor* will not be applicable and the contract will be voidable at the option of the buyer.

(*ii*) **Concealment of defects:** Where the seller makes active concealment of defects in the goods or makes any false representation regarding goods amounting to fraud, the above rule will not be applicable. The contract of sale is voidable and the buyer can claim compensation from the seller for the loss.

(*iii*) **Condition as to fitness for the purpose:** While making a contract of sale, the buyer discloses his purpose to the seller. He relies on the skill and judgment of the seller for the supply of the goods. And the seller happens to be a person who deals in those goods or whose business is to sell those goods. In this case, the seller is liable to supply goods fit for the purpose of buyer, and the rule of *caveat emptor* is not applicable.

(*iv*) **Sale by description:** In a contract of sale by description, where the goods are bought from the seller who deals in such goods, the goods supplied by the seller must be of merchantable quality. If the goods are not found to be merchantable, the seller cannot take defence of doctrine of *caveat emptor*, because it does not apply in such case.

(*v*) **Usage of trade:** According to Section 16 (3) of this Act, implied condition of quality or fitness for a particular purpose may also be inferred from the trade custom and usage. Well-established norms in a particular trade bind the seller to supply the goods which are suitable for the purpose of buyer, the rule of *caveat emptor* will not apply.

(*vi*) **Wholesomeness of the goods:** In a contract of sale of eatables and provisions the seller has to ensure that the goods supplied are free from any infection and dangerous adulteration which may make them unfit for human consumption. In such case the above rule is not applicable.

REVIEW QUESTIONS

1. Define the terms 'condition' and 'warranty'. Distinguish between them and explain those situations when breach of condition can be treated as breach of warranty.
2. What is the 'Doctrine of *caveat emptor*'? Discuss exception to this rule.
3. Explain two warranties in a contract of sale.
4. Explain the implied condition as to fitness for the purpose. Discuss the circumstances under which this condition is applied.
5. Define 'implied condition'. Explain condition as to sale by sample and sale by description.
6. Discuss various implied conditions which are applicable for the seller in a contract of sale.
7. Comment on:
   (*a*) Condition can be reduced to warranty.
   (*b*) Seller is not bound to supply goods fit for the purpose of the buyer.
   (*c*) Condition is essential for the purpose of contract of sale.
   (*d*) Implied condition are equally important, provided the parties had no contrary intention to them.
   (*e*) Goods sold must be under the ownership and right of seller to sell.

PRACTICAL PROBLEMS

1. Railway company has purchased timber for making railway sleepers. The timber supplied by the merchant was found unfit for the purpose of Railway Coy. Give legal advice to the Railway company.
2. A wanted to buy a car. He visited car dealer and told him that he needs a car which runs 30 km/litre petrol. The car dealer supplied a car to him. Later on, it appeared that the car hardly runs 15 km/litre petrol. Is it a breach of condition or a warranty? (Hint: Breach of condition.)
3. A purchased a ship from B, on the basis of representation that the capacity of the ship is 500 tonnes. But it appeared that capacity is only 400 tonnes. Can A avoid the contract? (Hint: No, it is breach of warranty.)

4. Ram purchased a second hand machine form Shyam for Rs. 10,000. He spends sum of Rs. 5,000 on its repair for making it usable. After sometime, it was discovered that the machine was stolen by Shyam. Consequently, Ram had to surrender the machine to the real owner. Suggest legal remedy available to A.
5. A agrees to buy 100 bags of 'Lalkila Basmati Rice' from B. @ Rs. 10,000 per bag. But B supplied 'Rajmahal Basmati Rice.' Can A rejects supply of Raj Mahal Basmati?
6. X purchased a piece of worsted coating by sample. Later on, it was found that there are some latent defects in cloth, which X could not discovered by making reasonable examination of that cloth piece. As a result of such defects it is not suitable for making coats. Is X entitled to reject the goods? (Hint: Yes).
7. N agreed to sell some oil to M, described as 'foreign refined rapeseed oil' equal to sample. N supplied that oil corresponding with sample, but adulterated with palm oil. Can M reject the supply of oil? (Hint: Yes, though it is in accordance with sample, it is not according to description.)
8. A lady purchased some cosmetic from a chemists shop in spite of knowing that her skin is sensitive to the use of such cosmetic. But she did not disclose it to the chemist. A used cosmetic and got some allergy. Can she claim damage from the chemist? (Hint: No).
9. A is in the retail shop of B and wants to buy some bottles of cold drink. He is examining some of the bottles, but the bottle exposed. He got injury in his hand. Can he claim damage from B? (Hint: No, because there is no contract of sale between A and B).
10. Certain goods were sold by A to B equal to sample. B in turn sold them to C by sample. But goods delivered to C were not according to the sample shown to him. Therefore C rejected the goods and gave a notice to B. Can B recover damage from A? (Hint: Yes).
11. A purchased an electric heater from B, under the impression that it is suitable for heating his room. But he finds that the heater is not fit for his purpose. Can A avoid contract? (Hint: No).

■■■

20

Trasfer of Ownership and Delivery of Goods

LEARNING OBJECTIVES

- Understand the concept of transfer of ownership and relate it with sale and agreement to sell.
- Get familiar with importance of transfer of ownership and apply it with regard to contract of sale and other civic rights.
- Examine various rules regarding transfer of ownership of goods in a contract of sale.
- Analyse those cases, when non-owner can pass valid title of goods to the buyer.
- Develop understanding about various types of delivery of goods.
- Remember rules regarding delivery of goods from the seller to the buyer.

MEANING OF TRANSFER OF OWNERSHIP

The phrase 'property in goods' means ownership in goods. The 'ownership' of goods is different from 'possesion' of goods. The 'possesion' of goods refers to the custody of goods. Every contract of sale involves transfer of ownership. The ownership is transferred from the seller to buyer. On such transfer, the seller ceases to be an owner of those goods. Transfer of ownership is different from transfer of possession. These are two different aspects of a contract of sale. The ownership of the goods may pass on from the seller to buyer, but the goods may remain in the possession of the seller. Similarly a person may have possession of goods, but he may not be the owner of those goods. For example, an agent, servant, bailee or pledgee etc., who may be in possession of goods of the owner.

Thus in a contract of sale, when the goods are sold to the buyer, the buyer becomes owner of those goods irrespective of the fact whether the buyer has taken delivery of goods or not. Therefore transfer of ownership means transfer of general right of ownership to the buyer. On such transfer, the buyer can enjoy peaceful possession, can use and can further sell those goods.

SIGNIFICANCE OF TRANSFER OF OWNERSHIP

The transfer of ownership of goods is primarily a concern of buyer and seller. It is up to them to provide when such transfer takes place. But rights and liabilities of the various other parties are related to such transfer. It is therefore very important to know the exact time of transfer of ownership. It is only on the basis of ownership, various disputes and claims regarding those goods may be settled. The following rights and obligations of the parties are affected by such transfer:

(*i*) **Risk passes with the ownership:** According to Section 26 of this Act, 'risk prima facie passes with property'. This rule states that, transfer of ownership of goods decides rights and liabilities of the seller and buyer. In case, the goods are destroyed, the real owner of those goods will bear the loss, regardless of the fact that who is having possession of those goods. Thus, when the ownership is transferred to the buyer, he becomes the owner of goods and if goods are damaged or lost, he will bear the loss.

According to Section 26 of this Act, 'unless, otherwise agreed, the goods remain at the seller's risk until the property therein, is transferred to the buyer, but when the property therein is transferred to the buyer the goods are at the buyer's risk, whether delivery has been made or not.'

However, if the delivery of goods is delayed due to fault of the buyer or seller, the goods are at the risk of the party at fault.

> ***Example:*** A purchased a car from the dealer. The ownership of the car has been transferred to A and he has made payment of price. But due to increased demand on account of festive season, the dealer could not supply the car within reasonable time. Meanwhile, godown catches fire and that car is damaged. The loss of such damage will fall on the seller, though ownership of that car has been transferred to the buyer.

(*ii*) **Right to take action against third party:** When the goods are damaged due to some fault on the part of third party, it is the owner who alone can take action and not the person who was in possession of the goods at that time.

> ***Example:*** A is a owner of a car. His brother B who is possessing that car drives it. Meanwhile he meets with an accident, in which the car is badly damaged due to fault of another party involved in that accident. It is only the A who can take action against that party.

***(iii)* Right to file suit for price:** In a contract of sale, ownership of the goods is transferred to the buyer for the payment of the price. It is therefore, the seller who becomes entitled to recover the price from the buyer only when the property in goods or ownership has passed on to the latter.

***(iv)* Insolvency of the seller or buyer:** After having made a contract of sale, the seller or buyer may become insolvent. In such situations, the right of official Receiver or Assignee to take over goods depend on the fact that whether the party declared insolvent, is the owner of the goods or not. If the buyer has been declared insolvent, and ownership has been transferred to him, the goods are still in the possession of the seller. The official receiver of the buyer will claim the goods from the seller.

RULES REGARDING TRANSFER OF PROPERTY OR OWNERSHIP

In a contract of sale of specific or ascertained goods, the property or ownership passes to the buyer, at the time, when the parties are intended to do so. Thus the whole question of transfer of ownership is left to the intention of the parties. The parties are free to determine any time for transferring ownership from the seller to buyer.

But sometimes, the intention of the parties may not be clear from the contract itself. In such cases, conduct of the parties, and the circumstances of the case would be given due consideration for ascertaining intention of the parties.

For the purpose of knowing the time, of passing of ownership from the seller to the buyer, the goods may be classified into three groups:

I. Specific or ascertained goods.

II. Generic or unascertained goods.

III. Goods sent 'on approval' or 'sale or return basis'.

Unless, a contrary intention appears, the following rules, which are contained in Sections 18 to 24, are applicable for ascertaining intention of the parties.

I. Specific or Ascertained Goods

Specific goods means goods, which have been identified and agreed upon at the time of making a contract of sale. According to Section 19 of this Act, "where there is a contract for the sale of specific or ascertained goods the property in them is transferred to the buyer, at such time as the parties to a contract intend it to be transferred." It further provides that, "for the purpose of ascertaining the intention of the parties, regard shall be had to the term of a contract, conduct of the parties and the circumstance of the case."

To know the intention of the parties, with respect to the time when the property in goods, is transferred to the buyer, the following rules are applicable:

(i) Specific goods in deliverable state: When the contract of sale is unconditional, is made for specific goods which are ready to be delivered, the ownership of goods passes to the buyer, when the contract is made. Delivery of goods and payment of price or both are posponed (Section 20).

By unconditional contract of sale, we mean that there is no condition regarding transfer of ownership of the goods.

> ***Example:*** A sells some specific goods to B. The goods are at deliverable state. A puts a condition that the ownership will be transferred to B when he accepts the Bill of Exchange. The contract of sale is conditional and therefore ownership will pass to B when he fulfils the condition of accepting that bill of exchange.
>
> Another essential point in this regard is that the goods must be in deliverable state. The goods are said to be in a deliverable state, when they are in such state that, the buyer would under the contract, be bound to take delivery of them. It means they are ready to be delivered then and there.
>
> ***Example:*** A purchases personal computer from B. He makes payment promptly and asks B to send the computer to his house. The ownership of that computer is passed on to B immediately at the time of making contract. But if A agrees to buy the computer assembled by the B, this case is different and ownership of goods is not going to be transferred immediately.

(ii) Specific goods not in deliverable state: At the time of making a contract, the goods may not be in a deliverable state. To make them ready for delivery, the seller has something to do to the goods such as packing sealing, polishing, extra fitting and filling them in containers etc. In such case, ownership will be transferred on the completion of such acts.

According to Section 21 of this Act, "where there is a contract of sale for specific goods and the seller is bound to do something to the goods for the purpose of putting them into deliverable state, the property does not pass until such thing is done and the buyer has notice thereof."

> ***Example:*** A agrees to buy golden ring from a jeweller. To put it in delivery state, the ring is got to be polished. While polishing the ring it is damaged. Since ownership of the ring is yet to be transferred to A, he will not be liable to bear the loss.

RUGG *vs* MINETT (1809, 11, EAST 203). In this case, A purchased certain quantity of oil from B. The oil was to be filled in tins to put it in deliverable state. B filled up some of tins and informed the buyer. In the meanwhile, godown catches fire and entire stock of oil was destroyed. It was held that A will bear the loss of oil which was filled in tins.

***(iii)* Specific goods to be measured or weighted for determining price:** Sometimes, the contract of sale is made for specific goods, which are in a deliverable state. But to determine the price of the goods, they are to be measured, weighted or tested. The ownership of such goods will be transferred when the task of weighting, measuring or testing is complete.

According to Section 22 of this Act, "where there is a contract of sale for specific goods, in a deliverable state, but the seller is bound to weight, measure, test or do some other act with reference to goods for the purpose of ascertaining the price, the property does not pass, until such act or thing is done and the buyer has notice thereof."

Example: A agrees to sell a heap of wheat at a particular rate to B. A had to weigh the wheat for ascertaining the price of wheat sold to B. The ownership of the heap of wheat will be transferred to B when A completes the task of measuring wheat and informs B about it.

ZAGUARY *vs* FURNELL (1809, 2, CAMP, 240). In this case, A sold to B 289 bales of goat skins. Each bale contained five dozens skins, and the price was for certain sum per dozen of skins. Before A could count goat skins in each bale, the bales were destroyed by fire. It was held that the property in goods had not passed to the buyer and therefore the loss caused by fire had to be borne by A.

II. Unascertained and Future Goods

Where there is a contract of sale for unascertained goods, no property in goods is transferred to the buyer unless the goods are ascertained (Section 18).

Thus, no ownership is transferred to the buyer, until the goods are identified and become ascertained.

Example: A is a dealer of rice. He agrees to sell 100 quintals of rice to B at a particular price. Unless the 100 quintals are not separated from the godown, the ownership will not pass on to B.

In the process of ascertaining the goods two sub-processes are involved *i.e.*, process of ascertainment and process of appropriation. In the process of ascertainment, goods are identified and separated from the lot. And through the process of appropriation, the goods are selected with an exclusive intention of using them for performing the contract with mutual consent of both parties.

Appropriation can be done by putting goods in suitable receptacles *i.e.*, by putting goods in bags or boxes or putting oil in bottles or casks. Sometimes, the seller delivers the goods to the carrier or to the bailee for transmitting them to the buyer, without reserving right of disposal the property in goods, it also amounts to appropriation.

The following points should be noted with regard to an appropriation:

(*a*) Appropriation is an act showing an intention to identify and determine specific goods.

(*b*) It is bilateral act which is done by mutual consent of the buyer and seller.

(*c*) The consent of the seller or buyer may be given before or after the appropriation is made.

(*d*) Appropriation of goods can be made either by the seller with the consent of the buyer or by the buyer with the consent of seller.

(*e*) The consent may be express or implied.

However it is to be noted that as soon as the goods are appropriated unconditionally either by the buyer with the consent of seller or vice-versa, the property in goods passes to the buyer.

With regard to unascertained goods, agreement to sell can be made. It becomes sale when the goods are appropriated to the contract.

III. Goods Sent 'On Approval' or 'On Sale or Return Basis'

Sometimes, a contract of sale is also made 'on approval' or 'sale or return' basis. In this case, the buyer has the option to return the goods to the seller if he is not satisfied with the goods.

According to Section 24 of this Act, "when goods are delivered to the buyer on approval, or sale or return basis or on other similar terms, the property therein passes to the buyer (*a*) when he signifies his approval or acceptance to the seller, or (*b*) he does any other act adopting the transaction, or (*c*) If he does not signify this approval or acceptance to the seller, but retains the goods without giving notice of rejection."

(*i*) When he signifies his approval or acceptance: On the approval or acceptance of goods, when the buyer informs the seller, the property in goods passes to the buyer.

Example: A delivered scooter to B on approval basis. As soon as B approves it and gives notice of it to A, ownership of scooter will be transferred to him.

(*ii*) **Adoption of transaction:** When the buyer does not send his express approval to the seller, but does some act regarding goods which shows that he has accepted goods, the property in goods will pass on such adoption.

Example: A delivers some jewellery to B on sale or return basis. B pledges that jewellery to C. It means he has adopted the transaction and therefore ownership is transferred to him.

(*iii*) **Failure to return the goods:** When the buyer does not intimate the seller of his approval or rejection and retains the goods, at the expiration of reasonable period of time the ownership passes to the buyer.

Example: A delivers a horse to B on approval basis for 10 days. On the expiration of 10 days, period B does not inform the seller about approval or rejection but retains the horse, B is deemed to have become owner of that horse.

SALE BY NON-OWNERS

Every contract of sale involves transfer of ownership of goods. The ownership is transferred by the seller or by his agent to the buyer for the payment of the price. The general rule of law, in this regard is that it is only the real owner of the goods or person authorised by him can sell the goods and thereby can transfer the title of those goods to another person.

Contrary to it, when the person is not the owner of the goods or he has no right to sell the goods, even if, he sells the goods, the buyer will not get any title. This is so because, 'no one can give what he himself has not got.' (*Nemo dat quod non habet*). Therefore, if the person deals with or sells the good without authority of the owner such transaction is not valid in the eyes of law.

Similarly, if the seller has no title or his title is defective, when it passes to buyer, all such defects will automatically be passed to the buyer. Hence the buyer either will not get any title or his title will also be defective.

Example: A has stolen a car from B and makes agreement to sell it to C. C buys the car in good faith, believing that A is a owner of that car. Later on, B recovers this car from C, because C had no title of that car.

According to Section 27 of this Act, "subject to the provisions of this Act, and of any other law for the time in force, where goods are sold by a person who is not the owner thereof and who does not sell them under the authority as, with the consent of owner the buyer acquires no better title what the seller had."

An interpretation of the above Section makes it clear that as per the law:

(*a*) Owner can sell goods and transfer title to the buyer.

(*b*) Any other person having authority and consent of the owner can sell the goods.

(*c*) In case, ownership is defective, such defects will also pass on to the buyer and his title or ownership will also be defective.

Exceptions to the Rule

The general rule regarding title of goods though protects the interest of real owner, it is subject to the following exception:

(*i*) *Title by stoppel* (Section 27): When the real owner of the goods makes any statement by the words of mouth or in writing or induces the buyer to believe that the seller has the authority to sell. Later on if the owner denies it, he will be stopped from doing so and the buyer will get good title of good purchased.

Example: A, who is a real owner of goods tells to B, who is a prospective buyer that C who is selling goods has been authorised by him to sell. B, will get good title of the good. In fact C is just an employee with A and has no authority to sell. But B, believing on the statement of A buys the good from C. B will get good title of the goods, though C had no authority to sell.

The following acts on the part of the real owner are fit to induce the buyer:

(*a*) The real owner is, standing by when the sale is affected.

(*b*) He is assisting in the process of sale.

(*c*) He is helping in putting goods into the possession of another person.

(*d*) He has made representation to the prospective buyer regarding authority of the person selling goods.

O' CONNOR *vs* CLARK (170, PA,ST. 318). In this case, M who was owner of the wagon, allowed one of his employee K to get his name painted on it, M did it for the purpose of inducing the public to believe that wagon belonged to K. C purchased a wagon from K in good faith and C acquires good title, as M is stopped from denying K's authority to sell.

(*ii*) *Sale by Mercantile Agent* (Section 27): Where the mercantile agent, with the consent of the owner is in possession of the goods or of a document of title to the goods, any sale made by him in the ordinary course of business, the buyer will get good title provided he buys goods in good faith and for value.

Thus, the buyer will get good title of the goods though the mercantile agent had no authority to sell, provided the following conditions are satisfied:

(*a*) Mercantile agent is an agent, who has an authority in a customary course of business as for the purpose of sale, or to buy goods or to raise money on the security of goods.

(*b*) The goods, which are being sold must be in his possession with the consent of the owner, or he must have documents of title of those goods.

(*c*) The agent has sold goods in ordinary course of business as an agent i.e., there should have been no emergency like situation.

(*d*) The buyer must have acted in good faith believing that the agent had authority to sell the goods.

Example: A was appointed as mercantile agent to buy raw material for B. But A has sold part of that raw material to C, who buys it in good faith believing that A who deals in that raw material will have authority to sell. C will get good title, though A was not authorised to sell the raw material.

FOLK *vs* KING (1923, 1, K.B. 282). In this case, F, the owner of a car delivered it to A, mercantile agent for sale on the condition that the car should not be sold at less than $ 575. A, however sold the car for $ 340 to K, who bought it in good faith without notice of any fraud. A, misappropriated the amount. F sued K to recover the car. It was held that since A was in possession of a car with F's consent for the purpose of sale. Thus K obtained good title of that car.

(*iii*) *Sale by one joint owners:* According to Section 28 of this Act, "if one of the several joint owners of goods, has the sole possession of them by the permission of other joint owners and he sells them to a person, who buys them in good faith and has, at the time of contract of sale, no notice of fact that seller has no authority to sell, the buyer will get good title of goods."

Example: A, B and C are joint owners of some furniture. And with the consent of B and C the furniture was kept in the possession of A. A sells the furniture to P who buys it in good faith and without notice that A had no authority to sell. P will get good title of the goods.

(*iv*) *Sale by person in possession under voidable contract:* According to Section 29 of this Act, "where a seller is in possession of goods under a voidable contract and he sells the goods to a bona fide buyer, before the contract is rescinded, the buyer gets good title to goods."

For applying this rule, it is necessary that the following conditions must be satisfied:

(*a*) The seller must be in possession of good under a voidable contract in which the consent of one party is caused either by coercion, undue influence, misrepresentation and by fraud.

(*b*) Buyer must have bought the goods, without having notice of seller's defective title.

(*c*) The goods are sold before the aggrieved party avoids the contract.

Example: A buys B's car by seeking his consent at gunpoint. On obtaining possession and ownership of the car from B, A sells it to C. And C buys the car in good faith believing that A is a real owner of car and A has sold the car to C before B rescinds the contract. C gets good title of the car.

However, this exception is valid only in case of goods obtained under voidable contract. But in void contract, an innocent buyer will not get good title of goods.

(*v*) *Sale by seller in possession after sale:* According to Section 30 (1) or of this Act, "where a person having sold the goods continues or is in possession of goods or of the document of title of the goods, if he resells the same goods to another buyer, the buyer shall get good title to the goods, provided he buys them in good faith and without notice of previous sale."

For the application of this exception it is necessary that the seller must possess the good as a seller. If he holds the goods as bailee or hirer or in any other capacity the innocent buyer will not get good title of such goods.

Examples: A buys some goods from B and leaves them with B for time being. Meantime, B resells same goods to C, who buys them in good faith and had no knowledge of previous sale. C will get good title of the goods, though A had no title to those goods.

Shyam buys a refrigerator set from Ram and asks him to retain possession of that set as a bailee for 2 months period. In the meanwhile, Shyam who is holding that set as a bailee resells it to Mohan who buys the set in good faith having no notice of previous sale. Mohan will not get good title, because Shyam was holding refrigerator set as a bailee.

(*vi*) *Sale by the buyer in possession after sale:* According to Section 30 (2) of this Act, "where the buyer has bought the goods in agreement to sell and has got possession of goods or document of title on those goods with the consent of the seller. Such buyer sells those goods to the second buyer, who buys these goods in good faith and has no knowledge of any right of original seller on those goods, he will get good title to the goods."

For applying this rule it is essential that the first buyer must have obtained possession of the goods or document of title with the consent of original seller.

Example: Ram buys a scooter from Shyam on instalment basis. In the contract, they agreed that Shyam will continue to be owner of that scooter till the payment of last instalment. Ram sold the scooter to Mohan, before the payment of last instalment. Mohan buys that scooter in good faith and has no knowledge about the arrangement between Ram and Shyam. Mohan will get good title, though Ram had no title of that scooter.

However, it is to be noted that if the person buys the option for purchasing goods and gets possession of those goods, with the consent of seller, and if he sells those goods, the buyer, who buys in good faith having no information on that arrangement will not get good title.

(vii) Sale by unpaid seller: In a contract of sale, the unpaid seller has got a right to resell the goods. According to Section 54 (3) of this Act, "where an unpaid seller, exercised his right of lien or stoppage in transit and gets back possession of the goods, if he resells such goods the subsequent buyer gets good title of the goods as against the original buyer." To apply this Section it should be noted that a reasonable notice must have been given to the first buyer for paying the price or the goods must be of a perishable nature.

Example: A sold a car to B and A becomes unpaid seller on sale for Rs. 1.5 lakh. B did not pay the price. A resells that car to C. C will get good title as against B.

(viii) Sale by finder of goods: When the person finds the goods belonging to another and takes custody of those goods, spend some money on the maintenance. He can sell the goods under the following situations:

(*a*) If the goods are of perishable nature and losing their value day by day.

(*b*) The money spent by the finder of goods exceeds 2/3 of the total cost of the goods.

(*c*) On tracing the real owner of those goods, such owner refuses to pay lawful maintenance charges.

On selling the goods under any above situation the buyer will get good title to the goods, though the seller is not a bona fide owner of the goods.

Example: A lost his pet dog. B finds it and takes custody of the dog. He spent sum of Rs. 500 on the maintenance of that dog till the date he could trace its real owner. The real owner refuses to pay lawful maintenance charges. A sells the dog to D. D will get good title.

(*ix*) *Sale by pawnee or pledgee:* When the debtor makes default in repaying debt or performing the promise on due date, the pawnee or pledgee has a right to sell the goods which have been pledged against the debt after giving reasonable notice of this fact to the debtor. Though, the pawnee is not a owner, if he sells goods, the buyer will get good title.

Example: Ram borrows sum of Rs. 5,000 from Shyam by pledging some goods to him. On due date Ram fails to repay the debt. Shyam gives reasonable notice to Ram for repaying debt, otherwise, the goods will be sold by him. Still Ram does not repay, Shyam sells the goods to Manohar, who will get good title to such goods.

(*x*) *Sale by official receiver or assignee:* In case, the person is declared insolvent by the court, his property is handed over to the official reciever or assignee. Though they are not owners of the property of insolvent but they can pass on good title to the buyer of that property.

DELIVERY OF GOODS

Definition of Delivery

In a contract of sale, not only ownership but also physical possession of the goods sold is handed over to the buyer. Though it is not necessary to do it at the time of making a contract, it is to be done for performing a contract. Thus, it is a duty of the seller to deliver the goods to the buyer or to his agent. The goods are said to have been delivered if they get into the possession of another person.

According to Section 2 (2) of this Act, delivery is a voluntary transfer of possession from one person to another. The person giving delivery must have parted with possession of the goods voluntarily.

Delivery of the goods sold, may be made by doing anything which the parties agree or which has the effect of putting the goods in the possession of the buyer or any person authorised to hold them on his behalf.

Section 32 of this Act deals with basic rules regarding delivery of goods. This Section provides that "delivery and payment are, by default, two concurrent conditions and must take place at the same time, provided the parties had no contrary intention to it."

Types of Delivery

Delivery of goods may be of following types:

(*i*) **Actual delivery:** In case of actual delivery, the goods are physically handed over to the buyer or to his authorised agent. Thus it involves removal of goods from the possession of the seller and putting them in a possession of the buyer.

(*ii*) **Symbolic delivery:** It is different from actual delivery. Such mode of delivery is used, where the goods are bulky and heavy. In such case, it is not possible to hand them over physically to the buyer. It is therefore some thing or some symbol which carries real possession with it, is given to the buyer. As a result of it, the goods are put under the control of the buyer.

> ***Example:*** A agrees to sell 100 cotton bales to B which are lying in his godown. A instead of physically handing over these to B he hands over key of godown to B, so as to facilitate delivery of those bales. It amounts to symbolic delivery.

(*iii*) **Constructive delivery:** It is different from actual and symbolic delivery. In such delivery, the person who is holding goods acknowledges that he is in possession of the goods on behalf of the buyer. It is known as 'constructive delivery'.

> ***Example:*** X sells 100 bags of wheat to Y the wheat is lying in the godown of Z. X gives an order to Z to deliver wheat to Y. Z agrees to hold the 100 bags on behalf of Y and makes necessary entry in his books. It amounts to constructive delivery of wheat.

Rules Regarding Delivery of Goods

The following rules are applicable with regard to delivery of goods:

(*i*) **Types of delivery:** Goods may be delivered by the seller to the buyer by giving actual, symbolic or constructive delivery. The important thing in this regard is that buyer or his authorised agent should get possession of the goods.

(*ii*) **Delivery and payment are concurrent conditions:** Unless, otherwise agreed, the delivery of goods and payment of price are concurrent conditions. The seller should be ready and willing to handover possession of the goods to the buyer and the buyer should also be ready and willing to pay the price to the seller.

(*iii*) **Buyer to apply for delivery:** Unless contrary intention appears the seller is not bound to deliver the goods, until the buyer applies for it. In case of future or contingent goods which are yet to be procured by the seller, it is the duty of the seller to inform that goods have been procured. Even in such case, the buyer has to apply for the delivery. In case he fails to apply, he has no remedy against the seller.

(iv) Effect of part delivery: Unless contrary intention appears, when in the process of delivery, part of goods has been delivered. For the purpose of ascertaining time of passing property in goods, it will be assumed that whole lot has been delivered. But, when part delivery is made with an intention to separate it from remaining lot, it will not be considered as delivery of entire lot.

(v) Place of delivery: While marking contract of sale, the parties may decide about place of delivery and the goods must be delivered accordingly. But if a place has not been decided, the following rules will apply:

(*a*) The goods sold are to be delivered, at the place, at which they are at the time of sale.

(*b*) Goods agreed to be sold are to be delivered, at the place at which, they are at the time of agreement to sell.

(*c*) If the goods are not in existence at the time of agreement to sell, they are to the delivered at the place, at which they are being produced.

(vi) Time of delivery: In case, time is fixed for the delivery, the goods should be delivered accordingly. But if no time is fixed and the seller is to deliver goods. He must make delivery of goods within reasonable period of time. Reasonable period of time is a matter of fact, varies from situation to situation depending on facts and circumstance of the case.

(vii) Manner of delivery: When the goods are in the possession of third party, such goods cannot be delivered, unless, third party acknowledges that he is holding the goods on behalf of the seller.

(viii) Expenses of delivery: Unless, otherwise agreed, expenses and incidental charges, which the seller incurs for putting the goods in to deliverable position, shall be borne by the seller.

(ix) Delivery of wrong quantity: When the goods are delivered in short quantity or in excess or mixed with other goods, the following rules will be applicable:

(*a*) When the goods delivered, are shorter than contracted quantity the buyer has a right to reject delivery. But if he accepts the goods, he will have to pay for that according to contract rate.

(*b*) When the seller delivers larger quantity more than contracted quantity, the buyer can:

- Reject delivery of goods.
- Accept contracted quantity and reject the excess.
- Accept whole quantity, he will have to pay for extra quantity according to contract rate.

(*c*) When the seller has mixed other goods with the goods for which contract is made and other goods are of different description. The buyer, either can reject whole lot, or can accept the goods according to contract and can reject remaining goods of different description.

(*x*) *Instalment delivery:* Unless, contrary intention appears, the buyer is not bound to accept delivery by instalments.

But, where, the contract of sale provides for instalment delivery which have to be separately paid for, the seller fails to deliver instalment or the buyer fails to pay for that instalment. The question arises that whether such failure leads to repudiation of the whole contract or only that instalment should be repudiated in respect of which default is made. It depend on the fact of the case and the circumstances.

MAPLE FLOCK COY LTD. *vs* UNIVERSAL FURNITURE PRODUCTS (WEMBLEY) (1943, 1, K. B. 14). In this case, A agreed to supply B, 10 tonnes of flock in 20 instalments. First 15 instalments were satisfactory. But the 16th instalment was defective and subsequent deliveries were also satisfactory. The buyer wanted to repudiate the whole contract. It was held that the buyer could not do so, because the probability of default being made was negligible.

(*xi*) *Delivery to carrier:* The term 'carrier' means an agency to whom the goods are handed over for transmitting them to the buyer such as railway, shipping coy, transport agency and airways, etc.

In this regard as per Section 39(1), there is a general rule of law that delivery of goods to a carrier, whether named by the buyer or not, operates prima facie as delivery of goods to the buyer.

So far as transfer of property in good is concerned, it should be remembered that when the seller delivers the good to the carrier without reserving right of disposal, the property of goods passes to the buyer when the goods are handed over to the carrier. This is so because, the carrier is treated as an agent of the buyer.

Example: A of Delhi sells certain goods to B of Bombay. A sends the goods by railways and railway receipt was made in the name of B. In this case, as soon as goods are delivered to railways, the property in goods passes to B because A has not reserved the right of disposal with him.

However it should be noted that the liability of the seller is not over just by delivering goods to the carrier. Section 30 (2) of this Act clearly provides that, "unless otherwise authorised by the buyer, the seller must make a reasonable contract with the carrier or wharfinger for the safe carriage of the goods."

In case the seller fails to make such arrangement for safe carriage and the goods are lost or damaged in transit, the buyer will hold seller responsible for such losses.

Sometimes, the goods are sent by sea transit, wherein it is quite usual to insure the goods. In such cases, the seller should give to the buyer such notice as shall enable him to insure the goods. If the seller fails to give such notice and goods are not insured the goods will be deemed to be at the risk of the seller.

The liability of the seller to inform the buyer will arise in FOB contracts (Free on board) when the goods are delivered on board the ship. But in case of CIF contracts (cost, insurance and freight) the seller is required to insure the goods.

Reservation of right of disposal: In a contract of sale, when the goods are delivered to the carrier for the purpose of taking them to the buyer, the property in goods passes to the buyer, provided the seller has not reserved the right of disposal. This is the right which is given to the seller by which he does not part with control over the goods, until certain condition are fulfilled. In other words, if the seller does some act which shows his intention that he will pass on the control over the goods to the buyer only when the buyer satisfies some conditions.

Example: Ram agrees to sell the goods to Shyam on the condition that goods will be delivered to him on the acceptance of 'Bill of Exchange'. The property in goods will pass on to Shyam only when he accepts the bill.

In the following two cases, the seller is deemed to have reserved the right of disposal with himself.

(*a*) Where the goods are delivered to railways or shipping company for carriage, but bill of lading or railway receipt as the case may be, is deliverable to the order of the seller or his agent and not to the buyer.

Example: A delivers goods to Railway company for the purpose of carriage to B. But instead of sending railway receipt to B, it is sent to C, the agent of A and asking him to hand over it to B on the payment of the price. A has reserved the right of disposal.

(*b*) Where the seller draws a bill of exchange on the buyer for the price of the goods and sends it along with railway receipt or bill of lading on a condition that those documents will be handed over to the buyer on the acceptance of that bill.

Acceptance of Delivery

In a contract of sale, the goods are to be delivered by the seller to the buyer. Delivery of the goods becomes complete, when it is accepted by the buyer or by his authorised agent. Mere receipt of goods on the part of the buyer does not amount to acceptance. Rather acceptance of delivery is something more than this. In this regard, the following rules are applicable:

(*i*) When the goods are delivered to the buyer, which he has not previously examined, the buyer should be given reasonable opportunity of examining them as to ascertain that whether they are in conformity with the contract. He is deemed to have accepted delivery only onsuch examination.

(*ii*) The buyer is deemed to have accepted the goods when:

- (*a*) He intimates the seller that he has accepted the goods.
- (*b*) The goods are delivered to the buyer, and he does any act in relation to them which shows that he has accepted them such as he resells the goods or pledges the goods.
- (*c*) The buyer retains the goods, beyond reasonable time, without intimating the seller that he has rejected them.

(*iii*) Unless otherwise agreed, when goods are delivered to the buyers, and he refuses to accept them, he is not bound to return them to the seller. But the buyer must inform the seller that he refuses to accept the goods.

Liability of the Buyer

When the seller is ready and willing to deliver the goods and requests the buyer to take delivery. But the buyer does not, within reasonable period of time, after the request of the seller, take the delivery of the goods, he is liable to the seller for:

- (*a*) Any loss caused to the seller by the neglect or refusal to take delivery of the goods.
- (*b*) Reasonable charge for the care and custody of the goods.

According to Section 44 of this Act, "where the neglect or refusal of the buyer to take delivery, amounts to a repudiation of a contract, the seller may sue the buyer for the price or for damage."

REVIEW QUESTIONS

1. Define 'transfer of ownership'. Why it is important in a contract of sale?
2. Why it is important to know the exact time when the ownership passes to the buyer.
3. State briefly the rules regarding the transfer of ownership.
4. What is meant by 'reservation of right of disposal'? When is right of disposal deemed to be reserved?
5. 'Delivery does not amount to acceptance of goods.' Comment.
6. What are the legal remedies available to the buyer? When goods of wrong quality and quantity are delivered to him?
7. Explain briefly the rules relating to delivery of goods.
8. 'No seller can transfer better than the himself has.' Explain this rule and discuss various exception to this rule.
9. Write notes on:
   (*a*) Appropriation of goods.
   (*b*) Transfer of ownership of specific goods.
   (*c*) Modes of delivery of goods.
   (*d*) Instalment delivery.
   (*e*) Acceptance of delivery.
10. Comment on:
   (*a*) Risk passes with ownership.
   (*b*) Unconditional delivery to carrier is, prima facie, deemed to be delivery of good to the buyer.
   (*c*) Finder of goods can pass, goods title to the buyer.
   (*d*) Duty of the seller is not over, when the goods are delivered to the carrier.
   (*e*) Transfer of ownership is different from transfer of possession.

PRACTICAL PROBLEMS

1. A sold some furniture to B. B left the furniture in the shop of A. Meantime the shop sets on fire and that furniture is damaged along with other furniture. Who is to bear the loss of that furniture, which has been sold? (Hint: B will bear loss.)

2. Ram sold a machine to Shyam on instalment payment basis with a condition that the ownership will be transferred to Shyam on the payment of final instalment. Before making payment of final instalment, Shyam sells the machine to Manohar who buys it in good faith. Will he get good title of that machine? (Hint: Yes).
3. A is a owner of a car. His brother drives it. While driving on the road he meets with an accident with B's car. In the accident A's car was badly damaged with the fault of B. Can A's brother has any legal remedy against B? (Hint: No, he is not a owner.)
4. A delivered his scooter to B on approval basis. B kept that scooter with him for three months. He does not give any information regarding rejection of that scooter to A. In the meantime the scooter is damaged in the fire. Who is liable for loss? (Hint: B will be liable.)
5. Y delivers some pieces of jewellery to X on sale or return basis. X pledges that jewellery with Z and does not give any information to Y regarding acceptance or rejection. Can Y recover that jewellery from Z? Give reasons. (Hint: No.)
6. F is a owner of a car, instructed this agent A to sell the car at stipulated price, and not below that. But A sold the car to B at a price lower than the stipulated price and misappropriated that money. B bought the car in good faith, will B get good title of that car? (Hint: Yes.)
7. A purchased B's car at gunpoint. Before B could rescind the contract A sells this car to C who buys the car in good faith. Can B recover this car from C? (Hint: No.)
8. Ram sold a wristwatch to Shyam and same was delivered to him. Later on, he delivered that watch back to Ram for repair. Ram resells that watch to Manohar. Is it valid sale? (Hint: No.)
9. A sold raw material to B who is in Bombay, the raw material is to be delivered through Indian Railways. A handsover the raw material, to the Railways. The railway receipt is being sent to A's agent along with bill of exchange which is to be accepted by B. But in transit the raw material is damaged. Who will bear the loss? (Hint: A will be liable for loss.)
10. Karim delivers a horse to John on trial for a week. Without negligence on his part, the horse dies on third day. Is John liable to pay the price? (Hint: No.)

21

Unpaid Seller and His Rights

LEARNING OBJECTIVES

- Understand meaning and concept of unpaid seller in a contract of sale.
- Remember the various rights of unpaid seller and see that which one is used very often.
- Examine the nature and extent of right of lien and compare it with right of stoppage in transit.
- Analyse the rights of unpaid seller against the buyer of goods.
- Be clear about the concept of auction sale.

MEANING OF UNPAID SELLER

A contract comprises reciprocal promises. In a contract of sale, if seller is under an obligation to deliver goods, the buyer has to pay for it. In case buyer fails or refuses to pay, the seller, as unpaid seller, shall have certain rights.

According to Section 45 of this Act, the seller of goods is deemed to be an unpaid seller when:

(*a*) Whole of the price has not been paid or tendered.

(*b*) Bill of exchange or other negotiable instrument has been received as a conditional payment, and the condition on which it was received has not been fulfilled, by reason of the dishonour of the instrument or otherwise.

Thus to be considered as an unpaid seller, the following conditions must be satisfied:

(*a*) Whole of the price has not been paid. It implies that even if a major portion of the price has paid, still the seller remains an unpaid seller.

(*b*) Goods have been sold and the price must be due.

(*c*) Bill of exchange, or cheque or other negotiable instrument was received as payment of the price, but the same has been dishonoured.

Thus the seller becomes an unpaid seller only on account of non-payment of the price. If some expenses incurred by the seller has not been paid, he cannot be termed as 'unpaid seller'. Similarly, where the seller has sold the goods on credit again he cannot be treated as unpaid seller, till the date of credit.

In case, where whole of the price has been tendered by the buyer and the seller has refused, it cannot be treated as unpaid seller.

Example: A sold goods worth Rs. 5,000 to B on credit for three months. A will not be considered as unpaid seller during the period of three months. And he will become unpaid seller, when the price remains unpaid even after the expiry of credit period of three months.

RIGHTS OF UNPAID SELLER

The rights of unpaid seller can be put in two categories:

I. *Rights against goods*

(*i*) Right of lien

(*ii*) Right of stoppage in transit

(*iii*) Right of resale

II. *Rights against the buyer*

(*i*) Right to file suit for price

(*ii*) Right to file suit for damages

(*iii*) Right to file suit for interest

These rights of an unpaid seller do arise by operation of law, irrespective of the fact that whether they have made any agreement express or implied between them.

Rights of Unpaid Seller Against Goods

Where the ownership of goods has passed to the buyer:

(*i*) Right of Lien: Right of lien means right to retain possession of the goods, till certain debts or claims in respect of those goods are cleared. This right is related to physical possession of the goods. So any party who is entitled to it can use it only if he has got possession of the goods. So is the case with an unpaid seller, he can exercise this right if he has possession of the goods.

According to Section 47 (1) of this Act, "the unpaid seller of goods who is in possession of them is entitled to retain possession of them until payment or tender of the price is made." He can exercise right of lien under the following cases:

(*a*) Where the goods have been sold on cash basis, without any stipulation as to credit.

(*b*) Where the goods have been sold on credit, but the term of credit has expired.

(*c*) Where the buyer becomes insolvent.

To exercise rights of lien transfer of ownership is not significant, rather the seller needs to have possession of goods. Thus the right of lien will not be affected, even if the document of title such as bill of lading or railway receipt etc., have been handed over to the buyer.

Example: A sold 100 bags of cement to B on cash payment basis. The bags of cement have identified and separated out from the stock. But B fails in making payment. A is entitled to retain possession of these cement bags till the payment of price is made or offered.

***Rules Regarding Right of Lien*:** The rules regarding right of lien are as follows:

(*a*) To exercise the right of lien the goods must be in actual possession of the seller. Due to any reason if he loses the possession, the right of lien will also be lost.

(*b*) The goods were sold on cash payment basis, but price has not been paid or tendered. It is sufficient ground for using this right.

(*c*) The goods were sold on credit, but the term of credit has been expired and full payment has not been made, the seller can use this right.

(*d*) When the buyer becomes insolvent, the seller can retain possession of the goods till the payment of price. According to Section 2 (8) of Sale of Goods Act insolvent means, "a person who has ceased to pay his debt, in the ordinary course of business, or cannot pay his debts, as they become due, whether he has committed act of insolvency or not."

(*e*) The seller who is possessing the good in the capacity of bailee or agent or in any other capacity can exercise right of lien.

(*f*) In case documents of title have been handed over to the buyer, but possession of the goods lies with the seller who can exercise right of lien.

(*g*) The right of lien is available to the seller only for the price and not for any other charges such as godown charges and other maintenance charges.

(*h*) Right of lien is not divisible. Thus in case of part payment made by the buyer, the seller may refuse to deliver part of the goods to the extent of payment.

(*i*) In case the seller has already delivered part of the goods to the buyer, he has a right of lien over the remaining goods, provided he has not waived right of lien in favour of the buyer.

***Termination of right of lien*:** The right of lien terminates:

(*a*) On giving possession of the goods to the carrier for the purpose of taking them to the buyer, without reserving right of disposal. This is so because unconditional delivery to the carrier amounts delivery to the buyer himself.

(*b*) When the buyer or his authorised agent gets possession of the goods lawfully, the right of lien will come to an end.

(*c*) The seller has an option to waive his right of lien in favour of the buyer. He may do it expressly or it may be directly understood from his conduct and intention, such as extending term of credit may amount to implied waiver.

(*d*) When the buyer tenders the price but the seller refuses to accept it, the right of lien will be lost.

(ii). Right of stoppage of goods in transit: When the goods are on the move towards the buyer and the buyer becomes insolvent, the seller can exercise the right of the stoppage of goods in transit. By using this right, he can check the movement of the goods immediately and prevent the buyer from getting possession of the goods.

This right is considered as an extension of right of lien, because by using this right, the unpaid seller regains the possession of the goods.

This right of stoppage in transit arises, when the right of lien comes to an end, because the goods are no more in the possession of the seller. He has delivered them to the carrier. By using this right the unpaid seller may get those goods back from the carrier or may withhold delivery.

According to Section 50 of this Act, "Subject to the provisions of this Act, when the buyer of goods becomes insolvent, the unpaid seller who has parted with the possession of the goods, has the right of stopping them in transit, that is to say, he may resume possession of the goods as long as they are in the course of transit and may retain them until payment or tender of the price."

When can this right be exercised (Section 50): An interpretation of the contents of Section 50's provision makes it clear that the right of stoppage of goods in transit can be exercised by the unpaid seller under the following situations:

(*a*) The seller must be an unpaid seller.

(*b*) The ownership of the goods must have passed to the buyer.

(*c*) The goods must be in the course of transit *i.e.*, neither in the possession of the seller nor in the possession of the buyer.

(*d*) The buyer of the goods has become insolvent.

(*e*) Goods may be stopped in transit only for the payment of the price.

Duration of transit (Section 51): The unpaid seller can exercise this right only when the goods are in the course of transit. The goods are deemed to be in transit when they are neither in the possession of the seller nor in the possession of the buyer. Rather, they are in the possession of a carrier, who is holding them in his own name for the purpose of taking them to the buyer.

According to Section 51 of this Act, "goods are deemed to be in the course of transit, from the time when they are delivered to a carrier or other bailee for the purpose of transmission to the buyer. Until the buyer or his agent takes delivery of them from such carrier or other bailee."

Sometimes, the buyer may apply for the delivery of the goods, at a different place other than the agreed one, the goods are in transit, until they are received by the buyer or his agent at that place.

How the right of stoppage is exercised (Section 52): The unpaid seller can exercise the right of stoppage of goods in transit in the following ways:

(*a*) By taking actual possession of the goods from a carrier.

(*b*) By giving notice of his claim to the carrier or other bailee in whose possession the goods are.

Such notice may be given either (*a*) to the person in actual possession of the goods or (*b*) to his principal. After receiving such notice, it is the duty of a carrier not to deliver the goods to the buyer, but to deliver them back according to the instruction of the unpaid seller. The expenses of redelivering the goods to him will be borne by the seller. If the carrier after receiving such notice delivers the goods to the buyer or his agent, he shall be liable to the seller for conversion.

When the transit comes to an end (Section 51): The unpaid seller can use this right, so long as the goods are in transit. As soon as the transit ends, the seller's right of stoppage will be lost. Transit comes to an end under the following situation:

(*a*) *Buyer taking delivery:* Once the goods reach into the hands of the buyer or his agent, transit comes to an end. Even if the buyer or his agent takes delivery of the goods at some other place, before reaching to appointed destination, transit comes to an end. [Section 51(2)]

(*b*) *Carriers's acknowledgement to the buyer:* As soon as the goods reach to appointed destination and a carrier acknowledges to the buyer or to his agent that he holds the goods on his behalf, the transit ends. [Section 51(3)]

(*c*) *Wrongful refusal to the buyer:* After having arrived at an appointed destination, the carrier wrongfully refuses to deliver the goods to the buyer or to his agent, the transit is deemed to be at end. [Section 51(6)]

Example: A sold some goods to B, to be delivered to him in Bombay. A handed over the goods to a carrier for the purpose of taking them to B. On the arrival at Bombay the carrier refuses to deliver the goods, unless some additional payment is made to him. On the arrival at Bombay the transit comes to an end.

(*d*) *Goods delivered to a ship:* In case, the goods have been delivered to a ship chartered by the buyer, if the buyer is an owner of that ship, transit ends as soon as goods are loaded on the ship. But if the buyer has deployed the ship as a carrier, the goods continue to be in transit. [Section 51(5)]

(*e*) *Part delivery:* Where part delivery of the goods has been made to the buyer or his agent, the remainder of the goods may be stopped in transit. Unless such part delivery has been given in such circumstances as to show an agreement to give up possession of whole of the goods. [Section 51 (7)]

However, to exercise the right of stoppage in transit it is not necessary that the buyer must have been declared as an insolvent by the court. His unsatisfactory or bad financial position provide sufficient ground for using this right.

Lien *vs* Stoppage in transit

	Lien	Stoppage in transit
Possession of goods	To exercise right of lien the goods must be in the possession of the seller.	To exercise this right, the goods must be in possession of independent carrier or bailee.
Insolvency of the buyer	This right can be exercised for getting payment of the price. It is not necessary that the buyer must be insolvent. Even if he refuses to pay, the seller can use this right.	This right can be used only if buyer becomes insolvent. Or his financial position becomes unsatisfactory.
Termination	As soon as the seller parts with the goods, the right of lien will be terminated.	Right of stoppages will be terminated when the goods get into the hand of the buyer or his agent.
Nature	The right of lien is a right to retain possession of the goods until payment of the price is made to the seller.	This right is used to regain the possession of the goods.
Exercise of the right	The right of lien is exercised by the seller himself.	The right of stoppage in transit can be exercised by the selller through the carrier or the bailee in whose possession the goods are.

Effect of sub-sale or pledge by buyer: As stated earlier, right of lien and right of stoppage in transit of unpaid seller will not be affected by sub-sale or pledge by the buyer. It is because the second buyer cannot stand in a better position than his seller (first buyer). In the same way, where the sub-buyer produced delivery orders to the seller who indorsed them that he was willing to give delivery, but after delivery of part of goods he refused to deliver the remaining on the ground that first buyer has not paid the price. The seller will be stopped from doing so. Thus the right of sub-buyer will get legal recognition provided sub-sale must have been made with the consent of the seller.

Example: A sold 100 bags of wheat from his godown to B. B then sold 50 bags out of these to C. A told to C that the wheat bags would be delivered to him in due course. In the meantime B becomes insolvent. Thus A's right with regard to 50 bags which have been sold to C is lost because he has recognised sub-sale made by B to C.

In the same way where the documents of title such as bill of lading or railway receipt etc., has been lawfully transferred to any person as a buyer and the buyer, in turn transfers these to second buyer who buys them in good faith and for valuable consideration, the unpaid seller's right of lien or stoppage in transit would come to an end.

However, Section 53 (2) of this Act states that "if such transfer of documents of title is by way of pledge, then the unpaid seller's rights are not completely defeated, but he can exercise these rights subject to the right of pledgee."

Example: A sold some goods to B and sent railway receipt to B. B without paying for the goods pledged the railway receipt with C as a security for a loan of Rs. 10,000 becomes insolvent. A is entitled to get back railway receipt after paying Rs. 10,000 to C.

(iii) Right of Resale: After regaining possession of the goods by exercising right of stoppage, the unpaid seller can exercise right of lien by retaining possession till the payment of the price. Still the contract of sale is in force and the buyer may get possession after making payment of price to the seller.

The most important right available to the unpaid seller is right of resale of those goods. Instead of using the above rights, if the seller does not get the price he is entitled to resell the goods under the following situations:

(*a*) *Perishable goods:* Where the goods, being retained by the seller are of a perishable nature and lose the value and utility regularly, the unpaid seller can resell the goods for best obtainable prices. The goods are said to be of a perishable nature if they deteriorate physically and chemically and become commercially unmerchantable.

(*b*) *Reasonable notice:* The unpaid seller, after having exercised right of stoppage and right of lien, give reasonable notice to the buyer, the seller can resell the goods. By giving such notice the unpaid seller may express his intention that if price remains unpaid till the expiration of reasonable period of time, he will resell the goods.

Where the goods are resold under any above situations, and the unpaid seller fails to realise that much price, which he was expected to get from the original buyer. In this case he has right to claim any shortfall arising out of resale from the original buyer. But if he gets more than the original price he is not bound to return excess of the price to the original buyer.

However, if the goods are resold under any other situations except above mentioned, the unpaid seller will have no claim for short fall in price and if he gets more than original price he is bound to return the excess to the original buyer.

Notice of resale: Except in case of perishable goods, in all other cases the unpaid seller is under legal obligation to give reasonable notice of this fact to the original buyer. The basic idea of giving such notice is that, on the one hand the buyer be given an opportunity for performing the contract by making payment of the price and getting delivery of the goods. On the other hand the buyer, who is not in a position to pay the price may ensure that the goods are resold at reasonable price. This is so because, if any short fall arises, it is to be made good by him.

The second buyer of the goods will get good title as against the first buyer provided the goods were resold under any one of the situations mentioned earlier. But this rule is subject to the following exceptions:

(*a*) *Right to resell is reserved:* In a contract of sale, if the seller has expressly reserved the right of resale in case the buyer defaults in payment of price, he is not required to give any notice to the original buyer for resale of goods ownership that has not been transferred to the buyer:

(*b*) *Right of withholding delivery of goods:* In a contract of sale, if ownership of the goods has not been transferred to the buyer, the unpaid seller has a right to withhold delivery. This right is similar to and co-extensive with his right of lien and stoppage in transit.

II. Rights of Unpaid Seller Against the Buyer

In addition to the rights against the goods unpaid the seller has certain rights against the buyer. These rights are known as 'right in personam', because these rights can be used against the buyer personally. These rights are:

(i) Suit for Price: In a contract of sale, the buyer is under legal obligation to pay the price of the goods. Where under a contract of sale, the property in goods has passed to the buyer, and the buyer wrongfully neglects or refuses to pay for goods, according to the term of a contract, the seller may sue him for the price of the goods. [Section 55 (1)]

Section 55 (2) of this Act provides, "if the contract of sale stipulates the payment of the price on a certain day irrespective of delivery and the buyer wrongfully neglects or refuses to pay such price, the seller may sue him for the price, although property in goods has not passed."

Thus, the contents of this provision may be read as an extention of the contents given under Section 55 (1).

Example: A sold some goods to B for Rs. 10,000 and B agreed to pay the price after 10 days of the contract. B refuses to pay the price on due date. A is entitled to file suit against B. Though property in goods has not been passed to the buyer, but the buyer was to make payment of the price on a certain day, which he refuses.

(ii) Suit for Damages: In case the buyer wrongfully refuses or neglects to accept delivery of the goods and pay for it, the seller may sue upon him for damages.

According to Section 44 of this Act, "where the property in goods has passed to the buyer, the seller is entitled to recover:

(*a*) Any loss caused to him by the buyer's refusal or neglect to take delivery.

(*b*) Any reasonable charge for the care and custody of the goods."

The provisions of Indian Contract Act contained under Section 73 will be equally applicable for determining the account of damages.

THOMSON *vs* ROBINSON (1955, C.H. 177). In this case, T a car dealer contracted to supply a motor car to R. R refused to take delivery. It was found that supply of cars was in excess of demand at the time of breach of contract and thus there was no ready market for cars on the date of breach. It was held that T was entitled to recover damages for the loss of profit in the bargain.

According to Section 60 of this Act, "where the buyer repudiates the contract before the date of delivery, the seller may either treat the contract as continue and wait till the date of delivery or he may treat the contract as rescinded and sue for damage for the breach."

(iii) Suit for Interest: When in a contract of sale, the seller tenders delivery of goods to the buyer and the buyer wrongfully refuses or neglect to accept and pay the price, the seller has right to claim reasonable interest on the amount of the price. The interest may be calculated from the date of tender of delivery of goods or from the date on which the price was payable. In the absence of specific agreement, the court may award interest at such rate as it think reasonable and fit on the amount of the price.

RIGHTS OF THE BUYER

In case, the seller makes breach of contract, the buyer will be considered as an aggrieved party. He has the following rights against the seller:

I. Suit for Damage (Section 57)

Where the buyer is ready and willing to accept delivery of goods, but the seller wrongfully refuses or neglects it, the buyer may sue upon the seller to claim damages for non-delivery of the goods.

II. Suit for Specific Performance (Section 58)

In a contract of sale of specific goods if the seller fails to deliver the goods, the buyer may file a suit for specific performance. But the court will pass such order only in those cases where the damages are not a suitable remedy as such that the goods to be supplied were of unique nature etc.

Example: A made a contract of sale for selling rare piece of painting to B for Rs. 10,000. Later on, A refused to deliver that painting piece. On account of breach of contract, the loss suffered by B cannot be measured in terms of money, thus damage is not an adequate remedy. B can claim order of specific performance.

III. Suit for Breach of Warranty (Section 59)

In case the seller makes breach of warranty, or the buyer treats breach of condition as a breach of warranty, the buyer can claim damage for the loss suffered by him. However, in case of breach of warranty, the buyer has no right to reject the goods.

IV. Repudiation of a Contract (Section 60)

Where the seller repudiates the contract before the date of delivery, the buyer may either treat the contract as continuous and wait till the date of delivery or he may treat the contract as rescinded and can proceed against the seller for the damages.

V. Suit for Recovery of the Price with Interest (Section 61)

In case, the buyer has paid the price to the seller, on due and date, and the seller fails to deliver the goods the buyer has right to file a suit for the recovery of the price along with interest on the amount of price. The interest will be calculated from the date on which the price was paid by the buyer.

AUCTION SALE

One of the very popular way of selling the goods is to sell them by auction. A sale by auction is a public sale, whereupon, people are invited to compete for the purchase of property by successive offers of higher amount. The offer of the price is known as 'bid' and the person offering the price is known as 'bidder'.

Auction sale may be arranged either by the seller himself or he may appoint someone as 'auctioneer' to sell the goods on his behalf. The auctioneer will act as an agent on behalf of the owner.

In order to sell the goods in auction, the auctioneer makes wide publicity of time, date and place of the sale. The prospective bidders are provided an opportunity to inspect the goods. Since the auctioneer invites the public to make an offer, he is not bound to sell the goods at time, date and place as mentioned in the advertisement. In case the auctioneer postpones the sale, prospective bidders have no right to sue upon him.

According to the usual practice, auction sale programme is duly advertised and printed catalogue of the goods along with the conditions of sale are circulated among the prospective bidders. At appointed time and place the auctioneer invites bidder to offer the price. He announces the acceptance of the last bid by a tap with his hammer or by any other approved method.

Rules Regarding Auction Sale

(*i*) Where the goods are put up for sale in lots, each lot is prima facie deemed to be subject matter of a separate contract of sale.

(*ii*) The sale is complete when the auctioneer announces its completion by fall of the hammer or by any other approved method.

(*iii*) As soon as the auctioneer announces the completion of sale, property in goods passes immediately to the buyer.

(*iv*) Before the completion of sale, any bidder may withdraw his offer.

(*v*) A right to bid may be reserved expressly either by the seller or on his behalf by any person. It may be done for protecting the interest of the seller.

(*vi*) It is very usual to announce a 'reserve price' by the auctioneer. It is a price below which the auctioneer will not sell.

(*vii*) In case the seller makes use of pretended bidding to raise the price, the sale is voidable at the option of the buyer.

(*viii*) Damping is an unlawful act, because it intends to discourage the bidders from bidding. This is done by printing out defects in the goods or scaring prospective bidders away so that they may not participate in the auction sale.

(*ix*) The seller can appoint only one 'puffer'. He is the person employed by the seller for the purpose of raising the price but he has no intention to buy the goods.

REVIEW QUESTIONS

1. Define 'unpaid seller'. What are his rights?
2. Explain the rights of an unpaid seller (*a*) as against the goods, and (*b*) as against the buyer.
3. 'Right of stoppage in transit is an extension of right of lien.' Comment.
4. Distinguish between right of lien and right of stoppage of goods in transit.
5. Discuss the situation when the transit ends.
6. Explain the right to resell the goods by unpaid seller and discuss the situations under which resale in valid.
7. Explain the effects of sub-sale or pledge on unpaid seller's right of lien and stoppage in transit.
8. What is 'auction sale'? Discuss various rules regarding auction sale.
9. Comment on:
   (*a*) Seller becomes an unpaid seller only on account of non-payment of the price.
   (*b*) Right of lien is possessory in nature.

PRACTICAL PROBLEMS

1. A sold a machine part to B without any stipulation to deliver the goods until the price is paid. Advise A.
2. Ram sells the goods to Shyam. Shyam makes payment of the price by cheque. Before Shyam could obtain delivery of goods, his cheque is dishonored by the bank. Ram therefore refuses to deliver the goods until payment is made. Is Ram's action justified? (Hint: Yes.)
3. Sohan sells one hundred bags of cement to Mohan of Calcutta. He sends the goods by railways. The railway receipt duly made in favour of Mohan was sent to him. On the arrival of the goods in Calcutta, Mohan asked the railways to carry them to Durgapur. In the meantime, Mohan became insolvent. Sohan asks railways to stop the goods. Will he succeed? (Hint: No.)
4. A sells the goods to B worth Rs. 5,000 on credit. The goods were consigned to him by rail. B assigns railway receipt to C to borrow Rs. 2,000 on the security of that receipt. Before the goods reach the

appointed destination, B becomes insolvent. A gives notice to stop the goods in transit, but C claims them. Will A succeed in stopping the goods? (Hint: Yes, subject to condition of assignment.)

5. Roshan sells 50 bags of wheat to Rajesh. The wheat bags are lying in the godown of Roshan. It is agreed that Rajesh shall get one month's credit for payment. Rajesh allowed wheat bags to remain in the godown of Roshan. Before the expiry of one month's credit Rajesh becomes insolvent. Can Roshan refuse to deliver the wheat to the official assignee? (Hint: Yes.)
6. Amar of Delhi places an order with Basant of Bombay to deliver some goods to him at Delhi. Basant sent goods by railways. When the goods reach Delhi, the railway official informs Amar that goods are lying at station, at the risk of Amar. Meanwhile Amar becomes insolvent. Can Basant stop the goods in transit? (Hint: No.)
7. A participated in an auction sale and made a bid of Rs. 1,000 for a second hand typewriter. But he withdraws his bid, before the fall of hammer. As per the condition of auction sale which, A knows, that bidding once made will not allow to be withdrawn. The auctioneer sued upon A for Rs. 1,000 as his being the highest bid. Examine the case and advise A.
8. K sold some furniture to M by an auction. M, gave a cheque for the price and took the delivery of that furniture. One of the clause of the agreement was that property in goods will not pass to the buyer until the cheque was honoured. M sold the furniture to N. K wants to take back the furniture from N. Will he succeed? Advise him.
9. Ashok made a bid for a steel almirah in an auction sale but withdrew the bid before the fall of hammer. Can Ashok be entitled to do it? (Hint: Yes.)
10. A railway company is in possession of the goods as a carrier, when an unpaid seller gives notice of stoppage in transit. The buyer of the goods already owes some money to the railway coy. Can the railway company exercise right of lien over the goods in violation of the right of stoppage in transit of the seller? (Hint: No.)

■■■

Unit 3

Negotiable Instrument Act, 1881

Companies Act, 1956

22

Introduction to Negotiable Instruments

LEARNING OBJECTIVES

- Understand basic concept of negotiable instrument in terms of special features and presumptions.
- Compare bill of exchange with promissory note and cheque.
- Develop conceptual clarity regarding various types of bills.
- Compare bearer instrument with order instrument in terms of their legal implication.

INTRODUCTION

The law relating to negotiable instruments is primarily contained in the Negotiable Instruments Act, 1881, which came into force on 1 March 1882. The Act extends to the whole of India except the state of Jammu & Kashmir. It does not interfere either with the local usage of these instruments or with the relevant provisions of the Reserve Bank of India Act, 1934.

Bills of exchange, cheques and promissory notes have been dealt within considerable details in this Act.

Meaning of an Instrument

The term 'instrument' means any written document by which a right is created in favour of some person. The word 'negotiable' has a technical meaning whereby rights in an instrument can be transferred by one person to another. Thus, a negotiable instrument is a document by which rights vested in a person can be transferred to another person in accordance with the provisions of the Negotiable Instruments Act, 1881.

Justice Willis has defined it as, "a negotiable instrument is one, property (title) in which is acquired by anyone who takes it bona fide and for value, notwithstanding any defect of title in the person from whom he took it."

In the words of Elvyn Thomas, "Negotiable instrument is one which is, by a largely recognised custom of trade or by law, transferable by delivery or by indorsement and delivery in such circumstances that, (*i*) the holder of it, for the time being is made to sue upon it, in his own name, and (*ii*) the property in it passes free from equities and free from any defect in the title of the person from whom he obtained."

It follows from the above definitions that negotiable instrument is a written promise or order to pay which is transferable. It can be transferred either by giving delivery of it (if it is payable to bearer) or by indorsing and then delivering it (if it is payable to order). On such transfer the transferee gets better title than the title of transferor.

According to Section 13 (*a*) of this Act, "'Negotiable instrument' means, a promissory note, bill of exchange or cheque payable either to order or to bearer."

Though the definition given above includes only three documents in negotiable instrument. But in practice, many other documents which meet the basic requirements of a negotiable instrument are also considered as negotiable instruments. And any matter or dispute regarding these will be dealt with according to the provisions of this Act.

The following instrument are characterised as negotiable instrument either by law or by custom and tradition of a trade:

(*i*) Treasury Bill
(*ii*) Government Promissory Note
(*iii*) Dividend Warrant
(*iv*) Share Warrant
(*v*) Bearer Debentures
(*vi*) Hundies
(*vii*) Port Trust Bonds
(*viii*) Improvement Trust Debentures/Bonds
(*ix*) Bearer Railway Bonds

The following instruments, resembling with negotiable instrument but are not recognised as so:

(*i*) Money order
(*ii*) Postal order
(*iii*) Deposit Receipt
(*iv*) Share Certificate
(*v*) Bill of Lading
(*vi*) Railway Receipt
(*vii*) Wharfinger's Certificate
(*viii*) Letter of Credit

Thus the provisions of negotiable Instrument Act do not apply to these instruments.

BASIC FEATURES OF NEGOTIABLE INSTRUMENTS

Negotiable instruments possess the following features:

(*i*) **Transferability:** Negotiable instrument is transferable. If it is payable to bearer, it can be transferred simply by giving delivery of it to the party concerned. If it is payable to order, for transfering it, first it is to be indorsed in favour of that party and then it is delivered to him.

(*ii*) **Good title to transferee:** In negotiable instrument, transferee gets good title from transferor, provided he gets instrument before due date, for value consideration and in good faith. In other words, even if the title of transferor is defective, the transferee gets good title free from all such defects, it is considered as basic feature of negotiable instrument.

(*iii*) **Right of holder:** On the transfer of negotiable instrument its holder or transferee gets among other rights, the right of ownership. He has a right to sue upon in his own name for the recovery of amount. Thus the transferee who gets instrument, in good faith, for value consideration and before maturity he is technically known as holder in due course. He can possess an instrument, can get payment of it, as a owner of it and can further transfer it.

(*iv*) **Evidence of debt:**Any instrument which has been drawn according to the provisions of this Act, but fails to qualify as valid negotiable instrument, can be used as an evidence of debt.

Example: A writes a promissory note amounting Rs. 10,000 payable after three months, in favour of B. But due to inadequate stamp duty it is not enforceable. At this instance B can use this invalid promissory note as an evidence that A owes sum of Rs. 10,000 to him, therefore he has made out promissory note in favour of B.

(*v*) **Legal presumptions:** Sections 118 and 119 of this Act provide for certain presumptions, which apply to all negotiable instruments. These are:

(*a*) ***Consideration:*** It is presumed that every negotiable instrument has been drawn, accepted and transferred for value consideration.

(*b*) ***Date:*** There is presumption regarding date of negotiable instrument that, it is drawn or made/on the date which appears on it.

(*c*) ***Time of acceptance:*** In case of bill of exchange which acquires validity on acceptance, it is presumed that the bill has been accepted within reasonable period of time after its date but before maturity.

(*d*) ***Stamp duty:*** In case, the bill of exchange or promissory note, which require stamp duty, it is presumed that every lost bill and promissory note were duly stamped.

(*e*) ***Order of indorsement:*** Indorsement is recorded on the instruments. Thus legally it is presumed that the instrument has been indorsed in that order, which appears on it.

(*f*) ***Time of transfer:*** Negotiable instruments are freely transferable. In this regard, it is presumed that every negotiable instrument is transferred before the date of maturity.

(*g*) ***Proof of protest:*** In case an instrument is dishonoured, to file suit on such dishonoured, instrument the holder should obtain a certificate known as 'Protest' from Notary Public. On the basis of such certificate the court will presume that the instrument hasbeen dishonoured.

(*h*) ***Holder in due course:*** It is presumed that, every holder of an instrument is a holder in due course. But in case, it is proved that the holder has obtained an instrument from its lawful owner by means of offence, fraud or unlawful consideration the holder has to prove that he is a holder in due course.

The above presumptions are rebuttable by the defendant. It means, burden of proving that the above presumptions do not exist, lies upon the defendant and not upon plaintiff.

TYPES OF NEGOTIABLE INSTRUMENTS

According to Section 13 of this Act, negotiable instrument includes the following three documents: Promissory Note, Bill of Exchange and Cheque.

Definition of Promissory Note

According to Section 4 of this Act, "Promissory Note is an instrument, in writing (not being bank note or currency note) containing an unconditional undertaking signed by the maker, to pay certain sum of money only to or to the order of certain person or to the bearer of the instrument."

The person who promises to pay is known as 'the maker' or promisor, and the person to whom the payment is made is called 'the payee' and main content of the note is 'the promise' to pay.

With regard to these definition the following points must be taken care of:

(*i*) No person in India except Reserve Bank of Central Government, can make or issue promissory note 'payable to bearer'. Thus the words 'payable to bearer' included in the definition of promissory note become ineffective.

(*ii*) Promissory note does not include bank note and currency note. Bank note means promissory notes issued by the banker payable to bearer on demand. And currency notes means promissory notes issued by RBI or Central Government payable to bearer on demand.

Specimen of Promissory Note	
Rs. 5000-00	New Delhi,
	December 15, 2006
Ninety days after date I, promise to pay to Ram Mohan or order the sum of Rs. Five Thousand only, with interest thereon at 10% per annum for value received.	
To Ram Mohan	Revenue Stamp
Daryaganj	S/d. Shyam Mohan

Characteristics of Promissory Note

According to the definition of promissory note given under Section 4 of this Act, a valid promissory note has the following characteristics:

(*a*) ***It must be in writing:*** Promissory note to be legally effective must be made in writing. The writing may be in ink, or pencil or printing, engraving or lithographing. No particular form of words needs to be followed. And it is not necessary that the word 'promise' should be used. The following is a valid promissory note.

Example: I acknowledge, myself to be indebted to Ram Mohan a sum of Rs. 5,000 to be paid on demand for value received.

S/d. Shyam Mohan

(*b*) ***It must contain unconditional promise to pay:*** The promissory note is promise to pay, thus it must contain express promise to pay. A mere acknowledgment of debt by the maker is not sufficient. To make it valid promissory note, such acknowledgement must be backed by clear intention to pay.

Example: I am indebted to pay Ram Mohan, a sum of Rs. 5,000 s/d. by Shyam Mohan. It is not promissory note, because it simply amounts to acknowledgement of debt.

Thus, to make it valid, it should be made as, I am indebted to Ram Mohan, a sum of Rs. 5,000. I will pay him the same on demand s/d. Shyam Mohan. Similarly I owe you Rs. 1,000 is not promissory note.

(*c*) ***The promise to pay must be unconditional:*** While making a promise, the maker must not put any condition to it. The promissory note to be legally valid must contain unconditional promise to pay. This is so because, conditional undertaking may interfere with negotiability of instrument, therefore it must be payable absolutely.

However the promise to pay, at a particular place, or after specified time or on the happening of some event, which is bound to happen, is not conditional.

Example: I promise to pay Ram Mohan, a sum of Rs. 5,000; 10 days after A's death, s/d Shyam Mohan. This promissory note is valid, because it is not conditional. But had it been contingent on the marriage of A, which may or may not happen, it would have been considered as conditional promise and thus is invalid.

(*d*) ***It must be signed by the maker:*** The promissory note must be signed by the maker. It is only by signing it his acknowledgement of debt and promise to pay becomes complete. Signature means, the writing of person's name in order to authenticate and give effect to the contract contained in the instrument. It is at the same time essential that the mind of signer must accompany the signature.

Signature may be done at any place, even at the top or at the back of the instrument. It is not necessary that it should be done at the bottom. It may be in pencil, or ink, even rubber stamp may be used for signatures. When the maker of a promissory note is illiterate, his thumb mark is sufficient.

(*e*) ***The maker must be certain person:*** It must be clearly specified in the promissory note with certainty that who is liable to pay. The promissory note may be made by two or more persons jointly, or jointly and severally. The maker of promissory note who has a primary liability to pay must be capable of being ascertained. The golden rule of law in that 'where liability lies, no ambiguity must lie.'

(*f*) ***The payee must be certain person:*** The promissory note becomes complete when the payee is capable of being ascertained by name or by description. Thus it must be pointed out with certainty the person to whom the promise is made. In case, there is a mistake regarding name of the payee or his designation, note is valid, provided the payee can be ascertained by evidence. The promissory note may be made payable to two or more persons jointly.

(*g*) ***The sum payable must be certain:*** The amount payable in promissory note must be certain and not subject to any contigency, addition or substraction. In the following cases, the promissory note is not valid:

(*i*) I promise to pay B sum of Rs. 1,000 and all other sums which may be due to him.

(*ii*) I promise to pay Rs. 1,000 to A along with all fines as per the rules.

But following are valid promissory notes:

(*i*) I promise to pay Rs. 2,000 to B; with 10% interest per annum.

(*ii*) I promise to pay B Rs. 2,000 in two equal instalments per month.

(*h*) ***Promise to pay money only:*** The promissory note should contain a promise to pay money and money only. Money means legal tender money of the country. The promise to pay in kinds or to pay money and partly in kinds is not valid.

(*i*) ***Other formalities:*** There are many other formalities which should be met while making promissory note. The promissory note must be made in writing, must be duly stamped according to the provisions of Indian Stamps Act 1899. Similarly for the convenience of the parties, the promissory note should contain date on which it is made and the place where it is made. The words 'value received' are also not essential, but as a custom, these words are also mentioned.

BILL OF EXCHANGE

According to Section 5 of this Act, "A bill of exchange is an instrument in writing containing an unconditional order signed by the maker, directing a certain person to pay certain sum of money, only to or to the order of certain person or to the bearer of the instrument."

Bill of exchange is written acknowledgement of debt accepted by the debtor and written by the creditor. There are three parties in a bill of exchange—the drawer, the acceptor or drawee and the payee. The drawer is a person who draws or makes a bill, the drawee is a person on whom the bill is drawn and the payee is a person to whom the amount of the bill is payable. Sometimes, the drawer and payee may be the same person.

Characteristics of Bill of Exchange

To be effective and valid, bill of exchange should possess the following characteristics:

(*a*) ***It must be in writing:*** Like promissory note, bill of exchange must be drawn or made in writing. The oral or verbal order to direct someone to pay is not valid bill.

(b) It contains an order to pay: The bill of exchange must contain express order for the acceptor to pay certain sum of money. However, mere request or a reminder to pay money will not be considered as bill of exchange.

Specimen of Bill of Exchange	
Rs. 5,000	New Delhi
	January 2, 2007
On demand pay to Sh. Ram Mohan or order, a sum of rupee Five thousand only for value received.	
To: Manohar	s/d. Stamp
25, Avtar Enclave	Shayam Mohan
New Delhi	

(c) The order to pay must be unconditional: In a bill of exchange the drawer gives an order to the drawee to pay. This order must be unconditional and the bill must not be made payable on contingency.

Examples:

(*i*) Please pay 90 days after the arrival of ship 'Peerless' at Mumbai S/d.

(*ii*) I shall be obliged, if you make it convenient to pay sum of Rs. 2,000 to B, s/d A.

(*iii*) Please pay C when I marry s/d.

These are not valid bills of exchange.

(d) It must be signed by the maker: The person who makes or draws a bill is known as 'drawer'. The bill of exchange must be signed by him. And without signature of drawer, it remains incomplete instrument and no action can be maintained against the acceptor.

Example: A draws a bill on B for Rs. 1,000 but forgets to sign on it. B accepts it and gives it back to A, who in consideration indorsed it, in favour of C. This is not a valid bill, thus C cannot recover its payment.

(e) The drawee must be certain: The bill of exchange is accepted by the drawee. He is primarily responsible for paying the bill. Thus the drawee must be named, and indicated with certainty in the bill. So that the payee, on the date of maturity can present the bill to him for payment.

(f) The payee must be certain: Like drawee of the bill, the payee, who is entitled to get payment on due date must be identified and ascertained. So that the drawee knows it very well with complete certainty that to whom he may pay the bill and discharge his liability properly.

(*g*) ***The sum payable must be certain:*** In bill of exchange, the drawer gives an order to drawee for paying the amount. The amount to be paid must be certain one. Any uncertainty regarding that may invalidate the bill. Not only this, but also that payment is to be made in money and money only.

(*h*) ***Other formalities:*** The bill of exchange to be valid must be duly stamped. Like other instruments, it must bear date, place, consideration and attestation etc. Though these are not essential by law.

Acceptance of a Bill

According to Section 33 of this Act, the bill must be properly accepted. It can be accepted only by the drawee or by all or some of the drawees mentioned in the instrument as (*i*) by a drawee in case of need, or (*ii*) by a person who accepts it for the honour of the drawer.

Acceptance of a bill of exchange, may be given by drawee by writing the word 'accepted' and signing on it.

Drawee in case of need

According to Section 7 of this Act, "when, in the bill of exchange, the name of any person is given, in addition to drawee to be resorted to in case of need, such person is known as 'drawee in case of need.'"

The name of 'drawee in case of need', is mentioned either in the bill of exchange or in any indorsement made on it. The 'drawee in case of need', will accept the bill if the original drawee does not accept it. Where the drawee in case of need, is named in the bill of exchange, the bill is not dishonoured till such drawee refuses to accept or to pay the bill.

Acceptor for honour

Where the original drawee refuses to accept the bill or after having accepted the bill refuses to furnish 'better security' when demanded by notary public in case of need, any outside person may accept the bill for protecting honour of the drawer or any of the indorser and bind himself by the acceptance. Such person is called 'acceptor for honour'. Thus any person may voluntarily become a part to a bill as an 'acceptor for honour'.

DISTINCTION BETWEEN PROMISSORY NOTE AND BILL OF EXCHANGE

Though these two instruments are part of negotiable instrument and have many features in common, they differ on the following grounds:

(*i*) **Number of parties:** In promissory note, there are only two parties, namely promisor or maker and payee or promisee. But in a bill of exchange, there are three parties, named as drawer, drawee or acceptor and payee.

(*ii*) **Nature of contents:** Promissory note contains unconditional promise to pay to the payee or to his order, but bill of exchange, contains unconditional order of drawer to drawee to pay according to the direction of the drawer.

(*iii*) **Acceptance:** Promissory note does not require any acceptance. While as a bill of exchange, becomes legally valid and effective when it is accepted.

(*iv*) **Nature of liability of maker:** The liability of maker or promisor in promissory note is primary in nature, because on the date of maturity he has to make payment. But in a bill of exchange the liability of drawer is secondary in nature because it is acceptor or drawee who has to pay the bill. And the liability of drawer arises only when the drawee fails to pay the bill on due date.

(*v*) **Relationship between drawer and payee:** In a promissory note there is a direct and immediate relationship between drawer and payee. But in the bill of exchange, drawer does not stand in direct relationship with payee. Rather he has direct and immediate relation with the drawee.

(*vi*) **Payable to bearer:** A promissory note cannot be made 'payable to bearer' as per the law. But the bill of exchange can be made payable to bearer, but not on demand.

(*vii*) **Notice of dishonour:** In case, the promissory note gets dishonoured, there is no need to give a notice of dishonour to the maker. But when the bill of exchange is dishonoured, the notice of such dishonour must be given by the holder to all parties, prior to him, liable to pay.

(*viii*) **Copies:** A promissory note cannot be drawn in set i.e., in part, but foreign bills are drawn in triplicate.

(*ix*) **Noting and Protesting:** In case of dishonour of promissory note, the protesting and noting is not required. While as in case of dishonour of bill of exchange, the certificate of protesting is taken as an evidence for recognising fact of dishonour by the court.

CHEQUES

According to Section 6 of this Act, "a cheque is a bill of exchange drawn on a specified banker and not expressed to be payable, otherwise than on demand and it includes the electronic image of truncated cheque and a cheque in electronic form."

For the purpose of this Section, the expressions:

(*i*) 'a cheque in electronic form' means a cheque which contains exact mirror image of a paper cheque, and is generated, written and signed in a secure system ensuring the minimum safety standards with the use of 'digital signature' (with or without biometrics signature) and asymmetric crypto system.

(*ii*) 'a truncated cheque' means a cheque which truncated during the course of a clearing cycle either by clearing house or by the bank, whether paying or receiving the payment immediately on generation of electronic image or transmission, substituting the further physical movement of the cheque in writing.

Now cheques can be issued in electronic form including truncated cheque in its electronic image. The cheque can be signed using digital signature and asymmetric crypto system.

Specimen of a Cheque			
Allahabad Bank			Date 10-01-2007
Paschim Vihar			
Pay Mr. Ram Mohan or bearer			
Rupee five thousand only. (Rs. 5000)			
			S/d.
A/c No 719800			
052560	110026581	25.	Shayam Mohan

Cheque is basically a bill of exchange, which is drawn only on specified banker and not to be payable other than on demand. Thus all cheques are bill of exchange but all bills of exchanges are not cheques, because bill of exchange can also be drawn on other parties.

In addition to basic charateristics of a bill of exchange a cheque has following charateristics:

(*a*) Cheque is always drawn on a specified banker.

(*b*) Cheque is always payable on demand.

(*c*) Cheque is a bill of exchange, nevertheless it does not require acceptance.

(*d*) Cheque is valid for a period of six months.

DISTINCTION BETWEEN BILL OF EXCHANGE AND A CHEQUE

Although, cheque is a bill of exchange, but there is a difference between these two as follows:

(*i*) **Drawee:** Bill of exchange, is generally drawn on some individual or a firm, but cheque is a bill of exchange which is always drawn on a particular bank.

(*ii*) **Acceptance:** Bill of exchange, to be legally effective and valid must be duly accepted, before payment can be demanded. But cheque does not require any acceptance, but it is meant for immediate payment.

(*iii*) **Payable on demand:** Cheque is always payable on demand. But a bill of exchange can be made payable or demand or payable after a particular period of time on the date of maturity.

(*iv*) **Stamp duty:** Bill of exchange, to be valid must be duty stamped. But cheque does not require any stamp duty.

(*v*) **Crossing:** There is no provision in the Act for the crossing of a bill of exchange. But to ensure payment of cheque to a bona fide person, it can be crossed.

(*vi*) **Notice of dishonour:** In case a cheque gets dishonoured, the holder is not required to give notice of it to the drawer, but in case of dishonour of bill it is necessary for the holder to give notice of dishonour to parties liable to pay.

(*vii*) **Days of grace:** A cheque is payable immediately on demand without allowing any time period of grace. But in case of bill of exchange, three days of grace are allowed from the due date within which payment can be made.

(*viii*) **Payment stoppage:** The payment of bill cannot be stopped by the drawer, while as the drawer of a cheque can stop the payment of cheque by giving instructions to the banker.

(*ix*) **Presentation for payment:** In case of bill of exchange, it is necessary for the payee to present it to the drawee for the payment. In case he fails to do so, the drawer will be discharged from his liability in that bill. But if the cheque is not presented for payment, the drawer will not be discharged from his liability for that cheque.

(*x*) **Noting and protesting:** Where the bill of exchange is dishonoured, it requires 'noting and protesting' to record the fact of dishonour. But such noting and protesting is not required in case of dishonour of cheque.

(*xi*) **Liability of drawee:** Where the cheque is dishonoured, the holder has no legal remedy against the banker, but if the bill gets dishonoured, the drawee will be liable to holder.

CLASSIFICATION OF NEGOTIABLE INSTRUMENTS

Negotiable instruments can be classified as:

I. Bearer and Order instruments

II. Demand and Time instrument

III. Inland and Foreign instruments

Bearer Instrument

Any instrument is payable to bearer:

(*i*) Which is expressed to be so payable, or

(*ii*) On which the only or the last indorsement is an 'indorsement in blank' *i.e*, where the holder has just signed without writing transferee's name.

The payment of bearer instrument can be made to any person who has got lawful possession of an instrument. The bearer instrument can be negotiated simply by giving delivery of it to the party.

Examples: (*i*) Pay to A or bearer, (*ii*) Pay the bearer, and (*iii*) A gets a cheque from B. A further indorsed the cheque to C just by putting his signature on the back of cheque, but does not write the name of C.

Order Instrument

A negotiable instrument is payable to order, which is expressed to be so payable, or which is expressed to be payable to particular person and does not contain words prohibiting or restricting transfer. The order instrument includes:

(*i*) Instrument which is expressed to be payable to order.

(*ii*) Instrument which is express to be payable to a particular person and does not restrict its transfer.

Examples**:** (*i*) Pay to A, (*ii*) Pay to A or order, or (*iii*) Pay to the order of A.

An instrument payable to order can be transferred by an indorsement and delivery in favour of party concerned.

Instrument Payable on Demand

A promissory note or bill of exchange in which, no time of payment is specified and a cheque, are payable on demand.

In case of demand instrument, as soon as the holder gets its possession he can demand its payment. To make a bill or a note payable on demand 'at sight' or 'on presentation' words are added to them. Thus an instrument becomes payable on demand if:

(*i*) no time for payment is specified.

(*ii*) it is made payable on demand or at sight or on presentation.

Time Instrument

An instrument said to be 'time instrument' if it payable at some time in future. The following instruments are time instruments:

(*i*) A promissory note or bill of exchange, which is payable after fixed period. *i.e.*, 90 days after sight.

(*ii*) A promissory note or bill of exchange, which is payable on specified day *i.e.*, on 10 January 2007.

(*iii*) A promissory note or a bill of exchange payable on the happening of an event, which is certain to happen *i.e.*, on the death of a person.

FORMS OF BILL OF EXCHANGE

The use of bills of exchange has become a part of modern business. These bills are used in the form of trade bills both in domestic as well as foreign trade. Thus these trade bills are known as 'inland and foreign bills'.

I. Inland Bill

A Bill of exchange is said to inland bill, (*i*) if it is drawn and made payable in India, or (*ii*) drawn in India upon any person who is a resident of India even though it is made payable in foreign country.

According to Section 11 of this Act, "a promissory note bill of exchange or cheque drawn or made in India and made payable in or drawn upon any person resident of India shall be deemed to be an inland instrument."

Examples:

(*i*) A bill drawn in Delhi on a businessman in Agra payable in Agra or in Bangladesh.

(*ii*) A bill drawn in Delhi on a business of London but made payable in Bombay.

(*iii*) A bill drawn in Delhi on a merchant in Agra and payable in London.

Foreign Bill

According to Section 12 of this Act; "Foreign instrument is one which is not a inland instrument." Following are the examples of foreign bill:

Examples:

(*i*) A bill which is drawn in India on a person residing outside India and made payable outside India.

(*ii*) A bill drawn outside India, made payable in India.

(*iii*) A bill drawn outside India on any person residing outside India.

(*iv*) A bill drawn outside India, on a person residing in India.

(*v*) A bill drawn outside India and made payable outside India.

Bills in sets: Generally foreign bills are drawn in sets of three. It is done to ensure safe transmission of at least one set of bill. When the drawer and payee of a bill are in distant place or different countries, the practice of drawing bill in part is very common. This practice is known as drawing 'bill in set'. Each part of the bill is despatched by a seperate means of conveyance to ensure safe passage of at least one part or set. All the parts constitute one bill and therefore, required stamp duty is affixed only on one part of the bill. And only one part of the whole set is required to be accepted and paid. As soon as any one part is accepted or paid, all other parts of that bill automatically become inoperative.

Sections 132 and 133 provide the following rules to deal with 'bill in sets':

(*a*) Bill of exchange may be drawn in parts. Each part or set must be numbered and must contain a provision that, it shall continue to be payable only so long as the other parts remain unpaid.

(*b*) All parts form one bill. On the payment of any one of the part, the entire bill is discharged. Each part of the bill must contain reference to the other parts.

(*c*) The drawer should sign and deliver all the parts of the bill, but the acceptance is to be conveyed on only one of the parts.

(*d*) When a person accepts or indorses different part of the bill in favour of different persons, he and subsequent indorser of each part are liable on such part as if it were a separate bill.

(*e*) As between holders in due course of different parts of the same set, he who, first acquired a title to any one part is entitled to the other parts and is also entitled to claim the money represented by the bill.

II. Trade Bill and Accommodation Bill

A bill is known as trade bill, if it is drawn and accepted for a genuine trade transaction. It is also known as 'genuine bill'. Such bills are generally drawn by the traders who sell goods on credit.

Example: A sells goods to B amounting Rs. 2,000 on credit and draws a bill of exchange for two months on B, and B accepts the bill, it is a trade bill.

In addition to such trade bills, accommodation bills are also in use. Accommodation bill is one, which is drawn and accepted to provide financial help to some party—may be a friend or known party. Thus instead of lending money directly he may propose to accept the bill drawn on him. So the other party may discount that bill from his banker. On the date of maturity the party using the money of that bill may send necessary amount to his friend who has accepted the bill for accommodation, so that he pays out the bill presented by the banker.

However, it is to be noted that, an accommodation bill may be drawn and accepted for the mutual benefit of both the parties.

Example: A draws a bill on B for Rs. 5,000 payable after two months. B accepts it and gives it back to A who gets the bill discounted and uses the money of that bill in his business. B also draws bill of same amount on A for the same date and gets discounted it from his banker. On the date of payment both A and B will pay out the respective bills.

The party who is getting financial help through accommodation bill is known as 'accommodated party' and the party who is providing such accommodation is known as 'accommodating party'.

The following rules are applicable on accommodation bills:

(*a*) No, liability for accommodated party: Where the accommodated party continues to hold the bill till maturity, the accommodating party shall not be liable to him for payment. This is so because accommodation bill does not create legal obligation between the parties (accommodated and accommodating parties).

(*b*) Liability for subsequent holder for value: The accommodating party shall be liable on the bill to any subsequent 'holder for value' even if that holder knows that it is an accommodation bill. On making payment of bill the accommodating party is entitled to compensation from the party accommodated.

(*c*) **Negotiation after maturity:** Where an accommodation bill is negotiated after maturity to the 'holder in due course', he becomes holder as if holder before maturity and can recover the payment of that bill.

(*d*) **Non-presentation of bill:** Where the accommodation bill is not presented by the holder to drawee on the date of maturity, the drawer of such bill will not get discharged from his liability in that bill (as an exception to general rule contained in Section 76 of this Act).

(*e*) **Failure to give notice of dishonour:** In case of accommodation bill if the holder fails to give notice of dishonour to all parties liable to pay, they are still liable for the payment of bill (as an exception to Section 98 of this Act).

III. Documentary Bill

The bill of exchange is said to be documentary bill, if documents of title of goods are attached to it. Document of title is a document used in ordinary course of business as a proof of possession, or control of goods or authorisation, covered by it, such as bill of lading, railway receipt, invoice and dock warrant etc.

In case of documentary bill, the document of title are delivered to the buyer only on acceptance or payment of the bill. Documentary bills may be of two types—'Document againest acceptance' and 'Document againest payment'. In case of D/A of bill, the document of title is handed over to the buyer or his agent on the acceptance of the bill. Similarly in case of D/P of bill, the document of title is handed over on the payment of the bill.

Documentary bills are very much is use in a foreign trade.

IV. Fictitious Bill

According to Section 42 of this Act, when, in a bill of exchange the name of drawer or payee or both are fictitious, the bill is called 'fictitious bill'. Such bill is drawn by a fictitious drawer and made payable to the drawer's order. Fictitious person means a person who is not in existence, or who is imaginary or a pretended person.

A fictitious bill even if accepted by a genuine person docs not hold good in the eyes of law. But such bill becomes good bill in the hands of holder in due course. It means if the bill is drawn as fictitious bill and indorsed to the holder in due course who gets it in good faith for value consideration and before date of maturity. Such holder in due course can recover the payment of such bill from the drawee provided (*i*) he can prove that the signature of first indorser and signature of so-called drawer are in the same handwriting, and (*ii*) acceptor is genuine person and is liable on the bill, to him.

V. Bank Draft or Demand Draft

Bank draft or demand draft is bill of exchange drawn by one bank on another bank, or by a bank on its, own branch or by one branch of bank upon another branch of the same bank for a sum of money payable to order on demand. It is a negotiable instrument like cheque but with the following distinct features:

(*a*) Bank draft can be drawn by a bank on another bank.

(*b*) A bank draft cannot be countermanded either by the person purchasing it or by the bank to which it is presented.

(*c*) Bank draft cannot be made payable to bearer and it is always payable to order on demand.

IMPORTANT TERMS USED IN NEGOTIABLE INSTRUMENT ACT

1. Ambiguous Instrument

Where the instrument has been drawn according to the provisions of Negotiable Instrument Act but so worded that it can be treated either as a bill of exchange or as a promissory note, such instrument is known as 'ambiguous instrument'.

According to Section 17 of this Act, "Where an instrument may be construed either as a promissory note or bill of exchange, the holder may at his option treat it as a bill of exchange or promissory note, thereafter shall be treated accordingly."

From the contents of above Section it follows that:

(*i*) Ambiguous instrument has been so worded, it may be treated either a bill or promissory note.

(*ii*) When such instrument gets into the hands of the holder it is optional for him to treat it either as bill or a note.

(*iii*) Once he opted to treat it either as bill or note, he cannot change his option later.

If the amount in the instrument differs in figure and words, the amount stated in words shall be the amount payable.

Example: A draws a bill of exchange on himself. In this case, drawer and drawee are one and same individual. If the bill is negotiated to B, he can treat it either bill or a promissory note. Similarly if the bill is drawn on a fictitious person or the person having no contractual capacity, it would also be an ambiguous instrument.

2. Inchoate Instrument

Where the instrument is drawn according to the provisions of Negotiable Instrument Act either wholly or party incomplete it is known as 'inchoate instrument'.

According to Section 20 of this Act, "When one person signs and delivers to another a paper stamped, in accordance with the law relating to negotiable instruments, then in force in India and either wholly blank or having written thereon an incomplete negotiable instrument, he thereby gives prima facie authority to the holder thereof to make or complete, as the case may be, upon it a negotiable instrument for any amount specified therein not exceeding the amount covered by the stamp. The person, so signing shall be liable upon such instrument, in the capacity he signed the same to any holder in due course, for such amount provided that no person other than holder in course, shall recover from the person delivering the instrument any thing in excess of the amount intended by him to be paid thereunder."

It follows from the above contents that:

(*a*) Inchoate instrument is drawn as per provisions of Negotiable Instrument Act which may be duly stamped.

(*b*) Inchoate instrument may be either wholly or partly incomplete.

(*c*) The holder, who gets such instrument has a right to complete it.

(*d*) The holder can recover the amount specified therein but not exceeding amount covered by stamp.

(*e*) The person signing on such instrument shall be liable in the capacity in which he signed.

(*f*) Holder in due course has a right to recover the amount, may be more than intended by the person signing the instrument.

Example: A signs a cheque as a drawer, but does not mention amount payable on that cheque. He gives it to his servant asking him to buy goods from the grocery merchant and gives a blank cheque to him. The servant bought the goods amounting Rs. 5,000. But grocery merchant filled up a cheque for Rs. 8,000. It is an inchoate instrument and the merchant cannot recover more than Rs. 5,000 on that cheque. But if he endorses a cheque in favour of B, who gets it in good faith, for value consideration and of course before due date. He has a right to recover sum of Rs. 8,000 from A on this cheque.

3. Payment in Due Course

Negotiable instrument is said to be discharged when the payment of it is made in due course.

Section 10 of this Act provides that, "payment in due course means, payment in accordance with the apparent tenor of the instrument in good faith and without negligence to any person in possession thereof under circumstances which do not afford a reasonable ground for believing that he is not entitled to receive payment of the amount mentioned therein.

It follows from the above contents that, payment in due course, to be legally valid must satisfy the following conditions:

(*a*) **Apparent tenor of the instrument:** The payment of the instrument should be made according to the intention of the parties which appears on the face of the instrument. The payment must be made at or after maturity but not before the maturity.

(*b*) **Payment to the holder:** The person to whom the payment is made should be in possession of the instrument. It should be made to the holder of the instrument or some other person, who is authorised to get payment on his behalf so that it leads to a valid discharge.

(*c*) **Payment in good faith:** The payment should be made in good faith without negligence. There should be no reasonable ground to believe that the person to whom the payment is made is not entitled to receive it. In case of suspicious circumstance, if the person making payment does not make necessary enquiry, it will not amount to payment in due course. But if a cheque bears forged signature of the drawer and banker fails to exercise necessary care and makes payment, such payment is not considered as payment in due course.

ALLAHABAD BANK LTD *vs* KUL BHUSHAN (A.IR. 1961) PURI 571: In this case, the bank paid a cheque bearing forged signature of the drawer. It was held that payment was not a payment in due course.

(*d*) **Mode of payment:**The payment must be made in money only. But if the holder agrees to accept payment by cheque or draft it will be considered as payment in due course.

4. Maturity of Negotiable Instrument

The promissory note and bill of exchange may be payable (*i*) on demand, or (*ii*) on a specified date, or (*iii*) after a specified period.

Where the instrument is payable on demand or on presentation or at sight such a cheque becomes payable immediately and there is no need to work out its date of maturity.

The need of calculating date of maturity arises in case of promissory note and bill of exchange which are not payable on demand.

According to Section 22 of this Act, "every promissory note, or bill of exchange which is not expressed to be payable on demand, is at maturity on third day, after the day on which it is expressed to be payable."

Thus, to calculate date of maturity three 'days of grace' are added to the period stated in the instrument.

Example: A draws a bill of exchange on B amounting Rs. 5,000 on 1 January 2007, which is payable three months after date. As per the bill it is expressed to become payable on 1 April 2007. To calculate date of maturity of the bill, three days of grace are added to it and its date of maturity will fall on 4 April 2007.

The 'days of grace' are not allowed in case of:

(*i*) A cheque.

(*ii*) A bill or promissory note payable at sight/presentment or on demand.

(*iii*) A bill or promissory note in which no time is mentioned.

The 'days of grace' are allowed in case of:

(*i*) Promissory note or bill of exchange payable on specified date.

(*ii*) Promissory note or a bill payable after sight.

(*iii*) Promissory note or a bill payable after certain period of time.

(*iv*) Promissory note or a bill payable after certain period of time after the happening a certain event.

Rules Regarding for Determining Maturity of an Instrument

Sections 23 to 25 of this Act lay down certain rules, which are applied for calculating date of maturity of promissory note or bill of exchange. These rules are:

(*a*) If a promissory note or bill of exchange is made payable, a stated number of months after date or after sight or after certain event, it becomes payable three days after the corresponding date of month after the stated number of months (Section 23). A bill of exchange dated 1 January 2007 is payable three months after date. It will mature on 4 April 2007.

(*b*) If the month in which the period would terminate has no corresponding day, the period shall be held to terminate on the last day of such month. Such as a bill payable three months after date, and drawn on 31 August will be at maturity on 3 December.

(*c*) In calculating the date at which promissory note or bill made a certain number of days after date or after sight or after certain event is at maturity, the day of the date of presentation for acceptance or sight or of protest for acceptance or on which the event happens shall be excluded.

Example: A bill payable '30 days after sight' is presented for sight on 1 April. It falls due on 4 May.

(*d*) When the day on which a promissory note or bill of exchange is at maturity is a public holiday, the instrument is deemed to be due on next preceding business day.

Example: A bill of exchange dated 12 June is payable 2 months after date. The instrument shall fall due for payment on 16 August (15th August being a Public Holiday).

(*e*) If an instrument is payable by instalments, three days of grace are to be allowed on each instalment.

REVIEW QUESTIONS

1. Define 'negotiable instrument'. Explain the basic characteristics of negotiable instrument.
2. Discuss legal presumptions, which are applicable on a negotiable instrument.
3. What do you mean by promissory note? Discuss its characteristics and make out its specimen.
4. Define 'Bill of exchange'. Explain characteristics of bill of exchange.
5. Define the term 'cheque'. Enumerate various characteristics of a cheque.
6. Distinguish between a promissory note and a bill of exchange.
7. 'All cheques are bill of exchange, but all bill of exchange are not cheque'. Comment and write difference between these two.
8. What is an 'accommodation bill'? Discuss the various rules concering it.
9. What is 'date of maturity'? Explain the various rules regarding the calculation of date of maturity.
10. Write notes on:

    (*i*) Payment in due course (*ii*) Inchoate instrument
    (*iii*) Fictitious bill (*iv*) Order instrument
    (*v*) Time instrument (*vi*) Foreign bill
    (*vii*) Bill in set

PRACTICAL PROBLEMS

1. A draws a bill of exchange on B, amounting Rs. 5,000 payable after two months. B is a fictitious person. Although it is a bill and A indorsed it to C. Is A liable to pay to C? (Hint: Yes, Ambiguous instrument.)
2. A makes credit sale of Rs. 2,000 to B and draw a bill for that amount on B. B refuses to accept the bill. C, who knows A just to honour him accepts that bill. Can A recover the amount of that bill from C on the maturity? (Hint: No).
3. Ram gets signature of Shyam forged on a cheque and gets payment of that cheque from the bank. Is it payment in due course? Can Ram claim the amount of cheque from the Bank? (Hint: It is not payment in due course, Yes.)
4. A promissory note dated 10 January 2007 was made payable two months after sight. It was presented before the maker on 20 January 2007. When does the promissory note matures for payment? (3 days after 20th March *i.e.*, 23rd March.)
5. Y signs a cheque and gives it to his servant B asking him to buy the goods from C and give a cheque to him for that amount. B buys goods worth Rs. 1,000 and hands over a blank cheque to C. C who has a right to complete it writes Rs. 2,000 on it. Can C recover this amount from Y? (Hint: No). But it he indorses it to Z who takes it in good faith for value consideration and before maturity. Can Z recover this amount from Y? (Hint: Yes, because he is holder in due course.)
6. A firm has two branches, one in Delhi and another in Mumbai. Delhi branch has drawn a bill of exchange amounting Rs. 2,000 on Mumbai branch. The bill was duly accepted and indorsed to B in Delhi. Examine legal position of B regarding this bill.
7. A is in need of money. He draws a bill on his friend B. Who accepts it A indorses that bill to C, who gets it for value consideration. Is B liable to pay to C? (Hint: Yes, C is holder for value.)

23

Parties to a Negotiable Instrument

LEARNING OBJECTIVES

- Identity various parties involved in bill of exchange promissory note and cheque.
- Make comparison between holder and holder in due course in terms of special privileges of holder in due course.
- Analyse contractual capacity of a minor, agents, representative, joint stock company, and insolvent in the context of negotiable instrument.
- Remember liability of various parties of negotiable instrument.

INTRODUCTION

Every negotiable instrument has many parties, depending on nature of instruments. In addition to original parties like the maker, the payee and the drawee, there are many other parties associated with an instrument, such as indorser, indorsee and holder etc. As the instrument goes on negotiating, the number of parties also increases.

Following are the parties involved in various types of negotiable instruments:

(*i*) **Parties to promissory note:** Maker, Payee, Holder, Indorser and Indorsee.

(*ii*) **Parties to a bill of exchange:** Drawer, Drawee, Payee, Holder, Drawee in case of need and Acceptor for honour.

(*iii*) **Parties to a cheque:** Drawer, Drawee (Bank) Payee, Holder, Indorser and Indorsee.

Maker or Drawer of an Instrument

Negotiable instruments are always drawn or made. The person who draws is known as maker or drawer. In case of promissory note he is primarily responsible for making payment. In bill of exchange and in cheque, the liability of the maker or drawer is secondary in nature.

Drawee or Acceptor of an instrument

The drawee or acceptor is a main party in a bill of exchange and cheque. In case of cheque, the banker becomes drawee and in a bill of exchange the person who accepts it become drawee. In both the cases, they have primary responsibility to pay.

Holder or Indorser

The person is said to be a holder of negotiable instrument who is legally entitled to possess the instrument, in his name and to get its payment on due date or on demand, as the case may be. Thus the holder is either the original payee or indorsee.

Payee

Negotiable instruments are used to facilitate the payment and settlement of transactions. The person who is entitled to get the payment of negotiable instrument from the person liable to pay, is technically known as 'payee'. In case of a bill of exchange and cheque, drawer and payee may be same and one individual.

Acceptor for Honour

In case, the drawee refuses to accept the bill drawn by the drawer, any person, with the consent of holder may accept the bill to protect the honour of the drawer. He becomes party to a bill voluntarily and is known as 'acceptor for honour'.

Drawee in Case of Need

Sometime, the name of another drawee may be given in the bill of exchange, in addition to original drawee. Such person is known as 'drawee in case of need'. He may be approached for acceptance or payment on the refusal of original drawee.

HOLDER

Generally the holder is a person, who is bearing or holding an instrument and is legally entitled to get its payment from the party responsible to pay.

According to Section 8 of this Act, "the holder of a negotiable instrument means any person, entitled in his own name to the possession thereof and to receive or recover, the amount due thereon from the party liable thereto."

It follows from the above contents that, the person is said to be holder of negotiable instrument, if he satisfies the following two conditions:

(*i*) He should be entitled to possess the instrument in his own name *e.g.*, legal custody of an instrument.

(*ii*) He should have a right to receive or recover the amount due on the instrument from the party liable to pay.

However, it is not necessary that the instrument must be in his possession. Rather, to be a holder, he is required to have a right to possession under some valid and legal title. Thus, the holder should be 'de-jure' holder (holder in law).

Thus, for a holder to be entitled to the instrument in his own name, the holder must be named in the instrument either as a payee or the indorsee. The legal representative of the holder may also become the holder of instrument, by operation of law *i.e.*, on obtaining certificate of succession.

Where the person, is in possession of negotiable instrument without having a right to possess it, he cannot be considered as a holder. The finder of goods or thief of lost goods and endorsee under forged indorsement, though may be having possession of an instrument, but cannot be called the holder. This is so because, he does not acquire legal title thereto. Similarly a payee, prohibited by an order of court from receiving the amount of the instrument will not be a holder. In addition to it, an agent holding the instrument, and beneficial owners through 'Benamindar' are also not holders.

SARJOO PRASAD *vs* RAM PAYARI DEVI (1950, PAT 493): In this case, S advanced a sum of Rs. 2,500 under a promissory note. The note, however was executed not in the name of S, but in the name of P who was 'Benamindar'. On maturity S sued to recover the amount from the debtor. It was held that he could not recover as he was not a holder having a right of possession and payment.

To become holder, it is not enough to have lawful possession of the instrument. But the person must also have right to recieve or recover the amount from the party liable to pay so as to give him valid discharge. Thus, the holder of an instrument, must have:

(*i*) Obtained an instrument in a lawful manner.

(*ii*) Right to sue in his own name to recover the payment.

Rights of a Holder

The holder of a negotiable instrument, is a very important party to the instrument as such. He has the following rights:

(*a*) The holder has a right to possess the instrument in his own name.

(*b*) He is entitled to receive or recover the payment of the instrument.

(*c*) He has a right to give valid discharge of the instrument.

(*d*) He can further negotiate instrument in favour of another party.

(*e*) He is entitled to complete inchoate instrument with an amount as intended by the drawer.

(*f*) He is entitled to treat 'ambiguous instrument' either as a bill or a promissory note.

(*g*) He is entitled to convert 'indorsement in blank' into full indorsement.

HOLDER IN DUE COURSE

The holder in due course occupies key position in the instrument with regard to his relation with other parties of an instrument.

According to Section 9 of this Act, "holder in due course means any person who for consideration, becomes the possessor of a negotiable instrument if payable to bearer or payee or indorsee thereof if payable to order before the amount mentioned in it became payable and without sufficient cause to believe that any defect existed in the title of a person from whom he derived his title." Before a person can claim to be a holder in due course, he must satisfy the following conditions:

(*a*) ***He must be a Holder*:** He must have right to possess the instrument in his own name and to recover or receive payment thereof from the parties liable to pay.

(*b*) ***He must be a Holder for consideration*:** The holder must have given lawful consideration to acquire the instrument. In case if someone gets a cheque as a gift, he cannot become holder in due course of that cheque. Thus a person, who gets an instrument without consideration, cannot enforce it as a holder in due course.

(*c*) ***He must acquire the instrument before maturity*:** The holder must have acquired the instrument at or before the date of maturity. In case he acquires it after the date of maturity, he will not get better title than that of transferor.

However, an accommodation bill can be negotiated even after the date of maturity with all benefits of a holder in due course to the transferee. In case of instrument payable on demand e.g., cheque he must have got it within reasonable period of time of its issue.

(*d*) ***Instrument should be complete and regular*:** The holder in due course must take the negotiable instrument complete and regular on its face. He must examine its form, contents and material defects in the instrument such as defects regarding name of drawer, date, stamp duty etc.

(*e*) ***Holder must take the instrument in good faith*:** The holder must take the instrument in good faith without any negligence. But good faith, regarding title of transferor, on the part of the holder is not sufficient. Rather, he must have taken it without having sufficient cause to believe that any defect existed in the title of the person from whom he derived his title.

The circumstances leading to suspicion may be related to blank acceptance, incomplete bill, torn pieces of the bill pasted together, and improper indorsement etc. In all such cases, he must exercise reasonable care and due caution as to be on safe side.

Thus besides good faith, reasonable degree of care and diligence is to be exercised by him to hold his right good. A holder in due course occupies privileged position in Negotiable Instrument Act. He gets many special rights which are generally not available to an ordinary holder. He gets title of instrument free from all defects. The burden of proving his title does not lie on him. Once an instrument passes through his hands, it becomes clean and free from all defects.

Special Privileges of a Holder in Due Course

The following are the special privileges of a Holder in due course:

(*a*) ***Good title of an instrument:*** A negotiable instrument is transferred freely till maturity. Once it passes through the hands of a holder in due course it become free from all defects. A holder in due course gets good title from the transferor. Even if the title of transferor is defective, he will get a better title than that of transferor.

According to Section 53 of this Act "holder of a negotiable instrument who derives a title from a holder in due course has the right thereon of that holder in due course." It means a holder in due course is not protected only against the defects in title of the parties prior to him, but subsequent holder also gets better title.

Example: A has stolen a cheque of Rs. 2,000 from the pocket of his father. A indorsed the cheque to B, who takes it for value consideration, and in good faith believing that A is honest enough and therefore he must have got it from his father. Though the title of A is defective, B who is holder in due course gets good title and can recover the payment of that cheque from the bank.

(*b*) ***Rights in inchoate instrument:*** Where the party having a right to complete instrument makes it complete for the amount more than as intended by the drawer, such party has no right to recover that amount. But if that party transfers it to holder in due course, he can recover full amount as mentioned in that instrument.

In this regard, Section 20 of this Act clearly says that if the person signs and delivers inchoated stamp instrument, he cannot avoid his liability to holder in due course on the ground that instrument has not been filled according to authority given by him.

Example: A signs a cheque and delivers it to servant asking him to buy the goods and asks the seller to fill it for that amount. The servant bought the goods amounting Rs. 2,000 and hands over blank cheque to the seller who completed it at Rs. 3,000. Though not entitled to recover more than Rs. 2,000; if he indorses it to a holder in due course, he can recover the full payment as mentioned in the cheque.

(*c*) ***Right in case of fictitious bill:*** Where the fictitious bill is drawn, in which either the name of drawer or payee or both the names are fictitious, such bill is not good in the eyes of law. And it cannot be enforced for the payment. But if such fictitious bill comes into the hands of a holder in due course, the acceptor of such bill becomes liable to him. A holder in due course can recover the payment of such bill provided he proves that signature of drawer and first indorser are in the same handwriting.

Example: Bill of exchange is drawn in a fictitious name of A payable to A or to his order upon B. B accepts this bill. The bill is then indorsed to C who is a holder in due course, under the signature of fictitious person A. C who is a holder in due course can recover the payment of this bill from B provided he proves that signature of A in both capacities are in same handwriting.

(*d*) ***Liability of prior parties:*** Every prior party to a holder in due course in a negotiable instrument is liable to him until the instrument is duly satisfied. The term prior party means, the maker or drawer, acceptor, and all intervening indorser prior to a holder in due course. The holder in due course can file a suit in his own name against any or all prior parties liable to pay.

Example: A draws a bill on B who accepts it and returns it to A. A further indorses it to C who indorses it to D and D to E. E is a holder in due course. He can recover payment of the bill from B and in case of his failure all other parties including A, C and D will be liable for the payment in that bill to E.

(*e*) ***Right in case of conditional delivery of an instrument:*** Where a negotiable instrument has been indorsed and delivered conditionally or for a special purpose *i.e.*, as collateral security or for safe custody and not with the intention of transferring property therein absolutely. So property in instrument does not pass to the endorsee and he is merely a bailee having limited rights against that instrument. This however does not affect the right of holder in due course. If such an instrument is negotiated to him, the parties liable on the instrument cannot escape liability.

Example: A, who is a holder of a bill of exchange, gives it to B for getting it discounted from the bank. But B instead of discounting it, indorsed it in favour of C and he is holder in due course. C can recover the payment of that bill from the drawee and all other parties are liable to him.

(*f*) ***Instrument becomes free from all defects:*** As soon as an instrument comes into the hands of holder in due course it becomes free from all defects regarding its title. Not only this, but a holder of negotiable instrument who derives title from a holder in due course gets rights thereon that of holder in due course. Thus holder in due course is not only protected from the defects in the title of parties prior to him, but his position also provides protection to subsequent holders.

Example: Ram obtained a bill of exchange by fraud from the Shyam, who is drawer of the bill. Ram indorsed it to Mohan, who becomes a holder in due course. Mohan further indorsed it to Shohan as a gift. The Shohan has a right to get the payment of the bill from acceptor, because he stands on Mohan's title.

(*g*) ***Right as to title of an instrument:*** There is a legal presumption regarding the title of holder that every holder is deemed as holder in due course. Burden of proving his title does not lie on him. But in case an instrument has been obtained from its owner by fraud or unlawful consideration or by offence, burden of proof is shifted and thus the holder has to prove that he is a holder in due course.

Example: Ram draws a bill on Shyam. Ram indorsers it to Mohan, who fraudulently transfers it to Shohan who transfers it to Sirin. Sirin claims payment from Shyam and Shyam proves fraud of Mohan. Thus Sirin has to prove that he is a holder in due course.

(*h*) ***Estoppel against denying validity of an instrument:*** The drawer of a cheque or bill of exchange or acceptor for honour cannot deny or challenge validity of an instrument as against holder in due course.

However, if the instrument is void on the face of it, even holder in due course cannot recover the payment of such instrument.

Example: A draws a bill on B, who refuses to accept it. Rather C accepts it for the honour of A. A transfers it to D and he further transfers it to E who is holder in due course. In this case, C who is acceptor for honour cannot deny validity of the bill and is liable to E for the payment.

(*i*) ***Estoppel against signature and capacity of prior party:*** The indorser of negotiable instrument is not permitted to deny the signature and capacity to contract of any prior party to that instrument in a suit filed by the subsequent holder in due course. Even if the payee of instrument is not competent to contract the holder in due course can claim payment.

Example: A draws a bill on B. A transfers it to C who further transfers it to D who is a minor. D transfers it to E and E to F. The bill is dishonoured on the date of maturity. F is a holder is due course. Thus E cannot plead that D was a minor and not capable of negotiating the bill. E will be liable to F.

DISTINCTION BETWEEN HOLDER AND HOLDER IN DUE COURSE

Though the holder in due course is a special type of holder, who occupies a privileged position, he can be distinguished from mere holder of an instrument. The following are the differences between these two:

. (*a*) ***Meaning*:** A holder is a person who is entitled to possess an instrument in his own name and recover the payment from the party liable to pay. But holder in due course is a holder who gets an instrument before maturity, in good faith and for valuable consideration.

. (*b*) ***Consideration:*** For a holder it is not necessary that he must have given consideration for the instrument. But to be holder in due course consideration must have been given by him for acquiring an instrument.

(*c*) ***Maturity*:** A holder may acquire an instrument even after the date of maturity, but holder in due course must get it before the date of maturity.

(*d*) ***Title*:** A holder of an instrument will get same title as the transferor had. But the holder in due course gets title better than that of transferor.

(*e*) ***Liability of parties to pay*:** For a holder it is only drawer, drawee and transferor who are liable to pay. But for holder in due course all parties prior to him are liable to pay until the instrument is duty discharged.

(*f*) ***Privileged position*:** A holder does not enjoy special position or right. While as, the position of a holder in due course is privileged and he gets special rights.

Capacity of the Parties

The parties of negotiable instrument must have a contractual capacity. They should be of a major age, sound mind and not declared disqualified for making a contract. This is so because, the contractual capacity of a party of an instrument is coextensive with that of his liability towards other parties. Barring a few case, generally if the party has no contractual capacity, he cannot be held liable to pay to the holder of an instrument.

However, if any one or more parties of an instrument are not having contractual capacity, agreement remains void, but it does not reduce the liability of other competent parties thereto.

With regard to Negotiable Instrument Act, the legal position of various parties, having no contractual capacity, is as under:

(*a*) **Minor:** A minor has no contractual capacity. In any agreement made by him, he does not incur any liability. But at the same time the law does not debar him from getting benefit in an agreement. In connection with negotiable instrument, if a minor draws or makes or accepts or indorses an instrument, he does not become liable to the holder of an instrument for making payment. But the holder of such instrument can hold other parties liable to him except a minor. An instrument remains binding on all other parties.

Though the minor cannot bind himself by accepting a bill of exchange and drawing a promissory note, he can be payee or indorsee. *Thus the minor cannot originate a title, he can serve as a channel to pass it on to other.*

(*b*) **Person of unsound mind:** The contract made by the person who is not of a sound mind also stands on the same footing as that of a minor. Such persons include lunatic, idiot and drunkards. A negotiable instrument drawn or accepted by such person is void. Thus, a negotiable instrument drawn by a person when he becomes of a sound mind as in case of lunatic and drunkards may be enforced against him.

Where the person of unsound mind or his dependent has borrowed money and drawn a promissory note or accepted a bill for the fulfillment of basic necessities of life. On the date of maturity the holder of such instrument can recover reasonable amount from the property of such person.

(*c*) **Agent:** According to Section 27 of this Act, "a person capable of contracting may make, draw, accept indorse, deliver and negotiate a bill, note or a cheque either by himself or through a duty authorised agent acting in his behalf." The main job of an agent is to bring third party into contractual relationship with the principal. As soon as he does so, his role is over.

Thus the agent can bind his principal by the transactions on negotiable instrument provided he has been given authority for that.

However, it should be noted that, general authority to transact business does not authorise an agent to draw or accept or indorse a bill of exchange or promissory note on behalf of the principal. An authority to draw, does not mean authority to accept them. Similarly authority to accept them does not imply an authority to indorse them.

According to Section 28 of this Act, "an agent who signs his name on a promissory note, bill or a cheque without indicating that, he signs as agent is personally liable on the instrument." The agent therefore must make it clear that he is signing as an agent, if this is not done, he shall be personally liable for that transaction on negotiable instrument.

(*d*) **Legal representative:** A person is said to be legal representative who would legally inherit property of a deceased person or who represents the estate of such person. The legal representative is entitled to recover the amount of the instrument due to the deceased and can give a valid discharge.

According to Section 29 of this Act, "a legal representative, of a deceased person who signs his name on promissory note, bill of exchange or cheque is liable personally thereon, unless he expressly limits his liability to the extent of the assets received by him as such. He may also exclude him from liability by adding the word, 'without recourse', or 'without recourse to one personally' on the instrument. In case he fails to do so, he shall be personally liable."

(*e*) **Joint stock company:** A company is an artificial person created by law. Once company gets certificate of incorporation, it acquires legal entity. The company can make contract, can file suit and can be sued. But it has no physical existence, and therefore it exercises these rights through authorised official. The right to make contract by the authorised official is limited by Memorandum of Association. Within the limits of this document, the authorised official of the company can draw, accept and indorse negotiable instruments.

However, if the authorised official issues a negotiable instruments beyond the scope of authority as given by the memorandum of association, such instrument will be void. And even a holder in due course cannot make company liable for such instruments.

(*f*) **Insolvent:** On being declared as an insolvent by the court, the property of such person is handed over to an official assignee or receiver. And such insolvent cannot draw, accept or indorse any negotiable instrument until the order of discharge is obtained by him from the court. But if indorser of a negotiable instrument in which he is payee or indorsee to a holder in due course, the indorsement would be valid as against all prior parties except the insolvent person.

LIABILITY OF PARTIES TO NEGOTIABLE INSTRUMENT

With regard to liability of various parties in a negotiable instrument, the following provisions of this Act are applicable.

Liability of Drawer

The liability of drawer in a bill of exchange is secondary in nature. This is so because drawee or acceptor of these instrument has to make the payment on the date of maturity. But in case, the instrument is dishonoured by non-payment the drawer of a such instrument will be liable to compensate the holder of the instrument, provided due notice of dishonour has been given to him. However, in case of accommodation bill no notice of dishonour is required to be given to the drawer.

But if the bill of exchange has been dishonoured by non-acceptance by the drawee, the drawer will be primarily liable to the holder. Similarly, in case of cheque, the liability of the drawer is primary in nature. It is because, if the chequc is dishonoured, the legal remedy to a holder is available only against the drawer of a cheque.

Liability of Drawee of Cheque

A cheque is a bill of exchange which is payable on demand. Thus the drawee of a cheque (banker) must pay the cheque, when it is duly presented for payment provided drawer's account has sufficient credit balance for that purpose.

If the banker wrongfully dishonours the cheque he can be made liable for paying even exemplary damages to the drawer.

In case, the bank makes default regarding the payment of cheque, he is liable only to the drawer and not to the holder of a cheque.

Liability of Maker of Promissory Note and Drawee of Bill

The maker of a promissory note and drawee of a bill of exchange are the people, who are primarily liable for making payment of the instrument. They have the liability to pay the instrument at maturity according to its apparent tenor. If the maker of promissory note or drawee of a bill fail to pay it on due date, they will be bound to compensate any party to a note or a bill for any loss caused to them by such default.

However, if the instrument is duly paid before the date of maturity and the instrument is subsequently indorsed to a holder in due course, he would be entitled to recover payment from the drawee of a bill or maker of a note.

Liability of Indorser

The liability of an indorser in the instrument is secondary and conditional in nature. The indorser of an instrument, is liable to every subsequent holders, in case of dishonour of instrument provided the following conditions are satisfied:

(*i*) The instrument has been dishonoured by the party who is primarily liable to pay.

(*ii*) Due notice of dishonour has been received by such indorser.

(*iii*) He must have not excluded him from his liability by making "san recource indorsement."

(*iv*) The holder has not cancelled prior indorsement without his consent.

Liabilities of Intervening Parties

According to the relevant provisions of this Act, every prior party in a negotiable instrument is liable, thereon, to a holder in due course until the instrument is duty satisfied. The prior parties may include the maker or drawer, the acceptor and all other intervening endorsers to a negotiable instruments.

However, it is to noted that their liability toward a holder in due course is joint and several. The holder in due course can hold any or all the prior parties liable for the payment of the dishonoured instrument. Each prior party shall be liable as a principal debtor in respect of such succeeding party.

REVIEW QUESTIONS

1. Describe the various parties of a negotiable instrument.
2. What do you mean by 'a holder of an instrument'? Discuss his legal position.
3. Define the term 'holder in due course'. Explain the special privileges granted to him in this Act.
4. Distinguish between a 'holder' and a 'holder in due course'.
5. Discuss the liability of various parties in a negotiable instrument.
6. Explain legal position of:

   (*i*) Minor

   (*ii*) Agent

   (*iii*) Joint stock company

   (*iv*) Person of unsound mind in the context of negotiable instrument

7. Comment on:
   (*i*) Holder in due course gets title better than transferor.
   (*ii*) Capacity to incur liability is coextensive with a capacity to contract.
   (*iii*) The holder should be, 'de-jure' holder and not necessarily a 'de-facto' holder.

PRACTICAL PROBLEMS

1. A draws a bill of exchange on B, payable 2 months after sight. The bill passes through several hands, before E becomes a holder of that bill. On presentation by E, B refuses to accept it. Examine the rights of E on the bill.
2. A, obtains acceptance of B on a bill by fraud. A indorsed it to C who becomes a holder in due course. C further transfers the bill to D, who knows about the fraud. Can D recover the payment from A? (Hint: Yes)
3. Ram signs a cheque and gives it to his servant asking him to buy the goods and make payment of that amount through the cheque. The servant buys goods worth Rs. 2,000 and hands over the cheque to the merchant, who completes it by Rs. 3,000. The merchant later on transfers it to Shyam, who obtains it in good faith for value and before due date. Examine the right of the merchant and Shyam.
4. A draws a bill on B for three months. A indorsed it to C who further transfers it to D, and D to E. On the date of maturity B refused to pay and E fails to give due notice of dishonour to D. Discuss rights and liability of the various parties.
5. A, an employee of B, fraudulently represents to his employer that C has done some work on their account and asks B to draw a cheque in favour of C. Later on A forges the indorsement of C and negotiates the cheque to D, who is bona fide holder for value. The cheque was duly honoured by the bank. C is fictitions payee. Can B recover the amount of cheque from D? (Hint: No).
6. A, B and C, who is minor, executed a promissory note payable after three month of Rs. 1,000 in favour of D. On the date of maturity joint promisors including a minor refuse to pay. What is the legal remedy available to D. Are all joint promisors are absolved of their liability?

7. A who is a minor borrows sum of Rs. 5,000 from B and executes promissory note in favour of B payable after two month. Out of that amount A pays Rs. 3,000 as a fees for doing computer course. On due date A refuses to pay. Discuss the right of B.
8. Ram delivers a cheque amounting Rs. 10,000 to his employee for getting it deposited in his account. An employee manipulates to indorse it to Shyam, who in good faith and for value gets the cheque. Can Shyam recover the payment from the bank? (Hint: Yes).
9. Bill is drawn under a fictitious name of A for three months on B. B accepts the bill. The bill is indorsed in favour of C who is a holder in due course under the signature of fictitions person A. Can C, claim payment of bill from B? (Hint: Yes).
10. A gives promissory note to B without consideration. B further indorses it to C and C to D who is holder in due course. Can D recover the payment of the note from A? (Hint: Yes).

24

Negotiation and Assignment

LEARNING OBJECTIVES

- Compare negotiation with assignment.
- Learn how an Instrument can be negotiated.
- Understand the basic concept of indorsement with various types of it. Get familiar with any one of them with suitable example.
- Examine legality of an instrument without consideration.

NEGOTIATION

In business world, the use of negotiable instrument has become very common and popular. It is because these instruments are freely transferable by one to another party. The holder of such instrument, even before date of maturity can further transfer is or can get it discounted from the bank.

The ownership of negotiable instrument can be transferred either by (*i*) Negotiation or by (*ii*) Assignment.

According to Section 14 of this Act, "when a promissory note a bill of exchange or a cheque is transferred to any person so as to constitute that person as the holder thereof, the instrument is said to be negotiated."

Thus, when, negotiable instrument is transferred by a negotiation, the title or ownership of the instrument is conveyed from the holder to the transferee. And on negotiation, the transferee becomes the holder of an instrument, who can possess the instrument in his own name. He is also entitled to recover the payment of that instrument on the date of maturity from the party liable to pay.

Briefly speaking, negotiation is a process of transferring negotiable instrument by one to another person. The process of negotiation presumes an intention to transfer the ownership of the instrument by the holder to another person.

Negotiable instrument which is payable to bearer can be transferred only by giving delivery of it to the party. And if it is payable to order, it can be transferred by indorsement and delivery.

ASSIGNMENT

Assignment is also an important method of transfering negotiable instrument. Assignment means transfer of ownership of negotiable instrument through a written and registered document under the provisions of the Transfer of Property Act, 1882. By making such document, the transferee becomes entitled to possess the instrument in his own name and recover its payment on due date.

Where the ownership of negotiable instrument is transferred by assignment, the assignee of such instrument will get same title as the assignor has.

NAR SINGH PANDA *vs* N. NAR SINGH MURT (1966) ORISSA 194: In this case, M executed a promissory note for Rs. 1,000 in favour of A, who in turn sold the promissory note to P under a separate sale deed. P sued M for the recovery of the amount of the note. M pleaded that P could not recover the money as he was not a holder in due course of the note and the suit was not maintainable. It was held that it is true that P was not a holder in due course but he was a holder under Section 8 as he was in possession of the note and as an assignee he was entitled to recover payment in his own name. A transfer of promissory note by means of registered instrument is valid.

DIFFERENCE BETWEEN NEGOTIATION AND ASSIGNMENT

Negotiable Instrument Act does not allow transfer of an instrument only by a process of negotiation. Rather an instrument can also be transferred by assignment. Though these two processes lead to same end, they are different on the following grounds:

(*a*) *Process*

Though both negotiation and assignment involve transfer of ownership of instrument from one to another party, the process of negotiation is simple and has little formalities as compared to assignment. Negotiation can be made either by delivery or by indorsement and delivery of instrument. But assignment needs written and registered document to be prepared and signed by the assignor.

(*b*) *Consideration*

Transfer by negotiation is based on the assumption that there has been a consideration. But there is no such presumption as to consideration in case of transfer by assignment and therefore transferee must prove consideration.

(*c*) *Title*

In case of transfer by negotiation if the transferee gets an instrument before maturity, in good faith and for value, he will get better title than that of transferor. Even if the title of transferor is defective, the title of transferee will be good title. But in case of transfer by assignment, the assignee gets only the rights of holder *i.e.*, he will get same title as the transferor has.

(*d*) *Notice of transfer*

In case of transfer by negotiation, the holder is not required to give notice of transfer to the debtor. But in assignment, notice of transfer is required to be given by the assignee to the debtor and the debtor must have consented to it, for making such transfer binding and effective.

MODES OF NEGOTIATION

Negotiable instrument can be negotiated in the following two ways:

(*a*) *Negotiation by delivery*

According to Section 47, a promissory note, a bill of exchange or a cheque payable to bearer is negotiated by delivery thereof subject to the provisions of Section 58 of this Act.

Simply speaking if an instrument is payable to the bearer, it can be negotiated only by giving delivery of it to the party concerned. And the party to whom it is delivered becomes the holder of that instrument. In this case, the transferor of an instrument does not require to make his signature on the instrument. It is therefore that he is not liable either to immediate party or to a subsequent holder. Thus he is not liable to any party in case of dishonour of an instrument.

(b) Negotiation by endorsement and delivery

According to Section 48 of this Act, a negotiable instrument payable to order can be negotiated by the holder by endorsement and delivery thereof.

In other words, if an instrument is payable to order it can be transferred first by endorsing it in favour of that party and then delivering it to him.

Significance of Delivery in Negotiation

The process of transfer of negotiable instrument completes with delivery of an instrument to the person concerned.

Under both the modes of negotiation, delivery of an instrument is involved. To affect the transfer, delivery of an instrument is made voluntarily with an intention of transferring ownership to the transferee. Thus mere delivery of an instrument may not necessarily result in transfer of ownership. The instruments may be delivered for the purpose of safe custody, deposit or for any other purpose. It will not amount to transfer of ownership.

It is clearly mentioned in the Act that valid delivery of an instrument made with clear intention of transferring ownership will complete the process of negotiation. In case of an instrument payable to order if the indorser after having endorsed an instrument dies, the negotiation remain incomplete. Even the legal representation of deceased indorser cannot complete it by giving delivery.

Types of delivery

Delivery of negotiable instrument may be made in the following manner:

(*i*) Actual delivery in which actual possession of an instrument is removed from one person and is restored to another person.

(*ii*) Constructive delivery takes place without the change of actual possession. Rather the transferor does some act which has an effect of making a delivery to transferee, such as handing over an instrument to an employee or agent. But in the eyes of law constructive delivery is equivalent to actual delivery.

Example: A and B are having accounts in the same bank. A who is a holder of negotiable instrument payable to bearer directs the banker to transfer the instrument to the account of B. The banker does so and has a possession of that instrument on behalf of B. It would amount to constructive delivery.

(*iii*) Conditional delivery implies delivery of negotiable instrument based on the fulfillment of some conditions attached to it. In case of conditional delivery, the ownership of an instrument is not transferred to the transferee unless he fulfils that condition even though an instrument has been endorsed to him.

INDORSEMENT

Negotiation of an instrument payable to order can be made in two parts (*i*) indorsement, (*ii*) delivery. Generally indorsement means writing of a holder's name or signature on the back of an instrument with a view to transfer its ownership. According to Section 15 of this Act, "when the maker, or holder of negotiable instrument signs the same, otherwise than as such maker, for the purpose of negotiation, on the back or face thereof or on a slip of paper annexed thereto or so sign for the same purpose a stamped paper intended to be completed as negotiable instrument, he is said to indorse the same and is called the indorser." The person making an endorsement is called 'indorser' and the person in whose favour the instrument is endorsed is called 'indorsee'. Thus indorsement implies:

(*i*) Signature of a holder or maker or any party authorised to negotiate the instrument.

(*ii*) Signature may be made either on the face or back of the instrument or on a piece of paper known as 'allonge'.

(*iii*) Signature must have been made with a view to negotiate the instrument.

(*iv*) Mere indorsement is not sufficient, to complete it the instrument must be delivered to the 'indorsee'.

Who may Indorse Instrument

According to Section 15 of this Act, indorsement can be made by the holder of a negotiable instrument. The payee of an instrument makes first indorsement.

Thereafter an instrument may be indorsed by any party who is a holder of that instrument. In general, a maker of promissory note or drawer of bill of exchange cannot indorse an instrument. But if the bill of exchange is payable to drawer's order, he can indorse it.

According to Section 51 of this Act, every maker, drawer or payee or indorser all of them jointly can negotiate an instrument provided he is in lawful possession or is a holder of such instrument.

Rules Regarding a Valid Indorsement

With regard to a valid indorsement, the following rules should be followed:

(*a*) ***Signature of indorser:*** In order to indorse an instrument, a holder must sign either on the face or back or on the piece of paper attached to it

(*b*) ***Intention:*** Signature on the instrument is not enough to affect indorsement. Rather a holder must sign on instrument with an intention of negotiating it.

(*c*) ***Spelling:*** The indorser must use same spelling of his signature as appearing on the face of negotiable instrument.

(*d*) ***No prefixes or suffixes:*** The prefixes and suffixes to the name of the payee or indorsee should not be included in the indorsement.

(*e*) ***Use of ink:*** Indorsement must be in ink. Indorsement in pencil or by rubber stamp is not usually accepted.

(*f*) ***No particular form:*** Indorsement does not require any particular form of words. But it must contain an order to pay.

(*g*) ***Illiterate person:*** If the payee or holder is an illiterate person, he may indorse the instrument by putting his thumb impression thereon, in the presence of another person who should sign it as witness.

(*h*) ***Order of indorsement:*** Indorsement shall be presumed to have been made in the order which appears on the instrument.

(*i*) ***Time of indorsement:*** Negotiable instrument may be indorsed until its payment has been made or at or before its maturity.

Kinds of Indorsement

Indorsement may be of following kinds:

1. Blank or General Indorsement

According to Section 16 (1) of this Act, if the indorser signs his name only and does not specify the name of the indorsee, the indorsement is said to be in blank. The net legal effect of blank indorsement is to convert order instrument into bearer instrument, which may be transferred merely by delivery.

Example: A gets a cheque from B, which is payable to 'A or order'. A wants to transfer it to C. For the purpose of transfer A puts his signature on the back of a cheque and delivers it to C. Such indorsement is known as 'indorsement in blank'.

Indorsed

S/d A

2. Indorsement in Full or Special Indorsement

According to Section 16 (1) of this Act, if the indorser signs his name and adds a direction to pay the amount mentioned in the instrument to or to the order of a specified person the indorsement is said to be in full.

However, it is to be noted that no specific form of words is necessary for an indorsement in full.

Example: A, the holder of bill of exchange wants to make indorsement in full to B. He can do it by writing 'Pay to B or order' S/d A. After such indorsement it is only the 'B' who is entitled to receive payment of the bill or he can further negotiate it.

Conversion of blank indorsement into full indorsement

According to Section 49 of this Act, the holder of an instrument which is indorsed in blank may convert it into an 'indorsement in full', without signing his own name, by writing necessary direction for payment as above the signature of indorser (who has indorsed instrument in his favour). The holder does not bear the responsibility of indorser in that instrument. He is not liable to any party on the instrument.

Example: A has made indorsement of a cheque in favour of B. The indorsement is in blank.

Indorsed

S/d A

In this case B becomes a holder of that cheque. He wants to indorse it to C, he can do it just by writing some direction regarding payment of that cheque above the signature of A.

Indorsed to C

S/d A

B is not liable to A and C on this instrument. It is to be noted that, when indorsement in blank is converted into indorsement in full, the basic nature of an instrument gets changed. It ceases to be payable to bearer and becomes payable to order.

Effect of blank indorsement followed by indorsement in full

A proper distinction should be made between the blank indorsement converted into full indorsement and blank indorsement to be followed by indorsement in full.

In case of blank indorsement to be followed by indorsement in full an instrument continues to be payable to bearer.

As such the ownership of the instrument can be transferred by mere delivery and still remains *payable to bearer as against all parties prior to indorsement in full.* The indorser in full is only liable to a holder and person deriving title through such holder.

Example: A draws a bill of exchange on B, making it payable to C. C indorsed it in blank to D. D indorsed it in full to E or order. E transfers a bill to F without indorsement.

F is entitled to sue A, B and C, but he cannot sue D and E, because D is indorser in full and E derives title from D.

3. Restrictive Indorsement

By making restrictive indorsement the negotiability of an instrument is restricted and the instrument cannot be further negotiated.

An indorsement is said to be restrictive one when it restricts further negotiability of an instrument. It is done by mentioning express words in the indorsement. Such indorsement entitles the holder of an instrument to receive the amount for specific purpose. Thus under restrictive indorsement, the indorsee gets all the rights except the right to negotiate it further.

Examples:

(*i*) Pay the contents to A only.

S/d B

(*ii*) Pay C for my use.

S/d B

(*iii*) Pay C or order for the account of B.

S/d B

4. Partial Indorsement

According to Section 56 of this Act, "negotiable instrument cannot be indorsed for a part of the amount appearing to be due on the instrument. Thus partial indorsement which transfers right to receive on by a part of due amount is invalid."

Partial indorsement is not allowed because it may interfere with the free circulation of an instrument and may cause inconvenience to the parties.

However, where the amount on negotiable instrument has been partly paid and it has been mentioned on the instrument, it can be indorsed for the balance.

Example: A makes a promissory note of Rs. 2,000 in favour of B. B indorsed it to C. A pays Rs. 1,000 to C and this fact is noted on the instrument. C can negotiate it for remaining balance of Rs. 1,000.

Pay to D or order Rs. 1,000 being unpaid residue on the note.

S/d C

5. Conditional Indorsement

Every indorser has a liability in the negotiable instrument. When he indorses that instrument by excluding his liability or makes his liability conditional, it is also known as 'conditional indorsement'.

According to Section 52 of this Act, "Where the indorser of a negotiable instrument, by express words in the indorsement makes his liability dependent upon the happening of a specified event, such indorsement is called 'conditional indorsement.'"

The conditional indorsement, limits the liability of indorser without affecting negotiability of an instrument.

Examples:

(*i*) Pay to A or order san recourse.

(*ii*) Pay to A or order, without recourse to me.

(*iii*) Pay to B on his arrival in India.

(*iv*) Pay to B or order, on his marriage.

In case of conditional indorsement if the indorser excludes his liability entirely, he will not be liable to the indorsee or subsequent holders if the instrument gets dishonoured. It is also known as 'San recourse indorsement.'

However, if the indorser makes his liability conditional subject to happening of specific event, his liability would arise only upon the happening of that specified event.

6. Facultative Indorsement

When the indorser by adding express words, gives up some of his rights in favour of the holder of an instrument, it is known as 'facultative indorsement.' As a result of such indorsement, endorsee or a holder is relieved of his duty doing that act, for which waiver has been given by the indorser.

Example: Pay to A or order, 'a notice of dishonour waived.'

S/d B

In case, such instrument is dishonoured on the date of maturity A or holder is not required to give notice of dishonour to B as to make him liable. B will be liable if notice of dishonour has been given to him.

Effects of Indorsement

Indorsement is one of the mode or a method of transferring ownership of a negotiable instrument to another party, provided it is followed by proper delivery of an instrument.

According to Section 50 of this Act, "the indorsement of a negotiable instrument followed by delivery transfers to the indorsee the property therein with the right of further negotiation."

Thus a valid indorsement gives the following rights to the endorsee:

(*i*) He can possess an instrument in his own name.

(*ii*) He can recover payment from the party liable to pay.

(*iii*) He gets ownership right of that instrument.

(*iv*) He gets right to negotiate the instrument further.

(*v*) He has a right to take action against all parties whose names appear on the instrument.

By making an indorsement, the indorser represents to his immediate indorsee that the indorser will indemnify the indorsee, if an instrument, duly presented, gets dishonoured. But where the holder without the consent of indorser, destroys or impairs indorser's remedy against the prior parties, the indorser is discharged from his liability as such that the instrument has been duly paid on maturity.

Negotiation Back

Negotiable instrument is freely transferable. It can be transferred for any times unless its negotiability is restricted. During the course of negotiation, sometimes an instrument may come back to the person who had indorsed it earlier. This is called 'negotiation back'. It implies that an instrument has come back to the person who had negotiated it.

It may be regarded as a process, under which an instrument comes into the hands of indorser in his own right. In such case, the indorser becomes holder of an instrument before the date of maturity. In case of negotiation back, the intermediate parties of that instrument ceases to be liable to the holder.

But if the indorser had excluded his liability by making san recourse indorsement, and later on becomes the holder of that instrument in his own right under the negotiation back; all intermediate indorsers will remain liable to him and in case of dishonour of an instrument he can recover the amount from all or any one of them.

Examples: A draws a bill of exchange on B amounting Rs. 2,000; payable to C or order. C indorses it to D, D has indorsed it to E and E to F. F has again indorsed to C. This is known as 'negotiation back' and as a result of it C has come back to his original position. And D, E and F will not be liable to him.

In the above case, suppose C indorsed the bill in favour of D, san recourse and again the bill comes back into the hand of C. Though C is not liable to D, E and F, all of them along with A and B will be liable towards C in case the bill gets dishonoured.

NEGOTIATION BY UNAUTHORISED PARTIES

Sometimes, in the course of negotiation, an instrument may be lost, or may be obtained by unlawful means or for unlawful consideration. In these cases, the rights and liabilities of the parties may be affected. Some of the cases of unauthorised negotiation are as under:

1. Lost instrument

In case the negotiable instrument is lost or stolen, the rights and liabilities of parties to a lost negotiable instrument will be subject to the following rules:

(*i*) The holder of a lost negotiable instrument should give notice of the loss to all parties liable to the instrument. Such notice should also be given to a public through advertisement.

(*ii*) The person who finds lost negotiable instrument has no right to sue thereon in his own name.

(*iii*) The true owner is entitled to recover the instrument from the finder. In case the finder has obtained the payment of that instrument, he is liable to indemnify the owner.

(*iv*) Any acceptor, maker or drawee, who has made payment in due course of the lost instrument, which was 'payable to bearer' to the finder, will be discharged from the liability.

(*v*) In case the instrument is 'payable to bearer' and the finder of that instrument negotiates it to holder in due course, such holder in due course will get good title and will become rightful owner.

(*vi*) In case the instrument is 'payable to order', the finder of that instrument forges the indorsement and negotiates it to holder in due course. But such holder in due course will not get title to the instrument. In this case the golden rule that 'forgery confers no title in any case' will be applied.

(*vii*) Where, the bill of exchange is lost, the following provision will be applicable:

(*a*) The holder of a lost bill should make an application to the drawee for payment on the date of maturity. On refusal by drawee, he must give notice of dishonour to all other parties liable to pay.

(*b*) If the bill is lost before it is due, the person who was holder of it may apply to the drawer for giving another bill of same tenor. He may be asked to furnish security to the drawer for indemnifying him in case the lost bill is found again.

(*viii*) The legal position in case of stolen instrument is almost same as in case of lost instrument. But in case of stolen instrument, the thief is subject to criminal prosecution. However if the thief transfers a bearer instrument to a holder in due course, such holder will get good title to it.

2. Instrument Obtained by Fraud

It is a general rule of a contract that all kinds of contracts are made by the free consent of the parties. Thus where the person obtains a negotiable instrument by fraud he is not entitled to get its payment. The parties who are liable to pay will get sufficient protection on the ground of fraud being used to obtain an instrument.

Thus where a negotiable instrument was executed or made or obtained by fraud, the proof of such fraud is a sufficient ground to an action on the instrument. In case, the maker or acceptor proves that an instrument was obtained from him by fraud, the person defrauding is not entitled to recover the payment. In the same way, if the instrument was further negotiated it will not be valid. But if the instrument obtained by fraud gets into the hands of holder in due course, such holder will acquire good title or a subsequent holder deriving title from such holder will enjoy good title.

3. Forged Instrument

Where the writing on a negotiable instrument is made or altered to the prejudice of rights of the parties thereof, it is known as 'forged instrument.' In other words, if the signature of maker, drawer or acceptor is forged by someone it is considered as forged instrument. The instrument can be forged in the following ways:

(*i*) Fraudulently, writing the name of the person who exists.

(*ii*) Signing the name of a fictitious or a non-existing person with a fraudulent intention inducing to believe that the instrument was signed by a real person.

(*iii*) Signing one's own name with the intention that signatures are of another person of the same name.

Where the signature on a negotiable instrument has been forged, the forged signature is wholly inoperative and therefore, the title of an instrument remains with the person who was the holder at the time when signature was forged. It is however to be remembered that, a person who has paid money by mistake on forged signature may recover it from the person to whom he has paid it. In case of a forged instrument, even a holder in due course does not get good title to it.

This is so, because, forged signature is worthless and there is complete absence of title on that.

Forged indorsement: In the eyes of law forged indorsement is regarded completely null and void and as a result of it no one claiming through forged indorsement gets any right on that.

Thus a bill of exchange and a promissory note cannot be negotiated by making a forged indorsement. Even if the holder gets it for value and in good faith he is not entitled to any rights of ownership in that instrument.

Example: X is a payee of a bill of exchange. His signatures are forged by Y and then that bill was transferred to Z for value and he gets it in good faith. But in no case, Z is a holder in due course but if he gets payment of that bill on maturity, the drawee of the bill will not be discharged from his liability. X remains a bona fide holder having every right to recover the payment from the drawee.

However, if the instrument is payable to bearer or has been indorsed in blank, it can be negotiated by delivery. If such instrument is further negotiated on forged signature, the holder can claim the payment. It is because, such holder derives a title independent of the forged indorsement.

According to Section 41 of this Act, "Where a person accepts a bill of exchange already carrying forged indorsement, with knowledge of having reason to believe the indorsement to be forged when he accepted the bill, he is not relieved from liability by reason that such indorsement is forged."

But with regard to a cheque, protection has been given to the banker under Section 85 of this Act, "Where a cheque payable to order purports to be indorsed by or on behalf of the payee the drawee (banker) is discharged by payment in due course, although the signatures of the payee may have been forged."

4. Instruments without Consideration

Though, in case of negotiable instrument, consideration is presumed but such presumption is rebuttable. The total or partial absence of consideration, if proved may affect liability of the parties.

Total absence of consideration: According to Section 43 of this Act, "a negotiable instrument, made, drawn, accepted, indorsed or transferred without consideration or for a consideration which creates no obligation of payment between the parties to the transaction. But if any such party has transferred the instrument with or without consideration to the holder for consideration, such holder and every subsequent holder deriving title from him may recover the amount due on such instrument from the transferor for consideration or any prior thereto."

Examples: A draws a bill of exchange on B, payable to C or order. C indorsed it to D without consideration. On maturity bill is dishonoured and D cannot sue C for the payment.

A draws a bill on B and B accepts it without consideration. A indorses that bill to C without consideration. C indorses it to D for value consideration D can sue any of the parties A, B or C.

Partial absence of money consideration: According to Section 44 of this Act "when the consideration for which a person signed a promissory note, bill of exchange or a cheque consisted of money and was originally absent in part or has subsequently failed in part, the sum, which a holder standing in immediate relation with such signor is entitled from him is proportionately reduced."

Example: A draws a bill on B for Rs. 1,000 payable to the order of A. B accepts the bill but subsequently dishonours it by non-payment. A sued B on the bill. B proves that it was accepted for value as to Rs. 800 and as on accommodation to the residue. A can only recover Rs. 800.

The following parties stand in immediate relation with each other:

(*i*) The drawer of bill of exchange stands in immediate relation with the acceptor.

(*ii*) The maker of promissory note, bill of exchange or a cheque stands in immediate relation with payee.

(*iii*) Indorser stands in immediate relation with indorsee.

Partial Failure of Consideration not Consisting of Money

According to Section 45 of this Act, "where the consideration which has partly failed consists of things other than money and the value of that failed consideration, can be ascertained without a collateral enquiry, the parties, standing in immediate relation, can recover from each other only the proportionately reduced amount and not the whole amount of a bill."

However, if the value of that failed consideration cannot be ascertained without collateral enquiry the immediate parties to the bill are entitled to recover the full amount of the bill from each other.

AGRA AND MASTERMAN BANK *vs* LEIGH TON (1866, LR.2 Ex 56) In this case, A agrees to supply two bales of cotton to B. B accepts a bill for Rs. 1,000 drawn by A, being the agreed price of two bales. Later on, A delivers only one bale of cotton to B. A sues B on the bill. B can take plea of partial failure of consideration. It was held that A can recover only Rs. 500.

However, the above rule applies only in case of immediate parties and the right of holder in due course will not be affected.

Example: In the above case if A after having obtained a bill accepted by B indorses it to C for value and C further indorsed it to D for value D, who is holder in due course is entitled to recover entire amount of Rs. 1,000 from B.

REVIEW QUESTIONS

1. What is 'negotiation'? How negotiable instrument can be negotiated?
2. Define the terms 'negotiation' and 'assignment'. Distinguish between them.
3. Define 'indorsement'. Explain rules regarding to a valid indorsement.
4. Discuss various types of indorsement with suitable examples.
5. Discuss the effects of indorsement of an instrument.
6. Comment on:
    (*i*) Partial indorsement does not operate as negotiation of the instrument.
    (*ii*) Forged indorsement is regarded as no indorsement.
    (*iii*) Absence of consideration is material only between immediate parties of the instrument.
    (*iv*) Negotiation is incomplete without delivery of an instrument.
7. Write notes on:
    (*i*) Negotiation back
    (*ii*) Forged indorsement
    (*iii*) Lost instruments
    (*iv*) Restrictive indorsement

PRACTICAL PROBLEMS

1. A executed a promissory note for Rs. 500 in favour of B. B, through sale deed sold that note to C. Can C claim the payment of that note from A? (Hint: Yes).
2. A draws a bill of exchange on B payable to C or order amounting Rs. 2,000. C indorsed it in favour of D and made his signature on the bill to this effect. Before the bill is delivered to D, C dies. Can legal representative of C complete indorsement by handing over that bill to C? (Hint: No).

3. Ram is the payee of a bill. He indorsed it in blank and delivered it to Shyam. Shyam indorsed it in full to Sohan or order. Sohan without indorsement transfers the bill to Mohan. Examine the right of Mohan with regard to the payment of that bill.
4. A is a holder of a bill amounting to Rs. 2,000. He indorsed it for Rs. 1,000 in favour of B and for the remaining balance of Rs. 1,000 in favour of C. Examine legality of indorsement.
5. A has drawn a bill payable to C or order on B for Rs. 5,000. C indorsed it to D to E, and E further indorsed it in favour of F, who indorses it to C. Discuss the right of C.
6. Ram was a holder of a cheque of Rs.1,000 payable to order. The cheque was stolen by a thief who forged the signature of Ram and got the payment of that cheque from the bank. Can Ram recover the amount of the cheque from the banker? (Hint: No).
7. A draws a bill on B for Rs. 2,000 payable to A or his order. On the date of maturity B refuses to pay and the bill is dishonoured. A filed a suit against B. B proves that the bill was accepted for the value of Rs. 1,000. Can A recover Rs. 2,000? (Hint: No).
8. X agrees to supply 10 cotton bales to Y and Y accepts a bill for Rs. 10,000 being the price of 10 cotton bales. X delivers only 5 cotten bales and sues on Y for the bill. Examine the right of X regarding payment of the bill.

■■■

25

Presentment, Discharge and Dishonour of Negotiable Instrument

LEARNING OBJECTIVES

- Get conceptual clarity about presentment of instrument for acceptance and payment.
- Find out those situations when presentment of an instrument is not required.
- Understand the concept of discharge of negotiable instrument.
- Get familiar with dishonour of negotiable instrument and find out implications of notice of discharge on the liability of the parties.

INTRODUCTION

There are many parties involved in negotiable instrument. Someone draws it, another accepts it, and some others hold it and gets a payment of it on due date. In the entire life cycle of an instrument, the presentment of an instrument occupies very important place.

Presentment is a process of presenting or placing the instrument before the party who is supposed to accept liability on it or pay out it on the date of maturity. It is presented by the holder or payee of an instrument.

Presentment of negotiable instrument may be made for:

(*i*) Acceptance, in case of bill of exchange.

(*ii*) Sight, in case of promissory note.

(*iii*) Payment in case of a bill, note and a cheque.

PRESENTMENT FOR ACCEPTANCE

A bill of exchange, to be legally valid and effective must be duly accepted by the drawee. Thus after having drawn a bill, it will be presented to the drawee by the holder for acceptance.

An acceptance implies expression of intention to have accepted the direction given by the drawer for making payment. It is done by writing a word 'accepted' and sign the name below it.

Following types of bills need not be presented for acceptance.

(*i*) A bill payable on demand.

(*ii*) A bill payable certain number of days after date.

(*iii*) A bill payable on certain day. However, presentment for acceptance is necessary in the following cases:

(*a*) Where the bill is payable at a given time after acceptance or 'after sight'. Such bills must be presented to the drawee for his sight or acceptance as to determine maturity of the bill.

(*b*) Where the bill contains express stipulation that it shall be presented for acceptance. Such bills must be presented for acceptance before it is presented for payment.

ACCEPTANCE

A bill of exchange contains unconditional order, directing upon the drawee for making payment. Thus the direction regarding payment is to be consented by the drawee. The bill is said to be accepted, when the drawee signifies his intention for accepting directions of payment by writing a word 'accepted' and making his sign below it.

As soon as a bill is accepted, the drawee delivers it to the holder or gives a notice of acceptance to him. By accepting a bill, the drawee virtually becomes liable to pay on the bill to the holder.

Types of Acceptance

An acceptance of a bill of exchange may be either general or conditional or qualified.

(*a*) *General acceptance:* An acceptance of a bill is said to be general, if it is accepted without any condition. In other words, where the drawee does not impose or attach any condition while giving the acceptance. It means he accepts the direction of the drawer of the bill regarding the payment as it is. It is a usual type of acceptance and generally the bills are accepted this way.

(b) Conditional or qualified acceptance: Where the drawee gives his consent for accepting the bill subject to some condition such acceptance is known as 'conditional acceptance'. In other words, by giving conditional acceptance, the drawee admits liability for marking payment according to the direction of the drawer, provided some conditions are fulfilled.

In case of conditional acceptance, the holder of a bill has a right to reject it and treat the bill as 'dishonoured by non-acceptance'. But if the holder takes conditionally accepted bill the parties prior to him shall not be liable on the bill, unless they give their consent for that.

An acceptance may be made conditional by the drawee in terms of place, time, event and amount for payment etc. Some instances of conditional acceptance are:

(*i*) **Condition as to time:** Generally at the time of drawing a bill the time of payment is determined by the drawer. But, the acceptor may not agree with that time period. Thus he may deviate from that and put a condition to it.

(*ii*) **Condition as to amount:** The acceptor while accepting the bill may not agree with drawer about the amount to be paid by him. He may give acceptance for lesser amount.

(*iii*) **Condition as to place:** The drawee of a bill may specify particular place at which the payment will be made.

(*iv*) **Condition as to an event:** The drawee may give his acceptance for making payment subject to happening or non-happening of some specific future event.

RULES REGARDING PRESENTMENT

The presentment of a bill for acceptance is subject to the following rules:

1. Who may present the bill for acceptance

In fact, the right of presentment lies with the holder of a bill. The holder of a bill may be the drawer of the bill or indorsee to whom he has indorsed it. The authorised agent of the holder may also present the bill for acceptance.

2. To whom a bill may be presented

The following are the parties to whom, a bill may be presented for acceptance:

(*i*) The drawee or his authorised agent.

(*ii*) In case of two or more drawees, bill may be presented to all of them.

(*iii*) In case the drawee dies, a bill may be presented to his legal representative.

(*iv*) The drawee in case of need.

(*v*) An acceptor for honour.

3. Time and place for presentment of a bill

(*i*) In case, no time is fixed in a bill, it should be presented for acceptance to the drawee within a reasonable period after it is drawn. The reasonable period of time varies case to case depending on nature of a bill, trade usage and distance between the place, bill is drawn and the place at which it is to be accepted.

(*ii*) Where, the time has been specified in the bill for its presentment, it must be presented within that time period.

(*iii*) Some time presentment of a bill may be optional. If it is so, it must be presented for acceptance at any time before the payment.

(*iv*) A bill must be presented for acceptance before its maturity on a business day and within business hours.

(*v*) So far as the place of presentment is concerned, if it is specified, the bill must be presented at that place. In case, the place is not specified, it must be presented usually at business place, but it may also be residence of the drawee.

According to Section 63 of this Act, "the holder, if so required by the drawee of a bill presented to him for acceptance, allow the drawee forty-eight hours (exclusive of public holidays) or, 'conclusive of public holiday' to consider whether he will accept it." After 48 hours, the drawee must return the bill accepted or dishonoured as the case may be. In case he fails to do so, the holder may treat the bill dishonoured by non-acceptance.

There must be concrete evidence regarding the fact that the bill was duly presented for acceptance but it has been dishonoured. It is a duty of the holder to prove it before 'Notary Public' to get such 'dishonour by non-acceptance' recorded.

When Presentment is not Required

A bill must be duly presented for acceptance to hold the parties liable to pay, unless such presentment is excused. It is excused under the following situations:

(*i*) Where the drawee cannot be found after making reasonable search.

(*ii*) Where the drawee is a fictitious person or he has no contractual capacity.

In case of death or insolvency of the drawee, the bill may be presented to the legal representative of deceased or to the official assignee, if it is not execused to be presented. According to Section 61 of this Act, "where presentment for acceptance is essential, *i.e.*, where the bill is payable at a specified period after sight, and the holder fails to present the bill for acceptance, all parties thereto, *i.e.*, drawer and indorsers, if any are discharged from their liability to such a holder."

Presentment of Promissory Note for Sight

According to Section 62 of this Act, "a promissory note payable at a certain period after sight, must be presented to the maker thereof, for sight (if he can, after search be found) by a person entitled to demand payment, within a reasonable time after it is made and during business, hours on a business day."

The words 'after sight' imply after presentment for sight.

In other words, the payment cannot be demanded till the note has been exhibited to the maker. When a promissory note is not made payable at a certain period after right, it must be presented for sight in order to fix the maturity of that note.

If default is made in such presentment, all the antecedent parties are discharged from liability to the person making such default. No presentment is required for promissory notes payable 'at sight', 'on demand' or 'on a fixed day' or 'on the expiry of a fixed period'.

Acceptance for Honour and Liability of Acceptor

Where the drawee of a bill refuses to accept it or refuses to give better security when demanded by a notary, any person for the honour of drawer may accept that bill. Such acceptance is known as 'acceptance for honour'. The following points must be taken care of with regard to such acceptance:

(*i*) Such bill may be accepted by any person on the refusal of original drawee, with the consent of a holder.

(*ii*) An acceptor for honour must declare it in writing that he is accepting a bill for the honour of the drawer or any indorser named therein.

(*iii*) If he does not make such declaration, it will be deemed that he is accepting a bill for the honour of the drawer.

(*iv*) The protest for better security takes place where the acceptor becomes insolvent or suspends the payment of a bill.

(*v*) An acceptor for honour will be liable to all parties subsequent to the party for whose honour he accepts the bill.

(*vi*) All parties prior to the party for whose honour, the bill is accepted will be liable to compensate an acceptor for honour for all losses and damages sustained by him in consequence of such acceptance.

(*vii*) An acceptor for honour will not be liable to a holder of bill unless it is presented or forwarded for presentment not later than the day next after the day of its maturity.

Presentment for Payment

Like acceptance, the negotiable instrument must be duly presented for payment to the party liable to pay.

According to Section 64 of this Act, "promissory notes, bill of exchange and cheque must be presented for payment to the maker, acceptor or drawee thereof respectively by or on behalf of the holder."

Rules Regarding to a Valid Presentment for Payment

The following rules are to be complied with for presentment for payment:

1. *Who can make such presentment*

A negotiable instrument should be presented for payment by a person who can give valid discharge to the debtor. Thus holder of negotiable instrument or his duly authorised agent, who can give valid discharge, is entitled to present the instrument for payment.

2. *To whom it may be presented*

A negotiable instrument must be presented for the payment to the parties as:

(*i*) A promissory note must be presented to its maker.

(*ii*) A bill of exchange must be presented to its acceptor.

(*iii*) Cheque must be presented to its drawee (banker).

(*iv*) In case of death of maker in promissory note, acceptor in bill it should be presented to his legal representative.

(*v*) In case, the maker, acceptor and the drawee has been declared insolvent, it would be presented to his official assignee.

3. *Time for presentment*

Regarding the time for presentment for payment, the following rules are applicable:

(*i*) A negotiable instrument, payable otherwise than 'on demand' must be presented for payment at maturity. Thus, an instrument payable at a specified period 'after date', or 'after sight' or a bill payable on the lapse of a certain period after the happening of an event must be presented at maturity. A presentment earlier than this is premature and ineffective and a delay in presentment even of a day would discharge the parties from their liability except the maker or acceptor.

(*ii*) A negotiable instrument payable on demand must be presented for payment within a reasonable time, after it is received by the holder, otherwise the parties except the maker or acceptor, will be discharged from their liability.

(*iii*) A promissory note payable by instalments, must be presented for payment on third day after the date fixed for payment of each instalment.

(*iv*) A cheque should, in order to discharge the drawer, be presented for payment at the bank upon which, it is drawn, before the relation between the drawer and his banker has been altered to the prejudice of the drawer.

(*v*) A cheque, in order to discharge any person except the drawer, be presented within reasonable time, after delivery by such person.

(*vi*) All instruments must be presented for payment during usual hours of business. A cheque must be presented within usual 'banking hours'. Delay in presentment for payment may be excused if it is caused by circumstances beyond the control of the holder and not imputable to his default, misconduct or negligence.

4. *Place of presentment for payment*

The following rules are applicable regarding the place of presentment for payment:

(*i*) A promissory note, bill of exchange or a cheque made, drawn or accepted payable at a specified place and not elsewhere, must, in order to charge any party thereto, be presented for payment at that place.

Thus in such cases, if an instrument is not presented at that place, no party will be liable on the bill. But when the promissory note or a bill is made payable at a specified place, it must be presented for payment at that place in order to charge maker or drawer. If it is not presented at the specified place only the maker or drawer will be discharged from his liability to holder and other parties will remain liable.

(*ii*) Where the place of presentment is not specified in a note or bill, it must be presented for payment at the place of business (if any) or at the usual residence of the maker, drawee or acceptor thereof as the case may be. However, if the maker, drawee or acceptor of a negotiable instrument has no known place of business or fixed residence and no place has been specified in the instrument, an instrument must be presented for payment to him in person wherever he can be found.

(*iii*) In case of a cheque, in order to charge the drawer, it must be presented at the bank upon which it is drawn before the relation between the drawer and his banker has been altered to the prejudice of the drawer.

However, the crossed cheque can be presented to collecting bank for receiving payment.

The holder of an instrument is expected to exercise reasonable degree of diligence in finding place of business or residence of the maker, acceptor or drawee.

5. *Effect of non-presentation of instrument for payment*

According to Section 64 of this Act, "when a promissory note, bill or cheque is not presented for payment to the maker, acceptor or drawee thereof, respectively, other parties thereto are not liable to holder. These parties are all parties other than maker in a note, all parties other than acceptor in a bill and in case of cheque all parties other than drawee."

Therefore, indorser, in case of promissory note, and drawer and indorsers in case of a bill and cheque are discharged from their liability to the holder making default.

6. *When presentment for payment is excused*

According to Section 76 of this Act, under certain circumstances it is not necessary to present an instrument for payment in order to make parties liable thereto.

Under these circumstances, an instrument is deemed to be dishonoured at the due date for presentment. There are as follows:

(*i*) **Presentment prevented:** Where the holder has been prevented from the presentment of instrument by some act of the maker, acceptor or drawee, he gets excused for presentment.

(*ii*) **Business place closed:** Where the instrument was payable at the business place of maker, acceptor or drawee and he keeps such place closed on business day during usual business hours.

(*iii*) **Non-availability of a person at the place of payment:** Where an instrument is payable at some other specified place and no one of maker, acceptor or drawee or his authorised agent is available during usual business hours.

(*iv*) **A party liable to pay cannot be found:** In case the instrument is not payable at specified place, it is the duty of the holder to make reasonable efforts to find out the party liable to pay. Despite such efforts party liable to pay cannot be found.

(*v*) **Presentment is waived:** The party liable to pay may waive such presentment by writing the words 'presentment is waived' in the negotiable instrument.

(*vi*) **Non-acceptance of a bill:** In case the bill of exchange has been dishonoured by non-acceptance, the presentment is automatically excused.

(*vii*) **Impossibility:** Where the presentment of an instrument becomes impossible due to any reason beyond the control of holder or due to no fault of the holder, the presentment is excused.

Payment for Honour

After getting a bill noted and protested for non-payment, any person may pay it for the honour of any party liable on the bill. The person who is paying it must declare before notary public that on whose honour he is making payment. This fact must be duly recorded by the notary public.

When the bill has been paid for honour, all parties subsequent to the party for whose honour it is paid, are discharged from their liability on the bill. And the person who pays the bill for honour will get rights and duties of the holder towards the party for whose honour he pays and all other parties liable to that party. Thus he may recover from the party for whose honour he pays all sums so paid with interest thereon and with all expenses properly incurred in making such payment.

DISCHARGE OF NEGOTIABLE INSTRUMENT

A negotiable instrument creates rights and obligations among the parties involved in it. Some of the parties may have a liability to pay. On the basis of nature of liability certain parties *i.e.*, the maker of promissory note, and acceptor of bill of exchange have primary liability and others may have secondary liability which may arise in case of default of the party who is primarily liable on the instrument.

A negotiable instrument is said to be discharged when the rights and obligation created by it come to an end. It ceases to be a negotiable instrument and no action can be taken even by the holder in due course upon it.

In other words, negotiable instrument gets discharged when the party who is primarily liable to pay on the instrument is discharged from his liability.

A negotiable instrument is said to be discharged under the following situations:

(*i*) **Payment of instrument:** When the party primarily liable on the instrument *i.e.*, the maker of a note or acceptor of a bill of exchange or the drawee bank in case of a cheque makes the payment in due course, at or after maturity to the holder.

(*ii*) **Negotiation back:** When a bill of exchange, during the course of negotiation is negotiated back to the acceptor of the bill and he becomes the holder at or after maturity, the bill is said to be discharged.

(*iii*) **Release of debtor:** When the holder of an instrument releases the debtor who is primarily liable to pay, all other parties will automatically be released and an instrument gets discharged.

(*iv*) **Cancellation of instrument:** When the holder of an instrument gets an instrument cancelled and consequently the party primarily liable to pay is released, that instrument will be discharged.

(*v*) **Non-presentment of a bill for acceptance:** Where the presentment of a bill for acceptance is necessary, the holder makes default with regard to such presentment, it will be discharged.

(*vi*) **Mutual agreement:** A negotiable instrument creates rights and obligations between or among the parties. In case all parties to an instrument agree to discharge it will be discharged by mutual agreement.

Discharge of One or More Parties From Their Liability

Sometime, a few parties of negotiable instrument may be discharged from their liability on the instrument. But other still may be liable and as a result of which, an instrument remains negotiable. It does not lead to discharge of instrument.

One or more parties of an instrument may be discharged from liability, without affecting negotiability of an instrument, under the following situations:

(*i*) **By cancellation:** When the holder of an instrument cancels the name of any party to instrument, such party and all subsequent parties to him will get discharged provided cancellation has been done with intention to release that party from liability.

(*ii*) **By release:** A holder may discharge, the maker, acceptor or indorser of an instrument from his liability by any method other than cancellation. In such cases, party liable, is discharged from his liability to such holder and to all parties deriving title under such holder after a notice of such discharge.

(iii) **By payment:** In case a negotiable instrument is duly paid at or after maturity, it would automatically lead to discharge of the parties and instrument as well.

(iv) **Extension of time for deliberation for acceptance:** Usually the drawee or acceptor is allowed to retain a bill for acceptance up to 48 hours. In case the drawer or holder extend the time period of 48 hours, all previous parties who have not been consented for such allowance are discharged from liability to such holder.

(v) **Delay in presenting a cheque:** When the cheque is not presented for payment within reasonable time of its issue and the drawer suffers damage through such delay he is discharged from his liability to the extent of damage he has suffered.

(vi) **By qualified acceptance:** If the holder of a bill agrees on taking conditional or qualified acceptance, all parties prior to him, whose consent is not obtained to such conditional acceptance will be considered discharged from liability on that bill.

(vii) **By operation of law:** Sometimes, the parties of a negotiable instrument may be discharged from liability by operation of law. Such as debtor becomes insolvent, and remedy of the party becomes time barred as per the provisions of law of limitation etc.

(viii) **By material alteration:** Where any party of a negotiable instrument makes material alteration in the instrument without the consent of other parties; all such parties will be considered as discharge from liability in that instrument. Material alterations are those alterations, which in a significant way affect rights and obligations of the parties such as change in the amount, name of the payee, date of payment and place of payment etc. However, if change has been made to carry on common interest of the parties, such as correction of spelling and clerical errors, it will not affect validity of an instrument.

(ix) **By not giving notice of dishonour:** In case a negotiable instrument is dishonoured and the holder fails to give notice of dishonour to some of the parties. All such parties, not getting notice would be discharged from liability.

(*x*) **By delay in presenting cheque for payment:** The holder of a cheque is under obligation for presenting a cheque for payment within a reasonable period of time. If he fails to do so, in the meanwhile bank fails, as a result of it the drawer suffers a loss, he will be discharged from liability to the extent of loss suffered by him.

DISHONOUR OF A NEGOTIABLE INSTRUMENT

A negotiable instrument is said to be dishonoured, if the party liable to accept or pay, refuses to do so on proper presentation (for acceptance) or at or after maturity as the case may be (for payment). A bill of exchange may be dishonoured either by non-acceptance or by non-payment. But promissory note and cheque may be dishonoured only by non-payment.

1. *Dishonour by Non-Acceptance*

According to Section 91 of this Act, "a bill of exchange whether payable 'after date' or 'after sight' will be treated as dishonoured by non-acceptance under the following situations:

(*i*) Where the bill is presented properly to the drawee for acceptance, he refuses to accept it or does not give his acceptance within 48 hours.

(*ii*) Where the presentment for acceptance was excused and the drawee does not accept the bill.

(*iii*) Where the drawee is incompetent to contract.

(*iv*) Where the drawee gives qualified acceptance.

(*v*) Where the drawee is fictitious person or after a reasonable search cannot be found."

However, it is to be noted that in a bill, if the 'drawee in case of need' is named, it will not be treated as dishonoured unless such drawee refuses to accept the bill.

2. *Dishonour by Non-Payment*

According to Section 92 of this Act, "a promissory note, bill of exchange or cheque is said to be dishonoured by non-payment, when the maker, of the note, acceptor of a bill and drawee of a cheque makes default in payment upon being duly required to pay the same."

According to Section 76 of this Act, "an instrument is also taken as dishonoured by non-payment, when presentment for payment is excused and instrument when overdue remains unpaid."

Notice of Dishonour: According to Section 93 of this Act, "a promissory note, bill of exchange or cheque is dishonoured by non-acceptance or non-payment, the holder or some party liable thereon, must give notice of dishonour to all other parties to whom holder seeks to make severally liable thereon and to someone of several parties whom holder seeks to make jointly liable thereon."

In other words, in case an instrument gets dishonoured either by non-acceptance or by non-payment, the holder must give notice of dishonour to the parties liable to pay for making them liable jointly or severally.

By giving notice of dishonour the holder of an instrument, on the one hand maintains his right against the parties liable to pay. On the other, it provides the protection to the drawer of a bill against the drawee who has dishonoured the bill, drawn by the drawer.

Rules Regarding Notice of Dishonour

Following rules are to be complied with for making and giving notice of dishonour:

(*i*) Notice of dishonour must be given by the holder or by some party, liable on the instrument. Thus to make valid notice of dishonour, it must be given by the party, who was liable on that instrument at the time of giving such notice.

(*ii*) The party receiving notice of dishonour, must give notice of dishonour, to any prior parties for making him liable, within reasonable period of time.

(*iii*) If the instrument is deposited with an agent for presentment, he is entitled to give notice of dishonour to the parties liable on the bill or he may give notice to his principal.

(*iv*) Notice of dishonour must be given to all parties whom the holder seeks to make severally or jointly liable. Such notice need not be given to the parties who are primarily liable on that instrument, such as the drawee of a bill, maker of note and drawee of a cheque.

(*v*) Notice of dishonour may be given to duly authorised agent of the person to whom it is required to be given. When the party to whom notice is to be given is dead, notice may be given to his legal representative and in case of insolvency, notice may be given to his official assignee.

(*vi*) Notice of dishonour may be given in any form, written or oral. It may be given in person or by post. To make it valid it must be made with an intention to inform the party in express term that an instrument was dishonoured. It is said to be irregular, if it misleads the receiver of a notice. It must be given within reasonable period of time after dishonour at a place of business or at the residence of a person to whom it is given.

When Notice of Dishonour is not Necessary

According to Section 98 of this Act, notice of dishonour is not necessary in the following cases:

(*i*) **Waiver by the party:** A party to a bill or note may give up his right of getting notice of dishonour in favour of the holder, by writing the words 'Notice of dishonour is waived' at the time of making indorsement.

(*ii*) **Payment stopped:** When the drawer of a cheque after having drawn the cheque, but before it is presented for payment countermanded payment.

(*iii*) **Party not found:** When the party to whom a notice of dishonour is required to be given could not be found after making a reasonable search.

(*iv*) **Unavoidable circumstances:** Omission to give notice of dishonour is excused if the holder had been in unavoidable situations may be death, illness, accident or under other natural calamites.

(*v*) **Conditional promise:** When the party to whom, notice of dishonour is required to be given makes a conditional promise to pay, notice is not required.

(*vi*) **Where drawer and drawee are same person:** When the drawer and the drawee or the drawer and the acceptor are same persons, a notice of dishonour is not necessary.

(*vii*) **Not negotiable promissory note:** Where a promissory note is not negotiable, even then it has been indorsed. The indorser of such note has no right to claim notice of dishonour.

Noting

When a promissory note or a bill of exchange is dishonoured the holder of such instrument is entitled to sue the party liable to pay. He can exercise his right only after giving a notice of dishonour to them.

To get the fact of dishonour, authenticated, noting of an instrument is made. The noting on the dishonour of the instrument is recorded by 'Notary Public'.

According to Section 99 of this Act, "noting may be done upon the dishonoured instrument or upon a paper attached thereto or partly upon each." Such note must contain the following particulars:

(*i*) Fact of dishonour.

(*ii*) The date of dishonour.

(*iii*) The reason for dishonour.

(*iv*) The reason why the holder treats it as dishonoured.

(*v*) The notary's charges: Though noting is not obligatory on an inland bill or note, it facilitates further legal process to be adopted against the party liable to pay. And it becomes easy for the holder to prove dishonour of an instrument.

Protest

'Protest' is a formal certificate of attesting the dishonour of the instrument issued by a Notary Public to the holder. It is based on 'noting' of the dishonoured instrument.

According to Section 100 of this Act, "when a promissory note or a bill of exchange has been dishonoured by non-acceptance or by non-payment, the holder may, within reasonable time, cause such dishonour to be noted and certified by a notary public."

It is also provided in the Act that, the court shall, in a suit, upon an instrument which has been dishonoured, on the proof of the 'protest' presume the fact of dishonour unless and until such fact is disapproved.

According to Section 100 of this Act, a certificate of protest should contain the following particulars:

(*i*) The instrument or its copy.

(*ii*) The name of the person for whom and against whom the instrument has been protested.

(*iii*) The fact of dishonour and reasons.

(*iv*) Time and place of dishonour.

(*v*) Signature of the notary public.

(*vi*) In case of acceptance for honour or payment for honour, the name of the person by whom or the person for whom and the manner in which such acceptance or payment was offered and effected, must be stated.

Protest for better security: When the acceptor of a bill of exchange has become insolvent or his credit has been publicly impeached before maturity of the bill, the holder may cause notary public to demand better security of the acceptor. On the refusal, the holder may within reasonable time cause such fact to be noted and certified. Such certificate is known as 'protest for better security'.

However in spite of protest for better security the holder cannot proceed against the party liable before the date of maturity.

REVIEW QUESTIONS

1. What do you mean by 'a presentment of a negotiable instrument'? Discuss various types of presentment of an instrument.
2. Discuss various types of acceptance in relation to a bill of exchange.
3. Explain various rules regarding presentment.
4. What do you mean by 'acceptance for honour'? Discuss the liability of such acceptor.
5. Define presentment for payment and discuss various rules regarding a valid presentment for payment.
6. Discuss those situations under which presentment for payment is excused.
7. Define 'discharge of a negotiable instrument'. Under which circumstances negotiable instrument is said to be discharged?
8. Explain the situations under which one or more parties get discharged from their liability on the instrument.
9. Define dishonour of negotiable instrument. Discuss the rules regarding notice of dishonour.
10. Write notes on:

    (*i*) Noting and protest (*ii*) Presentment for acceptance

    (*iii*) Conditional acceptance (*iv*) Notice of dishonour

PRACTICAL PROBLEMS

1. A draws a bill of exchange amounting Rs. 1,000 on B, payable three months after date. B accepts the bill as payable after four months. Examine validity of the bill of exchange.
2. Ram draws a bill on Shyam for Rs. 2,000 payable after two months and gives it to Sohan. Ram mentions the name of Mohan on the bill as a 'drawee in case of need'. On the presentment of a bill for acceptance Shyam refuses to accept it. Can Sohan treat that bill dishonoured? (Hint: No).
3. X draws a bill payable after three months on Y, and indorsed it to Z and Z to R. R presents the bill for acceptance and Y accepts it as payable for two months. R further indorses the bill to S. Examine rights and duties of various parties on the bill.

4. A draws a bill on B payable to C after two months. On presenting the bill by C to B, B refuses to accept it. D accepts the bill for the honour of A. C indorses the bill to E who is a holder in due course. Can E recover the payment of that bill from the D? (Hint: Yes).
5. A draws a cheque of Rs. 5,000 in favour of B on 1 December 2006. B does not present the cheque for payment. And on 1 January 2007, the bank fails. As a result of it A suffers a loss of Rs. 10,000. Is he still liable to pay to B? (Hint: No).
6. X draws a bill for Rs. 1,000 on Y payable after two months. X has indorsed the bill to Z and Z to R. On the due date Y refuses to pay. R was under treatment for same ailment of serious nature. As a result of it he could not give a notice of dishonour to Z. Is Z liable to pay? (Hint: Yes).
7. A draws a bill on B payable to C after one month. On the date of maturity C presents the bill to B's wife for payment. Can she give valid discharge? (Hint: No).

26

Crossing and Bouncing of Cheque

LEARNING OBJECTIVES

- Understand the relationship between banker and customer in terms of rights and obligations.
- Develop conceptual clarity about crossing of cheque, its implications on the payment and liability of the parties.
- Analyse those situations when the banker may and must refuse to honour the cheques of customer.
- Get familiar with the concept of bouncing of cheque and identify legal consequences of it.

INTRODUCTION

Crossing of a cheque is a unique feature associated with a cheque affecting to a certain extent the obligation of the paying banker and also its negotiable character. It is a particular method of modifying the instructions to the banker for payment of the cheque. But to understand crossing and bouncing of a cheque, it is necessary to have a brief knowledge of banker, customer and their relationship.

Banker Defined

Generally speaking, a banker may be defined as one who does banking business. The ordinary course of business of the banker mainly consists of accepting and receiving deposits from the public lending and investing it and repaying them on demand.

Thus any institution or individual, who is engaged in banking business will be considered as bank. According to Section 5 (b) of the Banking Regulation Act

1949, the term banking is defined as "accepting, for the purpose of lending or investment of deposits of money from the public, repayable on demand or otherwise and withdrawable by cheque, draft, order or otherwise."

According to this definition, a banker mainly performs three primary functions:

(*i*) Accepting deposits from the public through various accounts such as current account, saving bank account, recurring deposit account and fixed deposit account.

(*ii*) Lending and investing money to the needy businessmen and business houses, and other individuals.

(*iii*) Repaying deposits accepted from the public on demand made by them through some order, draft or a cheque.

Customer Defined

Generally the person or the party who deals with bank in various transactions is known as 'customer'. The usual mode of dealing with the banker is making transactions through the account mainly by depositing money in or withdrawing money out from the account. It is therefore, the person who maintains an account with the bank and utilises the various services provided by the bank is considered his customer. To hold someone as a customer of the bank, these two factors must be taken together. It is because if somebody merely utilises the services of the bank may be for a longer period of time he may not be considered as customer such as if he borrows money from bank and repays it on due date, he is not a customer. Thus, to be a customer of a bank one has to satisfy the following conditions:

(*i*) He must have an account in the bank.

(*ii*) He must have been using various services being provided by the bank such as depositing money, withdrawing it, paying insurance premium, and other bills etc.

(*iii*) Casual transaction made with bank by utilising its services would not make him a customer. There must have been regular dealings on continuous basis with regard to his account and utilisation of banking services. The person who keeps his valuables in the safe custody of the banker does not become its customer.

Relationship between Banker and Customer

The customer who deals with the banker regularly, has many relationship including that of debtor-creditor, trustee-beneficiary, principal-agent and bailor-bailee. Among these the relationship of debtor-creditor is considered more important.

Due to these relationship certain rights and obligations arise on the part of banker. These are as follows:

(*i*) Obligation to honour cheques of the customer.

(*ii*) Obligation to keep proper record of the transactions made by the customer.

(*iii*) Obligation to collect cheques and drafts on behalf of the customers.

(*iv*) Obligation of maintaining secrecy of customer's account.

(*v*) Right of general lien.

(*vi*) Right of appropriation.

(*vii*) Right of set-off.

(*viii*) Right to charge interest, commission, incidental expenses and charges etc.

CROSSING OF CHEQUE

Crossing on a cheque is a direction to the paying banker by the drawer that payment should not be made across the counter. The payment on a crossed cheque can be collected only through a banker. The cheque is an unconditional order given to the banker by a customer to make payment on demand a certain sum of money to the person named therein or to order or to bearer.

A cheque may be of two types:

(*i*) An open cheque, which is to be paid at the counter of the bank such as 'bearer' and 'order' cheque.

(*ii*) A crossed cheque, which is to be paid only through a collecting bank.

Meaning of Crossing

Where two parallel lines are drawn across the face of cheque with or without certain customary words such as 'A/c Payee', 'And coy' etc., it is known as 'crossing of cheque'. The net legal effect of crossing is that the crossed cheque cannot be paid at the counter of bank. Rather it is to be deposited by the holder in his account. Then it is to be collected by the banker on behalf of the holder and proceeds are credited to his account.

Thus crossing is a direction to the paying bank to pay the money to a collecting banker and not directly to the holder at the counter.

Crossing is usually done across the face of cheque indicating specific mode of payment of the cheque, which compels the holder to present the cheque for payment through collecting bank.

Objects of Crossing

Generally, crossing is done to ensure safe payment of a cheque to the authorised person. It has the following objectives:

(*i*) It prevents the payment of cheque from being made to wrongful holder of the cheque.

(*ii*) It ensures the payment of cheque to the person who is legally entitled to get it.

(*iii*) It also ensures safety of a cheque in circulation.

(*iv*) It facilitate in tracing of wrong person who has received the payment of cheque.

Types of Crossing

Crossing of a cheque may be of the following types i.e., general crossing, special crossing, restrictive crossing and not-negotiable crossing.

1. *General Crossing*

According to Section 123 of this Act, "where a cheque bears across its face an addition of the word 'and company' or any abbreviation thereof between two parallel transverse lines either with or without the word 'not negotiable' the cheque shall be deemed to be crossed generally."

A cheque is said to be generally crossed if:

(*i*) Two parallel transverse line have been drawn on the face of cheque with or without the words 'not negotiable'.

(*ii*) The words 'and company' or '& Coy' or any such words between parallel line have been mentioned.

According to Section 126 of this Act, generally crossed cheque cannot be paid at the counter of the bank. Instead its payment can only be received through any bank and cash be deposited into depositor's account.

Thus where a cheque is crossed generally, the banker on whom it is drawn shall not pay it otherwise than to a banker.

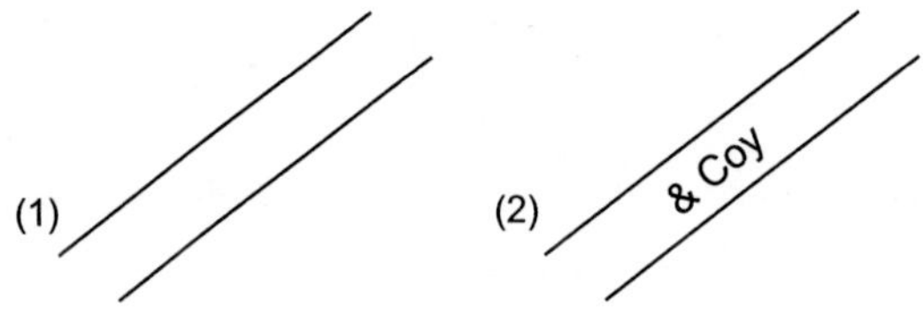

Specimen of general crossing

2. *Special Crossing*

According to Section 124 of this Act, "where a cheque bears across its face and addition to the name of banker, either with or without the words 'not negotiable', that addition shall be deemed a crossing and the cheque shall be deemed to be crossed specially and to be crossed to that banker."

Thus in a special crossing name of a particular banker is mentioned between the parallel line. As a result of it, that cheque can be collected only through that banker. And if the holder has no account in that bank he has to open it to get the specially crossed cheque deposited for collection. It is because when a cheque is specially crossed the banker upon whom it is drawn, will make the payment only to the banker in whose favour it has been crossed.

However, where the cheque is specially crossed, to more than one banker, the banker on whom it is drawn shall refuse payment thereof. But if the name of second banker is mentioned only for the purpose of collection it will not affect validity of special crossing.

Special crossing of cheque is considered safer than general crossing. Reasons being that the holder has to have account in the branch of that bank and payment of such cheque cannot be manipulated so easily.

(a)

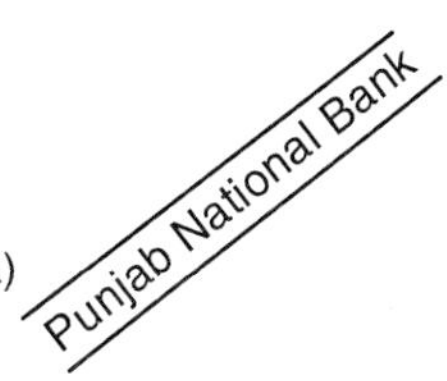

(b)

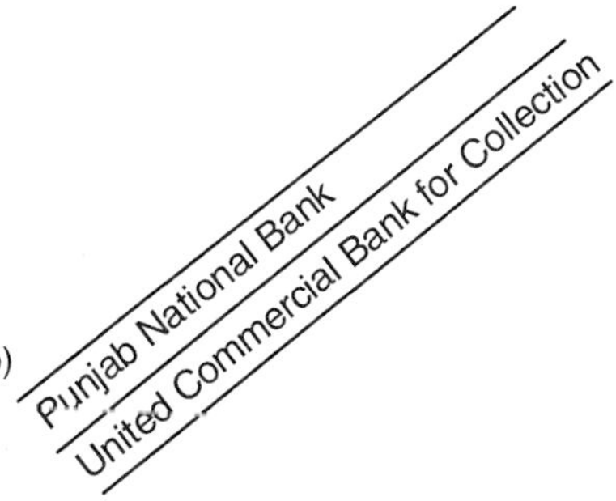

Specimens of special crossing

Thus in special crossing, mode of payment is changed, and the payment of a cheque is made only to the banker whose name is mentioned therein.

3. ***Restrictive Crossing***

Where a cheque crossed generally or specially also contain the words 'A/c Payee only' it is known as restrictive crossing. Restrictive crossing provides a direction to the collecting banker that proceeds of a cheque be deposited only in the account of 'payee' whose name is mentioned in the cheque.

Though restrictive crossing does not affect further negotiability, but collecting banker plays safe and collects the proceeds in the account of payee of the cheque. Thus where the collecting banker credits the proceeds in any account other than that of payee, the bank may be held liable for wrongful conversion of funds and would be deprived of statutory protections granted to the collecting bank under Section 131 of this Act.

However, it does not affect the rights of paying banker, who has to see that cheques have been presented to it for payment by the any bank in case of general crossing and by the particular bank (named therein) in case of special crossing.

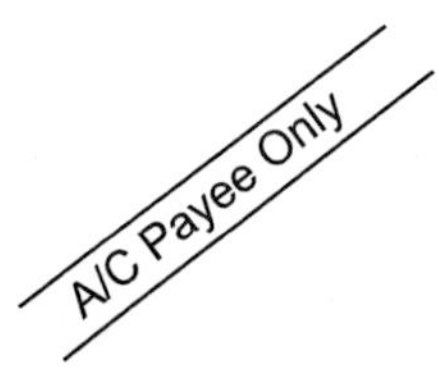

Specimen of restrictive crossing

4. ***Not Negotiable Crossing***

Where the cheque drawn by the drawer is made payable to payee and only to him, by mentioning the words 'not negotiable' between the parallel lines drawn for the purpose of crossing, such crossing is known as 'not negotiable crossing'.

The holder who gets, not-negotiably crossed cheque, cannot transfer better title to the subsequent indorsee than that of the holder prior to him. However, not negotiable crossing does not affect further negotiability of the cheque. Such cheque can be transferred. But net legal effect of such crossing is that the holder after such crossing cannot become 'holder in due course'. It means he will get same title of the instrument which the indorser had on that instrument.

Thus if the title of the transferor had been defective, transferee will also get defective title. The main objective of not negotiable crossing is to protect the rights of the holder.

Regarding 'not negotiable crossing', the following points should be taken care of:

(*i*) In 'not negotiable crossing' the words not negotiable is mentioned between parallel lines.

(*ii*) Not negotiable crossing can be done either with general crossing or with special crossing.

(*iii*) After such crossing the holder of cheque cannot become holder in due course, because he will get same title as transferor had.

(*iv*) Not negotiable crossing does not affect further transferability of a cheque, it can be transferred after such crossing.

(*v*) It protects the right of a holder of a cheque.

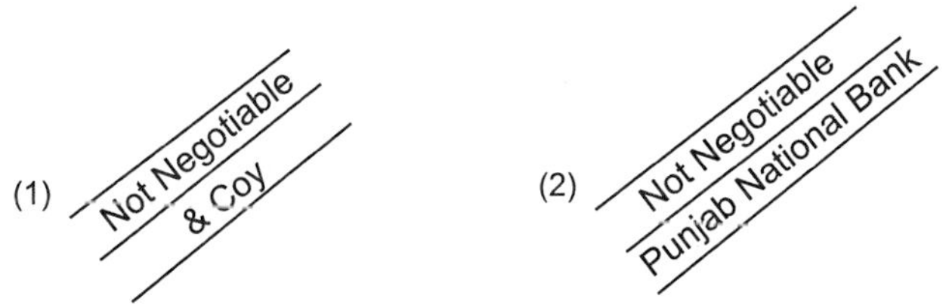

Specimen of not negotiable crossing

Who may Cross a Cheque

Section 125 of this Act provides that:

(*i*) A cheque may be crossed, generally or specially by the drawer.

(*ii*) Where a cheque is not crossed, when the holder gets it he can cross it according to his choice.

(*iii*) Where the holder gets a cheque which is crossed generally he may further cross it specially.

(*iv*) Where the holder gets a cheque crossed, generally or specially, he may add the words 'not negotiable'.

(*v*) Where a cheque is crossed specially, the banker on whom it is crossed may again cross it in favour of another bank for the purpose of collection.

LIABILITY OF PAYING BANKER

The drawee banker has an obligation for making the payment of cheques issued by the drawer. But such obligation is subject to some exceptions and it does not arise under the following situations. These situations may be placed in two categories: *i.e.,* when the banker may refuse to honour customer's cheque and when the bank must refuse to honour, cheques issued by his customers.

1. *When the maker may refuse to honour customer's cheques*

Under the following cases, the banker may refuse to pay customer's cheques. In these cases, if the payment is refused, the banker shall not be liable for damages. In case the banker honours cheques under these situations, it is up to the court to decide whether it amounts good payment as against the drawer.

(*i*) **Insufficient funds:** Where the banker does not have sufficient credit balance in the account of the customer, the banker may refuse to honour cheques.

(*ii*) **Post dated cheque:** Where the cheque, drawn by the drawer has become post dated *i.e.*, a cheque bears future date. If such cheque is presented for payment before date, the bank is justified in refusing to pay such cheques.

(*iii*) **Stale cheque:** Where a cheque is not presented for the payment within reasonable time which is considered to be a period of six months such cheque become stale cheque and the bank may refuse its payment.

(*iv*) **Irregular cheque:** Where the cheque is not properly drawn and is not complete in all respects, the banker may dishonour the cheque such as ambiguous cheque, mutilated cheque or cheque bearing irregular indorsement etc.

(*v*) **Undated cheque:** A cheque drawn by the drawer must be properly dated. The payment of undated cheque may be refused by the banker. But if the holder gets undated cheque, he may put date on that within reasonable period of time to get the payment from the bank.

(*vi*) **Other reasons:** The banker may also refuse to honour cheques of the customer under the following situations:

(*a*) Where signatures of the joint holders or their survivors do not appear on the cheque.

(*b*) Where a cheque is presented at a branch other than where the customer has his account.

(*c*) Where a cheque is not presented within usual banking hours.

(*d*) Where legality of a cheque has become doubtful.

(*e*) Where the crossed cheque is presented at the counter for the payment.

(*f*) Where the funds in customer's account cannot be applied for making the payment of cheques.

2. *When banker must refuse payment*

In some of the cases, the banker must refuse the payment of customer's cheques. On such refusal the banker has no liability towards the customer. These cases are:

(*i*) **Stop payment:** After having drawn a cheque, the drawer may instruct the banker to stop the payment of such cheque which is technically known as 'countermanding payment'. The drawer may give such instructions either in writing or by the words of mouth, but in every case it should be given well in time. The banker making payment, after receiving such instruction from the customer, will be solely responsible for that. It will not amount to good payment as against the drawer, the bank cannot recover that amount from the payee.

(*ii*) **Death or insanity of customer:** The banker, on receiving information that the customer has died or has become insane or insolvent, must refuse the payment of cheques presented afterward. The banker will have to bear liability similar as in case of stop payment.

(*iii*) **Garnishee order:** On receiving, Garnishee order or any other order of the court, which prohibits the banker from applying any payment from the account of a customer, the banker must refuse to honour cheques presented after such order.

(*iv*) **Notice of assignment:** The customer may assign credit balance standing in his account to some other person. After receiving information regarding such assignment of account, the banker must refuse the payment of customer's cheque.

(*v*) **Defective title of holder:** Where the banker is suspicious about the title of the holder, and has sufficient ground to believe that the holder, presenting a cheque has no title or his title is defective, the banker must refuse to honour such cheques.

(*vi*) **Closing of account:** When the customer has already given a notice to the banker for closing his account, after receiving such notice the banker must not make payment of any cheque drawn in that account.

(*vii*) **Lost cheque:** Where the customer has lost the cheque and has already given information about it to the banker; after receiving such information the banker is no more under obligation for paying the cheques drawn by the customer. In case, the banker makes payment, it can be recovered from the payee who has got the payment of the lost cheque.

(*viii*) **Irregular cheque:** When the banker has sufficient reason to believe that a cheque is irregular, due to an technical defect or cheque is materially altered or signatures of thc drawer are not tallying, the banker must dishonour such cheques.

WRONGFUL DISHONOUR OF CHEQUE

The banker is under legal obligation to honour cheques issued by the drawer. However, this obligation is subject to some exceptions which have been described earlier.

Barring those situations, if a cheque is dishonoured by the banker without any justification, the customer can claim compensation for the loss which he has suffered due to such unjustified dishonour.

In case the customer is trader, whose reputation and creditworthiness has been adversely affected by such dishonour, such customer is entitled to claim for punitive or vindictive damages. The amount of such damage exceeds actual loss of the trader. The golden rule in this regard is 'the smaller the amount of the cheque the larger the amount of damage'. But the customer other than traders has a right only to claim ordinary damage, the amount of which is equal to actual loss suffered by the customer due to such dishonour of a cheque.

Thus in case of wrongful dishonour of a cheque it is only the drawer who is entitled to initiate action against the banker. However, under the following situations, the holder or a payee may also sue the banker:

(*i*) Where, the holder fails to present a cheque for payment within reasonable time and as a result of it, the drawer gets discharged from his liability, such holder becomes creditor of the banker and has a right to get the amount from the banker.

(*ii*) Where the crossed cheque has been presented for the payment and the banker pays it at its counter, otherwise in due course, the holder is entitled to sue the bank for the recovery of such payment.

Protection to the Paying Banker

The paying banker means a banker upon whom a cheque is drawn by the customer. When the banker makes payment of customer's cheques in due course without having sufficient reasons to believe defects in the title of the holder, he is fully protected against the liability arising out of it. In addition to it, Section 85 of this Act provides the following protection to the banker:

(*i*) **Order cheque:** Where the banker makes payment of an order cheque in due course, the banker is discharged from the liability. Section 85 (1) of this Act also grants protection to the banker if he makes payment of an order cheque with forged indorsement on behalf of the payee, provided the payment made is in due course and the banker had no reason to suspect validity of indorsement.

(*ii*) **Bearer cheque:** According to Section 85 (2) of this Act, "where a cheque is originally expressed to be payable to bearer, the drawee is discharge by payment in due course to the bearer thereof, not withstanding any indorsement, whether in full or in blank appearing thereon, not withstanding that any such indorsement purports to restrict or exclude further negotiation."

In this regard there is a general rule that, 'once a bearer instrument' aways a bearer instrument. Thus the banker may ignore any indorsement full or blank or purporting to restrict or exclude further negotiation on the instrument.

Payment of Cheque on which Drawer's Signatures are Forged

However if the banker makes the payment of a cheque on which signatures of the drawer are forged he will not be discharged from his liability. This is so because the banker cannot debit customer's account by the payment of such cheques which are null and void and it will not be considered as payment in due course.

Payment of Materially Altered Cheque

Where the banker makes payment of materially altered cheques under the following situations, the banker will get protection:

(*i*) If the payment made by the banker is according to the apparent tenor of the instrument.

(*ii*) If the alteration is not apparent and noticeable and if does not appear to have been so altered.

Protection to Collecting Banker

The crossed cheque is to be deposited by the customer in his account for the purpose of collection. The collecting bank is one who receives the payment of a crossed cheque on behalf of his customer.

According to Section 131 of this Act, "a banker who has, in good faith and without negligence received payment for a customer, of a cheque crossed generally or specially to himself shall not, in case the title to the cheque proves defective, incur any liability to the true owner of cheque by reason only of having received such payment."

Thus, where the collecting banker has collected payment of crossed cheque without having sufficient reasons to, believe that cheque was defective, the bank will not be liable in 'conversion' to the true owner provided:

(*i*) The banker has acted in good faith and without any negligence.

(*ii*) The cheque was already crossed before it reaches his hands.

(*iii*) The banker received the payment, on behalf of a customer and not on his own account *i.e.*, he has acted as an agent for collection.

In order to get protection under Section 131 of this Act, the collecting banker must have received payment without any negligence. The banker may be held negligent under the following situations:

(*i*) The cheque has been collected without verifying indorsement thereon.

(*ii*) The banker has collected an order cheque without making enquires. Where the indorsement should have aroused the banker's suspicion.

(*iii*) The banker has collected a cheque for the account of a person other than payee.

(*iv*) The banker has collected a cheque payable to a company for the personal account of director or other official of the company.

(*v*) The banker collects a cheque payable to public official, but for personal account of the official.

(*vi*) A cheque was payable to partnership firm but has been collected for the personal account of the partner.

(*vii*) A cheque was payable to one company but has been collected for the account of another company.

(*viii*)Collecting a cheque for a huge amount for an account in which that much balance has never been maintained.

BOUNCING OF CHEQUES

The transactions regarding negotiable instrument assume great significance in mercantile community. This is so because these transactions, particularly related to cheque do provide alternative mode of payment. It is therefore to safeguard interest of the parties involved in these, the Negotiable Instrument Act, 1881 was enacted and necessary amendments were made in the Act far and again according to the requirements of the situation.

To ensure high degree of acceptability of these instruments particularly of a cheque, it is required that the instrument should be paid or discharged to the satisfaction of the parties. And dishonour of such instruments should be discouraged. It is therefore, the Negotiable Instrument Act, 1881 has been amended in 2002 with a view to promote the culture of using cheques as an alternative mode of payment and to promote and increase the acceptability of a cheque in settling business transactions.

A cheque is said to be bounced, when the banker returns it unpaid to the payee or the holder on presenting it for payment due to inadequate credit balance in the account of the drawer.

According to Section 138 of this Act, "Where any cheque drawn by a person on an account maintained by him with a banker for payment of any amount of money to another person from out of that account for the discharge, in whole or in part of any debt or other liability is returned by the banker unpaid, either because of the amount of money standing to the credit of that account is insufficient to honour the cheque or that it exceeds the amount arranged to be paid from that account by an agreement made with the banker." Thus bouncing of a cheque implies that:

(*i*) The drawer has maintained an account with the banker which can be utilised for paying cheques and discharging other debts.

(*ii*) A cheques drawn by the drawer being presented for payment, but the banker returns it unpaid because:

(*a*) The credit balance of customers account falls short of the amount of cheque to be paid, or

(*b*) The credit arrangement which the customer has made with the banker is less than the amount of a cheques presented for payment.

The drawer of such cheques shall be deemed to have committed an offence and will be punished

(*i*) With imprisonment for a term which may be extended to two years, or

(*ii*) With fine which may extend to twice the amount of a cheque, or

(*iii*) With both provided:

(*a*) The cheque has been presented to the bank within a period of six months from the date on which it is drawn or within the period of its validity whichever is earlier.

(*b*) The payee or the holder in due course of a cheque makes demand for the payment of said amount of money by giving notice in writing to the drawer within 30 days of the receipt of information by him from the bank regarding return of a cheque as unpaid.

(*c*) The drawer of such cheque fails to make the payment of the said amount of money to the payee or to the holder in due course within 15 days of the receipt of the said notice.

(*d*) The cheque has been dishonoured due to insufficiency of balance standing in the credit of customer's account on which the cheque is drawn.

(*e*) The payment for which the cheque was issued should have been for discharging legally enforceable debt or liability either in whole or in part.

Presumption of Discharging Debt or Liability

According to Section 139 of this Act, it shall be presumed that the holder of a cheque received the cheque for discharging whole or part of lawful debt or other liability. And this presumption can be rebutted only by the person who has drawn the cheque. This presumption is in favour of the holder of a cheque.

According to Section 141(1) of this Act if the person committing an offence under Section 138 is a company every person, who, at the time the offence was committed was incharge of and was responsible to the company for the conduct of business of the company as well as the company shall be deemed to be guilty of the offence and shall be liable to be proceeded againest and punished accordingly except the following cases:

(*i*) The offence was committed without his knowledge or he has exercised all due diligence to prevent omission of such offence.

(*ii*) If the person is nominated as a director of a company by virtue of his holding any office or employment in the Central Government, or state government or a financial corporation owned or controlled by Central Government or state government, shall not be liable for prosecution.

REVIEW QUESTIONS

1. What do you mean by 'crossing of cheque'? Discuss the various objects of crossing and examine its legal consequences.
2. Explain various types of crossing with suitable examples.
3. State those grounds under which the banker may refuse the payment of cheques drawn by the customer.
4. Explain those situations when the banker must refuse the payment of cheques drawn by the customer.

5. Discuss the liability of the banker for wrongful dishonour of cheque.
6. State the protection which the paying banker has got with regard to payment in due course.
7. What do you mean by bouncing of cheque? Discuss the quantum of punishment provided for this offence and which conditions must be satisfied for prosecuting the offender.
8. Write notes on:
   (*i*) Bouncing of cheque
   (*ii*) Protection to collecting bank
   (*iii*) Not negotiable crossing
   (*iv*) Restrictive crossing

PRACTICAL PROBLEMS

1. A draws a cheque payable to B or order upon State Bank of India amounting Rs. 10,000. C forged the signature of B and indorsed a cheque to D who presents it for the payment. The banker did not suspect any defect in the title of the holder and made payment in due course. Examine the extent of banker's liability in this regard.
2. A has drawn a cheque in favour of X and coy. The cheque was crossed 'not negotiable'. One of the directors of the company fraudulently indorsed that cheque in favour of Z, who presented the cheque and got payment of it. Can X and coy recover the amount from its director? (Hint: Yes, not negotiable crossing does not provide better title to the holder than that of the transferor.)
3. Ram draws a cheque payable to bearer. The payee or holder of the cheque makes out indorsement in full on the cheque in favour of Shyam Can the banker make payment of this cheque to the bearer? (Hint: Yes, 'a cheque drawn as bearer, will remain bearer.')
4. A draws a cheque amounting Rs. 2,000 payable to B or order. B presented cheque for payment to the drawee banker. The banker wrongfully refuses the payment of that cheque to B. Examine liability of the banker for wrongful dishonour of a cheque.
5. X has drawn a cheque of Rs. 10,000 in favour of Y or order on 1 January 2005. The drawer does not maintain sufficient credit balance for meeting requirements of payment of a cheque Y could not present cheque within

30 June 2005. When he presented it afterward, the banker refused the payment. Examine the liability of X towards Y.

6. A draws a cheque amounting to Rs. 5,000 payable to B or order on 1 March 2006 makes a cheque 'valid for two months'. B believing that he has time of six months to present it for the payment presents it after three month. The banker refuses payment. Can banker liable to A? (Hint: No).
7. A steals a cheque of Rs. 2,000 from the pocket of his father. The cheque is payable to bearer. A indorsed it in favour of C who get it in good faith and for value. Is C entitled to get the payment of this cheque? (Hint: Yes, he is holder in due course).
8. A has drawn a cheque of Rs. 2,000 in favour of his sister B or order and gifted it to her. B presented a cheque for payment but due to insufficient credit balance in the account of A the banker dishonoured the cheque. Is A liable for bouncing of a cheque which is an offence? (Hint: No, a cheque has been gifted).
9. Ram draws a cheque amounting Rs. 10,000 payable to Shyam. Shyam indorsed it to Mohan who further indorsed it to Sohan. The cheque was stolen by Ghanshyam, he crossed it and by making forged signature indorsed it to A. A deposited a cheque in his account. The banker collected proceeds without verifying signature of indorsee. Examine the liability of collecting banker.
10. A has stolen a blank cheque from the business of B. A forged the signature of B and got the payment of the cheques from the banker. Can B recover this amount from the banker? (Hint: No, in case payment is made on forged signature of the drawer, the banker would not get any protection.)

■■■

27

Meaning and Nature of Company

LEARNING OBJECTIVES

- Understand basic concept of the company.
- Find out its merits and demerits as compared to other forms of organisation.
- Make distinction between company and partnership.
- Develop conceptual clarity about 'lifting the corporate veil'.

INTRODUCTION

Company is an important form of business organisation. It is very popular and well established in modern economy. Due to certain special features and legal entity this form is preferred in comparison to other forms like sole-trade partnership and cooperative organisation etc., particularly for conducting business in large scale which requires huge amount of capital and lot of other resources along with managerial skill, the form of joint stock company is considered more feasible and suitable. The company is also known as a 'joint stock company', because it attracts capital in the form of stock or shares from large number of people.

Meaning and Definition of Company

Generally speaking the company refers to a group or association of persons which is formed for achieving some common objectives. It is that form of business organisation which raises capital from the public for commonly managed venture. More wide in scope, large in size and democratically managed it is different from other forms of organisation.

A company may also be defined as a body corporate or group of people, which has been brought into existence by fulfilling various prescribed legal formalities of Indian Company Act 1956.

The term company has also been defined by Lord Justice Lindley as, "by company is meant an association of many persons who contribute money or money's worth to a common stock and employ it in some trade or business and who share profit and loss arising therefrom. The common stock so contributed is denoted in money and is the capital of the company. The persons who contribute it or to whom it belongs are called members. The proportion of capital to which each member is entitled is his share. Shares are always transferable although the right to transfer them is often more or less restricted."

This definition emphasises on common capital of the company which is one of the important feature of company. But other important features have not been incorporated in this definition. And it is only in case of private company transferability of share is restricted but in public Ltd company, the shares are freely traded in the market.

According to Chief Justice Marshall a company is a person, artificial, invisible, intangible and existing only in the eyes of law. Being mere creature of law, it possesses only those properties which the charter of its creation confers upon it, either expressly or as incidental to its very existence.

In this definition one of the basic features of the company is that its legal existence has been explained. As compared to other definitions it is considered more elaborative.

In the words of Lord Haney, "a company is an incorporated association which is an artificial person created by law, having a separate entity, with a perpetual succession and common seal."

According to Section 3(1) of the Company Act a company means an association of individuals formed for some purpose and registered under the present Companies Act or an earlier Indian Company Act.

After taking into account all basic features of a company it may be defined as "an artificial person created by law. It is registered under Indian Company Act. It has its own legal existence perpetual succession and common capital divided in shares which are transferable. It also possesses a common seal."

Basic Features of Company

As analysis of the above definitions of the company bring out certain basic features. In fact these features distinguish company from other forms of business organisation. These basic features which make the company more popular and suitable form are:

(*i*) **Formation of Company:** In order to form a company, certain legal formalities which are prescribed under Indian Company Act are to be fulfilled. In other words, the company may be considered as a body corporate or group of person registered under Company Act. If it is not registered so it will not be considered as company in the eyes of law.

(*ii*) **Separate Legal Entity or Existence:** Once a group of people gets registered under Indian Company Act it acquires legal existence which means it exists in the eyes of law and the law gives recognition to it. Such existence or legal entity of the company is separate from the existence of persons who have formed it and who own it. The legal effects of such existence is that the company can make a contract, own property, borrow money, incur debts, can file suit against others and can be sued.

The separe legal existence of the company can be understood more easily with the help of one of the leading cases of **Salomon *vs* Salomon & Company Ltd.**

In this case Salomon, an individual doing sole trade converted it into registered company having seven members including his daughter, wife and four sons. The business of sole trade was sold to this coy for £ 30,000. The Salomon got 20,000 shares of £1 each and debentures of £ 10,000 as purchase consideration. After some time, due to some financial problem, the business of the company wound up and realised £ 6,000 from its assets. The company owed £ 10,000 to Salmon and £ 7,000 to unsecured creditors. After paying out to debenture holders nothing was left for unsecured creditors. But the creditors pleaded that they should get priority in repayment because Solomon, who is debenture holder, and Salomon & Company were one and same person.

But it was held that the business is owned by the company not by Salomon. The Company and Salomon are having separate legal entity. The Lord Halsbury, L.C. made it clear that, "the Act requires combining of seven persons to form a company. Once that condition is fulfilled it would not be competent to deny that they were shareholders."

In **T.R. Pratt (Bombay) Ltd *vs* E.D. Sasoon and Coy Ltd.**, it was observed that, under the law, an incorporated company is a distinct entity and although all the shares may be practically controlled by one person, in law, a company is a distinct entity.

In another case, **Abdul Haq *vs* Das Mal**, an employee of the company filed a suit against the director of the company for the recovery of outstanding salary due to him. It was held that remedy lied against the company, not against director or members of the company.

(iii) **Artificial Person:** A Company is an artificial person created by law. It is so because after the incorporation of the company it acquires legal status that of a person. It may enter into contracts, enforce these against other, it can sue others and can be sued. Being an artificial person, it cannot work at its own, rather some official who is authorised by the company uses the above rights on behalf of the company.

(iv) **Limited Liability:** The liability of the members of company is limited up to the face value of the shares held by them. In case the member pays off full amount of face value of his holding he cannot be called upon to share any losses, incurred by the company. This feature of a company attracts the persons to invest their money by buying the shares of company.

(v) **Transferability of Shares:** The shares issued by public limited company are freely transferable. Any person holding the shares of such company can transfer his share all or part thereof without consent of the company and other members of the company. However, the shares of a private limited company cannot be transferred because such transfer has been restricted under the provisions of Indian Company law. But it is widely accepted that transferability of shares provides benefit of liquidity to the investors.

(vi) **Perpetual Succession:** A company enjoys perpetual succession in its working life. It is because the legal entity of the company is separate from the entity of its members. The members may come and go and may transfer their holdings to others. But in no case it has any impact on the existence of the company. In an extreme case, if all members of the company become insolvent or die, the legal existence of the company is not going to be affected. Since the company is a creation of law, it is obvious that it can be brought to an end only by the process of law to which it is subject.

(vii) **Common Seal:** A company is an artificial person which exists only in the eyes of law. Having no physical existence it cannot use rights conferred on the company at its own. It is therefore, every company is required to have its seal, in which the name of the company is engraved. The seal, known as common seal has legal significance, because it is used as official signature of the company. Any agreement or any document of the company which does not bear the common seal will have no legal value and the company is not bound by it.

Evaluation of Company Form of Organisation

In modern business this form of organisation occupies important place. Particularly as compared to sole trade and partnership forms, the company form has certain additional advantages. These are:

(*i*) **Huge Financial Resources:** The capital of the company is contributed by public. Particularly in case of public limited company, any person may become member of the company by purchasing the shares of the company. On the one hand the company can mobilise public fund for its capital base, on the other it provides an opportunity to the public to become shareholders in the company and get benefit of prospering business of the company.

(*ii*) **Limited Liability of Members:** In joint stock company, those who purchase its shares become members of the company. The liability of the member of company is limited up to face value of the shares held by him. In case of financial losses or difficulties in the business of company, the shareholders cannot be called upon to contribute more than that. It provides benefit to the members who can enjoy prosperity of the company but with limited liability.

(*iii*) **Transferability of Shares:** In a joint stock company, the shares issued by it are transferable freely in the market. Any member can transfer his shares as per his choice as to get back his investment or to mobilise it towards more profitable companies.

(*iv*) **Continuous Existence:** Having separate legal existence, the company enjoys continuous as well as stable span of life. It is merely because after incorporation, the company acquires separate legal existence which is not affected by the existence of its members.

(*v*) **Economies of Large-scale Business:** The company having huge and sound capital base, generally conduct the business in large scale. As a result of it, all economies and cost effectiveness in business operations can be obtained which paves the way for further growth and expansion of business. It is only by using this form of organisation, business empires have been built around us.

(*vi*) **Professional Management:** The company having huge business resources at its disposal and doing business at large scale can afford to have a team of specialised and efficient managers to manage its affairs. The utilisation of management talent also provides further boost to its growth and prosperity.

(*vii*) **Protection of Investors:** The management and control of various operations and activities of the company is subject to legal provisions of Indian Company Act. The Act also provides extra cushion by empowering the Central Government to intervene directly in the affairs of the company for the protection of investors' interest.

Disadvantages of Incorporation

Undoubtedly, the company which has incorporated under the provisions of Indian Company Act has many advantages over other forms of business organisation. But in practice, the following disadvantages are also associated with it.

(*i*) **Difficult Formation:** The company is to be formed by fulfiling prescribed legal formalities of Indian Company Act. In this regard, many important documents are prepared such as Articles, Memorandum of Association and Prospectus etc., and are filed with the Registrar. It requires legal and technical knowledge on the part of the persons engaged in the formation of the company. Similarly many plans and reports are got to be prepared and agreements are entered into for acquiring various resources and judging economic feasibility of launching a company.

The completion of these formalities involves huge expenses and use of specialised and professional services. Not only this, whole exercise takes long time and requires continuous efforts at different stages on the part of promoters of the company.

(*ii*) **Lack of Secrecy:** The formation and management of a company is subject to the provisions of company law. As per law, every company requires to publish certain documents for giving full knowledge to the public about its functioning particularly management of resources. It also requires to file various returns documents from time and again which are also subject to public scrutiny. It has therefore, as compared to other forms, hardly any privacy for conducting the business.

(*iii*) **Separation of Control from Owernership:** In a public limited company, the equity shareholders are the real owners. But so far as management and control of the company is concerned it remains in the hands of professionally qualified managers working under the direction and command of the directors. These directors are elected not by all but by the group of equity shareholders those who are more active and interested in the management of the company. In this way management of the company based on the principles of democracy turns to be 'management by a few members'. And it is not considered healthy practice for managing public resources.

(*iv*) **Irregularities and Manipulation:** It is found in practice that in spite of excessive legal control, the directors of the company divert the fund of one company to an other companies in which they have personal stakes. There is no dearth of examples where companies are involved in the fraudulent activities at the cost of interest of innocent investors.

Distinction between Company and Partnership

Though these two are very important forms of business organistion, they differ with each other on the following points:

(*i*) **Formation:** The company comes into existence by fulfiling legal formalities prescribed in the Company Act. But to form partnership two or more persons have to come together and make agreement to this effect and registration of partnership is not legally compulsory.

(*ii*) **Number of Members:** Minimum number of members required in case of private and public company is two and seven respectively. Maximum number in case of private company is 50 (excluding past and present employees) and in case of public company there is no maximum limit of members. While as in partnership minimum number of person required is two and maximum number is restricted to 10 in banking business and 20 in other business.

(*iii*) **Legal Existence:** A company acquires legal existence in the eyes of law after obtaining certificate of incorporation from the Registrar, which is separate from its members. But partnership firm and partners are one and the same in terms of existence.

(*iv*) **Nature of Liability:** The liability of members in a company is limited up to the face value of shares held by them. And in no case they can be compelled to contribute more in the event of insolvency. While as in partnership, the liability of members in unlimited and joint and several also.

(*v*) **Transfer of Shares:** In a company, the members can freely transfer their shares, but the partners are not allowed to transfer their shares without consent of all other partners.

(*vi*) **Continuous Existence:** A company enjoys continuous existence. Its life and existence is not affected by the existence of its member. But in partnership existence of partners has impact on the existence of the firm, for example when partner dies, becomes insane or insolvent, the partnership comes to an end.

(*vii*) **Relationship:** In a company, the members are real owners of the company. But in case of partnership, the partners are having relationship of agent and principal with the firm and other partners.

(*viii*) **Ownership of Property:** In a company, the property acquired for business is in the name of company itself. During lifetime the members of the company has no stake on it. But the property of partnership firm is in the joint ownership of the partners.

(*ix*) **Management and Control:** The business of a company is managed by the board of directors and not by the members. While as in partnership, every partner has a right to participate in the management of business of the firm.

(*x*) **Dissolution:** The legal existence of a company comes to an end only according to the provisions of the Company Act. But partnership being creation of agreement can be dissolved at any time, by making another agreement.

(*xi*) **Application of Law:** A company is governed by the Companies Act 1956, but partnership is subject to the provisions of Indian Partnership Act 1932.

Doctrine of Lifting the Corporate Veil

As soon as a company procures certificate of incorporation from the Registrar, it acquires legal existence in the eyes of law. The legal existence of a company is separate from the existence of its members. This basic feature of a company has been established in the famous case of **'Salomon *vs* Salomon and Co. Ltd.'** According to this doctrine there is a veil or curtain between the company and its members. In case anything goes wrong with the management of a company or company comes under huge financial obligations, the members can take protection under this doctrine. They can plead that a company is a corporate personality solely responsible for its affairs.

But in reality, the members of a company are real beneficiaries, so they cannot completely disassociate themselves from the what is going on in a company. In case the members behind the company are legally considered as a part of corporate personality, it is said that veil or curtain between the members and company has been lifted. In other words, when the law disregards corporate entity separate from the entity of the members behind the legal facade it is known as 'lifting the veil of corporate personality.'

The corporate veil is lifted by the courts for protecting public interest by checking the members behind a company from committing any fraud or illegal acts.

Though it is discretionary for the courts to lift corporate veil, the circumstances and cases in which corporate veil will be lifted may be grouped into the following two groups:

(*i*) **Under Express Statutory Provisions:** The Company Act 1956 provides that under the following situations the directors or members are held personally liable along with the company. These situations are:

(*a*) ***When the number of members falls below statutory minimum number*:** Section 45 of the Company Act provides that in case the number of members of a company is reduced below the statutory requirement and the company carries on the business for more than six months, every person who was member of the company during that time when it carried on the business after those six months and who was aware of this fact, shall be severally liable for all debts of the company. It should be noted that personal liability of the members commences only after six months of carrying on business with reduced numbers of members.

(*b*) ***Non-disclosure of representative capacity*:** When an officer of a company or any person on its behalf signs or authorises to be signed on behalf of the company, any bill of exchange or a 'hundi,' promissory note, endorsement, cheque or order for money or goods, that he should clearly disclose name of the company on whose behalf he is acting. If the officer or person fails to disclose his representative capacity he will be personally liable for the amount due if the company refuses to pay it. For example, if bill of exchange is drawn upon the company and director of the company accepted the bill without disclosing that he is accepting the bill on behalf of the company, such director shall be personally liable for the bill.

(*c*) ***Holding and subsidiary company*:** When one company controls composition of the board of directors of another company or holds majority of its shares, the former is called 'holding company' and the later is called 'subsidiary company.' According to Section 212 of the Act, every holding company is required to disclose to its shareholders the accounts of its subsidiaries. It requires that the copies of balance sheet, profit loss account, director's report and auditor's report of each subsidiary company be attached to the balance sheet of the holding company. Thus companies under same group are treated as one entity disregarding the rule that each subsidiary had separate legal entity.

(*d*) ***For investigation into affairs of selected company*:** Under Sections 239 and 247 of the Act, corporate veil is lifted with regard to inspector's power to investigate related company. He can investigate affairs of related company under the same management for alleged mismanagement or oppression towards its members or to determine true ownership.

(*e*) ***Fraudulent conduct of business*:** Under Section 242 of the Act if in the course of winding up of a company it appears that any business of the company has been carried on with an intention to defraud its creditors or any other persons, in such case the persons who were knowingly parties to such acts may be held personally liable for any debts and liabilities of the company. In such case, the court may disregard the legal entity of the company and make the person involved in fraud personally liable.

(*f*) ***Failure to refund application money*:** In case a company fails to refund application money of unsuccessful applicants within 130 days of the issue of prospectus, the directors of the company shall be jointly and severally liable and the corporate veil is lifted.

(*ii*) **Under Judicial Interpretation:** In addition to these above mentioned legal situations, the courts have allowed lifting of corporate veil for proper administration of taxation laws, estate duty laws and wealth tax laws. Some of the instances are as follows:

(*a*) ***Determining character of the company*:** In case the war is declared between two countries, it becomes necessary to determine character of some companies which may be controlled by the residents of enemy country. For this purpose, the courts justify lifting corporate veil of such company as to ascertain identity of members, controlling the company. In **'Daimler Coy Ltd *vs* Continental Typer & Rubber Coy Ltd (1916) 2 A. C. 307.'** It was held that company, though incorporated in UK was an enemy company and the company was not allowed to proceed with an action to recover its debts. It was further upheld that company under the control of residents of enemy country may assume enemy character.

(*b*) ***Preventing of fraud or improper conduct*:** In case the purpose of the company is to avoid legal obligation or to defraud the creditors, the court will allow lifting of the corporate veil. In the case **'Gilford Motor Coy Ltd.,** Horne was appointed as managing director of the company with a condition that during his employment with the company and afterwards, he will not solicit the customers of the company.

After leaving the company, he formed another company to carry on same business and solicited the customers of Gilford Motor Coy Ltd. In a suit filed it was held that Horne had formed the company for his own benefit to solicit customers of his employer company. The court issued injunction against Horne and his new company, and he was prevented from making breach of contract with employer company.

Similarly in case of Jones *vs* Lipman the court lifted corporate veil, because dummy company was formed for avoiding legal obligations. Thus in case a company is formed to defraud, the court will lift the corporate veil and look into the true ownership of the company.

(iii) **Protecting the Revenue:** The court will allow lifting of corporate veil if it is of the opinion that the company has been formed for evading the tax or tax obligations. In such cases, the court will disregard corporate entity and would instead hold individual members liable to fulfil such revenue obligations. In, **'Sir Dinshaw Manakjee** case, Dinshaw, who was very rich person, was earning a lot of dividend and interest income has formed four companies as to divert his income and evade tax liability. The court ignored corporate entity of these companies and held that the company was nothing more than Sir Dinshaw and Dinshaw was held the owner of total income and liable to pay tax on it.

(iv) **Avoiding Welfare Laws:** The courts have disregarded the separate legal personality of the company when the company's independent legal entity was used as device to reduce the amount payable by the company to its workers as bonus etc. It is because such device would defeat provisions of welfare laws which are enacted for the benefit of the employees of the company.

(v) **Acting as an Agent of its Members:** As a general rule, no company can act as an agent of its shareholders or of another company. But under certain circumstances, a company may be regarded as an agent or trustee of its members or another company. In such situations, for all acts done by the company, the members of the company will be responsible and not the company.

In addition to the above mentioned situation, the courts may lift the corporate veil for protecting public policy and in all other quasi-criminal cases.

REVIEW QUESTIONS

1. Define 'company' and explain its main characteristics.
2. 'After being incorporated, the company gets certain advantages over other forms of business organisation.' Comment.
3. Discuss merits and demerits of joint stock company.
4. Explain the doctrine of 'lifting the corporate veil.' How does it ensure protection of interest of third party?
5. Distinguish between company and partnership.
6. Discuss the circumstances in which lifting of corporate veil is justified.
7. 'Company is an artificial person created by law having perpetual succession and is different from the personality of the members constituting it.' Comment.

PRACTICAL PROBLEMS

1. A is a director in X & Coy Ltd. The company needs to buy raw material for its plant. The raw material was purchased on credit. The supplier of raw material draws a bill of exchange in the name of the company. A gives his acceptance for that bill without disclosing that he is one of the directors of the company. Evaluate the liability of A in this case.
   (Hint: He is personally liable.)
2. B is a share broker and earns a lot of dividend and interest. He has formed a company and diverts his income from dividend and interest to this Coy. Expalin his libility taking into account the doctrine of 'lifting corporate veil'.
3. The number in a public limited company is reduced to 6 on 1st Jan., 2008. The company incurs trade debt on 2 January 2008, 31 March 2008 and December, 2008. How far the remaining 6 members of the company are personally liable for the above debts?
4. All members of a private limited company become insane and they are declared so by a competent authority. Does the company ceases to exist?
   (Hint: No, Company has separate legal entity.)

5. A and B sold a business to C on a condition that they will not compete with him for a certain period of time. After sometime, they formed a private limited company and became principal shareholders and directors and started a similar business to C's business. Explain legal remedy of C. (Hint: C can get order of injuction for that company.)
6. In a private limited company it is discovered that the total number of members is 60. On an enquiry it was found that 15 members have been employees of the company and they purchased shares when they were employees of the company. Is it necessary to convert this company into public limited company ? (Hint: Not necessary.)

■■■

28

Types of Companies

LEARNING OBJECTIVES

- Understand classification of companies.
- Develop conceptual clarity about public and private company.
- Remember distinction between these two and their conversion.
- Analyse functioning of Foreign Companies and Government Companies and Holding Companies.

Taking into account various basic factors such as number of members, their liability, mode of incorporation and control of companies, the companies may be classified as:

1. On the basis of incorporation.
2. On the basis of liability.
3. On the basis of control.

1. ON THE BASIS OF INCORPORATION

Depending upon manner and mode of incorporation, joint stock companies may be divided into the following:

A. **Chartered Company :** A company which is incorporated under a special charter granted by the king or queen of England is known as chartered company. These companies are governed and controlled by the provisions of charter under which they are formed. The provisions of the Company Act are not applicable on these companies. For example, East India

Company, Harts and Bay Company and Bank of England are examples of chartered companies. The charter under which the company is incorporated also prescribes nature of business and powers of such company. It is however to be remembered that such type of companies cannot be formed in India.

B. Statutory Company: A company which is brought into existence by passing Special Act in the Parliament or in legislative assemblies is known as 'statutory company'. Basically such companies or corporations are formed for achieving special purpose particularly with regard to public utilities. Such company or corporation enjoys similar legal status as being enjoyed by joint stock company. The Special Act under which such company is formed prescribes nature of business and powers of such company. The provisions of Company Act are also applicable on such company so far as they are consistent with the provisions of Special Act. Such companies do not require to have separate Memorandum of Association. So far as the management of such companies is concerned, an annual report regarding functioning of the company is required to be placed before the Parliament or legislative assembly as the case may be. The audit of such company is conducted under the control and direction of Auditor General of India. The employees working in such companies are not subject to Government rules and service conditions of government servant. The Reserve Bank of India, State Bank of India, Life Insurance Corporation, Food Corporation of India, Unit Trust of India, and Municipal Corporations are good examples of such company.

C. Registered or Incorporated Company: Generally the companies are brought into existence by fulfilling legal formalities prescribed in the Indian Company Act 1956. These companies are known as 'registered or incorporated companies. To bring a company into existence, the certificate of incorporation is obtained from the Registrar of the Companies. The management and day-to-day functioning of these companies is regulated by the provisions of Indian Companies Act.

Registered company may either be private limited company or public limited company.

Meaning of Private Limited Company: According to Section 3(1) (*iii*) as amended by Companies (Amendment) Act, 2000, a private company means a company which has a minimum paid up capital of Rs. 1 lakh or such higher paid up capital as may be prescribed and by its articles of association:

(*a*) Restricts the right of members to transfer shares, if any.

(*b*) Limits the number of members to 50 excluding the members who are or were in the employment of the company.

(*c*) Prohibits any invitation to the public to subscribe for any shares or debentures of the company.

(*d*) Prohibits any invitation or acceptance of any deposits from persons other than its members, directors or their relatives.

Although the shares of private company cannot be freely transferred as those of public company, the articles of a private company may provide that whenever a member of private company desires to transfer his shares he must offer these shares to the existing members at a price to be determined by the directors.

The Companies (Amendment) Act, 2000, provides that every private company existing on the date of commencement of this Amendment Act (13 December 2000) having a paid up capital of less than Rs. one lakh shall within a period of two years from such commencement enhance its paid up capital to Rs. one lakh. If it fails to enhance in paid up capital as specified above, such company shall be deemed to be a 'defunct company' under Section 560 of this Act and its name shall be struck off from the Register of Companies maintained by the Registrar of the Companies.

The minimum number of members required to form private company is two. Such a company must add the word 'private' in its name. Moreover, a private company enjoys some privileges over public company. In case a private company does not comply with any of the restrictions contained in the articles, it ceases to enjoy some of these privileges granted to it.

Meaning of Public Limited Company: According to Section 3(1) (*iv*) Companies (Amendment) Act, 2000, a public company means a company which:

(*a*) is not a private company.

(*b*) has a minimum paid up capital of Rs. five lakh or such higher paid up capital as may be prescribed.

(*c*) is a private company *i.e.*, which is subsidiary of a public company.

In other words, a public company is one which does not impose any restrictions on the rights of its members to transfer their shares, does not restrict the maximum number of members and which can invite general public to subscribe its shares. Hence any member of the public can purchase shares and debentures of public company. These shares and debentures can be traded on a stock exchange. It should however to be noted that minimum number of members in a public company must be seven.

Similarly according to Amendment Act 2000, every public company with a paid up capital of less than Rs. five lakh shall increase its paid up capital to Rs. five lakh within a period of two years from the commencement of

Amendment Act and failing which the company shall be deemed to be 'defunct company' and its name will be struck off from the Registrar of Companies maintained by the Registrar of Companies.

Distinction Between Private Company and Public Company

A private company can be distinguished from public company on the following grounds:

(*i*) **Minimum Number:** To form a private company minimum number of members is required to be two, but minimum number of members required to form public company is seven.

(*ii*) **Maximum Number:** In case of private company the maximum number of members is 50 (excluding past and present employees). While as there is no restriction on the maximum number of members in public company.

(*iii*) **Minimum Paid Up Capital:** A private company must have minimum paid up capital of Rs. one lakh, while as public company is required to have minimum paid up capital of Rs. five lakh.

(*iv*) **Name:** The name of public company, limited by shares or guarantee must use limited word at the end of its name. But private company must have 'Private Limited' words at the end of its name.

(*v*) **Minimum Number of Directors:** A private company must have at least two directors, but public company is required to have at least three directors.

(*vi*) **Transfer of Share:** The shares of a public company can be transferred freely and can be traded on stock exchange. But right to transfer shares in private company is restricted by its articles.

(*vii*) **Public Subscription:** A public limited company can invite general public for subscribing its share capital while as articles of private company prohibits to invite public for subscribing its shares.

(*viii*) **Acceptance of Deposits:** A public company can invite and accept deposits from public, but private company is prohibited to invite and accept public deposits.

(*ix*) **Commencement of Business:** To start business, a public company has to procure certificate of commencement of business. But a private company can start its business immediately after obtaining certificate of incorporation from the Registrar of Companies.

(*x*) **Articles of Association:** In case a public company not preparing its own articles of association, it is bound to adopt Table A of Companies

Act as its articles of association. In a private company, it is compulsory to prepare its own articles of association.

(*xi*) **Allotment of Shares:** A public company can allot the shares only after having received amount of minimum subscription. No such restriction is applicable on a private company.

(*xii*) **Statutory Meeting:** A public company is required to hold statutory meeting after one month and before six months from the date of obtaining certificate of commencement of business. A private company is not required to hold such meeting.

(*xiii*) **Issue of Prospectus:** It is obligatory for a public company to prepare prospectus or statement in lieu of prospectus and file it with the Registar. But a private company need not prepare and file it.

(*xiv*) **Managerial Remuneration:** In a public company total managerial remuneration cannot exceed 11 per cent of the net profit. This restriction is not applicable on a private company.

(*xv*) **Index of Members:** A public company is required to maintain index of members as it exceeds 50. But no such index is maintained by a private company.

(*xvi*) **Special Privileges:** A public company does not enjoy special privileges which are granted only to a private company.

Privileges of Private Companies

As discussed earlier, a private company basically differs from a public company. The private company cannot invite public to subscribe its shares capital, instead it raises its capital privately from a limited number of members. And the membership is usually restricted to the promoters, their friends and kith and kins. It is therefore the reason why many of the provisions of the Companies Act are not applicable on a private company. Such legal exemptions and privileges which are granted to a private company are:

(*i*) **Number of Members:** A private company can be formed with only two members.

(*ii*) **Commencement of Business:** A private company can start its business immediately after procuring certificate of incorporation from the Registrar.

(*iii*) **Minimum Subscription:** A private company is allowed to allot shares without complying with relevant provisions of minimum subscription.

(*iv*) **Prospectus:** A private company is not required to prepare and file a copy of prospectus or statement in lieu of prospectus.

(*v*) **Number of Directors:** A private company is required to have only two directors. They are not required to file their consent and hold qualification shares.

(*vi*) **Statutory Meeting:** A private company is not required to hold statutory meeting and file the report to the Registrar.

(*vii*) **Subsequent Issue of Shares:** In case a private company raises additional capital, it does not require to offer such issue to existing shareholders. Such shares can be issued even to the outsiders.

(*viii*) **Index of Members:** A private company is exempted from keeping index of members.

(*ix*) **Quorum:** The minimum number of members required to constitute quorum for a valid general meeting of the shareholders is two.

(*x*) **Managerial Remuneration:** The restriction on managerial remuneration of 11 per cent of net profit is not applicable on a private company.

(*xi*) **Provisions Regarding Directors:** A private company is exempted from the legal provisions of the Companies Act regarding number, appointment, retirement, granting loan to directors etc.

Conversion of a Private Company into a Public Company

A private company after incorporation, may get itself converted into a public company either by its own choice or by default in meeting the requirements of the provisions of Section 3(1) (*iii*). In addition, there are some other situations under which a private company is deemed to be a public company by operation of law:

(*i*) **Conversion by Choice:** A private company may itself choose to become a public company. The procedure for converting a private into a public company is prescribed under Section 44 of the Indian Companies Act which is as follows:

(*a*) The company desires to be converted must call a meeting of Board of Directors to consider and approve the proposal to convert it into a public company.

(*b*) The company must convene a general meeting and pass a special resolution for altering its articles of association. An alteration must be made in such a way that the articles does no longer contain restrictions of Section 3 (1) (*iii*) and articles are not inconsistent with the requirements of a public company.

(*c*) After having passed such special resolution within 30 days the company must file the following documents with the Registrar of Companies:

- A copy of special resolution.
- A copy of altered articles.
- A copy of prospectus containing the information required in accordance with Part I and Part II of the Companies Act or a statement in lieu of prospectus in the prescribed form.

(*d*) In case the minimum number of members is less than seven it must be increased to seven. Similarly the minimum number of directors should also be raised to three and paid up capital is raised to Rs. five lakh.

(*e*) After filing a copy of resolution and prospectus or statement in lieu of prospectus, the company must apply to the Registrar for a fresh certificate of incorporation.

The company becomes a public company from the date on which the special resolution is passed. However, change in its name becomes effective only after obtaining certificate of incorporation and the word 'private' will be deleted from the name of the company.

(*ii*) **Conversion by Default or by Operation of Law:** In case a private company makes a default in complying with essential legal requirements prescribed under Section 3 (1) (*iii*) of the Act, it is converted into a public company by operation of law. For example the number of members exceeds 15, it allows transfer of shares or invites or accepts deposits from the public, automatically it becomes a public company. The privileges granted to such company are no longer available and all the provisions of the Companies Act shall be applicable as if it was a public company. In this regard, it is however to be noted that the court has been given the power to grant relief in case provided the court is satisfied that the default in respect with the provision 3 (1) (*iii*) was purely accidental and not intentional.

Conversion of a Public Company into a Private Company

As a private company gets converted into a public company, similarly a public company may also be converted into a private company in the following manner:

(*i*) To convert a public company into private company special resolution shall be passed for making alteration in the articles so as to incorporate four restrictions imposed on a private company under Section 3 (1) (*iii*).

(*ii*) After having passed special resolution to this effect within 30 days of passing such resolution, a copy of such resolution will be filed with the Registrar of Companies.

(*iii*) The company will also reduce the number of members in accordance with the legal requirements applicable on a private company.

(*iv*) To this effect, sanction of the Central Government must be obtained for approving the changes in the articles of association of the company. The conversion shall become binding from the date of approval by the Central Government.

(*v*) After receiving such approval from the Central Government, within 30 days a copy of such approval with a copy of altered articles must be filed with the Registrar.

Every copy of articles of association issued after such conversion must include a copy of special resolution passed to the effect of such conversion and the company must add the word 'private' to its name.

2. ON THE BASIS OF LIABILITY

On the basis of a liability an incorporated company may be a public company or a private company (Section 12) may further be classified as:

(*i*) Company Limited by Shares: Such companies are known as 'limited liability companies'. In such companies the liability of the members is limited to the extent of face value of the shares held by them. In case the members acquire shares which are fully paid, the liability of such members will be nil. The liability can be enforced against the members in case the amount remain unpaid, during the existence of the company or during winding up of the company.

(*ii*) Companies Limited by Guarantee: According to Section [12 (2) (*b*)] of the Companies Act, a company having liability of its members limited by its memorandum, to such amount as the members may undertake to contribute to the assets of the company in case of its being wound up, is known as 'company limited by guarantee'. The liability of the members for the amount guaranteed can be enforced only during the winding up and not during the lifetime of the company. Such companies are generally formed for promoting art, culture, science and sports etc.

Such company may or may not have share capital. In case the company is formed without a share capital the members would be liable to pay only the guaranteed amount and that too when the company goes into liquidation. But if such company is formed with share capital, the members are also liable to pay unpaid amount on their shares and guaranteed amount can be demanded only in the event of winding up of the company. The memorandum of such company should state that each member of the company undertakes to contribute guaranteed amount to the assets of the company in case of winding up.

(*iii*) **Unlimited Companies:** A company where the liability of members is unlimited in known as unlimited company. In such companies, there is no limit on the liability of the members. The members of such companies may be required to pay the losses of company from their personal property. Every member is liable to contribute in proportion of his interest in the company towards the amount needed for paying of liabilities of the company. And if there is any deficiency that will be shared by the members in proportion of their capital in the company. Since the company has separate legal entity, the creditors cannot directly sue upon the members. It is to be noted that the liability of the members can be enforced only during the winding up of the company. Such companies may or may not have share capital. In case the company has share capital, it must be mentioned in the articles of association of the company. Such company must have its memorandum and articles of association. The articles of association must specify the number of members with which the company has got registered.

3. ON THE BASIS OF CONTROL

Management and control of the companies provides an important basis for classifying them. On the basis that who effectively controls the affairs, companies may be classified as:

(*i*) **Government Company:** According to Section 617 of the Act, government company means any company in which not less than 51 per cent of the paid up share capital is held by Central Government or by any State Government, or partly by the Central Government or partly by one or more State Government and includes a company which is subsidiary of a government company as thus defined. For example, Indian Telephone Industry, Hindustan Aeronautics Ltd., Hindustan Insecticides Ltd. are the government companies. A government company registered under this Act is a non-statutory company and is not an agent of the government.

A government company is subject to the following special provisions of Companies Act:

(*a*) ***Regarding auditor*:** The auditor of government company will be appointed by the Comptroller and Auditor General of India. He shall have a power to direct company's auditor for the audit and performance of his duties. He can also conduct supplementary test audit of the company's accounts.

(*b*) ***Regarding annual report*:** In case the Central Government is a member of the company, the Central Government shall prepare annual report on the working of the company and together with auditors report and the comment of Comptroller and Auditor General of India (if any) it will be placed in both Houses of Parliament.

(*c*) ***Regarding power of Central Government*:** The Central Government, may by notification in Official Gazette, direct that any of the provisions of this Act shall not apply to any government company or shall apply with such exceptions, modifications and adaptations as may be specified in the notification.

A government company registered in the Act shall have separate legal entity and will not be identified with any government. The employees working in these companies are not treated as government servants.

(*ii*) **Holding and Subsidiary Company:** Broadly speaking in case one company controls another company, the controlling company may be known as 'holding company' and the company so controlled is known as 'subsidiary company'.

According to Section 4 (4) of the Act, "company shall be deemed to be holding company of another, if that other is its subsidiary."

A company is to be subsidiary of another company only in following cases:

(*a*) When the company controls composition of board of directors of other company.

(*b*) When the company holds more than half of the equity share capital of a company in terms of a nominal value. In other words, a company has controlling amount of equity shares to have controlling power in other company.

(*c*) When company is a subsidiary of any company which in turn is subsidiary of a holding company.

It is however to be noted that holding and subsidiary companies do have separate legal entities in the eyes of law unless and until, there is a specific contract between two companies one does not become an agent of another. And subsidiary company cannot be treated to be a part of holding company.

According to Section 212 of the Act, holding company is required to present consolidated picture of accounts and will attach a copies of balance sheet, profit and loss account, directors, report and auditors, report in respect of each of its subsidiary companies for presenting true and fair picture of the state of affairs of a group as a whole for the benefit of its shareholders, creditors and prospective investors.

As per Section 213 of the Act, the Central Government has been empowered to extend the financial year of a holding company or subsidiary company so that the financial year of subsidiary company ends with the financial year of a holding company.

Under Section 214 of the Act, holding company may by a resolution authorise its representatives to inspect books of account of its subsidiaries. The members of holding company are also entitled to get the affairs of subsidiary companies investigated.

OTHER COMPANIES

(*i*) **Foreign Company:** According to Section 591 (I) of the Act, Foreign Company means "a company incorporated outside India but having place of business in India." It would be deemed to have establish a place of business in India, if it carries on business at some specified or identifiable place like godown, office, a place or a storehouse in India.

Within 30 days of its establishing business in India, a foreign company is required to file the following documents to the Registrar of Companies:

(*a*) A certified copy of charter/statues or memorandum and articles of the company. In case the instruments is not in English language, certified translation of the same will have to be furnished.

(*b*) A full address of the registered or principal office of the company abroad.

(*c*) A list of directors and secretary of the company along with their names, residential addresses, nationalities of origin, business occupations and directorship held by them.

(*d*) The names and addresses of person or persons authorised to accept on behalf of the company service of processes or any notices or documents required to be served upon the company.

(*e*) The full address of the office of the company in India which is to be deemed to be a principal place of business in India.

Any change in the above particulars must be notified to the Registrar within a prescribed time. The above mentioned documents must be delivered to the Registrar in New Delhi and also to Registrar of the State in which the principal place of business is situated.

In addition, the foreign company is subject to the following legal provisions of the Act:

(*a*) **Accounts (Section 594):** Foreign company is required to prepare profit and loss account and balance sheet in such form with such particulars as is required in case of another company under the Act.

(*b*) **Name (Section 295):** Every foreign company is required to state in its prospectus the country where the company is incorporated. It shall exhibit on the outside of every office or place, the name of the company and name of the country where it is incorporated. It will also state name of the company and name of the country in all business letters, bill heads, letter heads and in all official publications and notices.

(*c*) **Service of Notices and Process (Section 296):** Any process, notice or other documents which is required to be served on a foreign company shall be deemed to be served, if it has been addressed or sent by post to any person who is authorised to accept the same on behalf of the company.

(*d*) **Penalties (Section 598):** Any foreign company failing to comply with any of the above mentioned provisions the company or every officer or an agent of the company, who is in default shall be punishable with a fine which may extend to Rs. 1,000 and additional fine of Rs. 1,000 for each day during which default continues further.

(*e*) **Registration of Charges (Section 600):** Legal provisions of Sections 124 to 145 relating to registration of charges, appointment of receiver and books of accounts applied on Indian companies are also applicable to foreign companies.

(*f*) **Prospectus (Section 603):** No foreign company shall issue, distribute or circulate its prospectus unless the prospectus is dated and contains particulars about constitution of company, enactment under which it is incorporated, address in India where these can be inspected, address of principal place of business in India and date of incorporation.

(*g*) **Winding up (Section 584):** A foreign company, carrying on business in India, may be wound up as an unregistered company. It is only through the order of the court a foreign company can be wound up.

(*ii*) **Illegal Association:** According to Section 11 of Companies Act, no company, association or partnership consisting of more than 10 persons for the purpose of carrying on business of banking and more than 20 persons for the purpose of carrying or any other business shall be formed, unless it is registered as a company under this Act or is formed in pursuance of some other Indian law. If it is not registered it becomes an illegal association. The following points should be taken care of about illegal associations:

(*a*) An illegal association is not an association for illegal purpose.

(*b*) It remains an illegal association unless it is registered under Indian Companies Act or other Indian law.

(*c*) Illegality of an association cannot be cured even by subsequent reduction in the number of the members.

(*d*) Profits made by such illegal association are however liable to be assessed under Income Tax Act.

The consequence of forming such illegal association are as follows:

(*a*) It has no legal existence, it cannot enter into a contract and it cannot bring any legal action against its members and outsiders. No action can be taken against such association.

(*b*) Every member shall be liable for all liabilities incurred in the business.

(*c*) Every person who is member of such association shall be punishable with a fine which may extend to one thousand rupees.

(*d*) An illegal association cannot be wound up under the Company Act.

(*e*) No suit can be filed by any member for partition, dissolution or for taking accounts of illegal association.

(*f*) The offence under Section 11 is compoundable by the Regional Director under the provision of Section 621 of the Companies Act.

REVIEW QUESTIONS

1. Define 'private company'. Distinguish between private company and public company.
2. Discuss various privileges enjoyed by a private company. Why does law grants these privileges to a private company?
3. Describe the procedure for converting a private company into a public company.
4. Define 'public company'. Describe the procedure for converting public company into private company.

5. A private company cannot issue prospectus. Why?
6. Write a comprehensive note on Government Company.
7. Define 'foreign company'. Describe legal provisions relating to a foreign company.
8. Distinguish between holding company and subsidiary company. When can a company be called a subsidiary?
9. Explain company limited by shares, limited by guarantee and unlimited company.
10. Discuss the salient features of an illegal association. What are the consequences of forming such association?
11. Explain various legal obligations, which are imposed on a foreign company by the Companies Act.

PRACTICAL PROBLEMS

1. Forty per cent of paid up share capital of a company is held by the Central Government and 15 per cent is held by Life Insurance Corporation of India and Unit Trust of India. Is the company a Government Company? (Hint: No, because shares held by LIC and UTI cannot be taken to be held by the Government.)
2. X & Coy is a subsidiary company. To increase share capital it has offered shares to the existing shareholders. The holding company opposed the issue on the ground that it would dilute its control over the subsidiary company. Can holding company seek injunction to stop subsidiary company ? (Hint: No, subsidiary company has separate legal entity.)
3. A & Company was formed as a company limited by guarantee. The members of the company guaranteed a sum of Rs. 5,000; each share above the face value of each shares. The company suffer huge financial losses. Can the amount of guarantee be realised from its members? (Hint: No, it can be demanded only in the event of winding up.)
4. Fifteen persons formed a partnership firm. The firm has the main business of smuggling out some banned goods from our country to some other country. Is the firm an illegal association? (Hint: No, illegality of purpose does not make association as illegal one.)
5. The Central Government of India purchases 51 per cent of total shares of a British Company which is incorporated in UK. The company has a place of business in New Delhi. Is the company a Government Company? (Hint: Yes, it will be considered as Government Company.)

29

Formation and Registration of Company

LEARNING OBJECTIVES

- Examine various stages of formation of company.
- Analyse role of promoters in the formation of company.
- Get familiar with the process of registration of a company.
- Develop conceptual clarity about how to make company a going-on entity.

INTRODUCTION

Formation of a company is a lengthy and time-consuming process. From the very beginning of originating business idea and till it is implemented through the company form of business organisation, the whole process is to be meticulously planned. It requires preparation and filing of many legal documents, making out various plans and arranging all resources which are required for implementing business idea. Moreover, each and every activity to be performed with regard to formation of a company requires thorough knowledge of relevant provisions of the Company Act. And these provisions are to be complied with strictly. It is only after having fulfilled all legal formalities prescribed in the Company Act, the company comes into existence and acquires legal status in the eyes of law.

The whole process of formation of a company mainly involves the following three stages:

1. Promotion
2. Registration or Incorporation
3. Commencement of Business

Each of these stages consists of set of specific activities to be performed. These activities are discussed ahead.

1. PROMOTION

In the process of formation of a company, promotion stage is very important. It mainly involves the following set of activities. These activities are undertaken and performed by the individual or individuals popularly known as promoters. These activities are as follows:

(*i*) **Discovery of Business Idea:** The formation of a company begins with some business idea. It is because the company is formed to implement that business idea. The business ideas may have an origin in the mind of promoters either on the basis of their experience and knowledge or they may get help of some business analyst. The promoters may have many business ideas. They are supposed to look into each idea from the various perspectives as to find out and judge economic soundness and viability of each idea. The soundness may be judged in terms of present business trend, competition availability of resources and future prospects etc.

(*ii*) **Arrangement and Organisation of Resources:** An implementation of business idea requires various resources particularly capital, plant and machinery, man power and other assets. Although at this stage these resources are not actually procured, all necessary arrangements and agreements are made to ensure their availability at required time.

(*iii*) **Obtaining Consent of First Directors:** It involves seeking written consent of directors to act as such. The directors are required to give written undertaking to take up and pay for their qualification shares. In case of private company it is not required.

(*iv*) **Preparation of Documents:** Before filing an application for registration with the Registrar of Companies, the promoters shall take necessary steps for preparing important documents particularly memorandum of association and articles of association. In this regard, the promoters seek legal advice of solicitor or a company secretary. These documents should be duly printed. However, public company limited by shares need not prepare its own articles. It can adopt Table 'A' as given in Schedule I of the Act. These two documents are to be duly stamped.

(*v*) **Payment of Registration Fees:** At the time of filing these document together with other information, the company is required to pay prescribed registration fees. It differs from company to company depending on the amount of authorised capital of a proposed company.

(*vi*) **Application for a Suitable Name:** The promoters are also required to select suitable name of the proposed company, which must not be forbidden by law and undesirable. They will make an application for submitting tentative names to the Registrar of Companies. It is however to be noted that the name of limited company must have the word 'limited' at the end of its name. And names of private company and public company must be ended with the words 'private limited' and 'public limited' respectively.

(*vii*) **Preliminary Contracts:** The promoters may also be required to comply with other legal requirements of the Company Act. For this purpose they have to enter into the various contracts which are known as 'preliminary contracts'. Such contracts are to be entered into by the promoters for procuring assets and to secure services of the experts.

Promoters

The promotion is a first stage in the formation of a company. **Gerstenberg** has defined promotion as, "the discovery of business opportunities and the subsequent organisation of funds, property and managerial ability into business concern for the purpose of making profit therefrom." After having discovered business idea, the promoters make detailed investigations as to find out economic viability of the ideas and determine required amount of capital for getting that idea implemented.

The Company Act does not define the term 'promoters'. Generally speaking, the person or group of persons involved in performing various activities related to a promotion are known as 'promoters'. They are the people at the realm of promoting and forming a company. In the words of L.J. Bowen, "the term promoter is a term not of law but of business usefully summing up in the single word, a number of business operations familiar to the commercial world by which a company is generally brought into existence."

According to Justice **C. Cockburn** "a promoter is one who undertakes to form a company with reference to a given project and set it going and who takes the necessary steps to accomplish that purpose."

However, it is to be noted that everyone who is associated with the formation of a company is not a promoter. According to Section 62 (6) of the Act, "the person assisting the promoters by acting in a professional capacity *e.g.*, solicitors, accountant and other experts are not promoters."

A promoter may be an individual or a firm or association of person or even a company.

Legal Position of Promoters

In the entire process of forming a company, promoters occupy an important position. They enjoy wide ranging powers relating to the formation of company. Although the promoter stands in a fiduciary relationship (based on trust and confidence) with the company which he promotes, he is neither an agent nor a trustee of the company. It is merely because the company is yet to come into existence.

Lord Cairns has rightly pointed out the position of promoter in, **Erlanger *vs* New Sambrero Phosphate Co.,** "The promoters of a company stand undoubtedly in a fiduciary position. They have in their hands the creation and moulding of the company. They have the power of defining how and when and in what shape and under whose supervision, it shall come into existence and begins to act as a trading corporation."

It is clear from the above discussion that being in a fiduciary relationship with the company and original allottee of the shares, a promoter must make full and correct disclosure of the relevant facts including any profit made by him. He must not make any secret profit in all transactions made by him on behalf of the company.

Duties of Promoters

The promoter occupies the position of mutual trust and confidence with the company yet to come into existence and original allottees of the company. He has following important duties:

(*i*) **Not to Make Secret Profit:** In the process of formation of a company, the promoter makes many transactions and agreements. He is under legal obligation not to make direct or indirect profit out of these transactions. If at all he makes any profit it must be disclosed to an independent board of director or to the intended shareholders.

(*ii*) **To Make Full Disclosure of Relevant Facts:** A promoter is legally bound to make full and correct disclosure of all relevant facts including any profit made from the sale of his property to the company and his personal interest in a transaction with the company.

(*iii*) **To Give Benefit of Negotiation to the Company:** The promoter must pass on to the company, benefit of any negotiation and agreement entered into by him in a capacity of promoter. The promoter must act honestly and diligently to escape liability with respect to dealing with the company yet to come into existence.

(*iv*) **Duty of Promoter towards Future Allotees:** The promoters stand in fiduciary relationship not only with the company but also with future allottees of the shares. In this regard, the promoters must ensure that the prospectus issued at their instance contains all material facts and particulars and does not contain any mis-statement.

Liabilities of Promoters

The promoters stand in fiduciary relationship with company and as well as with future allottees of shares. The liability of the promoters arising out of the relationship is:

(*i*) Section 56 of this Act states that all matters and reports mentioned under this section must be set out in the prospectus. Failing to comply with the provision will make promoters liable toward the shareholder.

(*ii*) Under Section 63 of this Act, the promotor can be held liable for any false statement in the prospectus to a person who has subscribed for the shares and debentures of the company on the basis of that prospectus. On account of untrue statement made in the prospectus, if the person who has subscribed for shares and debentures suffers any loss or damage, the promoter is liable to pay compensation.

(*iii*) Section 63 of this Act describes the criminal liabilities for any mis-statement made in the prospectus.

It provides that in addition to the civil liability mentioned above, the promoter can be held criminally liable if the prospectus issued by him contained mis-statement. The punishment prescribed is imprisonment extending up to two years or a fine up to Rs. 5,000 or both. The promoter can however escape this liability if he proves that mis-statement was immaterial and he had reasonable ground to believe that the statement was true at the time of making it.

(*iv*) Section 478 of this Act states that in the event of winding up of a company if the liquidators find and report that fraud has been committed in the promotion and formation of the company, the court may order public examination of all promoters who arc found guilty for fraud in the promotion and formation of the company.

(*v*) Section 543 of this Act provides that, like any other directors or officers of the company, the promoters can also be held liable if they had misapplied or retained any of the property of the company or is found guilty of breach of trust or misfeasance with respect to the company.

(*vi*) Section 203 of this Act also provides that the court may suspend a promoter from taking post in the management of the company for a period of five years if he is convicted for any offence in connection with the promotion, formation or management of a company.

In case the number of promoters is two or more than two, they shall be jointly and severally liable. The right of contribution is applicable if any one of them has been compelled for paying total amount of damage.

Remuneration of Promoters

The promoter plays very important role in the formation of a company. Before a company comes into existence, he has to complete all legal formalities, use considerable amount of skills and efforts and arrange and organise necessary resources. For these valuable service, he is to be suitably remunerated. The remuneration may be defined as a consideration paid to promoter either in cash, or partly in cash and shares and debentures. But a promoter cannot claim, as a matter of right any remuneration from the company. He may be entitled for remuneration only when a company is formed and enters into a contract with a promoter for paying remuneration.

The remuneration may be paid to the promoters in any of the following ways:

(*i*) He may be allowed to sell his own property to the company for cash at a price higher than its value. But he has to make full declaration about valuation of the property and profit earned by him to an independent board of director.

(*ii*) If the promoter has purchased some business or some other property to be sold to the company, he may sell the same to the company at a higher price after making full and correct disclosure.

(*iii*) The company may allot fully paid shares to the promoter.

(*iv*) He may be paid a lump sum amount by the company as a remuneration for services rendered.

(*v*) The company may give him an option to subscribe for certain number of company's unissued shares at par.

(*vi*) He may be given commission at a fixed rate on the shares sold.

Position of Preliminary Contracts

In order to undertake and perform various activities involved in the process of formation of a company, the promoters of a company may enter into contracts for the company, yet to be incorporated. All such contracts made by the promoters with a third party for the proposed company (before incorporation) are called 'preliminary contracts'. However, the preliminary or pre-incorporation contracts are not legally binding on the company even after its corporation. Not only this, the company cannot ratify such contracts. It is simply because such contracts have been made when the company was not in existence.

The legal position of such contracts is explained as:

(*i*) On registration the company is not legally bound by the preliminary contracts made by the promoter during the process of formation of a company, even if the company has been benefited of the work or services provided on its behalf under these contracts. The company is not bound to pay for it.

(*ii*) The company cannot be held liable for such preliminary contracts and such contracts cannot be enforced against the company. On account of such preliminary contracts, the company does not get any right to sue upon the third party for performing the contract.

As an exception to above rules, the Specific Relief Act 1963 provides under Sections 15 and 19 of the Act that "where the promoters of a company, before its incorporation enter into contracts for the purpose of the company and such contracts are warranted by terms of incorporation, specific performance may be obtained by or against the company, if the company has accepted the contracts after incorporation and has communicated such acceptance to the other party."

(*iii*) The company cannot ratify the preliminary contracts. It is simply because the company has not been in legal existence at the time of making such contracts. In case of **Kelner *vs* Baxter,** it was held that the company was not in existence when the preliminary contracts were made, it could not be bound by any purported ratification. Thus the company may enter into new contracts with the vendors, after incorporation to give effect to the terms of contract made before incorporation.

(*iv*) The promoters are personally liable for preliminary contracts. It is because at the time of making such contract the company was not in existence and this fact was known to both the parties of a contract.

The preliminary contracts generally contain a provision that in case the company adopts such contracts on incorporation, the liability of promoters shall come to an end. In case the company does not adopt such contracts within specified period, either of the party may rescind the contract. In such case, the liability of the promoters will come to an end on the expiry of specified period.

2. REGISTRATION OR INCORPORATION

After having completed the stage of promotion, the company is got to be registered. In order to get the company registered the following steps are taken:

(*i*) **Application Form:** An application in a prescribed form together with prescribed fees is to be made with the Registrar of Companies, whether the name under which new company is to be started is available for adoption or not.

(*ii*) **Memorandum of Association:** Memorandum of Association of a company is a charter of the company. It needs to be prepared for every company. It defines the objective for which the company is being formed. Memorandum of Association describes basic character of the company. It prescribes extents within which the company does its business. For the purpose of incorporation, the promoters have to prepare and file with the registrar a duly signed, stamped and witnessed copy of this document.

(*iii*) **Articles of Association:** Preparing and filing of articles of association is optional for a public company with limited liability. Such company may adopt Table A Schedule I of this Act (model set of articles). Articles of Association contains the rules and regulations for managing internal affairs of the company. It defines relationship between the company and its members. However it is to be remembered that the articles of a private company impose restrictions on the right to transfer of shares, prohibit company to invite public for subscription, and restrict maximum numbers of members to 50.

(*iv*) **Copy of Proposed Agreement:** According to Company Amendment Act, if a company propose to enter into agreement with any individual for appointment as its managing director, or a whole time director or manager, a copy of such agreement should also be filed with the Registrar along with the other documents.

(*v*) **Written Consent:** A written consent of the directors to act in that capacity, duly signed by each director together with written undertaking by them to take necessary qualification shares if any, as provided in the articles is to be filed with the Registrar. However a company without share capital, a private company and a company which was a private company prior to its becoming a public company need not file this document with the Registrar.

(*vi*) **Notice of Address:** Notice of address of registered office is also to be filed with the Registrar. It is not required for the purpose of registration. It may however be filed within 30 days of incorporation.

(*vii*) **Statutory Declaration:** The promoters must file a statutory declaration in the prescribed form stating that all requirements of the Company Act and its rules relating to registration have been complied with. Such declaration may be signed by any of the following:

(*a*) an advocate of the Supreme Court or of a High Court, or

(*b*) an attorney or pleader entitled to appear before a High Court, or

(*c*) a secretary or a chartered accountant practising in India and who has been engaged in the formation of the company, or

(*d*) by a person named in the articles as a director, manager or secretary of the company.

On the filing of the above documents together with registration fees, to the Registrar, the Registrar shall scrutinise these documents and if he is satisfied that:

(*a*) all the documents are in order,

(*b*) all the requirements of the Company Act in respect of registration have been complied with,

(*c*) the objects for which the company is to be formed are lawful,

He shall enter the name of the company in the register of the companies maintained by his office. He would then issue a certificate under his signature certifying that the company is incorporated. This certificated is called a 'certificate of incorporation'. It contains the name of the company, date of its issue, and the signature of the Registrar with his seal.

The company comes into existence on the date printed on this certificate and the company becomes a legal entity with perpetual succession and common seal.

Conclusiveness of Certificate of Incorporation

A certificate of incorporation issued by the Registrar of Companies in respect with any association shall be a conclusive evidence that all the requirements of th Company Act have been fulfilled in respect of its registration as well as matters precedent and incidental thereto.

This in also known as rule in **PEEL's case.** In this case the memorandum was found materially altered after the signatories had signed, but before registration. It was held that corporate status remained unaffected and the certificate of incorporation was valid. It was made clear by the **Lord Cairns**, that once the Registrar has issued the certificate of incorporation, nothing further is to be inquired into and the validity of this certificate cannot be disputed on any grounds whatsoever. In another case, **Moosa Goolam Airf *vs* Ebrahion Goolam Arif,** the memorandum of association of a public limited company was signed by two adult persons and other five members of the company were minors. Their guardians made separate signature for each of the minors. The Registrar registered the company and issued certificate of incorporation. The incorporation of the company was challenged and the plaintiff pleaded that the certificate of incorporation should be declared void. The privy council rejected the plea and held that certificate of incorporation was valid.

The certificate of incorporation is also a conclusive proof of the fact that the company came into existence on the date mentioned on the certificate. In the case of **Jubilee Cotton Mills Ltd *vs* Lewis** the company filed documents required for the registration of the company to the Registrar on 6th January. On 8th January the Registrar registered the company and issued certificate of incorporation but dated 6th January. The company allotted few shares to Lewis on 6th January. The allotment of shares was challenged and the court was requested to declare the allotment as void. The court held that the certificate of incorporation is conclusive evidence of all that it contains. Hence the company shall be deemed to have been formed on 6th January and allotment of share was valid.

It should however be noted that the certificate of incorporation is not a conclusive proof of the legality of the objects of the company mentioned in the memorandum of association with which the company has registered.

3. COMMENCEMENT OF BUSINESS

A company comes into existence on obtaining certificate of incorporation from the Registrar. A private company can commence its business immediately after receiving certificate of incorporation. But a public limited company to commence its business has to procure certificate of commencement of business. However public company having no share capital can also commence business on receiving certificate of incorporation.

But a public limited company having share capital is required to fulfil a set of another legal formalities to obtain a certificate of commencement of business. Such company is required to file a prospectus or a statement in lieu of prospectus with the Registrar and fulfil the following formalities:

(*i*) The company has received in cash, the amount mentioned in the prospectus as minimum subscription and the shares up to the amount of minimum subscription have been allotted.

(*ii*) Every director has paid to the company, in cash, the application and allotment money on the shares taken or contracted to be taken by them.

(*iii*) No money is liable to be repaid to the applicants for failure to apply for or to obtain permission for the shares and debentures to be listed on any recognised stock exchange.

(*iv*) Where the shares of the company are to be quoted on the stock exchange, requisite application must be submitted to the stock exchange and approval must be obtained within stipulated time.

(*v*) The prescribed stamp duty as per Indian Stamp Act and as prevalent in that state in which the company is registered is paid.

(*vi*) A statutory declaration in the prescribed from duly verified has been filed with the Registrar. The declaration should specify that clause (*i*), (*ii*) and (*iii*) as above have been complied with. It should be verified by one of the directors or the secretary of the company.

The company having share capital but not issuing a prospectus inviting public to subscribe for its capital cannot commence business unless:

(*a*) The company files statement in lieu of prospectus with the Registrar along with the report given in Part II and Schedule III of the Act. Such statement must be filed with the Registrar at least three days before the first allotment.

(*b*) A declaration that every director of the company has paid to the company in cash, the application and allotment money on the share taken or contracted to be taken by them.

(*c*) A duly verified declaration in the prescribed form has been filed with the Registrar at least three days before the first allotment is made.

It should specify that the above conditions have been complied with and should be verified by one of the directors or the secretary of the company.

On the fulfilment of the above requirement, the Registrar shall issue a certificate knows as 'certificate of commencement of business'. The document certifies that the company is entitled to commence business and is also a conclusive evidence of the fact that the company is so entitled.

In case the company commences business in contravention of these provisions, every person who is responsible for the default shall be punishable with fine which may extend to Rs. 500 for everyday during the default continues. It should also be noted that the company must commence business within a year of its incorporation or otherwise it is liable to be wound up.

REVIEW QUESTIONS

1. What are the different stages involved in the formation of a company? Discuss.
2. List all the documents that are required to be filed with the Registrar of the Companies for the purpose of registration.
3. What do you mean by 'incorporation of company'? What are legal effects of registration of a company?
4. 'The certificate of incorporation is a conclusive proof that all requirements of the Act in respect of formation of company have been complied with.' Explain.
5. Define the term 'promoters' and explain the functions performed by them.
6. Discuss duties and liabilities of a promoter towards company promoted by him.
7. What do you understand by 'preliminary contracts'? Discuss the position of a company with regard to these contracts and the liability of the promoters for such contracts.
8. 'Promoter is not a trustee or an agent of a company, but he stands in finduciary relationship with the company.' Explain.
9. Why preliminary contracts are not binding on the company?
10. Explain the procedure for obtaining certificate of commencement of business by a public company having share capital and has issued prospectus.

PRACTICAL PROBLEMS

1. All legal formalities for the registration of a company were completed on 1 January 2010. The certificate of incorporation was issued to the company on 6th January bearing date of 3 January. Can company allot shares before 6 January 2010? (Hint: Yes, the date on certificate of incorporation is valid.)
2. The promoters of the company purchased some propety. Later on they sold the property to the company at huge profit. Can the company recover that profit from the promoters? (Hint: Yes, because they have not disclosed it).

3. Four signatories out of seven forged their signatures in a memorandum of association. But the company has been registered and certificate of incorporation was issued. Later on the legal existence of the company was challenged by one shareholder on the ground of forged signatures. Can he do it? (Hint: No, Registration of the company is valid.)
4. A company was formed with an object to produce coffee from dates on German patent. But German patent was not granted to the company and the company purchased Swedish patent for producing coffee from dates. Two shareholders filed petition for the winding up of the company. Is it valid? (Hint: Yes, Company can be wound up.)
5. The certificate of incorporation was issued to a company on 1 January 2008 and subsequently the company obtains certificate to commence business on 15 April 2008. But due to certain unavoidable circumstance, the company could not start business till the end of January 2009. Is the company liable to be wound up?

   (Hint: Yes, the company must have started business within one year from the date of certificate of incorporation.)

■■■

30

Principle Documents

LEARNING OBJECTIVES

- Understand importance of principle documents.
- Get clarity about memorandum of a company.
- Examine contents of articles of association.
- Develop conceptual clarity about prospectus.
- Remember how the contents of memorandum and articles can be changed.
- Understand the consequences of mis-representation and untrue statement in prospectus.

MEMORANDUM OF ASSOCIATION, ARTICLES OF ASSOCIATION AND PROSPECTS

For the formation of a company and the commencement of its business, a company has to prepare number of documents. Of these the main documents are:

1. Memorandum of Association
2. Articles of Association
3. Prospectus.

1. MEMORANDUM OF ASSOCIATION

Meaning and Nature

The Memorandum of association is a principle document of a company. Every company has to prepare and file it with the Registrar for getting it registered. It means the origin of the company is related to this document.

Under Section 2 (28) of the Companies Act, "Memorandum means the Memorandum of Association of a company as originally framed or as altered from time to time in pursuancc of any previous company law or of this Act." But this definition does not imply the meaning, nature and significance of the document. In this regard let us move to some other definitions.

According to **Lord Macmillan**, "The purpose of memorandum is to enable the shareholders, creditors and those who deal with the company to know what is its permitted range of enterprise." This definition describe basic nature of the document. According to this definition the memorandum prescribes scope extents and range of the business to be carried on by the company.

Lord Cairns, in the case, **Ashbury Railway Carriage Co *vs* Riche** has observed that "the memorandum of association of a company is its charter and defines the limitations of the power of company. The memorandum contains the fundamental conditions upon which alone the company is allowed to be incorporated."

On the basis of the above definitions it is clear that Memorandum of Association is a charter or constitution of a company. It contains those fundamental conditions and that structure upon which the company can be brought into existence.

The company can carry on the business which is mentioned in the object clause of this document. It prescribes and defines the sphere of activities of the company. In case the company does something beyond the prescribed limits, it will be considered beyond the power of the company and will be null and void.

This document establishes and defines the relationship of a company with the outsiders dealing with the company. Thus every outsider who deals with the company is supposed to go through the contents of this documents so as to ensure that the transactions made by him are within the power of a company. Therefore the memorandum of association is considered as a public document open for inspection by any member of the public.

The memorandum of association must be printed, and divided into paragraphs. It is to be signed by at least 7 persons in case of a public company and by at least 2 in case of a private company. The persons signing memorandum are known as 'subscribers of memorandum'. Every subscriber must give his address and occupation. Their signatures are required to be witnessed by at least one witness. Each of the subscriber must take at least one share and must mention number of shares subscribed by him opposite to his name.

Contents of Memorandum

According to Section 13 of this Act, the memorandum of a company contains the following main clauses:

(*i*) Name Clause
(*ii*) Situation Clause (Registered Office Clause)
(*iii*) Object Clause
(*iv*) Liability Clause
(*v*) Capital Clause
(*vi*) Association Clause (Subscriber Clause)

(*i*) **Name Clause:** The memorandum of every company must contain the name of the company. In case of public company the name must be ended with the word 'limited' and a private limited company must have 'Private Limited' word at the end of its name. The company may choose any name which must not be undesirable in the opinion of the Central Government. Section 25 of this Act permits Charitable Companies formed to promote art, commerce, religion, science etc., under the licence granted by the Central Government, registered with limited liability without the word 'Limited' as a part of its name.

The Department of Company Affairs (Government of India) has formulated certain guidelines for deciding cases of making a name available for the registration of the company. Also the proposed name should not be identical with or too closely resemble the names of an already existing company.

In addition, the name of a proposed company must not contravene the provisions of the Emblems and Names (Prevention of Improper use) Act 1950. This Act prohibits the use of certain names and emblem (*a*) UNO and WHO (*b*) Indian National Flag (*c*) the official seal and emblem of Central or State Government, and (*d*) the name and picrtorial presentation of Mahatma Gandhi and the Prime Minister of India.

Once the name of a company is registered, it must be printed or affixed on the outside of every office or a place of business in a conspicuous position, in letters easily legible, in the language in general use of the locality. The name of the company must also be engraved on the seal of the company and mentioned in all notices, advertisements, bills, letter heads etc. Non-compliance of these provisions renders the company and its officers in default liable to fine (Section 147).

(*ii*) **Situation Clause (Registered Office Clause):** Every company must have a registered office. It determines domicile of a company. It contains name of the state in which the registered office of the company is to be situated.

The registered office of the company is an address where company's statutory books including register of members, register of debenture holders, register of charges, minute books of general meeting etc., are kept. And all other communications including notices are sent in this address.

Though the address of a registered office of a company is not to be given in the memorandum at the time of incorporation, within 30 days from its incorporation the address of registered office must be communicated to the Registrar of Companies.

(iii) **Object Clause:** Undoubtedly a company is formed to achieve some objectives. These objectives are contained in an object clause. This clause prescribes scope of activities to be carried on by the company. The company cannot do anything outside its object clause any act done beyond it will be ultra-vires and void. Such act cannot be ratified even by the consent of all shareholders. However, a company can do all those activities which are incedental and consequential upon the objects maintained in this clause. For example, trading company has an implied power to borrow money, draw and accept bills of exchange. The object clause makes it clear to its members that for what purpose their money is going to be utilised and what is the area and scope of operation of the company.

The object clause must be carefully drafted and it must be clear and unambiguous. While drafting it, the following points must be taken care of:

(*i*) The object of the company must be legal one.

(*ii*) These objects must not be inconsistent to any provisions of this Act.

(*iii*) The object must not be against public policy.

(*iv*) Not only the main objectives, but also other objectives incidental and subsidiary to main objectives should be stated clearly in this clause.

However it is to be remembered that the main objective shall be pursued by the company immediately after its incorporation. But to start business included in other objectives, the company shall have to pass special resolution or an ordinary resolution and get the sanction of the Central Government.

(iv) **Liability Clause:** This clause contains nature of liability of the members of the company. It must specify whether liability of the member is limited up to the nominal value of shares held by them or to an amount of guarantee given by them. It means that in the former case liability of the members is

limited only up to unpaid value of the nominal value. In case fully paid shares are allotted, liability of the members will be nil. And in case of limited by guarantee, the liability of the members goes beyond the nominal value of shares up to the guaranteed amount which the company can demand only in the event of liquidation of the company. This clause shall not be included in the case of unlimited company.

(*v*) **Capital Clause:** Every company (whether limited by shares or limited by guarantee) having a share capital must state the amount of its share capital with which the company is proposed to be registered. Such capital is known as 'Authorised or Nominal capital'. This clause shall also state the number and value of shares into which the capital of the company is divided. These shares are of a fixed value or amount. This fixed value is known as 'Par' or 'Nominal' value.

The amount of authorised capital should be determined by taking into account future need of capital particularly in case of expansion of business. It is because the company cannot issue more shares than are authorised by the memorandum.

(*vi*) **Association or Subscription Clause:** In this clause the subscribers to the Memorandum of Association make the following declaration, "We the several persons whose names and addresses are subscribed are desirous of being formed into a company, in pursuance of the Memorandum of Association and we respectively agree to take number of shares in the capital of the company set opposite our respective names."

According to Section 12 of this Act, the memorandum must be signed by at least 7 subscribers in case of a public company and 2 subscribers in a private company. Each subscriber should sign in the presence of at least one witness. Each subscriber must take at least one share and write opposite his name in the memorandum, the number of shares he is subscribing for.

Alteration of Different Clauses in the Memorandum

Alteration in any one or more clauses of memorandum is very difficult task. According to Section 16 of the Act, "a company shall not alter the conditions contained in its memorandum except in case, in the mode and to the extent, for which express provision is made in the Company Act."

In other words, an alteration in any clause of memorandum can be made by adopting the following procedure laid down in this Act:

(*i*) **Change of Name:** The name of the company can be changed at any time by (*a*) passing special resolution at a general meeting of the company and with (*b*) the written approval of the Central Government.

But no approval of the Central Government is needed if the change of name involves only the addition or deletion of the word 'private' on the conversion of a public company into a private company or vice-versa.

In case a company is registered with a name which is considered undesirable by the Central Government, it may change its name only by passing ordinary resolution and obtaining the approval of the Central Government.

The change of name must be communicated to the Registrar of Companies within 30 days of passing of the said resolution. Consequently, the Registrar shall enter new name in the Registrar of Companies and shall issue a fresh certificate with necessary alteration.

(ii) **Change of Registered Office:** A company is at liberty to shift its registered office from one place to another within the same city by passing Board's resolution and informing the Registrar within 30 days of the change. But in case the registered office is to be shifted from one city to another with the same State, special resolution is to be passed by the company to this effect.

(*a*) In order to shift registered office of the company from one State to another, special resolution is to be passed in the general meeting of the company.

(*b*) This resolution is to be confirmed by the Central Government. The Central Government will ensure that sufficient notice has been given to the shareholders, debenture holders and to every person or class of persons whose interest will be affected by such change. The consent of every creditor has been obtained to such alteration or his claim has been either discharged or secured. The Central Government shall cause notice to be served on the Registrar who shall be given a reasonable opportunity of appearing before the Central Government and state his objections or suggestions, if any, with respect to the alteration. The Central Government may confirm alteration on such terms and conditions as it thinks fit.

(*c*) A certified copy of the order of Central Government together with printed copy of memorandum must be filed with the Registrars of both the States within 3 months of such order. The Registrar of each of the States shall register the same and certify under his hand the registration thereof.

(*d*) The registered office is shifted to its new location in the other State and notice of new address is given to the Registrar within 30 days of shifting the office.

(*iii*) **Change in Object Clause:** The object clause is very important having wider implications. It is therefore that some restrictions have been imposed on the company on its right to alter this clause.

According to Section 17(1) of this Act, the object clause and registered office can be altered only if the change enables the company:

(*i*) to carry on business more economically or more efficiently.

(*ii*) to attain its main purpose by new or improved means.

(*iii*) to enlarge or change its local area of operation.

(*iv*) to carry on some business which can be suitably combined with the present business of the company.

(*v*) to restrict or abandon any of its objects specified in the memorandum.

(*vi*) to amalgamate the company with any other company.

(*vii*) to sell or dispose of the whole or any part of undertaking of the company.

The change in object clause has now become internal matter of the company. A company may alter its objects by passing special resolution and filing the same with the Registrar within 3 months of passing, such resolution together with a copy of the altered memorandum of association.

(*iv*) **Change in Liability Clause:** Generally the company cannot alter the liability clause of memorandum for increasing liability of the members. The liability of the member can be increased only with their consent in writing. However, the limited liability of directors can be converted into unlimited liability only by passing special resolution. The alteration of liability clause requires confirmation by the Registrar of Companies.

(*v*) **Change in Capital Clause:** The nominal or authorised capital of a company can be increased as provided in Section 94 of this Act. A company limited by shares if so authorised by its articles, may alter the conditions of its memorandum so as to increase its share capital by such amount as it thinks expedient by issuing new shares. This power can be used by the company when it has issued all its authorised capital and requires more funds.

This alteration in the share capital must be made by the company in General Meeting by passing ordinary resolution to this effect. In case share capital is increased, notice thereof must be filed with the Registrar of Companies within 30 days of passing such resolution. The Registrar of Companies shall record the increase and make necessary alteration in the company's Memorandum of Association.

Doctrine of Ultra-Vires

A Memorandum of Association of a company is its charter or constitution. Particularly the contents of its object clause defines and prescribes the area and scope of the operations of the company. Therefore any act or transaction which is beyond or outside the scope of object clause is ultra-vire the company and therefore null and void.

Generally the term 'ultra' means beyond and 'vire' means powers. Thus the doctrine of 'ultra-vires' implies that any transaction and act which is outside the ambit of its object clause is deemed to be ultra-vire or beyond the powers of the company. All such transactions or activities are null and void and cannot be ratified by the company in spite of having consent of all shareholders of the company. Though the company has a separate legal entity, its powers are limited to the contents of various clauses of its memorandum.

The basic purpose of this doctrine is to ensure that the interest of members, creditors and outsiders is fully protected. It is because an application of this doctrine forces the company to use member's money for the object known to them and already mentioned in the memorandum. Similarly, the creditors are assured that the assets of the company are used for authorised purpose.

Ultra-vires acts can be divided into the following three categories:

(*i*) Ultra-vires the Company Act.

(*ii*) Ultra-vires the Memorandum of Association.

(*iii*) Ultra-vires the Articles of Association.

(*i*) Ultra-vires the Company Act: In case any act is done contrary to the provisions of the Act or which is inconsistent to these provisions, these acts are considered ultra-vires the Act and shall be void. These acts can not be ratified even by an unanimous resolution of all the shareholders. For example payment of divided out of capital, free distribution of bonus shares, purchasing its own shares and reducing the share capital without complying with legal formalities laid down in this Act, are ultra-vires the Act.

(*ii*) Ultra-vires the Memorandum: The memorandum is a constitution or charter of a company. It lays down and defines the powers of the company. The object of the company is also determined by it. A company cannot do anything beyond the purview of object clause, therefore any act done in contravention of the object clause shall be ultra-vires the memorandum and shall be void. It cannot be ratified even by passing unanimous resolution by all shareholders.

The doctrine of ultra-vires was first applied in the famous case of **Ashbury Railway Carriage And Iron Co *vs* Riche.** In this case the company was incorporated to make and sell or lend on hire railway carriages and wagons and to carry on the business of mechanical engineers and general contractors. The director of the company made a contract with Riche, a firm of railway contractors to finance the construction of a railway line in Belgium. The contract was ratified by the company by passing special resolution at its general meeting. The House of Lords held that the contract was ultra-vires the memorandum and therefore void. And it could not be ratified by the shareholders.

This doctrine was further affirmed by the Supreme Court in a case of **Mudaliar *vs* LIC of India.**

***(iii)* Ultra-vires the Articles:** The acts which are ultra-vires the articles of association but are within the powers of the company are considered as ultra-vires the articles. For example, payment of interest on advance calls at a rate higher than allowed by the articles. Such acts are also void, but the company in General Meeting may alter articles by passing special resolution and ratifing unauthorised acts.

Effects of Ultra-vires Transactions

(*i*) Any act ultra-vires the company shall be void and it cannot be enforced against the company.

(*ii*) An act ultra-vires the company cannot be ratified even by unanimous resolution of all the shareholders.

(*iii*) Not only outsiders against the company but also the company cannot enforce such transactions or acts against the outsiders.

(*iv*) When the ultra-vires acts have been done or is about to be done, the member of the company can approach the court and get an injunction restraining the company from proceeding with such acts.

(*v*) The directors of the company can be held personally liable for any loss caused by an ultra-vires transaction.

2. ARTICLES OF ASSOCIATION

Meaning and Nature

Articles of Association is also an important document of a company. Basically it contains rules relating to the management of internal affairs of the company.

According to Section 2(2) of the Companies Act, "Articles of Association of a company as originally framed or as altered from time to time in pursuance of any previous company law or of this Act."

The articles of a company contains detailed rules and regulations for carrying out the business of the company. Though every company need not register articles with the Registrar, the management of every company is governed by the articles.

Taking into account the role played by articles in the management of the company, **Lord Cairns** observed in **Ashbury's** case that "the articles play part subsidiary to the memorandum of association. They accept the memorandum as a charter of incorporation, so accepting it, the articles proceed to define the duties, the rights and powers of the governing body as between themselves and the company at large and mode and form in which the business of the company is to be carried on, and the mode and form in which changes in the internal regulations of the company may from time to time be made."

The articles contain the power of directors, officers and of the shareholders as to voting etc. The rights, duties and the powers of the company vis-a-vis the members are also included in the articles of association. The articles of association may be regarded as an agreement not only between the members and company, but members *inter-se* also.

Registration of Articles

According to Section 26 of the Act, every private company, an unlimited company and a company limited by guarantee must have its own articles and it should be registered along with the memorandum. But a public company limited by shares may either have its own articles or it may adopt Table A of Schedule I of the Company Act. The fact of adoption must be endorsed on the face of Memorandum of Association.

The articles of private company must contain three restrictions given under Section 3(I) (*iii*) of this Act.

The articles of association must be printed, divided into paragraphs, numbered consecutively and signed by each subscriber of the Memorandum of Association in the presence of at least one witness who shall attest the signature and shall likewise add his address, description and occupation if any [Section 30].

Contents of Articles

The articles of association of a company contains rules and regulations for the internal management of the company. These rules and regulations may be related to the following matters:

(*i*) The extent to which Table A is applicable.

(*ii*) Share capital shares and their value and division of shares into equity and preference shares, if any.

(*iii*) Rights of each class of shareholders and procedure for variation of their rights.

(*iv*) Increase, alteration and reduction in share capital.

(*v*) Procedure relating to allotment of share, making of calls and forfeiture of shares.

(*vi*) Transfer and transmission of shares.

(*vii*) Lien of the company on the shares allotted to the members for the amount unpaid in respect of such shares.

(*viii*) Appointment, remuneration, powers, duties etc., of directors and officers of the company.

(*ix*) Conversion of shares into stock.

(*x*) Notices of meetings, voting rights of members, quorum, poll and proxy etc.

(*xi*) Audit of accounts, transfer of amount to reserve and declaration of dividend etc.

(*xii*) Borrowing powers of the company and mode of borrowing.

(*xiii*) Adoption of preliminary contracts.

(*xiv*) Issue of share certificates.

(*xv*) Keeping of different registers.

(*xvi*) Use of common seal of company.

(*xvii*) Board meeting and proceeding thereof.

(*xviii*) Arbitration provisions, if any.

(*xix*) Winding up of the company.

However, the articles must not contain anything which is against the law of land and the Companies Act, public policy and ultra-vires the memorandum. Any such thing shall be inoperative and void. For example, the articles must not contain a rule permitting the payment of dividend out of capital because according to Section 205 the dividend can be paid only out of profits.

Alteration of Articles

According to Section 31 of this Act, a company has a statutory right to alter its articles of association. It empowers the company to alter or add to its articles of association. This Section further provides that subject to the provisions of this Act and to the conditions contained in the Memorandum, a company may by special resolution alter its articles.

However, alteration in the articles for converting a public company into a private company will be legally effective only on the approval of the Central Government.

Though the Companies Act gives wide powers to the members of the company to alter its articles, such alteration should be made bona fide for the benefit of the company as a whole and not only for the benefit of majority of the shareholders. It is however to be remembered that articles of association cannot be altered in such a way as to be contrary to whatever is given in the Companies Act or in company's memorandum. The alteration in the articles can be carried out subject to the following limitations.

Limitations or Restriction or Power to Alter Articles

(*i*) The alteration in the articles proposed to be made must not be in conflict with whatever is contained in Memorandum of Association.

(*ii*) The alteration in the articles must not be inconsistent with any provisions of the Companies Act.

(*iii*) The alteration in the articles cannot be made in such a way as to include anything which is illegal under the Companies Act and other law of land.

(*iv*) The alteration must be bona fide being made for the benefit of company as a whole and not for majority of shareholders.

(*v*) The alteration which has the effect of compelling members to take or subscribe for more shares or in any way increasing his liability will not be binding on the existing member unless he gives their consent in writing.

(*vi*) A company may pass special resolution and convert uncalled capital into reserve liability, to be called up only at the time of winding up. But reserve liability once created cannot be unreserved but may be cancelled on reduction of capital.

(*vii*) No alteration in the articles can be made for converting a public company into a private company without the approval of the Central Government.

(*viii*) No alteration in the articles can be made which results in discrimination between the majority shareholders and minority shareholders as to give benefit to the former.

(*ix*) No alteration to the articles can be made which enables the company to commit breach of contract with third party.

(*x*) An alteration must not be inconsistent with an order of the court.

In order to alter articles of association, a copy of special resolution authorising the alteration must be filed with the Registrar within 30 days of passing such resolution. According to Section 40, an alteration should be noted in every copy of articles of association issued after the date of alteration.

Distinction between Memorandum and Articles

The basic points of distinction between memorandum of association and articles of association are:

(*i*) **Nature:** The memorandum of company is a charter or constitution on the basis of which a company gets incorporated. But articles are basic rules for the internal management of a company which are considered to be subsidiary to the memorandum.

(*ii*) **Contents:** The memorandum contains fundamental conditions upon which alone the company is allowed to come into existence. While as articles of association contains rules and regulation which are to be followed in the internal management of the company.

(*iii*) **Agreement:** The memorandum of association is an agreement between a company and outsiders dealing with the company. Thus an outsider who want to transact with the company must go through the contents of the memorandum. But articles of association is an agreement between company and members of the company who form the company and who are the owners of the company.

(*iv*) **Scope:** The scope of memorandum is wider than the scope of article of association. The acts which are ultra-vires the memorandum are totally void and cannot be ratified even by all shareholders. But the acts which are ultra-vires the articles within memorandum are irregular and can be ratified by the shareholders.

(*v*) **Alteration:** Alteration in the clauses of memorandum is comparatively very difficult, while as articles of association can be altered easily by passing special resolution.

(*vi*) **Filing of document:** It is compulsory to file memorandum of a company with the Registrar to get the company registered. But a public limited company limited by shares need not file articles with the Registrar. It may rather choose to adopt Table A of the Companies Act.

(*vii*) **Purpose:** The purpose of memorandum is to ensure that the money of shareholders is being used for authorised object and to enable outsiders to make transaction with the company which are within its purview. But main purpose of articles of association is to provide rules and regulation to facilitate internal working of the company.

Construction Notice of Memorandum and Articles

In order to incorporate a company memorandum and articles of association are required to be registered with the Registrar of Companies. On registration these two document become public documents. These documents are available for public inspection either in the registered office of the company or in the office of the Registrar.

Every person who deals with the company, whether shareholders or outsiders is presumed to have read these documents and is deemed to know contents of these documents. This is called 'constructive notice of memorandum and articles of association'. The net legal effect of this doctrine is that if a person deals with a company in a manner which is inconsistent with the provisions contained in its memorandum or articles, he must be deemed to have dealt with the company at his own risk and loss and shall have to bear the consequences thereof. For example, if a person enters into a contract with the company and supplies some material to the company. But the company refuses to pay on the ground that this contract is ultra-vires the company, the supplier cannot plead that he did not know the provisions of the memorandum of association of the company.

Doctrine of Indoor Management

The doctrine of indoor management is an exception to the rule of constructive notice. It protects the interest of the person who deals with a company. According to the rule of constructive notice, a person dealing with the company is presumed to have read and understood the contents of these two documents. On the basis of information given in these documents if he is satisfied, that the company has got power to make proposed transaction, he is not required to do anything more in this regard. Even he is not bound to enquire into the regularity of any internal proceedings of the company. He is entitled to presume that the provisions of articles of association have been complied with by the company. This is known as 'doctrine of indoor management' which basically seeks protection of outsiders against the company.

According to the doctrine of indoor management if the transaction appears to be within the powers of the company, the company cannot escape liability by showing that there was some irregularity while following the procedure. And the outsiders dealing with the company cannot be presumed to have constructive notice of such procedural failure.

Example: In case the articles of association permits a company to borrow money by passing ordinary resolution in General Meeting, the lender of money is not presumed to have a constructive notice of prescribed procedure for holding a meeting and passing resolution. It will be deemed that the company must have complied with prescribed procedure. Thus the company cannot escape liability by pleading that the meeting has not been properly held.

In the case of **COUNTRY OF GLOUCESTER BANK *vs* RUDRY MERTHYR & CO.** A person was issued a mortgage deed to which the seal of the company has been affixed at a Board meeting at which no quorum was present. It was held that mortgage deed is valid because the mortgagee has no means of knowing irregularity in the internal management of the company.

Exceptions: The doctrine of indoor management is subject to the following exceptions:

(*i*) **Knowledge of Irregularity:** A person dealing with a company, having knowledge of an irregularity regarding the internal management of the company, cannot claim protection under this doctrine. In the case of **Howard *vs* Pokent Ivony**, the directors were empowered to borrow money up to of £1000 and for above they were required to get sanction of shareholders. The directors themselves lent money to the company in excess of borrowing powers without the consent of shareholders. It was held that the directors had a notice of the internal irregularity and therefore the company was liable to them only for £ 1000.

(*ii*) **Negligence:** In case a person who deals with the company does not take trouble of reading these documents to find out whether the proposed transaction is within the purview of the company, he is not allowed to claim any benefit under the doctrine of indoor management. In the case of **Anand Bihari Lal *vs* Dinshaw & Co.,** a person accepted a, transfer of company's property from its accountant, without verifying that power of attorney executed in favour of the accountant by the company before accepting a transfer. Since the transaction was apparently beyond the scope of accountant's authority, the transfer was held void.

(*iii*) **Forgery:** The doctrine of indoor management will not be applicable when the document relied upon by the outsider turns out to be forged one. The company is not liable for forgeries committed by its officers. In the case of **Ruben *vs* Great Fingall Ltd.**, the secretary of a company forged the signature of two directors on a share certificate issued to the plaintiff. The company refused to accept him as a shareholder. It was held that the forged certificate is a pure nullity and the doctrine of indoor management is not applicable to causes of forgeries.

(*iv*) **Circumstances Inviting Enquiry:** Where a person dealing with a company could have discovered the irregularity, but he did not do so; such person cannot get protection under the doctrine of indoor management. In the case of **Underwood Ltd.** ***vs*** **Bank Of Liverpool**, a director deposited cheques drawn in favour of the company in his personal account. The bank was held liable because the act of director was of unusual nature which should have been enquired by the bank.

3. PROSPECTUS

After having obtained certificate of incorporation from the Registrar, a private company can start business. But a public limited company, generally needs huge capital which is to be raised by inviting public for subscribing its shares and debentures. This is done by issuing a document which is known as 'prospectus.'

The main objective of issuing prospectus is to inform prospective investors about the business, its management, capital structure and financial position of the company. By doing so, they can be made interested in the company for making investment.

Meaning and Nature of Prospectus

According to Section 2(36) of the Companies Act, prospectus means any document described or issued as prospectus and includes any notice, circular, advertisement or other document inviting deposits from the public for the subscription or purchase of any shares in or debentures of a company."

In simple words, a prospectus may be defined as an invitation made to the public for subscribing the shares and debentures of the company. However, a prospectus must not be considered as an offer, rather it is an invitation to make an offer to a prospective investor.

Thus the person who is willing to subscribe shares and debentures of the company would fill up share application form and submit the same together with required application money. On receiving application forms, the Board of Directors of the company will make an allotment of shares. As soon as an allotment letter is communicated to the applicant, it amounts to acceptance on the part of directors and agreement is formed between the shareholder and the company.

In this way prospectus may be considered as an important document, which becomes the foundation of an agreement between the shareholders and the company.

In Section 67 of this Act the term public has been explained as, "it includes any section of the public whether selected as members or debenture holder of the company concerned or as clients of the person issuing the prospectus or in any other manner."

Thus any invitation made by the company even to a particular section of the public will be considered as a prospectus. However, a document is deemed to have been issued to the public if it is to be open to anyone who wants to invest his money in the company.

In a case, **Sherwell *vs* Combined Incandescent Mantles Syndicate** an invitation for subscribing shares of the company was made to a few friends of the directors. It was held not amounting to an offer to the public.

But the Company (Amendment) Act 2000 has amended Section 67, by adding a Sub-section (3) to it. According to this amendment, any offer or invitation for subscribing share and debentures, to 50 or more persons will be treated as an offer made to the public. However this stipulation will not apply to non-banking financial companies and public financial institutions.

When Prospectus is not Required to be Issued (Section 56)

A company need not issue a prospectus in the following cases:

(*i*) A private limited company.

(*ii*) When promoters and directors intend to raise the capital from their personal contacts without making offer to public.

(*iii*) When shares are offered to underwriters.

(*iv*) When the company intends to raise capital only from the existing shareholders through the right issue.

(*v*) When the shares and debentures to be offered are uniform in all respects with the shares and debentures issued previously and dealt in or quoted in a recognised stock exchange.

Registration of Prospectus

The prospectus must be registered with the Registrar on or before its publication. The registrar shall register it on the fulfilment of the following legal requirements:

(*i*) The guidelines of disclosure and investor's protection issued by SEBI (Securities and Exchange Board of India) with regard to public issue must be complied with.

(*ii*) That every prospectus must be dated and that date shall be taken as a date of publication provided nothing contrary is proved.

(*iii*) It must state all matters and reports which are required to be set out under Section 56 of this Act.

(*iv*) The prospectus shall not include statement purporting to be made by an expert, if he is in any way connected with formation or management of a company.

(*v*) In case such statement is included in the prospectus it shall not be issued without the consent of an expert and declaration about the consent and that he has not withdrawn his consent must also appear in the prospectus.

(*vi*) The prospectus shall also be accompanied by the consent in writing of the person if any, named therein as a broker, legal advisor, attorney, solicitor, banker etc., of the company or the intended company.

Contents of Prospectus

The information given in the prospectus becomes base for the prospective investors to invest their money in a company. It is therefore the Companies Act ensures that full and correct disclosure of all material and essential information regarding the company has been made.

The Act provides that every prospectus issued by or on behalf of the company must state the matters and set out reports specified in Schedule II of the Companies Act, 1956. This Schedule has been revised by the Central Government in 1991. As per the revised schedule the prospectus must contain the following information:

(*a*) Name of the company and address of its registered office.

(*b*) The names and addresses of the promoters.

(*c*) The main objects of the company.

(*d*) The names, addresses and occupation of manager, managing director and directors.

(*e*) The size of present issue and preferential allotment to the promoters and others.

(*f*) the date of opening and closing of subscription and date of earliest closing of the issue.

(*g*) The names and addresses of company secretary, legal advisor, auditor, banker and brokers to the issue.

(*h*) In case of issue of debentures, the name and address of trustee under debenture trust deed.

(*i*) Consent of directors, solicitors, managers, bankers, expert and banker to the issue.

(*j*) The provisions in the articles of a contract regarding appointment, remuneration or compensation for loss of office of directors, managing director and manager.

(*k*) The amount payable on application and allotment of each share.

(*l*) The detail of option to subscribe for securities in the 'depository mode'.

(*m*) The amount of minimum subscription, on the receipt of which the directors may proceed to allot shares.

(*n*) Names of regional stock exchange and other stock exchanges where application has been made for listing the present issue.

(*o*) Names and addresses of underwriters, underwritten amount, commission payable to them.

(*p*) Material details about the project, its location, plants, machinery, technology, process, collaboration, performance guarantee, infrastructural facilities, implementation of project and progress so far.

(*q*) The nature of product, consumer or industrial, approach to marketing, proposed marketing set up and export possibilities.

(*r*) The details of any public issue made by the company during the last three years or made by other listed companies under the same management.

(*s*) The details of outstanding litigations and prosecution.

(*t*) Management perception of risk factors including foreign exchange rate fluctuation, availability of raw material, and marketing of product.

(*u*) The disclosure of credit rating obtained from CRISIL (Credit Rating and Information Science of India Ltd.)

(*v*) Expenses about the present issue, including fee payable to advisors, registrar and managers to the issue.

(*w*) Particulars of property to be acquired by the company including names and addresses of the vendors, purchase price and mode of payment.

(*x*) An amount of benefit given to the promoters or officers of the company within two preceding years.

(*y*) A reasonable time and place at which the copies of all balance sheet and profit and loss account may be inspected.

(*z*) A declaration that all relevant provisions of the Companies Act, guidelines issued by the Central Government and SEBI (Security Exchange Board of India) regarding prospectus have been complied with.

Reports to be Set Out in the Prospectus

In addition to these matters, Part II of the Revised Schedule requires that the following reports to be set out in the prospectus:

(*i*) An auditor's report showing (*a*) profit or loss in each of the last five years, (*b*) assets and liabilities at the last date to which accounts were made up, (*c*) rate of divided paid by the company in respect of each class of shares during the preceding five financial years, and (*d*) similar details with regard to subsidiary companies.

(*ii*) In case the company proposes to acquire any business, a report should be made by the chartered accountant whose name should be disclosed upon the profit and losses and assets and labilities of the business for the preceding five years.

(*iii*) In case the proceeds or any part of proceeds of the issue of shares and debentures are or is to be applied directly or indirectly in the purchase of any business the report similar to the one in (*ii*) above is required to be set up.

Under the latest guidelines issued by the Central Government it must be printed in every prospectus and every application form issued by the company that (*a*) an applicant should submit only one application for the total number of shares required, (*b*) an application may be made in single or joint name (not more than three), (*c*) two or more applications in single on joint names will be deemed to be multiple applications, (*d*) the board of directors reserves the right to reject in its absolute discretion all or any multiple applications, and (*e*) where applications are signed under the power of attorney related documents must be submitted to the registrar for perusal and return.

Statement in Lieu of Prospectus

A public limited company may intend to raise capital from the private sources. In such cases, the company does not invite public for subscribing its capital, there is no need to issue prospectus, rather the company will have to file statement in lieu of prospectus with the Registrar of Companies at least three days before it can make any allotment of shares or debentures. The statement in lieu of prospectus must be prepared in accordance with Schedule III of the Companies Act 1956. This document contains information similar to the prospectus. It must be signed by all directors and copy thereof must be filed with the Registrar at least three days before the allotment of shares.

In case allotment of shares in made without filing this document with the Registrar of Companies, the allottee may avoid allotment within two months after the statutory meeting.

Misrepresentation in the Prospectus and its Consequences

Issue of prospectus by a company basically aims at subscribing its share capital. The information given in the prospectus is to be gone through and analysed by the prospective investors as to make decision to invest money in the company. The prospective buyers of the shares or investors are entitled to full and true disclosure in the prospectus.

As a matter of rule the prospectus must, therefore, tell the truth, the whole truth and nothing but the truth. It must present true picture of the company in terms of its financial position and management. In other words, it must not misrepresent or conceal material facts as to mislead prospective investors in making their decision for investing money in the company.

It was held in a case, **Peek *vs* Gurney** that a prospectus containing false, misleading, ambiguous or fraudulent statement of material facts will be deemed to the misleading prospectus.

In another case, **Rex *vs* Kylsant**, a company issued a prospectus, and did not contain any untrue statement. One of the statement given in the prospectus disclosed rate of dividend paid for a number of years. But actually, the dividends were paid not out of profit but out of capital gains. This fact was not disclosed in the prospectus. It was held that it was an omission of important statement, therefore, allottees of shares are entitled to avoid allotment and use another legal remedies under the Companies Act.

Legal Remedies Available to Allottee of Shares

In case an allottee of shares who had applied for the shares on the faith of prospectus containing untrue statement or omitting material facts has the following legal remedies:

(*i*) Remedies against the company.

(*ii*) Remedies against the directors and promoters.

(*iii*) Remedies against the expert.

(*i*) **Remedies Against the Company:** The person who has purchased the shares from the company on the basis of statements given in the prospectus has the following remedies against the company:

(*a*) ***Rescission of Contract:*** The contract of purchasing shares by the allottee on the basis of misleading and untrue statements given in the prospectus, is voidable at his option. He can repudiate the contract by returning shares to the company and getting back his money. The right to rescind the contract is solely governed by the rule of misrepresentation, which is applicable to a contract.

In order to exercise the right of rescission the following conditions must be fulfilled:

- The representation must be of a false nature. It includes positive misstatement or an active concealment of facts.
- The misrepresentation must be of material facts. The material facts are those which in a significant way affect judgment of a person to purchase or refrain from purchasing shares. However misrepresentation of law does not provide any remedy to the aggrieved party. For example, the statement given in the prospectus for issuing shares at a discount more than prescribed in the Act does amount to misrepresentation of law. And an aggrieved party has no remedy, because ignorance of law is no excuse.
- The aggrieved party in entitled to claim right of rescission provided he must have relied and acted upon such misrepresentation. This right is available only to original allottees and not to the buyer of shares in the open market.
- The right of rescission can be exercised by the allottee provided the prospectus which contained misleading statement must have been issued by the company or by someone authorised to issue, for example, board of directors.
- The suit for rescission must have been filed within reasonable period of time before the winding up of the company.

(*b*) ***Damages for Fraud:*** The aggrieved party who has purchased the shares of a company on the basis of misstatement or material omission in the prospectus can also claim damages. The company could be held liable for damages provided such prospectus was issued by the company or by someone authorised by the company and those acting on behalf of the company must have acted fraudulently and the aggrieved party has suffered a financial loss.

(*ii*) **Remedies Against Promoters and Directors of the Company:** According to Section 62 of this Act, where the prospectus is issued inviting persons to subscribe the shares and debentures of the company, the following persons shall be liable to compensate all those who subscribe for shares on the faith of prospectus for the losses suffered by them on account of untrue and misleading statement:

(*a*) Every person who is director of the company at the time of issue of prospectus.

(*b*) Every person who authorises himself to be named in the prospectus as director.

(*c*) Every promoter of the company.

(*d*) Every person including an expert who has authorised the issue of prospectus.

Defence Available: The promoters, directors or anyone who is responsible for issuing the prospectus may escape liability provided he proves anyone of the following:

(*a*) that he withdrew his consent to act as director before the issue of prospectus and that it was issued without his authority or consent, or

(*b*) that the prospectus was issued without his knowledge or consent and on becoming aware of it he gave reasonable notice of that fact, or

(*c*) that he withdrew his consent after the issue of the prospectus but before allotment and gave reasonable public notice to this effect, or

(*d*) that he had reasonable ground to believe that statements made were true and he honestly believed to be true, or

(*e*) the statement was correct and fair summary or copy of an expert report, or

(*f*) the statement was made by an official or is an official document.

(iii) **Remedies Against Experts:** The term expert includes an engineer, a valuer, an accountant and any other person whose profession gives an authority to a statement made by him.

An expert is liable in respect of his own untrue statement, wrong report or valuation made by him and included in the prospectus, to pay compensation to the aggrieved party. However he shall not be liable if he proves that:

(*a*) He withdrew his consent before filing a copy of the prospectus to the Registrar.

(*b*) On becoming aware of untrue statement, before allotment, withdrew his consent and gave public notice to his effect.

(*c*) He was competent to make statement and believed on reasonable grounds that it was true.

Criminal Liability for Misstatement in the Prospectus

Section 63 of this Act provides for criminal liability for misstatement. It provides that where as prospectus contains a misstatement every person who authorised the issue of prospectus shall be punishable with imprisonment for a term which may extend to two years or a fine which may extend to fifty thousand rupees, or with the both unless he proves:

(*a*) that the statement was immaterial.

(*b*) that he had reasonable ground to believe up to time of the issue of the prospectus that the statement was true.

However Section 63(2) exempts expert from this liability. Furthermore according to Section 68 of this Act, any person who knowingly or recklessly makes any statement, promise or forecast which is false, deceptive or misleading or dishonestly conceals material facts so as to induce another person to subscribe to the shares of the company shall be punishable with imprisonment for a term which may extent to five years or a fine which may extend 1,00,000 rupees or with both.

Self Prospectus

The provisions regarding shelf prospectus and information memorandum were included in Companies (Amendment) Act 2000 under Section 60A and 60B. The self prospectus means a prospectus issued by any financial institution or bank for one or more issues of securities or class of securities specified in that prospectus.

The basic objective of self prospectus is to minimise the repetition of issue of prospectus. It is because self prospectus remains valid for a period of one year. During the period of validity the company by issuing memorandum of information can make fresh issue without issuing fresh prospectus.

Section 60A of Companies (Amendment) Act, 2000

Section 60A of this Act provides that:

(*a*) Any financial institutions, public sector bank or scheduled bank whose main business is 'financing' shall file a self prospectus with the Registrar.

(*b*) Such shelf prospectus will be valid for one year from the date of first issue of securities under the prospectus. Thus the company need not file fresh prospectus when it makes new offer of securities during the validity of prospectus.

(*c*) At the time of making subsequent offer of securities within valid period of self prospectus, the company has to file information memorandum on all material facts relating to new charges created, change in financial position have occurred between first and subsequent offers of securities. The memorandum has to be filed, within such time, before the offer of securities as may be prescribed by the Central Government.

(*d*) An information memorandum shall be issued to the public along with self prospectus.

(*e*) An update information memorandum is to be filed every time, when an offer of securities is made. Such memorandum along with self prospectus shall constitute the prospectus.

Explanation: For the purpose of this Section 'financing' means making loans or to subscribing in the capital of a private industrial enterprise engaged in infrastructural financing or such other company as the Central Government may notify in this behalf.

Information Memorandum

Section 60B of this Act provides for the provisions regarding 'Information Memorandum'. Information memorandum means 'a process undertaken prior to the filing of a prospectus by which a demand for the securities proposed to be issued by a company is elicited, and the price and the term of issue for such securities is assessed, by means of a notice, circular, advertisement or document.'

The provisions regarding information memorandum are:

(*i*) A public company making an issue of securities may circulate information memorandum prior to filing a prospectus.

(*ii*) A company inviting subscription by an information memorandum shall be bound to file prospectus prior to the opening of the subscription list and the offer as a 'Red Herring prospectus' at least three days before the opening of offer.

Explanation: Red Herring prospectus means a prospectus which does not have complete particulars on the price of the securities offered and quantum of securities offered.

(*iii*) Any misstatement or omission of material facts in the information memorandum or the 'Red Herring Prospectus' will attract same civil and criminal liabilities as applicable in case of the prospectus.

(*iv*) Any variation between information memorandum and 'Red Herring Prospectus' shall be highlighted and individually intimated to the persons invited to subscribe the issue. Failure to intimate will amount to misstatement in the prospectus.

(*v*) In the event of issuing company or the underwriters to the issue have received advance subscription by way of postdated cheques or 'stock invest' they shall not encash such subscription without having individually intimated the prospective subscribers of the variation and without having offered an opportunities to such subscribers to withdraw their application. The prospective subscribers shall have a right to withdraw his application within 7 days of an intimation of variation.

(*vi*) Upon the closing of the offer of securities, a final prospectus stating therein the total capital raised whether by way of debt or share capital, the closing price of securities and any other details which were not complete in Red Herring Prospectus' shall be filed wih the Securities and Exchange Board of India (SEBI) and Registrar of Companies.

Deemed Prospectus

In order to prepare and file and issue prospectus, a number of legal formalities given in this Act are to be complied with. It is therefore, to avoid issue of prospectus a company may issue securities to 'Issue House', who would then make further offer of sale of these securities to the public by advertisement.

Any document by which the offer, for sale of shares and debenture to the public is made shall for all purposes be deemed to be a prospectus.

According to Section 64(2) of this Act an offer for sale shall be presumed if,

(*i*) The offer of sale is made within 6 months of the allotment to the issuing house, or

(*ii*) At the date of the offer for sale, the company has not yet been paid the whole consideration for the shares.

(*iii*) It must also state that the consideration received by the company for those shares and debenture, and the place and time at which the contract between he company and issuing house can be inspected.

(*iv*) An offer for sale is deemed to be a prospectus and therefore, any misstatement included therein will make the company and directors of the company liable the same way as they would be in case of misstatement in the prospectus. In addition, the issuing house would also be liable for such misstatement.

(*e*) an offer for sale made by a company must be signed by two directors or their agents authorised and it must be sent for registration.

REVIEW QUESTIONS

1. What do you understand by 'memorandum of association'. Explain the purpose of this document.
2. Discuss various clauses which are included in the memorandum of association.
3. Describe the procedure for changing the object clause of memorandum.
4. Explain the doctrine of 'ultra-vires'. Discuss the effect of 'ultra-vires transaction'.
5. Define 'articles of association'. Enumerate the contents of articles.
6. How the articles can be altered? Discuss the limitations on powers of the company to alter articles.
7. Explain the distinction between memorandum and articles of association.
8. What do you mean by 'doctrine of indoor management'? Explain various exceptions to this doctrine.
9. Define 'prospectus'. Explain the purpose of prospectus.
10. Enumerate some of the important particulars which are required to be included in a prospectus.
11. Discuss the situations when prospectus is not required to be issued.
12. Does prospectus require registration? Discuss the legal requirements which are to be fulfilled for the registration of the prospectus.
13. Write note on 'Statement in lieu of prospectus'.
14. Discuss the various legal remedies, which are available to an aggrieved party who has purchased shares on the faith in the statement given in prospectus which is untrue or false.
15. Explain the extent of criminal liability for misstatement in the prospectus.
16. 'A prospectus must state truth and nothing but truth.' Explain.
17. What is 'self prospectus'? Explain the legal requirements of the Companies Act regarding self prospectus.
18. Discuss 'information memorandum' and legal provisions regarding it.
19. What is deemed prospectus? When it issued?

PRACTICAL PROBLEMS

1. The articles of association of a company contained a clause that articles cannot be altered. Is this clause valid? (Hint: No, the company is empowered to alter its articles.)
2. Company 'A' lends money to company 'B' on a mortage of its assets and the procedure laid down in the articles was not complied with. The directors of the two companies were same. Is mortgage is binding upon company 'B'? (Hint: No, the directors had knowledge of irregularity.)
3. The articles of a company provided that the directors could allot shares to outsiders with the consent of the company in the general meeting. The directors allotted shares to the plaintiff without seeking consent of the company in the general meeting. Is allotment valid? (Yes, the allottee of shares could assume that the consent of the company had been sought in the general meeting.)
4. The secretary of a company issued a share certificate in favour of 'A'. The secratary has forged signatures of the directors on the certificate and affixed the seal without authority. Is certificate binding on the company? (Hint: No, A forgery is nullity.)
5. A public limited company was formed. The articles of association of the company provides that A would be the solictor for the company and shall not be removed except on the ground of misconduct. Can the company remove Mr. 'A' from his position though he is not guilty of fraud? (Hint: Yes, the company can remove him, because articles do not constitute agreement with outsider.)
6. The object clause of memorandum of association of an X & Coy. Ltd. authorised it to do trading in mangoes. The company entered into partnership with 'A' and traded mangoes. The company incurred a liability to 'A'. But the company refused to admit the liability. Is the stand of the company is legally valid? (Hint: Yes, company cannot enter into partnership with 'A'.)
7. The memorandum of association of a company contains object clause of improving and encouraging breeding of poultry. The clause also contains that no remuneration shall be paid to the members of the governing body. But later, the company passed special resolution for giving equitable remuneration to the members who are rendering services to the company. Is such alteraction valid? (Hint: Yes, it is covered under Section 17 of this Act.)

8. Ramesh applied for 100 shares in a company in pursuance of prospectus. He has already paid application money on the applied shares. Can he withdraw his application to buy the shares? (Hint: Yes, because shares have not been allotted to him.)
9. Ram applied for 200 shares in the company on the basis of prospectus which contained a misstatement. Shares were allotted to Ram who transferred them to Shyam. Can Shyam rescind the contract on the ground of mistatement ? (Hint: No, only the original allottee of shares can rescind the contract).
10. Suresh an allottee of shares came to know about misstatement in the prospectus. But he did not take any action against the company for nine months and attended general meeting of the company. Now he wants to rescind the contract. Will he succeed? (Hint: No, he cannot rescind the contract after nine months and by attending general meeting, he has lost his right.)
11. An advertisement in the newspaper that some shares arc still available for sale according to the terms of the prospectus of the company which may be obtained by making application on those shares. Can the offer be valid? (Hint: No, the directors of the company are liable for non-compliance with the requirements of the Act, because is was held to be a prospectus issued to the public.)
12. A prospectus containing untrue statement was issued by the directors on behalf of the company. The prospective buyer 'B' received copy of it but did not buy any shares originally in the company. The allotment was completed and several months afterwards, B purchased 200 shares of that company in open market. Has B got a right to rescind the contract on the ground of misstatement? (Hint: No, he has purchased shares in open market, he cannot rescind the contract.)

31

Directors

LEARNING OBJECTIVES

- Understand the basic concept of director.
- Examine position of director in company.
- Identify the role of directors in the management of the company.
- Analyse duties and powers of the director.

INTRODUCTION

The joint stock company commands huge public resources at its disposal. It is in the public interest that these resources must be utilised as efficiently as possible. In order to manage the business of a company which involves use of these resources some human agency is needed. It is because being an artificial person in the eyes of law, the company cannot act itself.

It is therefore the equity shareholders who are in large number and are real owners of the company, elect their representatives known as directors who are given the responsibility to direct, manage and control the business of the company.

Director Defined

According to Section 2(13) of this Act, "Director includes any person occupying the position of director, by whatever name called."

This definition is not complete in all respect but even then it makes clear that to determine whether a person is a director or not, it is the position he occupies and functions and duties he discharges, will therefore be taken into account

Little more legally, director may be defined as a person appointed for managing the affairs of the company with a complete sanction of articles of association of the company.

Thus, instead of name or designation, the definition of director is based purely on two factors namely his functions and duties and legal sanction of his appointment and other matters related to him. Indeed, the directors are brain of the company which makes the company functional.

According to this Act only an individual can be appointed as a director and no director is empowered to act individually unless permitted by the Board of Directors in respect of any power or powers delegated to him.

POSITION OF DIRECTORS

The Company Act is silent regarding the legal position of directors in the company. Though the directors are appointed to manage the affairs of the company and are given powers and duties together with liabilities, but in which capacity they perform their functions and do needful for the management of the company is not clear.

The director, however, has been described as agent, trustee, managing partner or an employee of the company.

Directors as Agents

Directors are regarded as the agents of the company. It is because the company is an artificial person and cannot act at its own and it functions through the directors, who act as its agent.

In a case, **Ferguson *vs* Wilson** the court has explained agency relationship of the directors. "They are merely agents of the company. The company itself cannot act in its own person; for it has no person, it can only act through directors, and the case is, as regards those directors, merely the ordinary case of principal and agent, for wherever an agent is liable those directors will be liable. Where the liability is of principal and principal only the liability is the liability of the company." On the basis of the above it is clear that the relationship of directors with the company is governed by the agency relationship. Thus whatever the directors do on behalf of the company within the perview of memorandum and articles of the company, all such acts are legally binding on the company and the directors will have no personal liability for those acts.

Similarly is another case, **Re Desiraju Venkata Krishana Sarma** a company defaulted in paying of sales tax to the government. It was an offence punishable under Madras General Sales Tax Act. In an action against a director for the recovery of sales tax dues, the court held that the directors as agents could not be held personally liable for the payment of such dues.

However, it is also to be noted that notice given or information obtained by the directors will be considered notice to the company and information to have been obtained by the company.

Directors as Trustees

In many cases, the directors stand in a fiduciary relationship with a company. It is, therefore, under these situations they may be considered as a trustees of the company.

(*a*) ***Money and properties of the company:*** The company commands huge resources including money and properties at its disposal. Regarding the use of these resources, the directors are considered as trustees of the company and would be liable for mis-application and mis-utilisation of the resources.

(*b*) ***Powers delegated to the directors:*** The equity shareholders, who are the real owners of the company delegate powers to the directors. They are supposed to exercise the power in the best interest of shareholders.

(*c*) ***Secret profit:*** The directors are under legal obligation not to earn secret profit in the transactions made by them. In case they have earned, they must account for such profits.

(*d*) ***Trustee for the company:*** The directors act as trustee only for the company and not for individual shareholders.

Director as Managing Partner

The directors are elected representative of shareholders. The are empowered to manage and control the company in which other shareholders are dormant partners. Thus the directors manage the affairs of the company on behalf of shareholders as a managing partner.

However, it is to be noted that the director has no authority to bind another directors by his acts. But the acts of one partner are binding on another partner.

Directors as Employees or Servants

Though the directors of the company perform basic functions regarding the management of the company, they are not the employees of the company due to the following reasons:

(*a*) A director is not employed by the company, rather elected by the shareholders.

(*b*) He is not entitled to any preferential claim in respect of his salary and debts.

(*c*) A director is allowed to hold the office of directorship in more than one company.

Thus in a nutshell, the role and position of directors in a company is multi-dimensional. They discharge their obligations and perform their functions in a combined role of agent, managing partner, trustee and employee.

MINIMUM NUMBER OF DIRECTORS

According to Section 252 of this Act, every public company (other than a public company which has become such by virtue of Section 43A) must have at least three directors. The Companies Act does not provide for maximum number of directors. Thus any company subject to above mentioned statutory limits may prescribe maximum and minimum number of directors for its Board. The company is at liberty to reduce or increase the number of directors within prescribed limits in articles, by passing ordinary resolution in the general meeting to this effect.

According to Section 259 of this Act, in case of a public company any increase in the number of directors beyond the maximum limit as prescribed in articles must be approved by the Central Government, except where the increase in number of directors does not make the total number of directors more than 12.

Directors Representing Small Shareholders

A public company having paid up capital of Rs. 5 crore or more and having 1,000 or more small shareholders may have at least one director elected by small shareholders to represent them in the Board. However appointment of such nominee shall be subject to the Companies (Appointment of Small Shareholders Director) Rule 2001, notified by the Department of Company Affairs. These rules are:

(*a*) Small shareholders who intend to propose a person as their representative on the Board must give 14 day's notice before the shareholder's meeting. Such proposal must be endorsed by at least one tenth of total small shareholders in the company.

(*b*) Nominee must be small shareholder in the company.

(*c*) In case of listed public companies, the nominee shall be elected through postal ballot and in other cases, such nominee will be elected by majority.

(*d*) Such nominee director would not be eligible for appointment as whole time directors or managing director of the company.

(*e*) Such director shall hold office for maximum of three years.

(*f*) A person cannot hold office as small shareholder's director in more than two companies.

(*g*) A person who fails to pay call money for a period of 6 months from the last date, would not be eligible to be appointed such director.

(*h*) Failure to attend three consecutive meetings of the Board of Directors or absence from all board meeting for a continuous period of three months, whichever is longer, such director would require to vacate the office.

QUALIFICATION OF DIRECTORS (SECTION 270)

Though the Companies Act does not prescribe that director must hold qualification shares, the articles of the company, generally, requires director to hold certain shares, which must be held by them within two months of their appointment.

Any provisions in the articles of the company which requires a person to hold qualification shares before his appointment as director or to obtain them with shorter time than two months after his appointment shall be void [Section 270 (B)].

A director may procure qualification shares either from company directly or from the open market. Shares held by a firm in which director is a partner shall be sufficient to qualify him.

The nominal value of the qualification shares shall not exceed rupees 5,000.

In case the shares are held jointly, any one of the joint holders is entitled to be appointed as director.

A director appointed by the Central Government under Section 408 of this Act need not hold any qualification shares.

The articles of the company may require some directors to hold qualification shares and exempt others from holding qualification shares.

Disqualification of Directors

According to Section 270 of this Act, a person shall not be capable of being appointed as a director of a company if:

(*a*) He has been found to be a person of unsound mind by court.

(*b*) He is an undischarged insolvent.

(*c*) He has applied for being adjudicated as an insolvent, but application is pending.

(*d*) He has been convicted to any offence involving moral turpitude and sentenced to inprisonment for not less than 6 months.

(*e*) He has not paid calls for 6 months on shares held by him alone or jointly.

(*f*) He has been disqualified in pursuance of Section 203 of this Act.

(*g*) He is the auditor of the company.

(*h*) He holds office of directorship in more than 15 companies.

(*i*) He has not filed annual accounts and annual returns continuously for three financial years on or after 1 April 1999.

(*j*) He has been removed from the office of director by the decision of the high court.

DIRECTOR'S IDENTIFICATION NUMBER (DIN)

Under MCA 21 e-Governance Programme, the Concept of Director Identification Number has been introduced. The Companies (Amendment) Act 2006 has included Section 266 A to 266 G which contain the following provisions regarding allotment of Director Identification Number:

(*i*) Every individual who intends to be appointed as director of a company, as well as every existing director [appointed before commencement of the Company (Amendment) Act 2006] shall make an application for allotment of Director Identification Number to the Central Government in a manner (including electronic form) along with such fee as may be prescribed.

(*ii*) The Central Government shall, within one month from the receipt of the application, allot a DIN to an applicant in such manner as prescribed.

(*iii*) No individual who has already been allotted DIN, shall apply, obtain or possess another DIN.

(*iv*) Every existing directors shall within one month of receipt of DIN, intimate his DIN to the company or companies wherein he is a director.

(*v*) Every company shall within one week of receipt of intimation, furnish the DIN of all its directors to the Registrar of Companies or any other officer as may be specified by the Central Government.

(*vi*) Every person or company, while furnishing a return, information or particulars required to be furnished under this Act shall quote DIN in such return, information or particulars in case they relate to the directors or contain any reference of the director.

(*vii*) Any individual, director or a company referred in the aforestated sections contravenes any provisions of these sections, every such individual, or director or the company, as the case may be who or which, is in default shall be punishable with a fine which may extend to Rs. 5,000 and where the contravention is continuing one, with a further fine which may extend to Rs. 500 for everyday.

APPOINTMENT OF DIRECTORS

First Directors

The first directors of a company are usually named in the articles of the company. In case the articles do not name them, the subscribers to the Memorandum of Association may appoint them according to the procedure laid down in the articles.

But in case, they are not named in the articles and subscribers to memorandum do not appoint them, the subscribers to the memorandum who are individuals, shall be deemed to be the first directors of the company (Section 254). Such directors will hold office till the first annual general meeting of the company.

It is however to be noted that it is only an individual subscriber who can be deemed to be director, because of requirement of Section 253. In case all subscribers to the memorandum happened to be body corporate, the company will then have to go without directors till the first directors are appointed under Section 255.

Subsequent Appointment

Unless the articles provided otherwise, all subsequent appointment of directors will be made in the general meeting which may be either annual general meeting or an extraordinary general meeting of the company.

Rotational Retirement of Directors

The articles of a company may provide for retirement of all directors at annual general meeting. In the absence of the provision in the articles, one third of total number of directors, in a public company or private company which is subsidiary of a public company, may be permanently appointed who shall not subject to rotational retirement. The remaining two-third of the total number of directors shall be subject to retirement by rotation (Section 255) of the two-third, one-third, must retire by rotation at every annual general meeting (Section 256).

However, directors nominated by financial institutions and those appointed by the Central Government under Section 408 of this Act shall not to be subject to retirement by rotation.

At the annual general meeting, at which the directors retire by rotation, the company may fill up vacancy by appointing retiring or some other person thereto.

A person, other than retiring director shall be eligible for appointment to the office of directors at any annual meeting, if he or other member who intends to propose him, has served upon the company a notice in writing at least 14 days before the meeting. The company will notify its members of his candidature at least 7 days before the meeting by serving them individual notices.

A person, who is proposed as a candidate for the office of directors is required to file with the company his consent to act as director, if appointed. However a person who has already served as director in the immediate preceeding term, need not furnish his consent.

Appointment of Directors by the Board

The Board of Directors of a company is empowered to appoint directors under the following circumstances:

(*i*) **Additional Directors:** In case the articles of the company permits, the board of director can appoint additional directors subject to maximum number prescribed in the articles. Such additional directors shall hold office only up to the date of next annual general meeting of the company.

(*ii*) **Alternate Directors:** The articles of association of company may also permit the board to makes appointment of alternate directors, during the absence of director the more than 3 months, from the State in which meetings of the Board are ordinarily held.

An alternate director shall not hold office for a period longer than that permissible to the original director in whose place he has been appointed. He shall vacate office as soon as original director returns to the State or the term of the original director expires.

(*iii*) **Causal Vacancies:** In case the office of the director falls vacant before his term expires (may be due to death or resignation or disqualification), the Board is empowered to fill casual vacancy. Any person so appointed shall hold office only up to the date up to which the director in whose place, he is appointed would have held the office. Such appointment can be made by the Board only with regard to vacant post of director appointed in general meeting.

Appointment of Directors by Debenture Holders and Financial Institutions etc: The directors may be appointed by financial institutions who have got stake in the company. They may do so by nominating a person to the board of the company. Such appointment will be subject to articles of association of the company and powers to nominate directors by the institution which is authorised to do so under the relevant Act.

However, the number of such directors cannot be more than one-third of the total strength of the Board. These directors are not subject to retirement by rotation. The articles of the company may also give such right of appointing directors to the debenture holders and other creditors.

Appointment of Directors by Central Government

In order to prevent oppression and mismanagement, the Central Government is empowered to appoint any number of directors on the order passed by Company Law Board as being necessary to safeguard the interest of the company, interest of shareholders or interest of public. This power can be exercised by Company Law Board either on the reference made to it by the Central Government or on the application of not less than one hundred members of the company.

The directors so appointed shall hold an office for a period of not more than three year on any one occasion. Such directors need not hold qualification shares and are not subject to retirement by rotation. They can be removed by the Central Government at any time. They will also not be included in the total number of directors for the purpose of counting two-third number or any other proportion of the directors.

REMOVAL OF DIRECTORS

By Shareholders

According to Section 284 of this Act, a company (whether public or private) by passing an ordinary resolution and giving a special notice can remove a director before expiry of his period of office. The shareholders who want to move resolution for the removal of director must give notice to the company at least 14 days before the meeting. The director, who is to be removed shall have the right of being heard at the general meeting.

On receipt of notice of resolution from the shareholders the company shall send a copy thereof to the director who is to be removed.

A vacancy created by the removal of a director may either be filled at the same meeting, provided special notice to this effect has been give, or, it may be filled as a casual vacancy.

A director, so appointed, will vacate the office on the expiry of the term of director so removed.

A director, who has been removed so, cannot be reappointed. But in case of this being wrongful termination of appointment, he can claim compensation. The shareholders, however cannot remove the following directors:

(*a*) Appointed by the Central Government.

(*b*) Director of a private company holding office for lifetime as on 1 April 1952.

(*c*) A director elected by proportionate representation under Section 265 of this Act.

(*d*) A director appointed by the Central Government under IDRA Act 1951.

(*e*) A special director appointed under Sick Industrial Companies (Special Provision) Act 1985.

(*f*) Is director appointed by any financial institutions.

(*g*) A nominee director.

(*h*) A director appointed by CLB Tribunal under Section 402.

Removal by Central Government

The Central Government can ask Company Law Board to enquire upon and order removal of a director under the following situations:

(*a*) That any person connected with, the conduct and management of the affairs of a company is guilty of fraud, misfeasance, gross negligence and breach of trust.

(*b*) A person has not conducted and managed a company in accordance with sound business principles or prudent commercial practices.

(*c*) A person has conducted and managed a company in a manner which is likely to cause or has caused serious injury or damage to the interest of trade, industry or business to which such company pertains.

(*d*) Such person has conducted and managed business of a company in a manner to defraud its members, creditors and prejudice to public interest.

Removal by Company Law Board

The Company Law Board is also empowered to terminate appointment of director on an application made to it for prevention of oppression or mismanagement. The Company Law Board can exercise this power provided it is of the opinion that company's affairs are being conducted in a manner prejudicial to public interest or in a manner oppressive to any member or members or that by reason of any material change in the management and control of the company. The director so removed cannot be appointed in any company for a period of five years, unless permitted by Company Law Board.

POWERS OF DIRECTORS

In a joint stock company, ultimate authority to manage and control the affairs of the company rest with the equity shareholders, who are real owners of the company. But they are in large number and not interested and capable of managing company. Thus they elect some of their representatives known as directors and delegate the power to manage and control the company's affairs to them.

However, it is to be noted that no director of a company in his individual capacity has power to act on behalf of a company in any way unless Board of Directors has given him authority.

In a case, **Shubh Shanti Service Ltd *vs*. Manjula. S. Agarwalla,** it was held that any director acting individually has no power to act on behalf of the company, in respect of any matters except to the extent to which any power or powers of the board have been delegated to him by the board as permitted by the Companies Act or any other law."

Thus it becomes clear that individual director has a power only as a member of the Board. The powers of the Board can be exercised by the Board of Directors in a collective manner through board meetings. And individual directors shall have only such powers as are vested in them by the Memorandum and Articles of the company.

General Powers of the Board (Section 271)

(*a*) The board is empowered to exercise all such powers and to do all such acts and things as the company is authorised to exercise and do.

(*b*) But the board cannot exercise any power or do any act or thing, which is directed or required whether by this Act or any other Act, or by memorandum or articles or otherwise to be exercised or done by the company in general meeting.

(*c*) No regulation made by the company shall invalidate any prior act of the board, which would have been valid, if that regulation had not been passed.

Powers to be Excercised at Board Meetings (Section 292)

The Board of Directors shall exercise the following powers on behalf of the company only by passing resolutions at the meetings of the Board:

(*a*) The power to make calls on shareholders, in respect of money unpaid on their holdings.

(*b*) The power to authorise the buyback.

(*c*) The power to issue debentures.

(*d*) The power to borrow money other than on debentures.

(*e*) The power to invest funds of the company.

(*f*) The power to make loans.

Other Powers Excercisable at Board Meetings

In addition to the power under Section 292 of this Act, the Companies Act provides some other powers which must be exercised only at the meetings of board. Such powers are:

(*a*) To fill up casual vacancy on the board (Section 262).

(*b*) Appointing additional directors (Section 260).

(*c*) Appointing alternate directors (Section 313).

(*d*) Giving consent to contracts in which director is interested (Section 29).

(*e*) Recommending the rate of dividend for shareholder's approval at the annual general meeting.

(*f*) Making declaration of solvency to make winding up of company as member's voluntary winding up (Section 488).

(*g*) Appointing first auditor of the company and filling up any casual vacancy in the office of the auditor (Section 244).

Restrictions on Powers of Board (Section 293)

This Section imposes certain restrictions on the powers of the Board of Directors. Such power can be exercised by the board only with the consent of a company in general meeting. These are:

(*a*) The power relating to the sale or lease or otherwise disposal of undertaking of the company (whole or substantial part).

(*b*) Remitting or giving a time for the repayment of any debt due by a director.

(*c*) Investing the amount of compensation received by the company on compulsory acquisition in securities other than trust securities.

(*d*) Borrowing money in excess of aggregate paid-up capital of the company and its free reserves.

(*e*) Contributing to charitable and other funds not directly relating to the business of the company or the welfare of its employees in excess of Rs. 50,000 in any financial year or 5% of the average net profit for the last three financial years.

DUTIES OF DIRECTORS

The directors occupy key position in the management of a company. In fact, Board of Directors, is considered as chief organ of the management of a company. A lot of powers of different nature have been vested in them. It is only under their direction and command, the business of the company is carried on. However it should also be noted that they may develop some personal interest out of their strategic position in the company. With a view to minimise misuse of power on their part specially for private gains, a number of duties have been imposed upon them. These duties may be grouped as under General duties and Statutory duties.

General Duties

The directors are overall incharge for the management and control of company's affairs. In this regard they have certain general duties to perform. These are:

(*a*) **Fiduciary duties:** The directors stand in fiduciary relationship (based on trust and confidence) with the company. On the one hand, a company procures funds on the goodwill of directors and on the other, investors and creditors repose confidence on them for an efficient utilisation of these funds. Thus they have a duty to act bona fide for the benefit of the company.

Where a director of a company procures some business from another company to which he has provided some business facilities of his company, he is under duty to account for such profits received by him.

Similarly he has a duty to hand over the profits to the company, which he earns on the sale of property which he has acquired only by reason of his being a director.

(*b*) **Duty of reasonable case:** While performing the various functions, the directors are under duty to exercise reasonable degree of care and diligence as the person of their knowledge and status normally does. Failing which, they would be held liable for negligence.

However, a mere error of judgment on their part will not amount to negligence and in this case they would not be held liable.

With reference to the duties of director, in case of **City Equitable Fire Insurance Co. Romer L.J.** made the following observation, "In ascertaining thc duties of a director, it is necessary to consider the nature of company's business and the manner in which, the work of the company is reasonably in the circumstances and consistently with the articles, distributed between the directors and other officials of the company."

(*c*) **Duty of attending board meeting:** Though it is not obligatory for directors to attend board's meeting, a director cannot afford to remain absent from the meetings of the board. According to Section 283 (g) of this Act, a director failing to attend three consecutive meetings of the board or absenting himself from all board meetings for three consecutive month, whichever is longer, without being on leave, shall be liable to vacate his office. Thus a director is under duty to attend board's meetings regularly.

(*d*) **Duty to disclose interest:** To manage the company's affairs, a director may be required to make many transactions. Being in a fiduciary relationship it is his duty to disclose his personal interest, if any to the board in any transaction made by him.

(*e*) **Duty not to delegate:** In order to manage a company, the directors get an authority delegated to them by the equity shareholders. Therefore they cannot further delegate, which is already delegated to them.

But in practice, they may allow, some of the officials of the company to share their workload. These officials are the employees of the company and not accountable to the directors.

However, the directors may delegate part of their authority to the officials of the company, provided, they are authorised to do so by the articles of the company or nature of business requires such delegation.

Statutory Duties

The management and control of a company is to be carried out strictly according to provisions of the Companies Act. The directors of the company have some statutory duties under the various provisions of the Act. These are:

(*i*) Directors are prohibited from getting any loan from a public company or its subsidiary of which he is director (Section 295).

(*ii*) Directors are required to obtain board's sanction and prior approval of the Central Government for certain contracts made with the company (Section 297).

(*iii*) Every director is required to give notice to the company regarding shares and debenture held by him (Section 308).

(*iv*) Directors must not receive remuneration in contravention of Section 309 and Section 198 of this Act.

(*v*) Directors cannot hold any office of profit without the consent of the company, by special resolution (Section 314).

(*vi*) Directors are not to receive any compensation of a loss of office, except in case of managing director, whole time director or director manager (Section 318).

(*vii*) Directors must not receive any compensation for transfer of the whole or any part of undertaking of the company (Section 319).

(*viii*) A director cannot receive any compensation from the transferee, for loss of office resulting from transfer of all or any of the shares of the company, unless it is approved by the company in the general meeting (Section 320).

LIABILITY OF DIRECTORS

So long as, a director acts within the scope of their authority under the provisions of the articles and the Companies Act, they do not incur any liability for that beyond that their liabilities may be classified as:

1. Civil liability
2. Criminal liability

1. Civil Liability of Directors

The directors have civil liability toward third parties and towards the company.

Liability to third parties: Since the directors act on behalf of the company as agents they do not have any personal liability to third parties. They would however, be personally liable to third parties in the following cases:

(*a*) When they make contract in their own name, or sign a contract without affixing seal of the company or agree to bind themselves for such contracts.

(*b*) Where they make pre-incorporation contracts.

(*c*) When the directors act fraudulently against third parties while dealing with them.

(*d*) Where the prospectus contains misstatement.

(*e*) Where the directors fail to refund application money in the event of the company fails to receive minimum subscription or where the company makes irregular allotment.

(*f*) When their liability is made unlimited.

(*g*) When they act beyond the scope of their authority.

(*h*) When they commit civil wrong against third party.

Liability to the company: The directors will be held liable to the company in the following cases:

(*a*) **Negligence:** While performing the duties, if the directors have been negligent, they will be liable to compensate the company for any loss which arises out to such negligence. However an error of judgment will not amount to such negligence, provided they acted bona fide for the benefit of the company and have taken reasonable care.

(*b*) **Misfeasance:** In case the directors are found quality for wilful misconduct they will be liable to company for any loss arising out of it. During the course of winding up, if the directors commit an act to misfeasance, the court may complete to repay the money or property or any part thereof respectively.

(*c*) **Break of trust:** The directors hold the position of trustee with regard to money and property of the company. In case they mis-apply or mis-manage the company's funds and properties, they will be liable to account for such misapplications.

(*d*) **Ultravires acts:** In case the directors act beyond the limits of memorandum or do any other prohibited acts, they will be liable for any loss to the company.

2. Criminal Liability of Directors

In case the directors of a company fail to comply with the provisions of the Companies Act, they incur criminal liability. They may be punishable with a fine or imprisonment or both under the following situations:

(*a*) The director, who fraudulently induces a person to invest money in the company shall be punishable with imprisonment for a term which may extend to 5 years or with fine of up to Rs. 1,00,000 or both (Section 68).

(*b*) In case, a prospectus includes any untrue statement or misstatement, the directors who authorises the issue of the prospectus shall be punishable with imprisonment up to 2 years or fine of Rs. 50,000 or both (Section 63).

(*c*) A director, who is responsible for destruction, mutilation, alteration or falsification of any book, paper or security shall be punishable with imprisonment for a term, which may extend to 7 years and shall also be liable for fine (Section 539).

In addition to these, the directors of a company may also be held criminally liable under the following situations:

(*i*) Default in filing return as to allotment (Section 75).

(*ii*) Supplying wrong information to the Central Government (Section 248).

(*iii*) Granting loans to the directors in violation of the provisions of this Act (Section 295).

(*iv*) Making false declaration of company's solvency [Section 488 (3)].

(*v*) Failure to attach board's report with the balance sheet (Section 217).

(*vi*) For holding office of director in more than 15 companies (Section 273).

(*viii*) Default in holding annual general meeting (Section 168).

REVIEW QUESTIONS

1. Define the term 'director'. Explain legal position of directors in the management of a company.
2. 'The role of directors is composite and multidimensional.' Comment.
3. The Companies Act does not provide for any share qualification for the director.' Comment.
4. The board of directors of the company can do all such acts and use powers as the company may do.' Comment.
5. What are the powers of board of directors? What restrictions have been imposed on them by the Companies Act?
6. How the directors are appointed in the company? Discuss.
7. Discuss legal provisions of the Companies Act regarding removal of the director from his office.
8. Explain various modes of appointment of directors.
9. Discuss legal provisions of the Companies Act regarding Director Identification Number (DIN).
10. Explain various duties of the director.
11. What are the general powers of board of directors? Which powers are to exercised only at a meeting?
12. Write note on the liabilities of the director.

PRACTICAL PROBLEMS

1. One of the directors of a company being interested in the allotment of shares to his nominees, not being entitled to vote at board meeting on this subject, but voted in the meeting. Excluding his vote, there was no quroum for passing resolution giving sanction to the above allotment. Can company avoid the allotment? (Hint: Yes.)
2. A private company having two directors at its board has been converted into a public company under Section 43-A. Is it obligatory for the company to appoint a third director, as required for a public company? (Hint: No, Section 25.)
3. A public limited company has 15 directors at its board, 4 of whom are not subject to retirement by rotation. Is the board constituted valid? (Hint: Yes, Section 252.)
4. X & Coy has 9 directors at its board. At a meeting of the board only 3 directors are present. One of the directors deemed to be interested in a contract to be approved and disclosed his interest and did not participated in the deliberation, thereafter. The board passed a resolution approving the contract. Is the action of the board valid? (Hint: No, due to lack of required Quorum of 1/3.)
5. The articles of the company exempted the directors of a company from liability for the act of default and negligence. Due to negligence of the director, the company was compelled to pay certain amount of compensation to third party. What is the liability of the director to the company? (Hint: No, director can escape his liability for the act of negligence.)

■■■

32

Meetings and Proceedings

LEARNING OBJECTIVES

- Understand basic concept of meeting.
- Get familiar with various types of meetings.
- Analyse the need and importance of these meetings.
- Remember requisites of a valid meeting.

Although the equity shareholders are the real owners of a company, they have ultimate command and authority for managing company. But these shareholders cannot act as an individual for exercising their authority. Rather they make decisions, transact business and do all other needful acts collectively in duly convened meeting by majority vote. Thus meetings are the means of action for the purpose of transacting lawful business and making decisions.

In a case, **Bying *vs* London Life Association Ltd.,** it is held that' the underlying reason for requiring a company to hold meeting is that members shall be able to attend in person so as to debate and vote on matters affecting the company.' It make clear that through such meetings every member can express his opinion, can participate in debate and finally can exercise his right of voting at the meeting.

Such meetings of a company can be grouped up in the following two groups:

(*i*) Class Meetings

(*ii*) General Meeting

The class meeting represent a particular class of shareholders in a company. Such meetings are held to pass resolutions which will be binding only on the members of that class who are eligible to attend the meeting. Such meetings are convened either by the company or by the court to affect variation in the rights of that particular class of shareholders or in connection with a scheme of arrangement. A scheme of arrangement may involve reorganisation of share capital by the consolidation of shares of a different classes or by dividing shares of a particular class into different classes.

Though class meeting is not a general meeting, legal provisions regarding holding and conducting of general meeting are applicable on class meetings.

'General meeting' may be defined as a meeting which shall be attended by all members of a company. The resolutions passed in such meeting are binding on the members as well as on the company. The general meetings may be of the following types:

1. Statutory meeting
2. Annual general meeting
3. Extraordinary general meeting.

1. STATUTORY MEETING (SECTION 165)

It is the first official general meeting of the shareholders of a company. It is held only once in the lifetime of a public company. It is legally compulsory for all public companies (except unlimited) companies to hold statutory meeting.

According to Section 165 (1) of this Act, 'every company limited by shares, or limited by guarantee having a share capital must hold statutory meeting of members of a company after one month, but within six months of obtaining a certificate of commencement of business.'

Though a private company is not required to hold such meeting, but if it becomes a public company, if must hold such meeting within six months of its incorporation.

The basic objective of holding such meeting is to make the members of a company well aware about the position of assets and other properties acquired by the company. Such meeting also provides an opportunity to the members to discuss any matters related to the formation of the company.

Statutory Report: The directors of a company are required to send a statutory report to every member of the company at least 21 days before the day on which such meeting is to be held. The report must be certified as correct at least by two directors, one of whom shall be a managing director and by the auditor, on various matters related to them.

The statutory report shall set out following particulars:

(*i*) The total number of shares allotted, amount paid up thereon, if allotted other than cash, the consideration for which they have been allotted.

(*ii*) The total amount of cash received by the company in respect of all the shares allotted.

(*iii*) The abstract of receipts and payments made by the company up to the date within seven days of the date of report, and an account or estimate of the preliminary expenses of the company, showing separately, any commission or discount paid or to be paid on the issue or sale of shares or debentures.

(*iv*) The names, addresses and occupations of directors, managers, secretary and auditor and the change, if any, which have occurred since the date of incorporation of the company.

(*v*) The particulars of any contract, the modification if any which is to be submitted to the meeting for its approval.

(*vi*) The extent to which each underwriting contract has not been carried out and the reasons thereof.

(*vii*) The particular of any commission or brokerage paid or to be paid in connection with the issue or sale of shares and debentures to any director or to the manager.

Default in Holding Statutory Meeting: Any default in holding statutory meeting and filing statutory report to the Registrar is punishable with a fine. If there is delay in filing statutory report, such delay may be condoned by all members present in the meeting. A default in holding a statutory meeting or in delivering statutory report may result in the winding up of the company. The petition for winding up may be filed by a contributory.

2. ANNUAL GENERAL MEETING (SECTION 166)

The equity shareholders of a company can exercise their powers through annual general meeting. It is the most important meeting of the shareholders. In this meeting, the directors retire and seek re-election. The shareholders get an opportunity to disapprove election of any of the directors who has not been working efficiently. The shareholders can also exercise their right of reappointing or replacing the auditor of the company in this meeting.

Legal Provisions Regarding Annual General Meeting

Every company must hold, in each year, in addition to any other meeting, a general meeting. It is held year after year with a view to review the overall functioning of the company. The legal provisions of this Act regarding the general meeting are:

(*a*) **First annual general meeting:** The first annual general meeting of the company must be held within a period of not more than 18 months from the date of its incorporation. If it is held within that period, it shall not be necessary for the company to hold any annual general meeting in the year of its incorporation or in the following year [Section 166 (1)].

(*b*) **Subseqent meeting:** Every subsequent annual general meeting must comply with the following requirements:

(*i*) It must be held once in a calender year.

(*ii*) The gap between two annual general meetings must not exceed 15 months.

However, the Registrar may, for any special reason, extend the time of holding the annual general meeting (not being first annual general meeting) by a period not exceeding three years.

(*c*) **Time and place of annual general meeting:** Every annual general meeting shall be called for during business hours, on a day that is not a public holiday and shall be held either at a registered office of the company or at other place within the city, town or village in which registered office in situated [Section 166 (2)].

(*d*) **Notice:** The company must give 21 days clear notice to all members of the company. A notice of less than 21 days may be validated with the consent of all members entitled to vote at the meeting. The notice must contain information regarding the place, the day and the time of holding meeting together with details of the business to be transacted [Section 171 (1)].

A copy of director's report, audited annual accounts and auditor's report must be attached with every such notice [Section 219 (1)].

To hold annual general meeting is a statutory requirement for a company. If default is made in holding annual general meeting as per Section 166 and 167 of this Act, the company and every officer of the company, who is in default, shall be publishable with a fine which may extend to Rs. 50,000 and in case of continuing default, with a further fine which may extend to Rs. 2,500 for everyday, after the first, during which the default continues (Section 168).

(*e*) **Business transacted:** In normal practice the following ordinary business is transacted in annual general meeting [Section 173 (1) (*a*)]:

(*i*) Election of directors.

(*ii*) Appointment and remuneration of auditors.

(*iii*) The declaration of dividend.

(*iv*) The consideration of accounts, balance sheet and director's and auditor's reports.

Any other items on agenda except listed above will constitute 'special business' For transacting a special business the company must annex a statement with the notice giving details about the nature of business to be transacted.

3. EXTRAORDINARY GENERAL MEETING (SECTION 169)

All meetings other than the statutory meetings and annual general meetings are the extraordinary general meetings. Such meetings are usually called by the board of directors at any time. The main purpose of holding extraordinary meeting is to transact some urgent business, which is required to be done before holding of next annual general meeting.

The board of directors must call such meeting when it is requisitioned by the holders of at least one tenth paid up capital, having a right to vote on the matters of requisition. In case the company having no share capital such requisition can be made by those holding at least one-tenth of the voting power. The business which is transacted in such meeting is called 'special business'.

On receiving requisition, which must state the purpose of requisition, within 21 days, the directors must proceed to call the meeting which must be held within 45 days.

Resolution must be passed at properly held board meeting for calling extraordinary general meeting. The power of directors to call extraordinary general meeting is a fiduciary power, which must be exercised by the directors bona fide in what they consider is in the interest of the company and not for any collateral purpose (**Pergamon Press Ltd *vs* Maxwell**).

Where the requisitionists call such meeting at their own, they are entitled to recover the necessary expenses from the company.

A meeting called by requisitionists must be held in the manner, in which it is called by the board and in the requisitioned meeting, only that business can be transacted for which it has been expressly convened. It means only special business can be transacted in such meeting.

But where sufficient notice of an additional business has been given, the meeting could deal with such additional business also.

The requisitioned meeting may be held at a place other than the registered office of the company.

The company law board can also call extraordinary general meeting. According to Section 186 of this Act if for any reason, it is impracticable to call and conduct the meeting, the company may apply to the Company Law Board, which may either at its own or on the application of any director or any member, entitled to vote, order a meeting to the called, held and conducted in accordance with its directions.

The Company Law Board can direct that even one person present or represented by proxy shall be deemed to constitute a meeting. A meeting held in pursuance of Company Law Board's order shall be deemed to be a meeting of the company duly called, held and conducted [Section 186 (1)].

Requisites of Valid General Meeting

Any general meeting is said to be valid one, provided it has been properly convened, properly constituted and properly conducted. For every company, it is necessary to comply with all relevant provisions given under Sections 171 to 186 of this Act for holding a general meeting. In addition to these, all rules included in the article of the company regarding general meeting must be followed. A valid meeting has the following requisites:

(*i*) **Properly Convened:** A valid meeting must have been convened by a proper authority e.g., the party or a person who is legally authorised to call such meeting. The board of directors is a proper authority to convene a general meeting of the shareholders. By passing a resolution at the valid meeting of board, such meeting can be convened. The members of a company, under certain circumstances may convene extraordinary general meeting by requisition.

In case, a default is made in holding annual general meeting according to Section 166 of this Act, the Central Government may not withstand anything contained in the Act or in the articles, on the application of any member, under Section 167 of this Act call or direct the calling of a general meeting of the company.

In addition, the Company Law Board is also empowered to make order that the meeting of the company to be called, held and conducted in such a manner, CLB thinks fit.

(*ii*) **Proper Notice:** While giving a notice of meeting, the general rules, the rules prescribed in the articles and the rules laid down in the Companies Act must be complied with.

Notice of a meeting must be issued by a person who is authorised to do so. The proper authority for issuing such notice rests with Board of Directors, who in turn, delegate this power to the secretary of the company.

A proper notice of a meeting should be given to every member, auditor of the company and each director of the company, to the legal heir of a deceased member and to the official assignee or receiver of insolvent member.

The notice must be given at least 21 days before the date of meeting. The meeting may be held with a shorter notice provided:

(*a*) All members entitled to vote in general meeting give their consent.

(*b*) Members holding not less than 95% of paid up capital give their consent.

(iii) **Contents of Notice:** Every notice of a meeting shall specify the place and the day and hours of the meeting along with the statement of the business to be transacted thereat.

Where any item of special business to be transacted at the meeting, it will be deemed to be special, and therefore, the statement setting out various details about that item must be annexed with the notice.

Where any item of business includes any document to be approved in the meeting, the time and place where the document can be inspected must be specified in the statement.

The notice of a meeting must be sent to the members either in person or by post in his registered address or the address given by him for sending notice to him.

No fresh notice is required to be given in case of an adjourned meeting, because such meeting is considered as continuation of the original meeting.

(iv) **Requisite Quorum:** A Quorum implies a minimum number of members whose presence is required for holding and conducting a valid meeting.

Unless the articles of a company provides for larger number, as per Section 174 (1) five members personally present in case of a public company [other than public company which has become such by virtue of Section 43 (A)] and two members personally present in case of any other company shall be the quorum for general meeting.

Such quorum is ensured at the general meeting only at the beginning and not throughout. If within half an hour from the time appointed for holding a meeting of a company, a quorum is not present, the meeting if called upon the requisition of members shall stand dissolved.

In any other case, the meeting shall stand adjourned to the same day the next week, at the same time and place, or to such other day and at such other time and place as the board may determine. If at the adjourned meeting also a quorum is not present within half an hour from the time appointed for holding the meeting, the member present shall be a quorum [Section 174) (5)].

The quorum for a board meetings shall be one-third of its total strength or two directors, whichever is higher. The total strength means the total strength of board of directors as determined in pursuance of this Act, by deducting, therefrom, the number of the directors, if any, whose places may be vacant at the time, and interested directors means any director whose presence, cannot, by reason of Section 300 of this Act, count for the purpose of forming a quorum at the meeting of the board, at the time of discussion or vote on the matter.

(*v*) **Chairman:** In order to preside over proceeding of a meeting there must be a chairman. He is in-charge of the meeting and is responsible for its smooth and proper conduct. With regard to the position of Chairman the following provisions of Section 175 of this Act are applicable:

(*a*) Unless the articles of a company otherwise provide, the members personally present in the meeting shall elect one of themselves to be the Chairman thereof on a show of hands.

(*b*) If a poll is demanded on the election of chairman, it shall be taken forthwith in accordance with the provisions of this Act, the Chairman elected on the show of hands exercising all the powers of the Chairman under the said provisions.

(*c*) If some other person is elected Chairman as a result of poll, he shall be Chairman for the rest of the meeting.

However, it may be noted that the provision of Section 175 will not apply, where the articles provide for the appointment of a Chairman. The article, usually provides for rules similar to those contained in Articles 50 to 52 Table A, which govern the appointment of Chairman. These provisions are:

(*a*) The chairman, if any, of the board shall preside as chairman at every general meeting of the company (Article 50).

(*b*) If there is no chairman, or if he is not present within 15 minutes after the time appointed for holding the meeting or is unwilling to act as a chairman of the meeting, the directors present shall elect one of their member to be the chairman of the meeting (Article 51).

(*c*) If at any meeting no director is willing to act as chairman, or if no director is present within 15 minutes, after the appointed time for holding he meeting, the members present shall choose, one of their member to be the chairman of the meeting (Article 52).

Duties of chairman: The duties of a chairman include the following:

(*a*) He must act bona fide and in the overall interest of the company.

(*b*) He has duty to maintain order at the meetings and to ensure that the meeting is conducted properly.

(c) He must act in an impartial manner, giving an opportunity to every member including the minority to express their opinion on the matter transacted at the meeting.

(*d*) He must ensure that all relevant provisions of this Act and the articles have been complied with.

(*e*) He has a duty to give his ruling over points of order and on all other emergent questions.

(*f*) He must ensure that the proceeding of the meeting is duly recorded in the minutes. He must certify the correctness of the minutes by putting his signature.

(*g*) He must not dissolve or adjourn a meeting in an arbitrary manner. If he does so, the members may elect a new chairman.

Powers of chairman: In order to conduct a meeting in a proper and impartial manner, the chairman may exercise the following powers:

(*a*) To decide points of order and maintain his ruling on those points.

(*b*) To decide about priority order of speakers, demand a poll, and expel any unruly member.

(*c*) He is a casting vote, if the articles authorises it. It is important when equal votes are cast in favour and against the particular matter.

(*d*) He has a right to adjourn a meeting for a short while, in case of disorder in the house.

(*e*) He reserves the right to give his verdict on all emergent and incidental questions or about inclusion or non-inclusion of any matter in the minutes.

PROXIES (SECTION 176)

Proxy may be defined as a person to act and vote on behalf of a member at the meeting. If the proxy is empowered to vote only on a particular resolution he is called a 'particular proxy'. He is said to be a general proxy if he is authorised to vote on all resolutions in the meeting. He has no right to speak at the meeting, but he can put a question in writing and sending the same to the chairman.

The following legal provisions of the Act are related to proxies:

(*i*) Every member of a company, having a share capital has a right to appoint proxies, provided nothing contrary to it is in the articles.

(*ii*) The proxy is not allowed to vote, except on a poll.

(*iii*) The member of a private company is not allowed to appoint more than one proxy, unless the articles otherwise, provide.

(*iv*) Proxy must be lodged in the prescribed form duly stamped and signed by the member.

(*v*) Proxy must be lodged at the office of the company not later than 48 hours before the commencement of the meeting.

(*vi*) For every meeting a separate proxy is required.

(*vii*) A proxy need not be a member of the company.

(*viii*) A proxy will not be entitled to speak at the meeting, but he can ask a question in writing and giving it to the chairman.

(*ix*) The member of a company has right to inspect proxies lodged with a company after giving three days notice to the company.

(*x*) A proxy can be revoked by giving a notice to the company at any time before it is acted upon. And the member can prevent proxy from using the right to vote by attending and voting at the meeting.

(*xi*) A proxy will be duty appointed agent of a shareholder at the meeting of the company.

(*xii*) A company must not issue an invitation to a member for appointing any person as a proxy at its own expense. And failing which, every officer shall be punishable with a fine up to Rs. 10,000.

RESOLUTIONS

After having made a discussion on the matter of agenda, a decision is made on it. To make a decision a proposal or a motion is put to vote and adopted by majority. It is known as 'resolution'.

In other words, resolution refers to formal decision of a meeting on any matter of agenda discussed in the meeting. The resolutions passed in the meeting of a company may be of three types as:

1. Ordinary resolution
2. Special resolution
3. Resolutions requiring special notice

1. Ordinary Resolution [Section 189 (1)]

A resolution is said to be ordinary resolution if it is passed at the general meeting by a simple majority of shareholders who are entitled to vote in person or by proxy. Such resolution is considered to have been passed, if the votes cast in favour of a resolution are more than the votes cast against it.

An ordinary resolution is required and passed for the matters of an ordinary business, which is transacted in the Annual General Meeting such as passing of annual accounts, declaration of dividend, appointment of directors in place of those retiring and appointment of auditors.

The general meeting in which an ordinary resolution is to be put to vote, must have been called after giving the usual notice of 21 days.

A company is not required to file an ordinary resolution with the Registrar. But in case ordinary resolution is passed for conferring powers upon the directors it must be filed with the Registrar within 30 days of passing it.

Special Resolution [Section 189 (2)]

A resolution passed by three-fourth majority is known as 'special resolution'. In other words, when the votes cast in favour of the resolution by the members present or proxies allowed in the meeting are not less than three times of member of votes cast against the resolution, such resolution is called 'special resolution'. A resolution shall be a special resolution when:

(*a*) The intention to propose the resolution as a special resolution, has been duly specified in the notice calling the general meeting.

(*b*) The notice of 21 days as required under this Act has been duly given. The notice must be accompanied with an explanatory statement, setting out the particulars of the special resolution, and whether any directors and managers have any interest in the resolution.

(*c*) The votes cast in favour of the resolution (whether by show of hands or on a poll) by members, who being entitled so to do, vote in person or where, proxies are allowed, by proxy are not less than three times, the member of votes, if any, cast against the resolution by members, so entitled to vote.

The special resolutions are passed for making all executive and administrative decisions, which directly affect the interest of the company and majority of shareholders.

Some of the matters, on which special resolution is required to be passed are:

(*i*) Alteration of memorandum and articles of association of the company.

(*ii*) Issue of further shares, without resorting to pre-emptive rights.

(*iii*) Creation of reserve capital.

(*iv*) Reduction of share capital.

(*v*) Variation of shareholder's right.

(*vi*) Shifting of registered office of the company from one State to another.

(*vii*) Payment of interest out of capital.

(*viii*) Requesting the government to appoint inspectors for investigation.

(*ix*) Authorising a director to hold any office of profit.

(*x*) Making the liability of any managerial personal unlimited.

(*xi*) For voluntary winding up of the company.

3. Resolution Requiring Special Notice (Section 190)

Whereby any provisions contained in this Act or in the articles, special notice is required for any resolution, notice of the intention to move the resolution shall be given to the company not less than 14 days before the meeting at which it is to be moved. It will be exclusive of the day on which the notice is served or deemed to be served and the day of the meeting.

The company shall immediately, after the intention to move any such resolution has been received by it, give its members, notice of the resolution. It will be given in the same manner as it gives notice of the meeting or if that is not practicable, shall give them notice thereof, either by advertisement in a new paper having an appropriate circulation or in any other mode allowed by the articles. It must be done in not less than 7 days before the meeting.

Under this Act, special notice is required, for moving and passing a resolution on the following matters:

(*i*) Appointment, of a person as auditor other than retiring auditor (Section 225).

(*ii*) Provision that, retiring auditor shall not be re-appointed (Section 225).

(*iii*) Removal of directors before the expiry of their term (Section 284).

(*iv*) Appointment of a person as a director in place of the director removed (Section 284).

Resolution by postal Ballot [Section 192 (A)]: The Companies (Amendment) Act, 2000 (w.e.f. 15.6.2001) has facilitated a decision making in a company through postal ballot which would also include voting by electronic mode.

The provisions of this Section are applicable w.e.f. 15 June 2001, which are:

(*i*) Postal ballot would also include voting by electronic mode.

(*ii*) Where a company decides to pass any resolution by postal ballot, it shall send a notice to all shareholders along with draft resolution stating reasons therefore, and requesting them to send their assent or dissent in writing on a postal ballot within 30 days from the date of posting of the letter.

(*iii*) The notice shall be sent through registered post or by any other method prescribed by the Central Government.

(*iv*) The company is also required to send pre-paid envelope, along with the notice, to all the shareholders.

(*v*) If the drafted resolution is assented to by a requisite majority of shareholders, by means of a postal ballot, it shall be deemed to have been duly passed at a general meeting.

(*vi*) If the shareholder sends his assent or dissent in writing on postal ballot and thereafter, any person defaces or destroys the ballot paper or declaration of identity of the shareholder, such person shall be punishable with imprisonment up to 6 months or with a fine or, both.

(*vii*) Failure to comply with the above provisions shall make the company and every officer in default punishable with fine up to Rs. 5 lakh in respect of each such default.

The Central Government has notified the following list of the matters on which resolution shall be passed through postal ballot:

(*i*) Alteration in the object clause of Memorandum Association and Articles of Association.

(*ii*) Buyback of own shares by the company.

(*iii*) Issue of shares with differential rights in terms of voting right or dividend.

(*vi*) Sale of whole or substantially the whole of undertaking of a company.

(*v*) Election of small shareholder's directors.

(*vi*) Corporate restructuring and entering in new business.

(*vii*) Matters regarding the change in management of a company.

MINUTES OF MEETING (SECTION 193)

The term 'minutes' may be defined as a brief and accurate official record of the matters transacted at the meeting. Generally, it includes only the resolutions passed in the meeting.

According to Section 193 of this Act, every company must keep minutes of the proceedings of general meeting and board meetings, within 30 days of such meetings entries of the proceedings must be made in the books kept for that purpose. Each page of every such book shall be dated and signed; (*a*) in case of minutes of proceedings of meetings of the board or of a committee, thereof by the chairman of said meeting or the chairman of next succeeding meeting, (*b*) in case of minutes of proceedings of general meeting, by the chairman of the same meeting.

The minutes of each meeting shall contain fair and correct summary of the proceedings thereat. The chairman has discretionary power of inclusion and non-inclusion of any matter in the minutes. For a meeting of the Board or Committee of the Board, the minutes must include the names of directors present in the meeting and names of the directors who have dissented a resolution passed in the meeting. The minutes of the meeting kept in accordance with the legal provisions of this Act shall be evidence of the proceeding recorded therein.

Once the minutes have been signed by the chairman, they cannot be altered. In no case should minutes be altered by striking off the unrequired portion for that, it would tantamount to falsifying the records.

The minute book of any general meeting of a company shall; (*a*) be kept at the registered office of the company, and (*b*) be open during business hours, for the inspection of any member without charge for not less than two hours in each day.

Any member shall be entitled to be furnished within seven days, after he has made a request, in that behalf to the company, with a copy of the minutes on payment of prescribed fees.

In case, the member is not allowed to inspect the minute book or is not furnished with the copy of minutes within specified time, the company and every officer of the company, who is in default, shall be punishable with fine up to Rs. 5,000.

However, the minute books of board meetings cannot be inspected by shareholders or by public. The proceeding of any general meeting of a company shall not be circulated or advertised at the expense of the company. Non-compliance shall attract a fine up to Rs. 5,000 for the company and its every officer who is in default.

REVIEW QUESTIONS

1. Define 'meeting'. Discuss the various types of meeting.
2. What is 'statutory meeting'? Explain the consequences of not holding such meeting.
3. What is 'annual general meeting'? Discuss the legal provisions regarding calling of such meeting.
4. Explain different types of resolutions which may be passed in the general meeting of the shareholders.
5. Discuss legal provisions for holding extraordinary general meeting.
6. Explain the requisites of a valid meeting.
7. Discuss the role, powers and duties of a chairman in the meeting.
8. State various matters on which an ordinary resolution and special resolution can be passed.
9. Write short note on:
   (*a*) Resolution requiring special notice.
   (*b*) Proxy.
   (*c*) Minutes.
   (*d*) Extraordinary meeting.
   (*e*) Statutory report.
   (*f*) Resolution by postal ballot.
10. What is 'Proxy'? Explain legal provisions of the Companies Act regarding proxy.

PRACTICAL PROBLEMS

1. Twenty members out of 50 numbers of a company submitted a requisition for holding extraordinary general meeting in order to remove managing director from the office. On the failure of the company to call the meeting, the requisitionists called the meeting at registered office. As registered office was locked and keys were with the managing director, the members held meeting elsewhere and adopted a resolution for removing the managing director from the office. Is the resolution valid? (Hint: Yes.)
2. X is a member of the company. He appointed A his proxy who attended the meeting and voted on a particular resolution. A, thereafter, claimed to exercise his vote. Examine his legal position. (Hint: A cannot exercise his right.)

3. Default has been made in holding AGM of a company, more than 18 months have been elapsed since the date of last meeting. What legal remedy is available to the members for calling such meeting? (Hint: Members can apply to Company Law Board for ordering to call meeting.)
4. A company has 100 members. The notice of meeting has been sent to all of them. Twenty members do not attend the meeting, out of 80 members, who were present, 20 abstain from voting. How many members should vote in favour of resolution to be passed as special resolution? (Hint: At least 45 members.)
5. The board of directors at their meeting held on 10.11.2009 called the annual general meeting to be held on 10.1.2010 at 3 p.m at the registered office of the company at Delhi. The notice were duly served on the members. On 26 December 2009, the State Government declared 10 January 2010 as public holiday. Advise the chairman. (Hint: Public holiday must be declared by the Central Government thus date of meeting is effective.)
6. Due to some internal conflict and deadlock in the management of X Engineering Co., no general meetings were held for more than two years. A group of shareholders, six in number holding 5% of the total paid up capital of the company, approaches to you for advice. What is to be done in this regard? (Hint: The members can apply to the Central Government to call or direct to call the AG meeting.)
7. Y and Co. failed to hold its annual general meeting at an appointed time, because the account books of the company had been seized by police and produced in the court. Can company be punished for not holding the meeting? (Hint: No.)
8. A resolution to make a call on shares, was passed but without stating the date of call. Thereafter the secretary of the company added the date in the minutes. Is the action of secretary legally valid? (Hint: No, it cannot be done without passing resolution.)
9. A annual general meeting was called by the company in December 2009. The meeting was adjourned to March 2009 and was held at that time. Subsequently next annual general meeting was held in February 2010. Is the company liable for any irregularity? (Hint: Yes, the company has failed to hold a meeting for the year 2009.)

33

Winding Up

LEARNING OBJECTIVES

- Understand the concept of winding up and dissolution of a company.
- Distinguish between compulsory and voluntary winding up of the company.
- Examine the role of liquidator in the process of winding up.
- Get clarity about the concept of winding up on 'just and equitable grounds'.

INTRODUCTION

A company is an artificial person, having existence only in the eyes of law. The existence of the company is perpetual with regard to the existence of its members, but it is not permanent in nature. In one way or other, a company may lose its existence and it may cease to exist due to many reasons, but only through legal process.

There are three legal processes for putting the existence of a company to an end:

(*a*) Process of reconstruction and amalgamation occurs when the undertaking or a business of one company is transferred to another company and the court gives an order for the dissolution of transferor company, without resorting to winding up.

(*b*) By striking off company's name from the Register of Companies, kept by the Registrar on its becoming defunct or non-existent.

(*c*) By restoring to winding up process.

Winding up or liquidation of a company is very popular legal mode for putting the existence of the company to an end.

According to Prof. Grover, "The liquidation or winding up (the two terms are used indiscriminately) of a company is the process, whereby its life is ended and its property administered for the benefit of its creditors and members. An administrator called liquidator, is appointed and he takes control of the company, collects its assets, pays its debts and finally distributes any surplus among the members in accordance with their rights."

In other words, winding up of a company is a legal process to put going concern to an end. By doing so, its all activities and operations come to halt, its assets are realised, and proceeds are distributed among the creditors and members of the company.

It is further followed by its dissolution as to end. It is its corporate existence and status.

WINDING UP AND DISSOLUTION

The term winding up and dissolution are not same, because these two have different legal consequences. The process of winding up implies, realisation of assets of the company and distributing the proceedings among the creditors and the members of the company. But the legal existence of the company does not come to an end automatically.

Thus the process of dissolution starts as soon as the process of winding up comes to an end. It is only after having dissolved the company its corporate status or legal existence also comes to an end. Therefore on the completion of compulsory or voluntary winding up under the supervision of the court, the official liquidator makes application to the court for getting the company dissolved.

Similarly in case of voluntary winding up, on the submission of satisfactory report by the liquidator regarding the conduct of the company on the proceedings of winding up the court may order dissolution of the company.

MODES OF WINDING UP

According to the Companies Act, company may get wound up through the following modes:

1. Winding up by the court or compulsory winding up.
2. Voluntary winding up.
3. Voluntary winding subject to the supervision of the court.

1. WINDING UP BY COURT OR COMPULSORY WINDING UP (SECTION 433)

This Section of the Companies Act states the circumstances under which a company may be wound up by the court. These are:

(*i*) **By Passing a Special Resolution:** In case the company has resolved by passing special resolution that the company be wound up by the court, the court may order for compulsory winding up of the company. But special resolution so passed by the company does not bind the court to order winding up. The court may refuse to pass an order of winding up, if it is likely to be against the public interest.

However, in practice, where members resolve to wind up the company, they prefer to adopt the mode of voluntary winding up instead of compulsory winding up.

(*ii*) **Default in Holding Statutory Meeting or Delivering Statutory Report to the Registrar:** To hold a statutory meeting and to file statutory report is compulsory for a company. Failing which, the court may pass an order of winding up on the petition filed either by the Registrar or by a contributory. However, the court is not bound to order winding up of the company on this ground. Instead the court may order the company to hold such meeting and file the report to the Registrar at the cost of the persons at default.

(*iii*) **Non-commencement of Business:** A company may get an order of winding up by the court, if it does not commence a business within a year of its incorporation, or suspends business for a whole year. Again in this case, power of the court is discretionary in nature, and the order of winding up may be passed by the court only if the company has no intention to carry on business, because the chances of resuming a business are bleak and all directors except one were found absconding.

(*iv*) **Reduction of Membership Below the Statutory Minimum:** If the number of members of a company is reduced in case of a public company below seven and in case of private company below two, the court is bound to make an order of winding up of the company.

(*v*) **Inability to Pay Debts:** Every company is supposed to honour its monetary commitments and pay out debts. In case, the Company becomes unable to pay out its debts, the court may order winding up of the company. According to Section 434 of this Act, the company is deemed to be unable to pay its debts in the following situations:

(*a*) If a creditor to whom the company is indebted for a sum exceeding Rs. 1,00,000; has served upon the company a notice requiring the company to pay such due and the company has for three weeks, thereafter, neglected to pay or otherwise satisfy him, or

(*b*) If execution or other process issued on a decree or order of any court in favour of a creditor of the company is returned unsatisfied in whole or in part, or

(*c*) Where it is proved to the satisfaction of the court that the company is unable to pay its debts. To determine it, the court shall take into account, the contingent and prospective liabilities of the company. And if its existing and probable assets are insufficient to meet existing liabilities, if would be deemed to be unable to pay its debts.

In the above cases, it is discretionary on the part of the court either to pass an order of winding up, or to postpone winding up for sometime or refuse to make such order of winding up. It all depends on the wisdom and satisfaction of the court regarding commercial solvency of the company.

(*vi*) **Just and Equitable:** In case the court is of the opinion that, it is 'just and equitable' to wind up, the court may pass an order of winding up of the company. The power of the court is discretionary depending on the merit of the situation. Up to so far under the following instances the court has ordered winding up on the ground of 'just and equitable' clause:

(*a*) ***Deadlock in the management*:** In case of deadlock in the management which is permanent in nature and severe hostility between or among the directors, the court may order winding up of the company. However, mere difference of opinion or lack of good relationship between the two groups of directors may not find favour with the court for issuing an order of winding up.

(*b*) ***Cannot achieve main object*:** Where a company's main object cannot be achieved, it would be deemed to have lost its 'substratum', and the court may pass order of winding up. In a case of **Re German Date Coffee Coy**, a company was formed for manufacturing coffee from dates under the patent be sanctioned by the German Government. But such patent was never granted. The court passed an order for winding up of the company. Similarly where the company proposed to acquire running business, but the vendor refused to sell the business, and where the whole or substantially the whole of the paid up capital of the company has been lost, these have been considered sufficient reasons for winding up of the company.

(*c*) ***Cannot carry on business except at loss:*** If the company has reached to such a state that it cannot carry on the business except at a loss or it has no reasonable prospects of running business at profit, the court is empowered to order winding up of the company. But suffering a loss or likely to suffer further loss in the business may not provide sufficient ground for winding up.

(*d*) ***A company formed for fraudulent purpose:*** In case, a company has been formed for some illegal or fraudulent object, the court may order winding up. In this regard, the court has ordered winding up of a company conducting lottery business on account of illegality of object.

(*e*) ***Oppression towards minority:*** In case the shareholders holding majority voting power use oppressive tactics towards minority, it will be 'just and equitable' ground for the court to order winding up of the company.

(*f*) ***Bubble company:*** A company, which has no real business or property is known as 'bubble company'. Since such company is without resources and business, it may be considered to be 'just and equitable' to pass the order of winding up for such company.

(*g*) ***Public interest:*** The court may grant an order of winding up if it is in the interest of public. For example where a company maintained no proper records, pretended to be an investment advisor though it was only a share vending company; the court ordered winding up in public interest.

(*h*) ***Private company similar to partnership:*** A private company which is working in the nature and style of partnership may be wound up by the court on the ground of 'just and equitable' clause. For example, if there is an abuse of power or lack of confidence which partners repose in each other or right to participate in the management of the business is denied to any partner etc., it may be possible ground for winding up.

Who May Present Petition for Winding Up?

According to Section 439 of this Act, the following persons can file petition in the court for obtaining an order of winding up of a company:

(*i*) **Petition by the Company:** A company is entitled to file a petition for winding up in the court. It may be done by passing a special resolution to this effect at the meeting of the members. Such petition must be filed by the company itself. The directors or managing director without the sanction of general meeting if files petition, it will not amount to be filed by the company.

(*ii*) **Petition by Creditor:** The creditor or creditors of a company are also entitled to present petition for winding up of the company on the ground of inability of the company to pay its debts. The term creditor includes secured creditor, debenture holders and trustee of holder of debenture. For the purpose of tax dues, the Central Government or the State Government or local body may be considered as creditor. The creditor can present a petition only on the undisputable debts.

(*iii*) **Petition by Contributory or Contributories:** The term contributory includes the members and the past members (who cease to be a member within one year preceding the commencement of winding up) who are liable to contribute to the assets of the company in the event of winding up. A contributory is entitled to file petition, even though he may be a holder of fully paid shares, or that the company may have no assets at all, or may have no surplus asset left for the distribution among the shareholders after the satisfaction of the liabilities. A contributory is entitled to present a petition provided:

(*a*) He is an original allottee, or

(*b*) He became holder of shares through transmission, or

(*c*) He has been the registered holder of shares for at least six months during the 18 months before the commencement of winding up.

(*iv*) **Petition by the Registrar:** The Registrar of Companies is also entitled to present a petition for the winding up of a company. He can do so under the following situations:

(*a*) Default is made in holding statutory meeting or in delivering a statutory report to the Registrar.

(*b*) Company fails to commence business within year of its incorporation and suspends its business for a whole year.

(*c*) Number of members is reduced below prescribed minimum.

(*d*) When the court is of the opinion that a winding up is 'just and equitable'.

The Registrar must seek prior sanction of the Central Government before filing petition under any aforesaid situations. Such sanction can be granted by the Central Government after having given an opportunity to the company for making representation, if any.

(*v*) **By a Person Authorised by the Central Government:** Section 243 of this Act provides that, if the report of the inspector appointed under Section 235 shows that the company's affairs have been conducted with a view to fraud its creditors, members or other persons, or the management of a company is found to be guilty of fraud, the Central Government may authorise any person, to present a petition for winding up, on the grounds of 'just and equitable' clause.

Powers of the Court on Winding up Petition: After having received the petition of winding up of the company, the court will decide about date of hearing on the petition. In this regard, notice will be issued to the company and to the public as to notify to all creditors and contributories, so as to give them an opportunity to register their objection, if any.

On giving hearing, to all concerned parties, the court may:

(*a*) Dismiss a petition, with or without a cost.

(*b*) Adjourn hearing conditionally or unconditionally.

(*c*) Make any interim order on the petition.

(*d*) Make an order for winding up of the company with or without cost.

Consequences of Winding Up Order: In case, the court has passed an order of winding up of a company, such order will have the following consequences:

(*i*) After having passed, winding up order, it must cause intimation thereof, to be sent to the official Liquidator and the Registrar.

(*ii*) After such order, the petitioner and the company are required to file, certified copy of the court's order with the Registrar within one month of passing such order.

(*iii*) On receiving copy of the court's order, the Registrar will then notify in the official Gazette that such order has been made.

(*iv*) The winding up order shall be deemed to be a notice of discharge to the officers and members of the company except the business of the company is continued for the purpose of beneficial realisation of assets.

(*v*) The powers of the Board of Directors are terminated and will be vested in the official Liquidator.

(*vi*) The winding up order shall operate in favour of all creditors and all the contributories of the company.

(*vii*) Any debt which is payable at future date will become immediately payable on the winding up order.

(*viii*) On making winding up order by the court, official liquidator shall become by virtue of his office, the liquidator of the company.

(*ix*) The court passing winding up order is empowered to entertain or dispose of:

(*a*) Any suit preceding by or against the company.

(*b*) Any claim by or against the company.

(*c*) Any application made under Section 391 of this Act (compromise or arrangement with creditors).

(*x*) Any disposition of company's property, transfer of shares in the company or alteration in the status of its members made after commencement of winding up is void.

(*xi*) No suit or legal proceeding can be commenced against the company without the leave of the court. Any pending suit against the company on the date of winding up order cannot be proceeded further without the permission of the court.

OFFICIAL LIQUIDATOR

After having passed an order of winding up of a company, the official liquidator is appointed by the Central Government. The basic job of the liquidator is to seek realisation of company's assets and distribute the proceeds among creditors and contributories. He is an officer, who shall conduct proceeding of winding up of a company and performs such duties as the court may specify in this behalf.

On the winding up order the official liquidator shall by virtue of his office, becomes the liquidator of a company. The official liquidator, who is appointed after the presentation of winding up petition but before passing final order by the court is known as 'provisional liquidator'. A provisional liquidator is appointed only under exceptional situations like:

(*a*) When the company is shown to be insolvent.

(*b*) When the petition is presented by the company itself.

(*c*) When the directors do not oppose the petition.

Duties of Liquidator

The liquidator conducts the proceedings of winding up and performs the various duties as specified by the court. The main duties of the liquidator are:

(*i*) **To Submit Preliminary Report to the Court:** The director, manager and secretary of the company are required to submit statement of affair of the company to the official liquidator within 21 days from date of winding up order, in the prescribed form. It is duty of official liquidator to prepare preliminary report on the basis of information given in the statement of affair and submit the same to the court within 6 months from the date of winding up. Such report includes, amount of issued capital, subscribed capital, paid up capital and estimated amount of assets and liabilities.

(*ii*) **To Take Custody of Company's Property:** After having received a copy of winding up order, the liquidator is required to take custody of all properties, books and other documents of the company. For taking such custody, he may take the help of concerned District Magistrate.

(*iii*) **To Comply with Directions of Creditors and Contributories:** To distribute the proceeds of realised assets, the liquidator must give due regard and follow the directions of the creditors and contributories, given to him in the form of resolutions passed by them in the general meeting.

(*iv*) **To Maintain Books:** The liquidator is also required to maintain books in the prescribed manner and must record entries or minutes of the proceedings at meeting, and of such other matters as prescribed.

(*v*) **To Submit Account of Receipts and Payment to the Court:** The liquidator in under legal obligation to submit account of receipts and payment to the court, at such time as may be prescribed but not less than twice in each year during the tenure of his office. For the audit of such account, the liquidator must furnish the court all the required information.

(*vi*) **To Determine Membership of Inspection Committees:** In case the committee of inspection is appointed on the direction of the court to act with the liquidator, the liquidator must convene a meeting of the creditors for determining membership of the committee.

(*vii*) **To Deposit Money into Scheduled Bank:** It is the duty of the liquidator to deposit all sums of money, which he receives on the realisation of assets of the company, into a scheduled bank.

(*viii*) **To Perform Duties as an Officer of Court:** The liquidator is also required to perform all other duties as specified by the court as an officer of the court. For example, duty of setting list of contributories, rectifying the register of members etc.

The liquidator must perform duties assigned to him, sincerely and faithfully, keeping in view the directions of the court and requirements of this Act.

Powers of Liquidator

The powers, to be exercised by the liquidator may be grouped up as:

(*i*) Powers, with the sanction of the court.

(*ii*) Powers, without sanction of the court.

(*i*) **Powers with the sanction of the court:** The liquidator can exercise the following powers with the sanction of the court:

(*a*) To institute or defend any suit, prosecution or any other legal proceeding, civil or criminal, in the name and on behalf of the company.

(*b*) To carry on the business of the company for the beneficial winding up of the company.

(*c*) To sell the movable and immovable property and actionable claims of the company through private contracts.

(*d*) To raise money required on the security of the company's assets.

(*e*) To do all other things as may be necessary for winding up the affairs of the company and distributing its assets.

(*f*) To appoint an advocate, an attorney or a pleader who may assist him in the performance of his duties.

(*g*) To compromise both with the debtors and creditors and take security for the discharge of, any call, debt liability or claim and give a complete discharge in respect thereof.

(*h*) To disclaim, in writing any part of company's property which will be of onerous and burdersome nature.

Powers without the sanction of the court: The liquidator can exercise the following powers without any prior sanction of the court:

(*a*) To do all acts in the name and on behalf of a company, to excute all deeds, receipts and other documents, for that purpose to use, when necessary, the company's seal.

(*b*) To inspect the records and returns of the company on the file of Registrar, without any fee.

(*c*) To prove, rank and claim in the insovency of any contributory, for any balance against his estate and to receive dividend in the insolvency, in respect of that balance as a separate debt, due from the insolvent, and ratably with other separate creditor.

(*d*) To draw, accept, make and endorse any bill of exchange, *hundi* or promissory note, in the name and on behalf of the company.

(*e*) To take out in his name, letter of administration, to any deceased contributory and to do in his name any other act necessary for obtaining payment of any money due from contributory or his estate.

(*f*) To appoint an agent to do any business which the liqudator is unable to do himself.

In order to check the abuse of powers on the part of the liquidator, Section 460 (6) of this Act provides that, any person aggrieved by any act or decision of the liquidator, may apply to the court, and the court may confirm, reverse or modify such act or decision and make further order as it thinks appropriate in the situation.

2. VOLUNTARY WINDING UP

In case, a company is wound up by the members or creditors without approaching to the court, it is known as 'voluntary winding up'. In this type of winding up, the company and its creditors settle their claims and resolve the various issues at their own, without any intervention of the court.

According to Section 484 of this Act, a company may be wound up voluntarily when:

(*a*) The period fixed for the duration of the company has expired, or the event on the occurrence of which, the company is to get dissolved, has happened, or

(*b*) The company passes a special resolution that, it shall be wound up voluntarily.

A company after having passed a special resolution to this effect, must give notice of such resolution, within 14 days of passing resolution, by advertisement in the Official Gazette and also in some newspaper, circulating in the district, where the registered office of the company is situated; failing which, the company and its every officer shall be punishable with fine up to Rs. 500 for everyday during which the default continues.

Consequences of Voluntary Winding Up

A voluntary winding up of a company results in the following consequence:

(*i*) A voluntary winding up commences, with a retrospective effect from the date when a special resolution is passed to this effect. The date of commencement of winding up is important for determining the liability of past members.

(*ii*) From the commencement of winding up, the company ceases to carry on its business, except so far as may be required for the beneficial winding up of such business. However, corporate personality exists, until the company is dissolved.

(*iii*) On the appointment of the liquidator, the powers of the directors, managing director or whole time directors come to an end, except for the purpose of giving notice of such appointment to the Registrar.

(*iv*) A voluntary winding up may or may not operate as a dismissal of company's employees. A winding up of a company on the ground of insolvency will discharge company's servants. But such winding up on the ground of solvency of the company will not lead to dismissal of employees, if it is meant to affect amalgamation.

(*v*) In case of a voluntary winding up, any proceeding against the company may be proceeded with or without the leave of the court until a stay is obtained.

(*vi*) All transfer of shares until a stay is obtained, of the members, made after the commencements of winding up of the company shall be void, except when it is made with the permission of the liquidator.

Types of Voluntary Winding Up

The voluntary winding up may be of the following two types:

- Members's voluntary winding up
- Creditor's voluntary winding up

Member's Voluntary Winding Up

Voluntary winding up of company by the members takes place, when the company is solvent and is capable of paying out its liabilities in full. For such winding up, (*a*) declaration of solvency is to be filed with the Registrar by the directors, and (*b*) passing of an ordinary or a special resolution as the case may be by the members at extraordinary general meeting and filing a copy of it with the Registrar.

Declaration of Solvency: In case of voluntary winding up of a company by members the majority of directors, must at a meeting of the board, make a declaration verified by an affidavit stating that they have made full enquiry in to the affairs of the company and that having done so, they have formed the opinion that the company has no debt or it will be able to pay its debts in full within such period not exceeding three years from the commencement of the winding up. Such declaration will be effective when (*a*) it is made within five weeks before the date of passing resolution for winding up, (*b*) it is accompanied by a copy of report of the auditor on the profit and loss account and balance sheet of the company, and (*c*) it contains statements of company's assets and liabilities.

In case the directors make false declaration of solvency, they are punishable with imprisonment up to six months or with a fine up to Rs. 50,000 or with both.

Other Legal Provisions Regarding Member's Voluntary Winding up: (Section, 490 to 498)

(*i*) **Appointment and Remuneration of Liquidator:** The company in a general meeting must appoint one or more liquidators and fix their remuneration. The remuneration so fixed cannot be raised at any cost even with the sanction of the court. However, it can be reduced. The liquidator must not take charge of their office unless remuneration has been fixed. The appointment of every liquidator must be notified by the company with the Registrar within 10 days of their appointment. Default in complying with the above shall make the company and its every defaulting officer punishable with a fine up to Rs. 1,000; for everyday during which default continues.

(*ii*) **Board's Powers to Cease on Appointment of Liquidator:** On the appointment of liquidator, all powers of board of directors, managing director or managers will come to an end except for the purpose of giving notice of such appointment to the Registrar.

(*iii*) **Power of Liquidator to Accept Share as Consideration:** In case a company is being wound up voluntarily for the purpose of amalgamation or reconstruction, the liquidator may receive shares, debentures, policies and other interest in the transferee company for distributing it among the members of transferor company. He may also enter into another arrangement by which the members of transferor company are to participate in the profits or other benefits of the transferee company, in lieu of or, in addition to receiving cash, shares, debentures or other interest.

(*iv*) **Duty of Liquidator to Call Creditor's Meeting in Case of Insolvency:** If the liquidator is, at any time, of an opinion that the company will not be able to pay its debts in full within the period mentioned in the declaration of solvency or that period has expired without the debts having being paid in full, he shall forthwith, summon a meeting of the creditors and shall lay before the meeting, a statement of assets and liabilities of the company.

(*v*) **Duty of Liqudator to Call General Meeting at the End of Each Year:** In case the winding up process continues for more than one year, the liquidator must call a meeting of the company at the end of each year passed on. He must lay before this meeting an account of his acts, and dealing and conduct of winding up during the preceding year.

(*vi*) **Final Meeting and Dissolution:** In case, company's affairs are fully wound up, the liquidator must make an account of winding up showing how the winding up has been conducted. He should also call a general meeting of the company for the purpose of laying the accounts before it. The meeting shall be called by making advertisement in a local newspaper specifying time, place and object of the meeting and should be published in a Official Gazettee at least one month before the meeting.

Within one week, after the meeting, the liquidator shall send to the Registrar and the official liquidator a copy of accounts and return of the meeting. The liquidator must make a return stating that the meeting was called and no quorum was present, if adequate quorum has not been present in the meeting.

The official liquidator, on receiving accounts and returns shall make scrutiny of books and papers of the company and report the result to the court. If the report of official liquidator shows that the affairs of the company have been conducted in a satisfactory manner taking care of public interest and the interest of the members, the company shall be deemed to be dissolved from the date of submission of the report to the court. In case he reports that company's affairs have been conducted in manner prejudicial to the interest of members or the public, the court shall direct the official liquidator to make further investigation. On receipt of the report, the court may order for dissolution of the company or make such other order as per the demand of the circumstance.

(*vii*) **Alternative Provisions:** During the voluntary winding up of a company by the members, if the company is found to be insolvent, the liquidator must call a meeting of creditors under Sections 508 and 509. And the winding up would proceed as if, it was creditor's voluntary winding up.

Creditor's Voluntary Winding Up

This mode of winding up is resorted by insolvent companies not capable of paying out debts is full. Such winding up takes place when 'declararation of solvency' is not made and delivered to the Registrar, by the directors. The following legal provisions of this Act are applicable on creditor's voluntary winding up:

(*i*) **Meeting of Creditors:** The board of directors must call separate meetings of the members and creditors to pass separate resolutions for voluntary winding of the company. The meeting of the creditors shall be held on the day or the day next to the day on which general meeting of the members is to be held. The notice of such meeting of creditors must be sent to them by post simultaneously with the notices of general meeting of the members. The notice of creditor's meeting must be advertised in the official Gazette and in two newspapers circulating in the district, where registered office is situated. The board of directors must lay before the creditor's meeting a full statement of company's affairs together with a list of creditors and the estimated amount of their claims. The notice of any resolution passed in the creditor's meeting must be given by the company to the Registrar within 10 days of passing the resolution.

(*ii*) **Appointment of Liquidator:** The creditors and the company may nominate a person to be liquidator for the purpose of conducting proceeding of winding up. In case, the creditors and the company nominate different persons, the person nominated by the creditor will be the liquidator.

(*iii*) **Appointment of Committee of Inspection:** The committee of inspection may be appointed in the meeting of the creditors. Such committee would supervise the proceedings of the liquidation. The Committee must not consist of more than five members. These members will bc appointed by the company at the meeting held for passing resolution of winding up.

(*iv*) **Fixation of Liquidator's Remuneration:** The committee of inspection may fix the remuneration payable to the liquidator. In case it is not fixed by the committee it will be fixed by the court. Remuneration fixed in aforesaid manner shall not be increased in any circumstance with or without the sanction of the court.

(*v*) **Board's Powers to Cease on Appointment of Liquidator:** As soon as, the liquidator is appointed, all the powers of the directors come to an end, except when sanctioned, either by the committee of inspection or by the creditors in general meeting.

(*vi*) **Filling the Vacancy in the Office of Liquidator:** In case, vacancy occurs in the office of liquidator by dealth, resignation or otherwise, the creditors, in a general meeting are authorised to fill such vacancy.

(*vii*) **Calling Meetings of the Company and Creditors at the End of Each Year:** The liquidator must call a general meeting of shareholders and creditors at the end of each year, if the proceedings of winding up continued for more than a year. The purpose of such meetings is to provide regular information to shareholders and creditors about the proceedings of winding up.

(*viii*) **Final Meeting and Dissolution:** Once the proceedings of winding up are complete, the liquidator will call final meetings as per the provisions of this Act, of both creditors and members.

3. VOLUNTARY WINDING UP UNDER THE SUPERVISION OF THE COURT

In case, the proceedings of winding up are already in progress and in the meanwhile the creditors, or contributories apply to the court, requesting that the winding up be proceeded further under the supervision of the court; the court may determine the extent of control which shall be exercised on the voluntary winding up proceedings. Such control of the court is sought under the following situations: (*a*) liquidator is partial and is found acting in a manner which prejudicial, (*b*) the rules relating to winding up are not being followed, and (*c*) the company managed, fraudulently, resolution for winding up.

On passing an order of winding up under the supervision of the court, the court may appoint additional liquidator and remove any liquidator. The court is also empowered to fill the vacancy caused by death or resignation of liquidators.

Effect of Supervision Order

(*a*) A liquidator is empowered to exercise all these powers which a liquidator in voluntary winding up enjoys. However, he will exercise these powers subject to the supervision of the court.

(*b*) Under supervision order, the court is empowered to use all those powers, which it might have used for making an order under 'winding up by the court.'

The court is empowered to pass an order for compulsory winding up superseding the supervision order. In this case, the court may appoint provisional or a permanent liquidator who will act as a liquidator in the winding up by the court. Such liquidator shall act is addition, and under the control of official liquidator.

REVIEW QUESTIONS

1. Define 'winding up'. Distinguish between winding up and dissolution.
2. Who can present petition for the winding up of a company? Explain effects and consequences of a winding up order.
3. What is winding up by the court? Under which circumstances the court may wind up a company?
4. Who is an 'official liquidator'? Discuss the power and duties of official liquidator.

5. Discuss the relevant provisions of the Companies Act, relating to member's voluntary winding up of a company.
6. Under what circumstances may the court pass winding up order, when the company is unable to pay its debts?
7. 'The court can also wind up a company on a 'just and equitable' grounds.' Comment.
8. Write notes on:
   (*a*) Declaration of insolvency.
   (*b*) Winding up of a company under the supervision of the court.
   (*c*) Creditor voluntary winding up.
   (*d*) Liquidator.
9. Distinguish between 'member's voluntary winding up' and 'creditor's voluntary winding up'.

PRACTICAL PROBLEMS

1. The petition for winding up of a company was presented on the ground of existence of friction among shareholders, bickering as between one group and another group of members of the company, exclusion of some person from management and mismanagement by the person in-charge of the company. Can court order a winding up of the company? (Hint: No, these grounds are not sufficient leading to just and equitable clause.)
2. The business of a company has been suspended temporarily due to economic recession going on in the world. But the company has an intention to continue. The petition was filed in the court for winding up the company. Can the company be wound up? (Hint: No.)
3. There are three directors in a company. All of them do carry different opinion in the management of the company so more so, they are not in speaking terms with each other and conducting company's affairs through their private secretaries. Can company be wound up on this ground? (Hint: Yes, deadlock in the management of a company.)

4. A company went into liquidation by an order of the court. The official liquidator during the scrutiny of books and accounts found that the promoters and directors of the company have committed irregularities and fraud in several instances. What is legal remedy for it? (Hint: Liquidator may approach the court for public examination of the promoters and directors.)

5. A transport company was incorporated for being a part of public transport system in Delhi. But later on, Delhi Goverment refused to give permit of plying buses in the different routes of the city to that company on the ground of some technical problems. Can the company be wound up? (Hint: Yes, the main object is being defeated.)

■■■

Unit 4

Consumer Protection Act, 1986

The Information Technology Act, 2000

34

Introduction and Application

LEARNING OBJECTIVES

- Understand basic concept of consumer protection.
- Analyse need and importance of consumer protection.
- Identify applications, features and various objects of Consumer Protection Act.
- Develop clarity how it will help in protecting consumers.
- Get conceptual clarity about various definitions given in the Act.

INTRODUCTION

In a modern business, a consumer occupies central place and is considered as a 'king of the market'. In order to provide maximum satisfaction to him, major policies and strategies of business organisations relating to production and distribution revolve around the consumers. All operations and activities of the organisation focus on the interest of the consumers. Whether it is a design of product, or its price, place of availability or durabelity etc., all are to be made according to consumer's preferences and priority.

But despite the progressive business policies, in many cases, consumer's interest is least protected and promoted, and he finds himself at the receiving end. An unethical and misleading advertisement, lack of purity in quality, adulteration, under weighing, black marketing, hoarding and profiteering etc., are not less common in business.The consumer is very often cheated particularly in respect with the quality and price of goods and services.

To survive the competition, instead of making production and distribution cost effective, inefficiency of the organisation is passed on to an innocent consumer through various undesirable and unfair practices. Even the world class organisations are not free from these exploitative business practices.

The lust for earning more, becoming big and growing, faster have driven these organisations to unhealthy and undesirable practices.

NEED AND IMPORTANCE OF CONSUMER PROTECTION

There has been a serious concern to protect the interest of consumers, all over the world including in our country. In our country the consumer movement started long back. In spite of many pieces of legislation, which have been enacted for giving fair deal to the consumers, the interest of consumers could not be protected effectively.

The need of Consumer Protection Act arises due to the following reasons:

(*i*) **Lack of Knowledge:** The consumer, who buys the goods and services to meet his needs, may not have adequate knowledge of these products particular the products which are very technical in nature. All the time it may not be possible for him to have full knowledge about the product. And the person who deals with the consumer finds it easy to misguide him.

(*ii*) **Lack of Awareness:** As stated earlier, we have many other legislations for safeguarding the interest of consumers, including Essential Commodities Act, 1955. Prevention of Black Marketing and Maintenance Supplies of Essential Commodity Act, 1980; Essential Services Maintenance Act, 1968, Standards of Weights and Measures Act, 1976. Prevention of Food Adulteration Act, 1954. But lack of awareness among the consumers about their right under these Acts and poor implementations of provisions of Acts has made the situation worse.

(*iii*) **Lack of Unity:** The consumers are widely scattered and belong to different income classes of the society. As a result of these wide ranging dissimilarities, they remain unorganised. Lack of unity among them has been one of the most effective factor, which does not allow them to assert their rights.

(*iv*) **Lack of Time:** The consumers are always considered to be very busy and having no time for asserting themselves on the sale, persons or organisations. They need to have enough time, courage and patience to take a fight against corrupt businessmen to a logical end.

(*v*) **Lack of Effective Legal System:** Though there have been many Acts enacted by the Government from time to time for protecting interest of consumers, the difficult and lengthy legal process for redressing the grievances of the consumers under these Acts makes it difficult for the consumers to protect themselves from unfair and exploitative marketing practices of these business organisation.

THE CONSUMER PROTECTION ACT, 1986

An enactment of Consumer Protection Act, in a real sense, is a milestone in the history of consumer movement in our country. This Act was made because the well-organised sections of producers, traders and service providers, having full knowledge of market and manipulating skills often, attempted to exploit the consumers for their personal gains. They have been indulged in such unfair practices, despite the existence of various other laws.

In addition to it, due to increase in population, cases of consumer disputes pending in civil courts went up. Unnecessary delay in the settlement of these cases even for small claims paved the way for the enactment of this Act.

Ultimately, the Consumer Protection Act was made in 1986 with an object of protecting the interest of the consumers. It is one of the most important and comprehensive piece of legislation. It provides protection to the consumers in respect to goods and service, purchased by them from producers, suppliers wholesalers and retailers.

The provisions of this Act came into force in April 1987, except the provisions regarding Consumer Dispute Redressal Agencies, which came into force in June 1987.

This Act extends to the whole of India, except the State of Jammu and Kashmir.

This Act shall apply to all goods and services expressly provided by the notification of the Central Government.

Features

The Consumer Protection Act, 1986, is the most progressive and appropriate piece of legislation for safeguarding the interest of the consumers. The main features of this Act may be enumerated as:

(*i*) The provisions of the Act are applicable on all goods and services as notified by the Central Government.

(*ii*) It seeks and promotes social purpose by taking care of the most important segment of the society *i.e.*, consumers.

(*iii*) This Act provides an alternative legal system, in addition to other Acts, for the redressal of consumers grievances.

(*iv*) It provides various rights to the consumers such as right to safety, right to be heard, right to education and right to seek redressal etc.

(*v*) This Act provides for the setting up of a three-tier judicial powers machinery, at the National, State and District levels.

(*vi*) The authorities under this Act exercise quasi-judicial powers for settling the consumer disputes.

(*vii*) The remedies, which are available to an aggrieved party under this Act are wider. Under this Act, in addition to granting specific relief, the consumer fora have jurisdiction to award compensation for the mental agony, sufferings etc.

(*viii*) This also provides for speedy and less expensive disposal of consumer complaints by the redressal agencies.

Objects of the Act

The Consumer Protection Act, 1986, was enacted as a result of widespread consumer protection movement in India. In this Act adequate provisions have been made taking into account the consumer movement and international obligations to protect consumer rights. The main objects of this Act are:

(*i*) This Act has been enacted to provide for the protection of the interest of consumers.

(*ii*) The Act also aims at promoting welfare of the society by enabling the consumers to participate directly in the market economy.

(*iii*) It also aims at removing the helplessness of a consumer, which he faces against the powerful business lobbies and network. The enactment of this Act is of course to be a silver lining, which has been successful in checking a lot and providing justice to the consumers.

(*iv*) This Act provides for giving various rights to the consumers and protecting those rights by implementing provisions of the Act.

(*v*) It also aims at setting up of consumer protection councils at the Central and State and District levels, which will act as an advisory bodies to promote and protect the rights of consumers.

(*vi*) The legal provisions of this Act also aim at providing simple and speedy redressal of consumer disputes through quasi-judicial machinery. While making settlement of dispute, the principles of natural justice and equality are observed.

The Rights of Consumer

One of the basic object of the Consumer Protection Act, 1986, is to provide and protect the rights of the consumers. It seeks *inter alia*, to promote and protect the rights of consumer, such as:

(*i*) The right to be protected against marketing of goods, which are hazardous to life and property.

(*ii*) The right to be informed about the quality, quantity, potency, purity, standards and price of goods, to protect the consumer against unfair trade practices.

(*iii*) The right to be assured wherever possible, access to an authority of goods at competitive prices. Under this right, the consumer must be assured access to varieties of goods and services available at competitive prices.

(*iv*) The right to be heard and to be assured that consumer's interest will receive due consideration at appropriate forums.

(*v*) The right to seek redressal against unfair trade practices or unscrupulous exploitation of consumers.

(*vi*) The right to consumer education *i.e.*, under this right, the consumers must be given an access to all type of information relevant to the goods and services, and his rights and remedies.

IMPORTANT DEFINITIONS

1. **Appropriate Laboratory** means, a laboratory or organisation:

   (*a*) Recognised by the Central Government.

   (*b*) Recognised by the State Government, subject to such guidelines as may be prescribed by the Central Government in this behalf.

   (*c*) Any such laboratory or organisation established under law, for the time being in force, which is maintained, financed or aided by the Central Government or a State Government for carrying out analysis or test of any goods for determining defects therein.

2. **Complainant** means:

   (*a*) A consumer, or

   (*b*) Any voluntary consumer association registered under the Companies Act.

   (*c*) The Central Government or any State Government.

   (*d*) One or more consumers.

   (*e*) In case of death of consumer, his legal heir or representative who makes a complaint.

3. **Complaint** means any allegation in writing made by complainant that:

(*a*) An unfair trade practice or restrictive trade practice has been adopted by any trader or service provider.

(*b*) The goods bought, or agreed to be bought by him suffer from one or more defects.

(*c*) The service hired or availed of by him suffer from deficiency in any respect.

(*d*) A trader or service provider, has charged for the goods or for the services mentioned in the complaint a price, in excess of the price:

- fixed by under any law for the time being is force.
- displayed on the foods or on the package containing such goods.
- displayed in the price list.
- agreed between the parties.

(*e*) Goods which will be hazardous to life and safety, when used, are being offered for sale to the public.

(*f*) Service which are hazardous to life and safety of public, when used, are offered by the service provider, which could have been known with due diligence to be injurious to life and safety.

4. **Consumer** means any person who:

(*a*) Buys any goods for consideration, which is paid or promised to be paid or deferred to be paid in future. But does not include the person, who obtains such goods for resale or for any commercial purpose.

Explanation: For the purpose of this clause, 'Commercial purpose' does not include, use by a person, of goods bought and used by him and services availed by him exclusively for the purpose of earning his livelihood by means of self-employment.

In a case **Shri Lakshmi Narayan Rice Mill *vs* Food Corporation of India** it was held that a person who purchased large quantity of rice cannot be considered as a 'consumer' as such a large quantityy cannot be for self-consumption, but for resale.

In a case **Dharam Chad *vs* Manjeep Gas Service**, it was held that, a person registering himself for release of LPG connection, with the distributor is a 'consumer' though at that time he pays nothing and payment is deferred till the time of release of gas connection.

5. **Consumer Dispute** means a dispute where the person against whom, a complaint has been made, denies or disputes the allegations contained in the complaint.
6. **Defect** means, any fault, imperfection or shortcoming in the quality, quantity, potency, purity or standard, which is required to be maintained by or under any law by the trader in any manner, whatsoever in relation to any goods.
7. **Deficiency** means, any fault, imperfection shortcoming or inadequacy in the quality, nature and manner of performance, which is required to be maintained, by or under any law, has been undertaken to be performed by a person in pursuance of a contract or otherwise in relation to any service.
8. **District Forum** means Consumer Disputes Redressal Forum, established under Section 9, Clause (*a*) of this Act.
9. **Goods** means goods as defined in the sale of Goods Act 1930.
10. **Manufactures** means a person who:
    (*a*) makes or manufactures any goods or part thereof, or
    (*b*) does not make or manufacture any goods but assembles parts thereof made or manufactured by others, or
    (*c*) puts or causes to be put his own mark on any goods made, or manufactured by any other manufacture.
11. **Member** includes the president and a member of the National Commission or a State Commission or a District Forum as the case may be.
12. **National Commission** means, the National Consumer Disputes Redressal Commission established under Section 9 and Clause (*c*) or this Act.
13. **Notification** means, a notification published in Official Gazette.
14. **Person** includes:
    (*a*) a firm whether registered or not.
    (*b*) a Hindu undivided family.
    (*c*) a cooperative society.
    (*d*) every other association of persons, registered under the Societies Registration Act, 1860.
15. **Prescribed** means prescribed by rules made by the State Government or by the Central Government, as the case may be.

16. **Restrictive Trade Practices** means a trade practice, which tends to bring about manipulation of price or its conditions of delivery, or affect flow of supplies in the market, relating to goods and services, in such a manner, as to impose on the consumers unjustified cost or restrictions and shall include:

   (*a*) Delay beyond the period agreed to by a trader in supply of such goods or in providing the service which has lead or is likely to lead to rise in the price.

   (*b*) Any trade practice which requires a consumer to buy, hire or avail of any goods or services as condition precedent to buying, hiring or availing of other goods and services.

17. **Service** means service of any description which is made available to potential users in connection with banking, financing, insurance, transport, processing, supply of electrical or other energy, board or lodging or both, entertainment, amusement or the purveying of news or other information. However it does not include the rendering of any service free of charge or under a contract of personal service.

18. **Spurious Goods and Services** means any such goods and services, which claim to be genuine, but they are actually not so.

19. **State Commission** means a Consumer Disputes Redressal Commission established in a State under Section 9 and Clause (*b*) of this Act.

20. **Trader** means, in relation of any goods, means a person who sells or distributes any goods for sale and includes the manufacture thereof and where such goods are sold or thereof and where such goods are sold or distributed in package form, includes the packer thereof.

21. **Unfair Trade Practices** means a trade practice which, for the purpose of promoting the sale, use or supply of any goods or for the provision of any service, adopts any unfair method or unfair or deceptive practice, including any of the follows practices:

Clause

1. The practice of making any statement, whether orally or in writing or by visible presentation which:

   (*i*) Falsely represents that the goods are of particular standard, quality, quantity, grade, composition, style or model.

   (*ii*) Falsely represents that the services are of a particular standard, quality or grade.

(*iii*) Falsely represents any rebuilt, second hand, renovated, reconditioned or old goods as new goods.

(*iv*) Represents that the goods and services have sponsorship, or approval, performance, characteristics, accessories, uses or benefits which such goods and services do not have.

(*v*) Represents that the seller or supplier has sponsorship, or approval or affiliation, which such seller or supplier does not have.

(*vi*) Makes a false or misleading representation concerning the need for, or the usefulness of, any goods and services.

(*vii*) Gives to the public any warranty or guarantee of the performance, efficacy or length of life of a product or any good, that is not based on adequate or proper test thereof.

(*viii*) Makes to the public, representation, in a form that purports to be:

(*a*) Warranty or guarantee of a product or of any goods or services

(*b*) Promise to replace, repair or maintain an article or any part thereof or to repeat or continue a service until it has achieved a specified result.

(*ix*) Materially mislead the public concerning the price at which a product, good or service have been or are ordinarily sold or provided.

(*x*) Gives a false or misleading fact disparaging the goods, services or trade of another person.

Explanation: For the purpose of Clause (1), a statement that is:

(*a*) expressed on an article offered or displayed for sale, or on its wrapper or container, or

(*b*) expressed on anything attached to, inserted to or accompanying on an article offered or displayed for sale.

(*c*) contained in or on anything that is sold, sent, delivered, transmitted or in any other manner, whatsover made available to the member of public shall deemed to be statement to public.

2. Permits the publication of any advertisement: Whether in any newspaper or otherwise, for the sale and supply, at a bargain price, of goods or services, that are not intended to be offered for sale or supply at a bargain price or for a period that is, and in quantities that are, reasonable, having regard to the nature of market, the nature and size of business and the nature of the advertisement.

Explanation: For the purpose Clause 2 bargaining price means:

(*i*) A price that is stated in any advertisement to be a bargaining price

(*ii*) A price that a person who reads, hears or sees the advertisement, would reasonably understand to be a bargain price, having regard to the prices at which the product advertised of like products are ordinarily sold.

3. Permits:

(*i*) The offering of gifts, prizes or other items with the intention of not providing them as offered or creating impression that same thing is being given or offered free of charge in the transaction as a whole.

(*ii*) The conduct of any contest, lottery, game of chance or skill for the purpose of promoting directly or indirectly the sale, use or supply of any product or any business interest.

(*iii*) A withholding from the participants, of any schemes offering gifts, prizes or other items free of charge, on its closure, the information about final result of the scheme.

The participants deemed to have been informed of the final result of the schemes, where such results are published prominently, with in reasonable period of time, in the newspaper in which scheme was originally advertised.

4. Permits the sale and supply of goods intended to be used byconsumers, knowing or having reason to believe that the goods do not comply with the standards prescribed by competent authority relating to performance composition, contents, design, construction, finishing or packaging are necessary to prevent or reduce the risk of injury to the person using the goods.

5. Permits, the hoarding or destruction of goods or refuses to sell the goods to make them available for sale or to provide any service, if such hoarding, destruction or refusal raises or tend to raise the cost of those or other similar goods and services.

6. Manufacture of spurious goods or offering such goods for sale or adopting deceptive practices in the provision of services will also amount to an unfair trade practice.

REVIEW QUESTIONS

1. What do you means by the 'consumer protection'? Discuss the main objects of consumer protection.
2. Explain the need and importance of consumer protection. Why does it arise?
3. Discuss the scope, main features and the object of the Consumer Protection Act.
4. Define the following terms:
   (*a*) Unfair Trade Practices
   (*b*) Manufacture
   (*c*) Consumer
   (*d*) Person
   (*e*) Defect
   (*f*) District Forum
   (*g*) Complainant
   (*h*) Consumer Dispute
5. Discuss the various rights of consumers provided in the Consumer Protection Act.
6. Define the term consumer. Explain main objectives of Consumer Protection Act 1986.
7. Explain the rights and problems of the consumer under Consumer Protection Act.
8. Explain various unfair trade practices given in the Consumer Protection Act.

■■■

35

Consumer Protection Councils

LEARNING OBJECTIVES

- Get clarity about the role of Consumer Protection Councils.
- Develop clarity about the functioning of such councils at grass root level.
- Analyse important and functioning of Central Consumer Protection Council.
- Find out how the State and Distinct Consumer Councils operate.

The Consumer Protection Act, 1986 provides for establishing consumer protection councils at the central, the state and district level. These councils are basically advisory bodies to promote and protect the rights of consumers. These councils play an important role in strengthening and broadening the base of consumer movement in India particularly in rural sector.

CENTRAL CONSUMER PROTECTION COUNCILS

The legal provisions of the this Act regarding the Central Consumer Protection Council are:

(*i*) **Establishment of the Central Council:** The Central Government shall by notification establish, central council, from such date as it may specify in such notification. [Section 4(1)].

(*ii*) **Composition of the Council:** Council shall consist of the following members, namely:

(*a*) The minister in charge of the Consumer Affairs in the Central Government, who shall be the chairman of the council.

(*b*) Number of other official or non-official members representing various interests groups shall be determined by the Central

Government [Section 4 (2), which shall consists of following members not exceeding 35. (excluding chairman].

(*c*) Minister of State or Deputy Minister, in-charge of Consumer Affairs in the Central Government shall be Vice-Chairman of the council.

(*d*) Minister in-charge of Consumers Affairs of two of the states from each region mentioned in Schedule I to be changed by rotation on expiration of the term of the council on each occasion.

(*e*) An administrator of a Union Territory, to represent Territory, as mentioned in Schedule II to be changed by rotation on expiration of the term of the council.

(*f*) Two Members of the Parliament, one from Lok Sabha and one from Rajya Sabha.

(*g*) Representatives of Central Government Departments and autonomous organisations, concerned with consumer interest, not exceeding five.

(*h*) The Registrar National Consumer Disputes Redressal Commission, New Delhi.

(*i*) Representatives with proven expertise and experience who are capable of representing consumer interest drawing from consumer organisations, consumer activists, woman, farmers, trade and industry, not exceeding five.

(*j*) The secretaries in-charge of Consumers Affairs in the State to be nominated by the Central Government, not exceeding three.

(*k*) Secretary-in-charge of Consumer Affairs in the Central Government shall be the Member Secretary of the Central Council.

(*iii*) **Term of the Central Council:** The term of council shall be three years.The Central Goverment must reconstitute the Council before the expiry of the term of existing council.

(*iv*) **Vacancies in the Central:** Any member may by writing under his hand to the Chairman of the Central Council resign from the council. The vacancies so caused or otherwise shall be filled from the same category by the Central Government.

(*v*) **Objects of Central Council:** The objects of the central council shall be to promote and protect the rights of consumers such as:

(*a*) The right to be protected against the marketing of goods and services, which are hazardous to life and property.

(*b*) The right to be informed about quality, quantity, potency, purity and standard and price of goods.

(*c*) The right to be assured, whenever possible, access to a variety of goods and services at competitive prices.

(*d*) The right to be heard and to be assured that consumers interest will receive due consideration at appropriate Forum.

(*e*) The right to seek redressal against unfair trade practices or unscrupulous exploitation of consumers.

(*f*) The right to consumer education.

(*vi*) **Procedure of Meetings of the Central Council:** Under Section 5 (2) of this Act, the central council will observe the following procedure in regard with the transaction of its business:

(*a*) The meeting of the central council will be presided over by the chairman, in his absence by the vice chairman and in the absence of both, the council shall elect any member to preside over the meeting.

(*b*) Each meeting shall be called by giving, not less than 10 days notice in writing to every member.

(*c*) Every notice of a meeting shall specify the place and day and hours of the meeting and shall contain statement of business to be transacted thereat.

(*d*) No proceeding of the central council shall be invalid merely by reason of existence of any vacancy or any defect in the constitution of council.

(*e*) The resolution passed by the central council shall be recommendatory in nature.

(*f*) For the purpose of performing its functions, under this Act, the central council may constitute a working group from among its members. Every working group shall performed such functions as are assigned to it by the central council.

(*g*) In connection with the journey undertaken to and from by non-official members for attending meetings of the council or its working group, they shall be entitled to avail first class or two tier, air conditioned class fare or cost of actual mode of travel, whichever is less.

STATE CONSUMER PROTECTION COUNCIL

The legal provisions of this Act regarding state consumer protection council are:

(*i*) **Establishment of the State Council:** The state government, by notification establish a council known as from state council such date as it may be specified in such notification. The State Government have been authorised to establish state councils in their respective states. The state government are fully empowered to determine number of members of the council, laydown the procedure for meetings and to decide rules as to term of the council. However, for maintaining uniformity in the functioning of these councils, the state government may adopt rules provided under the Consumer Protection Rules, 1987.

(*ii*) **Composition of the State Council:** The state council, shall consist of the following members, namely:

(*a*) The Minister in charge of Consumer Affairs in the State Government shall be its chairman.

(*b*) Such number of other official or non-official members, as may be nominated by the Central Government, not exceeding 10.

(*c*) Such number of other official or non-official members, representing such interest as may be prescribed by the state government.

(*iii*) **Meeting of the Council:** (*a*) The State Council, shall meet as and when necessary, but not less than two meetings shall be held every year.

(*b*) The State Council shall meet at such time and place as the chairman may thinks fit and shall observe such procedure for transaction of its business, as may be prescribed by the State Government.

(*iv*) **Objects:** The objects of every state council shall be to promote and protect, the rights of the consumers, laid down in Section 6, Clause (*a*) to (*f*).

DISTRICT CONSUMER PROTECTION COUNCIL

In order to promote and protect the rights of consumers at grass root level, the District Consumers Protection Councils are formed. The legal provisions regarding these are:

(*i*) **Establishment of the District Council:** According to Section 8A of this Act, the state government is authorised to establish for every district, a District Consumer Protection Council. These councils shall be established by the notification of the state government, in the 'Official Gazette'. The state government is empowered to prescribe the number of official and non-official members for the district council.

(*ii*) **Composition of District Council:** According to Section 8A (2), the District Consumer Protection Council shall consist of the following members:

(*a*) The Collector of the District (by whatever name called) who shall be its chairman.

(*b*) Such numbers of other official and non-official members, representing such interest, as may be prescribed by the state government.

(iii) **Number of Meetings:** According to Section 8A (3) of this Act, the District Council must hold at least two meetings in a year. This is minimum statutory requirement and district council is free to hold as many meeting as it thinks fit.

(iv) **Procedure of Meeting:** As per Section 8A (4) of this Act, the District Council shall meet at such time and place, within the district as the chairman specifies. The district council shall observe such procedure in regard to the transaction of its business as may be prescribed by the state government.

(v) **Objects:** As per Section 8B (1) of this Act, the object of every District Council shall be to promote and protect, within district, the rights of consumers laid down in Clause *(a)* to *(f)* of Section 6 of this Act.

REVIEW QUESTIONS

1. Define 'Central Consumer Protection Council'. Discuss the legal provisions of this Act regarding the central council.
2. What is 'State Consumers Protection Council'? Explain legal provisions regarding the working of state council.
3. Write note on 'District Consumer Protection Council' elaborating its working.

36

Consumer Disputes Redressal Agencies

LEARNING OBJECTIVES

- Understand three-tier judical machinery for disputes.
- Compare jurisdiction of Central, State and Commission and District forum.
- Examine the procedure used for settling complaints of consumers.
- Get idea about redressal machinery for settlement of consumer disputes.

As stated earlier, the Consumer Protection Act, 1986 provides, three-tier quasi-judicial machinery for redressing consumer grievances and settling complaints at the earliest and with least cost.

According to Section 9 of the Act, there shall be, established, for the purpose of this Act, the following agencies, namely:

(*i*) Consumer Disputes Redressal Forum, to be known as 'District Forum shall be established by the State Government', in each district by notification.

(*ii*) Consumer Disputes Redressal Commission, to be known as 'state commission', shall be established by the state government, in the state, by notification.

(*iii*) National Consumer Disputes Redressal Commission, shall be established by the Central Government by notification.

DISTRICT FORUM

(*i*) **Establishment of District Forum (Section 9):** Every district of the state shall have a District Forum, working at the lowest level of in the three-tier, Quasi-judicial machinery. Such forum will take care of consumer's complaints at the district level. Taking into account, the workload more than one district forum may be established in the district. For establishing such forum, the State Government shall make notification in its 'Official Gazette'.

(ii) **Composition of the District Forum (Section 10):** The District Forum will consist of three members to be appointed by the State Government on the recommendaton of a selection committeee to be formed under Section 10 (1A) of this Act.

Of these, one will be President, and out of remaining two one shall be a woman. Every member will have to give an undertaking that he or she will have no financial or other interest affecting the performance of their functions.

(*a*) ***Qualification:*** The President of the District Forum must be either a serving or retired District Judge. So far as the qualification of other members of the Forum is concerned, they must not be less than 35 years of age, must possess, bachelor's degree from a recognised university and the required ability, integrity, knowledge and experience of at least 10 years in dealing with the problems relating to law, economics, commerce accountancy, industry and public administration.

(*b*) ***Disqualification:*** According to this Act, a person shall be disqualified for being appointed as a member, if he:

- has been convicted and sentenced to imprisonment for an offence involving moral turpitude, or
- is an undischarged invosvent, or
- is of unsound mind declared by a competent court, or
- has been dismissed from the government service or from body corporate under the control of the government, or
- his interest, including financial one interferes in performing his functions, or
- has any other disqualification, prescribed by the state government.

(*c*) ***Selection committee for appointment:*** Every appointment of President and other members of the forum by the state government shall be made on the recommendation of a selection committee, which consists of the President of State Commission; Secretary, Law Department of the State and Secretary in-charge of the Department Dealing with Consumer Affairs in the State (President of State Commission will be a chairman).

(*d*) ***Term of office:*** Every member of the District Forum shall hold the office for a term of 5 year or up to the age of 65 years, whichever is earlier.

(*e*) ***Re-appointment:*** A member shall be eligible for a re-appointment for another term of 5 years or up to the age of 65 years, whichever is earlier, provided he fulfils eligibility criteria.

(*f*) ***Filling vacancies:*** The vacancies may occur in case of completion of term, death, resignation or removal of a president or member. In case such vacancy occurs in the office of President, the seniormost member shall perform functions of the President. And the vacancy in the office of a member shall be filled by appointing a person having required qualification as prescribed in this Act.

(*g*) ***Removal of the president and member:*** The state government may remove the President and members of the District Forum, who:

- has been declared as an insolvent; or
- has been convicted for an offence involving moral turpitude.
- has become, incapable, physically or mentally, of acting as a member or the President, or
- his interest including financial interest interferes in performing his functions, or
- has abused his position.

(*h*) ***Salary, Honorarium and Service allowances:*** The state government is enpowered to frame set of rules to deal with service conditions and salary and allowance payable to the President and members under this Act.

(*iii*) **Jurisdiction of the District Forum (Section 11):** The jurisdiction of the district. Forum inplies an area of its operations and extent of authority. The District Forum shall have a jurisdiction to entertain complaints where the value of goods or service and the compensation claimed, does not exceed Rs. 20 lakh.

In addition to it, a complaint shall be entertained by the District Forum provided the opposite party or parties involved in the complaint:

(*a*) actually or voluntarily resides, or

(*b*) carries on business, or

(*c*) has a branch office, or

(*d*) personally work for gain

within the local limits of jurisdiction of that District Forum.

(*iv*) **Procedure for Making Complaint (Section 12):** A complaint in relation to goods sold or delivered or agreed to be sold or delivered or any service provided or agreed to be provided may be filed with a District Forum by:

(*a*)
- the consumer to whom such goods are sold or delivered or service is provided.
- any recognised consumer association.
- one or more consumers (when they are many in numbers) on behalf of all consumers or for the benefit of all consumers with the permission of District Forum, individually.
- the Central Government or the state governments or as representative of consumers in general.

(*b*) Every complaint filed shall be accompanied with the amount of fee payable in such a manner as prescribed.

(*c*) On receipt of such complaint, the District Forum may allow the complaint to be proceeded within 21 days from the date of receipt of the complaint or may reject it after having heard the complainant.

(*v*) **Procedure on admission of complaint (Section 13):** On the admission of a complaint, it will be proceeded with by the District Forum, in the following manner, if it relates to any goods:

(*a*)
- a copy of admitted complaint, will be referred to the opposite party within 21 days from the date of admission, directing him to give his version of the case within a period of 30 days, which can be extended by next 15 days, by the District Forum.
- where the opposite party denies or disputes allegations contained in the complaint or omits or fails to represent his case, the District forum will proceed further in the following manner, (from *c* to *g*).
- where the defects in the goods alleged in the complaint cannot be determined without proper analysis and test, the District Forum shall obtain a sample of goods, will seal it and to refer it to the appropriate laboratory for finding the defects. The laboratory is required to submit its report to the District Forum within a period of 45 days from the reciept of sample.
- the complainant may be required to deposit prescribed fee with the District Forum payable to the laboratory for the analysis and test.
- on the reciept of report from laboratory, the District Forum will forward a copy of it, along with remarks to the opposite party.

- In case, the opposite party or complainant disputes the correctness of finding or method of analysis and test, the District Forum shall require the parties to submit their objection in writing to the appropriate laboratory.
- the District Forum shall provide reasonable opportunity to the parties of being heard as to their objections.

In case the complaint relates to goods, for which the above mentioned procedure cannot be followed or it relates to any servicc, the following procedure shall be followed:

(*b*)
- to refer such complaint to the opporite party within the period of 30 days, which may be extened by maximum 15 days by the District Forum.
- where the opposite party disputes or denies the allegations or fails to represent his case, the District Forum shall proceed to settle the dispute in the following manner:
- where the complainant fails to appear on the date of hearing, on the basis of evidence given by complainant the District Forum may either dismiss the complaint or decide it on merit.

(*c*)
- every complaint shall be heard as expeditiously as possible and efforts shall be made to decide it within a period of three months, if it does not require any analysis and test and within five months, if it requires, analysis and test.
- during the pendency of the case, before the District Forum, it may pass an interim order which is just and reasonable keeping in view the facts and circumstances of the case.

(*d*) The District Forum shall have same powers of the civil court under the code of Civil Procedure 1908 the respect with the following matters:
- to summon and enforce an attendence of defendent or witness and to examine the witness on oath.
- to discovcr and produce any document as evidence.
- to receive evidence on affidavits.
- requisitioning of the report of analysis and test from the appropriate laboratory.
- issuing any commission for the examination of any witness.
- any other matter which may be prescribed by the Central Government.

(*e*) Any proceeding before the District Forum will be considered as Judicial proceeding for certain purposes such as contempt to court, giving of false evidences and the Forum shall be treated as Civil Court for these purposes.

(*f*) With a view to avoid multiplicity of litigation and to facilitate decision on the complaint which involve the interest of large number of persons the class action complaint has been permitted. In 'class action' proceedings are brought by one or more consumers of a 'class' on behalf of numerous consumers, having common cause and interest to be protected. In case the claim is proved, it awards damage to all the consumers of that class.

(*g*) In the event of death of complainant or opposite party, the substitution of parties be made in accordance with the provisions of order XXII of the Schedule I of Code of Civil Procedure 1908.

(*vi*) **Remedies Available to Consumer (Section 14):** In case the allegations contained in the complaint are proved, the District Forum will issue an order for the opposite party to do one or more of the following things: [Section 14 (1)].

(*a*) to remove defect pointed out by the appropriate laboratory from the goods.

(*b*) to replace the goods with new goods of similar description, which shall be free from any defect.

(*c*) to return the price to the complainant or charges paid by him.

(*d*) to pay compensation to the consumer for the loss or injury caused to him due to negligence of opposite party.

(e) to remove defect or deficiency in the services in question.

(*f*) to discontinue the unfair trade practice or restrictive trade practice.

(*g*) not to offer hazardous goods for sale.

(*i*) to provide adequate cost to parties.

Every proceeding shall be conducted by the President of District Forum and at least one member thereof. And every order made by the District Forum shall be signed by its President and the member or members who conducted the proceedings.

(*vii*) **Appeal to the State Commission: (Section 15):** Section 15 of this Act provides that any person who is not satisfied or aggrieved by an order made by the District Forum may prefer an appeal against such order to the State Commision, within a period of 30 days from the date of the order. The appeal will be made in a form and manner as may be prescribed.

The 'State Commission' may entertain an appeal after the expiry of one month period, if it is satisfied that, there was sufficient cause for not filing it within the prescribed period.

An appeal filed by a person, who is required to pay any amount as per the order of the Forum, shall be entertained, if the appellant has deposited 50 per cent of that amount or Rs. 25,000, whichever is less.

Table showing amount of fee payable to District Forum

S. No.	Total value of goods a service and the compensation claimed	Amount of Fee Payable
1.	Up to one lakh rupees for complainant	Rs. 100
2.	Above one lakh up to five lakh rupees	Rs. 200
3.	Above five lakh up to ten lakh rupees	Rs. 400
4.	Above ten lakh up to twenty lakh rupees	Rs. 500

Note: The complainants who are under the Below Poverty Line shall be entitled for exemption of payment of fee only on production of an attested copy of the 'Antyodaya Anna Yojana' Cards.

STATE COMMISSION

(*i*) **Establishment of the State Commission (Section 9):** This Section of the Act provides that a Consumer Disputes Redressal Commission established by the State Government in the State, by notification, is known as State Commission. Every state shall have State Commission located at the capital of the State. The official seal and emblem of the State Commission shall be such as the State Government may specify.

(*ii*) **Composition of the State Commission (Section 16):** The State Commission shall consist of a President and not less that two members one of them should be a woman. Thus it may have more than two members subject to maximum number as may be prescribed.

(*a*) ***Qualification*****:** The President of the Commission should be a person who is or has been a Judge of a High Court.

The other members shall be the person of ability, integrity and standing and must have adequate knowledge and experience of dealing with problems relating to economics, law, commerce, accountancy, industry public affairs and administration.

(*b*) ***Appointment:*** The appointment of the President of the State Commission should be made by the State Government in consultation with Chief Justice of the High Court.

Every appointment of members of the State Commission, should be made by the State Government, on the recommendation of the selection committee.The selection committee shall consists of chairman and two members. The President of the State Commission will be the Chairman and Secretary, Law Department of State and Secretary in-charge of Department of Consumer Affairs in the State will be the members.

(*c*) ***Qualification for appointment of members:*** A person to be appointed as a member in the State Commission must possess the following qualification where he must:

- not be less than thirty-five years of age.
- possess a bachelor's degree from a recognised university.
- be a person of ability, integrity and standing and have adequate knowledge and experience of at least 10 years in dealing with problems relating to economics, law, commerce, accountancy, industry, public affairs and administration.

  The Amendment Act, 2002 provides limit that not more than 50 per cent of the members shall be from among persons having a judicial background.

Disqualification for appointment as member: A person shall be disqualified for appointment as a member if he:

- has been convicted and sentenced to imprisonment for an offence, which involves moral turpitude.
- is of unsound mind declared by a competent court.
- has been dismissed from the Government service or service in body corporate owned and controlled by the Government.
- has such financial or other interest, which may interfere in performing his functions as members.
- has such other disqualifications as may be prescribed by the State Government.

However, no such disqualifications have been prescribed for the appointment of the President of the State Commission. But the President is also a member thus, aforesaid disqualifications will be applicable for the appointment of the President.

(*d*) ***Term of office*:** Every member of the commission shall hold office for a term of five years or up to the age of 67, whichever is earlier.

(*e*) ***Re-appointment:*** According to the provisions of Amendment Act, 2002, a member shall be eligible for re-appointment for another term of five years or up to the age of 67, whichever is earlier, provided he fulfils the qualification and other conditions for appointment as mentioned earlier.

(*f*) ***Filling vacancies in the office:*** A vacancy in the office of the President or a member may occur due to expiry of term, or resignation or by removal. Such vacancies may be filled by appointment of a person possessing the prescribed qualification.

(*g*) ***Removal of the president or member:*** The set of consumer protection rules framed by the State Government are applicable for the removal of the President or a members of the State Commission. The State Government may remove President or a member from the office who:

- has been declared as an insolvent, or
- has become physically or mentally incapable of acting as a members, or
- has acquired financial or other interest which will interfere in performing his functions as a member, or
- has abused his position in a manner prejudicial to the public interest.

But to remove the member, position the State Government is required to hold an enquiry by prescribed procedure, and only in case, they are found guilty such removal can be done.

(*h*) ***Consititution of benches:*** According to the provisions of Amendment Act, 2002, a bench may be constituted by the President with one or more member. Such bench may exercise jurisdiction, power and authority of the State Commission.

The Consumer Protection Regulation 2005 lays down a provision, where a bench constituted by the President of the State Commission, does not have a member with judicial background to look into complex legal problems, the same may be referred to the President of the State Commission to constitute another bench.

(*iii*) **Jurisdicton of the State Commission (Section 17):** The State Commission has three types of jurisdiction, which are:

(*a*) The State Commission can entertain complaints, which involve the value of goods and services and compensation, if any, claimed exceeds 20 lakh of rupees, but not more than one crore rupee.

(*b*) The complaint shall be instituted in the State Commission within limits of whose jurisdiction the opposite party or parties, at the time of institution of the complaint:

- actually or voluntarily resides, or
- carries on business, or
- has a branch office, or
- personally works for a gain.

Every complaint filed in the State Commission shall be accompanied with a fee of Rs. 2,000 for the total value of goods and services and the compensation claimed up to Rs. 50 lakh and Rs. 4,000 for above 50 lakh and up to one crore rupees.

However, the complainants below poverty line have been exempted from the payment of fee on the production of an attested copy of the Antyodaya Anna Yojana Card.

(*c*) Under the provisions of this Act, the State Commission shall have a jurisdiction to entertain appeals against the order of any District Forum within the State.

The State Commission has also a jurisdiction to call for the records and pass an appropriate order in any consumer dispute pending before the District Forum, within the State.

(*iv*) **Procedure Applicable to State Commission (Section 18):** The Consumer Protection Act 1986, does not provide any specific procedure to be followed by the State Commission. According to Section 18 of this Act, the provisions of the Sections 12, 13 and 14 and rules made thereunder for the disposal of complaints by the District Forum shall be applicable to the State Commission.

Section 12 of this Act, provides the manner in which the complaint shall be made, Section 13 lays down the procedure for admittting of complaints and Section 14 provides for issuing an order directing the opposite party to do one or more things provided therein.

(*v*) **Appeals and Hearing of Appeal (Section 19):** According to Section 19 of this Act, any person, who is aggrieved or not satisfied by an order

made by the State Commission, may prefer an appeal against such order to the National Commission, within a period of 30 days from the date of the order.

Such appeal can be made in respect with those orders which have been passed by the State Commission under its original jurisdiction.

The National Commission may entertain an appeal after the expiry of a period of 30 days, if it is satisfied that there was sufficient cause for not filing it within that period.

The period of 30 days will be calculated from the date of acknowledging such order by the appellant.

[The appeal should be decided as far as possible within 90 days from the first day of hearing.]

The person who is required to pay any amount as per the order of the State Commission cannot file an appeal in the National Commission unless he has deposited in the prescribed manner 50 per cent of the amount or Rs. 35,000; whichever is less.

The National Commission ordinarily does not grant adjournment of case except only in exceptional situations.

NATIONAL COMMISSION (Section 9)

(*i*) **Establishment of National Commission (Section 9):** The Central Government shall establish a National Disputes Redressal Commission to be known as National Commission by making notification in Official Gazette.

The National Commission is an apex body in the judicial machinery for settling the consumer disputes.

(*ii*) **Composition of National Commission (Section 20):** The National Commission is to consist of a President and not less than four members one of whom shall be a woman. The maximum number of the members may be as prescribed by the Central Government.

(*a*) ***Qualification:*** The President of the National Commission should be a person who is or has been a Judge of the Supreme Court. The Central Government appoints the President of the National Commission in consultation with the Chief Justice of India.

Qualification for the appointment of the members: A person to be apppointed as a member, in the National Commission shall have the following qualifications:

- be not less than thirty-five years of age.
- possess a bachelors degree from a recognised university.
- be a person of ability, integrity and standing and possess required knowlege and experience of at least 10 years in dealing with problems relating to economics, law, commerce, accountancy, industry, public affairs and administration.

(*c*) ***Appointment of the members:*** Every member of the National Commission shall be appointed by the Central Government on the recommendation of a selection committee, which consists of the chairman and two members. The chairman, who is a Judge of Supreme Court, will be nominated by the Chief Justice of India. The Secretary in the Department of Legal Affairs in the Goverment of India, and the Secretary of the Department dealing with Consummer Affairs in the Government of India will be the members.

(*d*) ***Disqualification for appointment as members:*** According to the provisions of this Act, a person shall be disqualified for appointment as a member, if he:

- has been convicted and sentenced to imprisonment for an offence which involves moral turpitude.
- is of a unsound mind as declared by a competent court.
- has financial or other interest which interferes in performing his functions.
- has such other disqualificaitons as may be prescribed by the Central Government.

(*e*) ***Term of office:*** Every member of National Commission shall hold office for a term of five years or up to the age of 70 years, whichever is earlier.

(*f*) ***Re-appointment:*** A member shall be eligible for re-appointment for another term of five years or up to the age of 70 years, whichever is earlier, provided he fulfils the qualification and other conditions for appointment. Such re-appointment shall also be made on the basis of recommendation of the selection committee.

(*g*) ***Filling vacancies in the office:*** A vacancy in the office of the President or member may occur by the expiry of the term, or by death, resignation, or by removal. A vacancy caused shall be filled up by fresh appointment of a person who possesses the required qualification as prescribed by this Act.

(*h*) ***Removal of the President or Member:*** The Central Government may remove the President or any other members of the National Commission, who:

- has been declared an an insolvent, or
- has been convicted for an offence, which involves moral turpitude, or
- has been physically or mentally incapable of acting as President or the member, or
- has abused his position, in a manner which is prejudicial to public interst, or
- remained absent in three consecutive meeting except for reasons beyond his control.

The President or any member of the National Commission can be removed from his office only by an order made by the Central Government on the grounds specified above, after holding an enquiry by a sitting Judge of the Supreme Court.

(*i*) ***Power to constitute benches:*** The President of the National Commission may constitute a Bench, with one or more members. Such benches are empowered to exercise power and authority of the National Commission.

As per the Consumer Protection Regulations 2005, the bench constituted by the President does not have a member with judicial background. In case, any complex problem of law arises, it will be referred to the President to constitute another bench of which the President shall be a member.

(*iii*) **Jurisdiction of the National Commission (Section 21):** The National Commission shall have a jurisdiction:

(*a*) to entertain:

- Complaints, where the value of the goods or services and compensation, if any, claimed exceeds rupess one crore, and
- National Commission can admit appeals against the order of any state commission. An appeal may be preferred within a period of 30 days from the date of order of the State Commission. However, the National Commission may entertain such appeal even after the expiry of said period provided the Commission finds that there has been sufficient cause for not filing it within prescribed period.

(*b*) The National Commission can call for the records and pass appropriate order in any consumer dispute, which is pending before or has been decided by any State Commission provided it appears to the National Commission that:

- State Commission has exercised a jurisdiction not vested in it by law, or
- it has failed to exercise a jurisdiction so vested, or
- has acted in the exercise of its jurisdiction illegally or with material irregularity.

(*iv*) **Procedure to be Followed by the National Commission (Section 22):** According to Section 22 (1), the provisions of Sections 12, 13 and 14 of this Act and rules made thereunder for the disposal of complaints by the District Forum, shall be applicable to the disposal of disputes by the National Commission, with such modification as may be considered necessary by the Commission.

The procedure to be followed by the National Commission for the disposal of disputes is:

(*a*) A complaint containing the following particulars shall be presented by the complainant in person or by his agent or be sent by registered post to the National Commission:

- the name, description and the address of the complainant.
- the name, description and the address of the opposite party or parties.
- the facts relating to complaint and when and where it arose.
- documents in support of allegations contained in the complaint.
- the relief which the complainant claims.

The National Commission shall follow procedure and conditions laid down under Sections 12 and 13 of this Act for the disposal of complaints.

On the date of hearing it is obligatory for the parties to appear before the National Commission. In case the complainant or his agent fails to appear, the case may be decided 'ex parte'.

The National Commission may adjourn the hearing but the complaint must be decided within a period of three months from the date of notice received by the opposite party.

In case the National Commisson is satisfied with the allegations made in the complaint, it shall issue order for opposite party directing him to take one or more of the things as mentioned in Section 14 (1).

The National Commission shall have a power that any order passed by it (where no appeal is made against it or the Supreme Court affirms it) be published in the 'Official Gazette'.

The National Commision shall have the power to review any order made by it, when there is an error apparent on the face of the record.

On the application of complainant or its own motion, the National Commission may, in the interest of justice transfer any complaint pending before the District Forum of one State to the District Forum of another State or before one State Commission to another State Commission.

The National Commission is also empowered to set aside 'ex parte' order, against the opposite party or complainant in the interest of justice.

The National Commission shall ordinarily function at the New Delhi and perform its functions at such other place as the Central Government may notify in the 'Official Gazette' in consultation with the National Commission.

(*v*) **Appeal (Section 23):** Any person aggrieved by an order made by the National Commission may prefer an appeal against such order to the Supreme Court within a period of 30 days form the date of the order.

It has been held that the period of 30 days is to run from the date of 'knowledge of order'.

The Supreme Court may entertain an appeal after the expiry of 30 days, if it is satisfied that, there was sufficient cause for not filing it within that period.

An appeal made by a person, who is required to pay any amount on an order passed by the National Commission shall be entertained by the Supreme Court provided that person has deposited 50 per cent of that amount or Rs. 50,000; whichever is less.

(*vi*) **Finality of Orders (Section 24):** Every order passed by the National Commission, shall be final, provided no appeal has been filed against the order and the order has been passed under the provisions of this Act.

The National Commission, or the State Commission or the District Forum shall not admit a complaint unless it is filed within two years from the date on which the cause of action has arisen.

However, the complaint can be entertained even after the expiry of prescribed period, provided the complainant satisfies the Forum that he had sufficient cause for not filing the complaint within such period.

(*vii*) **Administrative Control:** The National Commission shall have administrative Control over all the State commissions in the following matters:

(*a*) Calling for periodical return regarding the institution, disposal, pendency of cases.

(*b*) Issuance of instructions regarding adoption of uniform procedures in the hearing of matters prior service of copies of documents produced by one party to the opposite parties, furnishing of English translation of judgments written in any language, speedy grant of copies of documents.

(*c*) overseeeing the functioning of the State Commissions or the District Fora to ensure that objects and purposes of the Act are best served without in any way interfering with their quasi-judicial freedom.

The State Commission shall have administrative control over all the District Fora within its jurisdiction in all matters referred above.

(*viii*) **Enforcement of Orders of the District Forum, the State Commission or the National Commission (Section 25)**

(*a*) ***Attachment of property:*** The property of the person, not complying with an interim order made under this Act, may be attached by the order of the Distric Forum or the State Commission or the Central Commission, as the case may be.

(*b*) ***Recovery of arrears:*** On the application of any person who is entitled to receive any amount from another person under an order made by the District Forum or the State Commission or the Central Commission, any of these as the case may be, issue a certificate to the collector for recovery of that amount as arrears of land revenue.

The main objective of attachment of the property is to take away power of alienation of the person concerned and also to give notice to the general public not to purchase or deal with the property attached.

(*c*) ***Sale of property:*** No attachment made, under the above section, shall remain in force for more than three months, at the end of which the property attached may be sold and out of proceeds thereof the District Forum or the State Commission or the Central Commission, as the case may be, may award such damages as it thinks fit to the complainant and shall pay the balance, if any, to the party entitled thereto.

(*ix*) **Dismissal of Frivolous or Vexatious Complaints (Section 26):** The District Forum or the State Commission or the Central Commission may dismiss a complaint which is found to be frivolous or vexatious. The Forum/Commission must record its reasons in writing for the dismissal of a complaint. The Forum/Commission may also pass the order that the complainant shall pay to the opposite party, such cost, not exceeding ten thousand rupees as may be specified in the order.

The term frivolous means, insignificant, futile having no weight or inportance, vexatious means causing or likely to cause any trouble or harassment or interference.

(*x*) **Penalties (Section 27)**

(*a*) Where a trader or a person against whom complaint is made or the complainant fails or omits to comply with any order made by the District Forum or the State Commission or the Central Commission, as the case may be, such trader, or person or complainant shall be punishable with imprisonment for a term, which shall not be less than one month, but which may extend to three years, or with fine which shall not be less than two thousand rupees, which may extend to ten thousand rupees, or with both.

(*b*) Notwithstanding anything contained in the Code of Criminal Procedure 1973, the District Forum, or the State Commission or the Central Commission, as the case may be, shall have the powers of first class judicial magistrate for the trial of offences under this Act. On the conferment of such power, on the Forum/Commission such Forum/Commission shall be deemed to be the judicial magistrate of the first class for the purpose of the Code of Criminal Procedure, 1973.

(*c*) All offences under this Act, may be tried summarily by the District Forum or the State Commission or the Central Commission as the case may be. A summary trial implies speedy disposal of the cases according to the procedure laid down in this Act.

REVIEW QUESTIONS

1. Explain briefly agencies working in the three-tier quasi-judicial machinery for the settlement of consumer disputes.
2. Discuss legal provisions relating to composition of the District Forum.
3. Explain the procedure followed by the District Forum for admitting consumer complaints.
4. Explain various legal remedies, which are available to consumer under the provisions of Consumer Protection Act, 1986.
5. What do you mean by the 'State Commission'? Discuss the jurisdiction of the State Commission.
6. What in 'National Commission'? Discuss legal provisions relating to composition of the Commission.
7. Discuss the procedure followed by the National Commission for the disposal of consumer disputes.
8. Explain legal provisions of Consumer Protection Act relating in inforcement of order made by Forum/Commssion.
9. Explain various penalties imposed on the person for not complying with the order of Forum/Commission.
10. Write notes on:
    (*a*) Dismissal of frivolous or vexatious complaints.
    (*b*) Legal provisions relating to appeal.
    (*c*) Jurisdiction of the District Forum.
    (*d*) Jurisdiction of the National Commission.
    (*e*) Composition of the State Commission.
11. Discuss the redressal machinery for the disposal of consumer complaints under Consumer Protection Act, 1986.
12. 'Forum/Commission working in consumer complaints redressal machinery are a quasi-judicial bodies and follow principles of natural justice.' Comment.

■■■

INFORMATION TECHNOLOGY ACT, 2000

37

Introduction and Application of IT Act

LEARNING OBJECTIVES

- Examine necessity of IT Act and find out areas of its non-application.
- Analyse the various objects of IT Act.
- Get conceptual clarity of the various terms, which are used in this Act.
- Get an idea about computer, computer system, computer network and computer resources.

INTRODUCTION

In the recent years, there has been tremendous development in the sector of information technology. Its worldwide use and applications have greatly affected business practices and state governance. On one hand business transactions within the country as well as among the various countries are being conducted and settled by using electronic devices and procedures. On the other, it has paved the way for e-Governance (Electronic governance).

In other words, information technology is being equally used by the states for conducting various operations and activities which are related to social, economic and political systems of the countries.

The use of information technology has in fact facilitated inexpensive and rapid communication, on line trading of goods and services, electronic transfer of funds and transmission and exchange of information among the various organisations.

In fact, paper based records of information is being replaced by electronically stored, processed and transmitted records. High degree of precision, lesser cost and high speed of conducting transactions are well-known features associated with the use of this technology.

NEED OF THE ACT

In order to use electronic devices and procedures in the area of business and state governance, a suitable legal framework consisting of 'cyber laws' and other regulatory measures is required to be built. With the help of such legal framework, the use of this technology particularly in the business will gain worldwide acceptability and recognition. Similarly by using suitable legal measures, Internet use may be made more popular and reliable.

INFORMATION TECHNOLOGY ACT, 2000

This is the cyber law, first of its kind in India. It was enacted in the Parliament with the consent of the Indian President on 9 June 2000. This act is based on the model law on Electronic Commerce prepared and adopted by the United Nations Commission on International Trade Law in 1997. The General Assembly of United Nations also recommended that all states should give favourable consideration to this 'Model Law on e-Commerce' at the time of enacting suitable piece of legislation for their country. It will bring uniformity with regard to the provisions applicable on e-Commerce and e-Governance.

To make an effective application of this law; it was also recommended that the state should also revise and amend other laws which are related to this law. In our country, Indian Penal Code, Indian Evidence Act 1872, Banker's Books Evidence Act 1891, and Reserve Bank of India Act 1934 may be suitably amended for facilitating an application of Information Technology Act.

It becomes clear that Information Technology Act, 2000 provides:

(*i*) Legal recognition to business transactions which are related to Electronic-Commerce.

(*ii*) Electronic filing of documents with government agencies and promote 'Electronic-Governance'.

(*iii*) Suitable amendments in the various existing Acts mentioned above, which are related to various provisions of this Act.

This Act shall extend to the whole of India. It also applies to any offence or contravention committed thereunder, by any person, outside India. This Act shall not apply to:

(*i*) A negotiable instrument as defined in Section 13 of the Negotiable Instrument Act 1881.

(*ii*) A 'power of attorney', as defined in Section 1A of the Power of Attorney Act 1882.

(*iii*) A 'trust' as defined in Section 3 of the Indian Trust Act 1882.

(*iv*) A 'will' as defined in Section 2, Clause (*h*) of the Indian Succession Act 1925.

(*v*) Any contract for the sale or conveyance of immovable property or any interests in such property.

(*vi*) Any such class of documents or transactions as may be notified by the Central Government in the Official Gazette.

OBJECTS OF THE ACT

Information Technology Act contains 94 sections. These sections mainly deal with electronic-commerce, electronic-governance, digital signature, role of certifying authorities and their regulation and cyber offences and penalties provided for. The Act aims at achieving the following objectives:

(*i*) To facilitate and promote electronic-commerce and provide legal recognition to all transactions made through electronic devices and procedures.

(*ii*) To facilitate electronic-governance by providing suitable electronic devices and procedures for performing various operations and activities related to state governance.

(*iii*) To provide legal recognition to digital signature at par with paper based signature.

(*iv*) To regulate and control the functioning of various agencies dealing with electronic transactions such as certifying authorities, controller of certifying authorities and controller, etc.

(*v*) To check and prevent cyber offences of various nature and prescribe suitable penalties for them.

(*vi*) To recognise electronic transactions and records at par with paper based documentation and records.

(*vii*) To provide legal framework within which electronic devices and procedures can be effectively used in every walk of life.

(*viii*) To bring uniformity with regard to the use and application of electronic devices and procedures for various purposes by international community.

DEFINITIONS OF IMPORTANT TERMS

Section 2 of the IT Act provides definitions of various terms or expressions which are commonly used in this Act. These definitions are as follows:

(*i*) ***Access:*** In order to work upon an electronic devices one must have access to that device.

Thus an 'Access' means "gaining entry into, instructing or communicating the logical, arithmetical or memory function resources of a computer, computer system or computer network."

It is therefore, an unauthorised access or use of the device without access that will lead to an offence.

(*ii*) ***Addressee:*** It "means a person who is intended by the originator to receive the electronic record, but does not include any intermediary."

In order to transfer or communicate information or record through electronic device two ends are needed. At one point there is a originator who originates and transfers information and at other point someone to receive it, is known as 'addressee'.

(*iii*) ***Adjudicating officer*:** It "means an adjudicating officer appointed under Section 46 (1) of this Act."

Thus such officer is appointed by the Central Government for adjudging whether any person has committed any cyber offence under this Act.

(*iv*) ***Affixing digital signature:*** It "means adoption of any methodology or procedure by a person for the purpose of authenticating an electronic record by means of digital signature."

Thus any person may transmit any information through electronic device. In order to authenticate information and to ensure that the information is same as being transmitted by the originator, digital signature method is used. It verifies identity of originator and authenticity of the information sent by electronic method.

(*v*) ***Asymmetric crypto system:*** It "means a system to secure key pair consisting of a private key for creating digital signature and public key to verify digital signature."

This system is also known as 'public key encryption'. It involves the use of private key and public key, which are simply two mathematically related numbers. A private key which is used for creating digital signature transforms message or data into coded form. And another key which is used for verifying digital signature brings coded data or message into decoded form or original form.

(*vi*) ***Appropriate Government:*** It "means as respect any matter",

(*a*) Enumerated in List II of Seventh Schedule to the Constitution. (*b*) Relating to any state law enacted under List III of the Seventh Schedule to the Constitution. The state government and in any other case, the Central Government.

(*vii*) ***Certifying Authority:*** It "means a person, who has been granted a licence to issue digital signature certificate under Section 24.

The certifying authority has an important role in verifying and identifying the person seeking a certificate, and in certifying that a public key is associated with him.

(*viii*) ***Certification Practice Statement:*** It means a statement issued by certifying authority to specify the practices that the certifying authority employs in issuing digital signature certificate."

(*ix*) ***Computer:*** It "means any electronic magnetic, optical or other high speed data processing device or system which performs logical, arithmetic and memory functions by manipulation of electronic, magnetic and optical impulses, and includes all input, output, processing storage, computer software or communication facilities which are connected or related to the computer in a computer system or computer network..

Thus a computer is a:

(*a*) Electronic device used for processing data.

(*b*) For processing data, it performs logical, mathematical and memory functions.

(c) It also include input, output, process, software and other communication facilities.

(*x*) ***Computer Network:*** It "means inter-connection of one or more computer through":

(*a*) The use of satellite, microwave, terrestrial line, or other communication media.

(*b*) Terminals or a complex consisting of two or more interconnected computers, whether or not the interconnection is continuously maintained.

(*xi*) ***Computer Resource:*** It "means, computer, computer system computer network, data, computer database or software."

(*xii*) ***Computer System:*** It "means a device or collection of devices, including input and output support devices, excluding calculators which are not programmable and capable of being used in conjunction with external files, which contains computer programme, electronic instructions, input data and output data that performs logic, arithmetic, data storage and retrieval, communication control and other functions."

(*xiii*) ***Controller:*** It "means the controller of certifying authorities appointed under Sub-section (1) of Section 17."

(*xiv*) ***Cyber Appellate Tribunal:*** It "means the cyber regulation appellate tribunal established under Sub-section (1) of Section 48.

(*xv*) ***Data:*** It "means a representation of information knowledge, facts, concepts, or instructions which are being prepared or have been prepared in a formalised manner and is intended to be processed or has been processed in a computer system or computer network or may be in any form (including computer printouts, magnetic or optical storage media, punch cards, punched tapes) or stored internally in the memory of the computer."

(*xvi*) ***Digital Signature:*** It "means authentication of any electronic record by a subscriber by means of an electronic method or procedure in accordance with the provisions of Section 3."

(*xvii*) ***Digital Signature Certificate:*** It "means a Digital Signature Certificate issued under Sub-Section (4) of section 35."

(*xviii*) ***Electronic Form:*** With reference to information means any information generated, sent, received or stored in media, magnetic, optical, computer memory, micro film, computer generated micro fiche or similar device.

(*xix*) ***Electronic Gazette:*** It means the Official Gazette published in the electronic form.

(*xx*) ***Electronic Record:*** It means data, record or data generated, image or sound stored, received or sent in an electronic form or micro film or computer generated micro fiche.

(*xxi*) ***Function:*** In relation to a computer, includes logic, control, arithmetical process, deletion, storage and retrieval and communication or telecommunication from or within a computer.

(*xxii*) ***Information:*** Includes data, text, images, sound, voice, codes, computer programs, software and databases or micro film or computer generated micro fiche.

(*xxiii*) ***Intermediary:*** With respect to any particular electronic message means any person who on behalf of another person receives, stores or transmits that message or provides any service with respect to that message.

(*xxiv*) ***Key Pair:*** In an asymmetric crypto system, means a private key and its mathematically related public key, which are so related that the public key can verify a digital signature created by the private key.

(*xxv*) ***Law:*** includes any Act of the Parliament or of a state legislature, Ordinances promulgated by the President or a Governor, as the case may be. Regulations made by the President under article 240, Bills enacted as Presidents Act under Sub-clause (a) of Clause (1) of Article 357 of the Constitution and includes rules, regulations, bye-laws and orders issued or made thereunder.

(*xxvi*) ***Licence:*** It means a licence granted to a Certifying Authority under Section 24.

(*a*) ***Originator:*** means a person who sends, generates, stores or transmits any electronic message or causes any electronic message to be sent, generated, stored or transmitted to any other person but does not include an intermediary.

(*b*) ***Prescribed:*** means prescribed by rules made under this Act.

(*c*) ***Private key:*** means the key of a key pair used to create a digital signature.

(*d*) ***Public key:*** means the key of a key pair used to verify a digital signature and listed in the Digital Signature Certificate.

(*e*) ***Secure system:*** means computer hardware, software and procedure that:

- are reasonably secure from unauthorised access and misuse;
- provide a reasonable level of reliability and correct operation;
- are reasonably suited to performing the intended functions;
- adhere to generally accepted security procedures;

(*f*) ***Security procedure:*** It means the security procedure prescribed under Section 16 by the Central Government.

(*g*) ***Subscriber:*** It means a person in whose name the Digital Signature Certificate is issued.

(*h*) ***Verify:*** In relation to a digital signature, electronic record or public key, with its grammatical variations and cognate expressions means to determine whether:

- the initial electronic record was affixed with the digital signature by the use of private key corresponding to the public key of the subscriber.
- the initial electronic record is retained intact or has been altered since such electronic record was so affixed with the digital signature.

REVIEW QUESTIONS

1. What do you mean by 'Information Technology'? Discuss its role in business and state governance.
2. Explain Information Technology Act, 2000. Discuss the need of enacting this Act.
3. Explain various objectives of Information Technology Act, 2000.
4. Write a note on the applications of Information Technology Act, 2000.
5. Define the following terms:
   (*i*) Addressee
   (*ii*) Computer
   (*iii*) Data
   (*iv*) Information
   (*v*) Digital signature
   (*vi*) Originator
   (*vii*) Certifying authority
   (*viii*) Computer system
   (*ix*) Computer network
   (*x*) Asymmetric crypto system

38

Digital Signature and Electronic Governance

LEARNING OBJECTIVES

- Get familiar with the concept of digital signature and find out its significance in business.
- Compare public key with private key.
- Analyse the system of making and using digital signature.
- Have a conceptual clarity about electronic-governance and remember legal provisions which facilitate electronic-governance.

INTRODUCTION

While using paper based documents, it is easy for the originator or sender of a message or information to put his signature on it. By signing the documents, the identity of the sender is being certified and the information or the message gets authenticated.

But in an electronic message it is not possible to affix a handwritten signature while transmitting it. Therefore, Information Technology Act has recognised digital signature so that the transactions made through electronic device is authenticated and gets legal consequences. A digital signature plays a key role in authenticating electronic records. Therefore digital signature are considered at par with paper signature. Like paper signature, it can be used as a proof of a contract or transaction between two parties. This is so because the party initiating electronic transaction cannot deny the contents of a document originated and transmitted through electronic device.

Due to digital signature, on-line trading and Internet contracts have been legally possible.

MEANING

According to Section 2 (1) (*d*) 'affixing digital signature' means, "the adoption for the purpose of authenticating or procedure by a person for the purpose of authenticating an electronic record by means of digital signature."

Thus digital signature means authentication of electronic record and transactions.

"According to the Information Technology Act, digital signature means, authentication of an electronic record in accordance with the provisions of Section 3. Subscriber means, a person in whose name the digital signature certificate is issued."

Digital signature is data item that accompanies digitally encoded message which can be used to ascertain an identity of originator and integrity of message.

AUTHENTICATION OF ELECTRONIC RECORDS (SECTION 3)

(Creating and verifying digital signature)

"Any subscriber in whose name digital signature certificate is issued may authenticate an electronic record by affixing his digital signature. The authentication of an electronic record shall be affected by the use of 'asymmetric crypto system' and 'hash function' which envelop and transform the initial electronic record into another electronic record."

In other words, digital signature is technically a 'message digest'. It is created by processing the contents of a message through special algorithm. It means it involves the transformation of message into 'message digest' by using a technical process called 'hash function', encoding it and sending it with the message which is also encoded.

***Explanation*:** For the purpose of this Section, 'hash function' means an algorithm mapping or translation of one sequence bits into another, generally smaller set known as 'hash result', such that an electronic record yields the same 'hash result' every time the algorithm is executed with the same electronic record as its input making it computationally infeasible.

(*a*) To derive or reconstruct the original electronic record from the 'hash result' produced by the algorithm.

(*b*) That two electronic records can produce same 'hash result' using the algorithm.

***Algorithm*:** An algorithm is a set of mathematical instruction used for finding out answer to a mathematical problem. It may also be defined as a finite set of instructions that accomplish a particular task. Thus it is with the help of a special algorithm the contents of message are processed to yield a value which is known as 'hash result'.

***Asymmetric crypto system*:** While transmitting information and making transactions through electronic device it is necessary to ensure that these are authentic and have not been tampered with by any intermediary in the process of transmission.

For this purpose, Section 3 of this Act provides that authentication of electronic record is to be affected by the use of 'asymmetric crypto system'. This system involves the use of 'encryption' (coding of message) and 'decryption' (decoding of a message) methodologies and other software tools.

According to Section 2 (1) (*t*), "asymmetric crypto system means a system of a secure key pair consisting of private key for creating digital signature and a public key to verify digital signature." These keys are like large passwords.

In asymmetric crypto system, each person will have two corresponding and matched keys-one called a 'private key' which is always kept secure with such person. And the others called 'public key' which the person shares with others and makes it available to them on specialised database called 'repositories' or through 'certifying authorities'.

These two keys public key and private key are used to encrypt and decrypt the message respectively. The sender or originator of message procures public key of the intended receiver from 'repositories' and by using this key he encrypts the message (Coded message). On receiving such coded message, the receiver or addressee use his private key (which is only with him) to decrypt (decode) the encrypted (coded) message.

The public key and private key of any person or organisation would be so mathematically linked that a messages encrypted using one key can only be decrypted by using corresponding other key. However, it is not possible to derive private key of a person from his public key.

***Verification*:** Any person by the use of public key of the subscriber can verify electronic record. The private key and public key are unique to the subscriber and constitute a functioning 'key pair'.

Difference between public key and private key

	Public key	Private key
Use	Public key is used for encrypting (coding) the a message.	Private key is used for decrypting (decoding) a message.
Availability	Public key is freely available on 'repositories' on through certifying authorities.	Private key is available only with the sender of message. It is always kept secure with him.
Function	Public key is used to verify digital signature.	Private key is used for creating digital signature.

ELECTRONIC-GOVERNANCE

Electronic device and procedures are also being used in the sphere of governance. To make its use more dependable, transparent and effective, the Information Technology Act has accorded legal recognition to electronic records, digital signatures, electronic form of dealing with government offices and its agencies. Not only this, but also the retention of information in an electronic format has also been given legal recognition provided such information remains accessible and usable in future.

The Act also provides for the filing of any form or application, creation, retention of records, issue or grant of licence, receipt and payment in government offices in electronic form. It has been primarily done with an object of facilitating electronic-governance.

The Act provides the following provisions to facilitate electronic-governance:

(*i*) ***Legal recognition of eleconic records*** **(Section 4)**

Where any law provides that information or any other matter shall be in writing or in the typewritten or printed form, then, notwithstanding anything contained in such law, such requirement shall be deemed to have been satisfied if such information or matter is:

(*a*) rendered or made available in an electronic form;

(*b*) accessible so as to be usable for a subsequent reference.

(*ii*) ***Legal recognition of digital signatures***

Where any law provides that information or any other matter shall be authenticated by affixing the signature or any document shall be signed or bear the signature of any person then, notwithstanding anything contained in such law, such requirement shall be deemed to have been satisfied, if such information or matter is authenticated by means of digital signature affixed in such manner as may be prescribed by the Central Government.

***Explanation*:**For the purposes of this section, 'signed', with its grammatical variations and cognate expressions, shall, with reference to a person, means affixing of his hand written signature or any mark on any document and the expression 'signature' shall be construed accordingly.

(iii) ***Use of electronic records and digital signatures in government and its agencies:***

(*a*) Where any law provides for:

- the filing of any form, application or any other document with any office, authority, body or agency owned or controlled by the appropriate government in a particular manner;
- the issue or grant of any licence, permit, sanction or approval by whatever name called in a particular manner;
- the receipt or payment of money in a particular manner, then, notwithstanding anything contained in any other law for the time being in force, such requirement shall be deemed to have been satisfied if such filing, issue, grant, receipt or payment, as the case may be, is effected by means of such electronic form as may be prescribed by the appropriate government.

(*b*) The appropriate government may, for the purposes of Sub-section(1) prescribe:

- the manner and format in which such electronic records shall be filed, created or issued;
- the manner or method of payment of any fee or charges for filing, creation or issue of any electronic record under Clause (*a*).

(iv) ***Retention of electronic records***

(*a*) Where any law provides that documents, records or information shall be retained for any specific period, then, that requirement shall be deemed to have been satisfied if such documents, records or information are retained in the electronic form, if:

- the information contained therein remains accessible so as to be usable for a subsequent reference;
- the electronic record is retained in the format in which it was originally generated, sent or received or in a format which can be demonstrated to represent accurately the information originally generated, sent or received;
- the details which will facilitate the identification of the origin, destination, date and time of despatch or receipt of such electronic record are available in the electronic record:

  Provided that this clause does not apply to any information which is automatically generated solely for the purpose of enabling an electronic record to be despatched or received.

(*b*) Nothing in this Section shall apply to any law that expressly provides for the retention of documents, records or information in the form of electronic records.

(*v*) ***Publication of rule, regulation, etc., in electronic gazette***

Where any law provides that any rule, regulation, order, bye-law, notification or any other matter shall be published in the Official Gazette, then, such requirement shall be deemed to have been satisfied if such rule, regulation, order, bye-law, notification or any other matter is published in the Official Gazette or Electronic Gazette:

Provided that where any rule, regulation, order, bye-law, notification or any other matter is published in the Official Gazette or Electronic Gazette, the date of publication shall be deemed to be the date of the Gazette which was first published in any form.

(*vi*) ***Sections 6, 7 and 8 not to confer right to insist document should be accepted in electronic form***

Nothing contained in Sections 6, 7 and 8 shall confer a right upon any person to insist that any Ministry or Department of the Central Government or the State Government or any authority or body established by or under any law or controlled or funded by the Central or State Government should accept, issue, create, retain and preserve any document in the form of electronic records or effect any monetary transaction in the electronic form.

(*vii*) ***Power to make rules by Central Government in respect of digital signature***

The Central Government may, for the purposes of this Act, by rules, prescribe:

(*a*) the type of digital signature;

(*b*) the manner and format in which the digital signature shall be affixed;

(*c*) the manner or procedure which facilitates identification of the person affixing the digital signature;

(*d*) control processes and procedures to ensure adequate integrity, security and confidentiality of electronic records or payments;

(*e*) any other matter which is necessary to give legal effect to digital signatures.

(*viii*) ***Attribution of electronic records***

An electronic record shall be attributed to the originator:

(*a*) if it was sent by the originator himself;

(*b*) by a person who had the authority to act on behalf of the originator in respect of that electronic record;

(*c*) by an information system programmed by or on behalf of the originator to operate automatically.

(ix) Acknowledgement of receipt

(*a*) Where the originator has not agreed with the addressee that the acknowledgement of receipt of electronic record be given in a particular form or by a particular method, an acknowledgement may be given by.

- any communication by the addressee, automated or otherwise; or
- any conduct of the addressee, sufficient to indicate to the originator that the electronic record has been received.

(*b*) Where the originator has stipulated that the electronic record shall be binding only on receipt of an acknowledgement of such electronic record by him, then unless acknowledgement has been so received, the electronic record shall be deemed to have been never sent by the originator.

(*c*) Where the originator has not stipulated that the electronic record shall be binding only on receipt of such acknowledgement, and the acknowledgement has not been received by the originator within the time specified or agreed or, if no time has been specified or agreed to within a reasonable time, then the originator may give notice to the addressee stating that no acknowledgement has been received by him and specifying a reasonable time by which the acknowledgement must be received by him and if no acknowledgement is received within the aforesaid time limit he may after giving notice to the addressee, treat the electronic record as though it has never been sent.

(x) Time and place of despatch and receipt of electronic record

(*a*) Save as otherwise agreed to between the originator and the addressee, the dispatch of an electronic record occurs when it enters a computer resource outside the control of the originator.

(*a*) Save as otherwise agreed between the originator and the addressee, the time of receipt of an electronic record shall be determined as follows, namely:

if the addressee has designated a computer resource for the purpose of receiving electronic records:

- receipt occurs at the time when the electronic, record enters the designated computer resource; or
- if the electronic record is sent to a computer resource of the addressee that is not the designated computer resource, receipt occurs at the time when the electronic record is retrieved by the addressee;

if the addressee has not designated a computer resource along with specified timings, if any, receipt occurs when the electronic record enters the computer resource of the addressee.

(*c*) Save as otherwise agreed to between the originator and the addressee, an electronic record is deemed to be despatched at the place where the originator has his place of business, and is deemed to be received at the place where the addressee has his place of business.

(*d*) The provisions of Sub-section (2) shall apply notwithstanding that the place where the computer resource is located may be different from the place where the electronic record is deemed to have been received under Sub-section (3).

(*e*) For the purposes of this Section:

- if the originator or the addressee has more than one place of business, the principal place of business, shall be the place of business;
- if the originator or the addressee does not have a place of business, his usual place of residence shall be deemed to be the place of business;
- usual place of residence, in relation to a body corporate, means the place where it is registered.

REVIEW QUESTIONS

1 What is 'digital signature'? How would you create and verify digital signature.

2. Define Asymmetric Crypto System and distinguish between 'Public key' and 'Private key'.

3. What do you mean by 'electronic-governance'? Discuss the various provisions of IT Act related to electronic-governance.

4. Write notes on:

   (*a*) Digital Signature.

   (*b*) Electronic-governance.

   (*c*) Asymmetric Crypto System.

   (*d*) Provision regarding retention of electronic records in Government offices.

■■■

39

Regulation of Certifying Authorities

LEARNING OBJECTIVES

- Examine the legal mechanism of regulation of certifying authoriies.
- Remember the procedure of appointment and functions of controller and other officers.
- Fxamine the legal provisions of this Act regarding issue of licence used for issuing digital signature, its renewal, suspension and rejection.
- Get an idea about operational responsibility of certifying authority.
- Analyse the procedure of issue, suspension and revocation of digital signature certificate.

INTRODUCTION

To encourage the rapid growth of e-Commerce and e-Governance, an effective legal environment and mechanism is required. It is necessary to build and strengthen proper legal infrastructure of various authorities to regulate the devices and procedures such as issue and use of digital signature certificate, use of public and private keys, use of Internet facilities and use of cyber space, etc.

With a view to regulate these, IT Act 2000, provides for an appointment, functions, powers and duties of the controller of certifying authorities. It also lays down procedure for issuing licence to certifying authority who grants digital signature certificate and seeks compliance of relevant provisions of this Act. It also deals with suspension, revocation and renewal of licence issued to these authorities. The Act also provides legal provisions regarding operational responsibilities, powers and functions of certifying authorities.

In brief, the regulation of certifying authorities or digital infrastructure in India consists of:

(*a*) Appointment of controller of certifying authority (CCA): The Central government has already appointed such controller for supervising and controlling overall functioning of certifying authorities.

(*b*) Certifying Authorities (CA): These authorities will get licence from the controller and will function under the supervision and directions of the controller. These authorities primarily deal with issues and use of digital signature certificate.

1. Appointment of Controller and other Officers

The appointment of controller and other officers takes place as follows:

(*a*) The Central Government may, by notification in the Official Gazette, appoint a Controller of Certifying Authorities for the purposes of this Act and may also by the same or subsequent notification appoint such number of Deputy Controllers and Assistant Controllers as it deems fit.

(*b*) The Controller shall discharge his functions under this Act subject to the general control and directions of the Central Government.

(*c*) The Deputy Controllers and Assistant Controllers shall perform the functions assigned to them by the Controller under the general superintendence and control of the Controller.

(*d*) The qualifications, experience and terms and conditions of service of Controller, Deputy Controllers and Assistant Controllers shall be such as may be prescribed by the Central Government.

(*e*) The Head Office and Branch Office of the office of the Controller shall be at such places as the Central Government may specify, and these may be established at such places as the Central Government may think fit.

(*f*) There shall be a seal of the Office of the Controller.

2. Functions of Controller

The Controller may perform all or any of the following functions, namely:

(*a*) Exercising supervision over the activities of the Certifying Authorities.

(*b*) Certifying public keys of the Certifying Authorities.

(*c*) Laying down the standards to be maintained by the Certifying Authorities.

(*d*) Specifying the qualifications and experience which employees of the Certifying Authorities should possess.

(*e*) Specifying the conditions subject to which the Certifying Authorities shall conduct their business.

(*f*) Specifying the contents of written, printed or visual materials and advertisements that may be distributed or used in respect of a Digital Signature Certificate and the public key.

(*g*) Specifying the form and content of a Digital Signature Certificate and the key.

(*h*) Specifying the form and manner in which accounts shall be maintained by the Certifying Authorities.

(*i*) Specifying the terms and conditions subject to which auditors may be appointed and the remuneration to be paid to them.

(*j*) Facilitating the establishment of any electronic system by a Certifying Authority either solely or jointly with other Certifying Authorities and regulation of such systems.

(*k*) Specifying the manner in which the Certifying Authorities shall conduct their dealings with the subscribers.

(*i*) Resolving any conflict of interests between the Certifying Authorities and the subscribers.

(*m*) Laying down the duties of the Certifying Authorities.

(*n*) Maintaining a database containing the disclosure record of every Certifying Authority containing such particulars as may be specified by regulations, which shall be accessible to public.

3. Recognition of Foreign Certifying Authorities

(*a*) Subject to such conditions and restrictions as may be specified by regulations, the Controller may with the previous approval of the Central Government, and by notification the Official Gazette, recognise any foreign Certifying Authority as a Certifying Authority for the purposes of this Act.

(*b*) Where any Certifying Authority is recognised under Sub-section (1), the Digit Signature Certificate issued by such Certifying Authority shall be valid for the purposes of this Act.

(*c*) The Controller may, if he is satisfied that any Certifying Authority has contravened any of the conditions and restrictions subject to which it was granted recognition under Sub-section (1) he may, for reasons to be recorded in writing, by notification in the Official Gazette, revoke such recognition.

4. Controller to Act as Repository

(*a*) The Controller shall be the repository of all Digital Signature Certificates issued under this Act.

(*b*) The Controller shall:

(*i*) make use of hardware, software and procedures that are secure from intrusion and misuse;

(*ii*) observe such other standards as may be prescribed by the Central Government to ensure that the secrecy and security of the digital signatures are assured.

(*c*) The Controller shall maintain a computerised data base of all public keys in such a manner that such database and the public keys are available to any member of the public.

5. Licence to Issue Digital Signature Certificates

(*a*) Subject to the provisions of Sub-section (2), any person may make an application, to the Controller, for a licence to issue Digital Signature Certificates.

(*b*) No licence shall be issued under Sub-section (1), unless the applicant fulfils such requirements with respect to qualification, expertise, manpower, financial resources and other infrastructure facilities, which are necessary to issue Digital Signature Certificates as may be prescribed by the Central Government.

(*c*) A licence granted under this Section shall:

(*i*) be valid for such period as may be prescribed by the Central Government.

(*ii*) not be transferable or heritable.

(*iii*) be subject to such terms and conditions as may be specified by the regulations.

I. Application for licence

(*i*) Every application for issue of a licence shall be in such form as may be prescribed by the Central Government.

(*ii*) Every application for issue of a licence shall be accompanied by:

(*a*) a certification practice statement;

(*b*) a statement including the procedures with respect to identification of the applicant;

(*c*) payment of such fees, not exceeding twenty-five thousand rupees as may be prescribed by the Central Government;

(*d*) such other documents, as may be prescribed by the Central Government.

II. Renewal of licence

An application for renewal of a licence shall be:

(*a*) in such form;

(*b*) accompanied by such fees, not exceeding five thousand rupees, as may be prescribed by the Central Government and shall be made not less than forty-five days before the date of expiry of the period of validity of the licence.

III. Procedure for grant or rejection of licence

The Controller may, on receipt of an application under Sub-section (1) of Section 21, after considering the documents accompanying the application and such other factors, as he deems fit, grant the licence or reject the application:

Provided that no application shall be rejected under this Section unless the applicant has been given a reasonable opportunity of presenting his case.

IV. Suspension of licence

(*i*) The Controller may, if he is satisfied after making such inquiry, as he may think fit, that a Certifying Authority has.

(*a*) made a statement in, or in relation to, the application for the issue or renewal of the licence, which is incorrect or false in material particulars;

(*b*) failed to comply with the terms and conditions subject to which the licence was granted;

(*c*) failed to maintain the standards specified under Clause (b) of Sub-section (2) of Section 20;

(*d*) contravened any provisions of this Act, rule, regulation or order made thereunder. The controller may revoke the licence, provided that no licence shall be revoked unless the Certifying Authority has been given a reasonable opportunity of showing cause against the proposed revocation.

(*ii*) The Controller may, if he has reasonable cause to believe that there is any ground for revoking a licence under Sub-section (1), by order suspend such licence pending the completion of any inquiry ordered by him:

Provided that no licence shall be suspended for a period exceeding 10 days unless the Certifying Authority has been given a reasonable opportunity of showing cause against the proposed suspension.

(*iii*) No Certifying Authority whose licence has been suspended shall issue any Digital Signature Certificate during such suspension.

V. Notice of suspension or revocation of licence

(*i*) Where the licence of the Certifying Authority is suspended or revoked, the Controller shall publish notice of such suspension or revocation, as the case may be, in the database maintained by him.

(*ii*) Where one or more repositories are specified, the Controller shall publish notices of such suspension or revocation, as the case may be, in all such repositories:

Provided that the data base containing the notice of such suspension or revocation, as the case may be, shall be made available through a website which shall be accessible round the clock.

Provided further that the Controller may, if he considers necessary, publicise the contents of database in such electronic or other media, as he may consider appropriate.

6. Powers of Controller

The controller of Certifying Authorities has the following powers:

I. Power to delegate

The Controller may, in writing, authorise the Deputy Controller, Assistant Controller or any officer to exercise any of the powers of the Controller under this Chapter.

II. Power to investigate contraventions

(*i*) The Controller or any officer authorised by him in this behalf shall take up for investigation any contravention of the provisions of this Act, rules or regulations made thereunder.

(*ii*) The Controller or any officer authorised by him in this behalf shall exercise the like powers which are conferred on Income Tax authorities under Chapter XIII of the Income Tax Act, 1961 and shall exercise such powers, subject to such limitations laid down under that Act.

III. Access to computers and data

(*i*) Without prejudice to the provisions of Sub-section (1) of Section 69, the Controller or any person authorised by him shall, if he has reasonable cause to suspect that any contravention of the provisions of this Act, rules or regulations made thereunder has been committed, have access to any computer system, any apparatus, data or any other material connected with such system, for the purpose of searching or causing a search to be made for obtaining any information or data contained in or available to such computer system.

(*ii*) For the purposes of Sub-section (1), the Controller or any person authorised by him may, by order, direct any person incharge of, or otherwise concerned with the operation of, the computer system, data apparatus or material, to provide him with such reasonable technical and other assistance as he may consider necessary.

Certifying Authority

Certifying authority may be defined as an individual or body corporate who has been granted licence by the controller for issuing digital signature certificate. Such individual or body corporate possess required technical skills. In our country, National Information Centre (NIC) and Tata Consultancy Services (TCS) are the leading certifying authorities.

Operational Responsibilities of Certifying Authorities

The certifying authorities have the following responsibilities:

(*i*) ***Every Certifying Authority shall:***

(*a*) Make use of hardware, software and procedures that are secure from intrusion and misuse.

(*b*) Provide a reasonable level of reliability in its services which are reasonably suited to the performance of intended functions.

(*c*) Adhere to security procedures to ensure that the secrecy and privacy of the digital signatures are assured.

(*d*) Observe such other standards as may be specified by regulations.

(*ii*) ***Certifying Authority to ensure compliance of the Act, etc.***

Every Certifying Authority shall ensure that every person employed or otherwise engaged by it complies, in the course of his employment or engagement, with the provisions of this Act, rules, regulations and orders made thereunder.

(*iii*) ***Display of licence***

Every Certifying Authority shall display its licence at a conspicuous place of the premises in which it carries on its business.

(iv) Surrender of licence

(*a*) Every Certifying Authority whose licence is suspended or revoked shall immediately after such suspension or revocation, surrender the licence to the Controller.

(*b*) Where any Certifying Authority fails to surrender a licence under Sub-section (1), the person in whose favour a licence is issued, shall be guilty of an offence and shall be punished with imprisonment which may extend up to six months or a fine which may extend up to ten thousand rupees or with both.

(v) Disclosure

(*a*) Every Certifying Authority shall disclose in the manner specified by regulations:

- its Digital Signature Certificate which contains the public key corresponding to the private key used by that Certifying Authority to digitally sign another Digital Signature Certificate;
- any certification practice statement relevant thereto;
- notice of the revocation or suspension of its Certifying Authority certificate, if any;
- any other fact that materially and adversely affects either the reliability of a Digital Signature Certificate, which that Authority has issued, or the Authority's ability to perform its services.

(*b*) Where in the opinion of the Certifying Authority any event has occurred or any situation has arisen which may materially and adversely affect the integrity of its computer system or the conditions subject to which a Digital Signature Certificate was granted, then, the Certifying Authority shall:

- use reasonable efforts to notify any person who is likely to be affected by that occurrence; or
- act in accordance with the procedure specified in its certification practice statement to deal with such event or situation.

DIGITAL SIGNATURE CERTIFICATES

The basic function of certifying authority is to issue digital signature certificate to the applicants.

Procedure to Issue Digital Signature Certificate

The following procedure is used for this purpose:

(*i*) Any person may make an application to the Certifying Authority for the issue of a digital Signature Certificate in such form as may be prescribed by the Central Government.

(*ii*) Every such application shall be accompanied by such fee not exceeding twenty-five thousand rupees as may be prescribed by the Central Government, to be paid to the Certifying Authority:

Provided that while prescribing fees under Sub-section (2) different fees may be prescribed for 'different classes of applicants'.

(*iii*) Every such application shall be accompanied by a certification practice statement or where there is no such statement, a statement containing such particulars, as may be specified by regulations.

(*iv*) On receipt of an application under Sub-section (1), the Certifying Authority may, after consideration of the certification practice statement or the other statement under Sub-section (3) and after making such enquiries as it may deem fit, grant the Digital Signature Certificate or for reasons to be recorded in writing, reject the application:

Provided that no Digital Signature Certificate shall be granted unless the Certifying authority is satisfied that:

(*a*) the applicant holds the private key corresponding to the public key to be listed in the Digital Signature Certificate;

(*b*) the applicant holds a private key, which is capable of creating a digital signature;

(*c*) the public key to be listed in the certificate can be used to verify a digital signature affixed by the private key held by the applicant:

Provided further that no application shall be rejected unless the applicant has been given a reasonable opportunity of showing cause against the proposed rejection.

Representations upon Issuance of Digital Signature Certificate

A Certifying Authority while issuing a Digital Signature Certificate shall certify that:

(*i*) It has complied with the provisions of this Act and the rules and regulations made thereunder.

(*ii*) It has published the Digital Signature Certificate or otherwise made it available to such person relying on it and the subscriber has accepted it.

(*iii*) The subscriber holds the private key corresponding to the public key, listed in the Digital Signature Certificate.

(*iv*) The subscriber's public key and private key constitute a functioning key pair.

(*v*) The information contained in the Digital Signature Certificate is accurate.

(*vi*) It has no knowledge of any material fact, which if it had been included in the Digital Signature Certificate would adversely affect the reliability of the representations made in Clauses (*a*) to (*d*).

Suspension of Digital Signature Certificate

(*i*) Subject to the provisions of Sub-section (2), the Certifying Authority which has issued a Digital Signature Certificate may suspend such Digital Signature Certificate.

(*a*) on receipt of a request to that effect *from*:

- the subscriber listed into Digital Signature Certificate, or
- any person duly authorised to act on behalf of that subscriber;

(*b*) if it is of opinion that the Digital Signature Certificate should be suspended in public interest.

(*ii*) A Digital Signature Certificate shall not be suspended for a period exceeding fifteen days unless the subscriber has been given an opportunity of being heard in the matter.

(*iii*) On suspension of a Digital Signature Certificate under this Section, the Certifying Authority shall communicate the same to the subscriber.

Revocation of Digital Signature Certificate

(*i*) A Certifying Authority may revoke a Digital Signature Certificate issued by it:

(*a*) where the subscriber or any other person authorised by him makes a request to that effect, or

(*b*) upon the death of the subscriber, or

(*c*) upon the dissolution of the firm or winding up of the company where the subscriber is a firm or a company.

(*ii*) Subject to the provisions of Sub-section (3) and without prejudice to the provisions of Sub-section (1), a Certifying Authority may revoke a Digital Signature Certificate which has been issued by it at any time, if it is of opinion that.

(*a*) a material fact represented in the Digital Signature Certificate is false or has been concealed;

(*b*) a requirement for issuance of the Digital Signature Certificate was not satisfied;

(*c*) the Certifying Authority's private key or security system was compromised in a manner materially affecting the Digital Signature Certificate's reliability;

(*d*) the subscriber has been declared insolvent or dead or where a subscriber is a firm or a company, which has been dissolved, wound-up or otherwise ceased to exist.

(*iii*) A Digital Signature Certificate shall not be revoked unless the subscriber has been given an opportunity of being heard in the matter.

(*iv*) On revocation of a Digital Signature Certificate under this Section, the Certifying Authority shall communicate the same to the subscriber.

Notice of Suspension or Revocation

(*i*) Where a Digital Signature Certificate is suspended or revoked under Section 37 or Section 38, the Certifying Authority shall publish a notice of such suspension or revocation, as the case may be, in the repository specified in the Digital Signature Certificate for publication of such notice.

(*ii*) Where one or more repositories are specified, the Certifying Authority shall publish notices of such suspension or revocation, as the case may be in all such repositories.

DUTIES OF SUBSCRIBERS

The individual or organisation who has been granted digital signature certificate in known as 'subscriber'. The subscriber has the following duties which are laid down under Sections 41 to 43 or this Act:

I. *Generating Key Pair*

Where any Digital Signature Certificate, the public key of which corresponds to the private key of that subscriber which is to be listed in the Digital Signature Certificate has been accepted by a subscriber, then, the subscriber shall generate the key pair by applying the security procedure.

II. *Acceptance of Digital Signature Certificate*

(*i*) A subscriber shall be deemed to have accepted a Digital Signature Certificate if he publishes or authorises the publication of a Digital Signature Certificate.

(*a*) to one or more persons;

(*b*) in a repository, or otherwise demonstrates his approval of the Digital Signature Certificate in any manner.

(*ii*) By accepting a Digital Signature Certificate the subscriber certifies to all who reasonably rely on the information contained in the Digital Signature Certificate that:

(*a*) the subscriber holds the private key corresponding to the public key listed in the Digital Signature Certificate and is entitled to hold the same;

(*b*) all representations made by the subscriber to the Certifying Authority and all material relevant to the information contained in the Digital Signature Certificate are true;

(*c*) all information in the Digital Signature Certificate that is within the knowledge of the subscriber is true.

III. *Control of Private Key*

(*i*) Every subscriber shall exercise reasonable care to retain control of the private key corresponding to the public key listed in his Digital Signature Certificate and take all steps to prevent its disclosure to a person not authorised to affix the digital signature of the subscriber.

(*ii*) If the private key corresponding to the public key listed in the Digital Signature Certificate has been compromised, then, the subscriber shall communicate the same without any delay to the Certifying Authority in such manner as may be specified by the regulations.

***Explanation*:** For the removal of doubts, it is hereby declared that the subscriber shall be liable till he has informed the Certifying Authority that the private key has been compromised.

REVIEW QUESTIONS

1. What do you mean by 'controller of certifying authorities'? Explain his functions.
2. Explain the procedure to be followed by the controller for issuing licence and suspending its use.
3. Discuss the various powers which are given to the controller under the provisions of IT Act.
4. What do you mean by 'certifying authorities'? Discuss the operational responsibilities of such authorities.
5. Define 'digital signature certificate'. Explain the procedure followed by the certifying authorities to issue digital signature certificate.
6. Who is a 'subscriber'? Discuss his duties regarding digital signature certificate.
7. Explain the main provisions of the IT Act with respect to digital signature certificate.
8. Write notes on:

   (*a*) Digital signature certificate.

   (*b*) Certifying authorities.

   (*c*) Subscriber.

   (*d*) Revocation of digital signature certificate.

40

Cyber Contraventions, Adjudication and Offences

LEARNING OBJECTIVES

- Understand the basic concept of cyber contraventions and compare these with cyber offences.
- Analyse the penalty prescribed for cyber contraventions and get to know how these contraventions are adjudicated.
- Examine the necessity of having Cyber Regulations Appellate Tribunal.
- Analyse the various cyber offences and penalties prescribed for these offences.

INTRODUCTION

In spite of adequate security measures adopted by an owner of computer, computer system and computer network, its unauthorised and illegal use can not be checked completely. Any illegal act or unauthorised use of the computer system amounts to cyber crimes. The terms cyber crime includes both cyber contraventions and cyber offences. Under Information Technology Act, penalty is imposed on the person who commits such crime. He may be compelled to pay compensation to the affected party or may be awarded imprisonment as the case may be. The cyber crimes may be in the form of contravention or offence.

(*i*) ***Contraventions:*** A contravention is a mere violation or breach of cyber rules or procedures used in computer system or network such as to gain unauthorised access to computer system, introducing computer virus, disrupting the use of system etc. The person who is found guilty for such acts may be liable to pay damage as compensation to the affected person not exceeding rupees one crore. Sections 43 to 47 of this Act deal with contraventions, penalties and their adjudication.

According to Section 43 of this Act, if a person, without permission of the owner or any other person who is in-charge of a computer, computer system or computer network does any of the following act, he shall be guilty of a contravention of the Act.

(*a*) ***Accessing or securing access to such computer, computer system or computer network*:** This contravention can be considered as something similar to the trespass of a person's property. The term 'access' defined in Section 2(1)(*a*) would mean gaining a possibility of instructing or communicating with the logical, arithmetical or memory resources of a computer. The access may be secured in an, actual physical sense or from a distance.

(*b*) ***Downloading, copying or extracting any data, computer database or information from such computer, computer system or computer network including information or data held or stored in any removable storage medium.***

This provision would cover situations similar to theft or violation of a person's copyrights.

(*c*) ***Introducing or causing to be introduced all computer contaminant or computer virus into any computer, computer system or computer network.***

These two terms 'contaminant' and 'virus' have been used in the Act. Although these two differ in their technical meaning, their consequences are similar. The terms have been defined and explained later.

(*d*) ***Damaging or causing to be damaged any computer, computer system or computer network, data, computer database or any other programs residing in such computer, computer system or computer network.***

(*e*) ***Disrupting or causing disruption to any computer, computer system or computer network:*** The disruption may be caused by doing anything stated in earlier provisions, such as introduction of virus, etc., or a damage to any computer resource, or it may be done in any other manner.

(*f*) ***Denying or causing the denial of access to any person authorised to access any computer, computer system or computer network by any means:*** Such denials may be attempted by the person by flooding the Internet networks with unnecessary traffic so as to disrupt their normal functioning. Such disruption prevents the authorised users from utilising the services of these Internet service providers (ISPs). In addition to it, there may be other methods also to cause a denial of access to an authorised user to a computer resource.

(*g*) ***Providing any assistance to any person to facilitate access to a computer, computer system or computer network in contravention of the provisions of this Act, rules or regulations made thereunder:*** This provision implies the owners and users of computer resources not to help any other person in gaining an access to a computer resource in violation of the provisions of this Act.

(*h*) ***Charging the services availed of by a person to the account of another person by tempering with or manipulating any computer, computer system or computer network.***

Explanations: For the purpose of this Section.

(*i*) ***Computer contaminant:*** means any set of computer instructions that are designed:

(*a*) to modify, destroy, record, transmit data or program residing within a computer, computer system or computer network, or

(*b*) by any means to disrupt the normal operation of the computer, computer system, or computer network.

(*ii*) ***Computer database:*** means a representation of information, knowledge, facts, concepts or instruction in text, image, audio, video that are being prepared or have been prepared in a formalised manner or have been produced by a computer, computer system or computer network and are intended for use in a computer, computer system or computer network.

(*iii*) ***Computer virus:*** means any computer instruction, information, data or program that destroys, damages, degrades or adversely affects the performance of a computer resource or attaches itself to another computer resource and operates when a program, data or instruction is executed or some other event take place in that computer resource.

(*iv*) ***Damage:*** means to destroy, alter, delete, add, modify or rearrange any computer resource by any means.

PENALTY FOR THE CONTRAVENTIONS

The person guilty of a contravention as described above shall be liable to pay damages by way of compensation not exceeding Re. 1 crore to the person so affected.

Penalties for Certain other Contraventions

Section 44 has described certain other contraventions also and the penalty for each of them as follows:

(*a*) Failure to furnish any document, return or report to the Controller or the Certifying Authority when required to do so.

The penalty shall be a fine of an amount not exceeding Rs. 1,50,000 for each such failure.

(*b*) Failure to file any return or furnish any information books or other documents within the time specified thereunder in the regulations.

The penalty shall be an fine of an amount not exceeding Rs. 5,000 for everyday during which such failure continues.

(*c*) Failure to maintain books of account or records as required under law.

The penalty shall be a fine of an amount not exceeding Rs. 10,000 for every day during which the failure continues.

Residuary Penalty

Section 45 of this Act provides for various other possible contraventions which may not have been included in the Act specifically. It states: "Whoever contravenes any rules or regulations made under this Act, for the contravention of which no penalty has been separately provided, shall be liable to pay a compensation not exceeding Rs. 25,000 to the person affected by such contravention or a penalty not exceeding Rs. 25,000."

ADJUDICATION ON CONTRAVENTIONS AND APPOINTMENT OF ADJUDICATING OFFICER

Section 46 of this Act provides that where a need arises to find out whether any person has committed a contravention of any of the provisions of this Act or of any rule etc., made thereunder, the Central Government shall appoint an officer to be an adjudicating officer for holding an inquiry in the manner prescribed by the Central Government.

The adjudicating officer shall give to the accused person a reasonable opportunity for making representation in the matter. If he is satisfied that the person has committed the contravention, he may impose such penalty or award such compensation as he thinks fit.

No person shall be appointed as an adjudicating officer unless he possesses such experiences in the field of Information Technology and legal or judicial experience as may be prescribed by the Central Government.

Where more than one adjudicating officers are appointed, the Central Government shall specify by order the matters and places with respect to which such officers shall exercise their jurisdiction.

Every adjudicating offer shall have the powers of a civil court which are conferred on the Cyber Appellate Tribunal.

Factors to be taken into account by the adjudicating officer

While determining the quantum of compensation under this Act for contraventions, the adjudicating officer shall give due consideration to the following factors:

(*a*) The amount of gain of unfair advantage, whenever quantifiable, made as a result of the default.

(*b*) The amount of loss caused to any person as a result of the default.

(*c*) The repetitive nature of the default.

THE CYBER REGULATION APPELLATE TRIBUNAL (CRAT)

A Certifying Authority or a subscriber may feel aggrieved by the order of the Controller of Certifying Authorities or of an Adjudicating officer and may like to appeal against the order. The Act provides for creation of a suitable machinery for the speedy disposal of such appeals, in the form of Cyber Regulations Appellate Tribunals (CRAT).

Establishment of Cyber Appellate Tribunal

According to Section 48 of this Act:

(*i*) The Central Government shall establish one or more appellate tribunals to be known as the Cyber Regulation Appellate Tribunal.

(*ii*) The Central Government shall also specify, in the notification, the matters and places in relation to which the Cyber Appellate Tribunal may exercise jurisdiction.

A Cyber Appellate Tribunal shall consist of one person only called the Presiding Officer of the Tribunal.

The Act has laid down detailed provisions regarding the qualifications, terms of office, salary, etc., vacancies, resignation and removal of the Presiding officers of the Tribunals.

Appeal to Cyber Appellate Tribunal

Section 57 of this Act provides for the rules relating to appeals before an Appellate Tribunal. These are:

(*i*) Any person aggrieved by an order made by Controller or an adjudicating officer under this Act may make an appeal to a Cyber Appellate Tribunal having jurisdiction in the matter. However, there can be no appeal against an order made by an adjudicating with the consent of parties.

(*ii*) An appeal shall be filed within a period of 45 days from the date on which a copy of the order made to be challenged is received by the person aggrieved and it shall be in such form and be accompanied by such fee as may be prescribed.

The Tribunal may extend this time period if it is satisfied that there was sufficient cause for not filing it within that period.

(*iii*) The Tribunal may, after giving the parties to the appeal, an opportunity of being heard, pass such orders thereon as it thinks fit, confirming, modifying or setting aside the order appealed against.

(*iv*) The Tribunal shall send a copy of every order made by it to the parties to the appeal and to the concerned Controller or adjudicating officer.

(*v*) The appeal filed shall be dealt with as expeditiously as possible and endeavour shall be made to dispose of the appeal finally within six months from the data of receipt of the appeal.

Procedure and Powers of the Cyber Appellate Tribunal

Section 58 of this Act lays down provision regarding the procedure to be followed by the Tribunal and the powers available in the discharge of its duties.

The Cyber Appellate Tribunal shall not be bound by the procedure laid down by the Code of Civil Procedure, 1908, but shall be guided by the principles of natural justice and shall have powers to make its own procedure including the place at which it shall have it sittings.

The Cyber Appellate Tribunal shall have, for the purpose of discharging its functions under this Act, the same powers as are vested in a civil court under the Code of Civil Procedure, 1908, while trying a suit, in respect of the following matters:

(*i*) summoning and enforcing the attendance of any person and examining him on oath.

(*ii*) requiring the discovery and production of documents or other electronic records.

(*iii*) Receiving evidence on affidavits.

(*iv*) Issuing commissions for the examination of witnesses or document.

(*v*) Reviewing its decisions.

(*vi*) Dismissing an application for default or deciding it *ex parte*.

(*vii*) Any other matter which may be prescribed.

Civil Courts Barred

"No civil court shall have jurisdiction to entertain any suit or proceeding in respect of any matter which an adjudicating officer appointed under this Act or the Cyber Appellate Tribunal is empowered to determine" (Section 61).

Appeal to High Court

Any person aggrieved by any decision or order of the Cyber Appellate Tribunal may file an appeal to the High Court within 60 days from the date of communication of the decision or order to him on any question of fact or law arising out of such order.

The High Court may, if it is satisfied that the appellant was prevented by sufficient causes from filing the appeal within the said period, allow it to be filed within a further period not exceeding 60 days (Section 62).

Compounding of Contraventions

Section 63 provides for the possibility of a compromise between the Controller or Adjudicating officer and the accused person regarding the quantum of the penalty.

Any contravention under the Act by a person may, either before or after the institution of adjudication proceedings, be compounded by the Controller or by the adjudicating officer, as the case may be. But, the compromised amount shall not, in any case, exceed the maximum amount of the penalty which may be imposed under this Act for the contravention so compounded.

This facility will not be available to a person who commits the same or similar contravention within a period of three years from the date on which the first contravention, committed by him, was compounded.

***Explanation*:** Any second or subsequent contravention committed after the expiry of a period of three years from the date on which contravention was previously compounded shall be deemed to be a first contravention.

Recovery of Penalty

According to Section 64, a penalty imposed under this Act, if it is not paid, shall be recovered as an arrear of land revenue and the licence or the Digital Signature Certificate, as the case may be, shall be suspended till the penalty is paid.

CYBER OFFENCES AND PENALTIES FOR CYBER OFFENCES

The use of computer, computer system and computer network is subject to legal provisions of Information Technology Act. Where the person commits any act which is prohibited by law or which defeats the provisions of this Act, it will amount to cyber offence. In other words, cyber offence implies direct violation of legal provisions of this Act. A criminal intention on the part of the person committing illegal act constitute an offence. He intends to commit such offence with a view to cause loss to another person.

Sections 65 to 76 of this Act deal with the offences and provide for penalty of imprisonment or imposition of fine or both on the person committing such offences.

The Act has recognised the following offences and has prescribed a quantum of penalty for the person committing such offences:

(i) Tempering with computer source codes (Section 65)

This offence takes place when a person tampers with the valuable computer programs of another person.

The provision states that a person shall be guilty of an offence if he knowingly or intentionally conceals, destroys or alters or intentionally or knowingly causes another to conceal, destroy or alter any computer source code used for a computer, computer program, computer system or computer network, when the computer source code is required to be kept or maintained by law for the time being in force.

***Penalty*:** Such a person shall be punished with imprisonment up to three years, or with fine which may extend up to Rs. 2 lakh, or with both.

***Explanation*:** For the purposes of this provision, .computer source code. means the listing of programs, Computer command, design and layout and program analysis of computer resource in any form.

(*ii*) *Hacking with computer system (Section 66)*

This provision declares 'hacking' as a punishable offence.

This offence take place when a person with the intention to cause or knowing that he is likely to cause wrongful loss or damage to the public or any person destroys or deletes or alters any information residing in a computer resource or diminishes its value or utility or affects it injuriously by any means.

***Penalty*:** Whosoever commits hacking shall be punished with imprisonment up to three years, or with fine which may extend up to Rs. 2 lakh or with both.

Originally, the term 'hacking' was used for the efforts of computer-savvy people to make experiments with computer operations to, explore and exploit the, maximum abilities of the computer hardware and software. In course of time, the term 'hacking' has become a technique of indulging in certain types of cyber crimes.

'Hacking' involves a planned attempt to penetrate the security systems of a computer network and, having gained this unauthorised access into the system, causes a distortion or damage to the contents and functioning of the system. The damage may be caused to the hardware or to the software of the system. This may be done from a distance or by gaining a physical closeness to the system.

(*iii*) *Publishing of obscene information (Section 67)*

This offence takes place when a person publishes or transmits or causes to be published in the electronic form, any material which is lascivious or appeals to the prurient interest or if its effect is such as to tend to deprave and corrupt persons who are likely to read, see or hear the matter contained or embodied in it.

***Penalty*:** The guilty person shall be punished on first conviction with imprisonment for a term which may extend to five years and with fine which may extend to Re. 1 lakh and in the event of a second or subsequent conviction with imprisonment for a term which may extend to 10 years and also with fine which may extend for Rs. 2 lakh.

(*iv*) *Failure to comply with controller's directions (Section 68)*

When the Controller directs Certifying Authority or any employee of such 'Authority' to take such measures or cease carrying on such activities which are necessary to ensure compliance with the provisions of this Act, the concerned person is bound to comply with them. Any failure to do so will be an offence.

***Penalty*:** Any person who fails to comply with any such order shall be liable on conviction to imprisonment for a term not exceeding three years or to a fine not exceeding Rs. 2 lakh, or to both.

(*v*) *Failure to decrypt information (Section 69)*

The controller may direct any agency of the Government to intercept any information transmitted through any computer resource of any person, if he is satisfied that it is necessary or expedient so do to in the broad national interest. The government agency under the direction may call upon the person to extend all facilities and technical assistance to decrypt the information. Any failure to do so by the person shall be an offence.

Penalty: The person guilty of such an offence shall be punished with an imprisonment for a term which may extend to seven years.

(*vi*) *Breaking into protected System (Section 70)*

A Government may find it essential sometimes to declare any computer, computer system or computer network to be a protected system. The Government may, in such case, authorize specific person only to access such protected system.

It would be an offence for any unauthorized person to secure access or attempt to secure access to a protected system in contravention of these provisions.

Penalty: The guilty person shall be punished with imprisonment for a term which may extend to 10 years and shall also be liable to pay fine.

(*vii*) *Misrepresentation before CCA (Section 71)*

This offence is committed when a person makes any misrepresentation to, or suppresses any material fact from, the Controller or the Certifying Authority for obtaining any licence or Digital Signature Certificate, as the case may be.

***Penalty*:** The guilty person shall be punished with imprisonment for a term which may extend to two years, or with fine which may extend to Re. 1 lakh, or with both.

(*viii*) *Breach of confidentiality or privacy (Section 72)*

Under the provisions of this Act, a person representing an authority may have the powers to secure access to any electronic record and other information etc., of a person without his consent. If he, on obtaining this access to the information, discloses such electronic record or other information to any other person, it shall amount to an offence.

Penalty: The person guilty of this offence shall be punished with imprisonment for a term which may extend to two years, or with fine which may extend to Re. 1 lakh, or with both.

(*ix*) *Publishing erroneous digital signature certificate (Section 73)*

It may happen that a Digital Signature Certificate gets issued even while some error had crept in the whole process of issuing it. No person should make a public announcement of such an erroneous certificate knowingly. If it is done, it shall amount to an offence. Section 73 states as follows:

"No person shall publish a Digital Signature Certificate or otherwise make it available to any other person with the knowledge that:

(*a*) the Certifying Authority listed in the certificate has not issued it; or

(*b*) the subscriber listed in the certificate has not accepted it; or

(*c*) the certificate has been revoked or suspended;

unless such publication is for the purpose of verifying a digital signature created prior to such suspension or revocation."

Penalty: Any person who contravenes this provision shall be punished with imprisonment for a term which may extend to two years, or with fine which may extend to Rs. 1 lakh, or with both.

(*x*) *Publication for fraudulent purpose (Section 74)*

This offence takes place when a person knowingly creates, publishes or otherwise make available a Digital Signature Certificate for any fraudulent or unlawful purpose.

Penalty: He shall be punished with imprisonment for a term which may extend to two years, or with fine which may extend to Re. 1 lakh, or with both.

(*xi*) *Failure to surrender the licence (Section 33)*

As was discussed in the previous chapter, when a Certifying Authority's licence has been revoked or suspended, the person in whose name the licence is issued must surrender it before the Controller.

Penalty: On failure to do so, he shall be liable for imprisonment up to six months or a fine up to Rs. 10,000; or for both.

Other Rules

(*ia*) ***Offence or contravention committed outside India:*** The provisions of this Act shall apply also to any offence or contravention committed outside India by any person irrespective of his nationality, if the act or conduct constituting the offence or contravention involves a computer, computer system or computer network located in India.

(*b*) ***Order for confiscation:*** Any computer hardware, in respect of which, any provision of this Act has been or is being contravened, shall be liable to confiscation.

But, where it is established to the satisfaction of the court adjudicating the confiscation that the person in whose possession, power or control of any such computer hardware is found is not responsible for the contravention of the provisions of this Act, the court may, instead of making an order for confiscation, make such other order authorised by this Act against the person contravening of the provisions of this Act, as it may think fit.

(*c*) ***Penalties of confiscation not to interfere with other punishment:*** No penalty imposed or confiscation made under this Act shall prevent the imposition of any other punishment to which the person affected thereby is liable under any other law for the time being in force.

REVIEW QUESTIONS

1. Define the term 'Cyber Contravention'. Explain various cyber contraventions which are mentioned under Section 43 of IT Act.
2. Discuss the penalty for certain other contraventions laid down under Section 44 of IT Act.
3. How does adjudication on contravention take place? What factors would be taken into account by adjudicating offices for determining quantum of compensation?
4. How is Cyber Appellate Tribunal is formed? Discuss various rules for making appeal to such tribunal and explain powers of the tribunal.

5. Define 'Cyber Offence'. Discuss various offences with penalty prescribed for such offences.
6. Write notes on:
   (*a*) Adjudication Officer
   (*b*) Cyber Appellate Tribunal
   (*c*) Compounding of Contraventions
   (*d*) Publishing Obscene Information

■■■